THE ADDISON
GAYLE JR. READER

The Addison Gayle Jr. Reader

Edited by
NATHANIEL NORMENT JR.

UNIVERSITY OF ILLINOIS PRESS
URBANA AND CHICAGO

Library of Congress Cataloging-in-Publication Data
Gayle, Addison, 1932–
The Addison Gayle Jr. reader / edited by Nathaniel Norment Jr.
p.   cm.
Includes bibliographical references and index.
ISBN 978-0-252-03408-4 (cloth : alk. paper)
ISBN 978-0-252-07610-7 (pbk. : alk. paper)
1. American literature—African American authors—
History and criticism—Theory, etc.
2. African Americans—Intellectual life.
3. African Americans in literature.
4. African-American arts.
5. Aesthetics, Black.
6. Gayle, Addison, 1932–
7. Critics—United States—Biography.
I. Norment, Nathaniel. II. Title.
PS153.N5G299   2009
810.9'896073—dc22   2008049083

. . . the Black Aesthetic has as its fundamental thesis that there are cultural streams dividing blacks from whites in this country. At that point, the idea that the Black Aesthetic will become simply another literary movement misses the point. We're not talking about literary movements in that sense at all. The Black Aesthetic will exist until the liberation of black people is assured, because the Black Aesthetic is as much a political movement as it is a literary one. I think of the Black Aesthetic as nothing more than the cultural arm of Black Nationalism.

—Addison Gayle Jr.

Dedicated to

Addison Gayle Jr.

Lou Ethel Roliston, his widow

His family

His friends

His students

His colleagues

CONTENTS

PREFACE

Nathaniel Norment Jr.

> The Negro writer who seeks to function within his race as a purposeful
> agent has a serious responsibility. In order to do justice to his subject
> matter, in order to depict Negro life in all its manifold and intricate
> relationships, a deep, informed, and complex consciousness is
> necessary; a consciousness which draws for its strength upon the fluid
> lore of a great people, and molds this lore with the concepts that move
> and direct the forces of history today . . . to do no less than create values
> by which his race is to struggle, live, and die . . .
> —Richard Wright, *Blueprint for Negro Writing*

More than forty years ago, in the midst of the Black Arts/Aesthetics Movement,
black and Puerto Rican students forced the central administration of the City
University of New York (CUNY) and the City College of New York (CCNY) to
begin a policy of open admissions. Many prominent black scholars, historians,
literary artists and critics, and political scientists taught at the college. In 1969, I
began teaching Pre-Baccalaureate English in the S.E.E.K. program of the English
department. At different times, our colleagues at CCNY included Barbara Christian, Charles V. Hamilton, Allen B. Ballard, Dennis Brutus, Toni Cade Bambara,
Wilfred Cartey Jr., Audre Lorde, James Emanuel, Michele Wallace, Eugene Red-
mond, David Henderson, June Jordan, Larry Neal, Raymond Patterson, Stanley
Macebuh, Gwendolyn Brooks, Ishmael Reed, Ntozake Shange, Chinua Achebe,
and a host of others who contributed to the development, direction, and destiny
of African American/black arts and aesthetics.

At the same time I started teaching at CCNY, Addison Gayle Jr., who had
taught in the same Pre-Bac program for three years (1966–1969) was appointed
as an assistant professor in English at Baruch College–CUNY. He and the other
black and Puerto Rican faculty had had a difficult struggle within the English
department at City College. Between the years of 1969 and 1972 I had been in the
company of Gayle on several occasions. The most memorable experience I had
of him took place at the inaugural Langston Hughes Festival in 1972, which was
started by our late colleague and my close friend, the poet Raymond Patterson.
Both Raymond and Gayle were admirers of Paul Laurence Dunbar, and the first
Hughes festival was actually a celebration of Dunbar's hundredth birthday coordinated by Raymond and several black faculty (Jerome Brooks, Stanley Macebuh,
James Emanuel, and me) in the English department.

Shortly before the opening program, held at CCNY's Findley Hall, Wilfred Cartey Jr. and Gayle had adamantly refused to appear on the same stage with then-Chair of City's English department, Theodore Gross. At the time of this event, I was unaware of Cartey and Gayle's intense conflicts with and dislike of Gross. After much discussion with and appeasement of all three men, Raymond convinced Cartey and Gayle to let Gross welcome everyone and then leave the stage. It was only after this compromise that both Cartey and Gayle agreed to partake in this opening festival, which is still held every year in honor and recognition of black writers. The essays "White Experts—Black Subjects," "Separate, Not Mutual Estates," and "Cultural Strangulation: Black Literature and White Aesthetics" all provide Gayle's strong opposition to and opinions of Gross's (and other white critics') conferred expertise in black literature. Not long after Gayle's departure, it became clearly evident to me that while at City, he enjoyed a reputation as an outstanding, effective, and caring teacher by students who went on to become artists, doctors, lawyers, teachers, and writers themselves (e.g., Tony Medina, Charles Powell, Lottie Wilkins, Louis Rivera, and Sekou Sundiata).

Throughout the sixties and seventies, Gayle was widely recognized as the academic leader and one of the architects (along with Hoyt W. Fuller, Larry Neal, Sonia Sanchez, Amiri Baraka, Stephen Henderson, Askia Muhammad Toure, and Haki Madhabuti) of the Black Arts and Aesthetics Movement. Striking, then, is the fact that almost forty years later, Gayle is not seriously discussed or studied today, even within many African American/Black Studies departments and programs (which is ironic, considering that the modern Black Studies movement began at the apex of Gayle's output). In the recent history of African American literary criticism there has not been any work (save Toni Morrison's *Playing in the Dark: Whiteness and the Literary Imagination*) that critically interrogates and analyzes the misinterpretation, misappropriation, and misrepresentation of black characters, life experiences, value systems, and overall culture by white authors and literary critics—those presumed "white experts" on "black subjects."

In 2001, at the annual banquet of the College Language Association, I was sitting at a table with ten to twelve recently conferred African American PhDs who had written their dissertations on African American literature (from Duke, University of North Carolina–Chapel Hill, Harvard, Yale, and Princeton) intently listening as they discussed who were the best African American literary critics of the past thirty years; Gayle was not even mentioned. Disturbed, I inquired as to their opinions regarding Addison Gayle Jr. Their responses were alarming, to say the least: "Who is/was he?" "What did he write?" and the like. Not one knew about the man or his work. I stated that Gayle was one of the leaders of the Black Arts and Aesthetics Movement and that his contributions to black literature and literary criticism were among the most significant in the late twentieth century. A number of these young "literary scholars" suggested that if I felt so strongly about Gayle, and if his contributions were so monumental, I should write a book about him. Not long after this encounter, I phoned three of my friends (Jerome Brooks,

Annette Oliver Shands, and Margaret Reid) who knew Gayle and his works quite well and shared this incident with them, asking them the same questions posed to me.

I began research for this book in the summer of 2001 with the intent of answering for myself—as I thought—"who was Gayle, and, if he is so important, why have his contributions to African American literature and criticism remained so overlooked?" I also wanted to introduce his writing(s) to the new generation of undergraduate and graduate students in all fields. Most troubling to me as a professor of African American Studies is that there has not been a single dissertation or thesis written on either Gayle or his works, nor is there in existence a collection or anthology with an ample cross section of his works. However, I must note that Gayle has not been completely overlooked or forgotten. A few scholars (notably Houston Baker, Henry Louis Gates Jr., and Arnold Rampersad) occasionally make passing mention of or cite Gayle in some of their own works. Additionally, John Edgar Wideman and Arnold Rampersad have spoken at the Addison Gayle Memorial Lecture, held annually at Baruch College–CUNY.

In the field of African American literary criticism, the name Addison Gayle Jr. has become synonymous with the term "black aesthetic." No other literary theorist has provided the cultural and intellectual perspectives to black aesthetics on the scale of Addison Gayle Jr. His 1971 landmark text, *The Black Aesthetic,* a collection of essays on theory, music, poetry, drama, and fiction by prominent black artists and critics, remains the definitive source for a definition of a concept that is, perhaps, the most provocative issue in African American literary history.

Gayle wrote in several genres. His essays and articles on black aesthetics and black writers had a tremendous impact on cultural, literary, and political debates. The great bulk of his writings were in personal essays, literary history, biography, and literary criticism. In 1969, he edited *Black Expression: Essays by and about Black Americans in the Creative Arts,* followed by a collection of personal essays in 1970 titled *The Black Situation,* which covered a wide range of issues. *Bondage, Freedom and Beyond* was also published in 1970.

In addition to his autobiographical and personal writings, Gayle wrote a number of important biographies: *Oak and Ivy: A Biography of Paul Laurence Dunbar* (1972), *Claude McKay: The Black Poet at War* (1972), and *Richard Wright: Ordeal of a Native Son* (1980). In 1975, he published a significant analysis and history of the African American novel titled *The Way of the New World: The Black Novel in America.* In addition to his books, he contributed articles, short stories, and reviews to numerous anthologies, journals, and magazines such as *Negro Digest, Black World, Liberator, Amistad I,* and the *College Language Association Journal.* Gayle developed an ideological perspective for black literature, critics, and writers that was created through *Black Aesthetics.*

In this reader, Gayle's influence on black literature is presented through his personal essays, criticisms, and biographical works. This is a comprehensive representation of his writings. This is the first book about the intellectual founder of black aesthetics. As a key figure in the Black Arts/Aesthetics Movement, Gayle did not hesitate to project blackness and "African centeredness." The volume contains selected essays and articles that represent the range of Gayle's writing on such subjects as relationships between father and son, cultural nationalism, racism, black aesthetics, black criticism, and black literature. The volume includes definitive essays such as "Blueprint for Black Criticism," "The Harlem Renaissance: Towards a Black Aesthetic," and "Cultural Strangulation: Black Literature and the White Aesthetics." A chapter from his autobiography, an interview, and introductions to biographies he wrote are supplemented by his literary criticism.

Why has Gayle not yet received the proper recognition he so deserves within the literary world in general and circles of African American social and cultural thought (especially among "Afrocentrists" and "cultural nationalists") in particular? It is my sincere hope that this collection of Addison Gayle Jr.'s work presents and demonstrates his commitment to preserving African American culture, defending African American voices, and advancing the development of new black writers committed to "the way of the new world."

Nathaniel Norment Jr.

Philadelphia, Pa.

2009

ACKNOWLEDGMENTS

Early on and throughout my research, I spoke with a number of people who knew Addison Gayle Jr. both professionally and personally (Jerome Brooks, Annette Oliver Shands, Brenda Wilkinson, Margaret Reid), and recently discussed Gayle's legacy with John Todd, chair of the Department of English at Baruch College, and his widow (now my friend), Ms. Lou Ethel Roliston. Their words of encouragement to diligently pursue this project have not gone forgotten. I am indebted to them as well as to Sharon Howard (Reference Library of the Schomburg Center for Research in Black History and Culture) and the spirits of our Literary Ancestors—Raymond Patterson, Langston Hughes, Paul Laurence Dunbar, June Jordan, Chester Himes, Barbara Christian, Claude McKay, Jean Toomer, Wallace Thurman, Zora Neale Hurston, Larry Neal, Hoyt W. Fuller, Toni Cade Bambara, Gwendolyn Brooks, Henry Dumas, Ralph Ellison, James Baldwin, Richard Wright, Margaret Walker, Lorraine Hansberry, John Oliver Killens, Dudley Randall, and Wilfred Cartey Jr.

My personal gratitude goes to Dr. Greg E. Kimathi Carr of Howard University and Dr. Daniel Black of Clark Atlanta University, two of the earliest and most vocal supporters of this work, and Jason B. Neuenschwander, who was stalwart in giving me more of his time than he had to spare. I would like to express my gratitude to many colleagues at Temple for their assistance that helped me complete this project; special thanks to Carolyn Adams, Richard Englert, Jasion Kurichi, William Wilkinson, and Gloria Basmajian for their professional assistance and friendship.

Many, many thanks to the librarians at the City College of New York–CUNY, Temple University, Fordham University, Hofstra University, Westchester County Library System, University of Pennsylvania, Emory University, University of Georgia, University of Buffalo, Howard University, Penn State University, New York University, City University of New York Graduate Center, Baruch College–CUNY, Old Westbury–SUNY, and University of Maryland–College Park. Special thanks to Susan Howard of the Schomburg Center for Research in Black Culture, Marie Brown and Ashleen Ollivierre of Marie Brown Associates, Renee Cogdell Lewis, Esq. Corporate Counsel (Johnson Publishing Company, Inc.), Al Vara (Reference Libarian) at Temple University, and Aslaku Berhanu of the Blockson Collection at Temple University.

Additionally, I would like to thank the many people who helped and supported me in some way in making this book a reality: Brian Jones, Assata Rose Norment, David Norment (for his advice and counsel), Sanaya Marie Norment, Michael Norment (for his courage and tenacity), Natalie Norment, Rosemarie Norment, Suzzette Spencer, Jae Hardaway, Beverly Norville, Dr. Jerome Brooks, Janice Vincent, Moziah Nathaniel Norment, Toeanzar Norment, Jeanne Harris, Morgan Penn, Courtney M. Javois, Elexis A. DeGale, Porsche Blakely, and Jessie Norment. Special thanks are due to Paul Cyphers, Daphne Jarrett, and Marybeth Sweetra (Temple's Barnes & Noble bookstore), who provided "a table" for me when I needed a creative space and atmosphere, and Jaya Swamickannu and the staff of Temple University's Instructional Resource Center.

I owe a large debt to the University of Illinois Press, Joan Catapano (Associate Director and Editor in Chief), Dawn McIlvain (Associate Editor), Alison Goebel (Editorial Assistant, Acquisitions), Rebecca Schrieber (Assistant Editor), Rebecca Crist (Managing Editor), Abraham Millar (Copy Editor), and the staff at Publication Services for their patience and support.

CREDITS

I would like to express my gratitude to all of the authors, journal editors, literary agents, publishers, and permission and copyright specialists who so kindly granted their permission to reprint works in this book. Every effort was made to contact copyright holders of articles reproduced in this volume. Any rights not acknowledged herein will be acknowledged in subsequent printings if notice is given to the author and publisher. The author and publisher are grateful for permission to reprint the following copyrighted material:

"Addison Gayle Jr.: 'The Consummate Black Critic' 1932–1991" is used with permission of the College Language Association Journal. Copyright © 2005.

"White Experts—Black Subjects" is reprinted by permission of Marie Brown Associates. Copyright © 1970 by Addison Gayle Jr.

"Letter to a White Colleague" is reprinted by permission of Marie Brown Associates. Copyright © 1970 by Addison Gayle Jr.

"The Cabinet of the Mind" is reprinted by permission of Marie Brown Associates. Copyright © 1970 by Addison Gayle Jr.

"Nat Turner and the Black Nationalists" is reprinted by permission of Marie Brown Associates. Copyright © 1970 by Addison Gayle Jr.

"Black Power and Existential Politics" is reprinted by permission of Marie Brown Associates. Copyright © 1970 by Addison Gayle Jr.

"Black Power or Black Fascism" is reprinted by permission of Marie Brown Associates. Copyright © 1970 by Addison Gayle Jr.

"Hell No, Black Men Won't Go!" is reprinted by permission of Marie Brown Associates. Copyright © 1970 by Addison Gayle Jr.

"Racism and the American University" is reprinted by permission of Marie Brown Associates. Copyright © 1970 by Addison Gayle Jr.

"Dreams of a Native Son" is reprinted by permission of Marie Brown Associates. Copyright © 1970 by Addison Gayle Jr.

"The Harlem Renaissance: Towards a Black Aesthetic" is reprinted by permission of Midcontinent American Studies Journal. Copyright © 1970.

"The Black Aesthetic: The Defender" is reprinted by permission of Johnson Publishing Company, Inc. Copyright © 1974.

"Cultural Nationalism: The Black Novelist in America" is reprinted by permission of Marie Brown Associates. Copyright © 1970 by Addison Gayle Jr.

"Cultural Strangulation: Black Literature and the White Aesthetic" is reprinted by permission of Marie Brown Associates. Copyright © 1971 by Addison Gayle Jr.

CHRONOLOGY

1932   Addison Gayle Jr. born June 2 in Newport News, Virginia, to Addison and Carrie (Holloman) Gayle

1950   Graduates from Phoenix High School, Newport News

1952   Addison Gayle Sr. dies

1955   Gayle arrives in New York

1960   Enrolls in the City College of New York at age 28

1964   Graduates with B.A. in English from the City College of New York

1965   Marries Rosalie Norwood on September 12, 1965
        "The Literature of Protest"

1966   Receives M.A. degree from the University of California Los Angeles
        Lecturer in English/S.E.E.K. Department (1966–69)

1967   "A Defense of James Baldwin"
        "I Endured! But"
        "The Dialectic of *The Fire Next Time*"

1968   "Richard Wright: Beyond Nihilism"
        "Perhaps Not So Soon One Morning"
        "The Quiet Revolution: The Pre-Baccalaureate Program of the City College"

1969   Joins faculty of English department at Baruch College–CUNY
        Publishes *Black Expression: Essays by and about Black Americans in the Creative Arts*
        "Cultural Strangulation: Black Literature and the White Aesthetic"
        "The Critic, the University and the Negro Writer"
        "Langston Hughes: A Simple Commentary"

1970   Publishes *The Black Situation*
        "Cultural Hegemony: The Southern Writer and American Letters"
        "Integrating Negroes with Black People"
        "The Harlem Renaissance: Towards a Black Aesthetic"
        "The Expatriate"

1971   Signs three-book contract with Doubleday
        (Summer) visiting Professor of English University of Washington–Seattle
        Publishes *The Black Aesthetic*
        Publishes *Bondage, Freedom, and Beyond: The Prose of Black Americans*
        Publishes *Oak and Ivy: A Biography of Paul Laurence Dunbar*
        "What We Must See/The Hungered Ones"

Blueschild Baby (Book Review)
(1971–72) Assistant Professor of Creative Writing, Rutgers University
"Cultural Nationalism: The Black Novelist in America"

1972   Publishes *Claude McKay: The Black Poet at War*
        "The Politics of Revolution: Afro-American Literature"
        "The World of Gwendolyn Brooks"
        "Black Aesthetic"

1973   "Under Western Eyes"(Book Review)

1974   "Reclaiming the Southern Experience: The Black Aesthetic 10 Years Later"
        Debate: "The Black Aesthetic" (Defender)

1975   Publishes *Way of the New World: The Black Novel in America*
        "Literature as Catharsis: The Novels of Paul Laurence Dunbar"

1976   "Two Views of Winesellers"
        "The Function of Black Criticism at the Present Time"
        Eva's Man (Book Review)
        Flight to Canada (Book Review)
        "Notes from an Armchair Philosopher" (Book Review)

1977   Publishes *Wayward Child: A Personal Odyssey/Addison Gayle, Jr.*
        "Blueprint for Black Criticism"

1980   Publishes *Richard Wright: Ordeal of a Native Son*
        Love Story Black (Book Review)

1982   Appointed Distinguish Professor English Department, Baruch College–
        CUNY

1984   "Gwendolyn Brooks: Poet of the Whirlwind"

1986   W.E.B. DuBois—Literary Biography
        "Right of Baraka"

1988   Marries Lou Roliston

1991   "Should the Cannon Be Revised?"
        Dies, October 3, 1991
        His obituary in the *New York Times* read, "The students, faculty, presi-
        dent, trustees, alumni, friends of Baruch College, The City University
        of New York mourn the passing of our Distinguished Professor of
        English, Addison Gayle, Jr. For 21 years he taught generations of students
        of Baruch to love Literature, to think freshly about their own possibilities,
        and to appreciate the importance of African-American writers."

Addison Gayle Jr.:
"The Consummate Black Critic"
1932–1991

Even when their subject has been literature by Afro-American writers, Black critics have failed to make America see them, to say nothing of reading or hearing their words. The best known critics of Afro-American literature are white. . . . The fact is ironic and regrettable, since Black American critics can offer insights into the language, styles, and meanings intended by Black writers, insights frequently denied to those who have not shared the experience as living as Black people in the United States of America.

—Darwin T. Turner, "Afro American Literary Critics: An Introduction," in Addison Gayle Jr. (Ed.), *The Black Aesthetic* (1972), 57

Black critics have the responsibility of approaching the works of Black writers assuming these qualities to be present, and with the knowledge that white readers—and white critics—cannot be expected to recognize and to empathize with the subtleties and significance of Black style and technique. They have the responsibility of rebutting the white critics and of putting things in the proper perspective.

—Hoyt W. Fuller, "Towards a Black Aesthetic," in *The Black Aesthetic,* 11[1]

The dimensions of the Black artist's war against the society are highly visible. . . . The question for the black critic today is not how beautiful is a melody, a play, a poem, or a novel, but how much more beautiful has the poem, melody, play, or novel made the life of a single black man? How far has the work gone in transforming an American Negro into an African-American or a black man? The Black Aesthetic then . . . is a corrective—a means of helping black people out of the polluted mainstream of Americanism, and offering logical, reasoned arguments as to why he should not desire to join the ranks of a Norman Mailer or a William Styron.

—Addison Gayle Jr., "Introduction," in *The Black Aesthetic,* xviii

The above expressions are of a generation of black literary critics who initiated alternative artistic visions, created aesthetical and cultural redefinitions that denounced assimilationist precepts, and demanded a black art unspoiled by Americanization. In conjunction with large segments of black America, they started to question the efficacy, disadvantages, and the possibility of racial integration, in terms of black cultural hegemony, as well as black self-determination.

For black people in 1965, the American sociopolitical climate demanded that the fight against white racial oppression and injustice would have to move beyond the traditional Civil Rights Movement's philosophy of nonviolent direct action and the tactical sit-ins, boycotts, protests, and marches. "Black Power" was created out of the internecine ideological tensions between the integrationist tendencies of the old guard and the Pan-African-inspired, nationalist-oriented younger generation. While the Black Power Movement[2] raged under the tutelage of the Kwame Tures and Huey Newtons across a racially divided country, its sister movement in black arts[3] was parented by Sonia Sanchez, Amiri Baraka, Ed Bullins, Askia Muhammad Toure, Haki Madhubuti, Sarah Fabio, Hoyt Fuller, Larry Neal, and Addison Gayle Jr. Larry Neal proclaimed black arts the "aesthetic and spiritual sister of the Black Power concept."

Informal networks of black artists in Chicago, Detroit, New Orleans, New York, San Francisco, and many others cities presented the spectrum of political, religious, and cultural doctrines from Black Nationalism to Marxism and from Black Power to Islam endorsed by the black community in its search of the most effective means for resistance and empowerment. But despite their manifold backgrounds, the black writers, poets, dramatists, and critics of the era were rooted in and unified by one shared conviction—the liberation of black people was of unrivaled importance, and the culture needed to collectively construct a destiny separate from that of the American society that had made a tradition of ostracizing and abusing blacks: "For what Black Power means for many Negroes is a repudiation of the values, morals and ethics of a white majority. . . . More significantly, however, Black Power is a creative concept aimed at destroying one hundred years of mental enslavement, distorted images, and meaningless clichés. As such Black Power is a rebuke to white experts who do not realize that to be black in America is to journey through the fiery, labyrinthine corridors of hell; and only those who are capable of embarking on such a journey can fulfill the first requisite for competent scholarship: to know one's subject intimately and well."[4] Moreover, the dominating culture was not going to give up its perception of self as superior without a real, protracted political-cultural fight. The black community had to unify around a different set of sociopolitical, economic, and, above all, cultural principles; thus, the emergence of Black Power.

However perceived, Black Power was a call to action inspiring some to take up arms, compelling others to take on public address, and motivating still others to take to artistic platforms to express their "blackness"[5] through literature, poetry, drama, and art. The initial thrust for the black arts ideological framework emanated from the (revolutionary) nationalist organization, the Revolutionary Action Movement (RAM).[6] It was on this creative and sociopolitical stage that Addison Gayle Jr. found his voice in an artistic and cultural revolution: "No philosophy which does not demand change in the American power structure for the benefit of all the victims can be called revolutionary in any sense of the term. The Black Power proponent, like Nat Turner, realizes this fact, and for this reason he is the only true nihilist in twentieth-century America, believing with his heart, head, and soul that the conditions which exist at this moment are the worst."[7] In conjunction with the revolutionary efforts waged by fellow Black Nationalists, he argued: "For we are today in a Black cultural renaissance, in which, for perhaps the last time, Black Nationalist writers will be able to project—to Black people—a sense of our unique, separate, cultural identity by resolving the dichotomy between art and function, thereby making art functional and relevant to the Black community."[8]

It is important to understand the dynamics of the historical relationship between black authors and white literary critics,[9] because it mirrors that of larger society. Besides pointing out that our literature needs its own critics, Gayle noted, "In the America of today, renowned . . . for its great criticism, Negro critics have died the death of the public and academic anonymity. Why? . . . his [the Black critic's] is the predominant voice in America criticism which calls upon the Black writer to dedicate himself to the proposition that literature is a moral force for change as well as an aesthetic creation. In so doing, he risks not only continued invisibility, but denigrating charges that he does not know enough, coupled with insistent attacks upon his credentials as a critic."[10]

Like his contemporaries, Gayle understood that most white critics[11] historically judged works written by black authors on the basis of their own prejudices and out of fear that their fellow critics would castigate them, more concerned with their own image and maintaining a system of superiority than with the production of truly meaningful, critical literature: " . . . the literary image of the Negro was determined by white authors; and that image was largely comic. Writers rarely conceived of the Negro as a person and thus could not inform him with anything resembling a tragic sensibility: the mask of laughter was no different from the face of the man. So long as the Negro was not human, so long as his suffering was unexplored, the Negro did not threaten assumptions about his humanity; even writers like Twain and Faulkner could not escape the burden of inherited stereotypes. When the Negro himself began to write fiction and poetry, he did not challenge the images that had been created by white authors—for economic as well as social reasons."[12]

Historically, there were, and still are, a body of black authors who long for the praise of the white critics at the expense of their community, arguably because most white critics would never hold a black author with the same regard as the "best" of the white authors. This is a process by which these white critics "who, writing from a liberal and at times sentimental point of view, see masterpieces where none exist at all. Much of this criticism is of little intrinsic significance, and one need not document its unimpressive record; but the dangers can most clearly be measured."[13] Gayle noted, "A Black intellectual searching for some meaning to his existence and endeavoring to make peace within a society which he cannot comprehend, is forced to choose between two opposing philosophies."[14] These philosophies according to Gayle were that of the *accommodationist*[15] and that of the *nationalist*.[16]

Knowing that racism and oppression are rampant and blacks typically bear the burden of these societal ills, some black authors were not deterred from writing in an accommodationist style. Black accommodationists are far more likely to receive praise than those whose political slant is *nationalist*. According to Gayle and other *auteurs* of the Black Arts Movement, black authors who choose the accommodationist philosophy fail to have a connection and understanding of black history and are deluded to think that they could ever be fully included and accepted in the mainstream of American letters and life: "For what is the first obligation of any black writer in this country? It should be towards those from whom he gains his artistic strength; towards those whose lifestyle, language, culture, and history he uses; towards those for whom intentionally, or not, he is viewed as spokesman. And despite his flights into fantasy (those times during which he imagines that he is not a black writer, but an American writer), both the American society and black people know better."[17] It can be argued that some authors choose the method of inclusion to overcome barriers, yet Gayle and others in the Black Arts Movement argued that these authors had internalized the hatred they are the brunt of and had chosen to play it safe within the boundaries of the system. These authors, in Gayle's eyes, are counterrevolutionary and had chosen to become like their oppressor.[18]

Gayle believed that an impenetrable link must be established between the arts and the black community in order to foster social change. He believed, in his contemporary setting, that revolution could take place in all realms—the streets, as well as the galleries and the bookstores,[19] defining a *revolutionary* as one who is "an African in America, knowledgeable of his history and culture, who loves his people and who is determined to fight for their survival as a nation."[20] From this then, it is clear Gayle was not an accommodationist and held firmly to the beliefs in the Black Power Movement, especially ideas regarding self-reliance and self-actualization. With a firm belief in the need for black literary critics[21]—not only to critique the works of fellow black authors but those by white authors as well—he believed that, when it comes to black literary works, opinions of white critics were not as important as the opinions of the black community. Gayle didn't put much credence in the critiques of black literary works by white critics given their tendency to praise the "safe" content in black works and the Eurocentric perspective that some black authors utilized, as opposed to the creative and more socially significant works.[22]

Gayle never suggested that there were no standards for black literature. He believed that the lens through which black literature was viewed had to take into consideration the social and political context that determined its content and style: "When it's white novels that are concerned, then form becomes subsidiary to content. When it's black novels that are concerned—and I can understand it because they can't deal with the content—content becomes subsidiary to form. I keep seeing it in that sense."[23] In his essay "Cultural Nationalism: The Black Novelist in America" he posited, "It is not too far wrong to suggest that Afro-American literature awaits its Whitman. . . . Young black writers for whom the city is home are attempting to create a revolutionary literature[24] which moves beyond Richard Wright,"[25] echoing Wright's earlier assertion that "the Negro writer who seeks to function within his race as a purposeful agent has a serious responsibility. In order to do justice to his subject matter, in order to depict Negro life in all of its manifold and intricate relationships, a deep, informed, and complex consciousness is necessary; a consciousness which draws for its strength upon the fluid lore of a great people, and moulds this lore with the concepts that move and direct the forces of history today; . . . a new role is devolving upon the Negro writer. He is being called upon to do no less than create values by which his race is to struggle, live and die."[26]

A new generation of proactive artists fueled by the spirit of Black Power emerged—such as Henry Dumas, John Oliver Killens, Ed Bullins, Julius Lester, Ishmael Reed, Sonia Sanchez, Amiri Baraka, Dudley Randall, Mari Evans, Haki Madhubuti, June Jordan, Larry Neal, William Kgositsile, John A. Williams, Etheridge Knight, Calvin Hernton, Raymond Patterson, and Nikki Giovanni, to name but a few—to deliberately reject any relationship with the white and European standards that they believed had too heavily influenced (whether true or not) the work of literary and artistic forebears such as Gwendolyn Brooks, James Baldwin, Lorraine Hansberry, and Ralph Ellison. Creatively capitalizing on the socially and politically charged atmosphere that defined the era, the black artist reborn harvested inspiration from the black community it represented and addressed while the leaders of the Black Arts Movement focused not on idle intellectual exchange among themselves but pursued open communication with the black masses.

These new black artists embraced the basic premises of Black Nationalism—that black people are different and unique from other Americans and therefore such difference mandates a different literature. The Black Aesthetic Movement dictated that black literature champions the causes of black people and encourages them to define their own realities. Like the Black Power Movement, its social component, the Black Aesthetic Movement was not just a manner of being oppositional to the white aesthetic[27] and power structure. It was about building a community based upon a common value orientation, while working toward common goals. Subsequently, this renewed effort toward a black cultural autonomy helped spawn institutional resources such as African American Studies departments and black student unions at both historically black and predominately white colleges and universities nationwide. Black theaters, black art galleries, and black community/ neighborhood cultural organizations[28] appeared in black communities to evidence the change and realize the utopian vision for black unity: "To espouse and exult in a Black identity, outside the psychic boundaries of white Americans, was to threaten the pretension and hypocrisies upon which the American ideal rests. To advocate and demand love between one Black and another was to begin a new chapter in American history. Taken together, the acknowledgement of a common racial identity among Blacks throughout the world and the suggestion of a love based upon the brotherhood and sisterhood of the oppressed were meant to transform Blacks in America from a minority to a majority, from world victims to, to use Madhubuti's phrase, 'world makers': 'We want a black poem and a black world,' sang Baraka, 'let the world be a black poem.'"[29]

Breaking with the tradition that encouraged black writers to address a white audience, Gayle urged black writers to address their own people, making no attempt to disguise the hostility they felt. A frequent target was the liberal white intellectual, the sum of whose actions reveal his or her true bigotry. The purpose of such literature, however, is not to convert the liberal but rather, as Gayle suggested, to point out to black people the true extent of the control exercised upon them by American society, in the hope that a process of de-Americanization will occur in every black community in the nation: "So long as he [Black writer] builds his experiences upon a white western intellectual tradition, the Negro author speaks to whites-intellectually: and he speaks to Negroes-intellectually and empirically."[30]

However, it was the opposition to the white critics' artistic influence of habitually strangling black creativity that was one of the most lasting effects of the movement, and the distinction of an intrinsically black aesthetic became the career-defining mission of Addison Gayle Jr. The resulting product of his leadership in literary criticism and social commentaries were several editorial and anthological compilations—*Black Expression: Essays by and about Black Americans in the Creative Arts* (1969); *The Black Situation* (1970); *Bondage, Freedom, and Beyond: The Prose of Black America* (1970); *The Way of the New World: The Black Novel in America* (1975). But the 1971 publication of *The Black Aesthetic* was Gayle's signature work, considered by many to be the (unofficial) manifesto for the Black Arts Movement and its spirit of black self-realization.

The Black Aesthetic is a collection of essays by prominent writers and critics in the Black Arts Movement. Gayle set a combative tone for the book in his introduction, which proclaims that "the serious Black artist of today is at war with the American society." Quoting white critics who suggested black artists fall back on anger and rhetoric to mask literary deficiencies, Gayle refuted these assertions by negating the very premise on which they rest—that white aesthetics are a valid basis for judging black art: "In order to cultivate an aesthetic sensibility, given an oppressive society, the first prerequisite is that the oppression must end; to pave the way for the possibility of an ars poetica, the oppression must end; in more concrete terms, before beauty can be seen, felt, heard, and appreciated by a majority of the earth's people, a new world must be brought into being: the earth must be made habitable and free for all men. This is the core of the Black Aesthetic ideology and forms the major criterion for the evaluation of art: How much better has the work of art made the life of a single human being upon this planet, and how functional has been the work of art in moving us toward that moment when an ars poetica is possible for all?"[31]

Because aesthetics have traditionally been the domain of white poets, philosophers, and critics, Gayle argued that literary standards reflect Caucasian biases in which white is associated with beauty and goodness, and black with evil and ugliness.[32] Many critics asserted that there is no such thing as a white aesthetic and that, as Americans, black writers share with their fellow citizens a common cultural heredity. In a scathing indictment of American values, Gayle denied any association with the mainstream culture, in fact, maintaining that the standards set by white society are irrelevant to black works of art: "A critical methodology has no relevance to the Black community unless it aids men in becoming better than they are.... Not only have such elements been lacking in the critical canons handed down by white aestheticians, but consciously or unconsciously, critics have promoted works that 'keep the nigger in his place.'"[33]

The political and sociological implications of Gayle's philosophy did not escape critics. While most reviewers endorsed the concept of black unity achieved through black literature, several objected to Gayle's vision of separatism in art. Jerry H. Bryant, in the *Nation,* wrote, "A good deal of this irritates me.... No white man, any more than a black man, likes to be told that the color of his skin automatically disqualifies his insight, his sensibility, his intelligence from rendering valid judgments about a whole art.... Many of the Black Aesthetic proponents in this volume seem to be fighting the clubbiness of the white man with a clubbiness of their own.... Furthermore, there is no criticism of any black art in this book demonstrating that reliance on the Black Aesthetic or one's blackness discloses interpretations that can't be got at by honesty, intelligence and earnest and sincere effort."[34] Thomas Lask asked in the *New York Times,* "Why is not the Black experience, repellent, inhuman and destructive as it was, part of the American experience that we all share?"[35] Carolyn F. Gerald raised a similar point in her review in *Negro Digest* when she noted, "Because we begin to realize that contact with white culture has been tantamount to self-annihilation, it is normal that we would try to withdraw ... or ... refuse to adapt any forms from white culture to our own world view. The problem remains that neither position will lead us toward a more mature aesthetic realization, nor comes to grips with the enormous borrowings that have already taken place back and forth."[36]

Despite their objections, reviewers recognized the significance of Gayle's contribution. Bryant applauded the sense of purpose and set of values that black writers bring to American literature at a time when white writers seem aimless and exhausted, admitting forthrightly, "What these essays show is that the core of the Black Aesthetic is political. . . . And some of its most unequivocal spokesmen are not shy in saying so. In its most extreme form it implies Black Nationalism and separatism. . . . The Black Aesthetic is the means by which art accomplishes the political purpose of strengthening the unity between Blacks as a people."[37] Lask concluded that "in spite of its rancor and scorn and in spite of its attempted putdown, reading it is buoyant experience. The sense of engagement, of passionate caring runs like fire through the book. It has the feel of life itself."[38] Gerald pointed out that "without critical forums, such as *The Black Aesthetic,* we will become hopelessly lost in the maze. So we must credit Addison Gayle with a sense of the needs of the time and a talent for doing something about it."[39]

Gayle challenged a tradition of criticism and academic work, which, in his words, "strangled black cultural and literary creativity." The West's dual offensive strategy was to claim *universalism*—which, according to critic George Kent, "packs concealed cultural referents,"[40]—whilst simultaneously engaging in the popularization of negative images, myths, and symbols of African and African American life in the United States: "The Black writer at the present time must forgo the assimilationist tradition and redirect his art to the strivings within the race—those strivings that have become so pronounced here, in the latter half of the twentieth century. To do so, he must write for and speak to the majority of black people; not to a sophisticated elite fashioned out of the programmed computers of America's largest universities."[41]

Therefore, the committed black writer was enjoined by Gayle to accept the proposition that "black is beautiful" and to craft images commensurate with this proposed positive image of a real African American life of struggle and achievement. Gayle envisioned the role of the black artists as "providing us with images based on our own lives," encouraging them to "wage war against every institution which influences the actions of Black people."[42] Gayle's ability to formulate his critical polemics in an elegant, almost 18th-century prose made him a formidable opponent of and equal to his white contemporaries in the status quo and warrants placement in the pantheon of American letters and literary criticism: "Despite the historical fact that assimilation has worked no better for the Black critic than it has for the masses of Blacks. Recognition by the literary establishment has not been granted to those who champion its canons. Criticism written to impress the 'establishment' with the critic's intellectual acuity has not helped black writers either to clarify their literary visions or to move towards an understanding of their function as writers here in the latter half of the twentieth century."[43]

* * *

Addison Gayle Jr. did not deliver fiery speeches designed to rouse the black masses to active resistance. Nor did he lead protest rallies or martyr his personal freedom in support of the Black cause: "I could not allow myself to be distracted by them, could not become so obsessed with the drama of the sixties that I would forsake what, for me, was my life-saving occupation. . . . I praised their actions, worried about their deaths, wrote poems and essays about their gallant struggles; beyond this, I could not, would not go. Being so engaged, so preoccupied with my private war, I could not wholeheartedly join the other, though I was well aware that that too, was my war."[44]

Yet Addison Gayle Jr.'s contribution in his 25–year career as educator and critic, writer and editor was as essential to the reconstruction of black art and culture hampered by a homogenous "American" aesthetic as the teachings and leadership of Malcolm X and the Black Panther Party were to the reformation of America's sociopolitical climate. Addison Gayle Jr. was an activist; his thoughts and theories were nationalistic. According to novelist John A. Williams, Gayle was "the Miles Davis of the literary world. . . . His dedication was complete and unequivocal. If he demanded that writers and scholars act socially responsible, it is because he did not ask anything less of himself. . . . He insisted that Black literary critics and reviewers had as much right to critique writing by whites as whites had always had to critique writings by blacks. Obviously, the *Times* and many other individuals and publications did not agree. . . . There were publications for which he was no longer invited to write, but Addison's integrity remained intact. He could be botheringly insistent about integrity."[45]

Neither the man nor his writings and theories were without flaw. Besides sometimes being without just provocation, dismally morbid, and antagonistic in his pro-black recitations, Gayle also battled ghosts from his past that seemingly affected his work. While *The Black Aesthetic* was a tremendous influence in the black social and artistic revolution and propelled Addison Gayle Jr. to the status of a leading black literary and artistic authority, he endured his own lifelong struggles with demons of inferiority and self-hatred that began as a child and continued to evidence in his successful adulthood. In 1973, at the age of 40, Gayle began to explore the root causes for some of his emotional demons: "My days and nights changed little. . . . I moved always close to mental catastrophe, buttressed by alcohol and tranquilizers. My journal of the period—I managed to keep one, though I wrote only occasionally—is filled with notations on my lack of appetite, my long periods of sleeping, waking, and sleeping again, the decrease of my work output from twelve hours to half an hour daily, from twenty pages to one, and is capped by the admission of June 21, 1973: 'Life in a flux, I am, I know, a sick man. I must unravel my life . . . I must become well."[46] His eventual ascension to the consciousness that birthed *Black Expression: Essays by and about Black Americans in the Creative Arts, The Black Situation, The Black Aesthetic,* and *The Way of The New World: The Black Novel in America* marked a victory in his personal revolution. But remnants of the confessed need to prove his intelligence in compensation for his poor black self-image as a boy were sadly manifested in his work, throughout his life and until the end of his career. Through persistent references to writers such as Wordsworth, Plato, and his favorite, Dostoevsky, all celebrated by white academia as intellectual and literary icons, Gayle demonstrated in essay after essay that he was, until his death, unable to completely step out from behind his personal reservations about ability and self-worth: "Was I really a good writer possessing talent, or was I a fluke, brought into being by the Black Power movement, which caused publishers and editors to acquire Black writers, as pimps acquired women for their stables? Did I deserve my professorship at the university or was this too a gift of the white people, an act of their condescension? I could not answer such questions, and that fact only intensified my fears, adding weight to my anguish."[47]

Born in 1932 and raised in Depression-era Newport News, Virginia, it was the childhood experiences of young Addison Gayle Jr. that would both introduce his intelligence and talent as a writer and haunt him personally and professionally long into his enviable career. As a boy, Gayle simultaneously battled the blatant antagonism between racist whites and blacks, and the color complex that had long been instituted by a white slave system, perpetuated by condescending, lighter-skinned black elitists[48] and socialites, and aggravated by his own arrogance and lack of identity.

A product of the notoriously inferior, segregated Southern public educational system and a victim of a Southern social caste system that pitted blacks against one another according to skin complexion, Gayle used his gifts in literature and language to offset the dark skin and thick hair he detested and set himself apart from other blacks that he resented as unrefined and common: "What did it matter that I enunciated my words more clearly and correctly than other Blacks, that I took two baths a day, that I used deodorant unsparingly, that I avoided slang, spoke softly, walked correctly, that I read books and wrote poetry and novels? It mattered little to the Mrs. Martins and to those like her, no, no more so than what I really thought myself had mattered to the people in Virginia. Like them, Mrs. Martin had been able to telescope beneath the camouflage, to reveal the man hiding within."[49] He admittedly used his intellect not only to genuinely expand his mind, but to belittle and deride other black students not as bright or as gifted as he.[50] By doing so, he elevated himself, in his estimation, above the curse of possessing physical African features and could escape the expectation that he, like most of the other young men in Newport News, would labor after graduation in the local shipyard: "Yes, by becoming a writer, someone whom the white people would notice and recognize, I would be forgiven ugliness. I could compensate for my lack of fine physical features [and] my dark skin would be welcomed, even among the mulattoes."[51] As a man in New York, Gayle only outwardly overcame the color-based and biased apprehensions that plagued him as a child.[52]

Although he lacked the light skin, small lips, and "good" hair of "mulattoes,"[53] he saw his intelligence as a means of mentally aligning himself with them. His desire to relate to a group with conditions similar if not more dubious than that of "pure" blacks dictated the friends he sought, the girls on whom he developed crushes, and the adults he respected and idolized. His infatuation with the local mulattoes affected not just his self-identity but the relationships with his mother, and especially his father, Addison Gayle Sr.: "Thirteen years ago, I sat in my father's small book-filled room looking up at this tired man who, I knew, still bore the scar of my dagger. We did not look each other squarely in the face, perhaps because he realized that there was no longer any equality between us. The roles had been changed. I was on my way to becoming the man that he had never been able to be, free in a way far beyond his wildest expectations. He was old, decrepit, and dispirited, clinging to life with that same selfish tenacity with which he had clung to his dream: that tomorrow the world would be better, and thus a good place in which to die. 'I hope,' he said to me, hardly above a whisper, 'that when you finish your education, you will go out and help your people, educate them, as I have tried to do.'"[54]

Another manifestation of Gayle's turbulent childhood broached in his essays "Dreams of a Native Son" and "Revolutionary Philosophy: Three Black Writers"— both inclusions in his 1970 publication, *The Black Situation*—was his antagonism toward the idea of a living God and any structured religion, specifically Christianity.[55] For whatever reasons, Gayle personally discredited the existence of God and made vociferous references to his lack of faith throughout his autobiography as well. It seems Addison Gayle Jr. might have failed to appreciate an element of the black experience in America critical not only to the perpetuation of the culture itself but that served as the foundation for the very ethics, values, and beliefs of the people. Black people are and have historically been perhaps the most spiritual racial body, and the church has served as a proverbial backdrop for nearly every monumental social, cultural, political, and historical experience witnessed by the black community. With much of black cultural history and aesthetics founded in the Christian church,[56] it seems that Addison Gayle Jr.'s atheism was a stark contrast to the soul of the people about and for whom he wrote.

In the introduction to his anthology *The Black Aesthetic,* Gayle captured the thematic spirit of the movement: "The serious Black artist today is at war with the society as few have been throughout American history"; and "The question for the Black critic today is not how beautiful is a melody, a play, a poem, or a novel, but how much more beautiful has the poem, play, or novel made the life of a single Black man."[57] Although Gayle adamantly refused the role of spokesperson for the black community in general and the writers of the Black Arts Movement specifically, he was, in spite of his reluctance, ultimately responsible for setting a diagnostic and combative tone in his fiery introduction for both the entire book and aesthetic argument: "But the Black Aesthetic has as its fundamental thesis that there are cultural streams dividing blacks from whites in this country. At that point, the idea that the Black Aesthetic will become simply another literary movement misses the point. We're not talking about literary movements in that sense at all. The Black Aesthetic will exist until the liberation of black people is assured, because the Black Aesthetic is as much a political movement as it is a literary one. I think of the Black Aesthetic as nothing more than the cultural arm of Black Nationalism."[58]

Gayle passionately denounced the consumption of black art into the American "melting pot" and specified the dangers of applying white cultural standards to black cultural production. "White aesthetic values have habitually encroached upon black culture, and like any other foreign psychological or genetic element infiltrating a collective body, many in the black community have succumbed to the ensuing disease while others have worked consistently in rejection of white beauty and art." Facing a barrage of criticism by naïve and oversighted reviewers who claimed that no white aesthetic even existed and the creation of a "black" one would be nothing more than unwarranted separatism from a greater society, Gayle responded, "To be an American writer is to be an American and, for Black people, there should no longer be honor attached to either position."[59] He charged against the existing white aesthetic its irrelevance to the black community and intentional degradation designed to undermine and dismiss black talent while smothering the black masses into prescribed roles: "Due in part to what these negro 'experts' have told them and to their own propensity for taking their truth as the truth for all men, white people have codified my life in terms of their own. They have separated me from the Blacks who riot, differentiated me from those in the ghetto who did not pull themselves up by their bootstraps, bestowed upon me the honorific title of 'Negro Intellectual.'"[60]

In his address to fellow writers and his reading audience, Gayle implored others to throw off the shackles of white oppression, embrace the richness and inherent beauty of the black culture, and make no attempt to disguise hostility and resentment against those who for so long practiced their own legal separatism through tyranny and violence: "My essays on literature and social events had brought me enemies, newer ones, whom I welcomed because they could be dealt with on intellectual grounds. They were primarily whites—critics and social commentators on Black literature and life—whom I had purposely, selectively, set out to attack. Essays were, as I saw them, weapons, more immediate and direct than fiction, and, perhaps, still smarting under my guilt from [being] absent from the Black struggle during most of the sixties, I surrendered the ambition to write fiction and dedicated myself to non-fiction prose, successfully joining others to wage warfare against white arrogance [and] hypocrisy."[61] Two consistent themes therefore permeate the collected works of Addison Gayle Jr.: the necessity of black literature and art to reflect the reality of black life, and the urgency to create an autonomous black aesthetic disencumbered and unhampered by the influences of European hegemony.

Attacking the symbolic perpetuation of white or light as purity, beauty, and innocence, and the traditional use of either black or darkness to embody evil, menace, and death, Gayle contends in "Cultural Strangulation: Black Literature and the White Aesthetic" that these representations are distinct configurations of racist white principles dating to early Greek and Roman civilizations. Thus, the notions of black versus white, inferior versus superior have been revisited time and again as the learned definitions of good and evil, beautiful and ugly, civilized and savage, even heaven and hell. Black art, in turn, has been regarded as substandard and unrefined because the art of the people captured the distinct physical and cultural attributes of those people.[62]

Therefore, according to the white aesthetic, not only is the dark art an abomination, but the people the art reflects are, under the scrutiny of their white standards, hideous, unsightly, and strange. Gayle argued that like other art forms, literature too suffered from the constraints imposed by white principles, and in a zealous conclusion urges his counterparts toward black artistic reformation: "For the crisis of bowing to other men's gods and definitions has produced a crisis of the highest magnitude, and brought us, culturally, to the limits of racial Armageddon. The acceptance of the phrase 'Black is Beautiful' is the first step in the deconstruction of the old table of laws and the construction of new ones, for the phrase flies in the face of the whole ethos of the white aesthetic. . . . Black critics must dig beneath the phrase and unearth the treasure of beauty lying deep in the un-toured regions of the Black experience—regions where others, due to historical conditioning and cultural deprivation, cannot go."[63]

Gayle's 1971 challenge to his reading audience and his literary colleagues is still relevant, because individuals continue to allow themselves to be degraded, dismissed, and devalued as black persons—shedding dignity and cultural identity in an effort to forge themselves into the round, gaping abyss of Americanization: "And do you know and believe still that it is the job of the writer, the poet, to make manifest this dignity, to imprison in words for the coming generations, the records of human triumphs and victories as well as setbacks and defeats? Do you know that it is the writer's job to define in the human personality, the heroic and enduring, thus assuring faith in the possibilities of the future? . . . Before we can bring the new world into being, we must shed the garments of the old."[64]

What has become of the cultural and aesthetic revolution designed in part by Addison Gayle Jr. and promoted by those passionate, enthusiastic activists of the Black Arts Movement? The present and immediately preceding generations of the 1980s and 1990s have seemingly dropped the proverbial torch passed from their proactive forbears. Houston Baker makes the astute observation, "One result of a class-oriented professionalism among Afro-American literary critics has been a sometimes uncritical imposition upon Afro-American culture of literary theories borrowed from prominent white scholars. . . . When such borrowings have occurred among the generation that displaced the Black aesthetic, the outcome has sometimes been disastrous for the course of Afro-American literary study."[65]

Addison Gayle's subsequent contribution to *The Black Aesthetic* and the concluding essay in the anthology, "The Function of Literature at the Present Time," is also a seemingly timeless work, which, despite its relevancy to the artistic landscape more than 40 years ago, still addresses issues very real to the contemporary black community. "The urge toward whiteness in the race, as evidenced by Fridays, past and present, has prevented the creation of a nationalistic art," he noted, continuing, "Moreover, because of it, Black writers have postulated an imaginary dichotomy between art and function that had made much of the writing of Black authors irrelevant of the lives of Black people."[66] The tendency of artists to polarize their work and the community not only still exists, but is manifold. This concern is prevalent to date, with the publication of volumes of books composed largely of fiction that contributes little more to the black community than the published work of another black-faced author and listing of a black name among the weekly best-sellers.[67]

Novels like Zora Neale Hurston's *Their Eyes Were Watching God,* Wallace Thurman's *The Blacker The Berry,* James Weldon Johnson's *The Autobiography of an Ex-Coloured Man,* Richard Wright's *Native Son,* Ann Petry's *The Street,* Ralph Ellison's *Invisible Man,* Gwendolyn Brooks's *Maude Martha,* John A. Williams's *The Man Who Cried I Am,* Paule Marshall's *The Chosen Place, The Timeless People,* Chester Himes's *If He Hollers Let Him Go,* Toni Morrison's *Sula,* John Killens's *Youngblood,* Ernest J. Gaines's *The Autobiography of Miss Jane Pittman,* and James Baldwin's *Go Tell It On The Mountain* are inarguably fictional masterpieces; they were also designed to convey a significant, influential message to their black audiences through the imaginary. They sought "to function within [their] race as a purposeful agent." They protested against racism, lynchings, and social, political, and economic inequality in American society. The characters in their novels depicted and represented courageous and strong black men and women who valued black cultural values in various life situations.

In addressing the issues of the Black Arts Movement and his generation's shortcomings, the arguments of Addison Gayle Jr. have also provided direction and inspiration to those following his precedent for black solidarity. Gayle would note that "there is no correlation to be made, however, between the black sycophants of the present time and the novelists, past and present, and thus, the renaissance wrought by the Black Aestheticians, the new sense of historical vision in the works of black poets and novelists, the progress made in gaining control over the images, symbols, and metaphors of black life are threatened by men and women of little talent and far less intelligence, whose objective is not to inform but to disparage, not to create positive images, but to recreate negative ones of the past, to glamorize the hustler and the hipster, to elevate ignorance and downgrade intelligence in a world in which intelligence, knowledge, and understanding are paramount for a people who must yet break the bonds of oppression."[68]

* * *

The death of Addison Gayle Jr. in 1991, like the passing of many of his colleagues[69] and revolutionary cohorts,[70] has left an ever-widening chasm unfulfilled by contemporary black writers, academics, and editors either unwilling to risk the classification of a "radical,"[71] too afraid to endanger their long-pursued contracts or tenure, or too concerned with the opinions of white "peers" to watch them shift nervously during discussions on race relations in the academy or the black community. The black liberal and conservative (critic), like his or her white counterparts, will be caught off guard when the "revolution" is resurrected, when the torch is again picked up to raze against the social, political, and cultural assaults still being waged on black people. In order to realize the objectives and goals initiated by the black activists during the 1960s and 1970s that would raise the community to a conscientious, solidifying reaffirmation of culture, the lessons of the past must be revisited.

What Addison Gayle Jr. contributed in his lifelong career as a literary activist for the black condition is a series of tangible guidelines[72] designed for the progression of the culture of black people. What he meant to the establishment of a measure of beauty indigenous to the black people who played such a pioneering role in the formulation of the art, music, and literature emulated to this very day by other cultures and ethnicities, even within America, and especially within America, is incomparable.

Despite the objections of reviewers and critics, his presence is in fact credited by all for instituting the effort to build and develop a black artistic consciousness easily recognizable in our sculptures, paintings, literature, poetry, and music, as well as standards of beauty. Gayle summed up his philosophy best when he stated, "What this means is that the Afro-American novelist must be part politician, part sociologist, part historian and part novelist. . . . But the function of the novel, the function of the Afro-American writer as I see it, is a political function, and that is the liberation of the minds of black people in this country. It's a weapon, and I make no bones about it."[73] For Gayle, in order for real, positive, lasting changes to occur, blacks must take control of their destiny as a unified group, and there should be no self-inflicted segregation between the various components of the community: The poor are no less important than the wealthy; the women[74] are just as important as the men; and, as Gayle might argue, the writers and artisans are as key to the movement as the politicians and academicians. At a time when black writers were dismissed for their radical ideas and concepts, Addison Gayle Jr. was applauded for his sense of purpose and a set of values he brought to define and guide the Black Arts Movement.

The "consummate critic," Gayle is considered by many in African American letters as the intellectual and theoretical architect of the Black Aesthetic Movement and forerunner of new black literary criticism. My wish is that Gayle be rightly recognized as one of the most important contributors to African American arts and letters of the 20th century. Gayle would wish for us to (re)devote our efforts toward honoring black pride, dignity, and values to achieve the goals of the Black Power, Black Arts, and Black Aesthetic Movements. Then, in the words of this generation, he too would be given his "props."

*   *   *

The Addison Gayle Reader comprises six sections designed to provide a comprehensive representation of virtually all of Gayle's writings.

The first, "Black Situations," focuses on the bulk of social essays Gayle wrote between 1967 and 1980, many of them published in *The Black Situation,* and range from commentary on the impact of racism in America, the racial conditions facing black students at predominately white American universities (especially at City College of the City University of New York) and the historical influence of Black Power politics on black creative production.

"Black Aesthetics," contains Gayle's foundational writings on the philosophy of the black aesthetic and examines his evolving views on the historical relationship between white racism, American arts and letters, and black literature as well as the function of black literature and aesthetics in the Black Arts Movement.

"Literary Criticism," section three of the reader, features critiques, interpretations, and analyses of the writings of African American authors such as Richard Wright, James Baldwin, Gwendolyn Brooks, and Paul Laurence Dunbar. In addition, the section defines the role of black literary criticism in relationship to cultural nationalism, as well as examines discussions of setting new standards in judging black literature.

Section four, "Book Introductions, Forewords, and Prefaces" consists of the prefatory material Gayle wrote for numerous novels and plays by prominent black arts artists such as Woodie King and John Oliver Killens, as well as the numerous anthologies he compiled and edited.

"Book Reviews" contains some of Gayle's most pertinent and trenchant review essays, in which he judges the value of works by black authors such as George Cain, William Demby, Brenda Wilkinson, Gayl Jones, and Ishmael Reed, according to the new standards and criteria set by the Black Arts Movement, responses to reviews of his own works, and his infamous letter to the *New York Times,* where he resigned as a contributing book reviewer.

Section six, "Autobiographies" includes excerpts from Gayle's autobiography, *Wayward Child: A Personal Odyssey,* a rare interview, and a number of autobiographical essays.

Notes

1. Two of the more recent examinations into the origins and evolution of the Black Arts and Aesthetics Movement may be found in James Smethurst, *The Black Arts Movement: Literary Nationalism in the 1960s and 1970s* (Chapel Hill, N.C.: University of North Carolina Press, 2005), esp. 23–99, 247–318; and Lisa Gail Collins and Natalie Crawford, eds., *New Thoughts on the Black Arts Movement* (New Brunswick: Rutgers University Press, 2006).

2. Long seen as an "offshoot" or "rupturing" of the more traditional, mainstream modern Civil Rights Movement, the sociopolitical concept of Black Power has been consistent in the history of black people in America since at least the 18th century. For the purposes of this work, Black Power can be defined as "a call for black people in this country to unite, to recognize their heritage, to build a sense of community. It is a call for black people to begin to define their own goals, to lead their own organizations and to support those organizations. It is a call to reject the racist institutions and values of American society." Stokely Carmichael and Charles Hamilton, *Black Power: The Politics of Liberation in America* (New York: Random House, 1967). See also John H. Bracey Jr., August Meier, and Elliot Rudwick, eds., *Black Nationalism in America* (Urbana: University of Illinois Press, 1972); Robert Allen, *Black Awakening in Capitalist America* (Trenton, N.J.: Africa World Press, 1990); William Van DeBerg, ed., *Modern Black Nationalism: From Marcus Garvey to Louis Farrakhan* (New York: New York University Press, 1997).

3. Perhaps the most salient definition of the interconnectedness between black cultural and artistic production and (Black Power) politics can be found in the work of Larry Neal: "Black Art is the aesthetic and spiritual sister of the Black Power concept. As such, it envisions an art that speaks directly to the needs and aspirations of Black America. In order to perform this task . . . a radical reordering of the western cultural aesthetic . . . a separate symbolism, mythology, critique, and iconology . . . relate broadly to the Afro-American's desire for self-determination and nationhood. Both concepts are nationalistic. One is concerned with the relationship between art and politics; the other with the art of politics." See Larry Neal, "The Black Arts Movement," *Drama Review* 12, no. 4 (1968).

4. Addison Gayle Jr., "White Experts—Black Subjects," in *The Black Situation,* ed. Addison Gayle Jr. (New York: Doubleday, 1969), 8. While Gayle was focusing on black literary criticism from his viewpoint, his audience was not, I believe, black people primarily, but rather his audience was white literary critics to whom he wished to inform, teach, and provide truths they could not obtain in their own institutions because those institutions neither valued black literary criticism nor attributed any value to black works of literature.

5. See Raymond Betts, *The Ideology of Blackness* (Lexington, Mass.: D.C. Health, 1971); George Kent, *Blackness and the Adventure of Western Culture* (Chicago: Third World Press, 1972).

6. See Kalamu ya Salaam, "R.A.M. Spanning the Period: From the Mid 1960s to the 1970s," *Chickenbones: A Journal;* see also Kalamu ya Salaam, "Historical Overviews of the Black Arts Movement," in Cathy N. Davidson, Linda Wagner-Martin, Elizabeth Ammons, Trudier Harris, Ann Kibbey, Amy Ling, Janice Radway, eds., *The Oxford Companion to Women's Writing in the United States* (New York: Oxford University Press, 1995).

7. Addison Gayle Jr., "Nat Turner and the Black Nationalists," in *The Black Situation,* 69.

8. Addison Gayle, Jr., "Black Power and Existential Politics," in *The Black Situation*, 75.

9. "In recent years (especially since the 1960s), the white critic has found himself increasingly under attack. His motives and qualifications for the assessment of Black literature has been called in question." C. W. E. Bigsby, "Introduction," in *The Black American Writer, Volume I: Fiction*, ed. C. W. E. Bigsby (Baltimore: Penguin Books, 1969), 1.

10. See "The Black Aesthetic, Defender/Opponent" *Black World* 24, no. 2 (Dec. 1974): 31–43.

11. The majority of mainstream criticism of African American literature as early as William Dean Howell and throughout the 20th century has been written by white critics such as Irving Howe, Theodore Gross, Robert Bone, Edward Margolies, Herbert Hill, Norman Mailer, Richard Gilman, Robert Penn Warren, and others who assumed and judged the content and purpose of writing by black authors according to the standards of the dominating white culture. See Robert Bone, *The Negro Novel in America* (New Haven, Conn.: Yale University Press, 1958); Edward Margolies, *Native Sons: A Critical Study of Twentieth Century Negro American Authors* (New York: Lippencott, 1968); Herbert Hill, *Anger and Beyond: The Negro Writer in the United States* (New York: Harper Collins Publishers, 1966); Norman Mailer, *The White Negro* (New York: City Lights Books, 1957); Robert Penn Warren, *Who Speaks for the Negro* (New York: Random House, 1984).

12. Theodore Gross, "Our Mutual Estate: The Literature of the American Negro," in *The Black American Writer, Volume I: Fiction*, 52.

13. Ibid., 55.

14. Gayle, "Nat Turner and the Black Nationalists," 12.

15. See "Addison Gayle, Jr." in *Contemporary Authors* (Gale Group Database, 2000). Paraphrasing Harold Cruse's opinions about the relationship between black writers and their white critics, Bigsby states, "According to Cruse the 'criticism of Negro writing is mainly the Negro's responsibility'—an attitude which is supported to some degree by the white former literary editor of the *New Republic*. Cruse is so violent in his demands that he comes close to seeing white criticism as an arm of political policy," Bigsby, "Introduction," in *The Black American Writer, Volume I: Fiction*, 20. For the original, see Harold Cruse, *The Crisis of the Negro Intellectual: From Its Origins to the Present* (New York: Random House, 1967), 182. See Gayle, "Nat Turner and the Black Nationalists," 64–70; Addison Gayle, "The Harlem Renaissance: Towards a Black Aesthetic," *Midcontinent American Studies Journal* 11(Fall 1970): 78–87.

16. See Richard Gilman, "White Standards and Negro Writing," in *The Black American Writer, Volume I: Fiction*, 35–50, where he comments on the evolution of black nationalism in black writing: "These Negro writers I speak of take their blackness not as a starting point for literature or thought and not as a marshaling ground for position in the parade of national images and forms, but as absolute theme and necessity . . . as weapon and seat of judgment, as strategy and outcry, source of possible rebirth, data for a future existence and agency of revolutionary change. For such men and women, to write is almost [a] literal means of survival and attack, a means—more radically than we have known it—to *be*, and their writing owes more, consciously at least, to the embattled historical moment in which American Negroes find themselves than to what is ordinarily thought of as literary expression or the ongoing elaboration of ideas." See also Earnest Mkalimoto, "Theoretical Remarks on Afro-American Cultural Nationalism," *Journal of Ethnic Studies* 2, no. 2 (1974): 1–10.

17. Addison Gayle Jr., "The Functions of Black Criticism at the Present Time," in

Houston A. Baker Jr., *Reading Black: Essays in the Criticism of African, Caribbean, and Black American Literature* (Ithaca, N.Y.: Cornell University Africana Studies and Research Center, 1976), 37–40.

18. See Addison Gayle Jr., *The Way of the New World: The Black Novel in America* (New York: Anchor/Doubleday, 1975), esp. 117–155, 246–267.

19. Since the 19th century, there has been a long and storied extra-academic, autodidactic tradition in many Northern and Midwestern black urban communities, rooted in the activities by black church book clubs, cultural literary organizations, reading groups to public speakers, and independent bookstores that helped fuel the Black Arts Movement as centers of political, artistic, and community information for gathering, organizing, and disseminating their ideas. Perhaps the best known of these were Lewis H. Michaux's National Memorial Bookstore, Richard B. Moore's Frederick Douglass Bookstore, and Liberation Books, as well as the Harlem History Club (later renamed the Blyden Society), all located in Harlem. See Colin Beckles, "Black Bookstores, Black Power, and the F.B.I.: The Case of Drum and Spear," *Western Journal of Black Studies* 20, no. 2 (1996): 63–71; W. Burghardt Turner, ed., *Richard B. Moore, Caribbean Militant in Harlem: Collected Writings, 1920–1972* (Bloomington: Indiana University Press, 1988); Elinore Des Vereney Sinnett, *Black Bibliophiles and Collectors: Preservers of Black Culture* (Washington D.C.: Howard University Press, 1990); Earl E. Thorpe, *Black Historians: A Critique* (New York: William Morrow and Co., 1971), 143–154; Cruse, *Crisis of the Negro Intellectual.*

20. Addison Gayle Jr., "The Politics of Revolution—Afro-American Literature," *Black World* 22 (June 1972): 12.

21. Although extremely variegated in their approaches and beliefs, there is in fact a long tradition of black literary critics, who, as early as the beginning of the 20th century were concerned with the development of standards for African American literature as well as the representation of black culture and history. Accompanied by many well-known, celebrated black authors such as Wallace Thurman, Langston Hughes, James Baldwin, Richard Wright, Zora Neale Hurston, and Jesse Fauset, essays by black literary critics Benjamin Brawley, William Stanley Braithwaite, James Weldon Johnson, W.E.B. DuBois, Arna Bontemps, J. Saunders Redding, James Emanuel, Sterling Brown, Alain Locke, Hugh Gloster, George Kent, Darwin Turner, Sterling Plumpp, Richard Long, Arthur P. Davis, Blyden Jackson, Nick Aaron Ford, and Nathan Scott argued that cultural production by black people in America was unique and different because of the historical and sociopolitical conditions, circumstances, and situations black people in America faced, and helped to construct a corpus of work for Gayle to draw from in formulating his ideas.

22. See Addison Gayle Jr., "Letter to the Editor," *New York Times Book Review,* March 13, 1972. Gayle's letter, which was a direct response to an article by John Leonard (February 13, 1972), levied a commentary in regard to the racial exclusivity he felt existed within the ranks of literary criticism, especially in regard to the way the *Times* approached black literature. Gayle felt that while white critics were given any and all opportunity to review and discuss black literature that the paper did not afford their black counterparts the same. See also, Addison Gayle Jr., "Interview with Saundra Towns," *Black Position* 2 (1972): 20–25.

23. Gayle, "Interview with Saundra Towns," 18.

24. Although the formal start of the Black Arts Movement is dated as 1965, with the establishment of the Black Arts Reperatory Theatre/School (BARTS) by Amiri Baraka (LeRoi Jones) after his move to Harlem from Greenwich Village, beginning as far back

as 1960, black artists, writers, poets, and playwrights began establishing the political-cultural framework that would coalesce into the Black Arts Movement. In 1960, On Guard for Freedom, a black (inter)nationalist literary organization had been founded by Calvin Hicks, and members included Harold Cruse, Amiri Baraka (then LeRoi Jones), Tom Dent, Nannie and Walter Bowe, and Rosa Guy, among others. From On Guard, in 1962, evolved Umbra, an organization spearheaded by Dent, James Johnson, Calvin Hernton, Ishmael Reed, musician Archie Shepp, Lorenzo Thomas, and Askia Muhammad Toure, to name a few. Umbra produced the journal *Umbra Magazine,* and was the first post–civil rights artistic and literary group led by blacks to define and make distinct their own voice from that of the prevailing white literary establishment. The merging of a black-nationalist-themed activist thrust with a (primary) artistic orientation caused a split in the organization, after which a number of former members, including Toure, Yusef Ruhman, South African Keorapetse "Willie" Kgositisle, formed the Uptown Writers Movement, performing all over Harlem. They later joined forces with Baraka and BARTS. Important to note, however, is that while much of the focus on black arts has historically been centered or confined to New York, it was a movement that was nationwide, with points of confluence in Chicago, Detroit, New Orleans, and San Francisco, where the work of Sonia Sanchez, Ed Bullins, Baraka, Marvin X (Marvin Jackmon), Jimmy Garrett, and Nathan Hare led to the establishment of the first African American Studies Department in 1968. See Larry Neal and Amiri Bakara, *Black Fire: Anthology of Afro-American Writing* (New York: Morrow, 1968); Abby Johnson and Ronald Maberry Johnson, *Propaganda and Aesthetics: The Literary Politics of Afro-American Magazines in the Twentieth Century* (Amherst: University of Massachusetts Press, 1979).

25. Addison Gayle Jr., "Cultural Nationalism: The Black Novelist in America," in *The Black Situation,* 208.

26. Richard Wright, "Blueprint for Negro Literature," in *Within the Circle: An Anthology of African American Literary Criticism from the Harlem Renaissance to the Present,* ed. Angelyn Mitchell (Durham, N.C.: Duke University Press, 1994), 102. The essay was originally written in 1937 and appeared in the journal *New Challenge* (11) and was expanded into a longer version for the edited periodical *Amistad I,* edited by John A. Williams and Charles F. Harris.

27. Gayle provides a clear explication of the historical relationship between so-called universal notions of beauty, art, and aesthetics and white cultural nationalism: " . . . the white aesthetic, despite the academic critics, has always been with us . . . poets of biblical times were discussing beauty in terms of light and dark—the essential characteristics of a white and black aesthetic—and establishing the dichotomy of superior *vs.* inferior which would assume body and form in the 18th century. Therefore, more serious than a definition, is the problem of tracing the white aesthetic from its early origins and afterwards, outlining the various changes in the basic formula from culture to culture and nation to nation . . . calling attention to the necessity of a more comprehensive study encompassing all of the nations of the world" (emphasis mine). See Addison Gayle, "Cultural Strangulation: Black Literature and the White Aesthetic," in *The Black Aesthetic,* 38–39.

28. See John Runcie, "The Black Culture Movement and the Black Community," *Journal of American Studies* 10, no. 2 (1976): 185–214; William Van DeBurg, *A New Day in Babylon* (Chicago: University of Chicago Press, 1992), 248–280; Komozi Woodard, *Nation Within A Nation: Amiri Baraka (LeRoi Jones) and Black Power Politics* (Chapel Hill: University of North Carolina Press, 1999).

29. Addison Gayle Jr., "Gwendolyn Brooks: Poet of the Whirlwind," in *Black Women Writers (1950–1980): A Critical Evaluation,* ed. Mari Evans (New York: Anchor/Doubleday, 1984), 86–87.

30. Gayle, *The Black Situation,* 192. See "Addison Gayle, Jr." in *Contemporary Authors.*

31. Addison Gayle Jr., "Afterword," in Addison Gayle Jr., ed., *The Black Aesthetic* (New York: Anchor/Doubleday, 1972), 313. See "Addison Gayle Jr. in *Contemporary Authors* (Gale Group Database, 2000).

32. Since the New Negro Movement and Harlem Renaissance, African American theorists, writers, and artists have fought to redefine the characteristics associated with the concept of "black" and "blackness," to ascribe positive associations with the term(s). See Ossie Davis, "The English Language is My Enemy," in *Language, Communication, and Rhetoric in Black America,* ed. Arthur L. Smith (New York: Harper & Row, 1972); Richard B. Moore, *The Name "Negro," Its Origins and Evil Use* (New York: Afroamerican Publishers, 1960); Raphael P. Powell, *Human Side of a People and the Right Name: The Great Book of New Education* (New York: Philomen, 1937). See "Addison Gayle, Jr." in *Contemporary Authors.*

33. Addison Gayle Jr., "Introduction," in *The Black Aesthetic,* xxxiii.

34. Jerry Bryant, "The Black Rebellion in Literature and Music," *Nation,* April 24, 1972, 535. See "Addison Gayle, Jr." in *Contemporary Authors.*

35. Thomas Lask, "Why Don't You Just Get Lost," *New York Times,* January 23, 1971, 27.

36. Carolyn Gerald, "The Black Writer and His Role," *Negro Digest* 18 (Jan. 1969): 42–44.

37. Bryant, "The Black Rebellion in Literature and Music," 535.

38. Lask, "Why Don't You Just Get Lost," 27.

39. Gerald, "The Black Writer and His Role," 42–44.

40. In discussing the *problematique* of the American literary *universalism,* Kent goes on to say, "And the problem with *universalism* is that its current use misdirects the writer and the critic, leads to vague abstractions (Man, the Human Condition). . . . Any universalism worthy of recognition derives from its depths of exploration of the density, complexity, and variety of a people's experience—or a person's. It is achieved by going down deep—not by transcending. Often, *universalism,* to the degree that it is being genuinely recognized, is simply an acknowledgement (by whites) that 'others' now have achieved the psychological readiness for entrance into the work." George Kent, *Blackness and the Adventure of Western Culture* (Chicago: Third World Press, 1972), 11.

41. Addison Gayle Jr., "The Function of Black Literature at the Present Time," *The Black Aesthetic,* 393.

42. Gayle, "Cultural Nationalism," 205.

43. Addison Gayle Jr., "The Function of Black Criticism at the Present Time" in Baker, *Reading Black,* 37–40.

44. Addison Gayle Jr., *Wayward Child: A Personal Odyssey* (New York: Anchor Press/ Doubleday, 1977), 96.

45. John A. Williams, "Addison Gayle: The Consummate Critic," *Black Books Bulletin* 1, no. 3 (1991): 14.

46. Gayle, *Wayward Child,* 136.

47. Gayle, *Wayward Child,* 125.

48. See Lawrence Otis Graham, *Our Kind of People: Inside America's Black Upper Class* (New York: Harper Collins, 2000); Kathy Russell, with Midge Wilson and John Hall,

Color Complex: The Politics of Skin Color Among African Americans (New York: Anchor/
Doubleday, 1993).

49. Gayle, *Wayward Child,* 65.

50. In the first chapter of his autobiography, *Wayward Child,* he recalls his experiences
in his black Virginia elementary schools: "I believed that I was better, much better. None
of the others—not even the mulattoes (but I never thought I was better than they were!)—
had read Dostoevsky . . . And the others, even the mulattoes, listened to me and noticed
me when I told them the story of *Crime and Punishment.*" Ibid., 5.

51. Ibid., 75.

52. Contrary to the logical conclusion, it was not white teachers, students, or college
admission committees Addison Gayle Jr. sought to impress with his expansive grasp of
literature and history. He ironically expressed hatred toward white people, even though he
was far into his teenage years before he had any real interaction with them. Instead, using
his self-education as leverage, he feverishly sought the acceptance and recognition of his
peers and elders from the black mulatto community whom he idealized as the epitome
of beauty, intellect, and success. See Ibid., 18–37.

53. One of the clearest examples of the social variants of race, class, and gender inter-
secting in American arts and letters was through the creation of the "mulatto" character,
beginning in the 19th century. Beginning first as a trope of abolitionist writing to elicit
sympathy from white readers, the mulatto figure was a nearly white, racially mixed, woman
who had been tragically victimized by slavery. It further degenerated into a cruder stereotype of the "tragic mulatto," whose fate was predictable, melodramatic, and often reflected
that of the general white female victim of sentimental romantic literature, along with the
internalization of white standards of beauty. Many African American authors employed it
to focus on the broader elements of self-hatred and a color caste system that was rampant
in many black communities. However, for Gayle it was an issue he dealt with throughout
his life. See Ibid., 81, 121.

54. See Addison Gayle Jr., "Black Fathers and Their Sons, I/II," in *The Black Situation,*
152. Despite the fact that Addison Gayle Sr. was a superior intellect, had played a credible
role in the social and political landscape of the local black community, and was obviously
respected among his peers, who expressed their admiration to his resentful son, Addison
Gayle Jr. found himself, for several reasons, constantly at odds with his father. In his biased
comparisons of his own father to those of his mulatto friends, Addison Gayle Sr. fell short
of his son's unarticulated definitions of achievement. See Gayle, *Wayward Child.*

55. Through his writings, Gayle confessed on more than one occasion his subscrip-
tion to atheistic beliefs, but nowhere in his essays or his autobiography did he cite the
cause(s) for his severance from spiritual doctrines. Many times, however, he referenced
his mother's fervent Christianity, resulting in her insistence upon his church attendance
as a child: " . . . I could not go to see my father until one o'clock, not, that is, until I had
gone to church, paid homage to the God of my mother. "See Gayle, *Wayward Child* and
"Black Fathers and Their Sons, I."

56. How then, can Gayle, as a critic of black literature and the promoter of a black
aesthetic, absently dismiss religion in statements such as "Those who told us the weak
would inherit the Earth are here revealed for the liars they are."? The liars to whom Gayle
so passionately refers are the authors of Pslam 37:11 ("But the meek shall inherit the Earth,
And shall delight themselves in the abundance of peace") and Matthew 5:5 ("Blessed are
the meek, For they shall inherit the Earth"), both of which proclaim the scriptures that
Gayle rashly determined to be untruths.

57. Gayle, "Introduction," in *The Black Aesthetic*, xviii.

58. Gayle, "Interview with Saundra Towns," 12.

59. Ibid.

60. Addison Gayle Jr., "The Children of Bigger Thomas," *Liberator*, August 1968, 5.

61. Gayle, *Wayward Child*, 118.

62. Prior to the Black Aesthetic Movement, more than anyone else, the work of Zora Neale Hurston and her arguments regarding the uniqueness of black art and culture and the relationship between creative production and black cultural tradition challenged both the black and white misconceptions of black life. Much of Gayle's work, especially his arguments in *The Black Aesthetic* and *The Way of the New World: The Black Novel in America*, echoes Hurston's contention(s). See Zora Neale Hurston, "Characteristics of Negro Expression," in *Negro: An Anthology*, ed. Nancy Cunard (London: Wishart & Co., 1934; rpt, New York: F. Unger, 1984]).

63. Gayle, "Cultural Strangulation," 46.

64. Gayle, *Wayward Child*, 166.

65. Baker continues, "In the recent criticism of Afro-American literature, there have been two distinct generational shifts. Both have involved ideological and aesthetic re-orientations, and both have been accompanied by shifts in literary-critical and literary-theoretical paradigms. The first such shift occurred during the mid-1960s. It led to the displacement of what might be described as integrationist poetics and gave birth to a new object or scholarly investigation. . . . A new order of literary-critical and literary-theoretical thought—one which sought to situate higher-order rules of the Black Aesthetic within a contemporary universe of literary-theoretical discourse—was signaled in the mid-seventies not only by Neal's essay, but also by symposia and conferences on the Black Arts that occurred throughout the United States." Houston Baker, "Generational Shifts and Recent Criticism of Afro-American Literature," *Black American Literature Forum* 15 (Spring 1981): 3–21.

66. Gayle, "The Function of Black Literature at the Present Time," 393. See also Amiri Baraka's *Raise, Race, Rays, Raze: Essays Since 1965* (New York, Random House, 1971), 129.

67. The bulk of black fiction produced by the contemporary generation is not unlike the works of many blaxpoitation authors of the late sixties and early seventies (e.g., Donald Goines, "Iceberg" Slim), as well as "drugstore" and "dime store" novelists whose work fails to express any sincere attempt to convey appreciation of the traditional or aesthetic sensibilities of their forebears.

68. Addison Gayle Jr., *The Way of the New World: The Black Novel in America* (New York: Anchor/Doubleday, 1975), 382.

69. Virtually all of Gayle's contemporaries in literary and artistic criticism have since died, including Hoyt Fuller, Margaret Walker, June Jordan, Audre Lorde, Toni Cade Bambara, Larry Neal, George Kent, Darwin Turner, Raymond Patterson, Henry Dumas, James Baldwin, Gwendolyn Brooks, Tom Dent, Etheridge Knight, and Calvin Hernton.

70. In addition to the untimely deaths of Huey P. Newton, Kwame Ture/Stokely Carmichael, Bayard Rustin, George Jackson, Fred Hampton, Eldridge Cleaver, Robert F. Williams, Fannie Lou Hamer, and James Forman, to name but a few, others who were activists during the time have either been effectively silenced or suffered irreparable damage.

71. Most recently, Amiri Baraka, designated poet laureate of the state of New Jersey came under fire for his poem "Somebody Blew Up America," and the state assembly voted to eliminate the position altogether rather than have him serve out his term. See Laura Mansnerus, "New Jersey Assembly Votes to Cut Embattled Poet's Job," *New York*

Times, July 2, 2003, B2. Incidentally, Baraka's work in terms of upholding the legacy of the Black Arts Movement has been *nonpareil,* and he remains the single most influential black radical in American letters today.

72. The bulk of Gayle's work can be viewed as a continuation in a long tradition of a series of social and artistic essays by black artists and writers who seek to forge viable, alternative theoretical approaches to interpreting and critiquing black creative production. See Langston Hughes, "The Negro Artist and the Racial Mountain," *Nation* no. 122: 1926; W. E. B. DuBois, "Criteria for Negro Art," *The Crisis: A Record of the Darker Races* no. 32: October 1926; Richard Wright, "Blueprint for Negro Literature," *New Challenge* no. 11: 1937.

73. Gayle, "Interview with Saundra Towns," 6.

74. Much as Gayle criticized white critics during the Black Arts Movement, and largely as a result of the very issues he raised in the call for an aesthetical reorientation of black cultural and artistic production, there has been the emergence of a cadre of black female literary critics and theorists—represented by the likes of Hortense Spillers, Hazel V. Carby, Nellie McKay, Trudier Harris, Carolyn Fowler, Eleanor Traylor, Thulani Davis, Sherley Anne Williams, Beverly Guy-Sheftall, Mae Henderson, Barbara Christian, Frances Smith Foster, Claudia Tate, Cheryl Wall, Mary Helen Washington, bell hooks, Barbara Smith, Patricia Bell Scott, and Gloria Hull—who posit not only that black women have been historically misrepresented in American arts and letters but have been omitted from virtually all discussions regarding the history and culture of black people. See Gloria T. Hull, Patricia Bell Scott, and Barbara Smith, *All the Women Are White, All the Blacks Are Men, But Some of Us Are Brave* (New York: Feminist Press, 1982), 157–208; Barbara Christian, *Black Women Novelists: The Development of a Tradition, 1892–1976* (Westport, Conn.: Greenwood Press, 1980); *Black Feminist Criticism: Perspectives on Black Women Writers* (New York: Pergamon Press, 1985); Deborah McDowell, *Changing Same: Black Women's Literature, Criticism, and Theory* (Bloomington: Indiana University Press, 1995).

THE ADDISON
GAYLE JR. READER

PART 1

Black Situations

> Everyone in the village knows my name, though they scarcely ever use it, knows that I come from America—though this, apparently they will never believe: black men come from Africa—and everyone knows that I am the friend of the son of a woman who was born here, and that I am staying in their chalet. But I remain as much of a stranger today as I was the first day I arrived, and the children shout Neger! Neger! as I walk along the streets . . . In so far as I reacted at all, I reacted by trying to be pleasant—it being a great part of the American Negro's education (long before he goes to school) that he must make people "like" him. This smile-and-the-world-smiles-with-you routine worked about as well in this situation as it had in the situation for which it was designed, which is to say that it did not work at all.
> —James Baldwin, "Stranger in the Village"

Like most black literary critics during the mid to late 1960s, Gayle did not limit himself to strictly literary criticism. The first section, "Black Situations," focuses on social essays Gayle wrote between 1965 and 1970—many of them published in his *The Black Situation* (1970). These social essays range from commentary on the impact of racism in America, the racial conditions facing Black students at predominately white American universities/colleges (especially at City College of the City University of New York) to the historical influence of Black Power politics on black creative production.

Gayle's heightened sense of racial consciousness surrounding the socio-political and cultural struggles facing black people at the time the essays in this section were written is evident, beginning with "White Experts—Black Subjects" and ending with "Dreams of a Native Son." In "Letter to a White Colleague," "Black Power and Existential Politics," and "Black Power or Black Fascism?" Gayle attempts to explicate his reasons for supporting Black Power politics as well as divulge the problematic elements he sees in the black leadership sector embracing and advocating (wholesale) integration: "The dedication must be to race. There must be an unashamed, unabashed commitment to race that admits the differences between blacks and whites, and explores these differences."

In "White Experts—Black Subjects" and "Racism and the American University," Gayle forcefully contends that the idea of American education has been anything but liberal, and instead promotes either white racial and cultural domination or subservience to the nation.

CHAPTER 1

White Experts—Black Subjects

(1967)

The first expert on Negro life was the plantation owner, who was called upon to evaluate his subject for pragmatic reasons. Viewing the Negro slave on the public auction block, the owner inspected his merchandise closely, feeling a plump limb here, probing for a broken one there, always cognizant that upon his expertise rode hundreds, sometimes thousands of dollars. Later the plantation owner made further evaluations: Which of his slaves would make the best house hands, which the best field hands? Which would require, to quote Frederick Douglass, "the most breaking" (the process of beating recalcitrant slaves into submission)? Which male would mate best with which female to produce the best stock? And finally, how much food and clothing would be necessary to sustain the slave during a long day in the fields?

Together with his colleagues, in group meetings or similar gatherings, the owner participated in seminars on the Negro wherein each owner contributed the facts revealed through his own scientific investigations. The subject himself took no part in these seminars. He had had little to say, thus far, concerning the voluminous amount of information supposedly held by other people concerning him. His job was merely to prove the experts correct: to be a good field or house hand as designated; to provide healthy offspring; to subsist on his allotted rations; and once broken, to remain broken.

To prove the experts correct, however, was ofttimes impossible. Frederick Douglass and Nat Turner, to name but a few, did not long remain broken. Some field hands were ill-equipped for their chosen tasks, as were some house hands. And the attempt at genetic experimentation ended, often enough, in such failure as that depicted by Saunders Redding in *No Day of Triumph*: "They kept us locked up in at ol cabin three nights." Julie Lively, a former slave confessed to Redding: "In the mornings they let me out an I done my work roun the house, but for three nights ol Doctor Smith lock me up with Bailey . . . [But] I didn't have no baby under Bailey."

Such failures, however, did not shake the confidence of the experts. As slavery became a national issue, experts on the Negro increased in number, gathering into their ranks politicians, ministers, intellectuals, and scholars.

The most famous of these was Harriet Beecher Stowe, whose novel, *Uncle Tom's Cabin,* became an immediate best seller. The Martin Luther King of her day, Mrs. Stowe set out to awaken the conscience of the nation to the evils of slavery and, in so doing, she created a character whose stereotype survives in the minds of Blacks and whites to the present day. Mrs. Stowe writes of Tom: "He was an expert and efficient workman in whatever he undertook; and was both from habit and principle, prompt and faithful. Quiet and peaceable in his disposition, he hoped, by unremitting diligence, to avert from himself at least a portion of the evils of his conditions."

Tom, then, is good personified, and Mrs. Stowe constructs her novel around the good–evil conflict by depicting the pious, loving black slave in symbolism so angelic that no such character could have existed upon earth. That Mrs. Stowe was able to palm such a fantasy off on her generation was remarkable in light of many contradictory examples presented by Negro slaves themselves. There was little of Tom's piety or love in Nat Turner, Denmark Vesey, Harriet Tubman, or Frederick Douglass.

Laudable though Mrs. Stowe's motives may have been, her portrait of the Negro was no more authentic than that of the plantation owners. She created the Negro not as he was, but as she wished him to be. Having no knowledge of what it meant to be either a slave or a Negro, Mrs. Stowe relied upon her creative imagination to probe dimensions beyond the depths of imagination. Like her present-day descendants, she viewed her Black subjects with the expertise of her own white experience and produced not real live people, but grotesque stereotypes, bestowing upon them her ideals, ethics, and values.

Present-day experts on the Negro differ from Mrs. Stowe only in methodology. Armed with the tools of research, financed by large foundations, and often members of Negro organizations, the modern-day Mrs. Stowe pretends to scrutinize his subject from an objective vantage point. No objective analysis of the Negro, however, can suffice. A present-day Joseph K, the Afro-American lives in the center of that dark mysterious abyss peopled by fantasies and illusions, where he is confronted by frustration and insecurity, and plagued by demons of persecution and oppression; and only those who are capable of plunging into the abyss, of living in that hell of anguish, despair, and pain; only those who are capable of dredging from the dank, musty interiors of their own wretched souls a vision of the human spirit in agony those and only those are capable of viewing the Black soul, stretched across the torture rack of history, in all of its power, beauty, and despair.

This is to say that most whites are incapable of portraying Blacks with any degree of reality. "The Negro," writes Saunders Redding in *On Being Negro in*

America, "lives constantly on two planes of awareness"; and Redding's statement has its antecedent in W. E. B. Du Bois' classic analysis of the Negro psyche in *The Souls of Black Folk:* "One ever feels his twoness; an American, a Negro; two souls, two thoughts, two unreconciled strivings; two warring ideals in one dark body, whose dogged strength alone keeps it from being torn asunder."

Like slavery, such a dimension constitutes a barrier beyond which the white mind cannot peer. The complexities of being Black in the American society are so varied that few Negroes are capable of interpreting them; and the day-by-day experiences of the average Black in America are such as to belie belief. These are unique experiences, and the Negro's reactions to them are unique reactions, owing little to white idealism, morality, or ethics. "This society," James Baldwin wrote to his nephew, "set you down in the ghetto to die"; and all Negroes have been enclosed in some such ghetto. To scale the walls of this ghetto, therefore, requires the kind of experience peculiar only to the ghettoized.

Negroes, at long last, are beginning to realize this fact. Lawrence P. Neal in an essay, "White Liberals vs. Black Community," in the July 1966 issue of *Liberator* magazine, asserts: "Presently, the dissemination and examination of the main features of Afro-American life and culture are not in the hands of Black people, but rather, in that of whites." And Neal further suggests that: "Black Intellectuals and artists cannot expect any meaningful development until we assume more power over all aspects of our culture. . . ."

No such realization, however, has occurred to whites. In an anthology, *Essays of Our Time,* edited by Leo Hamalian and Edmond Volpe, the essays selected to deal with Negro life are written by two white men: Norman Mailer and John Fischer. "Norman Mailer," write the editors, "has said that the function of a writer is to see life 'as others do not see it.' As the 'White Negro' indicates, he performs this function brilliantly and provocatively. . . ." Mailer's motives, like those of Mrs. Stowe, are perhaps laudable, yet his portrait of Negroes is no less fanciful or imaginative, and in no way does Mailer demonstrate the ability to see black life as others do not see it.

"Knowing in the cells of his existence that life was war," Mailer reports, "the Negro (all exceptions admitted) could rarely afford the sophisticated inhibitions of civilization, and so he kept for his survival the art of the primitive, subsisted for his Saturday night kicks, relinquishing the pleasures of the mind for the obligatory pleasures of the body. . . ." But Mailer's imagination knows no boundaries; and later he sees the Negro "forced into the position of exploring all those moral wilder-nesses of civilized society . . . [and] not being privileged to gratify his self-esteem with the heady satisfactions of categorical condemnation [the Negro] chose to move instead in that other direction . . . in the worst of perversion, promiscuity, pimpery, drug addiction, rape, razor-slash, bottle break, what have you. . . ."

One is never insulted by Mailer, only slightly amused. Yet one must question the judgment of scholars who fail to examine the credentials of their experts.

Mailer's characterization of Negroes, far from being unique, has its genesis as far back as the first white anthropologist. Moreover, the underlying thesis of Mailer's essay differs little from the underlying thesis of Richard Wright's *Native Son*. In Native Son, Wright suggests that the resurrection of white America rests upon the resurrection of America's Bigger Thomases, who are relegated to the bottom of the societal heap. Mailer, likewise, sees the Negro as the Christ-figure, resurrecting America by transforming her into the Negro's image.

Wright, however, living continually in that world of pessimism spurned by hatred, fear, anger, and bitterness which is a part of every Black's experience, could not possibly, for long, entertain such abstract ideals. Mailer, on the other hand, securely ensconced behind a white barricade, can continue to look at the Negro through eyes tinged with optimism.

If the choice of the "White Negro" by Mailer evidences an error in selection, the choice of John Fischer's "What the Negro Needs Most: A First Class Citizen's Council," represents a serious error in judgment. Whereas Mailer amuses, Fischer insults, not by his statements but, instead, by the posture of moral physician to the Negro people which he assumes for himself.

"So long," admonishes Fischer, "as the Negro blames his plight entirely on circumstances, history, and the white man, he is going to stay in that plight. He will get out of it only when he begins to change his circumstances, make new history, and shoulder a bigger share of responsibility for the fix he is in." (One is reminded of the story of the lynch mob, enjoying its beer and hot dogs, as the body of a Negro swung in the breeze. "You think God will blame us for this?" asked one of the members. "Hell no!" replied another, "God knows it's that nigger's fault for lettin' himself be lynched.")

Yet Fischer's prognostication is worse than his diagnosis. What the Negro needs, according to Fischer, in order to become a respected member of the American society is "A First Class Citizen's Council. Its purpose [will be] the genuine integration of Negroes into the normal streams of American life." A stream is like a looking glass. One looks at the images reflected and determines in his own mind whether they are true or distorted. Despite occasional ripples in "the normal stream of American life," Fischer concludes that the overall image reflected is that of an integrated society. Because the image is true for him, he assumes that it is true for most men. Such an assumption, fathered by arrogance, must be vigorously contested. Like his predecessors, Fischer has assumed that his truth, arrived at through years of bathing uninhibited in the "normal stream of American life," is one that Negroes can honestly embrace.

To many Negroes, however, the "normal stream of American life" is a stream polluted beyond the bounds of purification. It is a stream reeking with hatred and bigotry, and festering with racism. The waters of the stream have been muddied by one hundred years of lynching, brutalization, persecution, and every form of degradation which man has been capable of performing upon his fellow man.

The stream flows from North to South, East to West, and its waters are the same on each shore. To suggest that the Negro desires a cleansing bath in such a stream could be suggested only by one who has little knowledge of the complex psyche of an American Negro.

"We have been believers," intones Margaret Walker. But today, the belief in an America freed of racism, fear, and hate is a belief which few Blacks have either the time or interest to indulge in. Instead, Negroes, Ralph Ellison excepted, are more likely to be asking with the late Lorraine Hansberry, "Who wants to integrate into a burning house?" But, specifically, the black intellectual is more apt to be engaged in the serious task of reevaluating the values administered to him by such physicians as John Fischer.

The result can only be a repudiation of these values. Looking into the Black psyche, exploring the souls of his own people, and recognizing the distorted images propounded by experts from the plantation owners to the twentieth century physicians, the Afro-American has begun to piece together out of his own varied experiences, "a new table of the laws"; and, in so doing, he has begun to recognize the great disparity between his aspirations and those attributed to him by others.

That such a reevaluation is taking place in the Black ghettos of this country will come as a shock to many white experts. Many will recoil from the fact that the subject no longer looks at America through the rose tinted glasses of his ancestors. Even more will fail to understand why Frantz Fanon's *The Wretched of the Earth* has become a best seller among Black intellectuals; and none will wish to believe that, despite the opinion polls, the most powerful idea in the Black ghetto today is the idea of Black Power.

For what Black Power means for many Negroes is a repudiation of the values, morals, and ethics of a white majority. Black Power means an exploration of Black culture; and the realization that within this culture are those values which a Black minority can, without shame, embrace. Black Power means the coming together of men as brothers, in a way far beyond white America's ability to comprehend.

More significantly however, Black Power is a creative concept aimed at destroying one hundred years of mental enslavement, distorted images, and meaningless clichés. As such, Black Power is a rebuke to white experts who do not realize that to be Black in America is to journey through the fiery, labyrinthine corridors of hell; and only those who are capable of embarking upon such a journey can fulfill the first requisite for competent scholarship: to know one's subject intimately and well.

CHAPTER 2

Letter to a White Colleague

(1971)

Dear Lennie:

I have decided to answer your private letter in a public manner. I will attempt to do so without betraying the more personal aspects of your correspondence. My decision is dictated by my intention to clear the air—which has become excessively polluted over the past year—between myself and my friends, both Black and white. I find that their central questions are the same as those that you have put to me so eloquently in your letter; therefore in answering you, I shall also be answering them.

I said that this is a public correspondence, which does not mean in any sense that it is not personal. Indeed, it is personal in the most important sense, that is to say, it is personal to me. The statements I make here are binding upon no other Black man in this country, for, to paraphrase Saunders Redding, I have never been enclothed with the authority to speak for others. The truths which I record here are, therefore, personal—and may or may not find accord in the hearts and minds of the millions of Black people across this country.

I am very adamant on this subject. I remember all too well my own bitter and violent reactions to those who, over the years, have pretended to speak for me. I was incensed, I suppose, partly at the egotistical assumption of that being who attempts to speak for twenty million other beings; but more so, I was incensed because the society, in listening to such egoists, was communicating with me by proxy, which is the most effective way of denying my humanity.

I know that the society could not deal with twenty million of us individually. However, it could have dealt with us long ago (as it must deal with us now—as men of differing temperaments, persuasions, and ideologies in those areas so fundamental to our destiny), and listened, not to the solitary voices of specially bred and selected nightingales, but to the many voices of discord among us—those which dared to articulate truths profoundly believed by many of us. Such voices are not comforting to hear; they speak of turmoil, strife, and war, and herald the possible coming of an apocalypse; none of which is designed to placate or comfort white America.

But Americans desire comfort above all else, and it is indeed more comforting to listen to Booker T. Washington, A. Philip Randolph and Martin Luther King, rather than to W. E. B. Du Bois, Marcus Garvey and Malcolm X. And today, it is far more comforting to listen to the "responsible Negro leaders" than to those leaderless millions who voice their grievances in actions and terminology so different from that of their purported leaders.

It is this, I suppose, which causes me to be pessimistic. In the wake of the riots of the previous summer, the society still does business with the old combine that has returned nothing but empty dividends to its stock holders. Each Molotov cocktail thrown in the ghetto, each store looted, each sniper's bullet expended, gives the lie to the many assertions of Negro leaders, and reveals their influence to be bankrupt and impotent among all, save those who insist that Armageddon can be staved off forever by accepting myths and half truths which offer no more than a few months—maybe years—of comfort.

This is the best way of approaching your question regarding the importance of Black Power. Because white people have preferred to deal with certain members of the Black community as stand-ins, a serious effort at dialogue among Black people was averted. This was accomplished in the most insidious manner. That individual who more nearly articulated the grievances of the Negro upper and middle classes and who was, in turn, willing to accept the dictates of the white power establishment became the liaison between the Black and white communities. With this position went power, prestige, and money.

Such men, as Booker T. Washington proved, were remarkably capable of using that power; more often than not to stifle dissent. Washington, for example, marshaled, often by cajole and threats, the support of every Negro newspaper in America, with the exception of one, in his debate with W. E. B. Du Bois—and only Du Bois' strength and determination enabled him to carry on a struggle against such power.

Again, Malcolm X, who sought to produce among Black people a dialogue centered around those affairs which concerned Black people, was vilified in the Black and white press and attacked by Negro and white leaders. In both instances, such actions were possible only because the Negro leaders had the unqualified support of the white liberal establishment, which knew only one thing about the projected dialogue—that it would not be very comforting to white people.

What, you might ask, does this have to do with Black Power? For those of us who have demanded a debate between the ideological opponents in the Black community—Integrationist versus Nationalist—Stokely Carmichael's injection of the phrase Black Power into the civil rights struggle was the most important accomplishment in the history of this ideological war in the last one hundred years.

I am, to be sure, a Nationalist. And there has never been a day in my life during which I did not want Black Power. I did not call it by that name, and I had no formula by which it could be attained. Yet I thought seriously about it and I seriously desired it. When, at the age of six, I read articles and saw pictures of a Black man who had been lynched in Mississippi, I wanted Black Power. Much later, at the age of twenty-seven, when I was slapped by a racist policeman in New York City, I wanted Black Power. And even in college, confronting a professor who openly professed his bigotry, I wanted Black Power. In other words, I wanted some way of controlling my own life; but most of all, I wanted some way of controlling those who had control of my life.

I was not alone. Many young people thought as I did. Yet we had no forum and we had no power. The society dictated what it wanted to hear and appointed those whom it wished to hear. We, made impotent, carried on debates among ourselves, always in small numbers, knowing that the thoughts which other men attributed to us were false; but knowing too that we were powerless to expose the fallacy. The things which we say now with impunity, we did not say then—not entirely out of fear, but more out of a sense of futility. We were the young Davids. And the Goliaths were far too powerful.

What were the things we said? We uttered the same "Get Whitey!" and "Hate Whitey!" epithets which you so deplore today. Make no mistake about it: "Get Whitey!" is not a new phrase, not the exclusive property of poor and uneducated Negroes. Few of us in this country have not voiced such an epithet. And fewer still have not meant it. For my part, I do not apologize. This is a stage through which I had to go. To bypass it would have meant to deny a fundamental part of my experiences in this country and to be less than honest with myself. I could not realize that my hating whitey was unimportant to my functioning as a man until I had admitted that I hated him.

Today, more of us are admitting this fact, and perhaps here lies, if anywhere, our salvation. Once this step is passed, we can then proceed to the central issue confronting us as Black People—serious debate on what our collective goals are. We will no longer allow men who hold monologues only with themselves to decide for us the most important goals of our lives. This has been the situation since the close of the Martin Delany–Frederick Douglass debates one hundred years ago. Since that time Black people have been unable to carry on a debate among themselves, partly because white power would not allow it, but also because the time was not appropriate for an alternative to integration to be publicly enunciated and wholeheartedly supported.

The rebellions in the ghettos of the past summer brought about the appropriate time; and Black Power was born as the other alternative. Never mind that white people do not understand Black Power; never mind that many Negroes oppose it. Certainly it's no panacea, no magic key to Canaan, no paved stairway to paradise; but one thing it is; it is the other alternative to propositions put forward, debated and agreed upon by men who had little rapport with those whom they purported to represent. As such, it is a guarantee that, for some time to come, there will be a serious debate among Black people in this country concerning their own aims—one could expect far less from a slogan. No one has a right to expect more.

This leads me to your central question. What part can an individual such as yourself play at the present time? Granted that you are sincere; that your motives are impelled not by a search for power, nor by a wish to purge yourself of some unknown guilt; that you honestly see in your Jewish experience correlatives which enable you to equate, to a degree, some aspects of that experience with mine. What is your role at the present time?

Let me be very blunt. The answer, as far as the present dialogue is concerned, is that you have no role. This does not mean that you should not continue to teach Black children, to write about those conditions which produce poverty, crime, and rebellion; it does not mean that you should cease to work in any area or any organization dedicated to the alleviation of those ills which we both deplore. But it does mean that in the area of dialogue between Black man and Black man, none of your credentials—neither your sincerity nor your humanitarian interests—make you eligible to be a participant. Let me put it very candidly: The necessary requirement for participation in the dialogue is a black skin.

Many of us are convinced that the present debate will at long last clarify the goals of Black people in this country—not just for a few, but for many. It is incumbent then, upon every Black person, no matter his ideological persuasion, to take an active part in the debate. But the debate is a private, personal, family affair. A husband and wife, so to speak, are attempting to work out their relationship vis-à-vis the outside world. And only the husband and wife can determine what that relationship will be.

This should come as no surprise to you. It was Moses, a Jew, who had to lead the Israelites out of Egypt. The job could not have been entrusted to an Egyptian, no matter the degree of his sincerity.

It is Catholics who must choose a new pope, make dogma, pass on ideology, and formulate principles for the Catholic Church. No outsider can perform this function, for no outsider can have that information, varied as it must be, which will allow him to comment intelligently on issues important to the future of the Church. Indeed, the counsel of an outsider may be more disruptive than constructive.

Such is the position of the present debate in this country. It is one which, in the last analysis, only the Black people can resolve. White people, no matter how sincere, must remain outside as mere, interested observers. This is as true for white people who support Black Power as it is for those who oppose it. We demand the right to choose for ourselves the paths we wish to follow, whether integration or segregation, peace and tranquility or continued hostility and war, whether mutual co-operation or separate, individual endeavor. But most important, we reserve the right to choose those who will represent us, who will be emissaries from us to you.

Carmichael is correct. There will come a time in our history when dialogue between white and Black people is possible. But that time can come only when we ourselves have "Taken care of business," that is, transformed our inner dialogues into a realistic monologue, decided upon our goals, and are ready to present America with a list of demands that all of us accept—in the main, if not specifically.

Should we not have such an exclusive dialogue? It would seem to me that only men of narrow vision would attempt to prevent it. Yet, such men there are. One reads, in the white and Black press, daily vilifications of Black Power proponents and gross distortions of their ideas. We are constantly informed that "Black Power is disruptive," that it is separatism, that, in the words of one Negro leader, "it is an invitation to suicide." This may well be. But who can decide for another people, even and specially in the case of suicide, whether or not the act is desirable? Only the people themselves can decide. And they can decide only when men of differing ideas are willing to submit those ideas—in the market place, as it were—to be debated, agreed upon or rejected.

Let us suppose, for example, that the "Responsible Negro Leaders" who continue to see integration as the goal for twenty million people do not have faulty vision. Let us suppose that they are correct when they argue that the majority of Black people in this country support their "moderate leadership." What then should those leaders do? They should be willing to subject their ideas to the supreme test; that is, take their postulations to the Black churches, lodge halls, colleges, and ghettos of this country; and there have their positions authenticated by the only ones capable of honestly doing so; Black people themselves. This has not happened.

Negro leaders prefer instead to address their appeals to white America, to gain support from such men as you, who have no way of determining whether their claims are legitimate or not. Like Booker T. Washington, they exercise their power in the most negative way, attempting to silence those who refuse to accept their truths as gospel.

Some whites have been trapped into supporting them in this endeavor. The N.A.A.C.P. had every right to invite Vice President Humphrey to its annual convention. Vice President Humphrey had no right to castigate Black Power. In so doing, he infringed on a private debate—one of which he knows very little—and thus lost a chance at statesmanship—the chance to welcome a vigorous, healthy debate among a people seriously concerned with their own destiny.

Do not, my friend, make this mistake. At this stage of race relations, young and inquisitive men are conscientiously seeking a way out of that Götterdämmerung which confronts us. They are by no means homogeneous. There are great differences among them. But only when these young men have seriously debated the issues can there be any hope that you and I may live in a society where men are respected on the basis of individual worth.

Their task is difficult enough. It must not be made more so by men who are primarily interested in their own comfort. For these young men have arrived at a truth which their elders have not yet been able to grasp: In a society where some men are regarded as less than human, there should be no comfort for anyone. No, not for you, or for me. And certainly not for those millions of Americans whose only concern about the destiny of their country is reflected when they awaken one morning and are forced to dig themselves out of the rubble of a Detroit or a Newark.

Comfort is a luxury which must be earned, and America has not earned the right to be comfortable. Those of us who support Black Power are determined that she will not be until she has earned the right. This is, perhaps, a dangerous position for a member of a predominantly white university faculty to take in these troubled times. Yet, so high are the stakes that those of us who have welcomed in the new dialogue are prepared to make any sacrifice. But more important, we are prepared to bring the issues to debate; to bring our ideas before Black people and, if they are rejected, we are equally prepared, in the words of the poet, "to accept the verdict and the doom assigned."

CHAPTER 3

The Cabinet of the Mind

(1967)

Lately, I have sensed a strange uneasiness on the part of friends who still retain intellectual and physical contact with me. Some have read my writings and openly questioned my sanity. Others have spent long hours debating with me, attempting to convince me that I am a fraud, that I do not harbor the anxieties and hates which, in their opinion, make me a twentieth century monster. One suggested, quite seriously, that I leave the country.

These friends, Black and white, view me as a special kind of subversive agent, no challenge to them physically but an undeniable affront to their positions as intellectual prophets. Conceiving of Afro-Americans as things, these people have constructed special cabinets of the mind in which we, like fragile glassware, are assigned specific positions. One's position is dependent upon his success—or purported success, which means the same thing—in the American society. Having attained some measure of success, a higher shelf in that special cabinet of the mind has been reserved for me than, for example, some of my best friends in the ghetto.

I am an expensive piece of glassware, not because of my present success—professors are a dime a bushel—but, I am told, because of my promise, and my youth which makes it probable that my promise will be fulfilled. My only task, I am constantly reminded, is to rip away that aberration, that incestuous cancer, that demonic something within me which makes me fill the ears of my listeners with curses, the hearts of my well-wishers with despair and the minds of my sympathizers with anger and scorn. Still, I am an expensive piece of glassware, an object of value used only for the best courses—those dished out by Negro leaders and the society pages of Negro magazines. In all such propagandistic feasts I am exhibited—cautioned to be moderate, at least for now—praised for my unscarred countenance, marveled at for my sheen and polish ("you speak very well," remarked a lifelong liberal) and hailed for my endurance.

Lately, however, I have become restive, begun to fidget on the shelf, unable to remain moderate, and begun to suggest that my special niche is one of which

I am undeserving, that I belong on the bottom rung with the scarred, cracked, dust-colored glassware. At this point my friends start to drift away. For their "center," as Yeats says, "cannot hold." The demon within me cannot be exorcised, not by any medicine which they have so far produced; and this demon existing in me, threatening to erupt, is enough to bring chaos if not destruction to their mythological cosmic apparatus.

They have been the victims of myths. They have hypnotized themselves into believing myths not of their own concoction and certainly not of mine. Beset by stereotypes foisted upon them by the white world, like the early Black writers, they have attempted to destroy the stereotypes, not through reason and logic but, instead, by offering stereotypes of their own, usually more grotesque and imaginary than the ones they were designed to replace.

Denouncing Harriet Beecher Stowe's Uncle Tom as unrealistic and insulting, my friends have turned to the pages of Booker T. Washington's autobiography, echoing Washington in asserting that: "No white American ever thinks that any other race is wholly civilized until he wears the white man's clothes, eats the white man's food, speaks the white man's language, and professes the white man's religion." The New Negro, therefore, is no Uncle Tom, no cowering, pitying, tender-hearted old slave, "quiet and peaceable in his disposition, hoping by unremitting diligence to avert from himself at least a portion of the evils of his condition."

Instead, this New Negro is obsessed with his own peculiar manifest destiny, as prescribed by Washington during one of those interminable excursions into the backwaters of the South to bestow a benevolent smile upon the "culturally deprived masses": "The work to be done in order to lift these people up seemed almost beyond accomplishing—I wondered if I could accomplish anything, and if it were worthwhile for me to try."

Now begins the philosophy of the cabinet of the mind: the process of categorizing people as though they were pieces of china—a process begun in slavery where, like objects, Black men were shelved in terms of house niggers and field niggers, good niggers and bad niggers, objects usable either in the master's house or in the fields. The New Negro, however, like Washington, is capable of divining his own worth, of evaluating himself and thereby setting himself off from other Afros, thus refining that process begun by the white master. More sophisticated than Uncle Tom and more fearful of Black Simon Legrees than white ones, the New Negro has dedicated himself to mapping out a blueprint by which he and his white friends may live in peace and harmony. Though the stance is new, the old voice of the "great educator" echoes like a ventriloquist from their mouths: "—any individual who (learns) to do something better than anybody else—(learns) to do a common thing in an uncommon manner—(has) solved his problem regardless of the colour of his skin, and in proportion as the Negro (learns) to produce what other people (want) and must have, in the same proportion (will) he be respected."

The salient feature of the new stereotype was respect. Uncle Tom was pitied, mostly by white people who knew too little of Afro-Americans to discern fact from fiction, but what the New Negro demanded was respect, albeit a respect predicated upon the belief that in that vast world of inequality there were, still, some Black men who were more equal than others, and that these few could be granted their due recognition by appeals to a mythological American conscience. Washington's statement was written for white men and delivered before white men who Washington took to be representative of the American conscience. And it was these white men who chose Booker T. Washington as a Negro leader, thus elevating him above other Negroes and making him the personification of the New Negro, the living exemplar of the new stereotype.

The New Negro occupied the top shelf in that cabinet of the mind. He became the man with whom to do business, the man to control the Black militants—those insane men within the race who believed that the American conscience was more oriented toward the philosophy of the Ku Klux Klan than that of Jesus Christ. As a result, there came into being a combination of white and Negro leaders joined together by a pernicious contract which segregated Negroes within the race, forcing the dissidents underground, stifling debate, and destroying the Afro-American's initiative to assert himself individually.

In a Southern town, not atypical, my father and a small group of radicals confronted this combined white and Negro power in the summer of 1938. In the local shipyard, the sole reservoir for Black labor, Black workers were subjected to every conceivable form of indignity. They were forced to drink from segregated water fountains, to use dirty segregated latrines, to stand in segregated waiting lines for lunch; they were given the dirtiest jobs, fired more frequently, and hired at lower wages than whites of lesser schooling or experience.

This was possible because the shipyard had its own bargaining union which was more representative of the interests of management than of workers, Black or white. A mulatto was the liaison between the Black workers and the white management, though a white liaison official had as much power, or more, over the fate of Black workers as the mulatto official. In fact, Negroes often admitted that they would rather take their grievances to the white official from whom they could gain a measure of sympathy not forthcoming from the mulatto.

Together with an outside force, my father sought to have a national union, which would be more representative of the workers, substituted for the old management-dominated union then in existence. Black laborers, though not a majority, constituted a large percentage of those eligible to vote; if they were to combine with those whites who were aware of the advantages of an outside arbitrating body, the election could be won. To this end, rallies were held throughout the city, and many on both sides of the issue believed that the days of the old shipyard union were numbered.

None however, and especially the opponents of the old union, had accurately gauged the power—nor the determination to use that power—of the white and

Negro leaders in the city. In a post election letter, written to a friend in New York, my father explained: "Negroes, most of whom I had known all my life came to me, in shame, telling me that they knew we were right, but R—(the Negro banker) threatened to foreclose mortgages if the new union won, and to evict from those pigpens of homes around Warwick Avenue those who voted against the old union. Ministers denounced the new union from the pulpit—some seeming to discover for the first time that I am a Communist and labeling the new union Communist also—as troublemaking and anti-Christ. I would bet my life that the telephone lines between B—(the white dentist, Mayor of the city) and W—(a Negro leader) were on fire. We can do little here until we destroy this damn alliance."

Despite the costs to the masses—and the costs were great indeed—such alliances helped disseminate the stereotype of the New Negro. Whites were enamored of the patient, reasonable, rational Negro who realized that his fate was bound inextricably to that of whites and that furthermore some measure of recognition, of status, was available to those who adopted the Protestant Ethic, who struggled to disengage themselves from the uncivilized, culturally deprived masses. True to the Washington philosophy, such men pulled themselves up by their own bootstraps, showed what could be accomplished in America despite the racial band, displayed the frontier spirit, and emerged from the jungle of the past as living testaments to the future.

Such Negroes, victims of their own egotism, saw themselves in the role of Franklin Frazier's stereotype: descendants of those who "had been enslaved, and had suffered many disabilities since emancipation, (yet who) on the whole were well off economically, had gained civil rights, and had improved their status. Therefore what had happened to them during slavery, which was after all a mild paternalistic system, should be forgotten along with the other injustices which they have suffered since. Moreover, their economic position was superior to that of other peoples of the world, especially the colored peoples."

The significance of such a portrait of the Afro-American escapes no one. For in the first place, such portraits perpetuate the division between the house niggers and the field niggers, between the Black blessed and the Black damned, and construct status hierarchies by which men, robbed of human dignity, can find some modicum of security, retain some semblance of respect for their own worth as men, can sit securely upon some mountain top and peer down condescendingly upon their less fortunate fellows. Moreover, like all stereotypes, this new evaluation of the Black man serves to deny the realistic portraitures of the past, to erase from the minds of white and Black alike the reality of the existence of such men as Denmark Vesey, Nat Turner, Frederick Douglass, and David Walker. Such men become the invisible men of American history, far removed from the consciousness of the New Negro, existing, if at all, in the minds of a few Afro-Americans who feel more akin to them than to the new prophets.

Yet Vesey, Turner, Douglass, and Walker were revolutionaries—and in that cabinet of the mind which the New Negro has constructed there are no shelves for such men. Like white men, Black men also are suspicious of revolutionaries, those whose actions constantly challenge a philosophy of passivity and patience. Martin Luther King reached far more Negroes than Malcolm X, not because King's philosophy is sounder—safer maybe, but not sounder—but because King appealed to the dominant desire of the majority of Negroes to be good niggers as opposed to bad niggers, conformists as opposed to individuals, bourgeois as opposed to proletariat. "Negroes," some Negro leader (probably Wilkins or Young) has remarked, "are conservative on everything but the race issue." This is an understatement. The majority of them, even those in the Wattses and Harlems of America, are racial conservatives as well, aspiring more to become middle-class misfits than healthy, human beings.

The exploits of the Black revolutionaries of the past have been expunged from the minds of the majority of America's Black population. And it is this which makes my protestations suspect, my thoughts treacherous, and my opinions dangerous. For men possessing no knowledge of Nat Turner cannot begin, even in an infantile way, to understand me. Men enamored of the new stereotype who have lived so long in a hypocritical world peopled by Booker T. Washingtons are incapable of interpreting my world peopled by the ghosts of neurotic, troubled, desperate Nat Turners. Further, men unable to find meaning, hope and life in the futile, perhaps naive, yet brutal rebellion of Nat Turner, which was initiated in an orgy of blood and culminated in death by lynching—such men cannot possibly understand the meaning which the riots in California, Chicago, and New York hold for me.

Yet the riots do hold meanings, profound ones. They attest to the fact that a new generation of Afro-Americans is uncomfortable with the new stereotypes, unwilling to be considered little more than fragile glassware placed at random into cabinets constructed by the naive, fanciful minds of people who have no cognizance of human worth, no respect for human dignity, and utter contempt for the human spirit. Each Black soul in the ghetto who shouts out in a paranoiac frenzy of looting and rioting is shouting to a group of monsters who would categorize his humanity by transforming it into an object that the human spirit is never so depleted of hope, vigor, and anger that it cannot muster the strength for rebellion, even if—and all of us know this—rebellion must end in defeat, in mass murder by those who possess America's most important attribute—power.

Surely Nat Turner realized this fact. One could not exist in the era of slavery without realizing certain fundamental facts about one's existence: how much the continuation of existence depended upon the whims and fancies of one's master; how great, awesome and all-encompassing was the power of the master; how completely stifled, shut-in and hopeless one's own life was relative to ambition, growth and freedom of thought and movement.

Is it any wonder, then, that, like Sojourner Truth and Harriet Tubman, Nat Turner would hear voices and see visions urging him to undertake the liberation of his people? On August 21, 1831, Turner obeyed the dictates of these subconscious utterances and began the revolt which has now been all but wiped away from the pages of American history. The first to fall were those closest to the rebellion, the members of the family of Turner's master, John Travis. In addition, some sixty whites were killed before the rioters and their leader were hanged for the insurrection.

Too little has been written about the followers of Nat Turner. Seventy slaves joined the revolt; seventy men, not unmindful of the consequences, dedicated themselves to a hopeless, futile rebellion, engaged in an act of suicide and chose to gain freedom in the only way that freedom can be gained with honor—by wrenching it from the hands of the master through violence. There must have been those, nevertheless, who argued the pragmatic realities of the case: seventy men comprised a minuscule force in comparison to the majority number of whites; all the means of waging warfare were in the hands of whites—all power, all recourse to weapons, everything necessary to stop a rebellion; furthermore, given the tyrannical nature of the master in times of peace, what would that nature be in times of insurrection?

Each of the seventy knew the answer to such a question. Yet these men had heard voices and seen visions; and though to all rational men the utterances of the voices and the images projected by the visions were insane, to men for whom the rational and the irrational are one and the same, sanity and insanity are irrelevant terms. The voices and the visions were only secondary factors, wish fulfillments perhaps, of men who, though knowing, despaired of admitting the futility of their purported acts. For long before the sound of the first imagined voice, they had decided, in the chaotic jungle of horror and discontent where the Black soul nestles, that what existed was the worst, and that therefore nothing, not even death, could bring about a condition more terrible than that in which they daily lived.

Yet the New Negro, the maker of cabinets, sees no parallel between Turner's rebellion and the rebellions in the Black ghettos of present-day America. Such men are fenced in by their own constructions, forced to think in terms of criteria set up by their own minds, dedicated to distorting those truths which jeopardize their security, peace and comfort. They have acquiesced in the annihilation of the image of Nat Turner and his followers in an attempt to keep alive that stereotype which allows their narrow worlds to stave off destruction—a stereotype that omits the ominous truth that in American society today there exist hundreds of thousands of Nat Turners for whom no peace can be had, no calm can come, no sustenance found except in the final flaming Armageddon of violence and destruction predicted by the biblical prophets.

To these men the revolutionaries in America's ghettos are insane. And, certainly, according to the reality of the position of Black men in America—a condition analogous to that of Turner and his followers during slavery—violent rebellion

is suicidal, self-destructive, and fruitless. James Weldon Johnson summed up
the situation in 1928: "We would be justified in taking up arms or anything we
could lay our hands on and fighting for the common rights we are entitled to
and denied, if we had a chance to win. But I know and we all know there is not
a chance."

Johnson's prophecy is one for rational men capable of remaining so in a society
which exists on the irrational principle that some men are more human than
others. And though in his private heart each Black man agrees with Johnson,
still, to that scarred, bruised, desperate soul come voices and visions negating
rationality and propelling him to suicidal undertakings. Almost to the man, the
rioters in Watts, in Harlem, in Bedford Stuyvesant knew that rebellion would end
in injury, death, or jail. No one who concocted a Molotov cocktail was unaware
that to throw it meant to bring down annihilation upon him. Yet men made
Molotov cocktails, and men faced tanks and guns, taking the existential leap into
manhood by defying reason, logic, and history. "The lion is alone, and so am I,"
shouted Byron's Manfred. And each rioter, likewise, was aware of his alienation
even from those closest to him. For most Afro-Americans the journey to manhood is a lonely, solitary expedition over frightful, fear-laden passages of the spirit
and soul. More Joseph K than Bigger Thomas, the Black American has even been
deprived of the luxury of accidentally falling into manhood, of bribing his way in
with the currency of historical pride. Each step has been painful, grueling, and
torturous, and for only a few has the goal been reached.

Some, like the rioters, would know freedom and thus manhood for one short
moment, for the brief span of time between the rioting night and the daylight
calm. There in the darkness broken only by the flares of red, revolving lights from
police vehicles and the flaming, meteor-like tail of smoke of the Molotov cocktail,
in the still, hushed night interrupted by screams of terror, of curses, of jubilation,
some few Black men who had never before known freedom and who after tonight
would, perhaps, never know freedom again were enraptured by a maddening,
panoramic frenzy bordering upon mania. After long years of interment the ghost
of Nat Turner was revived, and men, drunk with frustration, fought their way
into that dream state of freedom so peculiar to the dispossessed of the earth.

Others, however, being trapped by their own psychology, will never know
freedom. Like most Americans the New Negro has misinterpreted the *Zeitgeist*
of the twentieth century. Being accustomed to categorizing people as things, the
cabinetmakers have built categories and erected criteria by which men and women
may be sorted and shuffled away into obscure niches oblivious to history.

These categories label certain Afro-Americans, rob those in the ghetto of visibility, depict those on the bottom shelves of the cabinets as things without substance, without feeling, without a claim upon normal life. Others in American
society, moving from this philosophical base into abstraction, view this "thing" as
dangerous—in which case one starves it, abuses it mentally in a million different

ways and, when in doubt, lynches it—or as loving, in which case one reveres it, looks upon it with paternal amusement, elevates it to the status of a redeemer: the Christ figure who will resurrect fallen America.

Few see the Black man as representative of modern man in the twentieth century, beset with all those problems which confront twentieth century man. The Afro-American is more alienated than Dostoyevsky's underground man because he has known loneliness for a much longer period of time; he is more terrified than Kafka's Joseph K because for a much longer time he has been the victim of forces beyond his control; he is more capable of murder than Richard Wright's Bigger Thomas because today the channels through which manhood is attained are more closed.

Each Black American, then, alone with his private soul, is closeted with a murderer, and no amount of distortion can erase this fact. The mania of twentieth century man is rebellion; and for the Afro-American, rebellion can only end in murder—his own or his oppressors'. Yet those given to sentimentality, those who catalogue the Afro-American in terms of love, meekness, and passivity, those makers of cabinets who would divide a race into categories, will vehemently dispute this argument. They will unpack the old clichés, drag out the old shibboleths, argue that "Negroes are people like everybody else"; "the Negro loves America"; "violence is futile"; "Negroes are not violent by nature"; "the Negro knows that he can only win his freedom in cooperation with well-meaning whites."

Such apologists should, however, closet themselves alone—as I have done—with their thoughts and, reinforcing those thoughts, the experiences of living in a society where every hour is one of torment, every day one of frustration, every waking moment beset with real and imagined horrors. Let each of them awaken, sometimes, as I have, in the middle of the night, and scream out to some nameless God to destroy his enemies, or to take that life which to him is meaningless, yet to which he clings so fervently.

Let the apologists confront themselves, own up to their Blackness and realize that the long years of chasing the stereotype, of attempting to appease an American conscience by deceit and by sacrificing freedom of emotion, of despair, of the thought of revenge, have resulted in an America grown sanguine, perhaps guilt-ridden, but nevertheless callous and unrepentant, toward its oppressed on the bottom shelf of those many cabinets of the mind.

The Afro-American is a tormented being, and these cabinet makers—especially the Negro carpenter—must realize this fact. A special shelf must be constructed to house a kind of chinaware no longer peculiar to America but representative of all the earths dispossessed. The New Afro is to be found, therefore, not in Booker T. Washington's *Autobiography,* but instead in Franz Fanon's *The Wretched Of The Earth;* and the character in these pages is to be found in the Black ghettos of America, where amidst the symbols of decay and death, the people themselves are the most vigorous, most dynamic exemplars of life. For such people are assured that what exists at present is the worst; the conditions of life under which they and their children now live have no parallels anywhere else in American society. Is it any wonder, then, that such men will set forward upon an adventure which can bring surcease to a tormented mind only through an orgy of violence and destruction?

When I make such statements, it frightens my friends, and causes them to hold me in disrepute, to question my sanity. They admit that they have taken no such excursions into themselves, as I suggest, never laid themselves open before the mirror of their own minds, never attempted to explicate their inner thoughts. In short, like most Americans they are aware of only one truth and desire neither to hear nor to believe in another.

My truth, they argue, will not make them free but, on the contrary, ensnare them more, cause the societal vise to tighten, close the few doors now open to them, reinforce the theories of white racists, and drive away their many sincere, white friends. Perhaps, they concede, they do exist in a half-hypocritical, half-deceptive world; yet the norm of their society is hypocrisy, and therefore hypocrisy and deceit are legitimized. Their goal, they proclaim, is to live and to let live, to achieve whatever possible, despite some limitations, in a society which, though oppressive, makes a show before world opinion of attempting to relieve their lot.

My truth, they say, is no private truth; for whether I intend it or not, each statement that I make rebounds upon them, inevitably saddles them with responsibilities which they do not want—responsibilities of explaining me away, of apologizing for my actions, and refuting me to their liberal friends. More precisely, however, they are angered because the cabinets which they have attempted to palm off on a naive society have not enough shelves to hold the likes of me. The stereotypes which they have attempted to foster are negated by me, one of their own, and my most treacherous act has been my refusal to be pigeonholed, to be categorized. Therefore, perhaps all the stereotypes are false, all the cabinets obsolete, and perhaps there are, out in that unknown where men plot murder by street light, more desperate men than myself.

"In the whole world no poor devil is lynched, no wretch is tortured, in whom I too am not degraded and murdered," writes Aimé Cesaire, voicing a truth which my friends have never deigned to explore. They do not yet realize that their fate is inseparably bound with the fate of those who suffer in every ghetto in America and that, in reality, in the minds of those who oppress others, cabinets are composed of one shelf and one shelf only. And in such a society where life can be so disregarded and humanity so often negated, no life, no humanity, is safe.

These are facts which my friends must eventually acknowledge whether they rationalize me away or not. They cannot, anyway, totally exile me from their minds, for to do so would be to deny too important a part of their private selves. My sickness is also their sickness, and because they too are sick, they are more capable of recognizing mine. In time, perhaps they will realize that the cabinets which they have constructed were predicated upon myth and fancy and that the New Negro, born of the Booker T. Washington stereotype, was a futile attempt to refute that terrible creature harbored in the dark caverns of their own minds—a creature as strange and as incomprehensible as I.

CHAPTER 4

Nat Turner and the Black Nationalists

(1968)

Ralph Ellison's *Invisible Man* returns to his underground retreat at the end of the novel, not because he is disgusted with the world, but instead because he has arrived at the conclusion that the world is impervious to change. A Black intellectual searching for some meaning to his existence and endeavoring to make peace with a society which he cannot comprehend, he is forced to choose between two opposing philosophies.

One philosophy, espoused by his grandfather, is that of accommodation: play up to white folks; don't question their assumptions of superiority; never challenge their assertions about being masters of the world—in short, coexist with white folks by "yessing them to death." The other philosophy, presented by the character Ras, the Destroyer, is nationalism: white men are the natural enemies of Black people, and only by removing them from the ghettos can Black men build a viable and fruitful society. Whites must therefore be driven from the ghettos and the economic, educational and social systems placed in the hands of Blacks.

The accommodationist philosophy was espoused by Booker T. Washington, "the first *Negro leader* chosen by white people" (italics mine); and Washington's philosophy, though couched in more sophisticated terminology, is advocated by the "responsible Negro leaders" today. At the core of Washington's philosophy was a demand for "a piece of this earth"; ". . . while the Negro should not be deprived by unfair means of the franchise, political agitation alone (will) not save him, and . . . back of the ballot he must have property, industry, skill, intelligence, and character, and . . . no race without these elements [can] permanently succeed." Acquiescence was the only legitimate means of attaining these ends. With the same self-righteous conviction of the so-called responsible Negro leaders of today, Washington kowtowed to the conscience of white America: "Casting down your buckets among my people, helping and encouraging them as you are doing on these grounds, and to education of head, hand, and heart, you will find that they will buy your surplus land, make blossom the waste places in your fields, and run your factories."

Warming to his subject, Washington continues: "While doing this you can be sure in the future, as in the past, that you and your families will be surrounded by the most patient, faithful, law-abiding and unresentful people that the world has seen. As we have proved our loyalty to you in the past . . . so in the future, in our humble way, we shall stand by you with a devotion that no foreigner can approach, ready to lay down our lives if need be, in defense of yours, interlacing our industrial, commercial, civil, and religious life with yours in a way that shall make the interests of both races one."

An expert at the game of "playing up to white folks," Washington believed that "no white American ever thinks that any other race is wholly civilized until he wears the white man's clothes, eats the white man's food, speaks the white man's language, and professes the white man's religion."

Washington has been echoed by the accommodationist leaders of today. Carl Rowan, writer, commentator, and spokesman for "moderate Negro leaders," has written: "A Negro man who cannot express himself adequately, orally or in writing, who has not achieved anything academically, who has not developed technical or scientific skills, and who, as a result, cannot compete in this . . . economy, is not going to have racial pride, or any other kind."

Roy Wilkins, the elder statesman of accommodationist Negro leaders, has said somewhat the same: "He [the Negro] is a very old American, and he's American in his concepts. I think he is a liberal only on the race question. I mean, I think he is a conservative economically. I think he wants to hold on to gains in property and protection. I don't see him as a bold experimenter in political science or social reform."

And Whitney Young, a self-professed "responsible Negro leader," has come closest of all to rendering a modern version of Washington's *Atlanta Address*. "Now I think Negro citizens in the face of the years . . . have shown an amazing restraint and an amazing loyalty. I give you only last year as an example. Last year, where you saw the March on Washington with its quiet dignity and its fervent pleading. Last year, where you saw Negro parents . . . after their children were bombed in a Sunday school, remain calm and cool and continued to pray. Last year, you saw in Jackson, Mississippi, Negro people in a church after their leader had been slain and after the widow of their leader addressed a meeting, a woman who had every right to hate, and she stood there and said, 'You mustn't hate, you must love.' And to see thousands of people in that audience . . . stand up and sing spontaneously . . . 'My country 'tis of thee, sweet land of liberty.' Now I don't know what simple element of testimony of faith in a system do you need on the part of people who have so little reason to have this kind of faith. . . . They have said to America, 'I believe in you.'"

Such statements by Negro leaders, past and present, have found accord in the hearts and minds of many Negroes primarily because Negroes, with few exceptions, have scorned revolution. For the most part, they have remained middle-class oriented either in actuality or in expectation. Here Jean Paul Sartre is correct: "What the American Negroes ... want is an equality of rights which in no way implies a change of structure in the property system. They wish simply to share the privileges of their oppressor, that is, they really want a more complete integration."

To achieve a "more complete integration," moderate Negroes and their leaders were willing to settle for the formula inherent in the Christian ethic—salvation for some of the people if not all of the people. Modern-day Noahs, Negro leaders are preoccupied with saving those few who come aboard the ark with a predisposition toward acceptance of gradualism, non-violence, integration, and the Democratic Party; and who unashamedly, unabashedly, support the war in Vietnam.

Theirs is the vision of America structured not upon race but upon class, one in which Black men, degrees in hand, meet frequently with their white counterparts over lawn tennis, golf, or mahjong to discuss ways of containing the legitimate rebellions of the Black people still left deprived, victimized and oppressed in the ghettos of this country. As one such "leader" recently remarked: "I am interested in getting more Negroes into policy-making positions." When I inquired about the fate of those who could not be put into policy-making positions, he retreated to a curious version of the Darwinian doctrine.

The formula—some if not all of the people—is not the exclusive property of the middle-class Negroes and their leaders. Black Nationalists, irrespective of ideology, have long taken such a formula for their rallying cry. Marcus Garvey propounded a "Back to Africa" philosophy, yet at the base of his philosophy was a materialism, a bourgeois mentality, as trenchant as that of one of his chief opponents, A. Philip Randolph. Because Garvey, too, desired a piece of this earth, he was willing to settle for the formula couched in the Protestant Ethic.

This is equally true of other Nationalist groups. The guiding ethos of the Moors was prudence and economy: own your own business, buy Black, keep your money in the Black ghettos. This means no more than each man getting his share of the "Gross National Product," thereby sharing in the capitalist system, embracing its economics while deploring its social arrangements, unable to realize that one is merely the result of the other. It is, therefore, no accident that the best dressed, often most prosperous members of the Black community are Black Nationalists, who are far more acquisitive and puritanical than the earliest white Puritan.

This dichotomy is proposed by Ralph Ellison's invisible man; he sees a world of extremes where one is forced to choose between Booker T. Washington and Marcus Garvey. But after close scrutiny the world is revealed to be one, without choice; for both men were controlled by the same ethic, both moved in the same direction, and both were bound together by the central fact that neither was willing to engage in revolution, to substitute for the formula "salvation for *some* of the people" that of "salvation for *all* of the people." Is it any wonder that a sensitive individual, caught in such a conundrum, would retreat to the safety and solitude of an underground dungeon?

The choices, however, have never been that restrictive. Like Americans in general, Ellison's protagonist was oblivious of the history of Black people in America. For within that history is another philosophy, that presented dramatically in action, not words, by Nat Turner. Turner left no philosophical system—that is, no written philosophy—but his actions dictated a philosophy which transcends the power of words.

Turner engaged in a violent revolution against the institution of slavery; and yet it is not the violent revolution that is most important. Black people have engaged in violent revolution before and since. Turner is important because he attempted to destroy an oppressive system totally; he saw himself always as one of the oppressed, and his actions were undertaken in the spirit of liberty for all, with the intent of bringing freedom to all. Turner demanded destruction of the oppressive apparatus not coexistence with it, realizing, as today's moderate Negro leaders do not, that coexistence (integration) is only another way of enabling the many—though many more many—to oppress the few.

But most important, Turner was able to say that that moment in history for him and his people was the worst, therefore negating a moral and ethical scripture against violence. The laws, morals, and ethics constructed by a totalitarian society are, due to their very nature, invalid. No victim has a moral responsibility to recognize the laws of the oppressor. And, in the same way, he owes no allegiance to a moral code which he did not help to construct, about which he was not consulted, and which operates continuously to keep him in his oppressed status.

In addition, Turner's actions negate the philosophy of the late Martin Luther King. Violence, argued King, binds the oppressor and the oppressed together, robbing the victim of that nobility inherent in suffering, pushing him further from his oppressor; and worst of all, the victim is psychologically damaged in the process. Undoubtedly, there is psychological damage incurred by the victim who engages in violence, but this must be measured against the psychological damage incurred by the victim who does not.

Was it psychologically healthier, for example, for the family of Emmett Till to watch passively as men led their son away to certain death? Is it psychologically healthy for young people today to accept non-violently the excesses of a system which ravages their minds, bodies, and spirits, bringing a more lingering and painful death than that suffered by Emmett Till? Alongside the psychic damage inherent in acts of violence must be placed, especially for the victim, what Franz Fanon has called the purgative effect of violence. Which is the more damaging is a question for psychologists.

Turner was restricted by no such philosophy. From that moment when he realized that the conditions which he lived under were the worst, he became a revolutionary in the true sense of the word; he dedicated himself to the elimination of the oppressive social and political apparatus, not in the interests of a few but in the interest of all. He envisioned a revolution which would free every man in chains, enable every victim to breathe the air of freedom, and grant every man the right to choose his own destiny. Thus Turner accepted the formula which has now become the guiding ethic of the Black Power revolution: salvation for all or salvation for none.

No philosophy which does not demand change in the American power structure for the benefit of all the victims can be called revolutionary in any sense of the term. The Black Power proponent, like Nat Turner, realizes this fact, and for this reason he is the only true nihilist in twentieth-century America, believing with his heart, head, and soul that the conditions which exist at the moment are the worst.

In this way the Black Power philosophy differs from philosophies espoused by other Black theoreticians, for its advocates envision a future—indeed the central meaning of the rebellion is predicated upon a future—in which the dignity of all men will have been restored. But the future is possible only after the complete and total destruction of the existing oppressive apparatus.

That the system is oppressive and has always operated to deny dignity to Black people, to rob Black people of any conception of themselves, of their worth, of their historical positions, and further, to deny them life, freedom of movement, and choice is a point which all moderate Negro leaders readily concede. Such leaders differ only in the means to correct the abuses, to so transform the system that it will remedy all defects, make some restitution—if not to the victims, then to the sons and daughters of the victims.

Their plans are well known. One calls for an economic miracle, a Marshall plan; another for increased legal, legislative, and political action; still another for mass assaults upon the American conscience. And the majority of Afro-Americans accept one, sometimes all of these plans simultaneously, primarily because most still believe in the American Dream, remain wedded to the Christian myth, and see salvation and redemption in the rhetoric of leaders who promise a piece of this earth not for all but for a chosen few.

Few are capable of believing with Nat Turner that the conditions under which they live at this moment are the worst, for dedication to such a belief mandates revolution. Only the advocates of Black Power have arrived at this position, and thus Black Power is the only philosophy in America demanding revolution in the common interest of all Black people.

The Black Power advocate seeks a higher meaning for man. He seeks a higher freedom. He seeks not only a more equal society, but a more just one, not a larger share of the fruits of production, but a more humane and precise definition of the human condition. As such, the advocates of Black Power are the champions of an ethic which goes far beyond existentialism, leading from property values to human ones, from degradation to dignity, from a preoccupation with some to a preoccupation with all. With Nat Turner, the Black Power proponent ignores the call of the Negro middle class and the Black Nationalists alike for a system which will only save some of the people, and demands instead a system in which no Black men will wear chains and all Black men will be free.

CHAPTER 5

Black Power and Existential Politics

(1969)

In the article "Farewell to Liberals: A Negro View," published in *The Nation* (October 1962), Loren Miller condemns white liberals for their failure to deliver the promises implied or stated in the liberal creed. The accusation is somewhat unjustified. The failure lies not with liberals, but with the liberal philosophy born in the fertile soil of Europe and transplanted to the arid wasteland of America. This philosophy, humanistic in intent, died an unnatural death in the racist, hate-filled climate of the United States. No more justified is the accusation that all liberals are hypocritical and insincere. The facts of history are otherwise, and no useful purpose is served by distorting such facts for propagandistic ends. The failure results neither from the insincerity of liberals nor from their failure to produce the great society; rather, failure should be attributed to their historical impotence in coping with those situations and conditions inimical to the lives of Black people in America.

The Civil War has been attributed, in part, to the humanitarian ideals born in France and England during the European Renaissance. If one accepts this argument, the "battle to free the slaves" received impetus from the writings of liberal intellectuals: Rousseau, Mill and Locke. Again, the facts are somewhat different, pointing up the early schism which existed in liberal ranks—a schism which pitted white abolitionists against those of liberal persuasion. The difference can be seen in the examples of two men: John Brown, an abolitionist, and Abraham Lincoln, a liberal.

John Brown probably never read Rousseau's *Social Contract;* Abraham Lincoln almost assuredly did. However, it was Brown who manned the barricades in an attempt to destroy slavery by the only means possible, whereas Lincoln was willing, even unto death, to bargain away emancipation for peace. The abolitionist spirit represented by John Brown was doomed to extinction soon after the Civil War, for liberals and abolitionists merged into one, wiping away all distinctions during the age of Booker T. Washington. It was the sons and daughters of the abolitionists who supported the Washington program with prestige and money, and it was the same abolitionists, now turned liberals, who enabled Washington to stifle any challenge to his authority.

This uniting of liberals behind a single, passive ideology accounts for their inability in the succeeding years to effect change in America in any meaningful way. Having given up the "sword and shield" of John Brown, liberals became castrated eunuchs, their power in the area of Black–white relations not much more potent than that of their Black wards. It is for this reason that during Reconstruction, when thirty-five hundred Black men, women, and children were lynched within a span of ten years, the liberal reaction was visible only in flowing, flowery rhetoric in which they condemned their fellow men from the safe distance of the university or the church.

Again, when Woodrow Wilson, an exponent of the new brand of liberalism, excluded Blacks from the body politic with is much ease as Robespierre effected when he condemned his fellow revolutionary, Danton, to the guillotine, white liberals excoriated these acts from the sanctuaries of the printing press, the public rostrum, and the church pulpit. It was not until the New Deal days of the Franklin Roosevelt administration that the liberals effectively used their power. It was during this period, also, that the major problems of Black America were enunciated and dealt with in a way which proved beneficial to both white liberals and Negro leaders. For the liberals, exercising their powers, hastened to construct the welfare state, giving form and substance to the welfare state mentality which was as old as Harriet Beecher Stowe, and thus cemented a Faustian pact between Negroes and themselves.

The pact offered something to each party. For whites, the programs of the welfare state made Black men dependent upon them, thus enabling liberals to pose as the benefactors of humanity—not withstanding the fact that the welfare state was overgenerous to some, criminal to many, and debilitating to most. For Negroes, the pact assured a return to the days of the Freedmen's Bureau when, after slavery, the job of rehabilitation was entrusted to whites who set policy, enunciated philosophy, and charted direction. But more important, the philosophy of the welfare state created an attitude of dependence in which men placed their faith in the mystical credo that others were capable of solving their problems. Such a creed robbed Black people of the propensity for sacrifice, of the willingness to mount realistic, sustained initiatives, of the ability to make a systematic, organized attempt to construct viable communities within those areas which were, physically at least, their own. Then as now, Blacks, divided and disorganized, either retired from the battle, proposed impossible schemes, or accepted the liberal thesis of the equalitarian society based upon integration.

Integration is a concept derived from the welfare state philosophy, and its greatest success has been in destroying initiative and stifling creativity on the part of men who need to control their own destinies. Moreover, the concept of integration—like the welfare state philosophy—was one which both Negro leaders and white liberals could live with. To be sure, there are white liberals who are charlatans and hypocrites; yet the essential characteristic of the white liberal is the need to save someone, preferably Black people, and integration, the best means of effecting this salvation, will transform twenty million Black men into carbon-copied white men. In such a society, in which all men were to be invisible, the humanistic principles applicable to the golden age could be operative. On the other hand, Negro leaders, much more sophisticated and less naively romantic, saw integration as the instrument by which—as Stokely Carmichael has noted—selected Blacks would become card-carrying members of the American Mainstream, while the mass would be pacified through the expansion of the welfare state.

This policy survived the years and has only recently been challenged by the concept of Black Power. Young people, in loud and uncompromising tones, have "sounded the death knell" of integration, and despite the protestations of Roy Wilkins and others of the antiquarian past, the idea of the egalitarian society in which Black men become the invisible men of the future now belongs to the cesspool of American historical thought. Integration is truly dead, and no more glorious a death has occurred since Adolf Hitler put a bullet into his own brain.

The death of integration, however, threatens to split the Black Power movement apart. In part this is due to the long years of the success of the welfare state ideology, which, transforming men into children, has made them subservient to the liberal fathers' image. Thus, the situation is analogous to that of a young child taken from his mother at an early age; such a rupture causes extreme frustration. The child may sulk in his special corner, bemoaning the passing of the comfortable old days; he may lash out in uncontrolled fury, mouthing slogans and shouting abusive epithets; or, close to the breaking point, he may dream impossible dreams to replace those of happier days.

This analogy between the child and many Black Power proponents is intentional. For many, incapable of accepting the concept of Black Power and all that the concept entails, have retreated to the sanctuary of "their piece of earth," there to brood about the past. Others, more distraught, excoriate "whitey" from one speaker's platform to another, "whipping that boy," to use Ralph Ellison's phrase, piling abuse upon abuse on the head of their favorite "honky."

Nowhere are these attitudes exhibited more blatantly than in some of the literature of the Black Power era. Some Black writers propound the most mystical of philosophies in poems, short stories, and plays, and their meanings are completely incomprehensible to everyone—one suspects even to the writers themselves. Others continue to present the same old stock characters, the same old plots, and the same old situations with the added dimensions of the theme "Black is beautiful."

Out of their frustrations, these writers have failed to realize that what is beautiful is the lives of Black people recorded simply, without mysticism, but with truth, and that the beauty of the Black spirit in this, the most oppressive of societies, is not only fertile ground for the writer to explore, but also the material from which he must construct and codify the theorems of a Black Aesthetic. For we are today in a Black cultural renaissance, in which, for perhaps the last time, Black Nationalist writers will be able to project—to Black people—a sense of our unique, separate cultural identity by resolving the dichotomy between art and function, thereby making art functional and relevant to the Black community.

But, too, there are the dreamers. Those who, incapable of confronting the world as it is, dream of the world as it should have been years ago. They are the octogenarians of the race, conjurors of old, outmoded ideas. Their greatest virtue is optimism; their greatest fault is ignorance combined with an arrogant disrespect for the intelligence of Black people. One needs no college degree to realize that Black Power is a goal yet to be attained, and that the Black masses, having been sold down the river by race charlatans so often in the past, will adopt no new philosophy without ample cause.

The dreamer, however, unlike the masses of Black people, believes that Black Power has been obtained. Moreover, he believes that he and his group have been instrumental in bringing this about. Therefore, if one accepts this misguided analysis, the dreamer is justified in condemning Black men of differing persuasion, of demanding that all Black men join him and his organization, and ordering that those who refuse be lined "up against the wall."

The reality is, however, that the goal of Black Power has not been attained. Were Black Power an actuality, Adam Clayton Powell would have his seniority in Congress; John Hatchett would be directing the Martin Luther King Center at N.Y.U.; John Carlos would not have been dismissed from the Olympic team; and the mayor of the city of New York would not be kowtowing to the racist-oriented United Federation of Teachers. Therefore, despite the fact that there are Blacks who are hindrances to the movement, no organization has accomplished enough to warrant the right to assign such men to the wall.

But dreams, as Sigmund Freud noted long ago, are wish fulfillments, and all Black men at some time have dreamed the impossible dream. What Black man has not imagined himself a Toussaint L'Ouverture doing to the Americans what the Haitians did to the French? What Black man, if he is honest with himself, has not dreamed of mass murder, of burning his way across America in an expedition that would make Sherman's march to the sea insignificant by comparison? And what Black man has not wished, deep in his private soul, that his people were the Viet Cong?

The awful truth of the matter is that Black people are not the Viet Cong. Despite the argument that "this is my land, too," this land belongs to the Indians, who are as powerless as Black people to dispel the invaders, and though the Viet Cong will eventually expel the invader from their soil, no such action is possible in the case of Blacks in America. Therefore, the revolution, which the rhetoricians tell us is on the way, can result in one thing and one thing only—the systematic extermination of Black people as a race.

Here the dreamers display that characteristic ignorance which stems from a lack of knowledge of history. For, behind their rhetoric lies the old belief in the potency of white liberalism and the philosophy of the benevolent state. They believe that, in the final analysis, either sympathetic whites in America, or non-whites of the Third World, or both, will prevent white Americans from carrying out the final solution. This, despite the fact that the Third World has yet to come to the aid of the Viet Cong, the Black South Africans, or Black Rhodesians, despite the fact that liberals have proved themselves, over the years, incapable of mustering any weapons more powerful than prayer and songs when Black life has been at stake. The truth is that we stand alone; and a nation capable of exterminating the Indians, putting Haitians into concentration camps, and lynching over a half million Blacks is not only quite capable of executing a large portion of the twenty million Blacks in this country, but capable also of *carrying out* such an act and *legitimizing* it throughout the world. Here is the evidence of real power—the power to control men, not by tanks and guns, but by the supremacy of the mass media, the domination of the instruments of propaganda, and control of the educational institutions, which are used to destroy one truth and replace it with another. American society is unique in this respect. It manufactures people as it manufactures things. Its power stems not from its vast military might, but instead from its ability to convince the victim that he deserves the punishment which it metes out. The white establishment, therefore, is not the classic example of the historical oppressor, for Blacks are controlled much more in a psychological than a physical sense, and one cannot fight ideas with Molotov cocktails.

The dreamers aside, Black people may indeed have to fight—given the intransigence of American society, the shift toward the right which will intensify once the Viet Cong victory is assured, and the racism which pervades every institution of American society. And if fight we must, then fight we will. But there is no room for romanticism; we will fight alone, and there will be no victors.

But neither will there be a victory attained in pursuit of the "New Colonization"—a thesis set forward by an increasingly large number of Blacks. That many Black people have been willing to leave America for other countries is a fact as old as Paul Cuffee, a wealthy Black shipowner who used his wealth and his ships to transport Blacks out of America. In addition, in the nineteenth century and well into the twentieth, the argument for colonization was so strong among Black people that hardly an issue of *The Anglo-American, Freedom's Journal,* or Douglass' paper failed to contain some article or letter to the editor on the subject.

The new version of the colonization theme proposes that America set aside a number of states for the exclusive use of Black people. Thus, one of the most expansionist nations in history, one which fought a war on its own soil to prevent white people from walking away with several states, is somehow to be coerced or persuaded to give away one fifth of its territory to Blacks. But no nation has ever given up its territory unless forced to do so. And there is, as of yet, no power on the horizon which seems capable of exerting enough pressure on the power establishment of America to force it to destroy the physical solidarity of this country.

This is not to condemn those who forward such proposals. It is to demand evaluation of such proposals in light of what Black Power, in its short history, has meant in terms of Black liberation, as well as what it must mean as a political instrument for the future. And here, of course, is the central problem. The breakdown of the old white liberal-Negro coalition has placed Black people in the most existential position of their lives. For the first time, Blacks are demanding real change, not the semblance of change, real power, not the illusion of power, and are attempting to construct real, viable alternatives to the programs of the past.

The death of God, wrote Nietzsche, means that man was thrown back upon himself. Concomitantly, the death of integration means that Blacks are thrown back upon themselves, forced to forge from the smithy of their Black souls the theories, forms, and institutions by which Black people are "to live or to die." This is, to be sure, an existential undertaking; for Black Power, in its realistic manifestations is an existential doctrine. The weight of survival has been placed upon the shoulders of Blacks, and only Blacks can determine their future.

That Black people are capable of this task needs no comment. We can build our communities and transform them into working, livable units. The only requirement is a complete break with the philosophy of the welfare state. For men who believe in the benevolence of government cannot believe in their own power; for them the politics of existentialism becomes the politics of dependence.

But the task requires, in addition, that Black theoreticians talk sense to Black people, that they tell it like it really is, that they bring home the hard, cold pragmatic facts of the situation in which we find ourselves at this stage. To control our communities is no easy task. We need not rhetoricians, but architects, planners and builders; not fire and brimstone orators, but teachers, entrepreneurs, historians and all that vast paraphernalia essential to the realistic operation and control of a community.

Such theoreticians must demand that our children get an education—as minimal as that may be—in the existing institutions, until such time as we have either transformed those institutions or created our own. They must demand that Black people be presented with the whole picture, and that the charlatan and the hustler be brought to task. They must criticize those who offer the worn-out theories of the past, as well as those whose satisfaction (sexual?) is derived from orgiastic, meaningless attacks upon "whitey"—attacks totally irrelevant to the problems at hand.

There must be a re-evaluation of values which entails a final and complete break with the liberal orthodoxy and methodology of the past. There must be total destruction of the welfare state and the welfare state mentality; the best in men must be called forth, and it must be demanded that Black men expend as much creative energy in building the Black community as they have expended throughout history in attempting to become good Americans. None of this is easy. Such undertakings entail frustration, bitterness, and disillusion. Yet sacrifice of the highest order is a necessary requirement: sacrifice and a dedication to Black people, not just to Blackness, which means more than wearing a natural hair-do or a dashiki. The dedication must be to race. There must be an unashamed, unabashed commitment to race that admits the differences between Blacks and whites and explores these differences.

This means that it is more important to write a Black novel than an American novel, more important to support a Black institution than a white one, more important to address Black problems than American problems. But above all, it is most important to realize that as an existential doctrine, Black Power demands the allegiance of men who are capable of transcending the past and challenging the future. For only such men can possibly confront the dangerous era that lies ahead.

> The old year is dying in the
> night/ring out wild bells and
> let him die.

CHAPTER 6

Black Power or Black Fascism?

(1968)

On a hot dusty road in Mississippi during the summer of 1966, men, women, and children—victims the night before of ruthless white power—responded to the question "What do you want?" of a courageous Black leader with the refrain "Black Power." Two years after this historic occurrence, the phrase Black Power has given impetus to a new kind of revolution, involving—as numerous Black Power conferences have shown—Blacks of all ideologies and persuasions. The revolution is discernible in such distant places as Mississippi, where young children tutored by members of S.N.C.C. are pursuing Black awareness, and the college campuses of America, where Black students are presenting instructors and officials with demands based upon Black Power concepts.

The revolution has been a long time coming. As far back as 1963, many of today's "militants" were still seeking the goals ardently pursued then as now by "responsible Negro leaders." Carried away by the rhetoric of the times, the slogans "Freedom Now" and "We Shall Overcome," and mesmerized by the seeming victories won through adherence to non-violence and the pursuit of integration, even many of those who were realists found themselves caught up in a Kafkaesque world in which reality gave way to illusion.

Yet the psychedelic state could not long remain. Reality—never far away—was revealed once the movement turned toward the North, toward the homes, jobs, and schools of those liberal proponents who, their voices raised as one with Blacks, had sung enthusiastically to Southern bigots: "We shall overcome." And once a commitment to see this reality was made, changes of far-reaching import were demanded and sought by young men who, unlike their parents, refused to chase that romantic illusion, an integrated society.

Many had refused to see the situation as it really was until after the "March on Washington." As thousands of Black people went to the shrine of the gods, offering libation and penance, many who had stayed away began to realize that neither God nor government would grant relief to an impotent army invading its domain with weapons no more powerful than spirituals and ministerial salvos to a non-existent white God. And they noted, too, that the Black people participating in the March on Washington represented less than one-fifth of one percent of Black people in the country—a statistic which illustrates that even before the Integrationist–Nationalist debate was brought into the open by Black Power, the majority of Black people preferred not integration but security, not Black–white brotherhood but food and education for their children, not assimilation (a means of transforming twenty million people into invisible men) but the means of living a decent life.

But it was in the aftermath of the March that many gained their most penetrating insight into the civil rights movement. Black people are not novices oblivious to the machinations of power politics. Our history has been filled with chauvinists and Uncle Toms who have allied themselves with white power in pursuit of selfish goals. Yet we were so mesmerized in the fifties that we ignored the lessons of the past. The March on Washington was a sobering reminder, pointing up the fact that the past was indeed very much with us, that Booker T. Washington was not yet dead, and that Negro power allied with white power could still be used to stifle dissent, to mute any voice which did not accept illusion as God-granted reality.

If the proceedings leading to this revelation had not been so serious, they would be ironic and pathetic—the stuff of which good comedy is made. There was the spectacle of Roy Wilkins, bowing his head, raising his arms, pointing in the direction of the buildings which housed Congress, and shouting to the absent congressmen (presumably the Southerners): "Give us enough time and we will liberate you, too."

It was to be discovered much later, however, that Wilkins and his associates, who had chided the country for denying freedom to Black people, had joined in an endeavor to deny freedom to one of their own colleagues. In *The New York Times* on the day following the march, there was a column dealing with a "rights leader" who had been forced to delete parts of the speech he had prepared for the march. John Lewis, the chairman of S.N.C.C., had planned to allude to the coming revolution which would burn its way across the nation, and in protest against this passage, some of the white participants threatened to pack their bags and go home, leaving the Afro-Americans to carry on their own show.

Rather than allow the white participants to withdraw from sponsorship, the "responsible Negro Leaders" chose to deny freedom to John Lewis—that is, they forced him to delete from his prepared text the passages considered offensive to whites. In so doing, white and Negro power were used in the most tyrannical manner. Once again, it was demonstrated that the historical alignment between Negroes and white liberals, which Booker T. Washington began in earnest, continued to dictate the tone, direction, and goals of Black people in America, primarily by silencing dissent and neutralizing opposition.

Yet the angry words which came forth from the men, women, and children during the "Meredith March" have proved immune to such coordinated efforts of white and Negro power. Despite the attempts by both civil rights leaders and white liberals to silence the proponents of Black Power in Black churches, colleges, lodge halls and the ghettos, Black Power has become a viable movement in which people of all persuasions have come together in a common undertaking.

No idea in America has caught the imagination of so many Black people in so short a time, brought awareness to individuals in so many different strata of life, and provoked responses and programs from so many people of diverse talents. It would seem that at this point—to use an old cliché—the only thing that Black Power has to fear is Black Power itself.

At a recent seminar on Black Power, a young student put the following question to a panel: "I believe in Blackness, but I don't identify with Africa, and there are other Black people who do not. Does this mean that I can't take part in the revolution?" The young lady was searching for answers. Like so many, she was unaware of what to do in these momentous times.

No one, however, attempted to answer her question. With few exceptions, the panel was convinced of its own righteousness—as if some Black god had ordained it with the power to speak the truth for twenty million people. The only answer forthcoming was not really an answer at all, but a number of clichés. "You have been brainwashed by white people," the panel declared, and "want to deny your Black heritage"—statements which proved that the panel had little understanding of the central issues of Black Power and was substituting emotionalism for reason and understanding.

Such has long been a characteristic of the fascist mind. Fascism as an ideology preys upon the purported ignorance of the people in the belief that all the people are ignorant. The emotional fascist, therefore, has no respect for the minds of other men, is convinced of their inferiority, and appeals to them only on the grounds of irrationality. Fascism is an important aspect of white power. John Lewis was denied the freedom to present his views because men believed that he should not think for himself; and the young student was attacked because men believed that she should have no opinion different from their own.

Such fascists have nothing but contempt for the people, though they attempt to compensate by sporting "au naturels" and dashikis. Like Father Divine, they believe that Black people can be moved only through emotionalism, and that the man who shouts the loudest is the wisest, best informed and best suited for leadership. They have only recently discovered that Africa is not a land ruled by Tarzan but instead by Black men like themselves, and that civilizations existed in Africa long before Columbus discovered America. Still, they berate others who have not yet discovered this, and instead of attempting to enlighten these others, they assume, *a priori*, like their white counterparts, that "them niggers can't learn anyway."

In addition, emotional fascists have a contempt for planning. Understanding neither revolution nor the nature of Black people in this country, they do not believe that we are capable of sustaining a social revolution. Not understanding the nature of white power, they are opposed to any long-range planning. What they want, they shout, is a violent revolution, not tomorrow but today, and they encourage young people to go out and "take care of business."

Yet they have taken care of no business themselves. Like the Negro leaders, the emotionalists are the last to know what is going on in the Black ghettos—because they listen to no voices but their own—and the first to leap under the bed when the action starts. They have the courage for one kind of action, and that is to shout "get whitey" and "hate whitey" slogans to people who are beginning to realize that shouting such slogans is as useless a preoccupation as shouting "we shall overcome" from the speaker's stand in front of the Washington monument. Perhaps, as one such individual told me, I do not know what Black Power is. I do know, however, what it is not: It is neither white fascism nor religious fanaticism.

But as dangerous as the emotional fascist may be, he is not so dangerous as the Professional Black Nationalist, who shows the same contempt for the people, but on a more sophisticated plane. The Professional Nationalist is the Black-by-Night missionary coming into the ghetto after sundown and intimidating others with his "more militant than thou" attitude. He has read Fanon—although he does not understand him—shuffled through a few pages of Guevara, knows something about Garvey—though not the whole story—and quotes Malcolm verbatim. This superficial machinery is designed to prove his militancy; yet, in effect, it allows him to serve as a liaison between the Black community uptown and The Man downtown. He has discovered, finally, that it pays to be Black, and he capitalizes on his Blackness to the utmost. No man is Blacker than he, none more dedicated to the "cause of the people," none has a better solution. He will disrupt the gatherings of others and even threaten their lives (Today some Black leaders who, unlike the "responsible Negro leaders," venture into the ghettos armed, not to protect themselves from the CIA but from other Blacks).

The Professional Nationalist is also the professional fascist. He is not interested in persuading men to accept his point of view through reason and logic—since his point of view differs little from The Man's. Instead, he hopes to establish a totalitarian apparatus wherein all proposals will be subject to his authority. He is not opposed to planning, for he has come to realize that there is money in planning, but he opposes any plan which he does not originate, sponsor and dictate.

Central to both the emotional and the professional fascist is their anti-intellectualism. The intellectual is always a danger to the fascist mind because the intellectual demands the right to think for himself. S.N.C.C. changed its orientation from integration to Black Power because Carmichael demanded the right to think for himself, to say things not sanctioned by the white and Negro power structure. We know how that power structure has reacted. It has not attempted to debate the issues fairly and squarely with Black people, nor has it been willing to bring its ideas before Black people in a serious attempt at honest discussion.

This is because the fascist mind, basically weak and insecure, cannot deal with issues through logic, reason, and persuasion. The Black fascists are no different, and in this respect they are joined by some Black leaders. They fear that the intellectual will take over their movement and render them impotent as leaders. In other words, the Black intellectual is as feared as the bubonic plague.

There are historical reasons for such fears. Black intellectuals have usually joined the civil rights struggle on the side of the integrationists. Too often they have pocketed their degrees, moved away from the ghetto, joined the N.A.A.C.P., and sold their skills and talents to the highest bidder, usually white. But this is equally true of most of Black America before the Black Power movement. Most Black men were caught up in the integrationist bag, seeing salvation only in terms of what Negro and white leaders said that it was. Whether or not the Black intellectual deserves more opprobrium than the rest of us is open to question.

The Black fascists are not opposed to intellectuals for these reasons. Men who are searching for personal power, whether through fantasy or political dealings with the power structure, they are opposed to those who have the ability to propose plans, methods, and goals different from their own. They refuse to understand that the intellectual, owing his allegiance to the people, must serve as a critic deriving his ideas from the people and putting them forth in favor of the people.

This, the Black fascist cannot understand. Neither can he understand the guiding ethos of every revolution from the French to the Algerian—that ideas are to be debated, then accepted or discarded not as a result of threats or emotional intimidation, but instead through working in an atmosphere of mutual respect and cooperation, realizing that in the area of truth there are no final dicta handed down by impotent gods.

The men, women, and children in Mississippi realized this fact. In the face of the most awesome power—the white Mississippi police and National Guard—they dared to choose Black Power. They did not choose the power which but a few hours before had denied them the right to express themselves in the way they deemed best; they did not choose the self-righteous power of narrow-minded, frustrated, paranoic, insecure little men whose only answer to any plea for understanding was a barrage of empty clichés and nonsensical epithets; they did not choose the power of those who attempted to persuade them, through sophisticated rhetoric, that they and only they had found the road to salvation.

They voted in favor of a free and open society in which men would come together, debate the issues, and sort out their differences, not as bewildered children, helpless without the sound of the master's voice, but as conscientious men truly concerned with their own destiny. Theirs was the spirit which dared to thunder forth in the face of oppression—while staring into the gun barrels of the oppressor: "We want Black Power!" Black Power and not Black Fascism.

And those of us who feel akin to this spirit have no recourse but to insist that it is Black Power which they shall have. We must demand this regardless of the consequences, for if the fascists are allowed to take over a movement begun by sincere and honest people, then we will have not Black Power but Black Fascism, differing in no respect from the white fascism against which Blacks have fought and died throughout our history in this country. At this point, it will then be incumbent upon those of us who are determined to destroy white fascism to oppose this carbon copy; for fascism must be opposed at all costs, whether it be white or Black.

CHAPTER 7

"Hell No, Black Men Won't Go!"

(1971)

At the height of the protest against the war in Vietnam in the summer of 1967, two Black soldiers on active duty in the battle zone appeared before the television cameras of the nation's major networks. Presumably, their appearance was to undermine the Negroes, here at home, who urge other Negroes of draft age not to participate in the war. This function was to be performed by rebutting two nationally known Negro leaders who had consistently urged Black men to answer their draft calls with the refrain, "Hell no, we won't go!"

Stokely Carmichael and the late Martin Luther King were the two leaders who most exemplified the Negro's opposition to the war in Vietnam. To many whites, they have been the apotheosis of Black resistance, and each has received insults, and threats of physical violence; however, the public viewed the two men quite differently. Carmichael was seen as a young, intellectual iconoclast, a hero out of the pages of Malraux's revolutionary novel, *Man's Fate*—a nihilist whose rashness knows no boundaries.

The view of Dr. King was exactly the opposite. Neither rash nor iconoclastic, and certainly not an intellectual, he was seen as a mild-mannered, reasonable, though impatient, Negro, embodying at times within his own person that moral fiber of which Blacks are supposedly constructed.

To rebut men whose ideals are so different, whose images, in the public mind, are so contrary, men had to be selected with consummate skill; chosen, not as the result of fortuitous fate, but as anti-images—as antagonists even—in order to effectively counteract what one correspondent has called, "the dangerous thinking of some American Negroes." Carmichael and King could be rebutted only by authentic, in-the-flesh heroes, men in the battle areas of Vietnam, doing their utmost for God, mother, and country.

The first soldier resembled Stokely Carmichael in everything except anger and rashness. Young, handsome, and vocal, attired in war gear, he was the perfect foil, and his pronouncements did the nation justice: No, he did not agree with Stokely

Carmichael. His country was at war, and as a loyal American, it was his duty to defend his country. Of course he was concerned about things at home, but after his experiences in Vietnam with people who thought of him as "just people," he knew that America would work out its problems at home. The important thing was that he had a job to do here, and he was determined to do it.

The foil for Dr. King was, naturally, a soldier of higher rank and educational status. A captain in the army, member of the N.A.A.C.P. in civilian life, mature, and apparently intelligent, he wished that people like Martin Luther King would realize the harm they do to their country's image. The country was engaged in a vicious war against communism, and every American should support that war. He was an American, and the enemies of his country were his enemies and the enemies of Black people. Moving beyond this, the captain aimed a few verbal blasts at the rioters in the nation's ghettos: Though things were bad in some parts of the country, riots were not a way of making things better. Negroes had to have more initiative, more concern for their own welfare, and they should not be influenced by demagogues—those who help to cause riots, and who tell them not to support the war in Vietnam.

As a Black man, my first response to these two spokesmen was to question the lack of opportunity for soldiers of differing persuasions and temperament to air their views. If my information is correct, there are many Black soldiers who do not share the views of these two men. On reflection, it became clear that the job of these two men was simply to rebut two popular figures in the Black community, not in an attempt to appeal to Black America, but rather to appease and comfort white America.

America is a country in which comfort is more important than anything else, and the statements of Carmichael and King regarding the Vietnam conflict have caused extreme discomfort. It is not comforting to know that a large number of Black men would prefer to die fighting tyranny, oppression, hunger and disease in the Black ghettos of America than to die in the jungles of Vietnam for an abstract freedom for the Vietnamese.

An increasing number of white people—even articulate and dedicated members of the liberal community—are becoming incensed upon realizing that Black men are not really grateful to the country which, according to eminent commentators on the American scene, has provided them with a higher standard of living than that enjoyed by any other Black people on earth. Such ingratitude distorts the image of an America constantly attempting, against historical odds, to live up to those ideals upon which it was founded.

To uphold these ideals and to assure white Americans a reasonable amount of mental comfort, the two soldiers in Vietnam were brought into the nation's living rooms, serving that function which Negro leaders have served so adequately before: pacification of the American conscience. Such is the mentality of white people regarding Black people: that a single Negro, echoing the words which find accord in white America's own breast, is taken as the metaphor for all Blacks—the spokesman who has really told it like it is.

This is no new phenomenon. Dick Gregory's idea of the "Hertz Rent-A-Negro Corporation," through which Negroes would be rented out to white people to tell them what other Negroes believe, is less a joke than a practiced reality. For a long time, white America has had at its disposal a cadre of Negroes whose function is to soothe the American conscience, to assure white Americans that things are not as bad as a few "irrational and irresponsible" Negroes would have them appear to be. Such Negroes serve America in much the same way that the *deus ex machina* served Greek theatergoers—as a reminder that things could never degenerate to the point of no resolution, and that, in the final analysis, good, justice, and reason would prevail.

The Negro who tells white America what it wants to hear has always been with us. Against the rational polemic of W. E. B. Du Bois, Booker T. Washington came forth to articulate the "real problem," advocating in his "Atlanta Exposition Address" the program which the white South had long before conceived and begun to implement. Against the postulations of Marcus Garvey, A. Philip Randolph became a constant scene-stealer, assuring America at every turn that, despite Garvey's enormous following, Negroes were immune to the attractions of Black Nationalism.

Malcolm X and the Black Muslims were subjected to perhaps the most serious scathing of all, drawing thunderous phrases of denunciation from established Negro leaders as well as some not yet established. An examination of the rhetoric of such leaders during the Malcolm X years will convince even the most disinterested observer that Negro leaders, reflecting white concern, had nominated Malcolm X public enemy number one. (This is understandable, though hardly excusable: It is a fact that when white people become paranoiac, some Negro leaders become hysterical, and proceed to act accordingly.)

Recent events prove that the Negro who tries to assuage the fears of whites is still in great demand. When Stokely Carmichael uttered the phrase, "Black Power," during the Meredith March, the words had hardly faded away before Negro leaders were beamed into every living room in the nation. So all-pervasive was the hysteria at this point, that even non-Black leaders like Vice President Humphrey felt compelled to join the fray—pacifying white America by offering assurances that Black people would not take this step into "romanticism and murder."

During the teachers' strike in New York City in 1967, many Black people, myself among them, joined with the Afro-American Teacher's Association in protesting the strike. Then, when the grievances of the Black community were articulated by such spokesmen as Floyd McKissick, H. Rap Brown, Charles Kenyatta, and Jesse Gray, the United Federation of Teachers dug into its files and brought forth its personal Negro leader: tired, old, metaphysical Bayard Rustin, whose following in the Black community numbers less than three.

Again, when Negro athletes agreed not to participate in the coming Olympic Games, the white press reached back into the past, dragging forth such now forgotten "Leaders" as Jesse Owens, Don Newcombe, and the perennial expert on Negro sports and sportsmen, Joe Louis, to assure America that the majority of Negro athletes did not hold such radical views and would not interject "politics into the sports arena."

Yet the most recent event demanding the continual involvement of the Negro leaders has been the war in Vietnam. Almost daily, "responsible leaders" of the Young–Wilkins variety are paraded before the American public, their statements taken as gospel by the American people—despite evidence to the contrary—much in the way that the statements of the two soldiers were taken as evidence that the overwhelming majority of Black people in America support the Administration's Vietnam policies, and that the statement made by Stokely Carmichael before nine hundred cheering students and faculty members in a speech at Hampton Institute in 1967—"Hell no, we won't go!"—represents little more than emotionalism, irrationalism, and youthful iconoclasm, completely lacking any basis in fact, and inapplicable to most Black Americans.

But still, more and more Black men in the ghettos are deciding that they will not go to the war in Vietnam, and their decisions are not the result of emotionalism nor youthful iconoclasm. Not only are their decisions derived from first-hand experience of the treatment received by them and their kinsmen at the hands of present-day white Americans; they are even more aware of the history of the participation of Black men in past American wars and the treatment accorded these men and their fellow Negroes once those wars had ended.

It is ironic that the first man gunned down by the British redcoats was a Black man. Crispus Attucks was, however, only one of the many Blacks who sacrificed their lives in the Revolutionary War for a freedom and liberty which their survivors and descendants would never know. Some of these men served as proxies for their masters, others were released from slavery specifically to take part in the war.

The decision to allow Negroes to participate in the war at all was reached only after serious deliberation. General George Washington, who at the outset had wanted no Black soldiers at all, relented to the point of accepting freed Negroes in his Revolutionary Army. His decree was soon amended, however, when Americans realized that many Negroes were escaping from slavery to join the British because the British promised them manumission. America followed suit, promising Black men who participated in the war that, after the war, their freedom would be assured. Thus began the first of a long series of broken promises made to Black men by white men; for once the war was over, many of the men who bad joined in the fight for American independence were re-enslaved.

This breach of faith did not prevent Frederick Douglass from petitioning President Lincoln, during the Civil War, to accept Black soldiers into the Union Army. Douglass saw the war between the states—despite evidence to the contrary—as a war to end slavery. But like Washington before him, President Lincoln, too, was reluctant to use Black soldiers. He was not eager to "loose that Black hand" which Douglass claimed lay impotent; not willing, that is, to allow Black men to kill white men, even in the interest of liberty. Only under the steady prodding of Douglass, and as a result of Confederate victories, did Lincoln finally accept Negro soldiers—at less pay, with fewer supplies, under segregated conditions—into his army.

The men fought well despite these handicaps, earning the respect of many of their commanders in the field; however, once the war was over, they became a part of that displaced mass of Black people, soon to be deserted by the very union forces they had aided. Left to the mercy, caprices, and devices of those whom they had fought against, their fight for liberty was, in the final analysis, no more than a fight for re-enslavement, this time by the "Black Code Laws"—chains more binding than those welded about their arms and ankles by callous masters.

Yet when the world plunged into its first global war, W. E. B. Du Bois urged Black men to close ranks and fight shoulder to shoulder with their white brothers in a common cause. This cause—"to make the world safe for democracy"—was a cause which so astute a scholar as Du Bois must have certainly suspected.

For President Woodrow Wilson had never even attempted to make America safe for democracy. Almost from the inception of his administration, he had begun to transform the nation's capital into the most segregated city outside of the deep South. Overnight, the civil services were resegregated, "colored" rest rooms were established in office buildings, restaurants, and government establishments, and the lynching rate climbed as high as two Blacks per month.

Despite Wilson's reputed declaration that "this is a white man's war," there was little resistance this time to accepting Black troops. In fact, the editor of the "Waterbury Times" considered the use of Black men a good thing: "It seems a pity to waste good white men in battle with such a foe. The cost of sacrifice would be nearly equalized were the job assigned to Negro troops. . . . An army of nearly a million could probably be easily recruited from the Negroes of this country without drawing from its industrial strength or commercial life. . . . We will be sacrificing white blood . . . and drawing on skilled labor when unskilled labor was available."

Still Black men heeded the call to participate in the "war to end all wars," serving in segregated units, most of them under the control of Southern officers, one of whom welcomed his troops with the following words: "[You] need not expect democratic treatment . . . White men made the division, and they can break it just as quickly if it becomes a troublemaker. . . . Don't go where your presence is not desired."

The only place, it seemed, that the presence of Black soldiers was desired was the battlefield. In America, their presence quickly became a signal for danger. Trained as men, the soldiers proceeded to act as such, rioting and even killing, retaliating against acts of barbarism directed against them, despite the uniforms they wore. When drum-major Noble Sissle of the 15th New York Infantry was assaulted by a group of white men for refusing to take off his army-issued hat in the presence of a white newspaper dealer, rumors of war swept Spartanburg, South Carolina, warning that the coming war was to be fought, not against the Germans, but against the enemy closer to home. The 15th was made a part of the 369th Regiment, another contingent of Black soldiers, and immediately shipped to the front.

Once again, Black men proved their valor, winning a considerable share of the victories, and receiving many decorations both individually and collectively. One such decoration was France's *Croix de Guerre,* awarded to foreign troops for the first time. Lauding the Black soldiers at this important ceremony, the French commander remarked: "You have won the greatest battle in history and saved the most sacred cause, the liberty of the world. . . . Posterity will be indebted to you with gratitude."

Perhaps posterity will repay its debt. But it seems evident that America will not. Hardly had the victory parade down New York's Fifth Avenue ended before the Ku Klux Klan arose, stronger than ever, to take advantage of a world now made safe for democracy. In the same year in which the war ended, seventy-six Negroes, many still in uniform, were lynched. That following year—one of those now forgotten hot summers of American history—Blacks were the recipients of America's indebtedness in Texas, Arkansas, Pennsylvania, Washington, and Chicago, Illinois, where in a twelve-day massacre, Black men, women, and children were maimed and murdered by mobs of whites, operating with tacit assistance from the legal authorities.

These facts notwithstanding, in World War II, Black men went forth once again, though with mixed emotions, to defend the freedom of their country. And this despite the fact that lynchings had now become an accepted part of the American Character, so much so that an anti-lynching bill could not be passed in the Congress, even though the rate of lynchings had gone up during the Roosevelt years to one per week.

Once again Black men acquitted themselves well on the field of battle, and once again after the battle was done, their heroism and sacrifice was forgotten. After helping to defeat the racist regime of Adolf Hitler, Americans returned to a position, vis-à-vis their fellow citizens, as severe as that of the Nazi racists. Black people were the first to be dismissed from the defense jobs, the last to receive training for the coming years of automation, still segregated in housing and public accommodations, and still victims of the rope, the torch, the firebomb, and the rifle at the hands of white Americans North and South.

Nor did the situation change after Korea. Black veterans returning to America found that they and their people were in the same predicament as before: still the recipients of inferior education, the worst jobs, the most degrading treatment, and still subject to acts of terrorism, physical assault, and murder. In exchanging the khaki brown for civilian clothes, they discovered what the compatriots of Crispus Attucks had discovered after the Revolutionary War—that the most cherished freedom which they had fought to preserve was the freedom of Americans to oppress them and their people.

This is a terrible truth to arrive at concerning one's country. And yet nothing, either in the past or in the present, has made it necessary for Black people to disavow this truth. And if indeed the future is merely a product of past and present, then the Black soldiers fighting and dying in Vietnam—including the two Negro representatives—can look forward to a future differing very little from that of their predecessors. Their people will still be oppressed, still given the worst jobs, their children still forced to attend inferior schools, and most of them still forced to live in crime-infested ghettos. They will continually be the victims of acts of violence—no longer the sole expression of the Ku Klux Klan, but now initiated by solid citizens, those of the suburbs of Chicago, Boston, Newark, and New York City, who will rationalize their actions with the assertion that they are fighting to preserve *their freedom.*

The Congress of the United States will reflect the consensus of such constituents and refuse to pass civil rights legislation, except the most meaningless kind; veto rat bills; dismiss a Black congressman with impunity; cut appropriations funds; refuse to enact open housing legislation—in short, refuse to accord Negroes, who have fought and died for this country, the elemental rights which it accords any fair-skinned foreigner who steps off any boat in New York City's harbor.

In addition, there is the fact that the most fervent supporters of the war in Vietnam are men and organizations whose names read like a Who's Who of racism in America: Congressmen Eastland, Thurmond, Rivers, and Stennis; Governors Wallace, Faubus, and Maddox; the Conservative Party, the American Nazi Party, the John Birch Society, and the Daughters of the American Revolution, which does not, even today, permit any of the daughters of Crispus Attucks to join its ranks.

Not even the two Negro soldiers can presume that such a coterie has the interests of Black people at heart. Such men and organizations offer evidence that America will, after this war is over, return once again to repressing Black people, rerunning the old film through the same old cameras, performing as the American people have always performed in the aftermath of every war in which Blacks have participated. The only difference this time will be that Black people will no longer passively and quiescently accept such oppression.

There comes a time in the life of a people, as in the life of an individual, when each says to the oppressor, "No more, you have gone far enough." That moment has now arrived for Black people. Young, articulate Black men, who are refusing to serve in the war in Vietnam, are the inheritors of an experience which Crispus Attucks did not possess. They know that America is a racist society and that the fight for liberty and freedom must begin here where liberty and freedom are so blatantly denied, and that it affords a man nothing to make another country safe for democracy only to live under totalitarianism in his own.

But also, these men have no illusions. They know that America will continue to listen to the self-appointed guardians of her conscience—those Negroes who pass their own truths off as the truths of twenty million people. They know also, as certainly the Greek theatergoers must have known, that the *deus ex machina,* is little more than a mechanical construction, not the voice of man, but the instrument of man; holding out the hope of salvation which no honest men would dare to vouchsafe.

And they know, too, that even as the *deus ex machina* is wheeled into the living rooms of America—whether from the nation's capital in Ivy League suits, or from the battlefields of Vietnam in khaki brown and war gear—in an attempt to comfort white America, an increasing number of Black men in the ghettos are refusing to join this war, refusing to once again become the laughing stock of history—fighting for a freedom which they themselves have never possessed—and refusing to allow nonsensical rhetoric and empty phraseology of the machine gods to drown out their short, eloquent statement, "Hell no, we won't go!"

CHAPTER 8

Racism and the American University

(1971)

Not since the eighteenth century has the American university been embroiled in more conflict than at present. In 1750 the conflict centered around control: Would the university continue to be dominated by church denominations or would control pass to the states? In the famous Dartmouth College case of 1819 in which Daniel Webster appeared as attorney, the ruling of the court established the right of private, sectarian universities to exist free of state control. "The way was therefore open," notes Russell Blaine Nye in *The Cultural Life of the New Nation*, "for public and private institutions of higher education to develop separately, with the victory to the most powerful. In the ensuing struggle for educational dominance of the United States, the religious institutions had by far the heavier guns."

The control of American higher education by religious denominations lasted until the middle of the nineteenth century. American colleges were little more than satellites of the Presbyterians, Methodists, and Baptists. They existed primarily to inculcate morals, dispense ethical values, and propagandize on behalf of God and nation. Disdaining the plight of the poor, they were primarily concerned with the sons of the wealthy whom they attempted to provide with "a body of knowledge that would assure them of entrance into a community of educated leaders." In *Political Inquiries*, written in 1791, Robert Coram voiced objections to this policy: "Education must not be . . . confined to the children of wealthy citizens; it is a shame, a scandal to civilized society, that part only of the citizens should be sent to colleges and universities."

Church domination of the institutions of higher learning meant that the university would be non-secular in mood as well as control. Ostensibly modeled after the universities of Europe—more specifically those of England—the early institutions did not encourage an atmosphere conducive to the free exchange of ideas. In a series of lectures given in 1852, John Henry, Cardinal Newman, proposed the basis for such an atmosphere, but these were found irrelevant in a society which did not believe, with the Cardinal, that knowledge, "considered in a religious aspect, concurs with Christianity a certain way, and then diverges from it; and proves in the event, sometimes its serviceable ally, sometimes, from its very resemblance to it, an insidious and dangerous foe."

The church leaders considered knowledge unrelated to Christianity "a dangerous foe," and they kept a tight rein on college curricula. Their autocratic control led to serious controversy. "The first revolt against the traditional curriculum began in the middle of the eighteenth century. Expanding horizons in both scientific and non-scientific knowledge called for a broader collegiate education for broader purposes. American colleges had failed to reflect the changing character of American life. . . ."

The failure "to reflect the changing character of American life" is a censure under which the twentieth century university still labors. The blame does not lie with the university alone. In the latter part of the eighteenth century, it reacted to intense pressure, not from students, but rather from the church fathers, politicians and wealthy citizens. Each of these factions wanted the university to cater to their interests, thus necessitating certain changes in the curricula. The church demanded a continuation of moral and ethical training; therefore, its members sought retention of curricula embodying moralistic themes. The politicians, acting out of a sense of nationalism, demanded a shift front the preoccupation with morals and ethics to the inculcation of ideals of patriotism. The importance of science and technology to the business world caused men of wealth to demand a curriculum more favorably disposed to these disciplines. The university, which had traditionally reacted more favorably to the demands of outside special interest groups than it had to those of its own students, complied with all three demands. Thus, the curriculum of the nineteenth century university differed radically from that of previous centuries.

For the university, the consequences were grave. In conforming to the wishes of special interest groups outside its structure, it surrendered all possibility of existing as an independent institution devoted to the pursuit of knowledge. During the nineteenth century, it became the pawn of forces far more dangerously sectarian than the most dogmatic religious order. In the Southern states, the policy which determined the content of the curriculum was dictated by politicians. In other parts of the country, the institutions came under the dictatorship of wealthy alumni whose control was often as tyrannical as that of the Southern politicians.

By the end of the nineteenth century, the university had ceased its attempt to become an independent agency for the dissemination of creative, independent thought. Outwardly it maintained its appearance of a cloistered monastery where wise monks, devoted to the pursuit of wisdom, discoursed with eager, inquisitive students; however, in reality, the university was the home of men whose political and religious attitudes were merely replicas of those in the world outside. The appraisal of American universities as liberal institutions remains one of the purest examples of the elasticity of the English language.

Far from being liberal, the universities have been the most conservative, reactionary and racist institutions in the American society. Like the tides, they demonstrate the remarkable ability to move back and forth with the varying times. After the Civil War, when the conservative movement dominated America politically, economically and socially, the trend of the university was toward conservatism. When Franklin D. Roosevelt's New Deal policies produced a new wave of liberalism, it executed an almost one-hundred-and-eighty-degree turn to the left. In only one area has the university maintained equilibrium throughout its history—the area of race relations.

There was no necessity to institute change in this area. The policies of the nation concerning Black people have changed little since the days of Reconstruction. No special interest group pressured the university to change policy or curricula in deference to Blacks. The "responsible" Negro leaders and their organizations, whose memberships usually include a large number of college professors, waged their war against state governments, primarily in the South, and ignored the university. Always few in number, Black college professors found themselves (those who made the attempt) unable to effect change.

Dr. Du Bois, who attempted to institute the first Black Studies program in America, although he did not call it by that name, was stymied in his efforts by a conservative faction in American education led by Booker T. Washington. Washington, who had long been the darling of the educational establishment, supplied, through his philosophy and work at Tuskegee Institute, the rationale which enabled the university to continue along its well-established route. Long before Washington enunciated his educational formula for the Negro in "The Atlanta Exposition Address," the men who controlled the institutions of higher education had put the theory into practice.

Washington was not an independent thinker. The policy he advocated and the formula he followed had been developed by General Armstrong at Hampton Institute. As a student at Hampton, Washington carefully observed the effect of industrial education upon Black and Indian students. He concluded that the Indians did not possess the capacity to learn technical skills, whereas Blacks showed great proficiency. No intellectual, having reached this conclusion and armed with a personal disdain for creative thought, he began to dream of a Black university in which the "practical and useful arts were to be taught."

The business and educational establishments were willing to help him realize his dream. They founded normal schools in the South and community colleges in the North. The aims of both institutions were similar: train Blacks to be the servants and lackeys of white America. In the South this meant education designed to produce carpenters, maids, agricultural workers and petty businessmen; in the North, to produce nurse's aides, orderlies, clerical helpers and lab technicians.

In addition, conforming to the ideals prevalent in the society outside its walls, the men from the universities developed not only the theories to justify their proposed educational program for Blacks, but also the theories which tended to validate the Black man's inferiority. A summary of the many arguments from university professors, North and South, was supplied by the educator Thomas Pearce Bailey in 1913. Bailey wrote: "The white race must dominate. The Teutonic peoples stand for race purity. The Negro is inferior and will remain so. This is a white man's country. No social equality. No political equality. In matters of civil rights and legal adjustments give the white man, as opposed to the colored man, the benefit of the doubt; and under no circumstances interfere with the prestige of the white race. In educational policy let the Negro have the crumbs that fall from the white man's table. Let there be such industrial education of the Negro as will best fit him to serve the white man. The status of peasantry is all the Negro may hope for, if the races are to live in peace. Let the lowest white man count for more than the highest Negro. The above statements indicate the leadings of providence."

To say that Bailey reflected the attitude of every college educator in America would be a gross distortion. To say that his opinions were held by a large number then and now is not. There have always been conscientious, dedicated men in the universities intent on moving it toward the fulfillment of its function of independent, creative education. Their attempts have been stifled, their idealism dissipated through their inability to deal with the Baileys who have the support of powerful interest groups, both in and out of the university. Men who hold Bailey's sentiments wield power in many universities, and although their language differs from that of the former educator (the City College of New York is an exception; there, the Baileys have not been reluctant to declaim in the language and tone of their predecessor), their aims remain the same. Furthermore, riding a wave of conservative reactionism, today they are in a position to fulfill their aims.

The student rebellions of the past few years have been ineffective because the rebels have not realized this fact. Those who sought to change the university, Black and white, neglected to do their homework. They chose targets of little real substance. The college administrator no longer exercises power as he did in the seventeenth and eighteenth centuries. At that time, his word was law. He could dismiss instructors and students with impunity; he could set arbitrary standards and demand that they be adhered to; his was the final word on curriculum. He answered only to the church authorities, who were usually in complete accord.

When the universities came under more ruthless secular control in the nineteenth century, the erosion of the administrator's power began. This change was completed by the institution of the tenure system, which allowed a group of individuals, reflecting the conservative nature of the society, to seize and maintain power. The result has been that, in the twentieth century, college presidencies have become ceremonial, not policy-making positions, and the occupants of these positions have no more power than the students.

Real power resides in the hands of the faculty. It is they who set policy, determine curriculum content, and develop admission requirements, More often than not, they run the university in a manner more dictatorial and capricious than the early church fathers would have thought possible. They are men of limited vision and questionable capacity, whose ideas of education belong to the age of Aquinas and the Scholastics. They are young and old, Black and white, and their most suitable metaphor is Dr. Bledsoe, the college president in Ralph Ellison's *Invisible Man.*

The controversy in higher education in the twentieth century centers about the arrogant use of faculty power to impede change and maintain the status quo in the political, economic and social areas of American life. This arrogant use of power, exercised in the interests of racism and reactionism, is, at present, nowhere exhibited more blatantly than at the City College of the City University of New York.

C.C.N.Y. has been designated—erroneously to be sure—as "a great liberal institution." This was due in part to the policy of the college, enacted at its inception, of enrolling the children of white minority groups. At the same time and ever since, it has practically closed its doors to the children of the Black and Puerto Rican minorities who live in the neighborhoods surrounding its Gothic buildings. The greatest enrollment of Black students in the college's history occurred in 1965, and the manner in which this token enrollment was effected evidences the power and racism of the faculty.

Despite the fact that Dr. Kenneth Clark, the well-known psychologist and advocate of integration, has occupied a prominent position on the faculty of the college for close to ten years, the initial impetus to enroll more Black and Puerto Rican students came not from the apostle of integration but from two white men, Bernard Levy and Leslie Berger. With little encouragement from Dr. Clark and no help, the two educators conceived the Pre-Baccalaureate Program. The program, to paraphrase Berger, was designed to offer minority students from New York City's ghetto areas an opportunity for a college education.

The program was begun during the summer when the majority of the senior faculty was on vacation. When the faculty returned to find the program in operation, in the fall of 1965, they began to develop stratagems to limit its effectiveness. Later, when the Pre-Bac Program became the model for the S.E.E.K. (Search for Educational Excellence through Knowledge) Program, the opposition increased. The threat of even greater numbers of Blacks and Puerto Ricans brought forth new stratagems, this time designed to destroy the program.

The proposals ranged from creation of a new community college in Harlem to which the students could be transferred, to the purchase of the Music and Art High School for the incarceration of the S.E.E.K. staff and student body. Another proposal was to keep the students on campus but to give them special courses for the entire four years, at the completion of which they would receive special degrees. The most effective plan was developed under the auspices of the English Department. Of all the departments, the English Department faced a special dilemma. It had opposed the Vietnam war and gained a reputation—in matters which did not pertain to Blacks—of being liberal. To have rejected the students outright would have been to reveal the racism which the members had assured themselves they did not possess. To have accepted the students into the educational life of the department would have forced the members to reveal their own deficiencies in educational skills and techniques.

The English Department moved in the direction which has been sanctioned ever since by departments and colleges searching for ways to minimize contact between whites and Blacks in an educational setting. It created a special branch of the department and hired a special staff of Black teachers. It attempted to discourage white teachers who applied to teach in the program and offered them positions in the regular department instead. It frowned upon those of its own members who were committed to true education and demanded to teach S.E.E.K. students. Therefore, within the English Department there existed a separate program with a staff and student body composed primarily of Blacks and Puerto Ricans. Dr. Clark, who resigned from the board of Antioch College due to an allegedly similar situation, retains his position on the faculty of C.C.N.Y.

During the uprising of 1969, Black and Puerto Rican members of the Student Coalition put forth as one of their five demands a greater voice in controlling the program. What they sought was the validation of the policy already being practiced by the English Department. Since the program was separate in every aspect except control, why not also relinquish this to Blacks and Puerto Ricans? In other words, extending the formula enacted by the English Department, why should a program primarily designed for Blacks and Puerto Ricans, which had been effectively transformed into a segregated program, not go all the way and become separate in every essential? The faculty balked. To maintain a separate program was one thing, to allow Blacks and Puerto Ricans to control it was another; however, with the exception of the question of control, the students and the faculty, to paraphrase William Blake, were both of the same devilish party without even knowing it.

What began as an attempt to legalize existing policy quickly degenerated into a conflict between Black and white. Black and Puerto Rican faculty and students became the objects of the type of verbal abuse which does honor to the memory of Senator Vardaman of Mississippi, who took great pride in his extensive vocabulary of racial epithets. Students were called "animals" and "misfits," faculty members were called "boys," "girls" and "niggers." The epithets were hurled by faculty members from the floor and rostrum during faculty meetings attended by Black and white students. Once, in my presence, the newly elected acting president, Joseph Copeland, referred to white students who supported the goals of the Blacks as "white trash."

Racist attitudes, which had heretofore been visible only to individual Black and Puerto Rican students in classrooms when papers were returned or their examinations marked, flared into the open, as the faculty could no longer restrain itself.

Much of it, to be sure, was occasioned by the student seizure of the south campus. But, this act alone does not suffice as an explanation of the terrible spectacle presented by college teachers shouting epithets at Black students, encouraging white students to display Nazi insignia, and performing with an hysteria and paranoia whose closest analogue is to be found in the lynch mobs, legendary in American history. The frenzied actions of the faculty mob were motivated by more threatening forces than the student occupation of buildings.

At the close of the fall semester of 1968, prior to the student revolt, the English Department hired Dr. Wilfred Cartey, the distinguished, internationally known scholar of Black history and culture, to institute a Black Studies Program. (During the turmoil when Professor Cartey was charged with being a tool of the Black Panther Party and having been brought to the college by this organization, the English Department did not attempt to clarify the issue or to refute the charges—the reason is clear: By that time, the English Department had had second thoughts about its choice.) Cartey was a scholar first, and with the keen analytical mind of the scholar; he divined the forces at work on the campus. They were the same forces that were at work on campuses throughout the nation. The rash of instant Black Studies Programs, ill-equipped, poorly organized and inadequately staffed, is merely a ploy of contemporary racists to perpetuate the miseducation of Black students, a policy which has been the hallmark of the American university.

Few of these programs are worth the paper they are drawn on. Designed to benefit neither Black nor white students, their objectives are to remove the burden of educational responsibility from the shoulders of the older, tenured faculty. To be effective, a Black Studies Program must be interdisciplinary. It must effect change in every liberal arts department in the university. In so doing, far from being, as Bayard Rustin insists, a cathartic exercise for Black students, such a program would radicalize the university and transform it into a truly educational institution.

To understand this statement, one must first be aware of the inadequacy of existing college curricula: In history courses on both the undergraduate and graduate levels, the contributions of Frederick Douglass, David Walker, Henry Highland Garnet, and Booker T. Washington to the making of the American nation are deleted; neither Phillis Wheatley, Paul Laurence Dunbar, Claude McKay nor Langston Hughes are read or studied in English courses, Students of sociology are not required to read Du Bois, E. Franklin Frazier, Weaver or Kenneth Clark. The same omissions are repeated in political science, music, and economics.

A realistic Black Studies Program would therefore force such delinquent departments to restructure their courses to include the contributions of minority groups. Far from being an isolated, segregated enclave existing somewhere in the hinterlands of the campus, the Black Studies Department would be a powerful institution capable of producing a renaissance in American thought and education.

Fred Cartey entertained such ideas. For this reason, he found himself caught between the Black and Puerto Rican student and faculty community and the white faculty. To once more paraphrase William Blake, the antagonists were working in the interests of the same deity. With few exceptions, neither the Black students nor faculty had the least idea of what a program of Black and Puerto Rican Studies entailed. In lieu of understanding, they substituted emotionalism which often took the form of demands for the improbable, incapable of being fulfilled by anyone—who did not have the power of Zeus, the wisdom of Apollo and, the patience of Job. They knew that they had been cheated out of their cultural heritage, but they did not know how to force the university to make amends.

On the other hand, the white faculty, old hands at deceiving Black students, knew what kind of Black Studies Program they would allow from the very beginning. Like the Pre-Bac Program, they wanted it to be separate. The teaching of Black history and literature in a separate institution, run by Blacks for Blacks, would lessen the pressure on the senior faculty members. Veterans of the white liberal tradition, having marched to Washington with Martin Luther King and attended meetings of the N.A.A.C.P., they knew how to mesmerize the natives by presenting the appearance of action without committing substantive acts.

Dr. Cartey's proposal called for the creation of a School of Black and Puerto Rican Studies, whose far-reaching effects would go beyond changing the traditional departmental curricula. More important, the program called for extensive exploration and study of areas of interest, not only to the student body, but also to the Black and Puerto Rican community outside the college. From the moment that such a program, designed to bring large numbers of Blacks and Puerto Ricans together in an educational setting to study not only their own history and culture but that of the oppressor as well, was unveiled, Cartey's days at C.C.N.Y. were numbered. The Black and Puerto Rican Faculty–Student Coalition and their white supporters whose impotence was displayed at each faculty meeting, found themselves with no program at all. In the absence of any restraining power, the new president, acting in behalf, if not with the full knowledge, of his reactionary faculty, arbitrarily dismissed Dr. Cartey, and, functioning as the hatchet man of the extremist faction, launched a verbal attack upon the scholar in the language fashionable among bigots from Mississippi to New York City.

The lesson to be learned from the C.C.N.Y. experience is important to students across the nation. The men who run America's educational establishment cover the spectrum from idealists to demagogues. At present, the political climate in America favors the demagogues. The special interest groups which influence educational policy from California to New York are dedicated to the proposition that the university will not change in any significant way. They are prepared only to offer palliatives instead of cures for the serious problems of the twentieth century.

Those most affected by this attitude are non-white minorities for whom the university has long been regarded as a stepping stone to success. They have watched colleges educate and prepare members of other minority groups to assume positions of importance in their communities. Three times within its history, City

College lowered its standards in order to enable members of white minority groups to enroll. Today, many members of those groups support the faculty's attempt to keep Black and Puerto Rican enrollment at a minimum. In addition, they constitute the special interest groups behind the politicians and college officials whose objective is to keep minority students within the limits of the Booker T. Washington formula.

They mask their racist attitudes behind seemingly legitimate reasons. The turn to repression and reaction on the campus, goes the rationale, is due to the student rebellions of the past few years. Most of these rebellions have been led and precipitated by white students, yet those who receive the brunt of the pressure are Black. This pressure was intensified when a group of Black students at Cornell University armed for self-protection after a fiery cross—the symbol of American tyranny which burns deep in the heart of every Black man—was placed in front of the Black women's dormitory. Denunciations came from Congress, the press and the more overt Negro haters across the country. The aim has been to depict Black students as disrupters of the peaceful university which existed, in the words of a white South Carolinian, "before they removed God from the schools and let the niggers in."

The peaceful university has never existed. As Nye notes, ". . . the history of almost any nineteenth century college shows at least one serious outbreak. In 1807, 125 of Princeton's total enrollment of 200 were expelled for rioting. Harvard freshmen and sophomores in 1817 smashed all the college crockery; that same year Princeton students broke the dormitory windows and threw wine bottles and firewood at the faculty. At Hobart students rolled red-hot cannonballs down a dormitory corridor and seriously injured a faculty member. At North Carolina students shot out windows with guns, and at Virginia, the high-spirited Southern boys horsewhipped several faculty members. In 1814 Princeton students constructed a giant firecracker with a hollow log and two pounds of gunpowder and nearly blew up Nassau Hall. The class of 1824, in preparation for graduation at Dartmouth, 'burnt one barn, stoned Professor Chamberlain, burnt him and tutor Parley and hung the President in effigy.' Three Bowdoin students were expelled and a score of others disciplined in 1827 for setting off powder charges under tutors' chairs."

Neither the university community nor the community at large responded with repressive measures. Unlike his counterpart in New York City today, the President of Hobart College did not threaten the students with the Army, Navy and Marines. They were white students; therefore, they were not placed in isolation, declared unworthy of an education, nor harassed by faculty members and fellow students. With far more limited resources than the college of today, the earlier institution moved to correct the problems which produced the disturbances.

That the same action will tape place in the reactionary atmosphere of the present is doubtful. Having proved that it is merely one more racist institution in the society, the university seems determined to continue those policies which can only hasten the coining of what James Baldwin has described as "the fire next time."

In 1965, in a moment of unfounded optimism, in an article in the *Journal of Human Relations,* I described the new Black and Puerto Rican students who had just entered City College in the following terms: "These young men and women are engaged in the process of ridding the American society of knot holes, of throwing open the doors of the world of intellect, of understanding through learning, scholarship, and perseverance, not for themselves alone, but for all of those in this country, Black and white, who comprise that segment of humanity which Franz Fanon has called 'the wretched of the earth.' I was correct about the students. I was wrong about the university. The metaphor of the twentieth century is a university impervious to change and, unlike its predecessors of the middle ages, incapable of bringing order out of chaos and establishing the rule of reason. Had I been more perceptive in 1965, 1 would have advised my students in the words which Matthew Arnold used to advise a college dropout in "The Scholar Gypsy":

> Fly our paths, our feverish contact fly!
> For strong the infection of our mental strife
> Which, though it gives no bliss, yet spoils for rest;
> And we should win thee from thy own fair life,
> Like us distracted, and like us unblest.
> Soon, soon thy cheer would die.
> Thy hopes grow timorous, and unfixed thy powers
> And thy clear aims be cross and shifting made:
> And then thy glad perennial youth would fade
> Fade, and grow old at last, and die like ours.

CHAPTER 9

Dreams of a Native Son

(1970)

I was introduced to the concept of the bogey man by my mother, a passionate believer in Christianity. Previously, she had attempted to discipline me by conjuring up images of the devil. When the attempt failed, she used her talent for metaphorical language and painted a frightening, vivid description of the bogey man. As she described him, he was ten times more vicious than the devil, five times more intent on devouring Black children and, whereas the devil was ugly, the bogey man was hideous. He had red eyes and red hair, redder even than the coals of hell, and a gray, fishy skin which shone bright and garish when illuminated by the sunlight.

She had not intended to supply me with a racial image. Yet, nevertheless, when the bogey man took form in my mind, the form was that of a white man. This may have been because the only white man I knew, the insurance man, had red hair and red eyes. And though he was not an ugly man, my imagination supplied those characteristics to his features which transformed him into an ogre.

Sometime later, having been threatened with the bogey man for perhaps the fifteenth time, I confronted the ogre in a dream. Here his hair was redder than in waking life and his eyes protruded like long binoculars from both sides of his face. In one of his fishy, gray hands, he carried a wide steel net which he threw over me again and again, as each time I miraculously made my escape. Finally he approached me with a net larger than any before, stalked me like a spider stalking its prey, and maneuvered me at last into a corner from which escape was impossible.

At this point I awoke in a cold sweat, and screamed into the darkness. "Don't let that white man get me! Momma, don't let that white man get me!" The dream has never recurred. And though I have often given much thought to it, I cannot begin to understand its meaning. One thing, however, seems clear: at the age of five, I was concerned about and frightened by the racial situation.

This is not surprising. By that time I had had my "Fire baptism" in the lava-hot waters of Southern racial prejudice. One day, while waiting for my mother in a department store, I stood against a table upon which various garments were arrayed. A white woman approached with a youngster not much older than myself. The young boy wandered over to the counter and, ignoring me, picked up a sweater and began to examine it. Suddenly, his mother, like an enraged, wounded beast, sprang to the counter, snatched the sweater from the child's hands, dropped it hastily upon the table, and pointed an accusing finger at me: "Can't you see that little nigger beside them clothes?" she screeched. "He probably been trying 'em on too. You want to catch germs?"

Records of such incidents would easily fill a library shelf. The naive see them as trivial, simply minutiae relative to the lynchings and bombings which are a part of many Negroes' experiences. Others, have yet to learn what the average Black has always known: Lynching is a word whose connotation cannot be restricted to assaults upon the body alone; brutal though such acts may be, the most vicious brutalization, the most terrible of all lynchings, are those which, in the long run, disfigure the mind.

For me, therefore, white people became natural symbols for things evil. And this symbolism manifested itself in the most trivial ways. Sitting on the backyard fence one Sunday morning, I watched two stray dogs in combat. One was almost pure black; the other dirty white. Neither dog was familiar, yet instinctively I sided with the black dog, egging him on with the epitaph: "Kill that dirty cracker!" I had no problem with identity.

Such incidents stand out in my mind, remembrances of things not really past but ominously ever-present, suggesting that for one Negro at least, to paraphrase Leopold Senghor, the past and the present must always be confused, and that not even in the unconscious can one be free of the realities of everyday life.

Yet the Black unconscious, in the main, lies immune to exploration. Psychologists, sociologists, and anthropologists are more interested in exploring the similarities between Black and white than in dealing with the universe of differences. Too often white and Black psychologists attempt to apply the rules of the academy equally to Black and white alike. As a psychologist, working in a college program with predominantly Black students, confided to me: "Race may be the most important thing to these students, but I doubt it. I think that I can deal with them on the same grounds that I deal with other students . . . at least, I have to; these are the only grounds I know."

By other students I suppose he meant white students, and beyond them, white Americans in general. If so, the argument is not feasible. Black Americans cannot be "dealt with" like white Americans, for despite the argument of the assimilationists, Black Americans are different from white Americans. In many subconscious utterances, Black people acknowledge this fact. Recently, a "Negro leader," addressing a gathering of Blacks in the hopes of quelling a riot, shouted consistently: "Mr. Charlie is armed baby! Them crackers is armed." A three-year-old Black child in the best furnished home in the suburbs could interpret the connotations of such perjorative synonyms as "Mr. Charlie" and "crackers." These synonyms are a part of the language of Blacks from every avenue of American life. In order to communicate with each other in the presence of the master, the slaves developed a system of signs and images. The system survived the institution of slavery. And until James Baldwin's play, "Blues for Mr. Charlie," the language was incomprehensible to most white Americans. Due to Baldwin and to the courage of today's young Black people who insist upon calling a cracker a cracker and a honkie a honkie out loud, white people have been made conscious of that metaphoric world of language in which they are condemned, castigated, and insulted by their porters, maids, countermen and orderlies. Now the world knows who Mr. Charlie is, and thus one of the most colorful symbols in the language has been negated.

The damage to the psyche is immeasurable. On the one hand, satisfaction is gained from mocking the enemy to his face while he, smiling all the while, sees in you only the stereotype of his American history. With a sense of joy, you vilify his family, race, and nation. On the other hand, you know that you must speak a language which he cannot comprehend; that you must wear "the minstrel's mask"; that you must guard against a slip of the tongue. Failure to do any of the above might bring down the apparatus, so carefully constructed by your ancestors during those first years on American soil and bring about your own destruction in one way or another.

Fear provided the structure of the apparatus—the metaphorical language, the wide, timid smile, the Uncle Tom mannerisms; fear keeps the mechanism secret and intact; fear forces a minstrel's mask upon every Negro. He lives in the American society by repressing his true instincts, suppressing his anxieties, and rigidly holding his emotions in check. I believe that unconsciously many Blacks have harbored the desire to pick up a gun, walk out into the crowd, and shoot "as often and as long as one can." Instead, the Negro goes passively to his job, to the theatre, to the corner store.

Such desires, therefore, find satisfaction in the unconscious, and this satisfaction is registered most often in dream phenomena. In the unconscious there is little need for a special apparatus, symbols, and metaphors designed to confuse whites; there is little need for fear. The Negro who dreams of murdering a white man is fulfilling a desire which he would not dare speculate upon in his waking moments. Conversely, the Black who dreams of being lynched by a mob, gives form and body to thoughts which have always been with him but which he has not dared to voice.

The meanings are ominous but clear. The only free Negro in America is a sleeping Negro. For in sleep, sublimated emotions are brought to the surface with a freedom impossible during waking hours. I have had such moments of freedom and I relate two of them here; not for the psychologically sophisticated, nor for the academic scholar, but because these two moments are perhaps the only ones in my life in which honestly, fearlessly, and with passion I could sincerely say with Goethe, "Verweile doch, du bist so schon."

This dream occurred in 1964 after a trip home to visit my family. My young sister was in a church play and I accompanied her to one of the performances. Because it was given during the Easter season, the play centered about the death of the Christ, and among the various stage props was a large oil portrait of Christ which stood in the center of the stage throughout the performance and around which the drama unfolded. During the rehearsal I sat fascinated by the portrait and, despite my atheistic views, was moved by the play. This was the first time I had been inside a church in fifteen years. Back in New York five days later, I had the following dream:

I found myself alone in the church, standing in the center aisle. The room was dimly lit by two lamps, one at the foot of the pulpit, the other, which gave forth a softer, yellower light was near the entrance. Shadows, gray, and ominous, descended upon the church, lighting momentarily—or so it seemed—the portrait of Christ, spraying it in garish colors: first white, then orange, then yellow. Moving slowly down the aisle to the foot of the pulpit, I stopped some few feet from the portrait.

They tell me, I thought, that I am made in your image. Yet I look at you, and I see the men who abuse me, who persecute me. I see the men who kill my children even before they are born, those children who you said were to come unto you. They say that you are my Saviour and you died for me. But if this is so, why did you not prove it, for certainly you must have known what would happen to me, what they would do to me. Why did you not once, just once, do something, anything, to prove that you acknowledged my existence? Why couldn't you have made one of your followers, one of those twelve—even he who was to betray you— why couldn't you have made one of them Black? And if not that, then when you asked the people that day on the mountain to step forward, to come to you and be blessed, why couldn't one of those men have looked like me? And on that last day, when they nailed you up and left you with two men and you said to them, "This day you will be with me in Paradise," why couldn't one of those who were the lowest of men—why couldn't one of those have been like me? Trembling, I moved closer to the rostrum.

No, I thought, it's a lie, all of it! All these years we've been kept in slavery. Yes, for you are the greatest slave master of them all. You taught us to be good to our enemies, to love them, to forgive them. Holding out promises of a heaven, you tied our hands and made us weak. Your words and promises kept us in bondage and prevented us from doing the things that those truly made in your image, have done to us. And so, whenever we look at you, we see them. Whenever we bow down to you, praise you, we are really bowing to and praising those like you, those with blue eyes, blond hair, and white skin. Whenever we worship you, we are, in reality, worshipping them.

My hands trembled violently. Tears sprang to my eyes. I slammed my fist into the palm of my hand. Giant hands tore a scream from my throat.

Yes, you are their saviour. It is they to whom you came and for whom you shed your blood. To them you have given your rod, your staff, and your power to enslave me, to bend me to their will, your power to rob me of life. They are your chosen ones, I your outcast. Yes, and so let it be. Let me not be tied to you. Let me not believe in you. Only in this way can I be free. Only in this way can I possess that freedom which you have granted to them.

With you, there is no freedom for me! No, no freedom and no hope. There is no heaven and no salvation! And until that day when I break away from you, when I hate your blue eyes, blond hair, and white face—until that day, I cannot really and truly hate them. It must begin with you. So let it be now, at this minute, when I can look at you and see them and hate you both, and I do, I hate you, yes!

My legs gave way and I fell at the foot of the platform. Harsh, guttural sounds wracked my body. Several times, a sharp scream came from my lips to reverberate from the walls of the church. I awakened to the sound of my own screaming.

The second dream occurred a few weeks after the death of Malcolm X in 1965. Malcolm had represented something important to me. To say merely that he was a man is not to explain his enormous influence upon those who, like myself, have lost faith in an American dream of egalitarian democracy. He was the first acknowledged prophet of our era to preach the moral decadence of Western civilization, to bring to the conscience of Black people the truth concerning that culture in which we seem bent on immersing ourselves, and to force us to question the idols which we had accepted without question from those who were said to be wiser than us: our leaders.

Despite our political persuasions, few of us had thought deeply about the country in which we found ourselves, about its people, history, and future. We accepted George Washington, Thomas Jefferson, and the other legendary founders of the "democracy" without considering the fact that their hands were wet with the blood of slaves. We accepted the words of the Constitution, notwithstanding the fact that this document, when first drawn up, excluded us from consideration, and that even later, amendments which did include us were purchased with the barrels of many rifles.

We believed in democracy without ever being its beneficiaries, in the dogma of Christianity without being accorded the elementary rights of a Christian, and in the conscience and good will of the American people, when the true nature of this conscience was revealed in lynchings, bombings, starvation, and acts of unbelievable torture. We believed the lies of the white writers, historians and missionaries who said that we had been rescued from a jungle, a nightmare of darkness called Africa from whence came the endless, monotonous, unproductive civilization of the tomtoms, where infested swamps and bushes hid fierce reptiles and savage beasts, and that this Africa was the other side of hell in contradistinction to this semi-paradise, this "Eden" to which we were transported.

Our desire was to be Americans, not understanding what that word connotes in the vocabulary of our short, yet grueling history. So many millions dead, so many millions still dying, and yet like men possessed, we rushed toward assimilation, toward integration, negating history, denying the present, and completely oblivious to the future.

But this rush to be Americans was, on a larger scale, to become part of Western civilization, which, we had been taught, was a product of Jewish and Christian thought derived from the intellectual and moral atmosphere of Athens where Socrates, Plato, and Aristotle held sway. We believed that scholar who wrote that "Western civilization is but a footnote to Plato" and stood awed at the might of Western thought, accomplishment, and success.

Like James Baldwin, we too admired symbols of Western achievement such as the cathedral at Chartres and hated our ancestors because they had not constructed it. Moreover, we traduced those ancestors who we were told were beating out weird mystical incantations upon hide-covered drums while the Hebrews were writing the great scriptures and the Greeks were producing timeless drama and thought. Not knowing who we were and afraid to attempt the discovery, we emulated those who were linked to the grandeur of the past by the color of their skins.

Some, like my father, never feared to explore that culture from which long-yesterday he had sprung. Yet even when the knowledge of the myth which had been foisted upon him was revealed, he, like others, could not forsake the dream of somehow being close to those who knew the wisdom of Socrates, the prophetic utterances of Solomon, or the sociology of Karl Marx.

Much before Ralph Ellison, he wanted to be an American Negro, some hybrid form of animal, a cross between something made and manufactured in America and something which, because it is American, is linked, no matter how tenuously, to the antiquity of Greece and Rome.

A man of great perception, my father was still unable to arrive at the most objective of all truths: that the inheritors of Western civilization have betrayed their heritage. The ideals of democracy, freedom, and equality handed down from the most famous sons of Greece have been turned into a mockery by those who have shamelessly colonized and exploited half the world. The teachings of the prophets which form the bulwark of Western ethics and morality, have been used as a pretext to enslave some, to burn others in gas ovens, and to lynch still more.

The predecessors of those to whom the tenets of justice, mercy, and honor were bequeathed, have honored their ancestors by anointing history with the blood of millions whose only crime was meekness, passivity, and trust. Like the men of old who subjected their God to ridicule and spectacle before riddling his body with nails, these, their historical siblings, have never allowed the God to be peacefully interred; but have dug up his body time and again to be ridiculed once more, to be drenched in blood and sweat yet another time, and to have nails driven into his flesh by even stronger arms than before.

Malcolm unveiled this history before us. "The white man is a devil!" he thundered. And in that statement is the most sincere indictment of Western civilization since that mob, in the shadow of the cross, broke into spontaneous applause as the martyr dropped his head upon his chest for the last time.

Moreover, Malcolm forced us to look at that with which we would integrate, to examine the history of those with whom we would assimilate, and to carefully observe this "burning house," which we sought so ardently, vigorously, and persistently to enter. He raised profound questions of morality, which our white anointed leaders refused to raise, and propounded the truth that not even the alleged savagery of our ancestors, those cannibals who ate other men, could stand equal to the acts performed by those who are purportedly the blessed of the Gods.

Malcolm thus sowed within our fertile minds the seeds of discontent—not with our treatment in the American society, such seeds had long ago blossomed into fruit—but with the idea of being part of all that has been instrumental in the wanton destruction of life, degradation of dignity, and contempt for the spirit. He caused us to question not what democracy could be but what it was; not the potential of Christianity but the actuality; not the ideals of Western culture but the reality; not the thoughts of the prophets but the practice of these thoughts. In so doing, Malcolm became more than just a representative of "Black masculinity"; he became the embodiment of an idea: that the new Canaan will not be built by those who are called the children of God but rather by those to whom the God in his apocalyptic fury never came.

I stood before a microphone. I was dressed in an African agbada, blue in color and embroidered in gold. A man stood on each side of me. Both were dressed in white robes with black cummerbunds. Beyond the speakers' platform were, it seemed, thousands of people, Black and white, some standing, some sitting, and some supported by some invisible force. Before this assembled multitude, I stood secure and comfortable. Somewhere in the back of the hall a voice shouted: "Indictment!" For the first time, I looked down at the notebook opened on the stand before me, flipped a page and began to speak.

"Two weeks ago, four Black children were murdered by bombs in this country. Like a fountain, the American conscience turned on, gushing out sympathy and anger. Yes, for approximately two weeks, the fountain bubbled forth. And then, suddenly, the faucet shut down and the incident was forgotten.

"Now we can assume—no, we can predict—that this is what white people will do time and again, for this is what white people have always done. They have short memories! But can we assume that Blacks too will forget? Can any Jew forget

Auschwitz and Dachau? No, they cannot and we cannot. Yet our Negro leaders say that we will forget; no, not only forget but also forgive. Now these are those Negro leaders that are called responsible, and I for one, must ask to whom they are responsible?

"They are not responsible to Black people, for all they ask of us is our patience, our tolerance, and our lives. And all this they ask in the name of God, truth, and right. We know too well how their argument runs: we are morally superior to those who butcher us, capable of loving them and thereby inoculating them with love so that one day love too will grow in their hearts and minds. This, supposedly, will happen because God is on our side. But what Black man sitting here today can claim that God is on our side? How many of us believe that he stands beside us? Well, maybe so, but if so, then he stands not beside us but behind us; yes, like a sniveling coward, behind us.

"Yes, because the white bigots have gotten to him too! They have frightened their God, and so we will get no help from him. But perhaps we can rely on the truth. But the truth is what white people say it is. And this is so because they have the power to make it so. And what is this power? It is nothing more than the power of life and death. There is no greater power that one man can have over another. So, my quarrel with the Negro leaders is that they have delegated that power exclusively to whites.

"Their dedication to love, God, and morality has given those who today destroy us, a covering of immunity. For we have been neutralized, our hands bound, while others commit murders and atrocities upon us. The Negro leaders have helped to make Black life the most inexpensive commodity in this country." I paused for the first time. Unconscious of time, it was as though I had said all of this and much more in the space of a few seconds. I wiped my face and flipped another page in my notebook.

"But my friends, white people have been deluded! They are still deluded. We Black people must not allow ourselves to be deluded also. Let us not be deluded about the American conscience. I spoke of this conscience as being like a faucet, and we know that when a faucet is shut off you don't know whether there is any water there or not. It may be dry. And so when the Negro leaders say that we will tap the American conscience, maybe there is nothing there to be tapped. Perhaps the truth is that the American people have run dry of decency, justice, and tolerance. And so from their hearts and minds, as barren as the driest deserts, we will get nothing, and until we realize that there is nothing there to get, we will remain deluded." I paused to flip another page.

"But white people too are deluded, and their delusion is by far the greater. You know they always call us boys and girls. No matter what our age, they regard us as children. And why is this? The reason is because we are children. Only children, boys and girls, allow themselves to be slapped down again and again by the enraged parent; only children bend their knees and dream of a thunderbolt from the sky; only children give up the power of life, the power not only to die for something but also to kill for it! Yes, to kill for it!

"Yes! For this is what it means to be a man in a world where there is no justice, where the law is prostituted. Yes, to be a man and not a child is to hold the power of life and death. And we will remain children until we take this power and use it. Yes, I say use it! Let the necks of white people crack under the pressure of the hangman's rope; let their flesh feel the sting, the force of hot, burning balls of metal; let their blond-haired, blue-eyed boys feel the knife cutting into their insides, slicing away the instruments of manhood.

"Ah, some of my white friends are twitching in their seats! How shocked, how sickened, how very frightened you are. But you have listened to the Negro leaders, and so it has never occurred to you that I have always wanted to do to you what you have done to me. But haven't you given me that right, shown me that only through violence can we communicate, man to man?

"Yes, in a thousand ways you have. It is your blueprint which stands before me. Yours is the example of what it means to be a man! Has it never occurred to you, never entered your mind, that that one dream of my life, salvation, will come for me when I cease to be a child and become a man on your terms: a man willing not only to die for freedom, but to kill for it? No, this has never occurred to you, and therefore this, this, is your delusion." I stepped away from the rostrum. The two men who had remained at my side throughout, stepped forward to shake my hand. "My brothers," I said, and woke up to the ringing of the alarm clock.

PART 2

Black Aesthetics

> When we speak of a "black aesthetic" several things are meant. First, we assume that there is already in existence the basis for such an aesthetic. Essentially, it consists of an African-American cultural tradition. But this aesthetic is finally, by implication, broader than the tradition. It encompasses most of the usable elements of Third World culture. The motive behind the black aesthetic is the destruction of the white thing, the destruction of white ideas, and white ways of looking at the world. The new aesthetic is mostly predicated on an ethics which asks the question: Whose vision of the world is finally more meaningful, ours or the white oppressors? What is truth? Or more precisely, whose truth shall we express, that of the oppressed or the oppressors?
> —Larry Neal, "The Black Arts Movement"

One of the primary purposes of this Reader is to present Addison Gayle Jr. as a key figure and intellectual architect of the Black Aesthetics Movement. More than anyone else during this period, Gayle provides a theoretical framework and critical blueprint for black aesthetics.

Section two, "Black Aesthetics," contains Gayle's foundational writings on his philosophy of the black aesthetic and examines his evolving views on the historical relationship between white racism, American arts and letters, and black literature as well as the function of black literature and aesthetics in the emergent Black Arts Movement.

In "The Harlem Renaissance: Towards a Black Aesthetic," Gayle provides a historical background for the dichotomy between the nationalists and the assimilationists and illustrates the direct relationship(s) between the Harlem Renaissance/New Negro Movement and the emergent Black Cultural Nationalism of the sixties.

"Cultural Strangulation: Black Literature and the White Aesthetic," "Separate, Not Mutual Estates," and "The Function of Black Literature at the Present Time" are directives about what Gayle views as the fundamental responsibility of black writers and critics to black communities, culture, and history: "Black writers, having adopted the political dicta of Black Power and, having moved beyond the pioneering position of Walker, Griggs, and Delany, have set about creating an aesthetic which has its genesis in the nationalism so very apparent in much of Black literature."

This section also introduces readers to Gayle's views on how black novelists and critics were received by mainstream white publishing houses, literary critics, and "liberal" white and black conservatives alike. "The Politics of Revolution: Afro-American Literature," "The Negro-Critic: Invisible Man in American Literature," and "Black Aesthetic: The Defender" reflect Gayle's ardent propositions on the importance for African American views and values to be representative of the literature and criticism that emanated from black communities.

CHAPTER 10

The Harlem Renaissance: Towards a Black Aesthetic

(1970)

During the Harlem Renaissance when Black people, as Countee Cullen notes, were only three generations removed from their ancestral homeland, a group of remarkable men and women converged on Harlem and transformed it into the literary capital of the world. They were a diverse group: They held different opinions concerning the function of art, their relationship with the United States and with each other. They were old and young, naive and sophisticated, college-educated, and self-taught, and they came from places as far away as the West Indies and as near as Washington, D.C. Yet, they had one thing in common—the determination, according to Langston Hughes, "to express our individual dark-skinned selves without fear or shame."

Such a determination may seem archaic in the nineteen sixties when Blacks have made expressing their dark-skinned selves into a religion; however, as late as 1925, to do so was not only unusual but revolutionary. To express one's dark-skinned self meant to seriously evaluate the myths and stereotypes foisted off on the race by Blacks and whites alike. "I never wanted to write dialect [poetry]," Paul Laurence Dunbar told James Weldon Johnson in 1990, "but I had to gain a hearing."

To gain his hearing, the poet catered to the desires of the white reading public by distorting the Black experience in the manner of Thomas Nelson Page, Thomas Dixon and Joel Chandler Harris.[1] In Dunbar's poetry and fiction, the simple, fun-loving, subservient Black becomes the metaphor for the dark race. He was prevented from expressing himself as he wished to and forced to adhere to the old myths and stereotypes by publishers and readers. The resultant damage to his self-esteem and his art is incalculable. In some of the saddest lines ever written by a Black writer, he tells of his personal despair:

> He sang of love when earth was young,
> And love, itself; was in his lays.
> But ah, the world, it turned to praise
> A jingle in a broken tongue.[2]

Dunbar sought the praise of the white world. Like many Black writers, past and present, he made the spiritual pilgrimage to the Cathedral at Chartres where he stood in awe before this symbol of the artistic accomplishment of the Western world. When the imaginary journey was over, having discovered the beauty and grandeur of Western civilization, like James Baldwin, he returned with the belief that civilization and whiteness were synonymous terms and that he who would be civilized must first shed his Black skin. For this reason, the heroes of his novels, Freddie Brent, Landry Thaler and Robert Van Doren, are white mirror images of himself.[3] [He] did not say that he was looking at white characters from a [Black] point of view," writes Saunders Redding, "he simply assumed inherent emotional, intellectual, and spiritual identity with his characters."

Dunbar was not alone. Phillis Wheatley, the second American woman to write poetry and the first Black poet to gain renown, wrote inspiring lyrics to George Washington and his troops during the Revolutionary War; however, she seldom noted the plight of her Black brothers and sisters under slavery, and when she did it was usually done in denigrating terms:

> Father of mercy! 'Twas thy gracious hand
> Brought me in safety from those dark abodes.[4]

William Wells Brown was the first Black novelist, the first Black playwright, one of the first Black historians, a runaway slave, an orator, and abolitionist. Yet, this gallant warrior, when dealing with Black people in fiction, adhered to the convention of the tragic mulatto established by the Plantation School of writers. In his two novels, *Clotel, or the Colored Heroine* (1853) and *Miralda; or the Beautiful Quadroon* (1861), his serious characters are quadroons, octoroons and mulattoes; those who, being closest to the gods, are worthy of salvation. Partly in reaction to this attempt by Black writers of the past to negate their "dark-skinned selves," *The Messenger,*[5] one of the most militant journals of the Renaissance period, adopted as its motto:

> I am an iconoclast
> I break the limbs of idols
> And smash the traditions of men.

The Renaissance writers were determined to adhere to the motto of *The Messenger.* Like Langston Hughes, the best of them sought a perch atop the racial mountain where, free in their own souls, they could express themselves and concomitantly, the hopes, aspirations, and fears of Black People. Living some twenty years prior to the advent of Richard Wright's *Native Son* (1940), many arrived at Wright's truth long before he became famous. Hughes, Locke, Fisher and McKay, any one of them might have written in the twenties, as Wright wrote in the thirties:

The Negro writer who seeks to function within his race as a purposeful agent has a serious responsibility. In order to do justice to his subject matter, in order to depict Negro life in all its manifold and intricate relationships, a deep informed and complex consciousness is necessary; a consciousness which draws its strength upon the fluid lore of a great people, and molds this lore with the concepts that move and direct the forces of history today. The Negro writer is called upon to do no less than create values by which his race is to struggle, live, and die. . . .

At no time in the history of Blacks in America has there been such an intensive campaign to create the values by which the race might survive than during the brief period knows as the Harlem Renaissance. Better educated and more sophisticated than those who preceded them, the Renaissance writers discovered new truths about America. Despite the servile posturing and proclamations of Booker T. Washington, the zenith of race relations had not been reached; despite the patience of Black men—sorely tested as a result of lynchings, bombings and burnings—racial harmony was farther away than ever; despite the heroism of Black men on the field of battle in Europe and that of their brothers and sisters on the home front, democracy was still a word which had meaning only for White Americans. Out of the realization of these new truths, McKay cried out in anger and desperation:

> Oh, Kinsmen; we must meet the common foe.
> Though far outnumbered, let us show us brave,
> And for their thousand blows deals one death blow!
> What though before us lies the open grave?
> Like men we'll face the murderous, cowardly pack.
> Pressed to the wall, dying, but fighting back.[6]

Perhaps in his calmer moments, the angry poet, like James Weldon Johnson, realized that "we would be justified in taking up arms or anything else if we could win, but I know that we cannot win." To be sure, the military battle could not be won. A people with little knowledge of the art of warfare, with no weapons and no allies could not look for victory against the forces of a country whose egotism had been increased by its victories—no matter how slight—in the first World War. This does not mean that Black men practiced passive resistance. Their backs pushed against the wall, they fought with the little they had at their command. In race riots in Chicago, Detroit, and New York City, they fought back and took a fair toll of the oppressor. However, there were no victories. Their losses were great. Although these warriors were courageous men, they fought a battle not of their choosing, at the wrong time and in the wrong places.

The decisive battle lay elsewhere. This was the opinion of Langston Hughes who, in "The Negro Artist and the Racial Mountain" (1926), wrote, ". . . it is the duty of the younger Negro artist . . . to change through the force of his art that old whispering 'I want to be white,' hidden in the aspirations of his people, to 'Why should I want to be white? I am a Negro—and beautiful.'" This was also the opinion of Alain Locke who wrote in *The New Negro:* "America seeking a new spiritual expansion and artistic maturity, trying to found an American literature, a national art, and national music implies a Negro-American culture seeking the same satisfactions and objectives. . . . Negro life is not only establishing new contacts and founding new centers, it is finding a new soul. There is a fresh spiritual and cultural focusing. . . . There is a renewed race-spirit that consciously and proudly sets itself apart. Justifiably then, we speak of the offerings of this book embodying these ripening forces as culled from the first fruits of the Negro Renaissance."[7]

The fruit was the pomegranate; for, like the pomegranate, the Renaissance had many seeds. There were those who continued to cling to the old values, who frowned on full scale war on tradition. They were writers of the stature of William Stanley Braithwaite, Benjamin Brawley and Jessie Fauset. Their position has been aptly summed up by Angelina Grimke:

> We ask for peace. We, at the bound
> O life, are weary of the round
> In search of truth. We know the quest
> Is not for us, the vision blest
> Is meant for other eyes. Uncrowned,
> We go, with heads bowed to the ground,
> And old hands, gnarled and hard and browned.
> Let us forget the past unrest,
> We ask for peace.[8]

For others—Locke, Toomer, Hughes, and Johnson—peace was an illusion. Not only did these writers declare war on tradition, but they also sought to re-evaluate the political, social and cultural values which had been handed down from the past. The position of this group has been recorded by Claude McKay:

> But the great Western world holds me in fee
> And I may never hope for full release
> While to its alien gods I bend my knee.[9]

The result was a split into two opposing groups. To place these groups into perspective the use of the terms "Nationalism" and "Assimilationism"—terms which should not be taken as all-inclusive—is necessary. Assimilationism, cultural or political, is an attempt at accommodation. Inherent in the assimilationist ideal is the belief that white American culture is the *sine qua non* of human existence, and that each Black man, to be civilized, must become a part of it. Politically it means, to use Ralph Ellison's phrase, "to be an American Negro." Culturally it means, in terms of Countee Cullen and James Baldwin, to be an American writer instead of a Black writer.

The major characteristic of Nationalism is its attempt to solidify the group conscience, to create unity among people of the same color, race, or locale. Accepting, *a priori,* the fact that Black men differ from white men, the nationalist argues against cultural sameness and in favor of cultural plurality. Therefore, politically, nationalism means gaining control of the institutions of the American society which control the lives of Black people; culturally, it demands an art which maximizes the differences between white and Black culture.

Central to both philosophies is the question of identity. Would the Black man negate his identity by assimilation so that his culture and that of white America would become one? Would he undergo a baptism in the American mainstream which would wash away his Blackness and transform him into a white man? Or would he find his identity in the artifacts of Black culture handed down from the spiritualists of the past to the present? Would he refuse to be baptized in the presence of alien gods and, instead, choose to be not an American Negro, but a Black man in America?

Two pre-Renaissance novels point up this dichotomy between the assimilationists and the nationalists, and an understanding of them is germane to an understanding of the major conflict among the writers of the Harlem Renaissance.

Marcus Garvey probably never read Sutton Griggs' *Imperium In Imperio,* but had he done so, he might have been accused of plagiarism. For the Imperium that Garvey desired to establish on African soil was established here in America in the novel of this virtually unknown nineteenth-century Black writer.

In *Imperium In Imperio,* published in 1899, a group of Black men, tired of their treatment by white Americans over the years, form a parallel government on American soil. This government also has a president, congress, and a constitution. After years of preparation, of checking out prospective members, the Imperium meets in a secret session to "decide what shall be the relations that shall henceforth exist between us and the Anglo-Saxon race of the United States of America."

Several proposals are put forth during the deliberations. One speaker offers the assimilationist point of view: "We must remain here. As long as we remain here as a separate and distinct race we shall continue to be oppressed. We must lose our identity. I, therefore, urge that we abandon the idea of becoming anything noteworthy as a separate and distinct race and send the word forth that we amalgamate." Another speaker "advocated emigration to the African Congo Free States," which, he argued, "was in the hands of the weak Kingdom of Belgium and could be wrested from Belgium with the greatest ease." The revolutionary argument was voiced by one speaker: "I am for war! . . . Whereas the history of our treatment by the Anglo-Saxon race is but the history of oppression, and whereas our patient endurance of evil has not served to decrease this cruelty, but seems rather to increase it . . . Be it resolved . . . That the hour for wreaking vengeance for our multiplied wrongs has come. Resolved secondly: That we at once proceed to war for the purpose of accomplishing the end just named, and for the purpose of obtaining all our rights due us as men." After much deliberation, the Imperium declares in favor of a separate state for Black people: "Resolved that we sojourn in the state of Texas, working out our destiny as a separate and distinct race in the United States of America." Conscious of American history, they did not expect to be given a state: ". . . let the troops proceed quietly to Austin, seize the capitol and hoist the flag of the Imperium . . . We will demand the surrender of Texas and Louisiana to the Imperium. Texas, we will retain. Louisiana, we will cede to our foreign allies. In return for their aid. Thus, will the Negro have an empire of his own, fertile in soil, capable of sustaining a population of fifty million people."

"I always confuse the present with the past," wrote Leopold Senghor. Knowing as much as we do about the Garvey movement of the 1920s and the movement for self-determination in the 1960s we are apt to confuse the events in *Imperium In Imperio* with those of the present. Certainly it is not too far wrong to suggest that political Black Nationalism had its genesis in the novel of Sutton Griggs. Move the clock ahead twenty-one years, change the setting and in place of the Black intellgensia, substitute the black proletariat of the Universal Negro Improvement Association; for Griggs' hero, Belton, president of the Imperium, substantiate the founder of the UNIA, Marcus Garvey; and we are in the era of the Harlem Renaissance wherein with the advent of the Garvey movement, the dichotomy between the nationalists and the assimilationists is weighted in favor of the nationalists. And no document is more important in understanding this shift than James Weldon Johnson's *The Autobiography of an Ex-Coloured Man*.

Johnson is the embodment of the dilemma of the Renaissance writer. Ostensibly, he is a conservative whose aesthetic and political beliefs are based on pragmatism. Nevertheless, he does more than any other black writer to break down the wall of tradition. In an introduction to *American Negro Poetry* published in 1992, he attacks the dialect tradition which was brought to the height of its popularity by Paul Laurence Dunbar. Realizing that behind the dialect tradition lay the stereotypes which depicted Blacks in pathetic and humorous terms, he sought to substitute a language which more closely resembled the language of black people. His volume of poems, *God Trombones*, published in 1927, is an attempt to return to the true rhythms, nuances and speech patterns of that language.

The 1917 reprint of *The Autobiography,* which was originally published in 1912, appeared five years before Claude McKay's *Harlem Shadows* and enhanced the cultural dichotomy so central to the Harlem Renaissance. Like James Joyce's *Portrait of the Artist, The Autobiography* is the picture of an artist trapped between two worlds. In Johnson's novel, the artist's dilemma is symbolized by a protagonist who is the illegitimate son of a White man and a Black woman. The father and mother symbolize two different worlds. The world of the father is that of Bach,

Beethoven and Mozart—that of the mother, the world of jazz, the blues and folklore. The question posed by the novel is clear: As an artist, more specifically a musician, to which world will the protagonist dedicate himself? He chooses the White world but does so with the realization that he may not have made the best choice. "I cannot repress the thought," he tells us at the end of the novel, "that, after all, I have chosen the lesser part, that I have sold my birthright for a mess of pottage."

Like Johnson's protagonist, the Renaissance writers were forced to choose between two worlds—one of opulence and splendor, already in existence, the other of poverty and hope, waiting to be born. They were confronted with the problem of breaking with tradition while having no substitute for it. They realized that the models handed down to them from the White world were inadequate for the creations of a nationalistic literature, yet they had little time in which to create new artistic forms and many of them doubted that such new forms could be created. This explains, in part, the continued adherence of Renaissance critics—Brawley, Braithwaite, Locke and Dubois—to the aesthetic criteria of the past. Again, as with Johnson's protagonist, they were not certain that the new world could be brought into being.

No one realized with fact more than Wallace Thurman, a bitter, frustrated man whose *Infants of the Spring* (1932) does as much to burlesque the novels of the Renaissance writers as Jane Austen's *Juvenile* does to burlesque the novels of her eighteenth-century predecessors. His portrait of his fellow writers is vivid and to the point: a group of men and women who, although possessing a great deal of talent, talk and dance away their creative energy. Having chosen to wage war by means other than physical confrontation, the Black writer did not bring his creative energies to this task and thus failed to create new images for black people. ". . . some Harlemites," wrote Langston Hughes, "thought the millennium had come . . . They were sure the New Negro would lead a new life from then on in green patures of tolerance created by Countee Cullen, Ethel Waters, Claude McKay, Duke Ellington, Bojangles, and Alain Locke."

The millennium did not come. The New Negro did not materialize in art. Despite innovations in traditional forms—Hughes' interjection of the blues into the poetic structure, McKay's use of the sonnet form to portray anger and protest, Toomer's explication of the rich possibilities of the language and Johnson's fusion of ancient oratorical patterns with the modern stanzaic structure—the Renaissance writers lacked an aesthetic which might have given from and direction to their art. This lack of an aesthetic prevented them from producing new art forms, creating new images and solving the problem of identity.

In reality—and especially is this true of the novelist—the image of the New Negro differed little from the stereotypic Negro of the works of Paul Laurence Dunbar. Of course, there were improvements over the old model: the New Negro was a man disgusted with western civilization and like Ellison's Invisible Man, wary of becoming part of a mechanized world. However, in the novels of McKay, Cullen and Hughes, the New Negro does not attempt to create new values, but rather, like Jake of McKay's *Home to Harlem* (1928), he searches for mystical, romantic ones whose only attraction is that they differ from those handed down by Booker T. Washington.

In *The Crisis of the Negro Intellectual,* Harold Cruse censures the writers of the Renaissance for their failure to produce a nationalistic literature[10] The censure is misdirected. Far more culpable than the writers were the critics who, imbued with archaic notions of what art should be, were incapable of laying down the theoretical guidelines for the evaluation of Black art. They failed to produce standards based on the artifacts of black life—from which the Black writer might create an indigenous literature—which had existed since slavery. Seeking accommodation with society instead of war, these critics demanded obedience to bankrupt critical standards and, in so doing, postponed the battle for cultural separatism now being waged in America by young writers of the Seventies.

However, despite the lack of these standards, much was accomplished and the Renaissance writer, although he did not travel the road to a Black aesthetic, at least mapped out the contours of such a road. As a result of the Garvey movement, the Black critic examined his African heritage; as a result of the large migration of Blacks from South to North, he examined the Southland—the first home away from the old world; as a result of the continued intransigence of White Americans, he questioned his loyalty to American society. Therefore, some writers were able to break with the White western world which for so long had held them in bondage.

The break was not complete. And even now, the Black writers of the Seventies remain as torn between the two worlds as were the Black writers of the Twenties. Once again, history repeats itself and the Black artist is forced to create in the absence of new and different critical criteria. Some—Ellison and Baldwin are the most well-known—still adhere to these canons of criticism vouchsafed by critics whose only contract with Black culture is through their Black servants. Others, like LeRoi Jones and Ishmael Reed, less concerned with white academic critics, deal with the artifacts of Black life realistically in an attempt to create images of the Afro-American in the 1970s.

Once again the critics are remiss. Many adhere to the standards erected by Archibald MacLeish, Robert Penn Warren and Allen Tate—standards applied to Black literature by Robert Bone, Theodore Gross and Herbert Hill. Unwilling to believe with Saunders Redding that Black men are different from White men, such critics continue to use an aesthetic which is inapplicable to Afro-American literature. They continue to adhere to the myth of the sanctity of Western values and ethics even though these values and ethics are being attacked by two-thirds of the people of the world. They refuse to believe with the youth of this nation that the time for change is long past and that the era of bending to other people's gods belongs to the slop jar of history. Like the critics of the Harlem Renaissance, contemporary black critics have refused to realize the most salient fact of the Black man's existence: to be Black in America is to be at war with the American society and of no man is this more true than the Black artist.

However, the situation is far from bleak. Across the country, Black critics are attempting to formulate new aesthetic standards. They have learned much from the artists of the Renaissance and steeped in the critical transactions of Sterling Brown, Arna Bontemps, Langston Hughes and Saunders Redding, they move beyond these critics to search for new codes by which to evaluate the literature of a great people. In this renaissance of the 1970s they remain the brightest hope; and although history may well record their failure to formulate new standards for Black artists, it must also note that, against superhuman odds, against assault from Blacks and Whites alike, they persevered and continued to "fight the good fight."

Notes

1. Thomas Nelson Page, Joel Chandler Harris and Thomas Dixon, White southern writers who gained eminence during the post-Reconstruction period, were instrumental in shaping and perpetuating, through their fiction, those myths about Black life which would dominate American literature for more than fifty years. In the ante-bellum novels of Page and Harris, Blacks were portrayed as docile, fun loving, rather simple-minded creatures, whose days on the plantation were one long series of "shuffles and songs." At the other extreme lay the stereotypes of Thomas Dixon, whose writings characterized Blacks as depraved and brutal sub-humans whose savage impulses were kept in check only by the presence of groups such as the Ku Klux Klan.

2. Paul Laurence Dunbar, "The Poet," *The Complete Poems of Paul Laurence Dunbar* (New York, 1913), Lines 5–8.

3. Freddie Brent is the protagonist of *The Uncalled* (1893), Landry Thaler appears in the *Love of Landry* (1900), while Robert Van Doren is the hero of *The Fanatics* (1901).

4. Phillis Wheatley, "To the University of Cambridge, in New England," *The Poems of Phillis Wheatley* (Philadelphia, 1930), Lines 5–6.

5. *The Messenger,* a monthly periodical, was edited by A. Phillip Randolph and Chandler Owen and published from November, 1917, through May/June, 1928. Its militancy can best be exemplified by a statement which appeared in its first issue (November, 1917, vol. I, no. II) in which the editors described their goal as, ". . . fighting for the economic and intellectual emancipation of the working man."

6. Claude McKay, "If We Must Die," *Selected Poems of Claude McKay* (New York, 1953) lines 9–14.

7. Quotation cited: Alain Locke, ed. *The New Negro* (New York, 1968) xvlxvll. *The New Negro,* originally the title of an anthology of the writings of young Blacks of the Renaissance, was published by Alain Locke in 1925. However, the phrase "New Negro" itself soon became synonymous with the literary movement more formally referred to as the

Harlem Renaissance. Of Alain Locke, author of the anthology just cited, historian Saunders Redding has said: ". . . Phi Beta Kappa Scholar, Rhodes Scholar, and professor of philosophy at Howard University, no man did more to stimulate, direct and stabilize the new intellectualism than he." (*They Came in Chains* [New York, 1950], 262.)

8. Angelina Weld Grimke, "Surrender," Caroling Dusk, ed., Countee Cullen (New York, 1927), lines 1–9.

9. McKay, "Outcast," op.cit., Lines 6–8.

10. Harold Cruse, *The Crisis of the Negro Intellectual* (New York, 1907), 519.

CHAPTER 11

The Black Aesthetic: The Defender

(1974)

Hoyt Fuller, who has withstood a fair number of attacks in his day, might have warned me that my policy of not responding to my critics would embolden some and spur others on to more, intensified attacks. Steve Cannon, who never fails to respond to his critics, once wondered aloud how I could allow tripe written by William Styron to go unanswered. Throughout the years, others have advised me that a vigorous defense is ofttimes the best offense. The advice notwithstanding, however, I have refused to answer criticism directed against me, first, because I have been reluctant to deal with trivia—and the criticism of most of my adversaries has been just that, trivia—and, second, because there is so much work to be done and so little time in which to do it, that to respond to each nonsensical critique would leave little time for much else. Again, I have always believed that people who read my books have a damn good right to criticize them, and that I, the author, have let myself in for it by subjecting my ideas to the marketplace.

This essay does not change any of that! I am, by nature, a peaceful man, a noncombatant, and I hope this is the last time that I will be forced to devote time and energy to answering nonsense, to coping with a very serious disease now infecting some segments of the Black community—a disease, I call Fridayism—which must be defined, analyzed, and rendered impotent, in order that others may continue the very important work, to quote Amiri Baraka, of creating a Black poem and a Black world. Martin Kilson is not half so important as the disease, but he is symptomatic of it, and his recent address, "What Is A Black Aesthetic?" illustrates the debilitating effect that the disease can have on the Black psyche, leading the infected to inveigh, hysterically, against the concept of the Black Aesthetic in general and its advocates in particular.

Were Kilson the only antagonist of the New Black Arts, there would be no need for rebuttal. After all, his constant attacks on any Black endeavor not meeting the approval of white Americans, and his continual fantasy in which he envisions himself as Black intellectual (?) ambassador to the white world or, more precisely, Black missionary to liberal whites, the sterling example of sanity and reason among Black insanity and unreason, in addition to his unimaginative, uncreative, unanalytical thinking, does not exactly qualify him as an opponent worthy of breaking a date with a pretty girl in order to do battle with. Moreover, in reading his statement in the *Harvard Advocate* (Spring 1974) ("It is, then the absence of a *discreet culture* among American Negroes that ultimately bedevils the new 'Black art.' This art, as it were, lacks authenticity. That is, 'Black art' is not valid *in itself.* Validity depends upon an *explicity antithesis* white America."), it is clear that the Black man in 1974, who believes that neither he nor his product has validity or sanction without the approval of white people is already so far gone that nothing I can say will help him.

The real issue, therefore, is much larger than Kilson. He and others have become dangerous, not because of what they say, but because they address Black audiences, who, often unable to hear the side of sanity and reason, are left no options but to accept flimsy premises leading to erroneous conclusions. Because no Black person should be left with nothing but the ideas of Kilson to enlighten him, this essay, though seemingly a response to charges made by Kilson is, in effect, a response to the arguments of others, who, incapable of dealing intellectually with the concept of the Black Aesthetic, attempt to do so through appeals to emotion and superficial arguments couched in the obtuse abstract jargon of the academics.

First: a definition of terms. The term, Fridayism, my own, is derived from Daniel Defoe's novel, *Robinson Crusoe.* Near the end of the novel, the Black Friday, having been civilized by Crusoe, joins the Englishman in repulsing an attack by other Blacks, lays his life on the line, so to speak, in order to protect, not only Crusoe, but his own newly won "civilized" status. Now one may rationalize Friday's actions by arguing that he had become, in effect, a slave of Crusoe, that he was a first generation Black man, thrust suddenly into contact with Western culture and technology, that his response, whether out of fear or gratitude, was to be expected. To explain similar actions by the sons of Friday, however, after centuries of immersion in the West, is a different matter. They, after all, have lived among the descendants of Crusoe, have witnessed their acts of inhumanity against man, whatever the color or religion, have witnessed their pragmatic attempt to destroy the human spirit. What then accounts for continual defense of Crusoe and, for obeisance to his wishes, even though he no longer constitutes a physical threat?

There are, one supposes, many explanations, but one that explains a great deal is what I have called Fridayism—a rationale based upon the Pavlovian theory of behavior. In the Pavlovian experiment, animals were conditioned to salivate at the ringing of a bell; food was the stimulus. In time, the food was removed, but the animals continued to salivate in its absence. Like Pavlov's model, the sons of Friday no longer need the stimulus—fear or gratitude—to propel them into action to protect the interests of Crusoe. Once Crusoe and his brood are attacked, from whatever source, the Fridays salivate in college journals, *The New York Times Book Review,* badly written books on Black authors, and public forums. They have concluded recently that the greatest threat to Crusoe comes from Black Nationalists, and *sans* food, they have rushed to his defense. Their line of defense is varied and concerted, including not only the Black cultural movement, but the political and social movements as well, and their objective, though seldom stated, is to return Black people to the romantic, myopic era of the "We shall overcome" years and "integration now." In short, they seek to protect the Crusoes of the world by depicting Black Nationalists as insane, irrational extremists, representative of only a minority within the race, who have, despite centuries of rebuff, not forsaken the goal of assimilation. Their defense in the cultural area centers specifically upon the Black Aesthetic Movement, and in each of their critiques, Imamu Baraka, Hoyt Fuller, Don L. Lee, and Addison Gayle are singled out for special opprobrium. Their charges range anywhere from the statement that Black Aestheticians are anti-Semitic—a non-literary evaluative term—to the argument that they are hopeless romantics. Neither of these statements, whether true or no, explains anything, therefore, in response—and using Kilson's address as a model—to insure that clarity and cogency prevail, I have had to place the charges into a framework which would allow for intellectual, rational discussion.

Foremost among the charges is that Black Aestheticians "shoot from the hip," do not do their homework, make *a priori* assumptions—in one word, they are unscholarly. Now scholarly, depending upon who defines the term, can mean one of two things: a search for truth, or validation of a truth already discovered. Carolyn Fowler Gerald's essay, "The Black Writer and His Role," which begins with a set of well thought out assumptions and moves intellectually to a valid conclusion, is illustrative of the first. Stanley Macebuh's book, *James Baldwin,* is illustrative of the second: "If one may go by Theodore Gross's observation on the matter," writes Macebuh (another antagonist of the Black Aesthetic), "there is hardly an American critic or teacher of literature who has not had to contend with the web of issues posed for criticism by Black Literature in this country . . ." What is important is not that the observation is erroneous, but that Macebuh has accepted the conclusion of a critic whose scholarly credentials are as dubious as his own. Thus, to be scholarly in the first instance means to sift through information, to accept nothing as given, to arrive at truth through one's own understanding and reason. In the second instance, to be scholarly means to accumulate the proper number of footnotes, quotes, addendums, and a bibliography which no ten men, let alone the author, could possibly read in a lifetime. Moreover, it means to accept as gospel, without question, the authority of white critics, whose own *a priori* reasoning has led to questionable truths. Such material is to be found in college journals, complete with style sheets which demonstrate the art of footnoting, spacing accurately, and paragraphing precisely. Missing, of course, is insistence upon creativity, upon using one's imagination, upon understanding, upon striving for clarity; academic jargon is the rule, abstract thinking a must, and total confusion a necessity. Needless to say, few Black Aestheticians would care to be "scholarly" in this fashion.

The essence of scholarship should be hard work, the kind of work which involves not only the search for truth, but the testing of these truths in the public arena, through experimental trial and error. No writers in America meet this criterium better than Askia Touré, Hoyt Fuller, Imamu Baraka or Don L. Lee. Their written works are testament to the depth of their reading and comprehension and exhibit a knowledge of the history and politics of the world that few writers in America possess. They are not, however, content to quote white authorities, to accept the dubious theorems of dubious critics, or to allow their newfound truths to gather dust on bookstore shelves. Askia Touré has long been engaged in work in the Black community; Hoyt Fuller is not only the guiding light behind the new Black Renaissance, but a force in OBAC, Chicago's outstanding cultural organization, as well as an active participant in planning for the forthcoming African Festival. The works of Baraka in Newark and throughout the Black communities of the world are well known, and Don Lee has established a publishing company and an institution for the education of Black children.

The argument that Black Aestheticians are unscholarly, however, is secondary to that which states that what these critics call an aesthetic is nothing more than a political, social movement, anti-white and anti-universal, completely parochial in design and practice. Their "outlook is based on the assumption," writes Kilson, "that no meaningful aesthetic exists outside of human or political needs, and thus the claim for a 'Black aesthetic' is valueless without linkage to the daily needs of Negroes . . . Now Addison Gayle's view of the 'Black aesthetic' as a creative act is excessively political."

The relationship between art and politics was enunciated long before Addison Gayle and the Black Aestheticians were born. In *The Republic,* Plato spoke at length concerning the threat posed by the artist to the utopian republic, believing that he could persuade men away from the ideology of the state. The art of the Bible is the art of persuasion, and the most lyrical passages are designed to move men in one direction as opposed to another. The conflict in Cervantes' *Don Quixote,* the first novel written in the Western world, is between illusion and reality, and Cervantes, opting in the final analysis for illusion, uses art to suggest to this audience that pragmatism, in a world ruled by men, is a necessity. The job of the novelist, to paraphrase English writer Henry Fielding, is to instruct and to entertain, and the instructions offered by Fielding and his contemporaries were designed to make the English middle class aware of its strength and power. Nathaniel Appleton, Noah Webster, and John Trumbull, among the earliest of American writers, saw no dichotomy between art and politics, each agreeing with the dramatist John Nelson Baker that America needed an art "to celebrate

American achievements and to record American events." The Black novelist, from William Wells Brown to Richard Wright, was engaged in the hopeless task of convincing the American public that Black men were not, as earlier writers had defined them, three-fifths of men, but human beings. Those, however, who have been most antagonistic toward art as politics—outside of Black opponents of the Black Aesthetic, who know little of literary history—were the writers who spearheaded "The New Critical" movement of the nineteen twenties.

Like Kilson and others, they argued that art should be autotelic, self enclosed, harboring no political or social message. The aesthetical qualities of a poem, novel, or play inhered in its form and style, principally, in the technique by which the artist, through dexterity of language and manipulation of lines, made us conceive the beautiful. Yes, these were the same men, who earlier thought of themselves as "The Southern Agrarians," and the political framework within which they operated is outlined in the book *I'll Take My Stand*—a racist, fascist document bearing great similarities to *Mein Kampf.* Their political program for America involved reincarnation, a return to antiquity, wherein, America might be reborn in the image of Greece and Rome. Here, they argued, was art at its best: simple, beautiful, exhibiting an aesthetic unspoiled by industrialization, technology, Northerners, and Black people. They sought a world of no conflict, struggle, or challenge, and they offered this prescription for an aesthetic "art," as one of them declared, "should not mean, but be."

Such an aesthetic, which conforms to Kilson's description of "disinterested attention," is one Black Aestheticians will have no part of. Despite the African influence upon Greece and Rome, the world of peace and tranquility, which sup-posedly existed in the Greek city-states, close to the Aegean, is not our world. Unlike Kilson, we cannot echo the sentiments of Angelina Grimké, "Let us forget the past unrest,—We ask for peace," for we know that peace is antithetical to the human condition, that so long as men be oppressed by other men, so long as hunger, poverty, and fear exist in the world, so long will peace remain an illusion, in which only white Don Quixotes and Black Sancho Panzas have the luxury to indulge.

For it is in one's perception of the world that leads to an aesthetic concerned only with form, structure, and technique, with being, not meaning, as opposed to one concerned with man's spiritual, political, and social needs. Kilson sees a world different from the one I see. In true scholarly fashion, he quotes me out of context: "To be an American is to be opposed to humankind, against the dignity of the individual . . . to be an American is to lose one's humanity." The America that I see, as the quote implies, is markedly different from that of my opponents; it is not the world of the integrationists, one in which a small band of *elite* Blacks achieve status by serving as mediators between the Black and white communities, not the America envisioned in the rhetoric of moving quickly to correct ancient injustices—not the America of freedom and democracy, of egalitarianism, where man is regarded with love and tenderness. The America I see is one in which Black people—whether they acknowledge it or not—are daily confronted with indescribable acts of inhumanity by other men, whose claims to superiority rest upon the ephemeral grounds of color, an America where men who dare to be different are stunted in their growth, never allowed to achieve full manhood, without undergoing the most terrible of struggles, an America whose sense of morality, justice, and decency is secondary even to that of the jungle cat, an America whose most appropriate metaphor is not the statue of Liberty, but Attica prison in New York.

Given such a world, how does one confront it? Integrationists, who admit part of this truth—even Kilson speaks of "white racist America"—caution patience and advocate appeals to conscience. The millennium, they tell us, though 300 years overdue, is just around the corner, and we must, therefore, continue to prove to the Americans that we are worthy of freedom, never let them believe that we are so ungrateful for the coming generosity that we could conceive of a culture, lifestyle, or world view different from theirs: "Addison Gayle and LeRoi Jones (Kilson is unable to believe that Imamu would discard his American name for an African one) want to politicize the creative energies of the Black people in a manner that excludes the possibility of white people from ever being able to discover some profoundly meaningful facet of their own white selves through an appreciation of the Black aesthetic."

To wage a campaign along Kilson's lines, one designed to convince white people of our communality, would, of course, constitute the very political and social aesthetic that, otherwise, he opposes. Thus, the Black writer believes that, through art, Black people might discover profound meaningful facts about *their* history and culture, is concerned not with art, but with politics, not with mankind, but with race. To be viable and noteworthy, in this infantile attempt at constructive reasoning, an aesthetic must be conceived by whites, legitimized by whites, or directed at whites. Here, Kilson and his supporters are at one with the New Critics.

In his charge, however, that Blacks are no more humane than whites, Kilson has left not only most of his supporters behind, but also the most racist historian. "The bitter truth is," he writes, and "and it must be faced gravely by all Blacks, that ruling *strata* in African societies willfully participated in the Atlantic slave trade during the 16th-19th centuries. . . . Without such willful participation of Africans in the slave trade, the brutal centuries that Negroes have experienced in the Black Diaspora would have been impossible." Racist historians have, at lest, assigned mutual culpability argued responsibility between the African chieftains who sold Blacks into slavery and the white invaders and colonists who bought some, stole others, and captured still more. Kilson, however, in an attempt to negate Black Nationalist charges of American immorality and inhumanity, is willing to rewrite history, to argue that slavery resulted from Black greed and treachery that were there no status-seeking Africans, Americans would have turned elsewhere for the brawn and muscle to build their cities and to harvest their cotton crops. Kilson and his supporters know more about the practice of selling out Black people than I do, yet, even if one indulges in this fictional account of history, how does this negate the contention that the last place in which one would search for decency and morality is among white Americans? Using Kilson's argument, it may be possible to contend that the slavery that existed among the Greeks and the early Christians was due to the collusion of African chieftains, yet the philosophers of Greece and the Christian religion, while acknowledging the existence of slavery in their orders, point out ennobling aspects of Grecian and Christian antiquity, never allow the world to forget that alongside slavery and brutality were concepts, practices, and theorems which, they claim, ennobled and dignified man. Kilson is unable to see such qualities in the ancient Africans, indeed, is blinded by their culpability in the slave trade, will not recognize that alongside those Africans who sold Blacks were those who did not, were those who constructed and developed humane societies, where each individual was regarded with decency and respect.

They need to prove white American innocence is all pervasive in Kilson's truncated theology; yet, if one accepts his contention of white American innocence in the slave trade, how does one continue to champion such innocence in light of the act of inhumanity practiced on the plantations and in the cities in an America far from the African chieftains, the indiscriminate murder and maiming of Black people, the purposive attempt to transform men, women, and children into chattel? How does one make the case for American innocence, today, when white racism destroys hope and faith, forces people onto drugs, keeps them inured in the welfare of poverty? How, again, does one explain away the atomic bombing of the Japanese, the centuries of lynching and castration of Blacks, the massacre at Attica prison, the napalm bombing of the Vietnamese, American support of regimes of terror and oppression like those in Rhodesia and South Africa? Kilson's rationale is the classic one: Blacks have not done these things because we have lacked the power: "Often, the victim is merely weaker, not morally superior."

Now the *intelligent* writer can never accept the argument that human nature, but for the pragmatic considerations of strength and weakness, is everywhere the same. To do so means to champion universal evil, to contend that people are incapable of change, and thus to espouse the ephemeral theory of art for art's sake. Kilson's conjectures concerning what the racial situation in America might be were the tables reversed for Blacks and whites demonstrates his ignorance regarding Black history and literature. Nowhere does the literature and history of Black people support the claim that murder and oppression are endemic to the Black character. Quite the contrary, our history and literature speak of man's belief and faith in man, of each person's commitment to the elevation of the human spirit, of love and fidelity to family and principle, of the belief that the New Jihad is possible even in the face of Armageddon.

To argue the contrary implies that centuries of brutality suffered at the hands of Americans, not African chieftains, was due to our weakness, our impotence, and yes, to our cowardice. I do not believe this! Those many thousand gone are testament to the courage and dignity of people who believed that through their struggles—ofttimes their martyrdom—they could change the institutions and people of America. I am convinced that they were misguided, that nothing short of a holocaust can change white America; yet the morality of Blacks from Harriet Tubman to Martin Luther King should be ample refutation to the arguments of those so desperate to enclothe themselves in the American flag that they are willing to accept American hypocrisy, oppression, and evil as their own. I have no quarrel with them. I believe still that Frederick Douglass' admonition in 1852 needs little emendation in 1974: "There is not a nation on the earth guilty of practices more shocking and bloody than the people of the United States, at this very hour." (African chieftains were not included in this statement.)

Of the charges leveled against the proponents of the Black Aesthetic, none receives such universal support as that which states that "these Black writers want to tell other writers how to write," want to dictate the form and content of the works of creative artists, and thereby relegate art to ideology: writes Kilson, "now it is precisely on this issue that I myself oppose the Black Nationalist spokesman of the New Black Arts and the new so-called 'black aesthetic.' This New Black Arts is nothing more than an ideology; it is an effort to subordinate the deeply profound and penetrating creative processes of Black people to an ideological movement."

Now those who contend that ideology and politics are antithetical to art know little of art, have read few novels and poems, and comprehend nothing of the little they have read. No matter the age in which they live, writers live in societies, non-autotelic, where ideology and politics enhance their perceptions, help to formulate their world view. That man is a political animal is a belief shared with Aristotle by writers throughout the world, and the most intelligent of them know that it was not due to the non-ideological components of their works that Cervantes was jailed, Pushkin hounded by the Czar, Byron feared by the British upper class, Wright forced to leave America, Baraka threatened with jail, or Solzhenitsyn exiled from the Soviet Union. Those who wield power, as opposed to those who theorize about it, have always understood that form and structure, style and manipulation of language, are only vehicles for forwarding political and ideological positions. This is a reality with which every critical movement—even the New Critical one—was forced to come to grips, to admit that, after all, the essence of a work of art lay, not in its being, but in its meaning.

But the opponents of the Black Aesthetic know all of this; they do not really discern an antagonism between art, politics, and ideology, are not opposed to critical systems that enunciate standards and guidelines; no, what they are opposed to is a particular kind of ideology and politics—Black Nationalism—and a Black critical system, as opposed to a white, which suggests guidelines and standards. Members of the "writer should be allowed to write anything he wants to school," they argue that the Black writer belongs to an *elite* group—he is not "a Negro writer, but a writer," and is responsible only to his art. The absurdity of this point of view was demonstrated some time ago, when I questioned a member of this school: "At a time when drugs are decimating many Black youngsters, should the writer be free to write poems and novels glorifying drugs, though this may lead in some small way to an increase in Black addicts?" The answer was an unqualified "yes."

Now freedom for the writer is one thing; nihilism is another. Freedom, after all, entails responsibility; nihilism, irresponsibility. To suggest that the Black writer owes no obligations to the Black community is not to champion freedom, but nihilism, to contend that though he gains his creative import, his nuances of thought and perception from the Black community, that even though the community conditions his way of looking and feeling, offers him a storehouse of material and experiences, that despite this, he owes nothing to the community, is free to indulge his fantasies at its expense. The best example of this kind of nihilism/irresponsibility are the Black films; here is freedom pushed to its most ridiculous limits; here are the writers and actors who claim that freedom for the artist entails exploitation of their artistic(?) existence.

Simply put, the advocates of freedom for the Black writer are convinced that he belongs to an *elite* club, that somehow, by becoming a writer, he has escaped the daily acts of terror and oppression faced by other Blacks, that he has, in a sense, become integrated into the American society. The Black writer, however, is no more than a Black man or woman who writes, and the same acts of inhumanity directed against other Black people by Americans are directed equally against him. His books are no antidote against American racism, do not immunize him against exploitation and brutality. Given these realities, his claims for freedom in light of the limited freedom of other Blacks is absurd, for his, whether he knows it or not, is irrevocably tied to that of others, and until other Blacks are free, he cannot be, neither as man, woman, nor artist.

Those who clamor for freedom for the writer, however, would add legitimacy to their cause, had they, historically, opposed the attempts of white critics to issue guidelines restricting them, had they, for instance, had the courage and the intellect to take on Robert Bone, Theodore Gross, Herbert Hill, Norman Mailer, Louis Simpson, and the reviewers of *The New York Times Sunday Review of Books*. Instead of taking them on, however, "the freedom for the writer advocates" quote them continuously, echoing their sentiments that Black writing must be "universal," and the Black writer must use his creative imagination to carry him beyond "the narrow parochialism of race:" Writes Kilson: ". . . It is necessary for those of us who truly believe in man's universal aesthetic capacities to respond to our Black separatist brothers by reaffirming the universal quality of humanity."

The "universal quality of humanity" is clearly visible in Sophocles' drama, *Oedipus Rex*, wherein the protagonist, white, wrestles with guilt and shame after seducing his mother and killing his father; not visible in Ron Milner's drama, *What the Wine Sellers Buy*, wherein the protagonist, Black, confronts old myths and sterotypes, masters them and moves forward to assert his manhood in a racist society; the universal quality of humanity is quite apparent in the Russian novel, which according to one critic, "speaks of the great Russian soul," in the Jewish novel, which treats the Jewish experience, in the English novel, which deals with the experiences of Englishmen; it is not apparent, however, in Black novels that deal with the Black experience, not in *Native Son*, nor *Youngblood*, nor *Captain Blackman*, nor *The Autobiography of Miss Jane Pittman*, despite the fact that the experiences depicted in these works are similar to those undergone daily by three-quarters of the earth's people.

Follow this reasoning to its most absurd conclusion, and the Black writer is free, can achieve universality, only when he is capable of distorting his experiences, of transforming them into non-recognizable abstractions, in order to appease and placate a white audience. Needless to say, Black Aestheticians have a different view of the humanitarian, universal aesthetic. We believe that it was demonstrated in the lives and experiences of Harriet Tubman and Denmark Vesey, Frederick Douglass and Martin Delany, Sojourner Truth, and Marcus Garvey, Malcolm X and Martin Luther King, H. Rap Brown and Ron Karenga, and that their struggles for humanity and justice, their dignity and courage under fire, make them paradigms for man's historical bout with the forces of racism, models for that three quarters of the earth's people, non-whites, who do not measure up to Kilson's definition of "universal."

Finally, this, in microcosm, is what concerns the antagonists of the New Black Arts movement. Charges that Black Aestheticians are unscholarly, advocate politics and ideology, and want to deny freedom to the writer all pale into insignificance alongside the fidelity of these self-appointed defenders of white American culture to white standards, white images, symbols and metaphors. Like Friday, they are those to whom the white god has come in all his fury and majesty, and upon whom he has bestowed his blessings. Centuries of Americanization have convinced them that the myths ring true, that Blacks are incapable of undertaking and succeeding in any endeavour, whether running Black Studies Programs or creating a New Black Arts— without the aid, support, and approval of whites. Having gained *entrée*, of sorts, into the world of the Americans, yet realizing, subconsciously, how precarious their own position is in that world, they devote much of their energy and what little creative potential they possess to assuring whites that they are different from other Blacks.

Their tirades against Black Nationalism, therefore, are to be found in the writings and rhetoric of their white ventriloquists, who oppose self determination for Black people, because, like Thomas Nelson Page and Thomas Dixon, they need the images of Blacks as impotent, docile children, helpless without the master's guiding hand. Their opposition to the New Black Arts, never stated, is due to the fact that it calls for re-evaluation of white values, a questioning and challenging of the ethics and morals of this country, a belief that man's humanity to man is possible once the symbols, images, and metaphors bequeathed by white men to Black men are redefined and restructured. For the Fridays, to move outside the voice of the ventriloquist would place them in a very precarious position indeed, for their sense of self, strength, and status is proportionate to their acceptance and approval by the white world, and without such approval and acceptance, like Freud's child, lost in the wilderness, they would have to confront the terrifying void of their own incompetence.

One final word: Nothing that I have said here will move the adversaries of the Black Aesthetic to attempt serious intellectual evaluation, and the reason is that Fridayism leads to terminal illness, not subject to cure by intellectual or rational reasoning. This does not disturb me. I know that Friday is nothing more than the surrogate for Crusoe, the complete personification of the Pavlovian model, who robot-like, responds upon impulse, and I have always preferred to deal with the Crusoes, with the ventriloquists, who at least, sometimes, demonstrate originality in thinking. The continuing attacks against me, however, coming not primarily from Crusoes, but from Fridays, have caused me to seriously evaluate this position, and though I still long for peace, for seclusion away from the noise of hysterical and paranoic adversaries, perhaps, such longing is wishful, is at the least quite unlikely; it may be, therefore, that as far as Martin Kilson and others are concerned, this is not the last word.

CHAPTER 12

Cultural Nationalism: The Black Novelist in America

(1971)

For the Western world holds me in fee
And I can never hope for full release
While to its alien Gods, I bend my knee.
—Claude McKay

We are familiar with the quest for Black Power in the political, social, and educational spheres of American life; however, few of us are familiar with the long struggle for Black Power or Black Nationalism in Afro-American letters. Yet in one important genre, the novel, cultural nationalism has not been explored since Martin Delany's fragment, *Blake or the Huts of America,* written in 1859. This quest—beginning early in Black literature when the majority of Black folk inhabited the rural areas of America—reached its apex at the time of the Harlem Renaissance when the greatest immigration in American history transformed a rural folk into an urban folk.

The ramifications of this statement cannot be properly appraised without an understanding of the cultural dichotomy which has existed for so long in the Black community; and a brief history of the Afro-American novel prior to the Harlem Renaissance is necessary to bring the novel of the city into sharper focus.

Clotel could have been written by any member of the Plantation School of writers, for in *Clotel,* William Wells Brown does not minimize the debt he owes to this school. His characters are equally romantic, his situations equally improbable, and his attribution of angelic qualities to those Afro-Americans who are white in every essential except color is in the best tradition of the Aryan supremacy mythologists. For Brown, as for his white contemporaries, the standards of beauty and excellence are white in every aspect.

The case is quite different with Martin Delany. Delany seeks to turn the Black novel inward, to deal with the Black experience as distinct, bordering only tangentially on the American experience. And what Frederick Douglass said about Delany sums up, I believe, Delany's attitude toward his race and his characters: "I wake up every morning and thank God for making me a man," wrote Douglass, "Delany thanks God for making him a Black man."

What is important here is that these two brother abolitionists viewed the function of Black literature in different ways. The novel for Brown was to be at one and the same time a vehicle for protest as well as a vehicle for cataloguing the achievements of the race. Those characters who survived the American racial inferno were rewarded with the artifacts of Western culture. The major thesis of the novel was the Horatio Alger motif done in colors of medium gray.

Delany, too, viewed the novel as a vehicle of protest, but even more as a vehicle for affirming the Black identity outside of the American context. For Delany, Black men were transplanted Africans, brought by misfortune to a strange land to sing their songs before alien gods. Therefore, these Blacks would have to make the group journey to identity outside the context of the American melting pot theory.

However, the history of the Black novel before the Harlem Renaissance is almost a complete negation of Delany's thesis, and the novel, as seen by Brown, would exist with slight variation for over fifty years. J. McHenry Jones (*Hearts of Gold,* 1898), Pauline Hopkins (*In Contending Forces,* 1900), and Paul Laurence Dunbar (*The Uncalled,* 1901) pay homage to the assimilationist motif. The experiences of their characters are shown to vary little from the experiences of white Americans. They argue, sometimes nauseatingly so, that the only difference between Black Americans and white Americans is the accident of color, and they come very close to arguing in fiction, as Phillis Wheatley does in poetry, that Blacks are little more than reformed savages brought to the altar of Christianity by the grace of Western civilization.

It is not surprising that such novels use as their setting a rural environment. The rural South is the basis of reference, and the romantic machinery of Southern life is a necessity for these writers. Mired in the South and steeped in the rural plantation tradition, these early novels were vehicles for the Black middle class in the same manner that the novels of Thomas Dixon and Thomas Nelson Page were vehicles for the Southern white aristocracy.

The break with the rural tradition came when the Black novel, following the exodus of Black people, came to the city. In the nineteenth century, Blacks poured into the nation's urban areas. They went as far west as California, as far north as Canada, and they settled in the Wattses, the Houghs, and the Harlems of America. They came, as W.E.B. Du Bois was to note, in search of Canaan, and they were sorely disappointed.

Into urban America, they brought their history, their folklore, their customs, and their anger. They demanded a religion which would suit their needs, and their ministers came north to minister to them in a new and different setting. They demanded a social structure based not upon caste and color but upon the brotherhood of one Black man with another. The similarities between the injustices, North and South, enabled them to pierce the veil of American mythology; and as a result, they demanded not a literature of manners and gentility, but one which would reflect their hopes, fears and anxieties, a literature which would be as forthright as the Garvey movement in presenting their demands and in helping them to achieve a sense of identity.

Alain Locke best summed up this new mood and its literary implications: "Of all the voluminous literature on the Negro," wrote Professor Locke in the introduction to *The New Negro,* "so much is mere external view and commentary that we may warrantably say that nine-tenths of it is about the Negro rather than of him. . . . We turn, therefore . . . to the elements of truest social portraiture, and discover in the artistic self-expression of the Negro today a new figure on the national canvas. . . ."

The "New Negro" was no longer the stereotype of the Booker T. Washington era; instead, he was the new Negro of the cities who, having deserted the farm, was rapidly becoming industrialized, and his earliest and most consistent supporter was the poet Langston Hughes.

"To my mind," wrote Hughes in "The Negro Writer and the Racial Mountain," "it is the duty of the younger Negro artist to change through the force of his art that old whispering 'I want to be white' hidden in the aspirations of his people to 'Why should I want to be white? I am a Negro and beautiful.'"

The spirit of Martin Delany is revived in the Harlem Renaissance; for Black was not only beautiful, but also different and distinct. With the acceptance of this fact, the Black novelist was forced to move away from romanticism and mythology and deal realistically with a people living, dying, hoping, and hating in the ghettoes of America. A cultural renaissance was in its earliest stages, and a new cultural awareness was evident in Afro-American life. The pioneers of the Harlem Renaissance did much to bring about this awareness, and in so doing, called for a commitment to reality which would be echoed by the young Black writers of the sixties.

The first Black writer to affirm this commitment to reality was a young man who, ten years after the Harlem Renaissance, would write in an article, "A Blueprint for Negro Writing": "The Negro writer who seeks to function within his race as a purposeful agent has a serious responsibility. In order to do justice to his subject matter, in order to depict Negro life in all its manifold and intricate relationships, a deep informed and complexed consciousness is necessary; a consciousness which draws its strength upon the fluid lore of a great people, and molds this lore with the concepts that move and direct the forces of history today. The Negro writer is called upon to do no less than create values by which his race is to struggle, live, and die. . . ." The young man was Richard Wright, and four years later he would write *Native Son,* create Bigger Thomas, and move the Black novel to a height of realism which, unfortunately, has not been surpassed to this day.

The plot of *Native Son* centers around Bigger Thomas, an uneducated Black youngster, born in a Chicago slum, forced to live in a one-room hovel with his

mother, sister and brother, and relegated to a life of frustration and futility because of the color of his skin. Given a job as the family chauffeur by Mr. Dalton,
a "white liberal" who owns the slums in which he is forced to live, Bigger accidentally murders Mary, the "liberal's" daughter. In addition, Bigger murders his
own girl friend, not gratuitously but by design, setting up the interesting angle
that he was responsible for only one murder—that of his girl friend—a fact which
has no bearing on the outcome of his trial for his life. Caught by the police, Bigger is tried and, despite pleas from his communist lawyer, sentenced to die. He
dies without repentance, without atonement for the death of the white girl. The
catalyst for the action in *Native Son* is the accidental murder of Mary Dalton.

We should not be swayed by the academic critics who, imbued with the notion
that "poetry should not mean but be," have dealt with *Native Son* in terminology
more appropriate for dealing with the plastic, not the literary arts. Nor should
we be swayed by the pseudo-moralists among us who attempt to find in Bigger
Thomas the epitome of man's degradation and inhumanity. Rather, let us put *Native Son* into proper historical perspective, and in so doing, deal with the period
of the nineteen forties when the novel was published.

In Europe, German aggression was well under way. In a short time almost the
whole of Europe would come under the sway of a tyranny as vicious as that under
which Blacks have lived in this country for over two hundred years. In America,
the detention camps would later house American citizens of Japanese descent,
who would be subjected to persecution and abuse. The paranoiac attacks on the
Jewish population of Germany would be reiterated in the propaganda attacks on
the Jewish population in America. For Blacks, the journey from South to North
would prove to be no more than a journey from one kind of oppression to another. For any sensitive individual living in this tumultuous period, the symbol
of man's reality was not the tragic clown, as Ralph Ellison would have us believe,
but rather the concentration camp. It is in this concentration camp environment
that Bigger Thomas was born.

The validity of Bigger Thomas and the test of his humanity must be examined
in light of the concentration camp metaphor. In so doing, we are forced to conclude that the murder of Mary Dalton, at one point so shocking and so senseless,
is, when viewed from a different perspective, so cathartic and so necessary. In a
world where the concentration camp is man's touchstone for reality, the values
by which men live and die are existential ones; and one must create his identity,
a sense of his own self-worth, out of the chaos and confusion inherent in living
as a victim in a dehumanized world.

We have come a long way from Martin Delany. Delany would have settled for
Black emigration back to Africa, to a place where men, free from arbitrary restrictions, might create their own identities. Richard Wright, on the other hand, would
settle for nothing less than a piece of this earth, where men would carve their
identity out of violence and despair, thereby transcending the limitations imposed

upon them. *Native Son* succeeds in destroying the American myth, in rending to shreds the make-believe world of the romantics, in leaving the American dream in shambles, and, finally, in presenting a portrait of reality which serious Black writers who followed would have to confront.

Two of today's most popular Black writers have had great difficulty in confronting the reality presented by *Native Son.* Neither has accepted the chaos and violence which the novel presents and neither has accepted Richard Wright's nationalistic formula as the best means for bridging the racial chasm and avoiding racial war.

James Baldwin wavers between the philosophy of assimilationism and that of nationalism unable, until *Blues for Mr. Charlie,* to examine American society in other than personal terms. No writer knows the ghetto or its people better than Baldwin, no one has a clearer insight into the alienation and despair of man in the twentieth century, and yet no writer has failed more miserably in depicting in fiction the plight of urbanized Black Americans.

Another Country, his most popular novel, serves as a case in point. The beginning of *Another Country* is to be found in the ending. Here one glimpses the New Society as Baldwin envisions it. At the end of the novel, three couples remain: a homosexual couple, a heterosexual couple, and an integrated couple. The emphasis should not be placed upon the makeup of the couples, but instead upon the tolerance each shows toward the differences of the others. In a sense, Baldwin would return us to the Garden of Eden before the fall when Adam and Eve, unconscious of their differences, accepted each other in terms of common humanity.

For Baldwin, however, to tread the road back to innocence entails great difficulty. Man must be created anew, and for the characters of *Another Country,* this implies that one must undergo a fire-baptism in which he either accepts his condition or forgoes it altogether. There is no middle ground. Man accepts himself for what he is and moves forward to reshape the world in his own image, or failing to accept himself, he attempts self-transcendence, which may lead to destruction.

Every man, argues Baldwin, has burdens to bear, and a man is distinguished by how well he stands up under his burden. In *Another Country,* the two characters who bear the heaviest burdens are Rufus Scott, Black, and Eric Jones, homosexual. Eric survives the end of the novel and emerges as the central figure in the new world. He learns to live with his condition, to accept himself for what he is, and thus he is able to pursue a career and carry on a meaningful relationship with others. Rufus, on the other hand, cannot rise above his condition. The Black skin is, symbolically, his shroud and his inability to shed it subconsciously leads him from poverty to degradation and finally to self-destruction. Unlike Eric, who is free to accept himself as a homosexual, Baldwin implies that Rufus, in accepting himself as a Black man, must accept the historical terms of degradation and distortion which circumscribe him: self-hate, self-abnegation, despondency, and frustration leading to vindictive acts toward others. Therefore one is led to believe that, in order to enter paradise, Rufus must discard his Blackness altogether. In accepting the myths of American society, Baldwin blames the victim for wearing the Star of David and suggests that for the sake of peace, the victim must thrust aside that which offends the victimizer. What emerges from *Another Country* is a subtle plea for integration which goes far beyond the scope envisioned by the early assimilationists.

Every institution in American society has been designed to substantiate the thesis that to be born Black is a sin. This is not so. The sin is not being born Black, but being born into a world in which to attain paradise one must pick up the instruments of war. "The symbol of the twentieth century," wrote Richard Wright, "is the man on the corner with a machine gun." In American society, one reaches the Garden of Innocence not through acquiescing in the destruction of his own heritage and identity but by constructing better machine guns than his enemies, or at least, learning to use them more efficiently. To offer Black people a Rufus Scott is to offer a Christ in black face, not withstanding the fact that both Christ and Rufus are doomed to die the death of cowards, and that neither the great society nor the Garden of Eden can be built upon a foundation whose chief architects are cowards.

To move from James Baldwin to Ralph Ellison demands that one clarify his own position in regard to the function of the Black writer in American society. Mankind exists in a world where injustice is the norm, where persecution is the measure of man's fidelity to his god, where human life is all too often sacrificed on the altar of power politics. Look upon this world of civilized men and your eyes will never fall upon a land where men are not victimized and persecuted by other men whose only claim to power is that they possess an abundance of the instruments of war. Given such conditions, the job of the writer is to wage total war against injustice; in American society this means that the Black writer must wage total war against the American system. This does impose a terrible obligation upon the Black writer; yet, persecution and oppression are equally terrible. None should argue with the assertion that the writer must be free to utilize his skill in the way he deems best. However, the same scripture holds true for all men, and in a society where some men are not free, freedom for the writer is based upon an absurdity. The Black writer in America can never be free until every Black man is free, and the obligation imposed upon the writer is no more severe than that imposed upon any man whose destiny is inextricably bound to that of his brother.

To wage total war against the American system does not mean that the writer will throw a Molotov cocktail or fire a rifle. (Although the time may come when he may have to do just that.) He has far more powerful weapons at his command, and these he must use not only to protest the injustices of the present but also to attempt to bring about those conditions in the future under which peace might prevail.

Such peace can come only when the last tyrant has disappeared from the earth, when the last hydrogen bomb has been dismantled, when the last concentration camp has been razed to the ground, when the last rifle has been broken, when the last man has been lynched because of his color, when the last patriot has died in defense of his Vietnam, and when the last child has gone to bed hungry for the last time in a world rich in natural resources.

Foremost among Black writers today, Ralph Ellison is perhaps the best equipped to analyze the precarious peace upon which the American system rests. There is no writer in America who possesses a finer temperament, none with a more thorough knowledge of Black history and culture, and none with more devotion to the perfection of the writer's craft. His *Invisible Man,* is a masterpiece, unsurpassed by those of his contemporaries, white or Black, American or European. Having said this, however, one asks certain questions, and these questions inevitably lead one to the conclusion that masterpieces may sometimes be irrelevant to the lives of men and nations. The portrait of the Mona Lisa belongs in a museum; in a concentration camp, it would be out of place. Men who live on the edge of desperation are not likely to be enthusiastic about the Mona Lisa or comparable "works of art."

When one begins to examine the theory of the masterpiece, he finds that it was put forth by men who sought to erect a barrier between themselves and other men. Traditionally, works of art were the private property of the aristocracy, and a Reubens or a first edition of Pope, differentiated the haves from the have-nots; in the same manner, poverty and starvation serve a similar function today. The creator of such masterpieces was in turn set off from his brother craftsmen, his nation, and his race, and admitted to the economical, social, and educational elite. However, the Black writer can never accept elitism, or a barrier which separates him from other Black men. Whether he wills it or not, unless he is very lucky or very white, he is not an individual but part of a group, and his fate is mirrored in that of the group's. He is no sophisticated minstrel entertaining the sons and daughters of America's academic establishment, but rather a Black artist whose every waking moment is a preparation for war, whose every word is an utterance of defiance, whose every action is calculated to move man toward revolution, and whose every thought centers about the coming conflict. He replaces the formula "art for art's sake," as poet Don L. Lee has written, with the humane formula, "art for people's sake," and instead of entertaining Black men, he educates them, instead of appealing to their sense of aesthetics, he appeals to their instinct for survival, instead of reminding them of the rewards of heaven, he warns them of the realities of hell. There is no elite in the concentration camp, and the inmates of the camp demand not funeral dirges but martial marches.

In the opening pages of *Invisible Man,* the reader encounters the protagonist in an underground cellar. The protagonist relates the story of his life, taking the reader on a picaresque journey characterized by laughter, tragedy, and pathos.

At the conclusion of the final episode, the reader is capable of empathizing with the protagonist's commitment to live the life of an underground man. He is, as he relates, an invisible man, a faceless being in a world where the machine is king. His journey is an attempt to impose his consciousness upon the world, to force the world to acknowledge his existence. In the final episode of the novel, the protagonist is mistaken for a criminal, Rhinehart, who has learned to cope with his invisibility by being all things to all men. A world in which Rhinehart is the symbol for every man is an absurdity, and thus the protagonist returns to his underground retreat.

On a more basic level, Ellison's protagonist seeks to force the American system to validate his existence, to grant him recognition not as a Black man nor as a white man, but as an American. The fallacy of the white liberal's theory of integration and the fallacy of the argument of *Invisible Man* are the same: that the Black American can find his identity only in a metamorphosed society in which the melting pot, having bubbled over, has fused the disparate cultures within and produced a product labeled American. In this analysis, one does not seek to destroy evil but to join forces with it. Like James Baldwin, Ellison wants racial peace and he is willing to purchase it at the expense of negating race and culture.

But the road to racial peace lies not through the negation of one's race and culture but through the affirmation of it. What Black men demand from America is not validation of their identity as Americans, which would only assimilate them into the resent society, but freedom and justice which would lead to the creation of a new society. If one accepts the argument offered by white liberals that the concentration camp metaphor of Richard Wright is no longer valid, one must argue concomitantly that the symbol of a Black Rhinehart, he who creates and re-creates his identity with each new experience, is invalid in Black America where the individual identity cannot exist apart from that of the group.

It is not too far wrong to suggest that Afro-American literature awaits its Whitman and the chances of this Whitman appearance are better today than at any time before. Young Black writers, for whom the city is home are attempting to create a revolutionary literature which moves beyond Richard Wright. They accept the basic premises of Black Nationalism—that Black people are different from other Americans—and they echo Edward Channing in arguing that such differences mandate a different literature. They are reexamining their own culture and finding it rich and diverse. They do not deny the relevance of American history to their lives, but they would not change their history by merging them into one. Unlike the Ralph Ellisons of the world, these young writers would never trade Frederick Douglass for a Thomas Jefferson, for they know that one was a slaveholder and the other a crusader against slavery and that, in such an exchange, they would get the short end of the bargain.

They are such men as Ed Bullins in drama, LeRoi Jones in poetry, and John

Williams in fiction; and though I have spoken of them as new, their spirit is not new at all. It is the spirit exemplified by Martin Delany, Walt Whitman and Richard Wright. And each has this in common: he realizes with Nietzsche that the old tables of the law have led us to corruption and oppression and must therefore be replaced by new ones. But more important, in adopting the tenets of Black Nationalism, he realizes with James Joyce that the writer can have no greater task than "to forge from the smithy of his soul, the uncrated conscious of the race."

CHAPTER 13

Cultural Strangulation: Black Literature and the White Aesthetic

(1969)

> This assumption that of all the hues of God, whiteness is inherently and
> obviously better than brownness or tan leads to curious acts. . . .
> —W. E. B. Du Bois

The expected opposition to the concept of a "Black Aesthetic" was not long in coming. In separate reviews of *Black Fire,* an anthology edited by LeRoi Jones and Larry Neal, critics from the *Saturday Review* and *The New York Review of Books* presented the expected rebuttal. Agreeing with Ralph Ellison that sociology and art are incompatible mates, these critics, nevertheless, invoked the clichés of the social ideology of the "we shall overcome" years in their attempt to steer Blacks from "the path of literary fantasy and folly."

Their major thesis is simple: There is no Black aesthetic because there is no white aesthetic. The Kerner Commission Report to the contrary, America is not two societies but one. Therefore, Americans of all races, colors, and creeds share a common cultural heredity. This is to say that there is one predominant culture—the American culture—with tributary national and ethnic streams flowing into the larger river. Literature, the most important by-product of this cultural monolith, knows no parochial boundaries. To speak of a Black literature, a Black aesthetic, or a Black state is to engage in racial chauvinism, separatist bias, and Black fantasy.

The question of a white aesthetic, however, is academic. One has neither to talk about it nor define it. Most Americans, Black and white, accept the existence of a "White Aesthetic" as naturally as they accept April 15th as the deadline for paying their income tax—with far less animosity toward the former than the latter. The white aesthetic, despite the academic critics, has always been with us: for long before Diotima pointed out the way to heavenly beauty to Socrates, the poets of biblical times were discussing beauty in terms of light and dark—the essential characteristics of a white and Black aesthetic—and establishing the dichotomy of superior vs. inferior which would assume body and form in the 18th century. Therefore, more serious than a definition, is the problem of tracing the white aesthetic from its early origins and afterward, outlining the various changes in the basic formula from culture to culture and from nation to nation. Such an undertaking would be more germane to a book than an essay; nevertheless, one may take a certain starting point and, using selective nations and cultures, make the critical point, while calling attention to the necessity of a more comprehensive study encompassing all of the nations and cultures of the world.

Let us propose Greece as the logical starting point, bearing in mind Will Durant's observation that "all of Western Civilization is but a footnote to Plato," and take Plato as the first writer to attempt a systematic aesthetic. Two documents by Plato, *The Symposium* and *The Republic,* reveal the twin components of Plato's aesthetic system.

In *The Symposium,* Plato divides the universe into spheres. In one sphere, the lower, one finds the forms of beauty; in the other, the higher, beauty, as Diotima tells Socrates, is absolute and supreme. In *The Republic,* Plato defines the poet as an imitator (a third-rate imitator—a point which modern critics have long since forgotten) who reflects the heavenly beauty in the earthly mirror. In other words, the poet recreates beauty as it exists in heaven; thus the poet, as Neo-Platonists from Aquinas to Coleridge have told us, is the custodian of beauty on earth.

However, Plato defines beauty only in ambiguous, mystical terms, leaving the problem of a more circumscribed, secular definition to philosophers, poets, and critics. During most of the history of the Western world, these aestheticians have been white; therefore, it is not surprising that, symbolically and literally, they have defined beauty in terms of whiteness. (An early contradiction to this tendency is the Marquis DeSade who inverted the symbols, making black beautiful, but demonic, and white pure, but sterile—the Marquis is considered by modern criticism to have been mentally deranged.)

The distinction between whiteness as beautiful (good) and blackness as ugly (evil) appears early in the literature of the middle ages—in the Morality Plays of England. Heavily influenced by both Platonism and Christianity, these plays set forth the distinctions which exist today. To be white was to be pure, good, universal, and beautiful; to be black was to be impure, evil, parochial, and ugly.

The characters and the plots of these plays followed this basic format. The villain is always evil, in most cases, the devil; the protagonist, or hero, is always good, in most cases, angels or disciples. The plot then is simple; good (light) triumphs over the forces of evil (dark). As English literature became more sophisticated, the symbols were made to cover wider areas of the human and literary experience. To love was divine; to hate, evil. The fancied mistress of Petrarch was the purest of the pure; Grendel's mother, a creature from the "lower regions and marshes," is, like her son, a monster; the "bad" characters in Chaucer's *Canterbury Tales* tell dark stories; and the Satan of *Paradise Lost* must be vanquished by Gabriel, the angel of purity.

These ancients, as Swift might have called them, established their dichotomies as a result of the influences of Neo-Platonism and Christianity. Later, the symbols became internationalized. Robert Burton, in *The Anatomy of Melancholy,* writes of "dark despair" in the seventeenth century, and James Boswell describes melancholia, that state of mind common to intellectuals of the seventeenth and eighteenth centuries, as a dark, dreaded affliction which robbed men of their creative energies. This condition—dark despair or melancholia—was later popularized in what is referred to in English literature as its "dark period"—the period of the Grave Yard School of poets and the Gothic novels.

The symbols thus far were largely applied to conditions, although characters who symbolized evil influences were also dark. In the early stages of English literature, these characters were mythological and fictitious and not representative of people of specific racial or ethnic groups. In the eighteenth century English novel, however, the symbolism becomes ethnic and racial.

There were forerunners. As early as 1621, Shakespeare has Iago refer to Othello as that "old Black ewe," attaching the mystical sexual characteristic to Blackness which would become the motive for centuries of oppressive acts by white Americans. In *The Tempest,* Shakespeare's last play, Caliban, though not ostensibly Black, is nevertheless a distant cousin of the colonial Friday in Daniel Defoe's *Robinson Crusoe.*

Robinson Crusoe was published at a historically significant time. In the year 1719, the English had all but completed their colonization of Africa. The slave trade in America was on its way to becoming a booming industry; in Africa, Black people were enslaved mentally as well as physically by such strange bedfellows as criminals, businessmen, and Christians. In the social and political spheres, a rationale was needed, and help came from the artist—in this case, the novelist—in the form of *Robinson Crusoe.* In the novel, Defoe brings together both Christian and Platonic symbolism, sharpening the dichotomy between light and dark on the one hand, while on the other establishing a criterion for the inferiority of Black people as opposed to the superiority of white.

One need only compare Crusoe with Friday to validate both of these statements. Crusoe is majestic, wise, white and a colonialist; Friday is savage, ignorant, Black and a colonial. Therefore, Crusoe, the colonialist, has a double task. On the one hand he must transform the island (Africa—unproductive, barren, dead) into a little England (prosperous, life-giving, fertile), and he must recreate Friday in his own image, thus bringing him as close to being an Englishman as possible. At the end of the novel, Crusoe has accomplished both undertakings; the island is a replica of "mother England," and Friday has been transformed into a white man, now capable of immigrating to the land of the gods.

From such mystical artifacts has the literature and criticism of the Western world sprung, and based upon such narrow prejudices as those of Defoe, the art of Black people throughout the world has been described as parochial and inferior. Friday was parochial and inferior until, having denounced his own culture, he assimilated another. Once this was done, symbolically, Friday underwent a change. To deal with him after the conversion was to deal with him in terms of a character who had been civilized and therefore had moved beyond racial parochialism.

However, Defoe was merely a hack novelist, not a thinker. It was left to shrewder minds than his to apply the rules of the white aesthetic to the practical areas of the Black literary and social worlds, and no shrewder minds were at work on this problem than those of writers and critics in America. In America, the rationale for both slavery and the inferiority of Black art and culture was supplied boldly, without the trappings of eighteenth century symbolism.

In 1867, in a book entitled *Nojoque: A Question for a Continent*, Hinton Helper provided the vehicle for the cultural and social symbols of inferiority under which Blacks have labored in this country. Helper intended, as he states frankly in his preface, "to write the Negro out of America." In the headings of the two major chapters of the book, the whole symbolic apparatus of the white aesthetic handed down from Plato to America is graphically revealed: The heading of one chapter reads: "Black: A Thing of Ugliness, Disease"; another heading reads: "White: A Thing of Life, Health, and Beauty."

Under the first heading, Helper argues that the color black "has always been associated with sinister things such as mourning, the devil, the darkness of night." Under the second, "White has always been associated with the light of day, divine transfiguration, the beneficent moon and stars . . . the fair complexion of romantic ladies, the costumes of Romans and angels, and the white of the American flag so beautifully combined with blue and red without ever a touch of the black that has been for the flag of pirates."

Such is the American critical ethic based upon centuries of distortion of the Platonic ideal. By not adequately defining beauty, and implying at least that this was the job of the poet, Plato laid the foundation for the white aesthetic as defined by Daniel Defoe and Hinton Helper. However, the uses of that aesthetic to stifle and strangle the cultures of other nations is not to be attributed to Plato but, instead, to his hereditary brothers far from the Aegean. For Plato knew his poets. They were not, he surmised, a very trusting lot and, therefore, by adopting an ambiguous position on symbols, he limited their power in the realm of aesthetics. For Plato, there were two kinds of symbols: natural and proscriptive. Natural symbols corresponded to absolute beauty as created by God; proscriptive symbols, on the other hand, were symbols of beauty as proscribed by man, which is to say that certain symbols are said to mean such and such by man himself.

The irony of the trap in which the Black artist has found himself throughout history is apparent. Those symbols which govern his life and art are proscriptive ones, set down by minds as diseased as Hinton Helper's. In other words, beauty has been in the eyes of an earthly beholder who has stipulated that beauty conforms to such and such a definition. To return to Friday, Defoe stipulated that civilized man was what Friday had to become, [proscribed] certain characteristics to the term "civilized," and presto, Friday, in order not to be regarded as a "savage under Western eyes," was forced to conform to this ideal. How well have the same stipulative definitions worked in the artistic sphere! Masterpieces are made at will by each new critic who argues that the subject of his doctoral dissertation is immortal. At one period of history, John Donne, according to the critic Samuel Johnson, is a second rate poet; at another period, according to the critic T. S. Eliot, he is one of the finest poets in the language. Dickens, argues Professor Ada Nisbet, is one of England's most representative novelists, while for F. R. Leavis, Dickens' work does not warrant him a place in *The Great Tradition.*

When Black literature is the subject, the verbiage reaches the height of the ridiculous. The good "Negro Novel," we are told by Robert Bone and Herbert Hill, is that novel in which the subject matter moves beyond the limitations of narrow parochialism. Form is the most important criterion of the work of art when Black literature is evaluated, whereas form, almost non-existent in Dostoyevsky's *Crime and Punishment,* and totally chaotic in Kafka's *The Trial,* must take second place to the supremacy of thought and message.

Richard Wright, says Theodore Gross, is not a major American novelist; while Ralph Ellison, on the strength of one novel, is. LeRoi Jones is not a major poet, Ed Bullins not a major playwright, Baldwin incapable of handling the novel form—all because white critics have said so.

Behind the symbol is the object or vehicle, and behind the vehicle is the definition. It is the definition with which we are concerned, for the extent of the cultural strangulation of Black literature by white critics has been the extent to which they have been allowed to define the terms in which the Black artist will deal with his own experience. The career of Paul Laurence Dunbar is the most striking example. Having internalized the definitions handed him by the American society, Dunbar would rather not have written about the Black experience at all, and three of his novels and most of his poetry, support this argument. However, when forced to do so by his white liberal mentors, among them was the powerful critic, William Dean Howells, Dunbar deals with Blacks in terms of buffoonery, idiocy, and comedy.

Like so many Black writers, past and present, Dunbar was trapped by the definitions of other men, never capable of realizing until near the end of his life, that those definitions were not god-given, but man-given and so circumscribed by tradition and culture that they were irrelevant to an evaluation of either his life or his art.

In a literary conflict involving Christianity, Zarathustra, Friedrich Nietzsche's iconoclast, calls for "a new table of the laws." In similar iconoclastic fashion, the proponents of a Black Aesthetic, the idol smashers of America, call for a set of rules by which Black literature and art is to be judged and evaluated. For the historic practice of bowing to other men's gods and definitions has produced a crisis of the highest magnitude, and brought us, culturally, to the limits of racial armageddon. The trend must be reversed.

The acceptance of the phrase "Black is Beautiful" is the first step in the destruction of the old table of the laws and the construction of new ones, for the phrase flies in the face of the whole ethos of the white aesthetic. This step must be followed by serious scholarship and hard work, and Black critics must dig beneath the phrase and unearth the treasure of beauty lying deep in the untoured regions of the Black experience—regions where others, due to historical conditioning and cultural deprivation, cannot go.

CHAPTER 14

Separate, Not Mutual Estates

(1971)

> For I was born, far from my native clime,
> Under the white man's menace, out of time.
> —Claude McKay

"Of all the voluminous literature on the Negro," wrote Alain Locke in the foreword to the anthology *The New Negro* (1925), "so much is mere external view and commentary that we may warrantably say that nine-tenths of it is about the Negro rather than of him. . . ." Professor Locke was too kind a critic to specify that much of this "voluminous literature" was written not by Blacks, but by whites. Between the year of the publication of *Clotel* (1853), the first novel by a Black writer, by William Wells Brown; and the year of *The Survey Graphic* (1925) edition, which supplied most of the material for *The New Negro*, over one hundred and fifty volumes—primarily criticism—were published by whites about Blacks.

The most offensive of these publications came not from the pens of sentimentalists like Thomas Nelson Page or overt bigots like Thomas Dixon, but, for the most part, from well-educated, competent, academic scholars. A sample list of titles illustrates their critical temperament: *The Negro: A Beast in the Image of God*, *The Color Line: A Brief in Behalf of the Unborn*, and *The Negro, a Menace to Civilization*. The dean of these academic scholars was John Burgess who declared from his chair at Columbia University in *Reconstruction and the Constitution*: "A black skin means membership in a race of men which has never of itself succeeded in subjecting passion to reason, has never, therefore, created any civilization of any kind. There is something natural in the subordination of an inferior race to a superior race, even to the point of enslavement of the inferior race. . . . It is the white man's duty and his right to hold the reins of political power in his own hands for the civilization of the world and the welfare of mankind."

The social critics were joined by literary critics (also educated in "our best universities") who attacked the works of Black writers from a more benevolent, though equally abusive, perspective. "It appears to me now," declared William Dean Howells, one of America's few literary dictators, "that there is a precious difference of temperament between the two races which it would be a great pity ever to lose, and that this is best preserved and most charmingly suggested by Mr. Dunbar [Paul Laurence Dunbar] in those pieces of his where he studies the moods and traits of his own race in its accents of our English . . . he reveals in these a finely ironic perception of the Negro's limitations. . . ."

This "damning with faint praise" was not peculiar to Howells alone. In conversation with James Weldon Johnson, H. L. Mencken proved himself also a master of the art. In his autobiography, *Along This Way,* Johnson notes that: "He [Mencken] declared that Negro writers in writing about their race made a mistake when they indulged in pleas for justice and mercy . . . when they based their unjust treatment on the Christian or moral ethical code. . . ." And, with that characteristic arrogance of white critics from Howells to Theodore Gross, Mencken vouchsafed this directive: "What they should do is to single out the strong points of the race and emphasize them over and over."

The fatherly advice of Mencken, the feigned liberal criticism of Howells, and the overt, biased appraisal of Burgess spring from the same source—a contempt for Black people which, despite having been "educated in our best universities," sorely affected the judgment of these critics. For each believed that Black people were indeed descendants of Ham who, like Benedict Spinoza, were to be accursed by day and night, in lying down and getting up, in going out and coming in. These accursed people, therefore, were the stanchions of an idyllic utopia ruled over by a race of Aryan superiors. The logical conclusion to this premise is evident: The creations of such people, whether material or intellectual, are to be censured as inferior and unimportant in an America of superior cultural, intellectual, and artistic attainment.

These *a priori* assumptions made by men who, like Kyo in *Man's Fate,* must be the guardians of the destinies of other men as well as their own, are remnants of that curious duplicity of American social life born in slavery. Thomas Jefferson's encomiums on the rights of man and the equalitarian society were negated by the physical presence of the many slaves who maintained his Monticello home. William Lloyd Garrison, who declared his refusal to equivocate on the issue of slavery, nevertheless broke with Frederick Douglass, who had taken the radical position of John Brown, opting for revolution instead of "moral suasion."

Such duplicity evidences the "plantation mentality" codified in the writings of Dixon and Page and expropriated, almost *in toto,* by white critics today. In the modern version of the plantation credo, Black people are neither mysterious nor inscrutable; they are far from being wearers of the mask, as Dunbar asserts, or invisible men, as Ellison describes. At most, they are the wards of Western civilization, a simple folk whose ideas are primitive, whose morals are perverse, and whose manners are unrefined. Any white critic is therefore capable of interpreting the ways of such people to Black and white alike. ("I have told you my truth," shouted Nietzsche's Zarathustra, "and now you may tell me yours." However, white critics have assumed that their truths about Blacks are definitive.)

This arrogance, close to what George Meredith called "self importance born of excessive hubris," is nowhere more evident today than on the college campuses of America. The oracle has been shifted from Delphi to the classrooms of America's largest universities—though, the young Socrates who journeys here for enlightenment in the area of Black studies will find that the mistress of the oracle has fled, her seat now occupied by decrepit gnomes who dispense not wisdom, but falsehoods, moral platitudes, and nonsensical clichés.

Here, upon this Olympian tower, like Washington Irving's "headless horseman," the spirits of Howells, Mencken, and Burgess ride roughshod over the Black Ichabods. And here, too, sits Shelley's "winged hound" feeding on the heart of the prostrate Black Prometheus, while the gnomish gods formulate those theories and ideas by which Black people might "live and die." Steadily, increasingly, the heralds come from Olympus via periodicals and publishing houses to those mortals who consider the new gods—distinct from the old gods, Dryden, Pope, and Johnson—to be the "fountainhead of all wisdom and judgment."

There is this, however, about the new Olympians: Their flaws are even more pronounced than those of the mortals whom they purport to instruct. In a universe where racism is so all pervasive, contempt for Blacks so definitive, and the need of white liberals to serve as father figures so obsessive, the rulers of Olympus share the racist infection of the society at large with all its inherent biases and prejudices.

Nowhere is this more pronounced than in literary criticism, and nowhere shown more explicitly than in a recent article, "Mutual Estates," written by Theodore Gross and published in the winter edition of *Antioch Review*. Like most white critics, Gross pretends to view the works of Black writers from an objective vantage point, believing in the myth perpetuated by "The New Critics" of the nineteen twenties that a critic is capable of bringing to the work of art a judgment free of the influence of the political and social climate of his time. Such an assumption leads Gross to inveigh against W.E.B. Du Bois, James Weldon Johnson, Alain Locke, and Sterling Brown, competent critics whose only fault is that they "have been Negro social leaders." Believing that the two must be mutually exclusive, Gross exclaims, "In their desire to preserve the artifacts of a cultural past they have often acted as benevolent censors of their creative contemporaries."

Gross' thesis has been stated more honestly, forcefully, and explicitly before. In an article on two Black critics, Pearl Thomas and Carolyn Reese, in *The Teachers College Record* (1967), Robert Bone avows: "Miss Thomas is a birthright critic, miraculously schooled in Negro literature by virtue of her race alone," while Miss Reese, "cannot deal with Negro poetry because at bottom she has failed to acquire the necessary skills."

However, the salient characteristic of literary criticism from Sainte-Beuve to T. S. Eliot has been that all criticism begins from a subjective point of view; from—to use Alexander Pope's oftmisinterpreted word—taste, a starting point conditioned by the social, cultural, and political environment. For this reason, Aristotle chose a play by his countryman, Sophocles, to formulate a theory of tragedy; Dr. Johnson followed suit in expanding that theory; and Wordsworth, evaluating the poetry of his eighteenth-century predecessors, initiated the dialogue on poetic language begun in the "Preface" to *Lyrical Ballads.*

That each critic reacts to the social, cultural, and political mores of his time should be no surprise to scholars and, indeed, would not be if the implications for white American critics were not so damning. Now that the critic is forced to deal with the lives of a people immune to analysis from the Olympian tower, and disdaining to acquire "the necessary skills" through empirical investigation, he is either relegated to the staid, narrow criticism of the New Critics, or forced to hand down dicta which have no foundation in actuality.

White critics are forced to deal with Black literature in terms postulated by Archibald MacLeish, adopting completely the assertion that literature "should not mean but be." The literary work of art is thus transformed into artifact, and the written word subjected to the type of critical analysis forwarded by the Bell-Fry school in painting, where art as object is judged solely in terms of form, technique, and aesthetic structure. To be sure, the Bell-Fry theory of criticism, when applied to literature, mandates being "educated in our best universities" and, were it possible to apply, would obliterate the prejudice which each critic brings to a literary work; thereby allowing white critics to deal with Black literature through the "back door" approach.

Gross tells us: "Wherever Americans meet, the subject is race and one suspects not only because of the unsettling practical problems aroused by the subject, but because it threatens the very preconceptions that Americans have about their own morality." If this is true—and it is no more true today than in the days of Burgess, Howells, and Mencken—then no aspect of American life can be insulated from the climate produced by such discussion, and no American can bring pure objectivity to any endeavor undertaken by Black people. It is very important to hold fast to this with all candor: White critics are white first, and the term critic is easily discarded where Black literature is concerned. For in a society in which racism is so all pervasive, the present-day critic, like his counterpart of yesteryear, is unlikely to remain untainted.

Robert Bone, for example, proves incapable of discarding the robes of the past. With the arrogance of a Howells, he proposes to instruct Black writers not only on literary technique but also on their moral responsibility to "their country." "Let us hope," cries Bone in a critique of William Gardner Smith's *Last of the Conquerors,* "that it will not be taken as evidence of either Yankee or American chauvinism if we point out that there are in fact important differences between the Negro's status in Philadelphia and in Georgia; between the systematic genocide of the Hitler government and the Supreme Court decision of 1954."

The same "Yankee or American chauvinism" is evidenced in a recent review of *How We Live: Contemporary Life in Contemporary Fiction,* an anthology edited by Penny Chapin Hills and L. Rust Hills. "Of the seven selections devoted to the 'Negro,'" writes the reviewer, Fred Ehrenfeld, "two are by Jews and one by a Southern white writer. The editors feel the need to justify this by contending that there are few good Black writers." Ehrenfeld agrees: "There is truth in this . . . the growing militancy of American Blacks in liberating themselves from their oppression releases energies that must be directed toward political and social ends."

And too, there is Louis Simpson, "a fine contemporary American poet with a liberal and humane sensibility," displaying the degree to which racism has tainted that "sensibility" in a review of a volume of poetry by Pulitzer Prize winner Gwendolyn Brooks: "I am not sure it is possible for a Negro to write well without making us aware he is a Negro; on the other hand, if being a Negro is the only subject, the writing is not important. . . ."

The star of this Comedy of Errors, however, is Theodore Gross, who contributes the following lines: ". . . every important Negro writer including Malcolm X and Eldridge Cleaver, has been intellectually shaped by a white Western tradition. [Malcolm X, of course, is not an important "Negro writer" since, like Socrates, he had his Plato in Alex Haley.] Across all that he has learned—the words, the techniques, the ways of looking at character—fall his own experiences; and the friction of mind and fact creates the special tensions of Negro art. . . . So long as he builds his experiences upon a white Western intellectual tradition, the Negro author speaks to whites—intellectually; and he speaks to Negroes—intellectually and empirically."

Gross' statement is applicable only to those Black writers whose obsession to enter the "American Mainstream" is determined by economic and social considerations. For most Black writers, at the present time, such an argument is merely a restatement of the theses propounded by white liberals from Harriet Beecher Stowe to Robert Bone; and constant reiteration in either the social, political, or literary sphere, can only bring us closer to the brink of racial Armageddon.

"I want to be a [writer], not a Negro [writer]," remarked an earlier James Baldwin to Langston Hughes, leading Hughes to comment upon that "urge towards whiteness in the race" which pervaded so much of Black literature in the past. This "urge"—not a belief that he had "been intellectually shaped by a white Western tradition"—led the Black writer to dream of mutual estates. Preferring to believe that he could only "build his experiences upon a white Western tradition," the writer viewed himself in the mirror of American society and created from his fantasy those characters, images of himself, who accepted a subordinate status in the great American chain of being.

Feigning belief in the mythological American Creed, such writers were imbued with the humanistic rhetoric flowing from the pens and lips of the abolitionists. They were motivated, often by social and economic factors, to function not as

Black writers, nor as Black men, but instead as Americans despite tacit recognition of the disparaging difference in culture, history, and world view. There were, to be sure, exceptions: men who viewed the world from a realistic perspective, who spoke not to whites but to Blacks, and who introduced the first strain of Black Nationalism into the field of Black literature.

David Walker, author of *The Appeals,* was one such writer; Martin Delany, who wrote *Blake or the Huts of America,* was another; and Sutton Griggs, who wrote *Imperium In Imperio,* was still another. The first book is a collection of essays; the other two are novels. Despite these differences, they have this in common: They are free of the assimilationist bent of the works of their contemporaries, and each writer, in accepting the political tenets of the Black Nationalist ideology, put forth a formula from which a "Black Aesthetic" could be derived. In circumventing that "urge towards whiteness in the race," they evidenced in their works that concern for separate estates which is such a significant part of the literary and cultural sphere of the Black Power revolution today.

Black writers, having adopted the political dicta of Black Power and having moved beyond the pioneering position of Walker, Griggs, and Delany, have set about creating an aesthetic which has its genesis in the nationalism so very apparent in much of Black literature. They have moved toward solving the age-old dichotomies between being a Black man and an American and between art and function. Believing with Saunders Redding that "Negroes are different from other Americans; their historical and social position makes this so . . .," the Black writers of today assert that it is far more important to be a Black writer than an American writer. And believing with Jean Paul Sartre that the serious writer writes not for posterity but for today, they have concluded that literature, to be meaningful, cannot serve as mere artifact, but must instead be functional and relevant to a particular people, a particular era, and a particular place.

Central to this new literary creed is a revolt against the protest novel. Keorapetse William Kgositsile, one of the finest of the young writers, relates in *Negro Digest:* "I do not write protest poetry. My poetry is love poetry. . . . My poetry is that spirit throbbing with the love of millions of Black people all over the world. My stance is racial. . . ."

Kgositsile's observation goes beyond that made by James Baldwin in "Everybody's Protest Novel": ". . . the avowed aim of the American protest novel is to bring greater freedom to the oppressed. [However] the protest novel, so far from being disturbing, is an accepted aspect of the American scene, ramifying that framework we believe to be so necessary." This is true only in regard to protest novels written by Blacks. The novel as a vehicle of protest, when written by whites, has not only disturbed the American scene, but, according to critics like Edmund Wilson, has succeeded in altering it. The failure of the Black protest novel is not in aesthetics, as Gross would have us believe, but in the naive, futile attempts of "the Negro author to speak to whites."

Richard Wright shouted most consistently for white men to listen, and he acknowledged that he wrote not for Blacks who already knew about the conditions and situations which he described, but instead for whites whose knowledge was limited. He wrote *Black Boy* for white liberals not realizing that they would find the facts of his life to be little more than "mundane actualities" which had been "crudely recorded." *Black Boy* needs no defense. As a work of art, it stands that "test of time" which Dr. Johnson, a much more judicious critic than his American counterparts, demanded of a literary work. What is significant, however, is the fact that this autobiography failed in its objective—to rouse the conscience of white America.

Black writers, cognizant of Wright's failure, have moved beyond protest, have ceased appealing to "the conscience of white America," and have begun to explore the culture and lives of Black people in an attempt to delineate not the similarities between Blacks and whites, but the many differences. This leads to that "danger of parochialism" which concerns Gross so much. But the danger is not for Black people whose lives are fraught with dangers of every conceivable kind, but instead for white critics whose skills, shaped in the dusty furnaces of Olympus, are inadequate to deal with literature which seeks to produce, not catharsis for whites, but revelation for Blacks.

The codification of the Black Aesthetic is a first step in this endeavor. Denying the dichotomy between art and function, the Black Aesthetic, derived from the political basis of Black Nationalism, propounds the most simplistic of themes: Culture derives from the group experiences of a people, and separate experiences produce separate cultures. That the experiences of Black Americans are distinct from those of white Americans perhaps needs no further justification than William Faulkner's oft-quoted remark that he could not imagine himself to be a Negro for five seconds. These distinct experiences have mandated a distinct language, life style, and world view.

Englishmen and Americans, Winston Churchill is supposed to have said, are divided by a common language. The division is even sharper between Blacks and whites in America. On arriving in America, Black slaves were separated from their countrymen with whom they shared a common tongue. The newcomers were, therefore, forced to devise a means of communication with each other, and in addition, with the white master and overseer. Two sets of language were necessary. And what seemed a difficult task was accomplished when the slaves intuitively stumbled on an important concept of language, that it is both denotative and connotative. Though speaking in the same tongue to Blacks and whites, the words of the slaves differed not only in meaning, but in the metaphors, symbols, and images which derive from a unique group experience. This is what makes Ralph Ellison's novel *Invisible Man* so incomprehensible to sophisticated white critics, leading Herbert Hill to confess: "In *Invisible Man*, Ellison evokes a world which perhaps only an American Negro can fully apprehend."

In developing a distinct system of communication, Black people also developed distinct life styles. These styles are many and varied, yet all have this in common: They are part of an arsenal of weapons devised by the group to confront Americans in a manner that no white American is forced to confront another; and no better example need be supplied than the wide range of characters in the "Negro Novel." James Weldon Johnson's protagonist in *The Autobiography of an Ex-Coloured Man* chooses assimilation as a way of confronting the society; Sheldon Howard in Saunders Redding's *Stranger and Alone,* chooses resignation; Jake, of Claude McKay's *Home to Harlem,* chooses the hedonism of Epicurus; Bigger Thomas, of Wright's *Native Son,* chooses outright rebellion; and Dr. Bledsoe of *Invisible Man,* chooses guile and deception. These styles are used by every Black man sometime during his lifetime, for each style constitutes part of a unique cultural experience.

There can be little question that the Black man has a distinctive world view. "The white man wakes up in the morning and puts on his suit," declares Charlene Hunter, "the Black man puts on his armor." And, indeed, the armor is necessary, for few Blacks any longer succumb to American mythology, and view the American society through the eyes of white liberals, or see a society moving rapidly toward equalitarianism. In short, they no longer have faith in white Americans; they have realized, at long last, that white Americans are the spiritual descendants of that mob which shouted "Give us Barabbas!" choosing not only their savior and redeemer, but providing a metaphor of Western civilization—with its concentration camps, its colonial armies, and its hanging trees—which has survived the ages.

The unique language, life style, and world view present a conundrum which the white critic cannot possibly resolve. Serious white critics, such as J. C. Furnas, Nat Hentoff, and Milton Meltzer, have realized this fact, and Charles E. Silberman, in the introduction to *Crisis in Black and White,* is unusually honest: "There is a certain arrogance, I suppose, in any white man presuming to generalize . . . about how Negroes think and what they are likely to do. . . ." Others, like Richard Gilman, have arrived at this conclusion belatedly. Still others, Bone and Theodore Gross, seem destined to remain in purgatory, singing, much like Shelley's nightingale, to cheer their own sweet solitude.

"No one," cries Gross, "seems to question the human credentials of a twentieth century, urbanized American graduate when he evaluates some medieval tract in which the language is different, the country and time are strange, the religion of the author may be alien. . . ." As a justification for continued critiques by white scholars of Black literature, the analogy is inaccurate. To see the work of art as more than artifact demands a critical perspective based on the preconceptions and attitudes which the critic brings to his analysis. Like Johnson, Arnold, and Trilling, who brought their personal biases to the fore in judging the works of Grey, Byron, and Dreiser, the twentieth century American graduate will probably reflect an arrogant racial superiority toward medieval subjects and literature. That he will reflect such attitudes toward Black authors and Black literature is a certainty substantiated by numerous historical examples. Subjective criticism is as old as Plato's republic, and to suggest the possibility of a leap from subjective bias to objective appraisal in the racial climate of America is the greatest defect in the argument for "Mutual Estates."

One would hope that white liberals, at this juncture of the twentieth century, would realize this fact and begin to search for ways not of assimilating Blacks into American society, but instead, of perpetuating those differences between Blacks and whites which mandate two separate societies. This means, for the white scholar, a reevaluation of those values which have brought us all, Black and white, to the present crisis. It means also that Black and white critics, working in their separate spheres, may well help stave off a racial Götterdämmerung.

This advice will be lost upon the Grosses of this world, for America has always been a free society for whites who will, no doubt, continue to hand down pronouncements from the tower of Olympus. But, one thing is certain: The pronouncements will be important only to those who refuse to believe with Richard Wright that "Each day when you see us Black folk upon the dusty land of the farms or upon the hard pavement of the city streets, you usually take us for granted and think you know us, but our history is far stranger than you suspect, and we are not what we seem."

CHAPTER 15

Reclaiming the Southern Experience: The Black Aesthetic 10 Years Later

(1974)

"We are a Southern people," John Killens had said, "because that is where our people are closest to Africa. But our literature does not show this." I thought immediately about my own writing and discerned an almost purposeful absence of my Southern experiences, as if, somehow, what I had known there and endured there and hated there and loved there had been obliterated by my experiences in the North; I thought, too, of my contemporaries—novelists, essayists, poets, critics—and, with the exception of Killens and Ernest Gaines, I could recall none who dealt with the South in a significant way, though a great many of them, like myself, were Southerners. The last major novel to treat the Southern experience is Gaines' *The Autobiography of Miss Jane Pittman;* I cannot think of a recent volume of poetry dedicated exclusively to the Southern experience.

Many critics, social and literary, who associate themselves in some manner with the concept of the Black Aesthetic, are Southerners. Except for Houston Baker, however, in his recent book, *Long Black Song,* few have journeyed back to the South—to the sounds and smells, the folklore and music, the ribald jokes and the humane laughter, back to the culture which, as Killens noted, is close to the African experience—for the symbols and images, the paradigms of history which should form the underpinning of a people's literature. The reason is due, perhaps, to the fact that the Black Aesthetic movement was an urban phenomenon, pushed into actuality by the Black Power Movement of the nineteen sixties to serve as the cultural arm of the Black Nationalist Movement.

Despite its detractors, Black and white, the movement has produced a major upheaval in Black literature. Black novelists and poets, contrary to the suggestions of Robert Bone and Blyden Jackson, have not followed the example of Robert Hayden and Ralph Ellison, a path leading into obscurantism and indecision, but instead have moved steadily along paths carved out by Imamu Baraka and John Killens—paths which emphasize a fidelity to the Black as opposed to the American experience. On the pragmatic side, even the Black detractors have benefited immeasurably by the movement brought into being through Baraka's

Black Arts Theater experience and Hoyt Fuller's tireless efforts as editor of *Black World*: lecture platforms, once occupied exclusively by white experts on Black people, are now mounted by Blacks. The arrogance and boldness with which white critics once dismissed Black literature occurs now only at the peril of the white critic. And Black critics, who were almost totally ignored before 1960, have gained visibility in the eyes of Black writers and public alike.

The elevation of the Black critic and Black criticism into acceptance and respectability by the Black community is a major achievement, for the job of the critic, as Toni Cade avers, is to call a halt to madness, and it is primarily the critics of the Black Aesthetic persuasion who have attempted to fulfill this function. They have called a halt to the madness of the nineteen forties and nineteen fifties that propounded the idea that literature could serve as cartharsis for whites, that it might produce changes in them that would force them to move toward producing the "great society." They have called a halt to the madness demonstrated by those who argued that Black men were half men at best, ersatz Americans at most, and that, via the vehicle of protest literature, a transcendence might occur which would allow for the existence of whole men. They have called a halt to the themes of Black pity and gratuitous Black suffering, to the creation of castrated men [and of] children who existed in another country of self-pity and hopeless desperation. They have called for a halt to the madness of those who believed that writing was a vehicle for moving outside the Black community and that publishing a novel, play, or collection of poems moved one into higher status than other Blacks, shielded the writer from white exploitation and an oppression. They have called a halt to the madness of those who argued that writing made them less African-American, that, in writing itself, they achieved a sort of mutation—"I am a writer, not a Negro writer"—and assumed that the value of Black literature could be validated only by white critics and a white audience.

Yet, despite the achievements of Black writers in the era of the Black Aesthetic, a major area of the Black experience—the Southern—was almost totally neglected: not the now outdated South of Richard Wright novels, where Blacks were the eternal victims of whites, not the South in which Black people lived complacently with fear and oppression, but a Black South where Black Nationalism is closer to achieving actuality than anywhere else in America, where the old suspiciousness of the Americans still survives, where a people know only too well that the solution to social and political problems must be wrought by their own hands. That is the South where Black women still maintain their proud carriage, where our young people continue to look with defiance upon the white world; a South where the ghosts of Harriet Tubman and David Walker, Sojourner Truth and Martin Luther King remain omnipresent, constant reminders of the greatness of a race of men and women, who, forced to desert their god and their land, struggled and survived the American diaspora.

To neglect this area of our experience meant to ignore the one remaining link between Black people in America and those in the Caribbean, Africa, and throughout the world; for it is in the American South that a people, close to the land, are closer to the Africa of their ancestors, closer to the values and ethics of a society where people, not things, are supreme; where men and women, thank God, have no intentions of bringing their children up in the image of Richard Nixon, no intentions, that is, of capturing the American metaphor and making it their own.

Two recent books, however, serve to reverse the trend begun in the sixties, to move us form an all-pervasive preoccupation with urban America toward an exploration of other, equally meaningful, areas of the Black experience: Houston Baker's *Long Black Song* and Askia Muhammad Touré's *Songhai!* —two books different in terms of genre, emphasis, and theme, and yet comparably important departures in the area of Black literature and criticism.

Long Black Song is a scholarly critique, an examination of the roots/foundations of Black literature from the earliest folklore of the race to the literature of the nineteen sixties and nineteen seventies. *Songhai!* is a collection of verse/ prose—melodic, rhythmical—weaving fascinating images and metaphors of the new Black World a-coming. Together they tell the same truth: that the strength of Black people lay in a culture outside that of the American, and that the "New Jihad," to use Touré's phrase, is possible only after a return to the values and ethics of our African forefathers. *Long Black Song* is a descriptive of the odyssey undertaken toward reaching the new world; *Songhai* is a celebration, as much of the odyssey as of the new world itself.

The first book begins with a status report concerning the health of Black culture, and in a personal, analytical, and moving introduction, Baker validates the health of the culture by citing his own conversion: "Born in a racialistic former slave state, I was bombarded with the words, images, and artifacts of the white world. My parents had been bombarded with the same images, and the Black librarian was no better off . . . All of us had been lobotomized into the acceptance of 'culture' on the white world's terms; we failed to realize that the manner in which the white world used 'culture' only helped justify its denial of the Black man."

For many, conversion leads to an attempt to synthesize the white and Black cultures, to critiques designed to prove that Black culture differs little from the American. Baker, on the other hand, rejects this attempt at assimilation and offers a cogent, well thought out answer to the Black and white proponents of a joint American culture: "There are, of course, those who insist on unanimity of the two cultures: they say to Black America: 'We are all from the same land, and the form of your intellectual and imaginative works are the same as ours.' Yes, we are all from the same land: but, to go back to the beginning one must realize that you came as pilgrims and I came as a 'negre.' Yes, the forms of our intellectual and imaginative works do coincide at points, but the experiences embodied in some of the forms of Black American culture explicitly repudiate the whole tradition out of which those forms grow."

According to Baker, the forms of things unknown, to use Wright's description, comprise the body of African-American folklore, which "rests at the foundation" of a Black literary tradition: "for the customs, practices, and belief of the Black American race . . . are clearly and simply reflected in the folklore." Here is the central thesis of *Long Black Song*. In this first literature of the Africans away from the ancestral home are the paradigms, images, metaphors, and symbols which have formed not only the literature, but to a large degree the conceptions and perceptions of the race itself. And to return to the intellectual past, to undertake the odyssey back into one's culture heritage, guided by a sensitive, imaginative pilot, is to understand the genesis of a racial literature, to discover the cultural ethic which infuses the works of Black writers from David Walker to Imamu Baraka: "Only when we have arrived at some knowledge of the heroes and values that characterize the group in which the Black writer has his genesis, can we begin to discuss the work of conscious literary artists with some degree of authority."

What Baker discovers in the animal tales, the trickster tales, in Black ballads, blues, and the spirituals, is what Maulana Ron Karenga has called a new value system, one in which man, not things, are the center of the universe, in which man's liberation instead of his oppression is of the highest priority, one in which the morality of the Americans and their institutions are continually called into question. From these early beginnings come the outlines of the Black Aesthetic—an aesthetic which refuses to divorce man from art, which agrees with the best of the Black critics of the sixties and seventies that an aesthetic, which proposes guidelines for art, must insist that art serve not some higher metaphysical entity, but people.

This inspirational and informative discussion of Black folklore must be read in its entirety. For what one learns after careful reading is that the values to which the Black Aestheticians seek to return—those which pervade the works of present-day Black writers—is a sense of moral commitment to the sanctity and nobility of the human spirit, and a belief, unshakable, that art is an instrument for producing not a beautiful artifact but a beautiful world. The African-American folklorist, like the African artist, was one with his community, and his works were validated and legitimized by the community itself. How many of the tales and songs have become nonexistent because the community, in its role as critic, found them unacceptable by *its* standards?

Had Baker ended his analysis here, had he merely provided us with a scholarly treatise on Black literature and culture, he would have satisfied the requirement of the academic critics, Black and white, who seek to divorce literature from life. And though parts of *Long Black Song* are marred by the stilted language and jargon of the academicians, Baker has left such mediocrity behind and become a critic in the best sense of the word—challenging, inquisitive, and demanding:

"The question of the Black man's humanity recedes with the acknowledgement of his culture: passive, bestial victims and sambo personalities are not generally what one has in mind when he speaks of culture as a whole way of life. The goal of an investigation of Black American culture is to discover what type of man the Black American is and what values and experiences he has articulated that might be useful in one's attempt to make sense of the world."

This statement points to the heart of the Black Aesthetic. For it demands that the Black artist help us make sense out of the world we live in, help us achieve a sense of morality, not out of the values of the Euro-Americans, but out of those which spring from our own culture and history. To accomplish this does not necessitate, as some paranoid, hysterical critics have suggested, that one must find irrelevant and invalid every artifact of the Western world; it suggests only that the offerings of the West must be scrutinized in light of the question, "Is it good for Black people?" (We know, for example, that the Viet Cong did not return captured machine guns because they bore the label "made in America"; instead, they utilized them in their struggle to overcome the Americans.)

It is such a world to which the author of *Long Black Song* calls our attention: a world of diversity and change, where men and women, seen in the context of historical perspective, are paradigms of the courage, endurance, grace, and beauty to which a race of people must, as did Jean Toomer, return and then again return. Writing in the *New Negro,* in 1925, Alain Locke assured his audience that the day of Aunties and Uncles, Toms and Sambos was over. *Long Black Song* tells us, here in the nineteen seventies, that the days of darky entertainers, superflies, sweetbacks, and Melindas, if not over, are numbered, that an excursion into the cultural past can provide images by which we may measure ourselves as a people; it tells us that we are a people whose history and culture exemplify those values by which men throughout the history of the world have lived and died, and that these values found their greatest expression in the Western world in the South, in the first home away from home for the African-American. It is there, where men and women, having undergone the racial holocaust and survived, that the best examples of a viable Black literary and cultural tradition exist.

Unlike *Long Black Song, Songhai!* is an imaginative work overflowing with symbols, images, and metaphors of the new African world to come. History is as germane to Touré's work, however, as it is to Baker's, for it forms the central underpinning of the work. Touré, however, is not only an explorer and analyzer of words; he is also a creator of them. He envisions the world as Baker does: peopled by strong Black men and women equipped with the grace and endurance to survive the Americans. Analogously to Baker, Touré the poet/songster argues that we are better, even, than we think we are.

Touré is one of the finest poets in the language; his verse rings with the sound and timbre of Coltrane and Bird, with the lyricism of Toomer at his best, and contains the rich, symbolic import of the best of Claude McKay's Jamaican poetry.

One of the founders of the Black Aesthetic Movement, in his works he is an apt paradigm for that movement. *Songhai!*, his finest effort to date, is an intellectual as well as imaginative exercise, which shows us what we must become by reminding us of what we are, by calling upon us to achieve "Tomorrow Jihad": "Move towards the visions and dreams we half suppress. Shape those visions/dreams with Imagination's scalpel, dare, to soar beyond the Beast-filled Present—Free! —your mind gliding upwards on the wings of love to other universes filled with throbbing Spirit, tropic song. For the real liberation is within. Then, Lover/Warrior/Sista-woman, fling this pulsing freedom from your breast into the astonished eye of Man!"

Songhai!'s music/prose/poetry evidences through its structure—sides one through four, like a long-playing record—that the three art forms are inseparable; that the poet is musician, storyteller, and prophet combined; and that the new African-American form must encompass them all. Only from such a totality can men come to understand themselves in relationship, not to the Western ethic and its God, but to history and Islam—the religion of man—not to a dead past, but to a new birth: "The Spiritual Nation. Samurai/Scholar-warriors in the West, rising with the sun. Teaching. Confronting. Growing into Manhood/anticipating Dawn. *Songhai!* a new world progressing towards birth. Beloved! commune with us in the purifying flames of Tomorrow's Jihad."

Songhai! readily lends itself to the kind of critical evaluation that some Black critics, imitating their white academic mentors, deem indispensable to the analysis of literature. Touré is a master of the symbol and metaphor: "And Malcolm's blood is straining the asphalt ghetto skies/over Harlem in our minds in our hearts in our dreams/his Eagle-spirit flies away into Eternal Paradise/leaving us to wander blindly in the midnights of our pain." No poet gains so much from meter rhythms and can bend lines with such consummate skill and ease: "You walk in warm honeyed tones sheathed in red/wild as the landscape of our continent./ You smile and tom-toms beat their lovesong/joyously in my heart./ Rhythm in your soul/ rhythm in the way/your hips sway/Congo rhythm primed in Mississippi—*Soul sista*, come and go with me!"

Touré is an experimental poet, searching continually for new forms of expression, and he could be analyzed and re-analyzed to the point of meaninglessness by critiques that focus upon his technical dexterity with poetry, yet ignore the important social and political meaning of his work. (Such critics—those who mount the barricade against social art and criticism, like white critics, believe that there is something unique and distinctive about Black poets who are experts in the technical aspects of the genre.) Black poets, however, with Touré, have long been aware of the fact that form is little more than the instrument through which poet addresses his community—the conduit carrying the prophecy which alone can produce change in thought and perception. To analyze poetry by the scriptures of the academicians is to suggest, therefore, that Black poets have little that is important to say about the social and political ideas which in the West play such havoc with one's life. To evaluate Touré by his standard alone would be to do an injustice to a fine mind, to obscure the important message/prophecy, which lies beyond the form, the call for commitment, awareness, and action: "Ambush the Silver Screen. Rob it of its victims—/frightened coons and screeching Aunt Jemimas./Kidnap Birmingham/Stepin Fetchit/Beulah/Butterfly. /Nature them to life with the love-cry echoes/of your soul. /A new image like a diamond sparkling in an/ebony palm. A Congo-song for the multitudes."

Not surprisingly, the introduction to *Songhai!* is written by John Killens, and if Killens is, as I have written elsewhere, the novelist of love, Touré is the poet of love, and some of the best verse in this collection is that which speaks of love between Black men and Black women, and, metaphorically, between one Black and another: "Melodies harmonizing with other heats/minds/souls/all as One, One as all—a symphony of ecstasy, /the loving cosmic harmonies of earth/ Yes, make it summer. It would be summer: / golden sunlight, incense, flowers nourishing butterflies/ azure skies breathing love; my ebony darling laughing/softly beneath my touch. I veteran/older wiser greying at the temples/lounging on a persian rug, stroking my reward/for wading through sewers of bloody death/to come back whole and laughing in an Age/of possibility and love."

Such an age is only possible after the Apocalypse, after the cleansing of the Black mind and soul, after a people have undergone the inward odyssey, sifted through the lies and distortions of the past, come to view themselves as new men and women, as earth people, determined to transcend the images offered by the white West. To move through the pages of *Songhai!*, to read poems of examination and conflict—"Babylove," "Entertaining Troops," and "My Man"—poems of love and endurance—"The Birth of a Nation," "Africa: A Faded Summer," and "Green Edens Flourish After Storms," is to arrive, finally, at the poems of intellect and imagination, those more prose than poetry, where the prophecy is fulfilled, the world born anew, Black people at one with their ancestral past: "I see now how lucky we are," says Mustafa, future Black woman, after witnessing the apocalyptic end of the West, "having witnessed the rebirth of man, to be free, moving about with a high oneness, remolding the world in a righteous Age . . ."

Imamu Baraka wrote, "We want a Black poem and a Black world." Well, *Long Black Song* and *Songhai!* are literary maps, depicting the contours of the new poetry that leads on to the creation of the new world. The direction must, of necessity, be one which leads back to the Southern experience, for here is the prelude for the final journey to the new Jihad, the African from whence we came, cleansed of the disease of colonialism. For despite the fact that modernization, urbanization, and all the concomitant evils have come to the South, there still remains the spiritual resilience of a people who, having undergone numerous Waterloos, remain faithful to the belief that life can be lived wholly and fruitfully outside the ethical system of the West.

Long Black Song reminds us of those values, once so much a part of our existence—a commitment to man, to the eventual freeing of the human spirit, to the communality and brotherhood of all the earth's people; *Songhai!* speaks of those values regained, that will allow us to construct the New Jihad, to bring upon this earth a world, where poet and people feed into each other's creative ethos, where all men are poets, where love and fidelity to the human condition remain sacrosanct. This, to quote a recent critic, is Addison Gayle's idealism at its highest. True, yet it is an idealism which argues that sane men must never accept the Western indictum that "what is, is right," but that they must work creatively, politically and socially, to construct a world where people are most important, not technology; that, like the slaves of old, they must never accept the dictates of tyrannical men and tyrannical systems; that they must search outside the West for images, metaphors, and symbols which exhibit courage, love, endurance, fidelity, and commitment to the human spirit.

Such idealism still exists in the South, in the minds of the young, who—though all too ready to accept the romance of the North, to be dazzled by the Superflies and the Shafts, the pimps and the hustlers, the chameleon-like clowns clad in high-heel shoes and red suits—are still possessed of a hunger to understand this diverse and complex world in which they live. They do not yet know that this is possible only if they examine the richness of that region where our ancestors first lived and died, only if they understand the examples of Frederick Douglass, Sojourner Truth, David Walker and Nat Turner. They do not know this, and the Black writer must begin to inform them and, in so doing, inform Black people throughout the world. Only when this is accomplished, when the Black Aesthetic has been directed Southward, only then can we begin, with Mustafa, to construct the new society. *Long Black Song* and *Songhai!* are two important works, pointing us in that direction.

CHAPTER 16

The Negro Critic: Invisible Man in American Literature: An Essay Review

(1968)

Although the Negro novelist has made a breakthrough of sorts into the long barricaded halls of the universities, the Negro critic remains outside much like Shelley's nightingale, singing to cheer his own sweet solitude. As writers of fiction, Richard Wright, James Baldwin, and Ralph Ellison are studied in more college classrooms today than any Negro writers heretofore, and yet each of them has written competent criticism—a fact unknown to those who appreciate their creative efforts.

If, then, Wright, Baldwin, and Ellison are neglected as critics, the censure is much more severe in the case of such competent, professional critics as Alain Locke, Stanley Braithwaite, and Saunders Redding, to name but a few. Not only have these critics contributed to the understanding of Negro literature, but also they have contributed those ideas without which, to paraphrase Mathew Arnold, no creative epoch is possible. Yet, in the America of today, renowned, as one critic has remarked, for its great criticism, Negro critics have died the death of public and academic anonymity.

One may advance several reasons for the academic neglect of the Negro critic, yet three stand out with more prominence than the others. First and foremost is the incontestable fact that Negro literature has never been considered an integral part of American literature. Second, and an outgrowth of the first, is the consensus among Americans, Black and white, that whites are more capable of rendering objective, unbiased opinions about Negro literature than Negroes. (This idea pertains to every facet of Negro life. Books and magazine articles abound with self-appointed experts on the Negro—the majority of such experts being white.) And third, the persistence of the myth, in colleges and universities, that Negro critics lack the sensitivity and perception necessary for literary criticism.

In 1940, Richard Wright's *Native Son* was hailed as "a great American novel." In 1953, Ralph Ellison was awarded the National Book Award for *Invisible Man.* Gwendolyn Brooks won the coveted Pulitzer Prize for Poetry in 1950, and in 1956, James Baldwin was hailed as the "greatest American essayist since Ralph Waldo

Emerson." Despite these accomplishments, however, Negro literature remains an unwanted and unacknowledged appendage to the vast body of American literature.

In part, this results from the effective use of the term "protest literature," which is bestowed upon any work by a Negro author. It is as if white critics were capable, en masse, of undergoing the experiences of a John Howard Griffin, of viewing the Negro world from within, and thereby drawing the conclusion that anyone relegated to permanence in such a world cannot help but scream, yell, and shout.

However true this may be, in much of Negro literature, the shout of racial slavery, under conditions which necessitated protest, neither shout, yell, nor scream was heard. And in many contemporary Negro novels, the search for racial protest is unrewarded. Where is Baldwin's protest against the racial situation to be found, for example, in *Giovanni's Room*? Or in Willard Motley's *Knock on Any Door,* or *We Fished All Night*? Or in the novels of Frank Yerby, novels made conspicuous by their total neglect of Negro life experiences? Evidence of such protest is hard to come by; for to argue that the condition under which the Negro lives mandates a literature of protest is one thing; to argue that the Negro author will obey such dictates is another.

However, the most important reason for the inferior status of Negro literature stems from the social mores deeply embedded in the American psyche. A nation incapable of recognizing Negroes as other than inferior beings—hewers of wood and drawers of water—has been unable to transcend the myths used to buttress the arguments of slave-holders and modern-day segregationists. Even so gifted a writer and liberal thinker as Norman Mailer can be found parroting (in "The White Negro") the most popular of such myths: ". . . the Negro . . . could rarely afford the sophisticated inhibitions of civilization, and so he kept for his survival, the art of the primitive . . . he subsisted for his Saturday night kicks, relinquishing the pleasures of the mind for the more obligatory pleasures of the body."

Such concepts have led to certain corollaries: Negroes are unlikely to produce important literature, or to undergo the kinds of experiences, universal in character, which form the basis of competent literature. For if one views the Negro through the sociological microscope, his inferiority mandates that his progeny, too, will be inferior. The old myths, therefore, remain. Black is inferior, of a poorer quality than white; Black people, as a result, are different beings, existing in narrow worlds, enclosed by petty experiences—experiences unrelated to the national character.

Viewed in the light of such deeply ingrained concepts, Negro literature is simplistic, immature, and unimportant. A distinguished editor of numerous anthologies remarked caustically, when asked why no Negro writers were represented in his latest work: "I never thought about it." Neither, it seems, have other anthologists, for anthologies today are noticeable by their omission of selections by Negro writers. Well might Robert Bone lament in *The Record* a year ago: "For it is a fact that Negro poets are virtually unknown among the teachers of American literature. Their poems appear but rarely in the textbooks and the anthologies; and their voices are seldom heard in the high schools or the college classrooms."

An outgrowth of the concept of Negro literature being inferior is the widely held belief that Negroes are incapable of objectively criticizing efforts by other Negroes. Such a task, therefore, can best be performed by whites. Thus, a major publishing company, seeking an editor for a collection of Negro writings, settled upon a white man who had little or no previous literary experience. The most publicized study of Negro literature remains Robert Bone's *The Negro Novel in America,* whereas Saunders Redding's equally perceptive *To Make a Poet Black,* and Hugh Gloster's *Negro Voices in American Fiction,* have long been out of print, with no new editions in sight.

But Negro critics have seldom been partial to their brother writers. Indeed, some of their polemics are reminiscent of the days of John Dryden and Thomas Shadwell, of Alexander Pope and Lewis Theobald. For example, neither Baldwin nor Ellison have been reticent in attacking *Native Son.* John Killens' attacks on *Invisible Man* have been vehement, and no more scathing an attack has been made on any literary work than that by Saunders Redding on *Another Country.* Far, then, from being partial, Negro critics have assaulted the works of other Negroes with a vengeance that makes Samuel Johnson's critique of the works of Thomas Grey judicious by comparison.

However, the oft-stated argument that Negroes lack the sensitivity and perception indispensable to the critical appraisal of literature is of far more import than the preceding ones, if for no other reason than that such arguments are vigorously set forward by members of the academic community. In his *Record* article, "American Negro Poetry: On the Stage and in the Schools," critic Robert Bone becomes the Danton of the literary establishment. Bone writes of two Negro critics, Pearl Thomas and Carolyn Reese: Miss Thomas ". . . is . . . a birthright critic, miraculously schooled in Negro literature by virtue of her race alone"; and Miss Reese ". . . cannot deal with Negro poetry because at bottom, she has failed to acquire the necessary skills.

Bone's argument is that these critics approach literature from a sensitive and perceptive vantage point, sharpened primarily by their racial experiences, which to Bone are inadequate. What is demanded is a knowledge of the critical tools sanctioned by the academic establishment. Writes Bone: "For the poet . . . teaches us to recognize our murderous and self-destructive feelings and to master them through form." Ralph Ellison, Bone's personal Negro writer in residence, has said something of the same: "Since fiction is always a collaboration between writer and reader . . . if a moral or perception is needed, let them [the readers] supply their own. For me, of course, the narrative is the meaning."

Through form, through the aesthetic presentation of the work of art, the writer communicates with the reader, allowing the latter to share aesthetically the varied nuances of the writer's experience. Form thus becomes a *deus ex machina*, a mechanical construction leading to "a heightened appreciation and awareness of life." Another way of stating the same argument is that form is the most important element in a literary work, while content is only ancillary, a necessary appendage, yet useless as a monitor or approximator of life. Literature is, then, reduced to mere artifact, timeless symbols of enduring beauty, much like the artifacts of Yeats' "Byzantium," appealing to man's natural propensity for beauty, and thus, to paraphrase John Keats, truth. In the final analysis, art is a luxury, the sole prerogative of the aristocracy—a new aristocracy, born of the academies—to be judged and evaluated upon those canons established by the aristocracy whose needs it serves.

The Misses Thomas and Reese, like Negro critics in the main—and there are exceptions—begin from an entirely different concept of the function of Negro literature. They are one with critics from Aristotle to Tolstoy who have demanded that literature, above all else, be moral; and with Samuel Johnson, they would argue that the academic critics "seem to think we are placed here to watch the growth of the planets, or the motion of the stars . . . what we [have] to learn [is] to do good and avoid evil."

This emphasis upon a moral literature may appear medieval to many in the context of the amoral atmosphere of the twentieth century. For the Negro, however, and for the Negro writer, the emphasis upon morality, a clamor for men to do justice and avoid evil, has been the hallmark of his struggle in America, and his most fervent pleas to his country have been couched in moral terms. None of America's minorities believe more in the American creed; none have staked more upon the Constitution; none have depended more upon man's natural instincts for justice and tolerance; and none have shouted with more patience, with more passion, with more eloquence—white man, listen! The Negro has been concerned with the problem of life, in a physical and moral sense, in a society in which Negro life has been the most expendable commodity. Such a concern is a moral one, for "the question how to live is itself a moral idea."

In this context, the Negro critic approaches the work of art from a moral perspective, believing with Mathew Arnold that "It is important to hold fast to this; that poetry is at bottom a criticism of life; that the greatness of a poet lies in his powerful and beautiful application of ideas of life—to the question: How to live."

This is not to imply that the Negro critic eschews aesthetics. All realize, of course, that aesthetics are a necessary requirement of art. Most are opposed to the naive, unmeaningful, critical formulas vouchsafed by the academic community. Criticism which attaches importance to the investigation of the contortions of lines, the hidden meanings of punctuation marks, the ambidextrous usage of words may be of value to the "New Aristocracy," yet completely worthless to men and women seeking an affirmation of life in positive terms.

Again, criticism based upon the search for metaphysical themes—Who am I? What is my identity? What is my relationship to the universe, to God, to the existential other?—is of no value to a Negro community daily confronted by the horrors of the urban ghetto, the threat to sanity and life in the rural areas of the South, and the continued hostility of the overwhelming majority of its fellow citizens.

Though convinced of the importance of aesthetics—a point which has never been seriously contested—Negro critics are wary of theories applicable only to a nonexistent golden age. Believing with Robert Lehan that "the writer is the last remaining hope for the modern world . . ." the Negro critic has demanded that the writer concentrate on life, that life, despairing, laughing, hoping, and dying in the ghettos of this country. To be sure, the Negro critic has used his Negroness as a vantage point, a point which enables him, unless he has been quite lucky indeed, to view the American scene from a moral perspective. In so doing, his insights and perceptions have been sharpened to deal morally with that material which is, or which should be, the preoccupation of the Negro writer. And what Gwendolyn Brooks said in regard to the Negro poet is applicable to the Negro critic: "Every poet has something to say. Simply because he is a Negro, he cannot escape having something important to say."

Here, too, Robert Bone's statement is applicable: "By virtue of his deeper insight, he, the Negro writer, can exorcise the demons that threaten his people from within." But it is equally true that he can exercise those demons which, today, rend the American society. For the Negro writer is America's conscience, and the Negro critic must be the conscience of them both.

This role of the Negro critic as moral adjudicator has never been more necessary than at present. And no period of Negro literature has demanded that the Negro critic exercise his critical sensitivity and perception for more moral reasons. For today, a dialogue persists in the community of Negro writers, which threatens the moral foundation upon which Negro literature has, in the main, been predicated.

Alain Locke planted the seeds of the dialogue in 1925 in his introduction to *The New Negro*. Wrote Professor Locke: ". . . it is the Negro problem rather than the Negro that is known and mooted in the general mind. We turn therefore . . . to the elements of truest social portraiture, and discover in the artistic self expression of the Negro today a new figure on the national canvas. . . . In these pages . . . we have . . . commented upon self expression and the forces of determination. So far as he is culturally articulate, we shall let the Negro speak for himself."

The idea that the Negro should speak for himself was not new. Though much of early Negro literature was marred by propaganda, still Frederick Douglass, W.E.B. Du Bois, James Weldon Johnson, and Langston Hughes spoke from that deep well-spring of Negro experience which represented the extent of Negro culture of that time. What was new, however, was Locke's insistence that the time had come for Negro writers to turn from moralizing, from attempts to force their just cause upon the conscience of the nation. Because attempts to make white men listen had aborted, the New Negro was admonished to forgo such attempts and to turn inward to self expression.

To do so, however, called for a new kind of literature and a new Negro to write that literature. Albert Barnes (in *The New Negro*) characterized both the literature and its creator: "The later Negro has made us feel the majesty of nature, the ineffable peace of the wood and the great open spaces. He has shown us that the event of our everyday American life contains for him a poetry, rhythm, and charm which we ourselves had never discovered. . . . His insights into realities have been given to us in vivid images loaded with poignancy and passion. His message has been lyrical, rhythmic, colorful. In short, the elements of beauty he has controlled to the ends of art" And perhaps Stanley Braithwaite stated the argument more succinctly: "Negro poetic expression hovers for the moment, pardonably perhaps, over the race question, but its highest allegiance is to poetry. . . ."

This philosophy has been stated anew by Negro writers today. Ralph Ellison has written: "If *Invisible Man* is 'free from the ideological penalties suffered by Negroes in this country' it is because I tried to the best of my ability to transform these elements into art." And, demands Ellison, "I can only ask that my fiction be judged as art; if it fails, it fails aesthetically." James Baldwin, theoretically at least, was certain of the saving grace of art: For him the only concern of the artist was "to recreate out of the disorder of life that order which is art."

Not until 1940 were these arguments, first set forth by the proponents of the Negro Renaissance, effectively challenged. The challenge came from Mississippi-born Richard Wright, who as artist and critic, transformed a monologue into a dialogue by presenting dramatically, forcefully, and persuasively, the other argument. Wright argued, in essence, that conditions in America had not changed to the degree that the Negro could desert the race question, engage in an art for arts sake endeavor, or wander free in the sunny utopia of abstraction in an attempt to desert the harsh reality of being Black in the twentieth century. "The grinding process of history," wrote Wright in his 1945 introduction to *Black Metropolis*. "had forged iron in the Negro's heart [and therefore] we heard a new and strange cry from another Negro. And this cry came from the pen of Claude McKay, the *enfant terrible* of the Negro Renaissance, in bitter, vehement protest, in the militant poem, "If We Must Die."

Though certainly not antagonistic to artistic principles, Wright realized that an era of oppression was not one in which "art could be the only consideration." Negroes capable of ignoring the brutal, inhuman treatment of other Negroes, were, according to Wright, Negroes "who recorded the feelings of a Negro reacting not as a Negro."

So central a part does this thesis play in Wright's critical theory, that he returns to it in 1956: ". . . the fact of separation from his native land has now sunk home into the Negro's heart; the Negro loves his land, but that land rejects him. Here we can witness the emergence of a new type of Personality." That personality was George Moses Horton who: ". . . was an emotionally trapped man; he lived in a culture of which he was not really a part; he was a split man believing and feeling something which he could not live; . . . Horton's cry for freedom was destined to become the lament, was to roll down the decades swelling, augmenting itself, becoming a vast reservoir of bitterness and infrequent hope."

But Richard Wright died in 1960, and no other Negro writer of his stature has arisen to enjoin the dialogue, presented today by the new proponents of a Negro Renaissance. The New Negroes of the nineteen sixties, apropos of their namesakes of the ninteen thirties, have, as Herbert Hill puts it in *Soon One Morning*. ". . . made the creative act their first consideration. . . . As the Negro writer moves beyond anger, he develops a new concern for the writer's craft, for literary discipline and control and seeks an involvement in the larger world of art and ideology."

The Negro critic remains, then, to present the other argument. He must, like Richard Wright, take an active part in the dialogue, not as a Lycurgus dispensing arbitrary laws and rules, nor as Polonius brandishing answers and solutions, but instead as an engaged participant, fully respectful of both sides of the dialogue. His criticism must be guided by a temperament which allows him to explicate the work of art in terms of its contribution to the alleviation of those problems which have confronted humanity for too long a time. This entails a sensitive and perceptive awareness which can only, in part, be conditioned by the academic establishment. Robert Bone's cry of despair, therefore: "But you really must know Ezra Pound, Hart Crane, and Charles Olson if you hope to understand Melvin Tolson, Robert Hayden, and LeRoi Jones," is presumptuous; for the understanding of such poets depends equally upon a critical perspective conditioned by the many-faceted experiences of the Negro in the turbulent American society.

On this point, the Negro critic and the university will remain at odds. If the day ever arrives when Negro literature is accepted as an integral part of American literature, the Negro critic will still remain invisible. For his is the predominant voice in American criticism which calls upon the Negro writer to dedicate himself to the proposition that literature is a moral force for change as well as an aesthetic creation. In so doing, he risks not only continued invisibility, but denigrating charges that he does not know enough, coupled with insistent attacks upon his credentials as a critic.

This cannot be helped. Though the moral argument has little relevance in America at present, still, the Negro critic must demand that the Negro writer articulate the grievances of the Negro in moral terms; for the time is far distant when the Negro writer can cry out in sweet delirium with John Keats:

> Away: Away! for I will fly to thee
> Not charioted by Bacchus and his pards
> But on the viewless wings of Poesy. . . .

CHAPTER 17

The Politics of Revolution:
Afro-American Literature

(1972)

> Let our thinkers and creators of literature provide us with images based upon our own lives, but let them also destroy those other mirrors by waging war against every institution which influences the actions of Black people.

I believe it was Malcolm X who said that everyone talks about revolution, but nowhere is a revolution to be found. This statement is true if we think of revolution in the classic sense—small bands of desperate men engaging the forces of oppression in guerilla warfare by means of sabotage and acts of terrorism. This form of liberation—which enabled the Russians to overthrow the tyranny of the czars, the Cubans to overthrow the corrupt Batista regime, and African states to overcome the tyranny of colonial power—is, unfortunately, impossible within the American context.

Power comes from the barrel of a gun, and those who possess the guns in America are the oppressors. If the singular deaths of Blacks at the hands of whites throughout history have not taught us the extent to which white Americans rely upon such power, then surely the massacre at the Attica Correctional Facility in which over 30 Black men were gunned down in less than two hours, should leave no doubt as to the willingness and intention of Americans to commit genocide upon the Black population. Only men ignorant of these facts would think of patterning an Afro-American revolution after that of the Russians, Cubans, or Africans.

There are those who argue that there are other oppressed people in America, and that such people will align themselves with Blacks in the event of an armed struggle. That there are other oppressed people in America is true. That such people realize the extent of oppression against them is doubtful. When the governor of the state of New York, one of the world's richest men, orders the execution of over 40 people, he is supported and cheered by the exploited and exploiters alike. To expect an alignment between Afro-Americans, white leftists, and working class whites, is to negate the facts of history. The liberation of a people must be executed by the people themselves.

If we are to speak of an Afro-American revolution, therefore, we must speak of it in a more profound sense. In order to do so, we must carefully analyze the nature of the country in which we live. To compare America with Nazi Germany is far-fetched only in the sense that the American Nazis are more sophisticated than were the German ones. The apparatus of control exercised by whites upon the Black population is more ingenious, insidious, and destructive than utilized by the Germans over the subject people of Europe. Black people are not marched off into concentration camps *en masse;* except in times of rebellion, no tanks patrol the streets of the Black community; and the police forces, at least in larger cities, are made up of oppressed and oppressor as well.

The military machine which stands as a vivid reminder to the native of his impotence before the state in colonial countries is not on visible display here. In America, members of the oppressed sit in the councils of government, hold conclaves with the president of the United States, teach in prestigious universities, and sit on the boards of powerful industries. Quite correctly, Hoyt W. Fuller has remarked: ". . . a certain minority of Black people in this country have privileges and education and access that no other non-white people in the world have any place else."

The consequences of this benign despotism are readily apparent: Black college students believe that they, too, may become sharers of the nation's wealth; the Black masses dream, not of overthrowing the society, but of finding a comfortable niche within it; the *bourgeoisie* dream not of nationhood, but of moving from the status of lower middle class to middle class, with all the concomitant neuroses such a move entails.

The desire of Blacks from all groups to become one with the oppressor cannot be explained by labeling such people corrupt, anti-revolutionary, or Uncle Toms. The reasons lie deeper and are central to the mechanism of control exercised by white Americans over Black Americans. The mechanism is not new; the model was established in the early days of this republic; and if it has appeared so ominous and everpresent in the twentieth century, it is only because we are oblivious of our own history.

Upon debarking in America, slaves were separated from one another in terms of language and national origin. No two slaves from the same tribe or region were sold together; no two slaves who spoke the same language were sold to the same master. This practice, which succeeded to a limited degree in forestalling rebellion, was more successful in forcing the slaves to surrender his own culture and lifestyle, to lose all cognizance of the symbols, myths, and metaphors which he had used to define himself and his people. Whereas once he had looked into the mirror of his own psyche for a portrait of himself, he was forced now to look into the mirror of his captor, a mirror in which two images predominated. One image pictured the slave as uncivilized and nonhuman, and thus deserving of the position of hewer-of-wood and drawer-of-water. The other image depicted whites as powerful, divine, and cultivated and, thus, deserving of the position of master of men. No one has more accurately identified these images than Hinton R. Helper who, in the book *No Jocue* (1867), wrote that the color black "has always been associated with such sinister things as mourning, the devil, the darkness of night," whereas, the color white has always been associated with "the light of day, divine transfiguration, the beneficent moon and stars . . . the fair complexion of ladies, the costumes of Romans and Angels and the white of the American flag, so beautifully combined with the blue and red without ever a touch of the black that has been for the flag of pirates."

Because these images were validated and substantiated by the power of the state, it is not surprising that, in time, many Black people adopted the white image as their own, came to view their own family and race as nonhumans, desired to become one with the oppressor. Listen to one of our earliest poets, to Phillis Wheatley, and we are in that era when a people first move to surrender their own identity and adopt that of another:

> Twas not long since I left my native shore
> The land of errors and Egyptian gloom:
> Father of mercy: 'twas thy gracious hand
> Brought me in safety from these dark abodes.

The adoption of white images was so pronounced by 1852 that Martin R. Delany devoted a book to *The Condition, Elevation, Emigration and Destiny of The Colored Peoples of The United States,* in which he pointed out, among other things, that "our friends have for years been erroneously urging us to lose our identity as a race, declaring that we were the same as other people. . . . We have inherent traits, and native characteristics, peculiar to our race and all that is required of us is to cultivate these to make them desirable and emulated by the rest of the world."

To accept images created in American mirrors meant to accept the concomitant values which comprise the American system. For men like Frank Webb, this meant to accept wealth and status as the dividing line between men; for Charles Chesnutt, it meant to accept the argument that some men were blessed, others damned according to their ability "to pull themselves up by their own bootstraps." In the lexicon of the Americans, a man was defined in terms of physical characteristics, status, and wealth. All too soon, men who had once defined man in humanistic terms succumbed to the tendency to relegate him to the status of a useable object.

When one people are forced to accept the definitions and images vouchsafed by another people, serious repercussions result, becoming discernible in the history of the subject people. In the case of Afro-Americans, such results are highlighted in the literature from 1853 to the present time, and they are nowhere delineated more explicitly than in two novels—one written in the latter part of the nineteenth century, the other in the early part of the twentieth. The first, *The*

Garies and Their Friends, by Frank Webb (1858) follows *Clotel, or The President's Daughter* (1853), by five years.

For William Wells Brown, author of *Clotel,* the most important attribute of Black people was color; his novels, therefore, are peopled with mulattoes, quadroons and octoroons. For Webb, color is an important, though not a necessary, characteristic. One may approach the American norm by adopting the values of the majority group. His hero, Mr. Walters, therefore, is not mulatto, but black in color. One of the leading citizens of Philadelphia, he is the first Black capitalist in Afro-American literature, one who has managed to construct a better mousetrap than his neighbors, Black or white.

Confusion of images is apparent in Webb's description of his hero: "Mr. Walters was above six feet in height and exceedingly well proportioned; of jet black complexion, and smooth glossy skin. His head was covered with a quantity of wooly hair, which was combed back from a broad but not very high forehead. His aquiline nose, thin lips and broad chin *were the very reverse of African* in their shape, and gave his face a very singular appearance." (Italics mine.)

The image is clear to the audience, if not to Webb. We are confronted in this novel with a Black-white man, one who realizes: ". . . that in our land of liberty it is of incalculable advantage to be white; that is beyond dispute, and no one is more painfully aware of it than I . . . it is everything to be white . . . When I look around me, and see what I might have been beneath a fairer skin . . . I am almost tempted to curse the destiny that made me . . . There is no doubt . . . but what I full appreciate the advantage of being white."

Regrettably, for Webb, Walters cannot be white, cannot approach the American norm by means of skin color. He has other options, however, for he is cultured, wealthy, and refined. Such characteristics are depicted in a description of Walters' home: the "furniture indicated not only great wealth but cultivated taste and refined habits. The richly papered walls were adorned by paintings from the hands of well-known foreign and native artists. Rich vases and well-executed bronzes were placed in the most favorable situations in the apartment; the elegantly-carved walnut table was covered with those charming little *bijoux,* which the French only are capable of conceiving, and which are only at the command of such purchasers as are possessed of more money than they otherwise can conveniently spend."

The Garies and Their Friends is a manifesto for the Black middle class, one which points out "a different route to the approximation of the American image." Those who are not fortunate enough to be born mulatto may become like white men by attaining such artifacts as education, wealth, and refinement. The fact that such people gaze into distorted mirrors is lost on Webb and many of the middle-class Black writers who proceeded him. After the nineteenth century, the objective of too many Afro-Americans was to become white by one formula or another.

The Garies and Their Friends was written in 1858, one hundred years before the Supreme Court Decision in favor of the plaintiff in Brown vs. Board of Education, Topeka, Kansas. Thus, we are blessed with a truth that Webb and his generation did not possess: The problem of America is the problem of race, not class, and to be educated, cultured, and refined does not transform a Black man into an American. The argument is conclusive: Black men can never approach the image vouchsafed by white Americans, and the attempt to do so has brought us to the present impasse of division and internecine warfare and prevented us from embarking upon a truly revolutionary course.

The origins of the divisions and antagonisms which continue to concern us in the seventies are depicted in *Home To Harlem,* written by Claude McKay in 1929. The novel was published during the time in which the Garvey movement had projected new images of Black men, when such writers as W.E.B. Du Bois, James Weldon Johnson, and Alain Locke attempted to arrive at a newer, more humane definition of man. It points out the repercussions suffered by people who, in accepting images of themselves constructed by others, turn to self-hatred and destructiveness.

Jake and Ray are the heroes of *Home To Harlem.* Jake, an easy-living, good-natured Black character, exists with ease in a world of prostitution, gambling, and corruption. Ray, the intellectual, has little affinity with such a world. An alienated man, isolated from the world of Blacks and whites, he is unable to accept the definitions promulgated by either group. The two characters inhabit an atavistic world—one of wine, women, and song. Unfortunately, this world is one in which Black men, afflicted by confusion of images, unable to correlate visions of themselves with those in the societal mirror, turn upon each other in attempts at self-annihilation.

McKay has one of his characters remark: "Harlem is the craziest place . . . The stuff it gives the niggers brain fevah, so far, as I see, and this heah wold has got a big-long horizon. We'se too thick together in Harlem. We'se just all lumped together without a chanst to choose and so we natcherly hate one another . . . Why, just the other night I witnessed a nasty stroke. You know that spade Prof that always there on the avenue handing out the big stuff about niggers and their rights . . . He was passing by the poolroom with a bunch of books when a bad nigger jest lunges out and socks him bif: in the jaw, I tell you, boh, Harlem is lousy with crazy-bad niggers . . . and I always travel with mah gun ready."

The image is vivid and concrete. Filled with resentment and frustration, the victims wage war against one another. This warfare leads to the creation of the "bad nigger," and it is with this phenomenon that the world of *Home To Harlem* is concerned. At one time, it was possible to deny the existence of this character, a creation of the Southern Plantation School of writers. However, after the publication of *Native Son* in 1940, after Richard Wright paraded Bigger Thomas into the milieu of the Afro-American novel, to deny his existence was an impossibility. Unable to accept the image of himself as defined by white Americans, the "bad nigger" is a reality, no longer to be ignored, romanticized, or repudiated. His very existence can be explained in terms of confusion of images.

There are those, however, who postulate other factors. Sociologists argue that victims of the social order who war against others do so as a result of powerlessness; others attribute such actions to the stultifying effects of environment. That the powerless seldom ravage the powerful is true; that this can be attributed to powerlessness is doubtful. No Black man in the American society—with the possible exception of Elijah Muhammad—is free of the stultifying effect of powerlessness, and yet, most Black men do not engage in hostile acts against each other.

The environmental argument no longer has validity. The effects of environment upon the individual personality is difficult to determine, the specific results impossible to measure. What factors account for Richard Wright, James Baldwin and Don L. Lee, and differentiate them from friends who shred the same geographic environment? What accounts for the fact that the majority of Blacks in Harlem are nonrebellious followers of the *status quo,* while a minority openly advocate revolution? The sophistic argument that each lives in the same geographical area, but not the same familial one, cannot suffice as an adequate explanation.

The major factor in the creation of the "bad nigger" is confusion of images engendered by 300 years of American oppression and tyranny. Forced to look into a mirror passed from one generation to another, the "bad nigger," like the characters of *Home To Harlem,* has become bitter, frustrated, and resentful. He has come to hate the image of whiteness which he can never approach, and the image of Blackness which he does not want to approach. His ambivalence is explained by pushing Du Bois' thesis of psychological dualism to its logical conclusion. One cannot be both Black and American in a society in which the term American is defined as white. The tension between attempting to attain the impossible, and the inability to attain it, produces the bad nigger.

The bad nigger is not only one who engages in *physical* warfare against other Black people. Such a definition is too narrow and fails to account for those numerous unheralded acts committed by one Black man against another. The Black professor who fails to act in the interests of his Black students is a bad nigger. The Black student who wastes his time in card playing, partying, and mock revolution, when his talents are needed by the Black community, is a bad nigger. The Black shopkeeper who overcharges his brothers and sisters in order to make excessive profits is a bad nigger. The Black writer who insists upon adhering to the standards of white critics at a time when the question for Black people is survival is a bad nigger. Those who continue to distort their African features and adopt the manners and characteristics of whites, at the expense of their Black heritage, are bad niggers. Those who continue to posit the integrationist heaven in racist America are bad niggers.

What is needed, however, is not simply castigation of those who have gone astray, but, instead, a vehicle by which the bad nigger might be transformed into an Afro-American. This is possible only by tending to the true causes of affliction, confusion of images. It is at this point that talk of revolution ceases, and true revolution begins. The revolutionary course leads through the destruction of the images, metaphors, and symbols created by American mirror makers and forced upon Black people.

The vehicle, therefore, must help us to purge ourselves of those concepts which we have accepted, and which we use daily in dealing with one another. A race of people, in other words, must undergo a rebirth, examine themselves in a new and different light, undergo a process of de-Americanization, look at images propounded by new mirrors, and strut to the beat of different drummers. None are more equipped to provide a vehicle to accomplish these objectives than our thinkers and creators of literature.

It is with justice that we turn to them, for all too often, like Brown and Webb, sometimes without knowing it, they have been the most important propagandists for the American image. From 1853 to the present, far too many of our poets, novelists, dramatists and critics were proponents of the white aesthetic. What will still the anger and rebellion of Bigger Thomas? Only a changed society, one in which Bigger has become Americanized, has accepted the values and ethics of white America. Ellison's protagonist in *Invisible Man* will leave his underground sanctuary only when the integrated society is brought into being.

The task of creating new images, of discarding old definitions, and redefining values is not as difficult as was once believed. Paradigms already exist. Go back into Afro-American history and there are those whose words and actions contradict the American image makers: Harriet Tubman, Sojourner Truth, Frederick Douglass, Nat Turner, Henry Highland Garnet, and Marcus Garvey; and in our own time, there are Malcolm X, Stokely Carmichael, H. Rap Brown, Martin Luther King, Imamu Amiri Baraka, the men and women of the Nation of Islam, and those countless thousands who have accepted in their lives and in their hearts the reality of Black Power.

Let our thinkers and creators of literature provide us with images and symbols based upon the lives and exploits of such Afro-Americans, let them show us images of ourselves in mirrors of our own construction. Let them never lose sight, however, of that other mirror; let them never cease to attempt to destroy it by waging war against every institution in this country which influences the thinking and actions of Black people.

We have reached a serious impasse at this juncture of history. A people who have long desired peace, whose past has been distinguished by a reluctance to wage war, find that such a course has brought us to the brink of destruction as a race. The country moves as though some invisible hand guides its destiny, slowly, but inexorably along the path of genocide. The murder of George Jackson, the assassination of members of the Black Panther party, and the massacre at Attica are only a *few* examples.

Once again, as in the past, we face the gargantuan monster alone; however, knowing a great deal about this country and its people, we are less inclined to believe that our salvation rests in approximating the images reflected in mirrors of oppression. We know all too well that a people at war must know and understand themselves, what they are capable of. Knowing these things, with the aid of Black people from all walks of life, we move at this period of the twentieth century to redefine the word revolution, and to posit a new image of the revolutionary. He is an African in America, knowledgeable of his history and culture, who loves his people and who is determined to fight for their survival as a nation. He is outside of American morality, history, and culture and, in so being, he is one who, in the words of Don L. Lee, "walks the way of the new world," and charts a righteous path for Black people who follow him.

CHAPTER 18

Revolutionary Philosophy: Three Black Writers

(1971)

"Every INTELLECTUAL," writes Ignazio Silone, "is a revolutionary." We in the Black community know from empirical evidence that this is not so. We do know, however, that every reformer is a potential revolutionary, for revolution begins when reform proves to be impossible. The reformer is the prophet of the possible; he has unlimited faith in manmade institutions. He believes in the just society and that events will bring it into being. He dedicates himself to a future world ordained not by man but by God and time, and thus he is not outside of history but history's captive. Like Abraham, to quote Auerbach, "his soul is torn between desperate rebellion and hopeful expectation."

The moment arrives when this inner dichotomy is resolved, when the forces of "desperate rebellion" take possession of his soul. When this occurs, he breaks his pact with history, steps outside of it, becomes a proponent of the impossible, an outlaw; which is to say, he becomes a revolutionary.

There was Frederick Douglass, the young man who began as a disciple of William Lloyd Garrison in 1841 and became the voice of the abolitionist movement. He is not the same Douglass we meet ten years later. The earlier Douglass was a reformer, dedicated to bringing into being "the community of man." He advocated moral suasion, a program designed not to kill the master, but to transform him, and by so doing, to transform the society. The later Douglass, however, began to realize that the only justification for moral suasion is faith in history—an unsure faith, for history can sanction either justice or injustice. He therefore chose to step outside of history, to dedicate himself to the proposition that the master must die, that the old institutions must be gutted by fire, not eroded by time, and a new moral code created out of the ashes of the old. It is thus that he champions old John Brown, American history's first white outlaw who, with a Bible in one hand and a rifle in the other, pledged himself to revolution.

There were the freedom riders of the nineteen sixties, reformers who dared not call for the maximum—destruction of the existing social order—being denied the minimum decency, dignity, and justice, brooding like Douglass, going back to their colleges bruised, battered, jail-weary, and contemplating the step across the boundary line which separates reform from revolution.

There was Martin Luther King, dedicated to the things of the spirit, standing atop the mountain, saddened by the reluctance of his country to grant minimum reforms and thus make revolution unnecessary.

For if the minimum is impossible to achieve, why should men not dedicate themselves to securing the maximum? If Satan cannot gain a small part of heaven by petition, why not attempt to take all of heaven at the point of a gun? If societies are unwilling to accept the formula "some if not all," why should men not embrace the abolitionist formula of Ivan Karamazov, "all or none"? To such questions, the answer of the Black reformer is as positive as that of Frederick Douglass. The Black man who began as a reformer, pledging himself to some if not all, becomes a revolutionary, pledging himself to all or none. In so doing, he takes the first fateful step outside of American history, moving away from the influence of the gradualists and the integrationists, becoming an outlaw, one who seeks not only to create the new society, but also a new morality which will produce, to use Julius Lester's phrase, "the new man."

"He taught us nothing," Matthew Arnold wrote of Lord Byron in the nineteenth century, "but our soul has felt him like the thunderer's roar." We too, have our hero in the twentieth century, but unlike Byron, not only have we felt him in the deepest part of our souls, but he has also taught us a great deal. Martin Luther King was the apostle of reform and in his living and dying, he taught us that reform in American society is impossible. He taught us that the problem of the twentieth century is no longer, as Du Bois believed at the beginning of the century, the problem of the color line, for such is not a problem but a conundrum and incapable of solution. The problem is whether Black men will attempt a revolution based upon the highest tenets of morality—justice, brotherhood, and individual worth, or conform to American history by attempting a revolution based upon nihilism or gangsterism.

The society which crucifies the reformer and the revolutionary on the same cross makes reform impossible and violence inevitable. The sum total of King's non-violent life and his violent death reduces the options of Black Americans to two: revolution or nihilism; and even as the cortege follows his body to its final resting place, the chaos and confusion following his death tips the scale in favor of nihilism. The man who bore the cross as a shield is discovered to have had a less powerful weapon than the gun; thus the instrument of Martin Luther King's destruction becomes the symbol of the Black man's salvation. The stage is set for vengeance and redemption and upon this stage, gun in hand, the philosopher of nihilism appears.

"During my last stay in prison," writes Eldridge Cleaver, "I made the desperate decision to abandon completely the criminal path and to redirect my life." The new direction led to the publication of two books, *Soul On Ice* and *Eldridge*

Cleaver, a position as Minister of Information of the Black Panther Party, and a presidential candidacy on the slate of the Peace and Freedom Party in 1968.

Today Cleaver is hunted by a government whose morality is inferior to his. Even the crime of rape which sent him to so many prisons, San Quentin, Folsom, Soledad, pales into insignificance when measured alongside the rape perpetrated by the United States government, with the sanction of the American people, upon half the world; however, similarities between hunted and hunter are so great as to approach the height of irony. Cleaver is the American society in microcosm, a pragmatist whose years in prison have taught him how this "world goes." More so than any other man in the last 50 years, he has stripped America of her facade, removed the tinsel, and symbolized in his own person what she is now and has always been. The nation which traded the cross for the gun, now hunts a man who, gleefully, without embarrassment, welcomes the exchange.

In this context *Soul On Ice* becomes more than a personal document; its ramifications extend the width and breadth of America. For what comprises reality for the average American if not the belief that the world evolves around muscle, that at the apex of the universe is the gun, that American morality rests upon power, and that in America, as nowhere else, gangsterism is idealism pushed to actuality? Cleaver, in two essays in his first book, reveals his kinship with these "average Americans." In the first, "Notes On a Native Son," a vicious, unwarranted attack upon James Baldwin, one must dig deep for Cleaver's central thesis. This thesis is not James Baldwin's ambiguity concerning his racial identity. What annoys Cleaver, and occasions the essay, is the presence of homosexuality in a world ruled by "Supermasculine Menials." "Baldwin," writes Cleaver, "despised not Richard Wright, but his masculinity." For Cleaver as for America, masculinity, the essence of brute force, is the symbol of power. Those who wield the rifles or bang down the guillotine must be men with all the connotations the term implies in a masculine-oriented society.

A "student of Norman Mailer's 'The White Negro,'" Cleaver, like Mailer, asks us to journey back to the days of Neanderthal Man, to the noble savage whose most important characteristic was his toughness. Here among mankind's first gangsters, manhood is measured by the savagery each man displays toward the others. In this environment, Bigger Thomas becomes for Cleaver what he was not for Richard Wright, a glorified gangster seeking to wreak revenge upon a society in which brute force is the norm. The man who begins by raping people, argues William Strickland, ends by raping society.

Cleaver's thesis, although symbolic and metaphorical, is nevertheless more clearly stated in the essay, "The Primeval Mitosis." The debt to Mailer is still being paid. Society is torn apart by two opposing forces symbolic of the dual aspects of man's nature. The higher instincts, those of the mind, are characterized by the Omnipotent Administrator; man's basic, primeval instincts, those of the body, are characterized by the Supermasculine Menials. "Weakness, frailty, cowardice, and effeminancy are, among other attributes, associated with the mind. Strength, brute power, force, virility, and physical beauty are associated with the body." Those who told us that the weak would inherit the earth are here revealed for the liars that they are. The world, according to Cleaver, belongs to the Supermasculine Menials.

In "The Land Question and Black Liberation," the central essay in *Eldridge Cleaver*, the role of the Supermasculine Menials in the early stages of the revolution is clear: They will guide us to the first way station on the road to *Götterdämmerung*. "The violent phase of the Black liberation struggle is here, and it will spread . . . America will be painted red. Dead bodies will litter the streets and the scene will be reminiscent of the disgusting, terrifying, nightmarish news reports coming out of Algeria during the height of the general violence."

In this orgy of violence, however, we are comforted by the fact that we do not fight Goliath alone: "Not only would Black people resist, with the help of white people, but we would also have the help of those around the world who are just waiting for some kind of extreme crisis within this country so that they can move for their own liberation from American repression abroad."

[I stood, jolted by the naiveté of my father who refused to admit to himself that the white communists had sold him and his people down the river, that when the chips were down they had settled for Soviet-Communist unity rather than continue to confront oppression of Blacks in America. I am jolted too, here, twenty-five years later, when history is not only so blatantly ignored but discarded as irrelevant. The history of whites in this country—farmers of Tom Watson's day, communists of the days of my father, and liberals of Martin Luther King's day— has been that when the decision must be made between life and death, between stability and chaos, few have been willing, to quote Albert Camus, "to go to the bitter end." The concentration camp is a lonely, deadly place; and few whites have ever been *willing* to embrace Blacks there.]

Eldridge Cleaver, metaphor of American society, has accepted the moral formula of America's madmen—an eye for an eye—and proposed to deal with the madmen on their terms. Neither reformer nor revolutionary, he is a prophet of the Apocalypse, telling us not what we are destined to become but what we are. When he accepts the American reality for his own, when he chooses to champion the forces of American history instead of opposing them, when he accepts the gun and the world of the gun as the essential reality, he ceases to be an outlaw, and becomes what is infinitely worse, more American than the Americans.

The problem is not Cleaver's alone. It is endemic to the whole Black revolution and occasioned by men who, frustrated in personal life, seize upon the Black revolution as a cathartic exercise. The serious Black revolutionary has no conflict between mind and body. The conflict is a much more severe one. The most schizoid of men, he is destined never to be a whole man, to always be many men, forced to operate "upon two planes of reality." He must be aware of Cleaver's major thesis, that the American society is one of the gun and that it evolves around muscle and brute force; however, for him, this constitutes only one aspect of reality, never the ultimate, a dedication to which means to be dedicated to insanity.

It is incumbent upon him to believe that the opposite reality is equally true: that men are more the victims of systems than the originators of them, that no man is inherently evil, and that somewhere in the netherworld of man's psyche there exists a human being like himself. Based upon these two conflicting aspects of reality, the revolutionary sanctions the use of the gun while at the same time deploring its use, argues for violence while hating the necessity for it, wages war while declaring that all war is illegitimate. The essential justification for the Black revolutionary is to make Black people better than they are.

To make Black people better than they are would be a revolution in itself. The major characteristic of past revolutions is that each has become a carbon copy of the system it displaced. The revolutionary who begins by attacking corruption and abuse and demanding "all power to the people" soon discovers that the people are no more virtuous, no more moral, no more willing to exercise power judiciously than the culprits who were overthrown.

This naive, romantic belief in the virtue of the people has had serious repercussions for Black revolutionaries of the past. The failures of the rebellions of Denmark Vesey, Nat Turner, and Gabriel Prosser, and the decline of the Garvey movement can be traced to the betrayal of one Black man by another. Today, the infiltration of many Black nationalist organizations by agents of the city, state, and federal governments is made possible by a simple faith born out of a frustrated desire to regard all Black men as seekers after change.

What, then, would it mean to substitute hell for heaven when both are ruled by the same tyrant? The acquisition of a separate paradise, if possible, given the expropriation by Blacks of the worst characteristics of whites—greed, lust, and hypocrisy—would demand that the Black revolutionary once again strap his carbine about his shoulders. Before the phrase "power to the people" has any meaning beyond the metaphysical, the people must undergo a metamorphosis, must be cleansed of their Americanism, must become "new men." "Man," wrote the German philosopher, Friedrich Nietzsche, "is a link between the ape and the superman"; the Negro is a link between the slave and the new man; he is something that must be surpassed.

At this point, the Black revolutionary lays down his rifle, conscious that an important task awaits him. He who masters the gun is as important as the gun itself; for like a fickle woman, the gun does the bidding of tyrants and revolutionaries alike. The revolution which moved beyond reformism, denounced non-violence, and made the gun a part of the consciousness of Black people, turns now to Black people themselves to make them conscious of their past, of their historical value, and lays the cultural foundation from which the moral revolution must spring. In the shadow of the holocaust, we turn from the world of emotion to the world of reason, from the world of the primitive to the world of enlightened man. We travel but a few steps from the prophet of nihilism, and we encounter the prophet of cultural revolution.

Like Eldridge Cleaver, Harold Cruse is the author of two books, *The Crisis of the Negro Intellectual* and *Revolution or Rebellion*. And like Cleaver, Cruse had little formal education. That Cruse did not get lost in a sterile, academic atmosphere was perhaps for the better, when one realizes the extensive education he acquired on his own. His post-secondary school education was gained through serving in the United States Army during World War II, traveling from one point on the globe to another, digesting books in the libraries, or in the lonely solitude of a small room, and finally through membership in the Communist Party.

An intellectual, whose mind has been formed in the day-to-day world and heightened by contact with the minds of scholars, past and present, Cruse has a unique vantage point from which to peer down on his fellow Black intellectuals. His vision is too often clouded, especially in *The Crisis of the Negro Intellectual*, with personal invective, acrimonious insults, insignificant attacks upon insignificant figures, and an ego problem which would delight Freudians everywhere; however, when brought to bear directly upon the racial situation in America, his vision concerning the crisis of the Black intellectual is crystal clear. The crisis is one of soul. Having bartered away parts of his soul to numerous American Mephistophleles—Jews, white liberals, capitalists, and communists—the Black intellectual can become master of his soul once again only by acquiring complete mastery over his own cultural apparatus: "The path to the ethnic decentralization of American Society is through its culture, that is to say through its cultural apparatus, which comprises the eyes, ears, and the mind of capitalism and its twentieth century voice to the world."

In other words, the crisis can be resolved only when men, searching for their identities, delve deep into their past, attempt to find out from whence they have come. To move outside of American history, men must plunge into their past, sift through the centuries of lies and distortions, and be born again, not in the American image, but in that of their ancestors. In fact, not fiction, Cruse heralds the coming of the "new Negro," the breaker of icons, the smasher of "the old tables of the law," the remaker of men and societies.

"The Black revolt is as palpable in letters as it is in the streets . . ." writes Hoyt Fuller; and this revolt is being carried on not by the Supermasculine Menials, but by cultural scholars and analysts. For concurrent with the "war in the streets" is a cultural war waged not only for men's minds but for their souls as well. To return to the Black past, to forge a momentary concordat with history, is to renew one's forces for the final confrontation. Somewhere between the landing of the first slave ship and Reconstruction, the past of Black people was stolen away, much as Prometheus stole the sacred fire from Olympus, and the attempt to regain that

past has been frustrated by more powerful, less moral gods than Prometheus':
Black intellectuals, integrationists, and white liberals.

To regain this past, men must look beyond the gun to ". . . the new concept
of cultural revolution." In *Rebellion or Revolution,* Cruse writes: "We maintain
that this concept affords the intellectual means, the conceptual framework, the
theoretical link that ties together all the disparate conflicting and contending
trends within the Negro movement as a whole in order to transform the movement from a mere rebellion into a revolutionary movement that can shape ideas
to fit the world into a theoretical frame."

So far have we come from the year 1906 in which the architects of the N.A.A.C.P.,
plotting their skirmish with American Society, enunciated a platform whose major
planks may be reduced to two: the reformation of American Society, wherein the
Constitution would be applicable to all citizens of the republic, and an extension
of the Booker T. Washington program of racial uplift, a program with the osten-
sible purpose of making Black people worthy of the benefits gained as a result
of reform. The first plank was burned to ashes by the fiery rhetoric of Eldridge
Cleaver, who is after all merely the antithesis of Roy Wilkins. The other falls apart
under the careful analysis of Harold Cruse.

Cruse asks us to step back from the confrontation, to pause, to take stock of
ourselves, to reinvest ourselves with the verities of old, to wage cultural war and
in so doing, produce the new man and the true revolutionary. We are called to
an intellectual awakening where the intellectual, having resolved the crisis of
identity, becomes "nationalistic in terms of the ethnic and cultural attributes
of his art expression." The men who return to pick up the gun differ from those
who put it aside. Out of the clay of nationalism, a Black man is born anew, dedicated to revolution instead of nihilism. In making the existential leap outside of
American history, he has ceased to be its captive; in gaining mastery of himself,
he has ceased to be the servant of the gun, but vice versa. Realizing now that
guns without moral sanctions become instruments of destruction not salvation,
he moves further along the path which divides nihilism from revolution, and
there, at the crossroads, extending his hand in greeting, is the prophet of moral
revolution.

In the third of three books, *Revolutionary Notes,* Julius Lester writes: "The revolutionary must seize upon experience as an opportunity to make himself more
revolutionary, to make him self more the new man. The revolutionary's commitment is not to the destruction of the dehumanizing system . . . the destruction of
the dehumanizing system is only a prelude to the creation of conditions under
which man may be fulfilled. Even as the revolutionary plans his attack upon the
dehumanizing system, he keeps at the core of his being, not the destroying, but the
creating that must follow . . . We must destroy in order to live, but let us never enjoy
the destroying more than the New Life, the only reason for the destroying."

The revolutionary must always wage war with the madman inside of himself. In American society where gangsterism is all pervasive, each man begins adult life as a gangster. What distinguishes the revolutionary from other men is that he is committed to discarding the gangsterism in his makeup. Too often in America, the tendency has been to define Black revolutionaries in American terminology. Thus the difference between a Black revolutionary and a Black reformer was said to hinge upon the devotion of one to violence and the other to non-violence.

To devote oneself to non-violence, however, means to surrender to gangsterism, to lie impotent before the massive roll of the juggernaut of American history. To dedicate oneself to violence without the restraining influence of a moral code is to acquiesce in terror, and to champion the extension of the history of American oppression from the United States to Vietnam. As the Black revolution borders upon gangsterism, moves closer to defining itself in terms of American history, Julius Lester imparts a moral note, attempts to establish a golden mean. From confrontations with the racist structure in Mississippi, from living among the people of the Delta, working with them, sleeping with them, and fighting with them, Lester has carved out "of those most terrifying of Southern nights," a philosophy which calls Black men to the noblest of all endeavors—the creation of a new social order.

The philosophy takes shape in his first book, *Look Out Whitey, Black Power's Gon Get Your Momma,* and reaches mature form in *Revolutionary Notes.* In the first book, Lester, analogous to Cruse, councils the Black artist: "The artist is essentially a revolutionary whose aim is to change people's lives. He wants people to live better and one way of doing it is to make them see, hear, and feel what he has seen, heard, and felt. The artist is not concerned with beauty, but with making man's life better."

In *Revolutionary Notes,* the message, amplified, becomes one for all men: "But many Blacks see the struggle as Black against white. Perhaps it is, but if that is true, then nothing really matters. It is not enough to love Black people and hate white people. That is therapy, not revolution. It is incumbent upon the revolutionary that he not do to someone else what that someone may have done to him. . . . The revolutionary is he who loves humanity and hates injustice. It is only through a commitment of this kind that social change in America will result in revolution and not in another of the varieties of oppression."

Julius Lester is a good man, and like all good men, he asks us to be better than we are, to follow him outside of American history, outside of a nation which places a higher value upon material things than it does upon human life, which awards a higher honor to the hypocrite and the military murderer than to the priest and scribe. As we move forward toward Armageddon, Lester asks us to transcend gangsterism, to remember that the gun is merely a necessary instrument to be discarded once and for all when new men, having created a new morality, have brought the new society into existence.

"You Black militants," remarked a colleague, "are incurable dreamers." Perhaps we are! We began as slaves outside of American history, and we dissipated two hundred years of energy attempting to get inside, unaware that we were seeking to ally ourselves with evil. In 1965, Stokely Carmichael cast himself against the tide of American history, removed himself from the back of the diseased tiger, and many of us followed him. When we did so, we began to dream dreams different from those of our fathers. We dreamed not of integration but of nationalism, not of a melting pot theory but of a pluralistic theory, not of a great society but of a new one. More important, we dreamed of fashioning Canaan out of the debris of the American society, of erecting a nation predicated not upon the gun but upon morality, and if these dreams are hopeless, then so too is the future of mankind. We do not believe that they are hopeless. At this point of the twentieth century in this land of gangsterism, we remain committed to the proposition that man's highest allegiance is to man, that a new world is ours to construct, and amidst the roar of the bombs of hate and dissension, with Margaret Walker, we intone: "Let a new earth arise. Let another world be born. Let a bloody peace be written in the sky. Let a second generation full of courage issue forth, let a people loving freedom come to growth, let a beauty full of healing and a strength of final clenching be the pulsing in our spirits and our blood. Let the martial songs be written, let the dirges disappear. Let a race of men now rise and take control."

CHAPTER 19

The Function of Black Literature
at the Present Time

(1970)

"One of the most promising of the young Negro poets once said to me," Langston Hughes related in "The Negro Artist and the Racial Mountain," "I want to be a poet—not a Negro poet, meaning, I believe, I want to write like a white poet; meaning subconsciously, I would like to be a white poet; meaning behind that, I would like to be white. . . . This is the mountain standing in the way of any true Negro art in America—this urge within the race toward whiteness, the desire to pour racial individuality into the mold of American standardization, and to be as little Negro and as much American as possible."

We, too, have our literary assimilationists in the nineteen seventies. More sophisticated than their counterparts of yesteryear, they declaim in the language of the academic scholars. The Black writer, they argue, must "join the American mainstream"; he must "make his work more universal," and instead of "writing about Negroes all the time, he must write about people." "Your book" (*The Black Situation*), remarked a Black colleague, "is interesting; but you should've included more universal experiences."

"Black-Writing—The Other Side" (*Dissent,* May-June 1968) by Jervis Anderson is a case in point. One supposes that Anderson is an honest man and should not be held accountable for the unsavory company he keeps. Afro-Americans, however, do not publish in *Dissent,* edited by Irving Howe—a racist *par excellence*—unless they are content to play the role of Friday to Irving Howe's Crusoe.

Apparently, Anderson has few compunctions about playing such a role. As a prelude to his major thesis, he quotes William Melvin Kelley: "There's no basic reason why we should talk to white people. Dostoyevsky did not talk to the Germans but to the Russians. . . . And we have to talk to our own people." The voice of the rebuttal is that of Anderson; the theme, tone, and contempt belong to "Father" Howe, who, one supposes, smiles approvingly over the shoulder of his young protégé: "Dostoyevsky's importance in the tradition of Western writing rests as much on the fact that he made a *great and universal art* (italics mine) out of Russian experiences as on the fact that diverse peoples of diverse life styles were able to find in his work images of their own situation. Obviously, Black separatist writing has not left itself open to such accomplishments."

The "urge . . . toward whiteness" in the race, as evidenced by Fridays, past and present, has prevented the creation of a nationalistic art. Moreover, because of it, Black writers have postulated an imaginary dichotomy between art and function that has made much of the writing of Black authors irrelevant to the lives of Black people. In an attempt to curry favor with the Crusoes of America, such writers, like Anderson, negate the idea of a unique group experience, and deny that Black people, but for the accident of history and geography, would constitute a separate nation.

When put forward by Black people, the thesis of a separate nation is dismissed as an absurdity. Yet, the same thesis, argued by white men of the nineteenth century, is catalogued in American history texts as "sound, patriotic, idealism." The poet Philip Freneau was one of the most vociferous advocates of a break with the cultural traditions of Europe—he was only slightly more militant than his contemporaries Ralph Waldo Emerson, John Trumbull, and Noah Webster.

Another of his contemporaries was the Black poetess Phillis Wheatley. Like Freneau, she borrowed extensively from the poetical forms of the English neoclassicists; however, unlike Freneau, she failed to use these forms to call a new nation into being. Oblivious of the lot of her fellow Blacks, she sang not of a separate nation, but of a Christian Eden. She wrote, as Richard Wright so aptly put it, "as a Negro reacting not as a Negro."

In the main, Black writers have traveled the road of Phillis Wheatley. They have negated or falsified their racial experiences in an attempt to transform the pragmatics of their everyday lives into abstract formulas and theorems. They believe, with Margaret Just Butcher and Hugh Gloster, that there is a universal condition that transcends race and nationality, and that this condition is relevant to men of all colors. In this analysis, the function of the artist is to depict the unique manner in which each man reacts to his condition. Therefore, Eric Jones, of *Another Country,* is a more universal character than Rufus Scott, because he copes with his condition (homosexuality) in a way in which Rufus cannot cope with his (Blackness).

The degree of similarity between the conditions under which Blacks and whites live has been exaggerated. This exaggeration results from the tendency to regard American slavery as an economical, political, and legal institution, capable of being legislated out of existence by the thirteenth, fourteenth, and fifteenth amendments; however, under the creative aegis of the Americans, slavery assumed a uniqueness heretofore unsurpassed in the annals of slave institutions. Men were separated, not only in terms of laws and economics, but also in terms of basic human qualities. For Quaker and southern plantation owner alike, the Black man was a subhuman being whose condition could be alleviated—if at all—only by divine intervention.

He was not an American, nor was his condition analogous to that of Americans. To be an American was not to be censured with Benedict Spinoza: "Let him be accursed by day, and accursed by night; let him be accursed in his lying down, and accursed in his rising up; accursed in going out and accursed in coming in. May the lord never more pardon or acknowledge him; may the wrath and displeasure of the lord burn henceforth against this man, load him with all the curses written in the book of the law, and blot his name from under the sky. . . ." The criteria for defining an American went beyond accidents of birth, acts of immigration, or legal statutes erected during periods of national frenzy.

Nevertheless, with more zeal than whites, Blacks continue to flaunt their Americanism. Like Don Quixote, they insist that this earthly hell can be transformed into a heavenly paradise through the sheer effort of will power. No one is more culpable in this respect than the Black writer. He attempts to gain recognition as an American by arguing that there are no separate cultural streams dividing the two races. There is, he supposes, only one giant cultural ocean, in which white and Black experiences have been churned into one. The result of such assimilationism is the transformation of Black men into carbon copies of white men.

Nowhere is this attempt at cultural assimilation more readily apparent than in the Afro-American novel, of which the works of William Wells Brown are early examples. The first Afro-American novelist and playwright as well as one of the first historians, Brown was also an eloquent speaker, ranking—with Frederick Douglass, Charles Remond, and Henry Highland Garnet—among the giants of the Afro-American oratorical tradition. Yet, Brown the abolitionist orator differs noticeably from Brown the novelist.

The orator dealt with the American society in uncompromising terms, pointing out, in the vein of Douglass, the manifest differences in a nation composed of masters and slaves. However, in his novels—and the second, *Miralda; or The Beautiful Quadroon,* is a better example than the first, *Clotel, or The President's Daughter*—he attempted to convince his white reading audience that Blacks and whites, with few exceptions, were indistinguishable in terms of cultural artifacts. *Miralda* was written to prove that Blacks were willing to deal with their experience in terms of the American experience.

The function of the novel as delineated by Brown has survived the years. His ideas of cultural assimilation have been adopted and refined by writers more sophisticated—if not more talented—than he, and his thesis is restated in the twentieth century in three works that are considered among the best literary efforts by Afro-Americans: *The Autobiography of an Ex-Coloured Man,* by James Weldon Johnson; *Go Tell It on the Mountain,* by James Baldwin; and *Invisible Man,* by Ralph Ellison.

The Autobiography of an Ex-Coloured Man presents a portrait of the Afro-American artist as a young man. The child of a white father and a Black mother, the protagonist is forced to choose between two worlds—one Black, the other white. A man with no ethnic ties, he symbolizes what James Baldwin has called the "blood relationship" that exists between Blacks and whites in the American society.

The world of art is also delineated in terms of Black and white. Black art is to be found in the spirituals, in the surviving African cultural artifacts, and in jazz. White art is depicted in Bach and Beethoven, the paintings of Michelangelo, and the Chartres Cathedral. The protagonist, a concert pianist, makes a pilgrimage to Europe, where he plays the works of European composers.

His objective is to merge the two worlds into one, to saturate the white artistic world with the Black idiom. Like Dvořák, who synthesized symphonic music, spirituals, and jazz in the *New World Symphony,* the narrator will also attempt to assimilate the two in the hope of producing a new American product. How far we are from Stephen in Joyce's *Portrait of the Artist as a Young Man!* Stephen wanted to cultivate and hold on to the artifacts of his Irish heritage; Johnson's narrator wants to debase his by fusing it with another. After spending time in both worlds, the protagonist finds his identity in the white world. In so doing, he fails as artist and as man; for although he realizes the richness of his African heritage, he cannot allow himself to think of his culture as unique and distinct—he can accept it only as a submerged entity within a larger cultural sphere.

The theme of identity, so prevalent in the works of Brown, Baldwin, and Ellison, is presented in *The Autobiography of an Ex-Coloured Man* in terms of its varied dimensions. Forced to choose between a white world and a Black world, between a white culture and a Black culture, the narrator opts for the former. With the exception of Ellison's protagonist, who, by the end of the novel, is content to remain faceless, formless, and rootless as he hangs midway between heaven and hell, each protagonist chooses cultural sameness instead of cultural diversity, and surrenders his racial identity to the American Mephistopheles for a pittance that Faust would have labeled demeaning.

"One writes out of one thing only—one's own experiences," notes James Baldwin in *Notes of a Native Son.* For the serious Black writer, this means writing from a group experience, for, in the American society, the individual experiences of the Afro-American, unless he is quite fair or quite lucky, is indistinguishable from that of the group.

John Grimes of *Go Tell It on the Mountain,* however, is ashamed of his group (read racial) experiences and attempts to transcend them by negating his racial identity. On two occasions in the novel, he is confronted with the problem of choosing between the two worlds offered him by his creator.

The initial, and most important, confrontation takes place on the mountaintop—a hill in Central Park overlooking New York City. Young Grimes is tempted by Satan, who offers him "the pottage" of the world in exchange for his birthright: ". . . the gigantic towers, the people in their dark gray clothes: and Broadway. The way that led to death was broad, and many could be found thereon; but narrow was the way that led to life eternal; and few there were who found it."

There is this difference between the worlds: The white leads to death and decay; the black, to life and vitality. Nevertheless, Grimes ". . . did not long for the narrow way, where all his people walked; where the houses did not rise, piercing, as it seemed, the unchanging clouds, . . . where the streets and the hallways and rooms were dark."

Baldwin prefers light to darkness, life to death. The dilemma confronting his protagonist is the same as that confronting Johnson's: To what world am I morally and culturally bound? Like Johnson's narrator, John Grimes has also "been down to the valley" and received the message of the anointed: ". . . they move with an authority which I shall never have; . . . they have made the modern world, in effect, even if they do not know it. The most illiterate among them is related in a way that I am not to Dante, Shakespeare, Michelangelo, Aeschylus, Da Vinci, Rembrandt and Racine. . . . Out of their hymns and dances come Beethoven and Bach. Go back a few centuries and they are in their full glory—but I am in Africa, watching the conquerors arrive."

These are the words of John's creator in the essay "Stranger in the Village." The tone of assimilation, the obsession with fusing the Black and white cultures—even at the risk of destroying the Black—is as pervasive in the novel as it is in the essay. At the outset, John will settle for nothing less than a colorless world. Unable to bring this about, eventually he will sell "his birthright for a mess of pottage."

On the first reading, *Invisible Man,* by Ralph Ellison, does not appear to be a novel in the assimilationist tradition. Ellison is a student of Black literature and history, and his novel illustrates a remarkable grasp of the Afro-American's historical past. No other writer has presented so well, in fiction, the vicissitudes of "The Age of Booker T. Washington"—an age that is fundamental to an understanding of Black Nationalism.

Ellison's knowledge of Black culture might have enabled him, with Joyce, to "forge in the smithy of [his] soul the untreated conscious of [his] race." However, the assimilationist aspirations are as strong in Ralph Ellison as in Black writers of the past: "When I began writing in earnest," he relates in *Shadow and Act,* "I was forced, thus, to relate myself consciously and imaginatively to my mixed background as American, as Negro American, and as Negro from what in its own belated way was a pioneer background." In addition, there was "the necessity of determining my true relationship to that body of American literature to which I was most attracted and through which, aided by what I could learn from the literatures of Europe, I would find my own voice, and to which I was challenged by way of achieving, myself, to make some small contribution, and to whose composite picture of reality I was obliged to offer some necessary modification."

We are again with James Baldwin, and the Chartres Cathedral stands before us, dazzling in its ancient beauty, striking in its reminder of the genius, mastery, and artistic superiority of white, Western man. Although Ellison's journey was only spiritual, like Baldwin, after the pilgrimage to Gethsemane, he, too, was able to stare "down the deadly and hypnotic temptation to interpret the world and all its devices in terms of race."

"It is quite possible," he writes after the baptism, "that much potential fiction by Negro Americans fails precisely at this point: through the writers' refusal (often through provincialism or lack of courage or opportunism) to achieve a vision of life and a resourcefulness of craft commensurate with the complexity of their actual situation. Too often they fear to leave the uneasy sanctuary of race to take their chances in the world of art."

Such statements do little justice to Brown, Johnson, and Baldwin, who, like Ellison, have not only refused to use race as a sanctuary, but instead have attempted to negate race either by integrating the racial idiom with that of whites, or by obliterating racial characteristics altogether. The narrator of *Invisible Man* is a good example. He is—to be sure—a Rinehart, the identity he assumes near the end of the novel. A man without a distinctive identity, he is all things to all men, and after the excursion through the Black world, he retreats to his dungeon to await the coming millennium, when race will have become irrelevant.

"Dr. Johnson," T. S. Eliot wrote of Samuel Johnson, "is a dangerous man to disagree with." The same may be said of Ralph Ellison. For this reason, among others, academic critics have been reluctant to meet the author of *Invisible Man* on his own terms. Ellison traces his literary lineage to the "comic tradition inherent in American literature"—one critic has called him "the Negro Mark Twain"—irrespective of the fact that there is no comic tradition in American literature. There is what can be labeled, at best, a tradition of minstrelsy, slapstick, and buffoonery. In terms of the comic tradition, therefore, it is in Europe, not in America, that Ellison's predecessors must be found; and *Invisible Man,* to get a fair hearing in the court of "mainstream criticism," must be evaluated in light of the comic tradition handed down from Aristophanes through Cervantes to Fielding, Thackery, Dickens, and Meredith.

Dickens, Thackery, and Meredith, England's nineteenth-century masters of the comic tradition, postulated no dichotomy between art and fiction. The Preface to *Joseph Andrews,* by Henry Fielding, is as nationalistic a tract as there is to be found in literature, surpassed, perhaps, only by sections of *The Republic,* and the Preface to *Lyrical Ballads.* The English novelists did not use the novel form to negate their identity as Englishmen. The pride in English cities, churches, and towns, the love for England's cultural past, and the sense of the Englishman as different from other Europeans led Dickens to create his people and his cities.

As a result of English nationalism, a comic tradition was continued and a comic theory was enunciated—a theory to which American writers have only in part been attuned. "Comedy," writes George Meredith, "is an interpretation of the general mind. . . . The comic poet is in the narrow field, or enclosed square of the society he depicts; and he addresses the still narrow enclosure of man's intellect, with references to the operation of the social world upon their characters. . . . To understand his work and value it, you must have a sober liking of your kind, and a sober estimate of our civilized qualities."

The function of comedy—"the perceptive or governing spirit"—is to awaken and give "aim to the powers of laughter." Laughter is, then, the cathartic instrument, capable of deflating egos, of forcing the individual to laugh at himself, and by so doing, force him to relate to others. On this level, comedy is the saving grace—the *deus ex machina* for man and society alike. Instead of laughing themselves to death, men will laugh themselves into greater unity with their fellows.

Meredith, the Englishman, spoke to other Englishmen. His faith in his countrymen led him to believe that they were endowed with that "sensitiveness to the comic laugh [which] is a step in civilization. . . ."We know," he argues at one point, "the degree of refinement in men by the matter they will laugh at; but we know likewise that the larger natures are distinguished by the breadth of their laughter. . . ." Such statements have little relevance in America, where historical racism occasions—in the majority group—contempt instead of understanding, barbarity instead of refinement, and an animosity toward the minority group that renders the term "civilized" obscure and irrelevant.

The lack of an American comic tradition "which feeds upon civilized and sensitive natures" makes Bret Harte so unreadable, Joel Chandler Harris so contemptible, and Mark Twain such a sentimentalist and buffoon. America is the last place to which one would go to find laughter. For instead of being transformed by the comic spirit, Americans, when gazing at the reflection of their egotistical selves, are more likely to be inflated than deflated. Richard Wright knew this very well, and thus there is no laughter in his fiction.

"If my work fails," writes Ellison, "it fails on artistic grounds alone." When *Invisible Man,* like its American mainstream predecessors, is evaluated by the criteria established by England's comic artists, the verdict that Ellison demands can then be rendered. There is, however, an Afro-American comic tradition, as manifested in the works of George Moses Horton, the best of Paul Laurence Dunbar, Langston Hughes, George Schuyler, Wallace Thurman, and Ishmael Reed. In this tradition, despite its assimilationist denouncement, *Invisible Man* ranks high indeed. This will bring little satisfaction to Ellison, who, like Brown, Johnson, and Baldwin, remains wedded to the concept of assimilation at a time when such a concept has ceased to be the preoccupation of the Black writer.

"Season it as you will," writes Saunders Redding, "the thought that the Negro American is different from other Americans is still unpalatable to most Negroes. Nevertheless, the Negro is different. An iron ring of historical circumstance has made him so." This difference is manifested in our cultural and social institutions. Although most Black institutions are photographic copies of white ones, each has its own uniqueness—white form with Black content. An example is the Afro-American church, which though white in form—Methodist, Episcopalian, Baptist—differs in ritual and message.

Black artists of the past expropriated and remodeled the forms of white America to fit the needs of Black people. Nowhere is this more evident than in the letters, speeches, and essays of David Walker, Henry Highland Garnet, Charles Remond, and Frederick Douglass. But not all was expropriation! The earliest Afro-American artists—the creators of the spirituals—constructed new forms with which to deal with their racial experiences. Not having been seduced by the scholastic Merlins, they were free from the myth that Black manhood was attainable only if one transcended his race and group experiences. ". . . The nationalistic character of the Negro people," wrote Richard Wright, in 1937, "is unmistakable. Psychologically, this nationalism is reflected in the whole of Negro culture, and especially in folklore. Let those who shy at the nationalistic implications of Negro life look at this body of folklore, living and powerful, which rose out of a unified sense of common life and a common fate."

The Black writer at the present time must forgo the assimilationist tradition and redirect his art to the strivings within the race—those strivings that have become so pronounced, here, in the latter half of the twentieth century. To do so, he must write for and speak to the majority of Black people; not to a sophisticated elite fashioned out of the programmed computers of America's largest universities.

For here we stand, acknowledging those truths we would not admit at the beginning of the twentieth century: that the problem of the color line is insoluble, that the idea of an egalitarian America belongs to the trash basket of history, and that the concept of an American melting pot is one to which sane men no longer adhere. In light of such realities, the literature of assimilationism belongs to the period of the dinosaur and the mastodon.

To return to Richard Wright: "The Negro writer who seeks to function within his race as a purposeful agent has a serious responsibility. In order to do justice to his subject matter, in order to depict Negro life in all of its manifold and intricate relationships, a deep, informed, and complex consciousness is necessary; a consciousness which draws for its strength upon the fluid lore of a great people, and moulds this lore with the concepts that move and direct the forces of history today; . . . a new role is devolving upon the Negro writer. He is being called upon to do no less than create values by which his race is to struggle, live and die. . . ." This is no easy task. To create such values, the writer must undergo a baptism in thought and spirit. He must descend into the pit of the mountain and rise to the top with a clearer vision than before; he must have a greater understanding of the task that lies before him; and above all, if he is to function effectively as a Black writer, he must believe with Don L. Lee: "Black! Poet. Black poet am I. This should leave little doubt in the minds of anyone as to which is first. Black art will elevate and enlighten our people and lead them towards an awareness of self, i.e., their Blackness. It will show them mirrors. Beautiful symbols. And will aid in the destruction of anything nasty and detrimental to our advancement as a people."

PART 3

Literary Criticism

> In the recent criticism of Afro-American literature, there have been two distinct generational shifts. Both have involved ideological and aesthetic reorientations, and both have been accompanied by shifts in literary-critical and literary-theoretical paradigms. The first such shift occurred during the mid-1960s. It led to the displacement of what might be described as integrationist poetics and gave birth to a new object of scholarly investigation . . . one which sought to situate higher-order rules of the Black Aesthetic within a contemporary universe of literary-theoretical discourse . . .
>
> —Houston A. Baker Jr. "Generational Shifts and the Recent Criticism of Afro-American Literature"

"Literary Criticism," section three, features Gayle's critiques, interpretations, and analyses of the writings of African American authors such as Richard Wright, James Baldwin, Gwendolyn Brooks, Paul Laurence Dunbar, and Langston Hughes, in addition to defining the role of black literary criticism in relationship to the evolution of black cultural nationalism.

"Blueprint for Black Criticism," "The Function of Black Criticism at the Present Time," and "The Critic, the University and the Negro Writer" set and demand criteria for black literary critics and writers in the fight to defend and determine the parameters of black reality in America as well as refute the gross misrepresentations of black culture by white authors and critics.

In "Cultural Hegemony: The Southern White Writer and American Letters," Gayle extensively discusses setting new standards in judging black literature and illustrates the relationship between white, racist, and cultural norms, which are perpetuated by the so-called New Critics in American arts and letters, and black people: "To demand a realistic portrayal of Blacks by whites is to demand the impossible; for whites are neither mentally nor culturally equipped for the task. The plantation sentiments are too strong in white America, the influence of the New Critics too pervasive. Their approach to black people can only travel the gamut from crude distortion to condescension occasioned by racism either unconscious or overt."

CHAPTER 20

Blueprint for Black Criticism

(1977)

Critics of the Black Aesthetic movement have demanded a formalized, programmatic approach to Black Criticism from those of us who support the movement. Though our practice has been to do the opposite of what our critics suggest, we realize now that the absence of specific criteria has enabled our opponents to substitute their own and to attack the movement, using their criteria as gauge. Enough has been written and said about the Black Aesthetic approach to art at this time to allow an attempt at synthesis of the varied theories proposed in such books as Stephen Henderson's *Understanding the New Black Poetry,* Baraka and Neal's *Black Fire,* Houston Baker's *Long Black Song,* and such articles as Julian Mayfield's "You Touch My Black Aesthetic and I'll Touch Yours," Hoyt Fuller's "Toward A Black Aesthetic," James Emanuel's "Blackness Can: A Quest for Aesthetics," Ron Karenga's "Black Cultural Nationalism," and Carolyn Fowler Gerald's "The Black Writer and His Role."

Before proceeding with such a synthesis, however, a historical perspective is necessary. Critic Georgi Plekanov has written: "When society at large, at a given stage presents certain problems to its spiritual representatives, these problems hold the attention of outstanding minds until they succeed in solving them." For Plekanov's term "spiritual representatives" we may substitute "Black Artists," and we may define "these problems" as assaults upon human dignity by the racist and oppressive nature of the American society. Such problems have preoccupied most Black Americans, including our spiritual representatives, since 1614. If the term "outstanding minds" is expanded to include critics of art and culture, we discover that for most of Black History, the critical approach to art has been less aggressive and imaginative than the creative. Indeed, with few exceptions, Black critics of the past may be likened to the leader of the French Revolution, who ran through the streets of Paris trying to catch up with his followers. A Benjamin Brawley, a W. E. B. Du Bois, an Alain Locke often made challenging observations about Black Art; for the most part, however, until the publication of Richard Wright's *Native*

Son in 1940, Black critics were little more than court followers of one school of writers or another.

Jessie Fauset's ideas concerning the nature and function of Black Art—ideas identical to those of such earlier novelists as Frank Webb and Charles Chestnutt— were received without question or alteration from such critics as Du Bois, James Weldon Johnson, and Locke. Her literary credo was and remains the integrationist–accommodationist expression on Black Art, and is to be found in the introduction to her novel, *The Chinaberry Tree:*

"There are breathing spells in between spaces where colored men and women work and love and go their ways with no thought of the race problem. What are they like then? So few of the other Americans know . . . (Their) early forebears are to (them) quite simply the early settlers who played a pretty large part in making the land grow . . . (Their) sons and daughters date their ancestry as far back as any. (Like their) white compatriots (they) speak of (their) 'old Boston families,' 'old Philadelphians,' 'old Charlestonians' . . . (They are) dark Americans who wear (their) joy and rue very much as does the white American . . . it is the same joy and rue."

For critics of Ms. Fauset's persuasion, the function of Black literature is to demonstrate the similarities between the Black and white middle class; it is a tool to be used in resolving the problems of racism and oppression by emphasizing class similarities as opposed to racial differences. Those writers who refused to accept Ms. Fauset's revisionist ideas, who sought to create a special kind of "Negritude," championed Langston Hughes manifesto as presented in "The Negro Writer and the Racial Mountain": "But then there are the low down folks, the so-called common element, and they are the majority—may the lord be praised. The people who have their nip of gin on Saturday nights and are not too important to themselves or the community, or too well fed, or too learned to watch the lazy world go round . . . they do not particularly care whether they are like white folks or anybody else. Their joy runs, bang! into ecstasy. Their religion soars to a shout. Work maybe a little today, rest tomorrow. Play awhile. Sing awhile. O, lets dance." Singing, dancing, playing, intuitive and instinctual in nature, constituted what Carl Van Vechten called "those qualities which all the civilized races were striving to get back to." In codified form, "those qualities" will find expression in the Negritude concepts of Aime Cesaire and Leopold Senghor and would be offered as tools of liberation by such Black writers as Claude McKay, Rudolph Fisher, Clarence Major and Ishmael Reed. In a world where racism and oppression are viewed as the step-children of rationalism, science, and technology, we are led to believe that liberation is possible for those who retain those intuitive (read primitive) characteristics of man in his natural state.

That both of these positions—that forwarded by Ms. Fauset and that forwarded by Hughes—distorted the actualities of Black life, that neither led to a realistic confrontation with racism, seemed to escape the notice of most Black critics of the time. Of the two positions, Hughes' was attacked most often, not by critics attempting to arrive at an independent position, but by those who championed the position of Ms. Fauset. Neither position, however, demanded that "call to arms," that tenacious aggressive evaluation of Black literature, warranted of Black criticism.

But Black critics *could* be tenacious and aggressive, and they demonstrated this by their critical assaults upon *Native Son,* published in 1940. Zora Neale Hurston and Du Bois launched early attacks upon the new novel; later, with vehemence akin to that of the earlier criticism, attacks were leveled by James Baldwin and Ralph Ellison, by Cecil Brown and Blyden Jackson. Such criticism, by the earlier and later critics, centered upon Wright's major character, Bigger Thomas; on behalf of the Black middle class, the critics rushed to deny Bigger 's authenticity, arguing with James Baldwin that the Blacks around Bigger—his mother and sister—were more accurate depictions of American Blacks.

Cecil Brown and Blyden Jackson have painted Bigger as a madman, a neurotic, created from Wright's own peculiar neurosis, and Ralph Ellison has attempted to deny the authenticity of Bigger as accurate paradigm by one of the most curious twists of logic in the history of literary criticism: I knew Wright, Ellison has argued, and he was nothing like Bigger Thomas. In other words, Wright could imagine a Bigger Thomas, but Bigger Thomas could never imagine Richard Wright, which is analogous to the argument that John the Baptist could imagine Jesus Christ, but Jesus Christ could never imagine John the Baptist. Both statements are equally meaningless.

There was, however, searching, perceptive Black criticism following the publication of *Native Son,* and Saunders Redding and Nick Aaron Ford, among others, supplied it. For the most part, however, the novel and its controversial character served only to demonstrate how closely allied Black criticism remained to Black middle-class aspirations and how subservient to white academic judgment.

If a novel like *Native Son,* which seeks in its dénouement not the dismantling of the American society but the liberalization of it in order to prevent multiplication of the Bigger Thomases in its midst, could receive such limited support from Black critics, and if in the main these critics remained wedded to the concept of art as nonpolitical and noninvolved—who could not gauge their reaction to writers who, inspired by Malcolm, Garvey, and Fanon, wrote such lines as these from Amiri Baraka:

> We are unfair
> And unfair
> We are black magicians
> Black arts we make
> In black labs of the heart
> The fair are fair

and deathly white
The day will not save them
And we own the night.

Such lines as these from Haki Madhubuti:

Change
create a climate for
change.
yesterdays weather has been un-
unchangeable
there is a dark storm coming;
has nappy-hair.

Such lines as these from Sonia Sanchez:

I'm blk, livin in a
white/psychotic/neurotic
schizophrenic/society where
all honkies have been plannen
my death since . . .

That such words, in isolated instances, had been written before, we know from the examples of McKay, Du Bois, Fenton Johnson, and Hughes. The circumstances during the nineteen sixties, however, were different from those during the period of the revolutionary sonnets of McKay or the angry poetry of Du Bois. The nineteen sixties were the years of "Black and white together," "integration by Sixty Four," "We shall overcome," and "one nation, indivisible, under God." Further, most Black writers and critics were unabashed integrationists, whose faith, if it ever faltered, had been renewed by the token victories which the early efforts of those years produced. Certainly, the young Black writers who gathered around Baraka and the Black Arts Theater in 1964 and who had earlier begun to write for *Liberator* and *Black World* magazines, would find little support among the Black literary establishment.

The reason was that their view of the nature of art and its function was based upon a political premise—Black Nationalism—which was and is anathema to both some Black and white Americans. These new writers rejected not only the idea of an integrated America, but even the value of it. In the words of Etheridge Knight, they denounced protest literature designed to change the attitudes of whites:

Now any Black man who masters the techniques of his particular art form, who adheres to the white aesthetic, and who directs his work towards a white audience is, in one sense, protesting. And implicit in the art of protest is the belief that a change will be forthcoming once the masters are aware of the protestor's 'grievance' (the very word connotes begging, supplication to the gods). Only when that belief has faded and protesting ends, will Black art begin.

The new art would be devoted to explaining the world in which Black people lived, to bringing about a new relationship between one Black person and another, to redefining the definitions handed down by Western philosophers and intellectuals concerning the Black experience. The essence and importance of a work of art, argued the proponents of the new Black Art, resided in its ability to move men toward changing the oppressive conditions under which they lived. In this sense, with this view in mind, Maulana Ron Karenga writes that a work of art must be committed, and committing must "expose the enemy, praise the people and support the revolution."

Against the noninvolvement, static notion of art as defined in the critical articles of the American academicians, the Black Aestheticians demanded an art that was involved, that was dedicated to change. They spoke of an art, Promethean in nature, generating its own *elan,* by going to the real source of its power—the experiences of the people; and they knew with Etheridge Knight that the adoption of a Black Aesthetic was to choose life over death: "Unless the Black artist establishes a 'Black aesthetic' he will have no future at all. To accept the white aesthetic is to accept and validate a society that will not allow him to live. The Black artist must create new forms and new values, sing new songs (or purify old ones); and along with other Black authorities, he must create a new history, new symbols, myths and legends (and purify old ones by fire). And the Black artist in creating his own aesthetic must be accountable for it only to the Black people." These non-Marxist critics had seized the Marxian postulate and amended it: "The philosophers," wrote Marx, "have only interpreted the world in various ways, the point, however, is to change it."

The Black Aesthetic movement began as an attempt to protect new, young writers who, in terms of form, content, and objective were revolutionizing Black Art. In articles, lectures, prose, poetry, and fiction, these writers, joined by a new breed of Black critic, produced critical material, offering support and guidelines for writers intent upon moving outside the American literary mainstream. In addition, they began a frontal assault upon the detractors of Black Art, both Black and white, realizing the necessity for defending a new and vulnerable art against the combined power of the white media and Black representatives of the critical *status quo.* Equally important was the necessity of emphasizing racism as opposed to class, in the Marxian formulation, as the major impediment to Black freedom. This statement must be explained in some detail.

The Black Aesthetic movement has been labeled Marxist, usually by those who have read neither Marx nor such Marxist aestheticians as Plekanov, Mehring, Thomas, Brecht or Caldwell. To be sure, there are similarities to be found in the critical works of Marxist and Black aestheticians. Many of the theories concerning the nature and function of art, its relationship to man and society, postulated in the writings of Black aestheticians can be found in the critical works of Malraux, Sidney Finkelstein, and George Lukacs. That which differentiates Black from

Marxist aestheticians, however, is the idea that the major factor in oppression is economic determinism, leading to class hierarchies and finally to class struggle. That economic exploitation has led to man's tyranny over other men is a given. The Third World was subjugated in the seventeenth and eighteenth centuries because of economic motivations; it was such motivations which determined, to a large extent, the slave trade in America and the Western Hemisphere. *Yet, historically more important, the motivating rationale behind the continual suppression of non-Europeans by Europeans has been and remains racism.*

The defection of some Black intellectuals, including two of the leading Black Aesthetic theoreticians, to the Marxist view mandates that this essential difference be clarified. An aesthetic based upon economic and class determinism is one which has minimal value for Black people. For Black writers and critics the starting point must be the proposition that the history of Black people in America is the history of the struggle against racism, and against this postulate a work of art must be judged and evaluated. For in all its manifest forms, Black Art has no function more important than this: to intensify the struggle against American racism. And a Black artist, to be deserving of such a designation, must be in continual warfare against the American society.

Based upon this premise, it is now possible at this point in time, by sifting through the critical pronouncements of those capable young men and women who follow the Black Aesthetic banner, to arrive at a blueprint for Black criticism. Among the major tenets of such a blueprint must be included the following:

1. Black artists must refuse to accept the American definition of reality and propose a Black definition instead.
2. Black Art must offer alternatives to the stereotypes of Blacks created by white Americans and validated in the works and critical offerings of Black fellow travelers.
3. Black Art must emphasize those paradigms of the Black past that enabled Black people to survive the American nightmare.
4. Black Art must create images, symbols, and metaphors of positive import from the Black experience.
5. Black Art must be written for, by, and about Blacks and the Black American condition.
6. Black Art must redefine the definitions handed down from the Western world.
7. The objectives of Black Art must be to inculcate the values of communality between one Black person and another.
8. Black Art must be critical of any and all actions detrimental to the health and well-being of the Black community.
9. Black Art must divorce itself from the sociological attempt to explain the Black community in terms of pathology.
10. Black Art must be in continual revolt against the American attempt to dehumanize man.

Most of these tenets are self-explanatory. A few, however, deserve further explanation.

The Artist, historically, has been concerned with the problem of reality, the attempt to communicate a sense of the real to his fellows. In the extreme, in the case of the surrealists and the abstractionists, this attempt takes the form of vast distortions; in other instances, as with the naturalist and the realist, the attempt to explain and to communicate a sense of reality is accomplished through an almost photographic rendering of it. For the Black artist, grasping and depicting reality demands constant struggle. Living in a society in which the very terms of life itself are defined by persons and forces antithetical to his being, the Black artist must hold on to his own sense of reality, while vigorously denying that offered by the society. For him, the overwhelming question is whether or not the reality of the oppressed and the oppressor are fundamentally the same; or whether the rigors of living in a tyrannical society do not force upon the oppressed experiences, perceptions, and ways of viewing man and the world that are contradictory to that of those who are not oppressed. For certainly, the reality held fast by Thomas Jefferson and Frederick Douglass concerning America are everywhere incompatible. The first prerequisite, therefore, for changing reality is to admit that which exists at the moment and to refuse to accept a distorted vision, due to personal accomplishment, which does not in the main alter reality for most of the people.

The refusal to accept white American definitions of reality leads to a refusal to accept its definitions of such concepts as manhood, heroism, beauty, freedom, and humanism. All such definitions are colored by the fact of American racism; they are constructed out of the desires, needs, and obsessions of the white society. For the West in general and for America in particular, manhood, beauty, freedom, humanism are the property of those who possess nordic skin, nordic eyes, and nordic hair. Yet, why should it be otherwise? A people have the right—no, the obligation—to create their god in their own image, to define reality according to their own life experiences, and to create terminology which enables them to believe in their own humanity. And their "spiritual representatives" are but their cultural protectors, barricading them against the destructive images, symbols, and definitions of others.

For most of Black history, however, there has been a maddening obsession to expropriate the terminology in all of its awesome connotations. With few exceptions, our "spiritual representatives" have not protected the culture of the people, but have bartered it away through the process of assimilationism. This Quixotic attempt notwithstanding, American definitions for the most part cannot be useful in a Black context. George Washington and Thomas Jefferson (rightly so) are heroes for white people; for Black people, they remain slaveholders, and this carries its own connotations.

That Black Art must offer alternatives to the stereotypes created by white

Americans and validated in the works of Blacks should require no explanation ". . . (T)he Negro," wrote Norman Mailer, "in the worst of perversion, promiscuity, pimpery, drug addiction, rape, razor slash, bottle-break, what-have you, discovered and elaborated a morality of the bottom . . ." These inhabitants of "the bottom," the hip and the cool, return us to the primitives of Van Vechten, Gertrude Stein, Vachel Lindsay, Jean Toomer, Langston Hughes, and Claude McKay, and they are reborn, here in the twentieth century, in *Manchild in the Promised Land, Another Country, Corregidora, Sula,* and *Eva's Man,* and in the Black exploitation movies from *Sweet-Sweetback* to *Superfly.*

Mailer did not create the type, and one should not denounce either his vision or his obsession for Black primitives. After all, he knows nothing of the Black Experience. No, censure must be leveled, not against the denuded white liberal, but instead against those spiritual representatives of a people who distort the Black condition for the 30 pieces of silver offered by a sensationalistic-starved society. And Black people must demand realistic paradigms from Black artists: they must demand that characters be modeled upon such men and women as Sojourner Truth, Harriet Tubman, Martin Delany, H. Rap Brown, Fannie Lou Hamer, and those countless mothers and fathers who sacrificed dignity and manhood in order to prepare their young to deal with a nation which ranks among the most tyrannical in history. Here and elsewhere are images, symbols, and metaphors of heroism, beauty, and courage to last a generation of Black youth for a lifetime.

Such views concerning the obligations and responsibilities of Black artists lead, logically, to the conclusion that Black Art must be created for and by Black people, and that one of its major objectives must be to inculcate a greater sense of communality between one Black person and another. Such suggestions, however, cause some of our critics to raise their collective spears. Black Aestheticians, they argue, are demanding a "separatist art," are neglecting the universal quality of art, are denying that "great art" reaches beyond race and color, beyond nationality and religion. The major proponents of such positions are Martin Kilson and Stanley Macebuh—men, limited in imagination, who have spent so much time in libraries copying words and facts that they have lost the capacity to think creatively or intelligently. They are, thus, unable to believe with Herbert Marcuse that,

> Reality is other and more than that codified in the logic and language of facts. Here is the inner link between dialectical thought and the effort of avante-garde literature; the effort to break the power of facts over the word, and to speak a language which is not the language of those who establish, enforce, and benefit from the facts.

Macebuh demands special censure. Kilson, after all, is a political theorist, and may be excused for his ignorance of literary theory and history. Macebuh, on the other hand, is a professor of English who might be expected to possess the tools necessary to acquire that knowledge which he does not have. His criticism demonstrates a total inability to understand, even in elementary terms, the concept of the Black Aesthetic. For Black Aestheticians believe—no, demand—that art seek to ennoble and inspire man, that it attempt, in Malraux's phrase, "to bring man back into the community of man." This has been the success of much of Greek literature, of Russian literature, of the German literature which so influenced the English Romantics, of the literature of the Harlem Renaissance school of writers that influenced the African proponents of *Negritude*.

It is equally true, however, that the literature of these diverse nationalistic and racial groups anchored its soul and being in the experiences of the particular race and nation, in its mythology and its collective conscious. "Greek art," wrote Marx, "presupposes the existence of Greek mythology. Not, however, a mythology taken at random. Egyptian mythology could never be the soil or womb which would give birth to Greek art." Concomitantly, Black Art must, by necessity, find its nourishment in the Black Experience, and the Black artist, by sifting these varied experiences through the creative imagination, enriches them and reproduces them in changed and ordered form. And if others are able to move beyond their own "narrow parochialism," they can find in Black Art those ennobling truths about the human condition peculiar to all mankind. It is no accident that *Native Son* has found a home in the libraries of readers throughout the world.

Despite the Macebuhs and the other Black neostructuralists, what is needed in American art at the present time is the kind of self-criticism which leads to a confrontation with tradition-bound truths. To speak of America as a land of justice and freedom, of opportunity and hope, might ring true if Black people were not here. To talk of humanism and the American commitment to the sanctity of the human spirit is revealed as meaningless cliché by the sight of one hungry Black child from the inner city. Thus, the conditions under which most Black people live in America serve as a critique of this society's postulates: our ways of living and our struggles for liberty and human dignity offer the kind of criticism that should emanate from the colleges and universities. Historically, by serving as the interpreter and analyzer of the Black Experience, Black artists have described and articulated those values which contest the society's attempt to dehumanize man, and have remained, in lieu of aggressive criticism from white Americans, the bulwark against the attempted reduction of man to object and the sustainers of the ideal of man as a spiritual being.

A blueprint for Black criticism must, necessarily, contain more postulates than those that I have offered. By synthesizing the theories of others, I have attempted to present only the basic outline of a starting point. In so doing, I have not been unaware of those arguments which will continue to be raised by our carping critics. Two of the major ones deserve special mention: the first is that concerning the supposed dichotomy between beauty and art, and the second concerns the false issue of freedom of the writer.

On the first point, the neo-structuralists argue: "You have offered a program which politicizes art and defined aesthetics in such a way as to leave aside its most important characteristic—the beautiful—that which appeals to and unites man through the intuitive instead of rational sense."

Such critics state their own position and not ours! Bedmates of "The New Critics," they argue, for a dichotomy between the political and the beautiful components of art, and we do not. They would remove politics from art, but we have never attempted to remove from art that sense of beauty that art at its best conveys. We believe that both components are necessary dimensions of the work of art, that art without politics becomes little more than the opiate of the people, and that art without beauty is little more than sterile propaganda. Picasso's "Guernica" and Romare Bearden's "Amistad" are, undoubtedly, works that convey a powerful sense of beauty. The critic of art can discern this in terms of color and line, shadow and tone, brush stroke and clarity of images. To view these paintings is to feel a sense of beauty—of terror and fear, of sublimation and exaltation. Still, the political significance of these works cannot escape us: Both point to a period of man's depravity and both, by dramatizing this, call upon us collectively to guard against a recurrence.

The "Spirituals," too, demonstrate this wedding of beauty and politics, and the best works of art have always contained a marriage of these two dimensions. What else is one to say of *Don Quixote, War and Peace, Paradise Lost, Man's Fate, Native Son, Ludell, Invisible Man,* or *The Autobiography of Miss Jane Pittman?* The beautiful and the political are necessary dimensions of each. There is beauty in the form of presentation, in the individual style of the artist, in the skillful usage of language which makes us see, hear, and feel through words that force our emotional identification with characters and their situations. But the political is there, also, in the expert usage of symbols, images, and metaphors, in the juxtaposition of characters and events, the nuances of plot, the content, and subject matter of the work itself. Each work demonstrates that the "true beauty" of art is of creation, but in the potential of that particular work to make more meaningful and more beautiful the lives of people. This, of course, is the function of politics at its best.

Vigorous arguments are also waged by our critics concerning the question of freedom for the writer. "You would deny," they contend, "the writer the freedom to exercise his creative imagination in the way he deems best. You demand that he be selective about his subject matter, careful about his use of figurative language, that he present positive characters, engage in warfare against injustice, racism, exploitation, *etc.* And you construct a supposed 'blueprint,' telling him how to do this. You are trying to rob him of his freedom."

The truth of the matter is that we are reminding him of the importance of freedom. We are saying that, contrary to the philosophy of Dostoyevsky's Grand Inquisitor, man's need for freedom is as great as his need for bread; that freedom cannot be parceled out to this group or this individual and denied to mankind as a whole. And we are telling him that the only safeguard for freedom for the writer is a free society, and that in those places where such a society does not exist, it is the job of the writer to help to bring it about. A man in a concentration camp, with his fellows being daily tortured before his eyes, might write odes of love to his tormentors. We might call this an exhibition of freedom; we could also label it perverse. For Black people, freedom for the writer is linked to freedom for Blacks in general, and the writer can be free only when the people are free. Racial, social, and economic freedom, to paraphrase Slochower, are prerequisites for human and artistic freedom.

I have discussed the critics of the Black Aesthetic at some length, primarily because they exemplify what we suggest to be at the core of the American dilemma: the inability to demand drastic and meaningful changes in the social fabric of a society built and constructed upon racial inequality and injustice. Our critics come mainly from such "prestigious institutions of higher learning" as Harvard and Yale, and this fact serves to highlight the problem confronting those who would propose a cultural solution to the Black situation in America. For it is in the academies that the great retreat from the age-old quest for human dignity and freedom has begun, and an acceptance of detente between liberty for some and denial of liberty for others has been validated. Christopher Jencks, Daniel Moynihan, and Sidney Hook are the new philosophers of this great retreat, and our Black critics have, perhaps unknowingly, become their unacknowledged disciples. Thus Black criticism has begun to retreat into neo-structuralism— aesthetics of the literary right wing—and moved away from concern with man and back to a concern with such mundane concepts of literature as paradox and ambiguity, irony and tension, the intrinsic and extrinsic nature of art.

That movement, however, is small and manned, mainly, by the least imaginative and creative: far from offering an alternative to the Black Aesthetic, their statements, public and published, serve only to lend added authority and prestige to those many talented men and women who, over 10 years ago, had the courage and the determination to chant with Baraka: "We want a Black poem and a Black world: let the world be a Black poem."

CHAPTER 21

The Function of Black Criticism
at the Present Time

(1976)

The upheaval in Black criticism and literature of the past few years, occasioned in part by the Black Aesthetic Movement, suggests that the age-old dichotomy between literature as artifact and literature as vehicle for the liberation of a people has been resolved. Among contemporary Black writers—John Williams, Louise Meriwether, Don L. Lee, Mari Evans, Gwendolyn Brooks, and Askia Touré, to name but a few—the debate his been consigned to the value of irrelevance. In the area of criticism—and here George Kent, Stephen Henderson, and Houston Baker come readily to mind—black critics have ceded to the disciples of Aristotle that which they claim as their own, and have moved to establish new criteria for black criticism and literature, criteria concerned more with improving the human condition than with achieving questionable status for the writer.

Yet, Stanley Macebuh, in his biography, *James Baldwin,* seeks to rekindle the debate of old: to postulate a meaning and function for literature and criticism consistent with the dictates of the academic followers of the New Critics. Writes Macebuh: "The point is that Black writing in America has not been distinguished, until quite recently, for its preoccupation with questions of 'aesthetics,' nor in the matter of content, has a compulsive concern with 'universal' themes been one of its significant characteristics." It should be noted that Macebuh displays the usual ambiguity of Black academicians, attempting to walk a tightrope between the new critical ideas generated by proponents of the Black Aesthetic, and those of the academicians in whose vineyard he toils. A full explication of his thought may be found in the introduction to his book.

The importance of Macebuh's study lies in the portrait he paints of the critic as dispassionate observer, whose function is not prescriptive, but descriptive; who—Samuel Johnson and Matthew Arnold, Benjamin Brawley and Saunders Redding to the contrary—must not suggest to the writer that he devote himself to those ideas which constitute the best that has been said and thought in the world, let alone suggest that he devote himself to the liberation of Black people in America. And this is so despite the fact that Black literature, according to Macebuh, has not concerned itself with either aesthetics or universal themes.

If one accepts this narrow, parochial view of criticism, then the work of art must be evaluated, not on its own terms, but on those prescribed by academicians who, more often than not, view the relevance of literature in terms of such abstract principles as "universality" and "endurance"—terms the academic world has never applied to artifacts by Blacks. The demand, therefore, is to bring back the days of old, when men agreed with those who demanded an objective criticism, despite the fact that no such criticism has ever existed. For criticism has, does—and if human beings are practicing critics in the future—will always begin at the point of taste—Do I, or do I not like the work? and sometimes, Do I, or do I not like the author?—a critical perspective that is subjective in nature. There are, however, those like Macebuh, who argue in favor of a criticism that will closely follow the orthodox party line held dear by the disciples of he who proclaimed that "literature must not mean, but be."

Plato, a much more thoughtful, if not more judicious critic, opted for a critical system that, in the main, celebrated life; Auerbach demanded that criticism and literature enable men to better function as human beings; Samuel Johnson, Matthew Arnold, and George Meredith, believed in a literature dedicated to producing a better world; John Trumbull, Noah Webster, and Nathaniel Hawthorne demanded a literature that would function in the interests of the new American nation. The works of Shaw, Dickens, Tolstoy, and Thoreau (not to mention those of Black writers) suggest that only among the academics was there support for the assertion that literature divorce itself from life, that it should concentrate on being rather than meaning.

Macebuh's literary and critical attitudes are representative of those held by a small coterie within the Black critical population, primarily by those intent upon assimilating into the literary mainstream, despite the historical fact that assimilation has worked no better for the Black critic than it has for the masses of Blacks. Recognition by the American literary establishment has not been granted to those who champion its canons. Criticism written to impress the "establishment" with the critic's intellectual acuity has not helped Black writers either to clarify their literary visions or to move toward an understanding of their function as writers here in the latter half of the twentieth century.

But despite Macebuh and those of his persuasion, the proponents of the Black Aesthetic are aware that questions concerning the function of Black criticism are inseparable from those concerning the function of Black literature in general. Black writers—from William Wells Brown to those of the present time—have varying ideas of what that function should be. Some believed that the function of Black literature was to convince the dominant white population of our common humanity others believed that it should explore the life style and culture of Black people. Richard Wright thought that Black writers should inform the general population of the truth concerning our condition in this country, and James Baldwin has argued persuasively that the job of the writer is to disturb the peace.

My own views are based, in part, upon a statement from Carmichael and Hamilton's *Black Power*. ". . . We must redefine ourselves," write the authors, "Our basic need is to reclaim our history and our identity from what must be called cultural terrorism from the degradation of self-justifying white guilt. We shall have to struggle for the right to create our own terms through which to define ourselves and our relationship to the society and to have these terms recognized. This is the first necessity of a free people, and the first right that any oppressor must suspend." My own pronouncement on the function of Black literature and the Black writer has been stated before: "[he must] wage unlimited, continual warfare against the American society—against its values, its morals, its ethics." The task of the Black critic is to make sure that the writer fulfills this function.

The reason, at least to his writer, is clear. Words, as Richard Wright noted some forty years ago, are indeed weapons. The most lethal warfare ever waged against a people has been waged against Black people through the medium of words. No armored vehicles patrol the Black community. Except in rare instances, Black people are not spirited away in the dead of night or placed under house arrest by this government. Yet, sane men must agree that in this country there is racism which stultifies the human spirit, oppresses human endeavors, and distorts human emotions and sensibilities. Such racism has produced the condition in which the majority of Black people find themselves in this country: poorly housed, inadequately educated, filling the prisons and welfare rolls, caught up in the vicious cycle of poverty.

It would be simplistic to argue that such conditions result only from the historical practice of white Americans of defining the terms by which Black people are to live their lives; however, it is not wrong to argue that we have not seized the opportunity to create our own terms and thus, to define ourselves. If a race of people allows an oppressive society to define its children as culturally deprived, without challenge or rebuttal, the overwhelming odds are that such a prophecy will become self-fulfilling. If a people allows an oppressive society—again, without challenge or rebuttal—to define them as inferior, in the end they will become so.

And despite Macebuh and others who would have us believe that words are instruments for depicting the beautiful, progressive, and affirmative in the human condition, we know all too well that in the lexicon of the Americans, words have been weapons of warfare intended to destroy human potential.

It would be simplistic, even fatuous, to suggest that sole culpability for the distortion of Black life through the "propaganda of the word," is attributable to whites in America and abroad. It would be fatuous, simplistic—and untrue. Those who have waged warfare against Black people through the medium of words have often been black artists and writers themselves. The "Black exploitation" films and the Black television shows, peopled by brainless, untalented Blacks, have presented images of Black life as distorted, insulting, and degrading as those presented by the American propagandists from Thomas Jefferson to Norman

Mailer. Nor is the Black writer immune to such criticism. To read *Manchild in the Promised Land* and *Another Country*—to point out the most flagrant examples—is to be in the company of a people who possess no values, no history, no sense of cultural identity—a people, in short, who exist as extensions of the perverted imagination of the Americans. And the Black critic—to return to Macebuh—in an attempt to gain prestige, recognition, and status, has all too often succeeded only in sanctioning the denigrating images and stereotypes offered by both Black and white writers.

Yet—and I am constantly being reminded of this fact—those who adhere to the concept of the Black Aesthetic have no monopoly on truth. Some critics argue that our romanticism and dedication to an "alien philosophy," Black Nationalism, cause us to attempt to formulate ironclad rules for Black writers, which originate from our own misunderstanding of the nature of the American society. Such critics do not deny that continual warfare rages between Blacks and this country. They do, however, deny our assessment of it tenacity and pervasiveness. They argue that the American society is moving steadily toward fulfilling the promise suggested in its laws, that tremendous progress has been made by Blacks. One critic summed it up this way: "Negroes are more literate now than they ever were. They earn more money. They are better housed. They dress better. They certainly look better. And none of these changes came overnight. . . ."

Others contend that the problems confronting Blacks in the American society demand no special attention from the writer, for he is neither politician nor revolutionary, but seer and prophet, dedicated only to the revelation of those truths which involve all men irrespective of race or color. For such people, the Black Aesthetic Movement is more political than aesthetic, importuning the writer to direct his truths toward a particular people— Black people—rather than toward "people in general." One critic of this persuasion has written: "Addison Gayle and Amiri Baraka want to politicize the creative energies of Black people in a manner that would exclude the possibility of white people ever being able to discover some profoundly meaningful facet of their white selves through an appreciation of the Black aesthetic."

Those who hold such views are honorable men. They are men of principle and integrity. Although one questions their ignorance of history in general, and of literary history in particular, their truths illustrate their concern. Yet, the primary question centers upon meanings: What do they mean? Those who argue that Black Aestheticians are hopeless romantics; that by focusing upon "the Black nationalist star in the heavens," that have been binded to the objective realities of this pragmatic world—what do they mean, if not that they see a world different from that viewed by Black Aestheticians?

Romanticism, after all, is endemic to those who wage continual warfare against insuperable forces. Such romanticism motivated Douglass and Delany, Sojourner Truth and Harriet Tubman, Malik El-Shabazz and Martin King, and those many thousands of Black people, past and present, who refused to adhere to the proposition that the seeming omnipotence of the enemy and his awesome power, mandated that they cease dreaming of liberation, of attempting to rescue themselves and their progeny from tyranny and oppression. In a world ruled by the Euro-Americans, the call for pragmatism is all too often nothing more than a rationale uttered by those who seek to join forces with men who, at a particular moment in history, possess tremendous power.

The same accusation may be leveled against those who today raise the banner of "artistic freedom," arguing that Black Aestheticians seek to ensnare the Black writer in an ideological iron curtain, thus negating his creative potential. Such an argument is not directed so much toward the question of freedom as it is toward that of obligation. For what is the first obligation of any Black writer in this country? It should be toward those from whom he gains his artistic strength; toward those whose lifestyle, language, culture, and history he uses; toward those for whom, intentionally or not, he is viewed as spokesman. And despite his flights into fantasy (those times during which he imagines that he is not a Black writer, but an American writer), both the American society and Black people know better. And twenty-four hours in any city in this country is enough to convince even the most neurotic among them that they are Black men and women first, and writers second.

Those who attempt to minimize the evils of the American society, who seek to rationalize its immorality, find today, more so than ever, that they stand on very shaky ground, indeed. Recent revelations of the tyranny and corruption of the "law and order" administration of Richard Nixon and Spiro Agnew, of the shoddy activities of the secret police systems—the CIA and the FBI—of the lynch mob mentality of the people of South Boston and Brooklyn, and the deprivation imposed upon thousands of black people in these months of recession, point up the veracity of the argument raised by Black Aestheticians in a way that no critical article ever could. There is no attempt in this analysis to deny progress; yet, progress does not justify a defense of the American society by Black writers whose primary responsibility is to sift through the lies and distortions and to arrive at a truth applicable to all Blacks in this country.

To do this necessarily demands a close correlation between literature and politics, and this writer will not retreat one inch from the proposition that literature and politics complement one another, and that in a war such as Black people are forced to wage against this country, politics constitutes an important area. Therefore, the Black writer, master of the word, must be our most consummate politician.

Nor do I retreat from the proposition that Black literature must be directed, not toward those with a vested interest in preserving the American society, but toward those whose salvation lies in its radical restructuring. The vogue of protest literature, designed to convince Americans that Blacks were human beings, is over. We no longer feel the necessity to convince others of our humanity. Attempts to convince the American literary establishment that those of us who write are different from the "uneducated, unlettered herd" have ceased because we know that in a totalitarian society man's worth is measured by neither his intellectual attainments nor his artistic creations.

We direct our energies and talents toward explicating the culture and history of Blacks; toward redefining the definitions handed down from the slave owners to present-day white politicians; toward recreating paradigms of the Black past—images of those who symbolized the struggle of a people to withstand the pragmatic realities of the society in which they lived, dreaming romantic dreams of a new world, a new Jihad, one outside the madness and sickness of those who believe that the universal essence of mankind is not the desire for liberty or freedom, but the selfish pursuit of material things. We write about the reality of this country, realizing as we do so that liberation for a people can occur only when they have understood reality and moved to change it. We argue fervently against the proposition that mankind must everywhere remain the same, that the evolution of man stopped with the birth of the Euro-American, and that beyond him lies only the deluge. We are, instead, convinced that Euro-American man is merely the flimsy structure which one crosses to reach the new man, and that this new man, compassionate, caring, dedicated to things of the spirit, should be found in the works of those free enough from American power and persuasiveness to envision him and call him into being.

The critic, to paraphrase Macebuh, seeks to undertake the prerogative of the creative writer. In the main, this is not true. This much of the assertion, however, is: The function of the critic is to demand that the writer adhere to the proposition that a sane universe is possible, that a new morality and a new ethical system are possible only when the new man has come into being, and that the writer must devote his talents to these ends. At every stage of human history, there have been those, romantic in nature, who envisioned a world of principle and justice against the overriding pragmatic considerations of the moment. This must be the position of the Black writer. The function of the Black critic at the present time is to see that he accepts this position. The critic will fulfill his function by devoting himself, not to spurious theories of art for art's sake, but to art for the sake of Black people everywhere.

CHAPTER 22

The Critic, the University, and the Negro Writer

(1967)

Thomas S. Eliot's classic statement on the "metaphysical" poets in an essay by that title in 1921 is too well known to warrant explication here. Yet, besides contributing to, or, more accurately spearheading the impetus for the revival of the "Metaphysicals" as objects of study, the essay stands as a classic example of the power and influence wielded conjointly by the critic and the university. Eliot's essay gave rise to a new group of critics, who, less judicious than either Dr. Samuel Johnson or Matthew Arnold, have dictated the tastes and forms of English Literature (mainly in America) for over a decade, and those "New Critics," in most instances were connected with the university, either in teaching positions or through prestige and influence.

The trend in recent years toward a different type of orientation (in most cases going back to the biographical-historical method of Taine and Saint Beuve) only serves to point up the importance of both the critic and the university in determining not only literary standards, but to a great degree, the works which in the judgment of the "Combine" (critics-English professors) meet these standards. The result has been, of course, a dictatorship which makes the dictators of old—Pope, Dryden, Dr. Johnson—seem like "New Deal Democrats."

Those who have been damaged most severely under the iron rule of this combine are Negro writers. Never taken seriously in the American society, never conceived of as much more than a protester, the Negro writer today, despite James Baldwin and Ralph Ellison, fares little better among the men of the "ivory tower" than his predecessor.

Saunders Redding has adequately summed up the argument against anthology writers who refuse to anthologize selections of Negro authors,[1] yet the nucleus of the problem lies in the classroom itself. And here, the Negro members of the combine are as guilty as the white members. Recently, a young graduate of a distinguished Negro college in the South, who had majored in English Literature and had taken several courses in American Literature, asked me, after thumbing through one of the books on my shelf, "Who is this man?" I never heard of him before!" "This man" was James Weldon Johnson, and the book was his *Autobiography of an Ex-Coloured Man.*

To document the ignorance of the white collegian would be needless, for few white students to whom I have talked have knowledge of any Negro writer outside of the "Big Three," Wright, Baldwin, and Ellison; however, the example of a professor may serve as a case in point. The professor, holding a doctorate in English Literature and at one time chairman of the department of a university renown for its English department, on reading a paper of mine with Saunders Redding as the subject, implored me to find out if the works of Saunders Redding could be found in the University Library. "I think," he remarked, "that every student should read the works of this man. Thank you for bringing him to my attention." This was in 1965, and Saunders Redding's first book appeared in 1939.

But more than ignorance of the works of Negro writers is involved here; much more pernicious are the concerted efforts by critics and professors to dispute the charges brought against the American Society by the Negro writer, without having to engage in a dialectic. The concept of the liberal professor, willing to acquiesce in change and to examine the new and different, is a concept nonapplicable to the professor of English Department. For the most part, English professors are the most zealous, conservative upholders of the *status quo,* more inclined, to quote Dr. Johnson, to champion that "which is right because it is established," than that "which is established because it is right."

A case in point is Professor Robert Bone's book, *The Negro Novel in America* which, for some years now, has served as a source book for any study dealing with Negro Literature. Professor Bone pretends to examine his subject with the scrutiny of the objective literary historian, yet, throughout the book, Bone drops his mask to record his personal reaction to any statement, or any work as a whole, that dares to point accurately to the reality of the American society. "Let us hope it will not be taken as evidence of . . . American Chauvinism if we point out that there are in fact important differences between the Negro's status in Philadelphia and in Georgia; between the systematic genocide of the Hitler government and the Supreme Court decision of 1954," he writes, in explicating William Gardner Smith's *Last of the Conquerors.*[2]

If we concede that Professor Bone is not being chauvinistic, we must then assume that—for want of a better word—he is being naive. If we substitute New York for Philadelphia (not the Philadelphia of 1948 when Smith's book was published, but today, when according to Bone, great progress has been made) and accept the basic contention of Bone's argument that the Negro is better off in New York than in Georgia, then we would be hard put to explain why the most vocal voice of protest against the American society are the voices of two New Yorkers, James Baldwin and LeRoi Jones.

But the second half of the statement is not only naive, but ludicrous, in that Bone attempts a feat of logical legerdemain, which would not deceive even a first-year philosophy major: The analogy between "the systematic genocide of the Hitler government," and "the Supreme Court decision of 1954" is no analogy at all; better would be the analogy between the genocide of the Hitler government and the lynching of over 4,000 Negroes (a recorded number, which does not include "justifiable homicide"—a favorite phrase of Northern police courts, or deaths from "unknown causes," such as bodies found in the Mississippi River during the search for the bodies of Chaney, Goodman, and Schwerner).

But this is an analogy which Professor Bones cannot bring himself to make. And those Negro writers who make such analogies receive the most devastating attacks in Bone's anthology. Nothing better illustrates this fact than the works of James Baldwin.[3] In less than 25 pages, Bone asserts that Baldwin is everything from a sexual maniac to a psychopath. Indeed, sex becomes the organizing principle around which Bone bases his criticism of Baldwin, but clear to the reader is the fact that Bone has undertaken a defense of the sexual and racial mores of the American society. James Baldwin, in particular, and the Negro "protest" writer in general, is then, his dragon, and he, Bone, is the society's St. George. (For an example of how Baldwin can be criticized sanely, and from an unbiased point of view, see Saunders Redding's "Since Richard Wright" and "The Problem of the Negro Writer.")

But Bone, at least, has the courage of his convictions. Unlike other instructors and critics, Bone brings his contentions out into the open, and he discusses, ofttimes skillfully, the deficiencies of many Negro novels. Yet the majority of the instructors of English Literature, those in positions of responsibility, make no such effort. In many universities, both Negro and white may receive a doctorate without having read one line by a Negro author. In a Western university whose English department ranks among the best in the country, the only Negro author included in the syllabus is Ralph Ellison.

In fact, the selection of Ellison evidences the fact that tokenism is not confined only to the industrial and social sphere of the American society. Some time ago, when an English department wished to display its propensity for taking all literature as its province, Richard Wright's *Native Son* was ushered forth to prove that the university had its one Negro representative; for some reason the Wright stock has nose-dived, but a successor, in the form of James Baldwin, was quickly ushered in to retain the university's "image"; but, alas, the Baldwin stock proved to be even less solvent than the Wright stock (Baldwin lasted only about three years) and, to fill the gap, Ralph Ellison was quickly brought forth.

The reasons for Ellison's ascension to university eminence range from the oft-quoted but true statement that *Invisible Man* is a supreme accomplishment in its own right, to the assertion (an assertion which both Irving Howe and Ralph Ellison have given credence to) that *Invisible Man* is not a "protest" novel. ("Invisible Man," remarked a college professor, "deals with modern man in the universe, not an isolated Negro in an oppressive society.") Nearer the truth is the fact that

Ellison's novel, no less that the novels of James Baldwin, is a "protest" novel; the only difference, and an essential one, is that Ellison has clothed his novel in myth and symbolism so skillfully that the average critic is unable or unwilling to search for the protest beyond the symbol and myth. (Another user of symbols and myths, William Blake, has not been as fortunate in this respect as Ellison; scholars have looked for the meaning behind the Blakean symbols and have discovered that poor old Blake was an avid protestor after all. This has not, however, caused his literary demise, but instead has added to his prestige.)

The ability to deal with Ellison, then, by skirting the indictment of the American society means that Ellison will be read in universities for a long time to come. Yet, the majority of Negro writers, and I mean the good ones (though being good has been no criterion for the selection of white authors for college syllabi), will remain unread in colleges, both Negro and white. For the American society is not yet capable of looking at the Negro through glasses cleansed of 150 years of prejudice, and the combine which controls the selection of the material which could do most to erase this distorted impression exercises its vast power in a negative manner.

Notes

1. Saunders Redding, "The Problems of the Negro Writer," *Massachusetts Review,* VI, No. 1 (1964–65).

2. Robert Bone, *The Negro Novel in America,* Yale University Press, 1958, p. 178.

3. Ibid., 215–39.

CHAPTER 23

Cultural Hegemony: The Southern White Writer and American Letters

(1970)

Movements in literary history are difficult to discern and the influences which give rise to and sustain them are not easy to trace. The movement from Classicism to Neo-Classicism in seventeenth and eighteenth century English literature cannot be traced to one particular work, although Dryden's *An Essay of Dramatic Poesy,* Samuel Johnson's "Preface to Shakespeare," and Gotthold Lessing's "Laocoon," must be noted. The movement from Neo-Classicism to Romanticism is equally difficult to pinpoint despite the poetry of Thomas Gray, Oliver Goldsmith, and William Blake, which point to the theories enunciated by Samuel Coleridge in *Biographia Literaria,* William Wordsworth in the preface to *Lyrical Ballads* and Shelley in "A Defense of Poetry."

In America, where little of a national literature existed until the latter part of the eighteenth century, any discussion of literary history centers upon the established traditions of Germany, France, and England. So great was the foreign influence on American letters that Nathaniel Appleton, Noah Webster, David Ramsay, and others demanded a literature of their own. John Trumbull summed up their nationalistic arguments in couplet form:

> This land her Swift and Addison shall view
> The former honors equaled by the new
> Here shall some Shakespeare charm the rising age
> And hold in magic chain the listening stage.

David Ramsay demanded a decisive break with the old world. The models to be followed were those of nations that had existed on the shores of the Aegean long ago: "It is hoped that the free government of America will produce poets, orators, critics, and historians equal to the most celebrated of the ancient commonwealths of Greece and Italy." Ramsay's call for an indigenous literature based upon the Greek ideal was not answered until 1830. Cooper's two novels, *The Spy* and *The Last of the Mohicans,* moved the American novel away from the influence of Samuel Richardson and Henry Fielding; Philip Frenau, "the first real poetic voice to be heard in the U.S.," broke new grounds in the field of poetry; and the Transcendentalists attempted to lay a philosophical foundation for a national literature. Yet, despite these specific movements, the literary tradition destined to survive the influence of Walt Whitman and William Dean Howells was brought into being by Southern writers who, in crossing Aristotle and Plato with Sir Walter Scott, produced a tradition which not only, in Dr. Johnson's words, stood the test of time, but has dominated American cultural thought from 1830 to the present.

The Plantation Movement occurred almost simultaneously with the Transcendental Movement. The latter, dying with Emerson, never reached the status of a tradition, but the former continued to grow and develop. The rise of the one movement and the demise of the other can be attributed to the fact that the Plantation Movement went back, as Ramsay had suggested, to the Aegean for confirmation of its faith, while the Transcendental Movement went to Germany for its confirmation. Between Immanuel Kant and Plato lay a world of difference, not only in philosophical approaches but in views of man and society. The voice of Kant calling upon men to be open-minded, to be inquisitive, to approach the complex problems of men in humanitarian terms, fell on deaf ears in a nation where prejudice, dogmatism, and simplistic approaches to problems, human and social, were and still are the norm. Given the choice between Platonic idealism and Kantian transcendentalism, the South chose to ally itself with the Greek mind and thus became the embodiment of the American myth.

The earliest proponent of this myth was the statesman-philosopher, John C. Calhoun, and American cultural thought is more indebted to Calhoun than critics and teachers care to admit. In defending the plantation system, Calhoun championed a republic modeled on the Greek ideal, one with a strong class structure. He devoted himself, according to Parrington, "to set class economics above abstract humanitarianism . . . He undid for the plantation South the work of his old master [Jefferson]. Speaking in the name of democracy, he attacked the foundations on which the democratic movement in America had rested, substituting for its libertarian and equalitarian doctrines conceptions wholly alien and antagonistic to Western democracy, wholly Greek in their underlying spirit."

With Calhoun, the defense of the plantation system passed from Virginia to South Carolina. Virginia, inoculated with the philosophy of Thomas Jefferson, and with her plantation system working at peak performance, had settled down to the complacency of an affluent Greek city-state. With abolitionism on the rise in the North, the *Appeal* of the Black writer, David Walker, calling for slave insurrections flooding the South, and the plantation system under daily attack, Calhoun appears to present the rationale for what Thomas Nelson Page called "the purest sweetest life ever lived."

In "A Disquisition on Government," Calhoun declared: ". . . it is a great and dangerous error to suppose that all people are equally entitled to liberty. It is a reward to be earned not a blessing to be gratuitously lavished on all alike—a reward reserved for the intelligent, the patriotic, the virtuous and deserving—and not a boon to be bestowed on a people too ignorant, degraded and vicious, to be capable either of appreciating or of enjoying it . . . Nor is it any disparagement to liberty that such is and ought to be the case. On the contrary, its greatest praise—its proudest distinction is, that an all-wise providence has reserved it, as the noblest and highest reward for the development of our faculties, moral and intellectual." Having carried us thus far in pursuit of the Greek ideal, having paid his debt to the early Plato of *The Republic,* Calhoun turns to invoke the spirit of the later Plato whose last dialogue, *The Laws,* is a treatise on despotism: "A reward more appropriate than liberty could not be conferred on the deserving—nor punishment inflicted on the undeserving more just, than to be subject to lawless and despotic rule."

For an accurate summation of Calhoun's thought on this point, one must turn to Vernon Parrington: "Democracy is possible only in a society that recognizes inequality as a law of nature, but in which the virtuous and capable enter into a voluntary copartnership for the common good, accepting wardship of the incompetent in the interests of society. This was the Greek ideal and this ideal had created Greek civilization."

In "Remarks on the States Rights Resolutions in Regard to Abolition," Calhoun describes the new Republic: ". . . The Southern states are an aggregate, in fact, of communities, not of individuals. Every plantation is a little community, with the master at its head, who concentrates in himself the united interests of capital and labor, of which he is the common representative. These small communities aggregated make the State in all, whose action, labor, and capital is equally represented and perfectly harmonized. Hence the harmony, the union, the stability of that section which is rarely disturbed, except through the action of this government."

John Pendleton Kennedy, William Alexander Caruthers, and Nathaniel Beverley Tucker, among the South's earliest literary lights, accepted the Calhoun sociological doctrine totally and lent their talents to extolling the virtues of the plantation system. Contrary to popular belief, their major efforts were not spent in defending the institution of slavery but in praising the virtue of the concept on which the plantation system rested. The defense of slavery by Calhoun and Albert Taylor Bledsoe in the social, political, and theological realm was not undertaken in earnest by poets and writers until after the publication of *Uncle Tom's Cabin* in 1852. Until then, the men of letters had been content with propagandizing the virtues of the Greek ideal.

The Southern mind was attracted to this ideal partly because of the justification for slavery offered by the world's first "democracy"; it was not attracted by what Matthew Arnold called the humane principles handed down from the Aegean—principles which distinguished man as the center of the universe. To the Southern mind, historically incapable of dealing with complexity, and seeking a stable, ordered society free from the disruption occasioned by the intrusion of enlightened ideas, Greece offered a model of the agrarian society, Athens, a universe where each man, awarded his place in society, lived by a set of norms which defined his daily existence and by extension defined him.

Plato's *The Republic* and Aristotle's *Politics,* not the King James version of the Bible, are the ancient tracts from which the Southerners gleaned their theology. Central to each of these works is the idea of the planned society in which men and women function as a unit—a world of superiors and inferiors, each cognizant of his particular niche in the social, political, and cultural hierarchy. Having laid the sociological and political basis for such a utopia, John C. Calhoun turned his attention to the coming break between North and South and left the task of singing its glories, of recording it in verse, prose, and song to poets and novelists. When these "legislators of the world," as Shelley called them, took up their pens to describe Calhoun's world, the plantation system became the model for the plantation school of writers who originated a tradition destined to survive for over two hundred years.

In this literature, one finds almost everywhere the dramatization of the perfect society whose closest analogue is Lovejoy's theory of the "Great Chain of Being." At the apex of the chain was the master, God's vice-regent on earth, Solon and Christ combined, bold, generous, and philanthropic, bending man and beast to his will with cajolery if possible, with the whip if necessary. The lesser plantation owner, whose wealth calculated in terms of number of slaves, was insufficient to grant him top status, was next. Next came the farmer, and following him were the peasants, the poor whites who, due to lack of ingenuity, were incapable of surviving in a Darwinian world. At the bottom were the slaves, upon whose shoulders the task of maintaining the plantation system rested. They were the inferior element, and a modern-day supporter of the plantation system, John Gould Fletcher, has justified their existence at the lower rung of the hierarchy: "The inferior, whether in life or in education, should exist only for the sake of the superior. We feed and clothe and exercise our bodies, for example, in order to be able to do something with our minds. We employ our minds in order to achieve character, to become the balanced personalities, the 'superior men' of Confucius' text, the 'Gentlemen' of the old South."

The "superior men of Confucius' text" remain the heroes of plantation literature. Their most important characteristics are devotion to region, duty, and loved ones. The loved ones are often fair damsels, ladies whose material possessions are fans, musical boxes, billets-doux, and perfumed handkerchiefs. In addition to Plato and Aristotle, the influence of Sir Walter Scott, Samuel Richardson, and Alexander Pope is apparent everywhere. The idyllic utopia, the paradise on earth, is re-created in poetry and fiction with the authenticity vouchsafed it by the rhetoric of John C. Calhoun.

Calhoun died in 1850, two years before the plantation tradition came under assault from Harriet Beecher Stowe. Although based upon slavery, one must not think of the plantation system and the institution of slavery as one and the same. In so doing, critics have attributed motives to Harriet Beecher Stowe which she did not entertain. Mrs. Stowe had no intention of "starting the big war," nor did she seek to do away with the slave system. Unlike her father, Lyman Beecher, and her brother, Henry, Mrs. Stowe was not an abolitionist. What bothered her was not slavery but the immorality of the institution which offended her Quaker sensitivity and led her, without realizing it, to explode the myth the plantation system rested upon.

The society of Southern mythology could be justified by its apologists only if it rested on a high plane of morality. Inferiors had to be treated humanely or proved deserving of punishment then inflicted upon them by loving masters, pushed beyond the limits of patience. Rewarding instead of abusing those who "stayed in their places" was an unwritten law of the ideal republic which, when violated, introduced chaos into the system. No slave was more conscious of his position than Tom, none accepted so readily the "place" to which providence and ill fortune had doomed him, and none was more obedient, loving, or submissive.

Tom's treatment at the hands of Simon Legree, who, as Edmund Wilson points out, is the plantation owner, a yankee, not an overseer and a Southerner as most people have been led to believe, does irreparable injury to the ideal which Southern writers had been propagating and reveals the plantation system to have been modeled less upon Plato and Aristotle than upon Epicurus and Heraclitus. He is not the victim of "the most pernicious institution known to man," but the victim of an imperfect social order, one which fails to live up to its promise. Whatever others might make of *Uncle Tom's Cabin* for abolitionist ends, Mrs. Stowe would have settled for a world in which the justice and humanity espoused by Southern writers was an actuality; one in which an "inferior" like Tom, who never violates the norms of his condition, is accorded due treatment for loyalty, devotion, and piety.

Southern writers have always been aware of the underlying thesis of Mrs. Stowe's novel. Their counterattack was not ostensibly based upon a defense of slavery but upon a defense of the plantation system. They went to great lengths to prove that the Simon Legrees were anomalies, and that the black Toms of the South fared better than the white Toms of the North. The tenacious zeal displayed in articulating the virtues of Calhoun's "near perfect society" was now marshaled in defense of it.

Less than one year after the publication of *Uncle Tom's Cabin,* William John Grayson, who with George Fitzhugh formed a two-man truth squad dedicated to correcting the falsehoods of Mrs. Stowe, used the heroic couplet as the medium for his rebuttal. Black slaves in the South, he argued in "The Hireling and the Slave," fare far better than the Northern poor; and after cataloguing the abuses of the poor in the North, he contrasts their plight with that of the slaves in the South:

If bound to daily labor while he lives,
His the daily bread that labor gives:
Guarded from want, from beggary secure,
He never feels what hireling crowds endure,
Nor knows like them, in hopeless want to crave,
For wife and child, the comforts of the slave,
Or the sad thought that, when about to die
He leaves them to the cold world's charity
And sees them slowly seek the poor-house door—
The last, vile, hated refuge of the poor.

George Fitzhugh, choosing to mount his defense in prose, based his argument in *Cannibals All/or Slaves Without Masters,* on the same theme. In "Slavery—Its Effects on the Free," he meets the moral argument posed by Mrs. Stowe without retreating one step from the Greek ideal: "Now at first view it [slavery] elevates . . . whites; for it makes them not the bottom of society, as at the North—not the menials, the hired day laborers, the work scavengers and scullions—but privileged citizens, like Greek and Roman citizens, with a numerous class far beneath them." And reminiscent of Grayson, Fitzhugh concludes: "Our slaves till the land, do the coarse and hard labor on our roads and canals, sweep our streets, cook our food, brush our boots, wait on our tables, hold our horses, do all hard work, and fill all menial offices. Your freemen at the North do the same work and fill the same offices. The only difference is, we love our slaves, and are ready to defend, assist and protect them. . . ."

Such gallant defenses proved of no avail against the juggernaut now poised to move in the North. Three years after Fitzhugh's *Cannibals All,* "the irrepressible conflict" erupted into a violent conflagration in which men like William Tecumseh Sherman, riding the whirlwind of the Apocalypse, burned to ashes the physical props on which had rested the literature of the South. When chaos came, when peace and tranquility was disrupted, all that would survive of the Greek ideal was a record of what men believed had once existed.

The writers after Reconstruction—Thomas Nelson Page, Thomas Dixon, and Joel Chandler Harris—brooded over the past, attempted to resurrect it in fiction and poetry, to create the Garden of Eden once again. The paradise lost haunted them all of their lives, and they died, pitiable old men, clinging to the dream of ancient Greece which once flowered anew on American soil. The dream would not die with them. They lived during the years of "the bloody shirt" when every Northern politician singled out the South as villain, when John Brown replaced Davy Crockett as the national hero, and when the best literary talents of the North were celebrating the virtues of "old New England."

When the days of Northern vindictiveness were over, when the railroad men discovered new routes in the South, when the Supreme Court had struck down the last of the Reconstruction legislation, and when President Hayes had withdrawn the last troops from the South, other men, dreaming the dreams of Post-Reconstruction writers, awakened to ask with Fletcher: "How can we preserve what little is now left to us of the traditions of leisure, of culture, of intellectual tolerance and sane kindliness, which are all that our fathers had to give us as a legacy from the past that was broken in the civil war?"

No longer the interpreter of the system or its defender, the task for the Southern writer was now "to forge from the smithy of his soul the uncreated conscious of the race." He set out at first to justify the ways of Calhoun to his Southern brethren; and he was oblivious of the fact, until much later, that his appeal was listened to and applauded by those in the ranks of the enemy. Despite Parrington's attempt to subordinate the influence of the Plantation School to that of the Transcendentalists and the Realists, it has with its simplistic view of man and the world remained dominant in American literature.

Men like Fletcher, better educated and more sophisticated than their predecessors, discovered Matthew Arnold's truth—that great creative epochs demand great ideas to propel them into being and that to accomplish this task, an era of literary criticism is necessary. Such men, apostles of a modern romanticism who refused to believe that the Southern Athens was gone beyond recall, set out to seize the reins of literary criticism in America, to force it into new and different channels and to posit a romanticism far less humane than that which they set out to destroy.

The New Critics appeared at a time when complexity was the norm in American life. In the late twenties and early thirties, the society was undergoing spasms from forces as varied as race riots and industrial expansion. The influence and power of the priest had been dissipated; the politician had lost favor through perversion of his art. The social institutions everywhere seemed incapable of confronting the complexity of life in the twentieth century. There was an overwhelming moral and social void and, like the men of the Middle Ages, the men of twentieth-century America turned to the university, calling on it to wage war in the interests of progress, to construct the formulas by which a nation might rise or fall.

Men who held such naive faith in the universities learned the lesson that young college students are learning today: The most reactionary institution in American society is the university, and the last place that one will find enlightenment, morality, or redemption is within its ivy-covered walls. Nowhere outside of the university is the Southern myth of the simplistic universe more pervasive, nowhere the aristocratic ideal held so dear, nowhere the vision of Calhoun clung to so tenaciously, and nowhere are the Greeks treated with more regard as the accurate prophets of man's existence. The American university has not changed essentially since the founding of Harvard College in 1636. Its purpose then as now was "to provide for young gentlemen a body of knowledge that would assure entrance into a community of educated leaders."

Toward these ends the university channeled its energy and its resources. Obsessed with the idea of establishing an educational aristocracy, the men of the university hastened to defend the validity of tradition, despite the precarious position upon which it rested. Despite the efforts of a few professors—outcasts among their peers—the tracts, books and articles supporting the institution of slavery, and perpetuating the nonsense of the Black man's inferiority poured out of universities, North as well as South. For a while, the historians were the chief villains in this comedy of errors, but soon the torch was passed on to the teachers of literature.

The English departments were ready for the New Critics who, in the latter part of the nineteen twenties began to remodel literary criticism in their own agrarian (read plantation) image. They left the Southern universities, took up residence at the universities in the North, and proceeded to construct a republic in letters based upon the social republic which they outlined in *I'll Take My Stand*.

Sometimes called "the Bible of agrarianism," *I'll Take My Stand* is a racist, fascist document, equaled in the twentieth century only by Hitler's *Mein Kampf*. Among its contributors are men whose names are legend in the field of American literary criticism. Included are articles by Donald Davidson, who in 1954 "became chairman of the Tennessee Federation for Constitutional Government," a right-wing organization "formed to oppose desegregation on the principle of states rights"; Allen Tate, whose introduction to *Libretto for the Republic of Liberia* by Melvin B. Tolson surpasses William Dean Howells' "Preface" to *The Complete Works of Paul Laurence Dunbar* in racial bigotry and arrogant, Aryan superiority; and Robert Penn Warren, who has denounced his contribution to *I'll Take My Stand*, admitting that "it was written in support of segregation." However, in his conclusion to *Who Speaks for the Negro?* published in 1965, Warren evidences how far along the road to rehabilitation he has traveled, and shows to be not very far at all.

In *I'll Take My Stand*, the major thesis is a reiteration of the social thesis propounded by Calhoun in the eighteen thirties. We are called to a rebirth of the republic of Athens and asked to reconstruct the society formed along class lines which existed in the South before the coming modern evils, progress and industrialism, intervened. We are asked to follow the agrarians back to the time when ". . . the even-poised and leisurely life of the Greeks, their oratory, their philosophy, their art . . . appealed to the South. The Greek tradition became partly grafted upon the Anglo-Saxon and Scotch tradition of life."

"The remarkable society" of the old South (Allen Tate's terminology) was not defeated in the civil war. Actual defeat threatens it now. The modern invaders are a varied assortment of incompatible elements: factories, railroads, bureaucrats, and civil rights agitators. These seek to change the simplistic life of a simple people, to destroy the romantic past born of rich soil, cultured old gentlemen and docile slaves. Against this modern aggression, the twelve writers take their stand, prepared to defend "a special notion of tradition—a notion that tradition is not simply a fact but a fact that must be constantly defended."

For these twentieth century Southern writers, tradition means what it meant for the plantation writers of the eighteenth and nineteenth centuries: a theory of society which goes back to the founding fathers of the old South, one based on the doctrines of Plato and Aristotle, a tradition in which the great chain of being stands as the metaphor of man's hopes and strivings, where aristocrat, farmer, and especially the Black man know their places. "In the past," writes Robert Penn Warren, "the Southern Negro has always been a creature of the small town and farm. That is where he still chiefly belongs by temperament and capacity; there he has less the character of a 'problem' and more the status of a human being who is likely to find in agricultural and domestic pursuits the happiness that his good nature and easy ways incline him to as an ordinary function of his being."

How then, Allen Tate asks, can this tradition which survives in Southern letters be resurrected again in actuality? His answer is definitive: "The answer is by violence . . . Since he [the Southerner] cannot bore from within, he has left the sole alternative of boring from without. This method is political, active, and in the nature of the case, violent and revolutionary. Reaction is the most radical of programs; it aims at cutting away the overgrowth and getting back to the roots."

Like the novels of Thomas Dixon which sanctioned the activities of the Ku Klux Klan when other men believed that tradition should be defended to the death, the contributors to I'll Take My Stand provided the rationale for the violence enacted against Arthurine Lucy and James Meredith, for the murders of Emmett Till, Jimmy Lee Jackson, and Medgar Evers, for the bombing of five Black children in a Birmingham church, and for the elevation of the Bull Connors and George Wallaces to a national eminence approaching sainthood.

Tate and his fellow Southerners misjudged the American temper. The book was written as a defense of the Southern way of life and directed at a supposedly hostile audience in the rest of the nation. However, Americans, to paraphrase William Blake, were not only of the Devil's party, but with the exception of a few misguided liberals, recognized their close affiliation. America is most Southern in her inclination to favor Aristotle over Immanuel Kant, to opt for the simplistic life instead of the complex one, and to believe as passionately in the concept of the great chain of being as the most rabid Southern aristocrat. The true character of white America was difficult to analyze during the period of continual wars and migration from country to city and from city to suburbs.

The case is quite different today. Supplied with a life of affluence and leisure surpassed in American history only by the plantation owner and the managerial capitalist, Americans today look forward to peace, comfort, and security. Few would be shocked by the philosophy displayed in I'll Take My Stand; a great many would accept these fascist myths of the thirties as the truths for the seventies. The republic imagined in writing stands a chance today of being established in fact by the administration of Richard Nixon, whose architects seem determined to transform America into a shadow image of the plantation system of yesteryear.

The nation was thirty years late in recognizing its true character; however, the university principles fell sway to the sophistry of the agrarians in less than two years. The initial assault was made on the English departments. Guardians of the national taste, these men of letters determine what cultured Americans will or will not read, what work of art deserves or does not deserve the National Book Award or the Pulitzer Prize, what writer will or will not receive a fellowship to work in leisure or a seat at a renowned university. The control of the nation's cultural apparatus rests in the hands of English professors and critics who, more often than not, peer out upon the American society with a condescension usually reserved for idiots and half-wits.

Such men welcomed the attempt of the New Critics to establish an aristocracy in American letters equal to that which they envisioned in the social sphere. The days of Hyppolyte Taine and Charles Augustin Sainte-Beuve were no more. Literature which dealt with man in terms of "race, moment and milieu," which considered the life of the author as important as the work itself, which argued that literature should not only mean but have a moral function as well, was denounced as irrelevant in a society where the artist sought not the elevation of mankind but the cultivation of his art.

A poem or a novel, like a well wrought urn, was an "autotelic structure," governed by inner rules and conforming to verbal structures which only the chosen few could analyze or interpret. The function of the writer was not, as Henry Fielding had believed, to instruct, but to produce masterpieces which would satisfy the aesthetic tastes of the cultured elite tastes conditioned by four years of English courses "in the best colleges and universities."

If America is to again become the legendary Athens, a literature which serves the demands of the aristocracy is a necessity. Still dreaming of the past, still enamored of the theories of the utopian society propounded by J. C. Calhoun, the agrarians seized upon the psychological criticism of I. A. Richards, the ambiguous criticism of T. S. Eliot, imbued it with their own biases and formulated a theory of art for art's sake with the concomitant denial of the democratic spirit and disdain for the masses.

When the English departments accepted the "ars poetica" of the Southern Agrarians, they chose to deal with literature in terms applicable to the plastic arts; moreover, they substantiated the Southern myth and gave authenticity to a society constructed along class lines. Their hypnotic attraction to the Greek ideal led them to accept the agrarian formula of a master class for whose personal comfort a literature was created. In so doing, they championed the worst of the plantation tradition and preceded the rest of the nation in succumbing to the philosophy of the descendants of Calhoun.

Nowhere is the influence of the plantation tradition more pronounced than in literature which deals with Blacks. Afro-Americans are the descendants of those whose presence in America made the plantation system possible; and the literary tradition based upon it owes as much to their presence as to the works of Plato and Sir Walter Scott.

Assigned the lowest positions on the great chain of being, Blacks, in attempting to extricate themselves, have evoked repercussions from white Americans in social, political, economic, and cultural areas. After the Emancipation Proclamation, in order to preserve the legacy left by the Plantation School of writers, white writers and critics instituted cultural slavery to replace the chattel slavery ended by the guns of war.

In 1925, in the preface to *The New Negro,* Alain Locke noted the cultural servitude under which Blacks labored and attributed this to the efforts of teachers and critics to deal with them in stereotypic terms. Locke's solution was to have the Negro speak for himself; however, Americans turned to white oracles. They preferred to listen to voices more attuned to their own, to those who spoke of peace and tranquility instead of war, who sought to assuage their fears with romance and make-believe instead of presenting the true story of America in all of its "hideous fullness."

No two oracles were more soothing in this respect than William Faulkner and William Styron. Nowhere in American literature does the plantation tradition reach greater heights than in the portraits of Black characters drawn by these writers. White critics of William Faulkner and their Black fellow travelers—Ralph Ellison and Albert Murray are the best known—have praised him for his "realistic portrayal of Negro people." However, his Negro characters, whose function is to satisfy the demand of white Americans for racial peace, are remnants of the plantation tradition.

Dilsey of *The Sound and the Fury* is one example. Like the "mammies" of Paul Laurence Dunbar's *Strength of Gideon,* her literary lineage goes back to Thomas Nelson Page: She attempts to hold the white family together; she is the foundation of a dying institution; and, while suffering insult and abuse, she survives by virtue of patience and submissiveness. The Greek ideal is safe with the Dilseys of the earth. Knowing and accepting their places, they face each tomorrow with a Bible under their arms, not with Molotov cocktails under their skirts. They are, to be sure, far different from the Harriet Tubmans and Sojourner Truths of actual American history.

Dilsey is the prototype of the good nigger, the darling of the earlier followers of the plantation tradition. No threat to the institution of slavery, she accepts her position in the hierarchy as having been ordained by God, and she will never bring chaos into the republic. Faulkner displayed great enthusiasm for the Dilseys of the race who became his metaphor for those whom other Blacks should emulate: "The Negro . . . must learn to cease forever thinking like a Negro and acting like a Negro . . . What he must learn are the hard things—self-restraint, honesty, dependability, purity; to act not even as well as just any white man, but to act as well as the best of white men."

No Black should emulate Joe Christmas of *Light in August.* One cannot exist in Faulkner's world half white or half Black, and the mulatto, a man with no discernible place, is doomed to an ignominious existence and a tragic end.

Without roots in either Black society or white, he is an outcast. He is the tragic mulatto of the plantation tradition who comes to prominence after the Civil War. The bad nigger of Southern fiction, he survives in Faulkner as a reminder of the evils of miscegenation—that act for which J. C. Calhoun made no provisions and which may eventually bring about the destruction of the existing social order.

A reassurance and a warning, this is the sum total of Faulkner's contribution to American letters; and Americans are more likely to remember the reassurance (Dilsey) than the warning (Joe Christmas). This is due, in part, to *The Confessions of Nat Turner* by William Styron. Coming in the midst of the Black Revolution, Styron's novel reassures white Americans who had begun to believe that Malcolm X, Stokely Carmichael and H. Rap Brown posed a threat to the maintenance of the great society. These men who chose the philosophy of Sparta over that of Athens were, it was believed, prepared to lead the Spartan hordes from the ghettos on an adventure designed to destroy the caste and class system upon which the republic stands.

Nat Turner was thrust upon the national consciousness to remind white Americans that, historically, all Black revolutionaries have had Achilles heels. What they desire in actuality is not the master's life but his daughter, and they are so confused about their relationship vis-à-vis white society that any determined assault upon white America, if it comes at all, is many years distant. Therefore, these modern-day Nat Turners pose no real threat, for not only are they half men, but they are sexually disturbed as well, seeking to wage war not in the streets or behind the barricades but in the bedrooms of white women.

Nat Turner in the hands of Richard Wright, LeRoi Jones, or John Williams would have been altogether different. And those who condemn Styron for his portrait, who demand that he portray Nat Turner with some semblance of reality, demand the impossible. To demand a realistic portrayal of Blacks by whites is to demand the impossible, for whites are neither mentally nor culturally equipped for the task. The plantation sentiments are too strong in white America, the influence of the New Critics too pervasive. Their approach to Black people can only travel the gamut from crude distortion to condescension occasioned by racism either unconscious or overt.

This is readily apparent in the area of literary criticism. Theodore Gross, the new Robert Bone of Black literature, lauds Joel Chandler Harris for being "able to share the fears, laughter, and anger of the Negro; he contributed the most popular Negro characters to American fiction—Uncle Remus, Balam, Ananias, and Mingo." Richard Wright, according to the same critic, when writing of his life and experiences in *Black Boy,* is found to depict "mundane actualities."

The assumptions upon which Gross' critical thesis rests are stated in his essay, *Our Mutual Estates:* Whites, he argues, due to their training in "America's best universities," are better equipped to deal with Black literature than Blacks. His thesis is supported by, among others, Fred Ehrenfeld who, in reviewing the anthology, *How We Live: Contemporary Life in Contemporary Fiction,* finds that, "Of the seven selections devoted to the Negro, two are by Jews and one by a Southern white writer. The editor feels the need to justify this by contending that there are few good Black writers."

These are the disciples of the New Critics, the academic architects of a new aristocracy, and their arguments are cogently summed up by Seldman Rodman in a review of Melvin Tolson's *Libretto for the Republic of Liberia*. After noting that Black literature has been "praised for its moral intentions and excused for its formal shortcomings," Rodman writes ". . . most of this poetry has been second rate, and critics, partaking of the general responsibility for the Negro's unreadiness to take the 'Negro Problem' in his stride, have hesitated to say so. The Negro poet's attitude of resigned pathos was followed by one of tragic aggressiveness, and both, as Allen Tate says in his preface to 'Libretto for the Republic of Liberia' limited him 'to a provincial mediocrity in which feelings about one's difficulties become more important than poetry itself.'"

To end with a quotation from the dean of Southern literary criticism is a measure of the extent of the influence of the Southern writer upon American letters; and it is no misstatement to say that American culture today is little more than a fiefdom of Southerners who exercise more despotic control over the national literature than their forefathers exercised over their plantations. Against this cultural dominance stands a small band of Black intellectuals and writers whose history has been one of continual struggle against the Greek ideal. More Kantian than Aristotelian, their vision is grounded in the ideals of democracy; they believe in art for people's sake, as one of their most respected poets, Don L. Lee, has so aptly put it, and they argue for cultural freedom as opposed to cultural imperialism.

Nothing could be farther from the minds of these Black intellectuals than saving America from despotism of any kind; yet, in propounding the thesis of a Black Aesthetic, they offer an instrument as potent as that of the early American writers who sought to break the domination of their culture by Frenchmen, Englishmen, and Germans. In freeing American letters from Southern tyranny, in advocating critical rules opposed to the antihumanistic ones of the disciples of the New Critics, in postulating a literature which functions in the interest of all mankind, they may bring about a revolution in American letters designed to usher in a new freedom for all writers—white and Black alike.

CHAPTER 24

Gwendolyn Brooks: Poet of the Whirlwind

(1984)

"To write poetry after Auschwitz," writes Theodor W. Adorno, "is barbaric." "These," writes the poet Baron Ashanti, "are dangerous times for poets." Adorno, white, Marxist, intellectual, is a good man, an idealist, onetime believer in the paradise to come. He believes no longer! The holocaust has embittered him, taught him that one cannot impose order upon chaos, cannot, in the words of Gwendolyn Brooks, "medicate the whirlwind." At one time, before Auschwitz and Dachau, poetry had a reason for being; that reason exists no longer. Poems, Adorno now realizes, cannot prevent human catastrophe, cannot protect humankind from oppression and tyranny.

Ashanti does not share Adorno's sense of hopelessness, futility, and despair. Young, Black, gifted, he knows that times are and have always been difficult for poets; that those who would confront the whirlwind are and have always been an endangered species. Unlike Adorno, he has a cultural history that has helped him to ameliorate despair; he has a cultural legacy bequeathed by Black poets from Jupiter Hammon to Gwendolyn Brooks that has admonished him to "Live and have your blooming in the noise of the whirlwind." This legacy has helped to strengthen the survivors of many holocausts: the middle passage, slavery, lynchings, mob law, indiscriminate murder and maiming of men, women, and children; it has helped the Black poet to carve from his Auschwitzes and Dachaus a record of man's inhumanities, as well as a record of Black courage and determination. Adorno is, then, one more voice in a growing chorus chanting the destruction of Western civilization; Ashanti, however, bears witness to the survivability of the human spirit; he reminds us that no number of Auschwitzes can make either poetry or the poet irrelevant, that if we are sensitive enough, we can muster the strength to love, and that this strength, mined from the history of a people, can encourage us to ride the whirlwind.

No one has contributed more to the formulation of the world view of such young poets as Ashanti than Gwendolyn Brooks. Born in Topeka, Kansas, she has lived most of her life in Chicago; she had received awards and recognitions accorded few of her contemporaries, Black or white. Before publishing her first volume, *A Street in Bronzeville* in 1945, she won four Midwestern poetry awards. She has also received two Guggenheim fellowships, the American Academy of Letters Award, and has served as poet laureate of Illinois. For her second volume of poetry, *Annie Allen,* she was awarded the Pulitzer Prize in 1950. In 1960, she published *The Bean Eaters; In the Mecca* in 1968 was followed by *Family Pictures* and *Riot.* In addition, she has published the fictional work *Maud Martha* (1953), an autobiography, *Report from Part One* (1972), and a collection of her works, *The World of Gwendolyn Brooks* (1972).

Brooks has labeled much of her work before 1967 "conditioned," "based on an assumption that her selfhood as a Black woman was defined, or at least conditioned, by the white world." Poet Haki Madhubuti writes of the early poetry that it "is fatless." And Brooks, in an interview in 1969, comments on changes in her work: "There is something different that I want to do. I want to write poems that will be non-compromising. . . . I want to write poems that will be meaningful to those people (Black people) I described a while ago, things that will touch them." For her supporters and critics and even for Brooks herself, this conversion to "the new poetry" ("Her new work," notes Madhubuti, "resembles a man getting off meat, turning to a vegetarian diet") began in 1967.

"Suddenly there was New Black to meet," Brooks recalls, when she stopped by a writers' conference at Fisk University in the spring of that year. There she met the energetic prophets of a new era: David Llorens, Hoyt Fuller, Ron Milner, John Killens, and Imamu Baraka. There were none among this assemblage who believed any longer with Dorie Miller from *A Street in Bronzeville:*

> Their white-gowned democracy was my fair lady.
> With her knife lying cold, straight, in the softness
> of her sweet-flowing sleeve.
> But for the sake of the dear smiling mouth and the
> stuttered promise I toyed with my life.
> I threw back!—I would not remember
> Entirely the knife.

There was, instead, the substance of the Baraka shout, "Up against the wall, whiteman." Whatever Brooks' assumptions, however, this was not history reborn but history in progress. There were few among the new prophets—Baraka in particular—who had not cried out at one time with Dorie Miller: "I had to kick their law into their teeth in order to save them." No, Dorie Miller was not irrelevant, only outdated. His cry had transcended the centuries, been echoed in the despair and longing of the spirituals, in the joy and resignation of the poetry of Hughes, McKay, and Toomer and in the muscular assertive poetry of the present, in that of Margaret Walker, Margaret Danner, Gwendolyn Brooks, Sonia Sanchez, Mari Evans, and Baron Ashanti.

Conditioned or no, the cry had to be issued, and it has been heard in the best works of our poets: In Claude McKay's *Harlem Shadows,* in Hughes' *The Panther and the Lash,* in Baraka's *The Dead Lecturer.* Each of these poets, in one way or another, recapitulate the exploits of many Dorie Millers, realizing that such was necessary in order to create the new sensibility. But necessary also were commentaries upon those "Whom the higher gods forgot/Whom the lower Gods berate." Only such commentaries could lead to a realistic confrontation with color caste the central problem of Black life. Writes Brooks: "Stand off daughter of the dusk/ And do not wince when the bronzy lads/Hurry to cream-yellow shining/ It is plausible. The sun is a lode."

"We know that we are beautiful," Langston Hughes declared, and these were and are stimulating words. For so long a period of our history, however, they were untrue to reality, the fantasy and wish-fulfillment of a poet, who all too often accepted the dreams that propelled his own metaphors as those of his people. "Throw the children into the river," sings Fenton Johnson. "Civilization has given us too many. It is better to die than to grow up and find that you are colored." "Yet do I marvel," Countee Cullen cries in astonishment, "at this curious thing./ To make a poet black and bid him sing." Such utterances do not remind us that we are beautiful, but instead suggest, and not so subtly, that we are ugly, that it is a terrible thing to be Black. If the whirlwind of the sixties was to be tamed, a return to the ethics of Du Bois was of primary importance: "Especially do I believe in the Negro Race: in the beauty of its genius, the sweetness of its soul. . . ." This has been the hallmark of the poetry of Gwendolyn Brooks, who has written of the beauty of Black people in kitchenettes, of Black mothers and daughters, of Lincoln West, Mathew Cole, and Satin Legs Smith, of those, metaphorically "Born in Alabama/Bred in Illinois,/ He was nothing but a/Plain black boy." Before the conversion, she had sought to help us to validate the sentiments of Hughes and Du Bois, and admonished us: "True, there is silver under/The veils of darkness./ But few care to dig in the night./For the possible treasure of stars."

It is not to be doubted that she learned from the new prophets at Fisk; learning has been and remains one of her strengths, has always been a growing process. She learned: "There is indeed a new Black today. He is different from any the world has known. He's a tall-walker. Almost firm. By many of his own *brothers* he is not understood. And he is understood by *no* white." Yet she had always understood, instinctively, with felt knowledge; had always known of our general universality; now, to that instinctive knowledge and generalized awareness of the hurts, pains, and joys of Black people, she added particulars, expanding the universal:

> Don Lee wants
> not a various America
> Don Lee wants
> a new nation

under nothing;
a physical light that waxes; he does not want to
be exorcised, adjoining, and revered

wants
new art and anthem; will
want a new music screaming in the sun.

From the writers' conference at Fisk, from her brief experience with the Black-stone Rangers, from her interaction with new, young enthusiastic Black people from all areas of Black life, she divined the energy, vitality, and certainty of the new art and anthem of such poets as Madhubuti, and incorporated them into her own canon: Amos from *In the Mecca* has transcended Dorie Miller. His prescription for America is bold and modern:

> Bathe her in her beautiful blood.
> A long blood bath will wash her pure.
> Her skin needs special care.
> Slap the false sweetness from that face
> Great nailed boots
> must keep her prostrate, heel grind that soft breast
> . . .
> Let her lie there, panting and wild her pain
> red, running roughly through the illustrious
> ruin . . .

The anger of Way Out Morgan, heard only as chorus in the early poetry, now becomes major anthem: Gun ready, Morgan "listens to Blackness stern and blunt and beautiful/organ rich Blackness telling a terrible story."

These vignettes are from *In the Mecca,* the long narrative poem published in 1968 which dramatizes events in the lives of people who dwelt, close, in compact quarters, like those on a slave ship, in "176 units" of a housing project established in 1891. Here are those who, like Madhubuti, clamor for the most part for "a new nation/under nothing." They are men and women, martyrs and poets, all locked behind the iron gates of Auschwitz, behind the doors "Of yelling pine or oak—the many flowers who start, choke, reach up, want help, get it, do not get it, rally, bloom, or die on the wasting vine."

We are all children of the poor, residents on the same slave ship, inhabitants of the same Dachaus and Auschwitzes, neighbors in the same Mecca. There is a sense, however, in which the analogy between the victims of the Mecca and those of Auschwitz and Dachau cannot be stretched too far. If we believe the chroniclers of the times—and Adorno is one such—the helpless of Dachau and Auschwitz revolted seldom, almost never, like Way Out Morgan, planned assault upon the dehumanizers. For the most part, those who inhabit the Mecca have purged themselves, of hopelessness and resignation, journeyed to the mountaintop and returned, prepared to usher in the final *Götterdämmerung*. There is something religious in the anger and intensity of such men as Malcolm X, Medgar Evers, Don L. Lee, Senghor—almost as if they prepare for a coming Jihad, having realized at long last that one's blooming must be fed and inspired by action, by movement, by dedication to the principle that only those die well who have lived freely. And to live freely is to interject chaos into the universe, to disrupt the pretensions of order and serenity, promulgated by those who man the concentration camps.

The symbol of the twentieth century, wrote Richard Wright, "is the man on the corner with a machine gun." "Not the pet bird of poets, the sweetest sonnet," chimes Brooks, "shall straddle the whirlwind." Though one poet speaks of guns and the other of sonnets, both address the same theme. Both are attuned to the absence of order and stability in the universe, and both argue for an ethic based upon chaos, realizing, with that intuitive gift of poets from time immemorial, that the growth of nations and individuals, as well, proceed upon chaos and disorder. This is the message of Brooks' volume *Riot* (1969), that which cements her ties to the new prophets: a realization that only through immersion in the fire this time can a new people and a new nation be born. It is a thought alien, however, to John Cabot and his many Black imitators, who reek of order, decorum, Jaguars, and Grandtully and are thus incapable of riding the red stallion of chaos: Such people are destined to go "down in the smoke and fire/and broken glass and blood . . ." to cry with disbelief, "Lord! Forgive these nigguhs that know not what/they do."

A riot, to paraphrase Martin Luther King, is the language of the unheard; it is also the painful language attenuating growth, the cries of a people wrenching themselves from the stultifying grips of a pained history. To the sensitive Black poets of the sixties and seventies, riots were metaphors of Black endurance, symbols of hope overpowering despair, similes—comparing birth to creation. At the vortex of the riot was the language of revolt and revolution, of promise and survival. "Fire./That is their way of lighting candles in the darkness," writes Brooks. "A White Philosopher said/'It is better to light one candle than curse the/darkness.' These candles curse—/inverting the deeps of the darkness." Not only does the riot purify the darkness; its sounds are piercing, soft, melodious, shattering, transforming the I into We, the individual into Us, the people into the nation: "The Black Philosopher will remember/there they came to life and exulted."

Exultation! Not resignation. We are far here from Adorno, who can see amidst chaos and disorder nothing but doom, destruction, and despair. For Brooks, however, these qualities produce revolutionaries, are the necessary ingredients for the new creation. For all new creations, despite the critics from the academics, whether human or artifact, are born only to be consumed in the flames of the new riot, the new birth. The poem, play, or novel that does its work well will shortly become extinct, pass on to a noble death, prepare the way for works more profound. "These Black writers," Brooks noted, writing of the talented young men and women, whom she anthologized in *Jump Bad,* "do not care if you call their products Art or Peanuts. Artistic Survival, appointment to Glory among the anointed elders, is neither their crevice nor creed. They give to the ghetto gut. Ghetto gut receives. Ghetto giver's gone." The riot reminds us, then, that there is no immortality, neither for systems nor for people; that change is endemic to the human animal and to the product that he or she produces. That which is immortal, that which continues *ad infinitum,* is contained in the best of literature and the riot alike: energy, vibrancy, challenge, daring, spontaneity, love: the propensity to engage in conflict and confrontation. The rioters, those in literature and in the streets, are the twentieth-century medicators of the whirlwind.

Such ideas concerning Black life and literature were promulgated and popularized during the sixties and seventies. Debts owed to many forerunners (Hughes, Du Bois, Margaret Walker, Richard Wright, Margaret Danner) come quickly to mind. Yet acclaim by a significant number of Black writers occurred among those whom Brooks hailed as "True Black writers [who] speak as Blacks about Blacks to Blacks. Boldly, daringly, innovatively they went to bars and cabarets, to places where residents of the Meccas lived and played, and read their poetry into Black consciousness and into the wind, affirming the fact that Black poetry belonged not to academic critics, nor to white and whitened Americans, but to Black people."

Their innovation and daring earned them little but scorn from those who believed/believe still that a poem, like a monument, is a sculptured artifact, created to last forever in the mausoleumlike minds of scholars and critics. Because they incorporated immediacy, energy, and innovation into Black poetry, the works of these talented young people were almost universally denounced by the literary establishment, Black and white. Part of the reason was that the new poetry interjected chaos and disorder into the ordered and structured cathedrals of American letters, in language understood only by fellow rioters. In those early years they had few allies: Hoyt Fuller, Dudley Randall, Lerone Bennett, James A. Emanuel, among them. When Brooks joined their ranks as supporter and participant, she offered inspiration and validity. The movement would have gone forward without her; it would not have gone forward so fast nor so well.

There was a price to be paid for joining the ranks of the literary rioters: ". . . Many people hated *The Bean Eaters.* Such people as would accuse me of forsaking lyricism for polemics, despised *The Bean Eaters* because they said that it was 'getting too social.'" The conversion of this master of the sonnet and ballad form whom the literary elite had acclaimed as its own brought forth worried, anxious questioning. The answers, however, were not difficult to come by, were not complex, metaphysical. For Brooks, to quote Blake, had always been of the devil's company, did not come to Fisk nor by way of Fisk to the ranks of the new prophets as an initiate. Despite her "integrationist philosophy," what was apparent to her young admirers were those qualities that abounded in her work: the search for a Black identity and love. The search had been carried on by Du Bois, Delany, and Sutton Griggs in the nineteenth century; Du Bois again, Hughes, and Rudolph Fisher in the early twentieth; in more recent times by James Baldwin, John Killens, and Sterling Brown.

For the writers of the nineteenth century, however, the search for Black identity and love was a prerequisite for entree into the American society. The writers of the twentieth century began to move away from such moorings, though for Baldwin, love in particular was a derivative of the Christian concept, the moral imperative that ranked Blacks higher on the scale of humanity than their oppressors. For Haki Madhubuti, Sonia Sanchez, Johari Amini, Askia Touré, and Mari Evans the search for a Black identity and the love of one Black person for another became political concepts. To espouse and exult in a Black identity, outside the psychic boundaries of white Americans, was to threaten the pretension and hypocrisies upon which the American ideal rests. To advocate and demand love between one Black and another was to begin a new chapter in American history. Taken together, the acknowledgment of a common racial identity among Blacks throughout the world and the suggestion of a love based upon the brotherhood and sisterhood of the oppressed were meant to transform Blacks in America from a minority to a majority, from world victims to, to use Madhubuti's phrase, "world makers": "We want a Black poem and a Black world," sang Baraka, "let the world be a Black poem."

Though Brooks had not traveled so far by 1967, she had always been among those who championed a Black identity and a communality of love between Black People and Black people. What the new poets gave to Brooks and to all of us was a transcendental ethic: Given the insane, racist nature of the American society, love and the acclamation of one's Black identity are political ideals, those which must precede revolution, whether in letters or in the streets of America. In other words, power comes, not from the barrel of a gun, but from one's awareness of his or her own cultural strength and the unlimited capacity to empathize with, feel for, care, and love one's brother and sister. "I mount the rattling wood," Brooks writes fondly in "The Wall." "Walter/says 'she is good.' Says/ 'she/our sister is' . . . In front of me/hundreds of faces, red-brown, brown, black, ivory/yield me hot trust, their year and their Announcement/that they are ready to rifle the high-flung ground." The giving and accepting of so much love, spontaneously, energetically, is difficult for the academic critics to accept or to understand. The reason is not that they are evil and calculating men and women, for most of them are not. The problem is that they have lived so long in America—an America whose most salient metaphor is the computer—that they have become enamored of the idea of an ordered universe, one governed by pragmatic, rational rules, codes, and laws. Their literature, therefore, is as deathly cold as their society, and products of the emotions, of the spirit, of the felt life, are anathema, even threatening. Better the poetry of a Carlos Williams, which says nothing, elicits not one emotional response, than "social poetry" which ordains love as a transcendental power. Not only love, therefore, but all of the emotions—anger, despair, joy, and hate—are equally suspect. Disciples of the New Critics of yesteryear, they demand poetry whose words demonstrate virtuoso feats of acrobatics, lines that dance like marionettes on a string, metaphors baked and tanned to obscurity, images that summon up—nothing at all. Little wonder, then, that sensitive, intellectual, well-meaning men like Adorno demand an embargo on poetry after Auschwitz. If art exists solely for itself and itself alone, it has little meaning, and thus no power to prevent other, more terrible Auschwitzes. It may well be, however, that the function of poetry is not so much to save us from oppression nor from Auschwitz, but to give us the strength to face them, to help us stare down the lynch mob, walk boldly in front of the firing squad.

It is just such awareness that the poetry of Gwendolyn Brooks has given us, this that she and those whom she taught/learned from have accomplished for us all. They have told us that for Black Americans there are no havens, that in the eyes of other Americans we are, each and every one of us, rioters, that the choice is clear: One may accept the fate of the victim or the creative birth of the rioter. One must do one or the other, for these are indeed, to paraphrase Ashanti, dangerous times for Black people. The sensitive Black poet realizes this fact, but far from despairing, picks up his pen, secure in love, Blackness, and hope, and echoes Gwendolyn Brooks: "My aim, in my next future, is to write poems that will somehow successfully 'call' . . . all Black people; Black people in taverns, Black people in alleys, Black people in gutters, schools, offices, factories, prisons, the consulate; I wish to teach Black people in pulpits, Black people in mines, on farms, on thrones. . . ."

CHAPTER 25

A Defense of James Baldwin

(1967)

In *Notes of a Native Son,* commenting on the dissatisfaction of Africans and American Negroes with Richard Wright, James Baldwin observed: "I could not help feeling: Be careful. Time is passing for you too, and this may be happening to you one day." The "one day" was not as far away for Baldwin as it had been for Richard Wright, for today American critics in general, and Negro critics in particular, are attempting to look behind what Irving Howe has called Baldwin's "brilliance of the language" and make that special effort which Howe sees as necessary "to attend the argument."

To attend an author's argument is a noble endeavor, but literary criticism from Plato to the present affords voluminous evidence that few critics are content to do so. As judicious a critic as irascible old Samuel Johnson may have been, he found it more appealing to discuss Gray personally than Gray's argument; and T. S. Eliot's "Shelley's ideas are silly," was an attempt to demolish the poet without seriously confronting his argument.

But this is true, even more so, in regard to the Negro writer. Critics, Black and white, usually find it uncomfortable to confront the argument of many Negro novelists, and their reasons are similar: Both would like to forget, to be able to nestle within the womb of their own illusions, clinging to that faith which has allowed them to live precariously in this society without, at present, attempting to exterminate each other en masse.

"Americans of all national origins, classes, regions, creeds, and colors have something in common: a set of beliefs, a political creed. This 'American Creed' is the cement in the diversified structure of this great nation." So writes Arnold Rose in *The Negro in America.* And Negroes and whites find it less painful to accept this bland declaration of solidarity than to face the real and uncontestable fact that the "American Creed" has not worked, and probably will never work for the Negro. And arguments to the contrary, far from being attended to, are simply not met at all; thus, in many instances, the critic zeroes in on some non-literary trait of the Negro writer (he hates white people, he hates Negroes, he hates his father, he hates himself), and from this evolves a literary theory.

In the chapter on James Baldwin in *The Negro Novel in America,* Robert Bone, like a modern-day Plato, endows Baldwin with all of the attributes of a mad man before finally expelling him from the Literary Republic: "On one side . . . we have adolescent rebellion and the smashing of taboo, hardening at times into Garveyism"; and again: ". . . we are dealing with an adolescent: who else gets his kicks from the violation of taboo?" And thus, oh Glaucon, let us say to the poet: "*Another Country* is not simply a bad novel, but a dead end. It is symptomatic of a severe crisis in Baldwin's life and art. . . . If he persists, he will surely be re-membered as the greatest American novelist since Jack Kerouac. The future now depends on his ability to transcend the emotional reflexes of his adolescence."

One thinks of Wycherley's *The Country Wife,* and the famous (or infamous, depending upon one's sexual mores) "china scene" in which, with the husband looking on, Horner and Lady Fidget dash into the china closet, not, presumably, to count china, and one wonders if Bone would have accused Wycherley of sexual rebellion! Or closer to our time, what does Professor Bone tell his students about filthy-minded Molly Bloom, whose inner thoughts are depicted in language which would not, perhaps, strike Wordsworth as the language of the common man, let alone the common woman.

Rebellion against sexual and social mores has been common in English lit-erature from Chaucer's *Canterbury Tales* to T. S. Eliot's "Love Song of J. Alfred Prufrock," and the critic who has not yet accepted such "rebellion" as one of the chief motifs of the artist of the twentieth century has ceased to dwell in the world of reality. The infamy of the twentieth century, its gas ovens, its hanging trees, and its concentration camps, has made morality, never an absolute, simply more relevant. Today we need no Nietzsche, "come back from the grave," to tell us that "God is dead." The very nature of the society in which we live makes rebellion mandatory, and in this world of sickness and insanity, rebellion may be seen as characteristic of health and sanity.

Professor Bone has his own ax to grind, and James Baldwin becomes his grind-ing stone, perhaps because Baldwin, more than any Negro writer since W. E. B. Du Bois, has rained such damaging blows upon the Northern-liberal construction which we call the "American Creed." Indeed, a fitting name for Bone's chapter on Baldwin may well have been, "A Defense of the American Society," for it offers us more of a critique of the mores of society than of Baldwin's works.

This is not to censure Bone for his defense (the American society needs all the defenders it can get), but it is to suggest that there is a line to be drawn between the extrinsic and the intrinsic approach to literature, and in the case of James Baldwin, Bone has stood solidly on the extrinsic side of the line. There are, how-ever, a number of students of literature who could not care less whether Baldwin hated his mother, his father, or both, or whether he slept with every eligible male on the continent.

But Bone is not the only critic to give Baldwin the "rainbow sign" in this manner! When Baldwin wrote: "This may be happening to me one day," he was, perhaps, thinking not of the Bones of this world but instead of the Eldridge Cleavers. In his article "Notes on a Native Son" (*Ramparts*, June 1966), after telling us of his experiences on first discovering James Baldwin (one is reminded of Keats: "And then I heard Chapman speak out loud and bold"), Cleaver writes: "I, as I imagine many others did and still do, lusted for anything that Baldwin had written . . . he placed so much of my own experience, which I thought I had understood, into new perspectives from which I derived new insights."

But Cleaver could not long sustain the Keatsian vision: Soon he was to feel no longer like some "watcher of the skies" who had found "a new planet" swimming in his ken. The planet turned out to be a man-made satellite which had taken him in, duped him into accepting it as the real thing. Chapman had lied to him, led him astray, seduced him: "Gradually, however," he writes, "I began to feel uncomfortable about something in Baldwin. I was disturbed upon becoming aware of an aversion in my heart to part of the song he sang. Why this was so, I was unable at first to say."

Had Cleaver read Irving Howe's "Black Boys and Native Sons," he might have been able "to say." In a statement quoted in part above, Howe writes: "James Baldwin's essays are superbly eloquent, displaying virtually in full, gifts that would enable him to become one of the great American Rhetoricians. But these essays . . . are marred by rifts in logic, so little noticed when one gets swept away by the brilliance of the language that it takes a special effort to attend their argument."

But Cleaver did not attend their argument, and what is more, no one knows this better than Cleaver himself. Like Bone, Cleaver has his ax to grind, but Baldwin is used here as a grindstone of far sterner stuff than Bone could have contemplated. For wherein Bone was content to defend the "American Creed," Cleaver, with nothing but contempt for the "Creed," is intent on defending Negro manhood, and avenging Richard Wright.

Cleaver's defense is both heroic and tragic. It is heroic in light of its historical perspective. Since Booker T. Washington, the Negro has been forced consistently to defend his manhood: Washington's "Atlanta Exposition Speech" may have been, as Rayford W. Logan termed it, a social and political compromise, but to the Negro intellectual it was a mental castration, reinforcing the myths which slavery and the white South had constructed. That the Negro was not a man in the eyes of white men was far less devastating than the fact that he was not a man in his own eyes. Before Washington, there had been the rebellions by Vesey and Turner, and the writings and speeches of Frederick Douglass, all attesting to the Negro's belief and pride in his own manhood. And those who still believe in

Washington's depiction of the slave who "entertained no bitterness against the whites before and during the war" and who grieved at the misfortune of "Mars Billy," if they have any wish to discern truth from fiction, have only to read in Frederick Douglass' autobiography: "Slaveholders, thought I, are only a band of successful robbers, who, leaving their own homes went into Africa for the purpose of stealing and reducing my people to slavery. I loathed them as the meanest and the most wicked of men."

But Washington and Tuskegee Institute managed to send, according to Washington's own account, "over six thousand men and women into the Southern states," all, presumably, well indoctrinated with Washington's teaching; and whether we like it or not, the Washington philosophy, to a large degree, is responsible for that self castration of the Negro which persists even to this very day. None saw this so clearly as Du Bois, and the reassertion of Black manhood became one of his major themes: "If," he wrote, "we make money the object of man-training we shall develop money makers, but not necessarily men: if we make technical skill the object of education, we may possess artisans, but not in nature men"; and Du Bois' *The Souls of Black Folk* abounds with metaphors and images of masculinity. And so, too, does Negro literature from James Weldon Johnson to James Baldwin, in all of which there is the attempt to negate the Washington philosophy.

But there is an element of tragedy also; for in being forced to defend his manhood, the Negro has been forced to compensate for what he considers his loss of it. The sexual myth of which Arnold Rose writes, the myth endowing Negroes with "large genitalia, and abnormal sexual prowess," may have been of white invention, but the Negro has acquiesced in the myth, and in many instances, taken pride in his purported sexual superiority. One has only to trace the concept of the hero in Negro fiction to find, looming almost everywhere, the fiber of the big, Black, powerful buck, a figure reflected in the Negro community in its idols from Jack Johnson to Willie Plays. Ironically, the Negro homosexual gives, in part, the lie to this concept, and thus challenges, once again, Negro manhood.

It is not surprising, therefore, to hear from Cleaver: "And then I read *Another Country*, and I knew why my love for Baldwin's vision had become ambivalent." For *Another Country* is the novel which demands that the Negro intellectual desert James Baldwin. More than *Giovanni's Room*, *Another Country* is Baldwin's most definitive statement on homosexuality. And the day is quite distant when Negroes will be found engaging in sit-ins for the rights of homosexuals. Without, perhaps, intending it, Cleaver has summed up the argument for the Negro on homosexuality: "I, for one, do not think homosexuality is the latest advance over heterosexuality on the scale of human evolution. Homosexuality is a sickness, just as much as baby-rape or wanting to become the head of General Motors." Perhaps, but we must not forget that there is still some truth in the old cliché, "One man's sickness may be another man's cure," and if we substitute "sin" for "sickness," there are many people in this society who would suggest that the analogy between Blackness and sin, woman-rape, baby-rape, and crime is just as valid an analogy as that between homosexuality, sickness, and baby-rape.

Cleaver writes of that "ubiquitous phenomenon in the Black ghettos of America: the practice by Negro youths of going 'punk hunting.'" And one cannot argue with Cleaver's seeming compulsion for "punk hunting" (I, for one, suggest that he be encouraged to get his kicks in the way he deems best), but one can and should argue with Cleaver's attempt to impose biography upon literature without attempting to differentiate the two. For by this approach, Cleaver comes to the conclusion that: "There is in James Baldwin the most grueling, total hatred of the Blacks, particularly himself, and the most shameful, fanatical fawning, sycophantic love of the whites that one can find in our time." Yet, Robert Bone, using much the same approach has found that "In the racial sphere, Baldwin employs defenses that go well beyond a healthy race pride"; and earlier, citing Baldwin's phrase "milk white bitch," Bone contended that Baldwin had evidenced his "hostility to both whites and women." Perhaps Cleaver has never read Bone, and Bone has never read Cleaver, but it seems clear that neither of the two is "attending the argument." And it is equally clear that Cleaver is a self-appointed defender of Richard Wright.

"Wright," says Cleaver, "has no need, as Caesar did, of an outraged Anthony to plead his cause," and then, however true this may be, Cleaver proceeds to negate the sincerity of his own metaphor by pleading Wright's cause, if not in the fashion of Anthony, at least in a manner which makes Tennyson's praise of the Duke of Wellington a feeble gesture in comparison. Cleaver intones: "Wright had the ability . . . of harnessing the gigantic overwhelming environmental forces and focusing them, with pin-point sharpness on the individuals and their acts as they are caught up in the whirlwind of the savage anarchistic sweep of life, love, death, and hate, pain, hope, pleasure and despair across the face of a nation and the world." (One can almost hear Tennyson wailing: "Mourn, for to us he seems the last / Remembering all his greatness in the past.")

One can understand if not sympathize with Cleaver's desire to avenge the name and honor of Richard Wright. Negroes have had few cultural heroes of the stature and magnitude of Wright, and, like Baldwin, every Negro boy who ever set pen to paper since *Native Son* has harbored a desire to grow up to be another Richard Wright. But it is one thing to admire Wright as a cultural hero, and quite another to deal with him as a novelist. Unlike the Negro-writer-aspirant, the critic owes no allegiance to Richard Wright, and if *Native Son* comes apart at the seams under close examination, then so much the worse for *Native Son*.

In "Everybody's Protest Novel," Baldwin's criticism is that of the critic, and he has hit at a fundamental weakness of *Native Son*. "The failure of the protest novel lies in its rejection of life, the human being, the denial of his beauty, dread, power, in its insistence that it is his categorization alone which is real and which cannot be transcended." And though one wishes that Baldwin had inserted "naturalistic novel" for "protest novel," the assertion holds true. And in effect, Cleaver fails to see that he is agreeing with Baldwin when he writes: "Bigger Thomas, Wright's greatest creation, was a man in *violent, though inept rebellion* [Italics mine] against the stifling, murderous, totalitarian, white world." For it is in the nature of the naturalistic novel that the individual be so categorized, that "the gigantic, over-whelming environmental forces" which Cleaver sees so plainly, dominate and determine his very existence. Thus, for Wright, Bigger's "violent rebellion" was to be inept from the very beginning, for all of Bigger's life is "dominated by rage," and that rage has its origin and its life in the society.

But if we think—and I think that we should—in this case of Camus' "Myth of Sisyphus," how is it possible to deny that man, trapped in an oppressive environ-ment does not have beauty, power, and life? I don't think that we can. The tragedy of Wright's Bigger Thomas is not that he rages, but that Wright allows him to rage on, implying that he does so as a result of environmental forces beyond his control, and that for this reason he will continue to do so.

At this point, the myth of the American Creed looms large in the eyes of both Wright and Cleaver. For all society has to do to stifle Bigger's rage is live up to its creed (treat me right, daddy, and I'll be yours, as the popular refrain goes). Neither Wright nor Cleaver makes allowance for the fact that the American people may never live up to such a creed. And Wright, finally convinced of this fact, in 1946 set sail for Paris, leaving the rest of us Bigger Thomases to rage on—perhaps till eternity.

But the rage has now died to a whimper, and American society seems no more frightened by the "coming . . . storm" of Mailer and Cleaver, than it was by *Native Son*.

The race will only be saved, argued Du Bois, by its "talented tenth," and Cleaver comes pretty close to arguing that it will be saved only by its "masculine" Bigger Thomases. Only Baldwin adheres to the historian's formula of predicting the future in light of the past and present, and in so doing, arrives at the conclusion that salvation is impossible. This is a dangerous position to take, for Negroes are accustomed to having their doom prescribed in the old hell and damnation curses of the evangelist preacher, and few would consider the fact that it takes far more courage to do a jackknife off of the Brooklyn Bridge than to utter futile, impotent curses from the cafes of Paris, or New York City.

CHAPTER 26

Richard Wright: Beyond Nihilism

(1968)

Richard Wright believed always in the 'community of man,' and he realized that complete dedication to nihilism would make impossible the building of such a community.

Richard Wright's revealing statement concerning the literature that he wrote had little to do with literature at all. In his autobiography, *Black Boy,* Wright recorded: "There are some elusive, profound, recondite things that men find hard to say to other men; but with the Negro it is the little things of life that become hard to say, for these tiny items shape his destiny. A man will seek to express his relations to the stars; but when a man's consciousness has been riveted upon obtaining a loaf of bread, that loaf of bread is as important as the stars."

Metaphorically speaking, the choice was one between the abstract and the pragmatic, between a literature which did not, in the words of critic Stanley Braithwaite, "hover over the race question," but instead, "owed its highest allegiance to poetry," and a realistic art which dealt with the fundamental problem of being Negro in America—art which refused to either ignore or subsume the problem through adherence to critical standards acceptable to the American academic community.

Having made his choice, Richard Wright refused to compromise. Believing always that words were weapons, he dared to probe levels of experience which more timid writers bypassed. Like Goethe's Faust, he was obsessed by an insatiable desire to delve into the pits of darkness and despair in an attempt to reveal the inferno of human discontent, fear, hatred, and violence which is the most telling characteristic of twentieth century man. Having himself undergone experiences which can only be called Kafkaesque in their grotesqueness, like Coleridge's Ancient Mariner, he was ravished with a passion to tell his story, to inform the naive of the malady of terror with which "everyman," trapped in a brutal, oppressive environment, is inflicted.

For this reason, his earliest fiction was naturalistic, and there was certainly a great deal of truth in his admonition that, "All my life had shaped me for the realism, the naturalism of the modern novel . . ." Yet, neither his writings nor his experiences can be so narrowly categorized. "The Negro," writes Saunders Redding, "lives on two planes of awareness," which is close to saying that the Negro's experiences are likely to be at one and the same time both realistic and existential. To be sure, the Negro lives in a society in which his outlook upon life, his personality, and his psychological make-up are predetermined to a great degree; however, each Negro (despite the disclaimers) envisions a coming Götterdämmerung, when, like the existential hero, he undertakes the establishment of his own identity by destroying in total the oppressive, restrictive societal apparatus which he secretly loathes.

It is not true therefore, as Ralph Ellison, among others, has intimated, that Wright was stifled and restricted by the form of the naturalistic novel; for in the light of his myriad experiences, Wright could not completely adhere to the naturalistic formula. Despite his indebtedness to Emile Zola, the father of the naturalistic novel, or to Theodore Dreiser whose *Sister Carrie* had a "tremendous effect" upon him, unlike his counterparts, for Wright there was always the insurmountable barrier of color which constituted a wedge of such fortitude between reality and illusion as to produce a fiction vastly different from that of other naturalistic adherents.

But insofar as a Black writer could be true to any formula, Wright was true to the naturalistic code. Yet, he never forgot his earlier injunction that a "loaf of bread is as important as the stars." His literature, therefore, would always contain a schizophrenic quality, wavering, as did the lives of those whom he wrote about, between pragmatism and transcendence. He never lost sight of the pull of "those tremendous forces upon the individual," yet he took cognizance of the individual's obsession to crush those forces. He never ceased to marvel at "how smoothly the Black boys acted out the roles that the race had mapped out for them. Most of them were not conscious of living a special, separate, stunted way of life. Yet . . . in some period of their growing—a period they had no doubt forgotten—there had been developed in them a delicate sensitive controlling mechanism that shut off their minds and emotions from all that the white race said was taboo."

Yet, he knew, and perhaps he was his own best example, that the personality had not been totally destroyed, that all emotions had not been channeled into a predetermined direction, that the social institutions had not completely transformed 20 million people into non-thinking, non-sensitive, non-feeling robots. And never mind that men wore masks. Never mind that men refused to articulate the truth; never mind that men practiced the art of mimetics—and American Negroes have made a profession of the art—the atmosphere of hatred and fear which created Bigger Thomas is still present in modern-day America, goading and pushing each Negro across the nihilistic brink where, in one transcendent moment, he is lifted above his predetermined state, gaining a sense of manhood, identity, and social worth, through the only means possible in an oppressive society—the medium of violence.

This is the reality of Bigger Thomas ignored by white and Black critics alike. There can, however, be no doubt of Bigger's transcendence. In Book One of *Native Son,* Bigger Thomas is, indeed, the mechanical robot, the prototype of the naturalistic character: "[He] had the feeling that the robbing of Blum's would be a violation of ultimate taboo; it would be a trespassing into territory where the full wrath of an alien white world would be turned loose upon [him;] it would be a symbolic challenge of the white world's rule over [him;] a challenge which [he] yearned to make, but [was] afraid." The Bigger Thomas of Book Two, however, transcends this fear. This section is appropriately labeled "Flight"—for it signifies not only Bigger's flight from the law, but also his flight from the frightened, unsure boy of Book One to whom "white folks formed a kind of superworld." "The thought of what he had done," Wright elaborates after Bigger murders Mary Dalton, "the awful horror of it, the daring associated with such actions, formed for him for the first time in his fear-ridden life a barrier of protection between him and a world he feared. He had murdered and created a new life for himself."

"Americans," Wright was to record much later—referring to *Native Son*—"have not been able to accept my vision," which is not completely true—Americans were capable of accepting the vision in part. Critics admit to the sanctity of the sociological argument, agree that the institutions of the American society have been repressive in regard to its Black minority; indeed, few would disagree with the indictment of the American social system leveled by Bigger's lawyer, Max. That part of the vision which Americans have not been able to accept—despite the recent yearly insurrections in the ghettos—is a nation of Bigger Thomases for whom no hope can be found, for whom no peace can come, for whom no transcendence is possible save through the flaming Armageddon of violent revolution. But on another level, as James Baldwin has pointed out, Americans have little to fear from Bigger Thomas.

The underlying thesis of *Native Son* offers hope to the American society if that society will come to the unmistakable conclusion that men live despicable lives of continuous desperation, and undertake those programs which, by resurrecting Bigger Thomas, will grant salvation to the nation as a whole. It is on this level, Baldwin's critique to the contrary, that Bigger Thomas serves as the Christ figure, the martyr to the hopes of desperate men everywhere, the catalytic agent by which a society can be redeemed.

But "Hope," writes Matthew Arnold, "once crushed is less quick to spring anew," and the Bigger Thomas of the nineteen forties is the embryo of the Bigger Thomas of the fifties and sixties. This is not to maintain, as Wright has been accused of doing, that Blacks have not made progress in the American society since the nineteen forties; but rather to suggest that progress must be measured not in terms of civil rights, material wealth, or governmental appointments but, instead, in terms of level of consciousness and the awareness by Black people of those tremendous forces of which Bigger could only conjecture—a realization that the human spirit must be free, unrestricted by either demagogic men or demagogic institutions. Wright was among the first to recognize such progress, and to create a character who serves as a footnote to Black men today—those for whom all hope has been dissipated, all optimism subsumed under the weight of constant rejection; men who see salvation not in terms of resurrecting the society, but in dismantling it *in toto* to produce a social order in which each individual will be the architect of his own destiny.

The Outsider, written twelve years after *Native Son,* is the archetype of the new spirit, the first Black character in American fiction to "dare all" in an existential attempt to stave off personal dehumanization. In Damon, the bridge from Bigger Thomas to nihilistic man is traversed, for "by the nature of things such a man sooner or later [was] bound to appear. Modern man sleeps in the myths of the Greeks and Jews. Those myths are now dying in his head and in his heart. They can no longer serve him. When they are really gone, those myths, *man* returns . . . and what's to guide him? Nothing at all but his own desires, which would be his only values."

Such a vision was totally rejected by Americans, both Black and white. A nation of men clutching a dream which has long since become a nightmare for most of its citizens, a nation whose people are daily tranquilized by the rhetoric of its leaders portraying a land of freedom, promise, and opportunity while one tenth of its population knows only misery, despair, and frustration—is it any wonder that such a nation would be incapable of accepting the existence of a character for whom the society is so degenerate as to produce a savage obsession to destroy everything that society has constructed?

Even Wright, himself, was ambivalent toward this vision. He could not accept Cross Damon as readily as he accepted Bigger Thomas, for it is Damon, not Bigger, who is the real monster, that "aberration," as one unkind critic has remarked, "upon humankind." Bigger blunders into murder, Cross skillfully executes it. Bigger's motives are guided by urges beyond his control; Damon's are premeditated, each step well calculated. Bigger desired to create a new identity; Cross desired no less than to create a new world. Bigger wants to share in the Protestant Ethic; Cross will settle only for an ethic devised by himself. Bigger is the disgruntled reformer; Cross is closer to being a nihilist, in the Camus sense, than any character in American fiction.

A "nihilist is not one who believes in nothing," writes Albert Camus, "he simply does not believe in what exists at the moment." And Wright's creation, but not Wright himself, could adhere to this philosophy. Wright believed wholeheartedly in the ethics and values which Damon—theoretically at least—wanted to destroy; and thus, Wright's most complex character got out of hand, refusing to allow his master to resurrect him even at the end of the novel. Damon remains the prophetic portrait of modern-day Black men who are putting forth the most nihilistic of questions—whether a nation which continues to physically and mentally murder and maim one-tenth of its people has any valid reason for existing.

Wright, himself, had asked a similar question before. In the short story, "Bright and Morning Star," Aunt Sue is forced to choose between saving her life and that of her son or protecting the movement which is to eventually usher in the new Jerusalem over the dying corpse of the old. Her hatred of the old system is so intense that she chooses in favor of the movement despite the tenuous position upon which the movement rests.

Wright never made such a choice. Despite periods of overwhelming doubt, he remained wedded to the theoretical concepts of Western democracy. Despite his brief excursion into the Communist party, despite his self-imposed exile, he remained convinced—as he argued in *Black Power*—that the survival of Western Civilization rested upon the co-existence and co-recognition of multi-cultures in which the sanctity of all would be inviolate.

His vision, though often varied, remained true to the theme of his earlier writings. He saw the possibility of transcendence in the Bigger Thomases of the nation, and he warned America that a nation in capable of putting its ideals into practice would produce Cross Damons seeking their manhood through a nihilistic attempt to negate the very structure of democracy itself. He reaffirmed this thesis in *White Man, Listen!* projecting his vision onto the world arena. Here he admonished the world powers, East and West, that at present the wretched of the earth could transcend their conditions only through violence, and if this remained the price that men would have to pay for individual freedom, then pay it they would.

This was Wright's final message to white men, and in light of the turbulence of the past years, the message is, perhaps, already outdated. For Wright is the last Black writer to admonish men to listen. Today, the representatives of that third force which Frantz Fanon envisioned as moving beyond existentialism to create a world order out of many varied identities no longer seek to communicate with those who continue the oppression begun by their ancestors. Each day, the lines of communication between Black man and white man in particular, and man and man in general, drift wider apart; and perhaps the telling mark of the twentieth century is the inability of one man to communicate with another.

This, Wright would not have liked. He believed always in the "community of man," and he realized that complete dedication to nihilism would make impossible the building of such a community.

True, then, to his basic ideals—to those ethics and values hewn out of the violence and terror of "those most darkest of Southern nights"—he would still believe, even at the time of his death, with André Malraux that "every man is a mad man; but what is a human destiny for if not to unite the mad man with the universe?"

CHAPTER 27

Langston Hughes: A Simple Commentary

(1967)

"The Poet of the People"

> From his writings, from his public lectures, from his private
> conversations, that enthusiasm, that love for the people, so
> Dostoyevskian in its intensity, pervaded everything that he said.

When I last saw Langston Hughes, he was off again on one of those endless odysseys to read his poetry and to make a little of that money which people always assumed, erroneously, that he had. I first met him on such an odyssey. He had traveled to our high school in Virginia, read his poetry and chatted with students and teachers. Though, to my knowledge, none of us had ever met a real live poet before, Hughes in no way measured up to our expectations of what a poet should be. Even in that segregated school, our models for literature and success were white; and we were led to believe that a poet could only be white—tall with blue eyes and a shock of long, black wavy hair. We read Emerson, Bryant, Wordsworth, and Coleridge and modeled our images of what a poet should be like upon the patterns presented to us by our teachers.

No place had been set aside in our world for a Hughes, and though we were amused and encouraged by him, still we felt somehow betrayed, for a Negro poet was as alien to our comprehension as a Negro President. Yet he stayed with us for a short time, laughing, talking, and assuring, and then he was gone. And we went back to Emerson, Bryant, Wordsworth, and Coleridge.

He was the only Negro poet who ever came to us, and though none of us realized it at that time, he destroyed something fundamental within us. Despite what our teachers told us, Emerson, Bryant, Wordsworth, and Coleridge would never again have the same effect upon us. For though we had excluded Hughes from our minds, shut him out like some Oedipus, still that distorted image of what constituted a literary figure was tarnished, if not completely negated.

Some time after his visit, many of us turned to Negro literature for the first time, to poems by McKay, Hughes, Johnson, and Dunbar, to novels by Wright, Redding, Himes, and Fauset. At each point of awareness, we became a little more embittered by the assumption that our elders had made about us, of our eagerness to accept their models without benefit of a personal choice; we became even more disheartened because there was a world of ours which was so alien to us, which had been carefully hidden from us by those who should have been instrumental in revealing it to us. In that world were people who shared so many of our own experiences, hopes, and desires, and, yes, our own anguish and pain.

The rivers of which Langston Hughes sang were more real to us than those of "limpid blue crystal-line streams" which flow through so much of English and American poetry; the yearning for "*das flie-gende stunde,*" the fleeting hour of fulfillment, in a world which promised nothing but chaos, confusion, and death— that yearning so peculiar to the literature of the Western World—was, for us, most profoundly expressed in Hughes, Johnson, and McKay. And no poet, neither a Bryant nor an Arnold would ever vouchsafe lines to us which portrayed our feelings of pessimism, despair, and fear so well as those of Langston Hughes:

> We cry among the skyscrapers
> As our ancestors
> Cried among the palms in Africa
> Because we are alone
> It is night
> And we're afraid.

Four months ago, at a party given by a mutual friend, I attempted to impart some of this to Hughes. Beaming as usual, a bright smile lighting up his tired face, he listened half-heartedly, and jokingly emitted some words of thanks. Perhaps I did not completely get through to him. It is difficult to praise a man to his face without becoming sentimental; but, moreover, it is difficult to tell a writer that his writing not only made you think, not only inspired you, not only encouraged you, but, in addition, gave you that strong, silent strength which only words can give to one who must face a stronger and noisier world; and again, it is difficult to tell any human being that his words made visible to you a new universe, aglow with promise and hope.

But, perhaps he would not have believed me. For years, critics had said that he was a simple poet, a folk singer, a mere teller of tales, lacking in profundity and complexity, the message he carried, the songs he sang, devoid of pathos, energy, meaning, and direction. He was a Negro poet who could not get beyond his Negritude; and thus, they said, he could never journey to the universal paradise where the aspirations of men soar far beyond race, creed, and color.

Like Richard Wright, Hughes, too, was a Negro writer, and like Wright, he never denied it. Therefore, readers Black and white allowed his books to gather dust on bookshelves, to be untouched upon library shelves across the country. From his writings, from his public lectures, from his private conversations, that enthusiasm, that love for the people, so Dostoyevskian in its intensity, pervaded everything that he said; and for this reason, he was, like Wright, an alien, a lonely man, invisible in the literature of that country which he loved so well, and of which he sang so eloquently.

His was the fate of the Negro writer. People who knew him by name, managed to get his autograph, never read his poetry; critics who read his writings did not understand it and, therefore, dismissed it as worthless; high school teachers who rushed to any gathering to come into contact with him never taught his poetry to their students; middle class Negroes who loved to have him, a great conversationalist, as an invited guest at their suburban affairs, never read his poetry aloud to their children; the colleges of this country, their English departments in particular, which have exalted Robert Burns, dismissed Hughes completely, uttering their synonym for Negro writers: simple.

He has remained alive in literature, not because people read what he wrote—few have—but because of his frequent excursions into towns and hamlets, bringing with him, in his own humble way, the message of a people. And yet these tireless excursions, these endless odysseys, robbed him of that vitality, that youth, which may have enabled him to last a few years more.

When I said goodbye to him for the last time, he was on his way to the University of California—a university whose English department would never include a poem of his in its syllabus for American literature—to lecture and to read his poetry. He was already an old man, and the age showed even beneath the spontaneous laughter and youthful joy which attempted to buttress it. At a time when white poets and writers of his stature had retired to their estates, become seers and honored prophets of literature, he was embarking upon yet another odyssey, because at sixty-five, he did not have the money to retire. Not even those people to whom he sang so long and so passionately had rewarded him for all of his long years, his endless devotion.

"The Negro," wrote Richard Wright, "is America's metaphor"; and Langston Hughes is the metaphor for the Negro writer. Far more than his poetry, his novels, his plays, and his countless lectures; his treatment by the academic establishment is the best example of what it means to be a Negro writer in America; and in many ways, he was more fortunate than most, for his name, among those of my generation, if not a household word, is known and respected. Yet, like other rewards, posterity will more than likely escape him. Those footprints which he etched upon the sands of time will be wiped away, no trace left of their imprint. Barring a mad dash for his books now that he is dead—a dash which might have helped to keep him alive—in but a short span of time, even his name, like that of Cullen, Toomer and Locke, will be unknown to any but those who prepare dissertations, give lectures on Negro literature, and nostalgically search for a new Negro Renaissance.

The high schools and colleges which denied him in life will continue, unless something radical happens to America's educational system, to deny him in death and, thereby, to doom him to extinction; for, unfortunately, literary figures are kept alive in our high schools, colleges, and universities. Another generation of

Negro youngsters, therefore, will not be as fortunate as those of my generation, will have no choice but Bryant, Emerson, Wordsworth, and Coleridge.

This is the tragedy of America; and it is this which causes the pain, the anguish, and the despair voiced by the Negro intellectual in the cry for "Black Power." We are denied our own heroes, our own prophets, our own songsters because of a group of narrow-minded, insecure little men have determined, *a priori,* that such songsters, prophets, and heroes are not good enough. In English departments across this nation, both Black and white, the shroud is wrapped securely around the corpse of the Negro writer.

Perhaps they are right. Perhaps, as they argue, Langston Hughes was not a great poet; perhaps he carried no message of profundity; perhaps his was a simple world unlike—and this will come as a surprise to many critics—that world of Jesse B. Semple. Perhaps! And yet, these are observations which no small group of men should be allowed to make arbitrarily; value judgments which should, at best, be made in concert with those who will be the beneficiaries of the judgment.

Instead, critics, Black and white, dismiss the Negro writer, hand down arbitrary judgments concerning him, in the same fashion in which Hughes has been arbitrarily dismissed on the college campuses of America. Hughes was a Negro poet, and therefore inconsequential; he was a poet of his people, and despite Robert Burns, John Millington Synge, and William Butler Yeats, a poet should not be a poet of a particular group of people, but of all the people; he wrote of drunken Negroes, of sad Negroes, of happy Negroes, of confused Negroes, in the same vein in which John Gay wrote of Englishmen with similar characteristics. Yet Hughes, but not Gay, was accused of writing of "trivial things." Like Wordsworth and Burns, Hughes' language was meant to be the "language of the people," yet unlike his "mainstream" predecessors, his verse was labeled simple. Yet, most Negroes know that his verse was not simple; neither was his life. He lived the role of the greatest tragedian on any stage, and throughout his writing, for the life that he lived, that life of joy sometimes, and sorrow sometimes, is the life that most Negroes live. Few can give voice to their anguish and despair as Hughes was able to do; none can so adequately justify the ways of Negroes to the world as Hughes does so well in all of his writings; none can keep him safe for posterity, for Negroes are powerless to do so against the army of academicians who wait like vultures to dismember his corpse still further. His reputation as "the poet of the people" cannot be kept alive in a world which seeks, as we rush faster toward the Armageddon of integration, to negate the people.

All that one can do is to remember that there once lived a writer, proud to be a "Negro writer," who never disowned either his heritage or his people; a poet who came before us, lived among us, and died. This is, no doubt, a simple commentary upon the life of so beloved and so generous a man; and yet, a commentary undeserving of many of today's writers who have found a haven among the English departments in our best universities, because, as they point out so vociferously, they are not "Negro writers" but "American writers."

CHAPTER 28

The Literature of Protest

(1965)

The Negro college student in the North is ofttimes completely uninformed about the history, trends, or value of Negro literature. This is attributable, in part, to the colleges themselves: their English departments, in particular, which are often all white. It is possible, as I did, to major in English Literature and not read one poem, essay, or novel by a Negro author.

The student, then, must on his own, and in addition to the tremendous amount of work which the curriculum itself demands, inform himself as to the newest in Negro literature. This often takes the form of literary criticism, which is derelict, usually, in both white and Negro publications.

The result, therefore, is a completely distorted picture, not only of the literature—but also of the ideas of the author himself. The distortion in these areas is propounded into a distortion of the society itself; and yet even more important is the effect upon the student, for what he derives from the literary criticism of Negro writers is the assertion that, far from being master craftsman, sensitive and thoughtful creators, the Negro author is a mere propagandist, a protester who cannot get outside of his own neurotic personality.

But in the final analysis, what does this really come to? It would seem—and many white literary critics are of this opinion—that Negro writers do not write about interesting subjects. (As one English instructor told me, "If you want to write, you have to move outside of your Negritude.") But if it is true that Negro writers do not write about interesting subjects, and if we remember that Negro writers write about Negroes, then the inescapable conclusion is that Negroes are unimportant people.

The assumption on both levels is a dangerous one. And what such an assumption does, more than anything else, is to indicate the all-pervasive nature of the discriminatory mentality of the American society. For, as Baldwin has pointed out, the saving grace for white Americans is the knowledge that despite any calamity, at least they are not Black; and I am sure that the white South African, and indeed white Europeans in general, at some point in their lives, gain solace from this fact. The result, therefore, is to make the Negro in particular and Black man in general, a separate entity within the universe, whose problems have no relevance to the larger world in which we live.

Thus, the Negro author is seen as propounding particular and not universal truths. Despite Auschwitz and Dachau, men would still, somehow, believe that suffering is germane to one particular group, that the victimization of men by other men, the destruction of men, women and children by forces beyond their control, which defy their concerted efforts of defense, are not universalized, but particular and peculiar to one group, one race or one individual.

And yet, if this is so, where does one draw the line between Ralph Ellison's invisible man and Kafka's Joseph K? Where does Joyce's *Portrait of An Artist* become more universal than Wright's *Black Boy?* And, finally, how do the countless number of themes which come out of Dickens' major novels differ in universality, in appeal to all men, from the themes that come out of the writings of James Baldwin?

Human Problems Portrayed

Yes, it is true that Baldwin says something for me that Ernest Hemingway could never say; and yet, Kafka says something for me that Frank Yerby could never approach. The belief that the Negro writer portrays an insulated world of his own construction is a myth which should no longer be propounded in the purported enlightenment of the twentieth century. There is no Negro problem, but instead a human problem, and those who fail to understand this are doomed to repeat the history of Hitler's Third Reich.

It may be possible that no white man can see himself as a Bigger Thomas; it may even be less possible that he could ever picture himself as living in the world of *Another Country;* yet if this is so, then he is unfamiliar with his own history. The overwhelming domination of an individual by his society, the power of that society to direct to a large degree his fate, and indeed to mold his character and being, is as old as Socrates. Man is not only a social animal, but even more so, he is an essential part of the conglomerate whole of the species called Homo Sapiens; and I, for one, happen to be naive enough to believe that the threat to one entity, to one individual is a threat to the whole. If I cannot feel with the Jews in Nazi Germany, and with the Black Africans in South Africa, then I am less than a human being. And too, though I have never lynched anyone, though I have never bombed a church, and though the victims of these atrocities are my own Black brothers, still I am as guilty and responsible for their occurrence as their white perpetrators, for actually, I have done nothing to stop this degradation, or perhaps, more explicitly—systematic extermination of a part of the human race. At the least, I have not done as much as I should have, because the conditions of which I write are still prevalent.

Within this naiveté, therefore, is the call for a collective responsibility, and though I am far too sophisticated—or cynical—to believe in its pragmatic application, still I know that the only hope for civilization lies in such a formulated, workable concept. Baldwin's assertion that only Negroes can understand how Negroes actually feel is correct, and yet, because it is correct, it is tragic. What it means is that whites do not understand Negroes—not that they cannot—and until they can, there will be no peace for any of us.

I cannot accept the theory that there is something peculiar about the obstacles placed against men and women in the world in which we live; suffering is common to all men and only the most inhuman of the species can look at a young Black child in the ghetto, and not think, if only subconsciously, there but for the goodness of some god, go I.

No, what happens to a Rufus or a Bigger Thomas can happen to us all; for in this age, this century, perhaps what happened to the uncle of Wright's *Black Boy*, or what happened to the four children of Birmingham, may not appear as possible to white people in this country. In some strange sense, they may feel completely alienated from it all; yet, the pendulum of history has swung backward and forward, and those who are safe today, need not be so tomorrow. Even William Faulkner was capable of envisioning that world in which the pendulum had swung back into ancient history; and the one third of mankind which is white may yet be petitioning Black governments for its human rights.

To contend, then, that the Negro writer is not a universalist is to contend that somehow, after all, men are basically different, that the Negro writer's protest against the American society is an isolated, selfish protest, applicable only to the Negro minority, that what J. Saunders Redding says about being a Negro in America stems lamely from Dr. Redding's own neuroticism, and that in the final analysis the protest is incompatible with the American Creed. ("That Baldwin," a white English instructor said to me after I had written a review on Baldwin's play, "should be taken down a peg or two; he uses white liberals to suit his own convenience. After all, what about the white liberals who agree with everything that he says?")

American Creed Attacked

The instructor was, as many are, visibly agitated about Baldwin's attack, not because the attack was not correct, but instead because the attack struck at the proponents of the American Creed. For the American Creed is a liberal, not a Southern-conservative manifestation, and any attack upon the liberals is an attack upon the ideals, aspirations and hopes expressed in the countless legislation, court decisions and documents which have proceeded since the Civil War.

Yet, no one with good conscience can disavow the legality of the attack; none of the literary critics, likewise, can disavow the legality of the Negro writer's protest. I suppose that the situation is similar in aspect to that of the young lady who, seated beside me during the showing of "Judgment at Nuremberg," turned her head and said aloud, during the showing of the films of the concentration camps, "Oh, for God's sake, they don't have to show these pictures all the time."

Thus, Negro writers should not write about American failures all the time. The remark appears to be cynical. If it means that things are not going to change anyway, no matter how much people are reminded of them, perhaps the history of America in its relationship to its Negro minority substantiates this conclusion. Yet, I think that much closer to the real answer is the fact that white Americans would rather live in what they consider to be their own reality, completely different from the reality of the other part of their society, and what the Negro protest does is to force a confrontation between the white idealistic conception of reality and the pragmatic conception which negates the American Creed. In so doing, the white American is forced to turn inward upon himself, to question his most sacred ideals, and if he is at all sensitive to admit that they are, after all, more imaginary than real.

If this is so, then, the Negro writer, and Negro protest literature in general, has made an important accomplishment. For only when men can begin to question their own truths can they postulate truths outside themselves; only then can a dichotomy between what is and what should be be initiated: and perhaps, from such a dichotomy can stem that unified vision of a world of law and justice applicable to the whole of mankind.

CHAPTER 29

Literature as Catharsis:
The Novels of Paul Laurence Dunbar

(1971)

The function of the novel as viewed by Henry Fielding—to entertain and to instruct—was one which William Wells Brown could not possibly adhere to. When he wrote *Clotel; or the President's Daughter* in 1853, he was on British shores, an exile from America; yet he remained conscious of the war for human dignity and freedom taking place in his native land. His awareness of, and his devotion to that war determined his outlook upon the new genre, the novel. Unfortunately, he left us no guidelines, no written instructions concerning the form which this new genre should take. If we look closely at *Clotel,* however, we might surmise that Brown viewed the novel as one more instrument in the abolitionist arsenal of weapons. His contemporary, Frank Webb, author of *The Garies and Their Friends* (1857), seems to come closer to accepting Fielding's stipulations; however, *The Garies and Their Friends* is as much protest against the plight of Northern Blacks, who undergo varied forms of discrimination, as it is instruction to the Afro-American middle class. With the publication of Martin Delany's *Blake, or the Huts of America* (1861), the notion that the Afro-American novelist would follow the prescription of Fielding, a proscription adopted by such American writers as James Fenimore Cooper and Nathaniel Hawthorne, is soon discarded. The novel is unmitigated protest, aimed at depicting the plight of Black men in America and abroad.

From the outset, then, the Afro-American novelist viewed the function of the novel differently than did his English and American counterparts. This view was shaped by the life he lived, a life which differed markedly from that of other writers. His was a life of chaos and turmoil, and, be he abolitionist or private citizen, the proscriptions which bound other black men applied equally to him: the lives of desperation lived by his fellows under bond were similar to his own, though his was lived, usually, on a higher plane of desperation. Spurred on by an atmosphere of revolt and pregnant with incipient revolution, when he sought to construct an art form, he forged it out of the steel and iron of his own experiences, thus creating a weapon of warfare to be used in the interest of black liberation.

Looking back upon these early novelists, we know that the direction in which they moved, away from the prescriptions of the English and American novelists, was the correct one. They thought of the new genre not as a vehicle for entertainment or instruction as such, but one to spur men to action; to move nations and races towards a new morality; and to prepare the way for the New Canaan soon to be erected—or so they believed—on American shores. Yet, innovative as they were, we know now that they failed to grasp the realities of the age in which they lived; that they were ignorant of the war being waged for the minds of men. More interested in freeing men's bodies than their minds, they were oblivious of the truth articulated by Richard Wright in 1936, that they had the ability "to fuse and make articulate the experiences of men," and "to create the myths and symbols which inspire a faith in life."

In other words, they were so obsessed with the novel as a weapon in the abolitionist struggle, that they did not realize its importance as a vehicle for creating positive images and symbols of black men, images for which paradigms existed in great numbers in black communities North and South. This failure accounts for the stultifying search for identity in the literature of many black writers who followed; and it contributed, in part, to the attempt of such novelists as Paul Laurence Dunbar to seek to escape what he believed to be images of degradation, and to adopt those of positive import. With the possible exception of Frank Yerby, no Afro-American novelist has been more confused concerning his true identity or worth as a black writer than was Dunbar. And none succeeded so well in using the novel form as a vehicle for vicarious identification with symbols drawn from an alien world.

What image was he attempting to escape? There were several, and Sterling Brown, in "Negro Characters as Seen by White Authors," has enumerated them for us. The one which stands out, however, is that enunciated by the narrator of John Pendleton Kennedy's *Swallow Barn:*

> I am quite sure they [black people] could never become a happier people than here. . . . No tribe of people have ever passed from barbarism to civilization whose . . . progress has been more secure from harm, more genial to their character or better supplied with mild and beneficent guardianhship, adapted to the actual state of their intellectual feebleness, than the Negroes of Swallow Barn.

It was this image—the black man as helpless, feeble-minded child—which so appalled Dunbar and caused him to seek to escape it in his novels. His dilemma is readily apparent. In most of his short fiction and in many of his poems, he championed such images with unmatched gusto, perhaps, even by the Plantation School of writers, who are credited with first creating the image. In his novels, however, he attempts to move outside of them in two ways: first, by adopting a persona; second, by confronting them and moving, existentially, beyond them. To suggest, with Benjamin Brawley, that he pandered to the popular taste in his short fiction and in his dialect poetry, seems too simplistic an explanation. The truth, I believe, is that he lacked literary models from his own contemporaries and forerunners. In addition, he lacked a literary tradition dedicated to validating the dignity and worth of the Afro-American. For a writer as sensitive as Dunbar, one so wracked by spiritual turmoil, such a lack produced, I believe, a schizophrenia causing him to question whether he would see himself as black man as represented in the fiction of the Plantation School or as "the American Man" in general—he who had built the great cathedrals and railroads, created the enduring literature, and established the "official" institutions. Out of this psychological dilemma, two images emerged to dominate his writing. One is found in his short stories, dialect poetry, and in two of his novels, *The Fanatics* and *The Sport of the Gods;* the other, in his poetry written in standard English and in his two other novels, *The Uncalled* and *The Love of Landry.* One image represents Blacks; the other, "man," as Paul Laurence Dunbar wished himself to be: free, white, and independent.

How much this dilemma was made more acute by William Dean Howells's critical appraisal of Dunbar's poetry, first issued in 1896, and repeated one year later, is difficult to estimate, though one suspects that the limitations and proscriptions which Howells, unknowingly perhaps, dictated, did much to force the writer to assess his own value as a man and a poet. Howells wrote:

> Yet it appeared to me then, and it appears to me now, that there is a precious difference of temperament between the races which it would be a great pity ever to lose, and that this is best preserved and most charmingly suggested by Mr. Dunbar in those pieces of his where he studies the moods and traits of his race in its own accent of our English. . . . In nothing is his essentially refined and delicate art so well shown as in these pieces, which, as I ventured to say, described the range between appetite and emotion . . . which is the range of the race. He reveals in these a finely ironical perception of the Negro's limitations. . . . These are divinations and reports of what passed in the hearts and minds of a lowly people.

To understand the slight here is to understand more about the dialect tradition than Howells probably did. We know, by the example of Douglass, Webster, and Abraham Lincoln, that one measure of intellect and manhood, for the eighteenth and nineteenth centuries, was language. At no time in American history had the old cliché that a man is known by the words that he speaks been better suited to actuality. Language, in many cases, therefore, was as indicative of the Black man's inferiority as was the color of his skin. As a consequence, the feeble-minded, half-witted man-child of the works of John Pendleton Kennedy, Irvin Russell, and Joel Chandler Harris was clearly identifiable by his "jingles in a broken tongue." But, while white practitioners of the Plantation Tradition could escape the stigma of guilt by association, Dunbar could not. When praised by Howells for revealing "a finely ironical perception of the Negro's limitations" simply by his facility with dialect verse, Dunbar was unable, without serious, mental difficulty, to dissociate himself from the images which he had propounded.

In *The Uncalled* (1898), written after Howells's review, he made the attempt at dissociation in the longer fictional form. The central metaphor of this first novel is rebellion from the restrictions of old mores and folk ways. It is, simultaneously, however, a metaphor for freedom—freedom from the restrictions of racial stereotypes. The plot itself is slight. Freddie Brent and his mother are abandoned in the town of Dexter, Ohio, by a wastrel father. When the mother dies, the orphan is adopted by the town spinster, Hester Prime, who, against the boy's wishes, educates him for the ministry. The thematic structure of the novel is now apparent: the conflict is between the young Brent and the religious parochialism of the people in the town. When Brent, having achieved ordination, refuses to preach a sermon against a "fallen woman," he surrenders the pulpit and a chance at marriage and success. In so doing, he moves outside the self-imposed code voiced earlier in the novel: "When fate is fighting with all her might against a human soul, the greatest victory that the soul can win is to reconcile itself to the unpleasant which is never so unpleasant afterwards."

Here is a strange intrusion in this naturalistic novel. The protagonist, destined to a life dictated by some "fate infinitely more powerful than his own," moves, in existential fashion, outside of his prescribed destiny. When he leaves the town of Dexter, he has moved toward redefining the terms which previously governed his existence, has stepped outside the traditional patterns, in order to create new ones—of his own making. The parallels between Brent and the author are unmistakable: Both had reached the threshold of success; one, the fictional creation, however, surrendered success in favor of individuality and freedom, while the other, the creator, could achieve freedom from tradition and restraint only through vicarious identification with his character. In private correspondence, in gatherings with friends, and in several of his poems in standard English, Dunbar openly revolted against what he viewed to be the limitations imposed upon him by Howells and his followers: "One critic says a thing," he related to a friend, "and the rest hasten to say the same thing, in many cases using identical words. I see now very clearly that Mr. Howells has done me irrevocable harm in the dictum he laid down regarding my dialect verse."

Instead of public revolt or confrontation with Howells, however, Dunbar sought to register his revolt by picturing himself as outside the negative images and symbols which the dialect tradition adumbrated. "He did not say," writes Saunders Redding, "that he was looking at white characters from a colored point of view. He simply assumed inherent emotional, intellectual, and spiritual identity with his characters." It is not too far wrong to suggest, therefore, that from Dunbar's perspective in *The Uncalled*, Freddie Brent was Paul Laurence Dunbar, and Paul Laurence Dunbar was Freddie Brent. In that unknown world where the author chooses his focus and point of view toward his characters, Dunbar associated himself with a character whose skin color moved him beyond the stigmata of inferiority and degradation; in so doing, he moved beyond the prescription of the Afro-American novel as handed down from Brown to Charles Chesnutt; he suggested, that is to say, that the function of the novel is to serve as the vehicle for catharsis.

This was possible, however, only in a personal sense. *The Uncalled* was published in the same year as a collection of short fiction, *Folks from Dixie* (1898). Most of the stories in this volume dealt with stereotypes; yet, *Folks from Dixie* received praise, whereas *The Uncalled* received disparagement. That Dunbar, a Black man, could masquerade as a white youth, struck his audience as insincere, and they quickly showed their preference for the old image by prating about the collection of short stories far in excess of its artistic merit. Far from dissuading Dunbar from other such ventures, however, the preference of his audience for traditional images exacerbated his own personal problems and caused him to seek to negate his identity all the more. The personal problems were pressing. Marriage difficulties had occurred as early as 1899; a terrible bout with pneumonia resulted in the weakening of his lungs, which made his body susceptible to tuberculosis—later the cause of his death. The inability of his public to award him praise and recognition for his verse in standard English helped push him into alcoholism. When he journeyed to Colorado, in 1899, to revive his health, be was an invalid, and the ills which beset him were both mental and physical. *The Love of Landry* (1900) his second novel, is the result of that illness.

If *The Uncalled* was naturalistic in form, veering sharply toward an existential bent at the end, *The Love of Landry,* a romantic novel, maintains its form throughout. In this shallowly plotted work, the conflict centers about a romantic triangle. Sought after by Arthur Heathcote, an Englishman who "smells of civilization," Mildred Osborne, daughter of wealthy parents, travels west, and falls in love with Landry Thayer, a ranch hand. Defying the wishes of her parents, and rejecting the attention of Heathcote, Mildred settles upon Thayer as her mate. In true Victorian fashion, this is not accomplished until Thayer has saved the heroine's life during a cattle stampede and is proved to be an heir and gentleman who had surrendered a fortune to fulfill his desire to live free of the restraints of civilization.

Dunbar's attempt to appropriate symbols and images for his fiction from his autobiography is even more discernible in his second novel than in the first. Mildred, like the author, suffers from tuberculosis. Despite her affliction, however, she is robust, spontaneous, and happy. Landry, whose name is too obviously a symbol of land, of earth, represents natural man in retreat from the "enslaving arms of civilization." Analogous to Freddie Brent, he surrenders one identity for another, and his daredevil rescue of the heroine evidences his freedom even from the fear of death. Though Heathcote is a poor stereotype of an Englishman, he is symbolic of an ordered, respected tradition, wherein a man's worth is evaluated in terms of his individual achievement. More personally, the attempt of the spinster aunt to separate the two lovers has its parallel in Dunbar's own life—his mother-in-law had led a long campaign to separate the poet and his wife.

The conflict, mirrored in the heroine and hero, who fight the lonely fight against tradition and restriction, is a conflict central to the author's life. A Black writer, seething with silent revolt, desiring freedom from rules and restrictions, he used the medium most natural to portray revolt—the novel. And as he had done in *The Uncalled,* in order to register his protest, he dons the mask of white men, thus lending his own weight to the negative images which he despised, validating the arguments of those who championed the superiority of white images over those of Blacks.

How far along this road of self-doubt and confused identity Dunbar had traveled can be seen when he depicts a major Black character in the longer fictional genre. Here the schizophrenia has reached acute form. Thus far, in *The Uncalled* and *The Love of Landry,* he had been free from confrontation with his Blackness; he had refused to allow Blacks entry into the genre. He wrote of Freddie Brent and Landry Thayer and affected an emotional identification with them, without being forced to disparage or denigrate the images and symbols of his Afro-American heritage. This problem was not acute in the short stories or in the dialect poetry. These were written for entertainment and held by the author in lower esteem than was the novel. Further, the poems in standard English, in their own way, satirized the material produced to satisfy the dialect vogue.

To interject a Black man into the novel alongside the images which he had appropriated from the outside world, however, presented a problem—how could he depict such characters and maintain his identification with the others? Having created Freddie Brent in the image of Paul Laurence Dunbar, could he now create a Black man in the same image without casting aspersion, in his own mind, upon his newly adopted identity? Such questions are answered in the negative in his third novel, *The Fanatics* (1901), where Nigger Ed, the Black character, is created in the images bequeathed Afro-American literature from the Plantation School of writers.

The Fanatics, a historical romance, centers upon events during the American Civil War. Two old Ohio families, the Van Dorens and the Waters, are on opposite sides in the contest. Bradford Waters sympathizes with the Union, Stephen Van Doren with the Confederacy. The conflicts between the two scions are reflected in the citizenry of the town, who are equally divided in loyalty toward the Union and the Confederacy. The tension generated by the conflict is exemplified in the affair between Mary, daughter of Waters, and Robert, son of Van Doren. When Robert joins the Confederate forces, Waters insists that his daughter break their engagement. Mary's rebellion against parental authority is explained by the author: "She loved Bob, not his politics. What had she to do with those Black men down there in the South, it was none of her business." Neither were "those men down there," the business of the town. When the escaping slaves attempt to enter the town, they are opposed by Loyalist and Union sympathizers alike: "For the time all party lines fell away, and all the people were united in one cause—resistance of the Black horde." Waters, Van Doren, and the townspeople are equally fanatical concerning the Black men and the war, and the keynote of the novel is sounded by the wife of Waters's son: "Every one is mad, you and I and all of us. When shall we come to our senses?"

Such a question is one which might have been asked of the age itself. Warfare between Blacks and whites on the social and political front had increased tenfold by 1901. The Black exodus from South to North had gained momentum; lynchings and mass murder, symbolized by the Wilmington, North Carolina, riot of 1898—the catalyst which propelled Charles Chesnutt to write *The Marrow of Tradition*—were almost daily occurrences. The compact initiated in 1895 between Booker T. Washington and the white industrialists had been all but nullified by young, courageous Black men like Du Bois and Monroe Trotter. Given these historical realities, the American Civil War, the product of national strife, might have served as the metaphor for a different kind of war—that between the races, which raged as intently in its own way as that between North and South during the eighteen sixties.

A novel of such dimensions might have been possible for a writer free from his own mental and spiritual dilemma. For Dunbar, however, beset with the old problems of marriage, identity, and the failure to achieve personal recognition commensurate with his expectations, the task was impossible. Fidelity to craft would have mandated that a novel dealing realistically with the Civil War accurately portray the Black man's part in it. To do this, Dunbar would have to step objectively away from his own problem of identity, and to project positive images of Black men and women. Such might have been possible before *The Uncalled*. By the time he wrote *The Fanatics,* however, he could look at Black people only through the eyes of Freddie Brent, and thus his perception, for all intents and purposes, was as distorted as those of his white contemporaries.

Take Nigger Ed, for example. The plan of the novel was to show Ed's evolution from town drunkard and buffoon to town hero. The character whom we meet in the beginning of the novel, who "has a picturesque knack for lying," is analogous to Nelse of *The Leopard's Spots,* and Thomas Dixon's description of his Black character is apropos Dunbar's description of Nigger Ed: "A Black hero of the old regime." What Dixon praised as heroic were obsequious behavior, childlike devotion and loyalty, and quirks of speech and gesture serving to entertain white people. Both characters were drawn from the Southern mythology and folklore which created the terms by which Black men were to be defined; both are the feeble-minded, darky-clowns of Southern literature. Viewed in this fashion, it is impossible to take seriously the proclamation at the end of Dunbar's novel that "there were women who begged him [Ed] to come in and talk to them about their sons who had been left on some Southern field, wives who wanted to hear over and over again the last words of their loved one"; nor is it possible to believe that the town buffoon, now become hero, is accepted by the same people who refused to accept Black contraband during the war: "They gave him a place for life and everything be wanted."

Dunbar himself could not have believed in the evolution of Ed; yet, in terms of his own problems of identity, he could have portrayed Ed no other way. In this first confrontation with a Black character in serious fiction, he moved to validate the stereotype, to cast his voice with those who averred that Mammy Peggy, Rev. Elisha Edwards, and Gideon, from the short fiction, were representatives of a unique species of humanity. Adhering to the truncated Darwinism of his old friend, Booker Washington, he suggests now, that there are superiors and inferiors, and he has answered the question which haunted him before—to which category did he belong? Freddie Brent may have been Paul Laurence Dunbar; Nigger Ed certainly was not. Ed was the key to the resolution of the artistic question of perspective. Dunbar, having come face to face with a Black man in his novels, and having portrayed him in the form of the old Plantation Tradition, could feel more secure in his own adopted identity, could pursue the route established in the short stories, step back from his material with that objective perspective which white critics deemed necessary to the creation of lasting and enduring art. *The Fanatics* freed the author to deal with Black men in novel form on the same terms that they were dealt with by white writers.

To substantiate this thesis, one need only turn to Dunbar's last novel, *The Sport of the Gods* (1902). The opening lines voice the author's intention to move away from the spirit of the Plantation Tradition: "Fiction has said so much in regret of the old days when there were plantations and overseers and masters and slaves that it was good to come upon such a household as Berry Hamilton's, if for no other reason than that it afforded a relief from the monotony of tiresome iteration." Once Dunbar begins to deal with his Black characters, however, the plan is laid aside.

Berry Hamilton, trusted, loyal, butler on the estate of Maurice Oakley, is the major protagonist. He and his wife, Fannie, their two children, Kit and Joe, are members of the Black middle class, increasing in number at the turn of the century. In contrast to the old Afro-American middle class, built upon caste, this new middle class is delineated by the power and influence it exerts in the Black community, and its close proximity to the real seat of power—white people. The Hamilton family are respected members of the Black community. They are pillars of the Black church, scions of Negro society, and they are admired and envied by Blacks of lesser attainments. Like the characters of Frank Webb's *The Garies and Their Friends,* they are content to rule in hell, while paying proper obeisance to heaven.

When Francis, wastrel brother of Maurice, steals money in order to finance his playboy activities abroad, disaster strikes the Hamilton family. The loyal servant for over forty years is framed for the theft, and the employer has little trouble in accepting his guilt: "The Negroes are becoming less faithful and less contented, and more's the pity, . . . more ambitious." Circumstantial evidence points toward Hamilton's guilt; the butler is remanded to jail, and his family expelled from the Oakley estate.

The incarceration of the breadwinner, and the expulsion of his wife and children, allows Dunbar to shift his characters from South to North, and to examine Black people in a new and different setting. Once again, the author travels the old Plantation Tradition road: away from the paternalistic arms of their white supporters, the family quickly disintegrates. Fannie is tricked into marriage with a brutal man; Kit enters upon a hapless career as a show girl; after succumbing to the temptation to become a dandy, Joe murders his sweetheart. Commenting on the disaster which overtakes the Hamilton family up North, Dunbar remarks, "Oh, is there no way to keep these people from rushing away from the small villages and country districts of the South up to tree cities, where they cannot battle with the terrible force of a strange and unusual environment? . . . The South has its faults . . . and its disadvantages, but . . . even what they suffered from these was better than what awaited them in the great alleys of New York."

When Dunbar invokes the aid of a *deus ex machina* to reunite Fannie and Berry and to return them to their Southern environment, the point is driven home. Hamilton is released from jail after a white reporter proves his innocence and Francis's guilt; the shock of the revelation sends Maurice Oakley to an early grave. Fannie's new husband is killed in a drunken brawl, and, reuniting with Berry, the two, minus their children, travel back to the waiting arms of the Widow Oakley, who "heard of their coming, and with her own hands re-opened and refurnished the little cottage in the yard for them. There the white-haired woman begged them to spend the rest of their days and be in peace and comfort."

Paternalism is the key to Dunbar's treatment of both Nigger Ed and Berry Hamilton, and this was an attitude devoted exclusively to Black characters. Both Ed and Hamilton are to be cared for by white benefactors, to be *given* everything they need for the rest of their lives. In a society of men, such charity is unthinkable, and it is not too far wrong to suggest that because Dunbar wanted to see himself as Freddie Brent, Landry Thayer, or the Waterses and Van Dorens, his psychological difficulties prevented him from regarding Black men as other than wards of American society. As a result, outside of his white personae, he was incapable of viewing himself as other than the sport of the gods, incapable of imputing heroism and grandeur to those made in his own image.

Dunbar was a victim of his age. His predecessors, who had wavered between formulating a theory of literature which would redefine the old definitions and one which would serve as an instrument to assault the conscience of white men, had failed him. The hard task of constructing new images and symbols had been left to their successors. Consequently, they failed to till the ground for such talented writers as Dunbar, who as a result, was forced to deal with the images and stereotypes of Black people as laid down in the literature of Southern and Northern propagandists.

What kind of instrument might the Afro-American novel have become had its first creators set out to depict the realities of Black life, to record the heroism of those who survived the holocaust of the middle passage and slavery, who lived and struggled despite terror and despondency, who dreamed always of a new world a coming for their successors? What models for positive images and symbols might have become the material of the novel had the artist drawn upon the experiences of those many thousands gone—of Frederick Douglass, David Walker, Harriet Tubman, Nat Turner, and others too numerous to list?

Dunbar had no such models, and this lack greatly affected his art, and his life. As he came to accept the images of the Plantation School of writers, as he continued to depict such characters in his own short stories and poetry, he was forced to confront a dilemma of schizophrenic proportions: Could he move outside the racial restrictions by adopting the mask of his oppressors? An examination of his life proves that he could not. For the characteristics which separated him from the Freddie Brents of the world went beyond color, to the depths of man's spiritual anguish and despair; to have surrendered this would have meant to have surrendered a body of literature still alive with meaning and promise for our times. Such a surrender would not have been salvation, but madness.

CHAPTER 30

The Dialectic of *The Fire Next Time*

(1965)

A philosophical approach to The Negro intellectual who is confronted with the fire next time and also faces a dilemma in the transformation of America.

"James Baldwin" wrote Langston Hughes, "is threatening America with the fire next time"; which is not an accurate statement, though a statement which reveals the state of mind of a majority of American intellectuals when confronted by the Baldwin dialectic.

Strangely enough, the confrontation is more difficult for Negro intellectuals who—contrary to Louis Lomax and John O. Killens—do not "see America as it really is." This is, simply, another myth added to that vast storehouse of myths which have enabled Negroes to survive in a hostile society. Supposedly, the Negro, in seeing America as it really is, is then the real American, a sort of Emersonian sage, capable of penetrating the veil of reality, but, even more so, a Christ figure who can resurrect fallen America, absolve her of her sins, and transform her—if not into another Eden—at least into another country.

But this myth, like all myths, disintegrates under the penetrating analysis of a James Baldwin, and the Negro intellectual, when confronted with Baldwin's prophetic utterances, can only rely on the feeble rationalization—"Baldwin doesn't really believe this."

"'My Dungeon Shook,'" remarked a friend, "is a good essay, but it has nothing to do with 'The Fire Next Time' (the second essay in the book), that is simply an exercise in rhetoric." My friend was unable to move beyond the myth propounded in the first essay to the prophesy which destroys the myth in the second. And this is because he refused to be drawn into the dialectic, refused, in other words, to confront the reality of *The Fire Next Time*.

For in one sense, the two essays represent two poles of a dialectic—the ideal as opposed to the real; and, in another sense, the second essay viciously satirizes the first. "My Dungeon Shook" could well have been written by Martin Luther King, and perhaps this is why the Negro intellectual is comfortable with it.

Here, the Negro is indeed the Christ figure, who can regenerate this sinful society through the power of love—"You must love them," writes Baldwin, in one of the most ironic lines in all of literature—and the Negro comes from a reading of this essay enthused with a feeling of power, harboring visions of himself as the great redeemer, if not creator, finding at last some rationalization for one hundred and fifty years of humility and subservience.

This is fine. If Baldwin had gone no further, he would have been considered a man of letters, capable of wearing the mantle of Emerson, as one of America's great essayists, instead of a poor man's Byronic hero, a propagandist, carrying, to paraphrase Matthew Arnold, the pageant of his bleeding heart throughout America.

But Baldwin wrote "The Fire Next Time" and completely demolished the idyllic vision propounded in "My Dungeon Shook." The Negro may well be Christ, but if so, he is a Christ who was a sunbaked fanatic, not a restorer or redeemer. And Baldwin makes Godhood so loathsome, that only a misanthrope would ascribe to the position.

"Perhaps," wrote Nietzsche, "Socrates really deserved his cup of hemlock," and Baldwin comes close to suggesting that the "fanatic" may well have deserved his cross. And it is here that the dialectic is forced. For the fire will come about, not at the given sign of a deity, but instead, because of the inability of the society to construct its principles upon a code of laws, which has nothing to do with deities. We are close to Nietzsche's Zarathustra, for only by erecting a new set of laws can the society be redeemed. And in such a society there is no place for gods. Indeed, in theme, Baldwin is, here, perhaps, borrowing from Thomas Hardy: America's initial mistake was slavery, and having made that mistake, she has been consistently drawn from one experience to another, almost fatalistically, toward that inevitable fire next time.

And those who suggest that Baldwin is positing an as-if dichotomy in the two essays are misreading Baldwin. There are no gods, Baldwin is suggesting, Black or white (isn't this what got us into all of this trouble in the first place?), and the society can only be redeemed by conscious acts of its own, but (and this is what makes Baldwin the greatest ironist since Jane Austen) the society is incapable of such acts.

In the final analysis, then, the fate of society rests upon people, and people, as history has shown, have always been pretty shaky resting places. But, more so, the Negro is an American, Baldwin pounds home in essay after essay, and—LeRoi Jones to the contrary—incapable of breaking the Faustian pact. To think of him, therefore, as an American on the one hand, and as a Christ figure on the other, is absurd.

The Negro cannot transform America, cannot redeem her, cannot absolve her of her sins; thus, we are again with the Negro intellectual who must break with Baldwin at this point. For, as Baldwin suggests—perhaps most explicitly in *Blues for Mr. Charlie*—whites will not resurrect their society, and Negroes cannot: therefore, the crushing realization that the society will not be resurrected.

The myth dissolves at this point, and the Negro intellectual, who must cling to the myth at all costs, utters his pitiable moan, "Baldwin doesn't really believe this," not realizing that whether Baldwin believes it or not, history supports the assertion. The problem, then, for the Negro intellectual is to confront the dialectic in *The Fire Next Time;* and perhaps in so doing, he will realize that the American dilemma cannot be solved by postulating a Black redeemer, who in all respects will probably turn out, under close scrutinization, to be as helpless—if not as fanatical—as the white one.

PART 4

Book Introductions, Forewords, and Prefaces

> Few, I believe, would argue with my assertion that the black artist, due
> to his historical position in America at the present time, is engaged
> in a war with this nation that will determine the future of black art.
> Likewise, there are few among them—and here again, this is only
> conjecture—who would disagree with the idea that unique experiences
> produce unique cultural artifacts, and that art is a product of such
> cultural experiences. To push this thesis to its logical conclusion, unique
> art derived from unique cultural experiences mandates unique critical
> tools for evaluation. Further than this, agreement need not go!
> —Addison Gayle Jr. *The Black Aesthetic*

Following his commitment to developing a blueprint for black literary criticism
and defining the function of the black critic, Gayle wrote introductions, prefaces,
and forewords for black writers he encouraged and for whom in his estimation
evoked aspects of the black aesthetic in their works.

Section four, "Book Introductions, Forewords, and Prefaces" consists of the
prefatory material Gayle wrote for numerous novels, biographies, plays, and collections by prominent Black Arts artists such as Woodie King, Charles Russell,
and John Oliver Killens.

Also included in this section are the introductions to Gayle's biographies on
Richard Wright, Claude McKay, and Paul Laurence Dunbar, along with the in-
troduction to collections of essays and cultural analyses he compiled and edited
such as *Black Expression* (1969), *Bondage, Freedom and Beyond* (1979), *The Black
Situation* (1970), *The Black Aesthetic* (1971), and the introduction and afterword of
Gayle's monumental historical analysis of the black novel—*The Way of the New
World: The Black Novel in America* (1975).

CHAPTER 31

Youngblood

by John Oliver Killens

(1982)

Foreword

"We must," wrote the novelist Louis Ferdinand Céline, "tell everything that we have seen of man's viciousness." For the French writer whose novel *Journey to the End of Night* explores the depths of man's depravity and inhumanity, human history was little more than a compendium of one atrocity after another. Unwilling to believe with Theodore Adorno that there should be no poetry after Auschwitz, Céline insisted that the function of the poet was to pass the record of man's failures from one generation to another. There have been few such theses in Afro-American literature, primarily, one supposes, because the many Auschwitzes undergone by Black Americans have simply strengthened the desire of Black poets to view humankind from many varied perspectives.

Few poets are more representative of this view than John Oliver Killens, whose novel *Youngblood,* published first in 1954, remains one of the classics of American literature. Coming at a point in time when the Afro-American novelist explored, almost exclusively, the Northern urban environment, when Ralph Ellison and James Baldwin were impressing many critics with their tales of alienated existential Blacks searching for a tenuous American identity, *Youngblood* returns to the terrain explored so well by Richard Wright and becomes a novel that serves as a symbol of the civil rights revolt, then in its infancy. Not willing, like Céline and Adorno, to accept modern history as a paradigm, Killens looked back upon Afro-American history with the penetrating, sensitive eyes of a talented poet, and divined in that history the counter thesis to the proponents of man's extinction and damnation. There were many monuments erected to human endurance in that history, foremost among which was courage.

And as courage is the unifying thesis of Afro-American history, it is also the unifying thesis of *Youngblood.* Around this concept men and women demonstrate their commitment to other human beings or acquiesce, cynically, in the belief that humankind is unregenerate: "Crackers been hard on me ever since I come into the world," announces a harried Joe Youngblood, "can't be no harder. . . . Made up my mind that I wasn't gonna take no more stuff from these crackers. Gon be a man by God, living or dead." Yet courage, as Killens knows so well, is not always so desperately or bitterly exclaimed; indeed, often takes the form of quiet concentrated effort. There is the courage displayed by Joe Youngblood, who refuses to allow a white paymaster to continue to cheat him of part of his wages; there is that displayed by Laurie Lee Youngblood, who lashes her son bloody-red on the orders of a sadistic policeman in order to save him. Courage is also displayed by Richard Myles, young Northern schoolteacher come South, in staging a Jubilee—a Black celebration of history—in the face of the anger of the white community. There is that of Robert Youngblood attempting to unite Black and white workers under the union banner, and that too of Oscar Jefferson, white, who casts his lot with the Black community.

Thus, contrary to the twentieth-century prophets of doom, Killens envisions a world not so much "red in tooth and claw" as one overflowing with limitless possibilities. It is a world populated by heroes, men and women who do not accept their fate but challenge it. "You bring your children into a white folks world," laments Laurie Lee Youngblood, "and you don't know what to tell them to live." The statement is not altogether true, and Laurie Lee, like others in her community, must realize that history has not begun with her generation in Crossroads, Georgia, for neither whites nor Blacks, that the ways in which men and women confront the terrors of living at present were prescribed by those who confronted similar terrors in the past, that the great Jubilee is as much an exercise in learning how courage was exhibited in the past as it is a reclamation of Black culture.

When Oscar Jefferson views the Jubilee, he is moved not so much because he has accepted Black history as his own, but by the courage displayed by men and women, mortal like himself. Because of his insistent struggle between the magnetic attraction of his white "tradition" and his humanity, he is able to perceive the "Sorrow Songs," as Du Bois called the Negro spirituals, as the poetry of the human heart and soul. It is the poetry of the Jubilee, then, composed after numerous holocausts, that espouses the best of the human condition; it is a vehicle of communication between individuals, highlighting a major tenet of Killens's poetry from *Youngblood* to the later novel *The Cotillion,* that the necessity for communication is paramount at this period of man's existence.

For it is this that motivated the freedom riders and the civil rights protesters, this need to construct lines of communication between one human being and another, that produced the rebellions in the streets from Watts to Harlem, and infused the rhetoric of Martin Luther King, Jr., and Malcolm X. Yet, the difficulty of establishing lines of communication cannot be understated: "Rob looked into the white man's face again, and he wanted desperately to trust this white man with the friendly face and the eyes that were crying out loud to be trusted, but how could he trust him in Crossroads, Georgia?"

It is the question raised today by individuals and nations alike, and the answer does not lie, Killens tells us, in a retreat into one's own ego, or into the philosophy of alienation. Existential man may be a product of the paradise lost, but his journey must be toward reclaiming that paradise, not for himself alone, but for all. Such a journey is undertaken by the Youngbloods and the gallant men and women of their community. It is a journey whose byroads, to be sure, are strewn with evidence of human viciousness, with fear, trepidation, and death. Still, it is a journey made by human beings who realize that manhood and womanhood are achieved not so much from reaching or not reaching a prescribed goal as by the courage displayed in moving toward it.

One comes away from the final pages of *Youngblood* having witnessed the death of the patriarch, gunned down by a white man, believing still in the nobility and sanctity of the human spirit. For the old man's death galvanizes the Black community into action, brings a partial reconciliation between Oscar Jefferson and the Blacks, and thus symbolically between whites and Blacks, and a promise of better things to come: ". . . Look all around you at your brothers and sisters," intones the minister after Joe Youngblood's funeral, "thousands of them, and great God-Almighty, fighting mad, and we're going to make them pay one day soon, the ones that're responsible. There's going to be a reckoning day right here in Georgia and we're going to help God hurry it up."

Looking back from our vantage point at the present time, we know that the "reckoning" day spread from the South to engulf the entire nation. The heroism and courage personified in the Youngbloods helped to move this nation toward a terrible confrontation with its own destiny. The mores and traditions that had bulwarked hundreds of towns like Crossroads were attacked and here and there people discovered sparks of humanity in others across the color line. The forces of hatred and racism—the forces of anti-man—were never completely vanquished, though the structure they had erected for centuries tottered precariously upon the brink of extinction. The Rubicon had not then been reached, and even today there is evidence that a resurgence of old traditions is at hand. Those who believe in the inalienable inferiority of other human beings now mount the barricades of bigotry and hatred across America. In the face of this new onslaught against the human spirit, few of the nation's poets, Black or white, are to be heard.

Thus the republication of *Youngblood* is necessary at this time. The novel is a kind of Jubilee of its own, calling us back to the fierce struggles of yesterday, while yet envisioning a future in which courage, struggle, and sacrifice will bring ample rewards in human terms. The novel reminds us of the enduring beauty and nobility of people and that human beings can create the great society. It speaks to what is good in the human character and encourages us to be ever hopeful about the human condition. It assures us that heroes and heroines abound still, and that to discover them we need only redefine our definitions. It assures us, in the words of the Negro spiritual, that the "great gettin' up morning" is possible for those with hope and faith.

One suggests, therefore, that even Céline, cynic, malcontent, would find much to admire about the human beings in *Youngblood*. They are noted more for their generosity than for their viciousness, more for their strengths than their weakness, more for their optimism than their pessimism. Throughout the history of this country, men and women very much like them have raised high the banner of freedom and democracy, and given real meaning to the Constitution and the Bill of Rights. It is little wonder, then, that wherever human beings gather in an attempt to rid themselves of oppression, the voices of Black poets from Claude McKay to Richard Wright have been heard. Foremost among those voices is that of John Oliver Killens. He has written a novel, timeless in evocations of the rights of humankind and unparalleled in its optimism concerning the human condition. *Youngblood* is a tremendous achievement.

CHAPTER 32

'Sippi

by John Oliver Killens

(1988)

Foreword

In Richard Wright's novel, *The Long Dream*, published in 1958, Fishbelly Tucker, the Black protagonist, upon learning of the brutal lynching of a friend by a white mob, seeks to steel himself against the barbarity of his Mississippi environment. When he finds a dead dog lying in the middle of a hot and dusty road he pulls out a knife, cuts the dog open—slitting the carcass down the middle—hacking through bone, gristle, and muscle. ". . . now," he assured himself, "when the whites came after him, he would know what death was." Such attempts at self education comprise part of the storehouse of Black folklore about Mississippi. Of those states which make up the Deep South—Georgia, Alabama, and South Carolina among them—Mississippi was the most feared. In many instances, rebellious Black slaves were silenced by masters who threatened to send them to this Southern state. After the Emancipation Proclamation, Mississippi was among the first states to enact the infamous "Black Codes" depriving newly freed Blacks of all political and social rights and the first to institute wholesale violence as a way of demanding compliance with the codes. Mississippi gained international notoriety during the nineteen sixties for the mob slayings of countless numbers of civil rights workers, including Mrs. Viola Liuzzo, Medgar Evers, James Chaney, Andrew Goodman, and Michael Schwerner. For this reason, one Black writer called the state "the most barbaric land outside of South Africa and the Germany of the Third Reich."

But another Black writer, though bearing witness to Mississippi as a land of oppression and brutality, expressed feelings of joy when thinking long and positively about the place of his birth: "There is," he is quoted in *Mississippi: Conflict and Change* (1974), "the feeling of love. Love of the land. To me Mississippi is the most beautiful country in the world. . . ." Even Richard Wright, the novelist whose testimony concerning the treatment of Blacks in Mississippi was documented for the world in the autobiography, *Black Boy,* envisioned his homeland as a place of hope and promise for humankind. This paradox—between the Mississippi that is and the Mississippi that might be—has caused Black novelists to shun the state as a subject of fiction. With the exception of *The Long Dream,* fictional works by Blacks about this Deep South state are almost nonexistent. The reason is, perhaps, that fiction demands a not-too-close identification of the writer with reality, and Blacks who live in Mississippi daily confront a reality so stark that description of it and the expression of feelings about it can better find expression in such nonfictional works as *Black Boy* and *Coming of Age in Mississippi* (1968) by Anne Moody.

John Killens is a notable exception among writers who have selected this Southern state as a subject for fiction. A Southerner—he was born in Georgia—who knows much about the ways of Blacks and whites in his native state, he makes his personal experiences those of every man and creates a novel that explores the lives of Blacks in ways that William Faulkner, the most famous of Mississippi's chroniclers, could not. With a perspective gained from involvement in the civil rights crusades of the nineteen sixties, In 'Sippi (1967) Killens returns to the terrain worked so well by Richard Wright and adds new and significant dimensions to the Black novel. 'Sippi focuses upon Wakefield County and the Blacks and whites who live and interact there. The county is ruled over by Charles James Richard Wakefield, who directs his many enterprises from a sprawling plantation upon which Blacks make a living through farming and working in the fields. He believes himself to be a representative of "a changing Mississippi," a progressive who argues that the "South must change" if it is to compete in the twentieth century. "Segregation in our modern society is impractical in the long run," Wakefield lectures a group of whites. "We can't run things like we used to. . . . The world won't stand for it. . . . It's world power we're negotiating for now." If Mississippi is to prosper and survive in a changing world, it too must change, must moderate the violent climate which makes it an outlaw state. He proves his devotion to this new policy by allowing Blacks who work for him and who live on his plantation greater freedom in terms of movement and political participation than do other white landowners. When trouble arises between Blacks and hostile whites, he intervenes on behalf of Blacks and he has arranged for Charles Chaney, the son of a lifelong worker and friend on the plantation, to attend college when he comes of age. The South must be made like the North, Wakefield tells his white colleagues. Blacks must be given the semblance of power, but not real power: ". . . Make the South like the North. . . . And niggers sure haven't got any power up there. We got to do the same thing down here. Appoint one Negro here and one over there and let the others have one great vicarious experience. That's what I'm preparing my Black boy for. Why do you think I'm sending him to college?"

Like Fishbelly Tucker, however, Charles Othello Chaney needs the kind of education not available in a college curriculum. He must learn the ways of white Mississippians; he must also learn the truth about white benefactors like Wakefield; he must learn the lessons graphically illustrated in the history of struggle by countless Black heroines and heroes, and he must learn the meaning and the power of love. The lessons concerning the ways of whites are easily, quickly learned. A brother who defends himself against a white man is forced out of the state into the army, where he dies in Korea. Another brother is not so lucky. For defending himself against an assault from a white man, he is lynched. These acts of violence are part of a general pattern of violent acts. They include bombings—in one instance an entire family, mother, father, and children, are the targets— beatings, and indiscriminate murder of Blacks, both the recalcitrant and those easily pliable. Through observing these occurrences, the young boy learns much about the world he shares with whites. In this world, divided between Blacks and whites, he learns that Wakefield—protestations to the contrary—owes allegiance to the white world. The white landowner admits as much. When Blacks begin to agitate for voting rights, Wakefield implores Chaney to tell them to shy away from Black power: ". . . Tell them . . . I'm working for them day and night. But they simply must not rock the boat . . . [or] I'll have to join up with the peckerwoods and shoot down Negroes on the streets of Wakefield City." The confession/dec-laration frees Chaney from debt to his benefactor and forces him to realize that he was being educated to serve the interests—not of Blacks, but of whites. This revelation intensifies his positive feelings about Blacks and makes him determined to join the process of integrating Black people with other Black people.

To begin this process, he had to learn the significance of the lives of men and women like Nat Turner, Harriet Tubman, Sojourner Truth, Fannie Lou Hamer, Paul Robeson, Martin Luther King, Jr., and Malcolm X. In so doing, he would master the most important lesson, necessary for growing up black in Mississippi, that would prepare him to undergo the barbarity and brutality fostered by the white world—the meaning of Black love and Black power. Both concepts were present in the historical attempt by Blacks to survive in Mississippi and both meant simply ". . . love of our own black selves." Having successfully completed this rigid curriculum, Charles "Chuck" Chaney is ready to vault into manhood, to form endearing relationships with men and women in the civil rights movement and to announce his independence to Wakefield: "At last we understand each other. Thank you for drawing the demarcation lines so clearly. You with yours [people] and I with mine." When the protagonist attains this level of conscious-ness, Killens brings the novel to its dramatic conclusion. The murders of such men as King, Malcolm, and the dedicated militant writer David Woodson (Killens?) brings the Black community together in violent revolution which, beginning in Mississippi, moves to embroil the entire world.

The ensuing bloodbath, however, is not for Killens, as such acts of vengeance and retribution were for Wright, a necessary occurrence if men were to learn to defend themselves against other men, but instead a means of bringing men and women together in a baptism of love in order to transform first the individual,

then the community, and finally the world. For this writer, who refused to retreat from the thesis that the writer has a social responsibility, art is as it was for
George Bernard Shaw, Richard Wright, Sonia Sanchez, Bertolt Brecht, and John
Williams, an instrument for improving the human condition. Thus, Mississippi
is symbolic not of a world hopelessly beyond redemption, but like South Africa
and Buchenwald, of a world where men daily assault human dignity and decency.
They are always talking about man, wrote Fanon about Westerners, but they kill
men everywhere they find them, "in all of their cities, on the streets. . . ." The
objective of literature, Killens realized and proclaimed publicly in *Black Man's
Burden,* was to attempt to reintegrate the murderer and outlaw, groups or individuals, into the "community of man." Paradoxically, because of its barbaric and
murderous history, a changed Mississippi would become an enduring model for
a society jointly ruled over by Blacks and whites for the benefit of all. Before this
society is possible, however, men and women must thrust aside the debilitating
myths of hostility and hatred that help to separate one from another and realize
the redemptive power of love. If love is strong enough, Chaney learns, nothing
is impossible. No, nothing! Not even the transformation of Mississippi into a
paradigm of decency and humanity.

Killens's final pronouncements on the state of Mississippi differ considerably
from those of Wright, who could hope for—but not totally believe in—its redemption. The lives of Blacks who chose to remain, Wright believed, would always be
circumscribed by hatred and fear. Killens disclaims this aspect of Wright's thought,
while retaining the former author's obsession with social conditions and his belief
that "words are weapons" to be used in the quest for liberation. His analysis of
those, Black and white, who struggle against tyranny from Mississippi to Vietnam
is as penetrating as that of Wright's. Here, however, most comparisons between
these two writers end. In the voluminous fiction of Wright, few instances of love
between one Black person and another are to be found. It is as if this native Mis-
sissippian was so scarred by his negative experiences that he came to believe that
the bond between man and man could be forged only through hostility, anger,
and rage. For Killens, on the other hand, love between Blacks is ever present,
and because this is so, they have been able to survive the worst of the Mississippi
nights. The men and women who people his novels—*Youngblood, And Then We
Heard the Thunder,* and *Cotillion,* as well as *'Sippi*—are not simply victims of the
social order but heroes, revolutionaries, whose love of life and of one another
enable them to mount the barricades in favor of universal justice. Thus, from his
first work to his last, he worked to establish a tradition in Black literature, moving beyond that initiated by Wright and practiced by such followers as Chester
Himes, Ann Petry, and William Gardner Smith. That tradition—based upon the
proposition that love is a more powerful and viable force for change than hatred
and hostility—remains strong in Black literature today. It is found in the works
of novelists and poets and in the works of young people in writers' workshops

throughout the country. These are men and women who, along with Charles Othello Chaney, have learned that Black people "are beautiful" and worthy of love. Throughout his rich and productive lifetime, Killens propounded this idea and *'Sippi,* a splendid novel and a great contribution to the nation's storehouse of classics, continues this effort.

CHAPTER 33

Five on the Black Hand Side:
A Play in Three Acts

by Charlie L. Russell

(1973)

Introduction

The problem of Black drama is the problem, in microcosm, of Black literature in general. All too often, the genre has swung between the poles of entertainment and protest, the former exemplified by the earliest successful Negro play, *Clorindy—The Origin of the Cake Walk* (1898), the latter by Lorraine Hansberry's *A Raisin in the Sun* (1959). The commitment to either of these themes was likely to appeal only to a limited audience of whites that in Sterling Brown's words, "wants stereotypes"; or to a Black middle class—to quote Brown again—that wanted "flattery instead of representation, plaster saints instead of human beings, drawing rooms instead of the homes of the people." The majority of Black people, those who opted for a realistic drama based upon the essentials of their lives, were neglected by the dramatist as they had been, with a few startling exceptions, by the poet and the novelist. Sensing this neglect, Brown suggested in 1937: ". . . If Negro playwrights could devote themselves to the observation of the lives of their people as well as to the more arduous business of learning technique, their work would be of the greatest importance."

The call here was not, as one might infer, for a simple commitment to stark realism. Rather, it was the acknowledgement that in the lives of Black people—those whose daily lives are filled with both hope and despair, struggle and sacrifice— lay the themes upon which a truly great drama might be constructed. In such a drama, entertainment and protest, though valuable ingredients, must give way to realistic depiction of the strength and courage which has enabled Black people to survive the American madness; and the stereotypes, whether of the dancing, singing "darky" of *Clorindy,* or the hard working, assimilation-bent darky of *Raisin,* must give way to those Black people who, as Langston Hughes wrote, ". . . have their nip of gin on Saturday nights and are not too important to themselves or the community, or too well-fed, or too learned to watch the lazy world go round ... they do not particularly care whether they are like white folks or anybody else."

The attempt to portray African Americans outside the stereotypes of the middle class is found in some of the poetry and fiction of the Harlem Renaissance. In Black drama, however, with the possible exception of John Matheus' *'Cruiter,* and Langston Hughes' *Jericho-Jimcrow,* the movement was not accepted until the resurgence of Black drama in the nineteen sixties. With the opening of Imamu Baraka's Black Arts Theatre in 1964, and the emergence of Black playwrights such as Ronald Milner, Ben Caldwell, Willie Branch, Ed Bullins, and Loften Mitchell, a new era in African American theatre was begun. The contemporary Black playwright is committed to a drama based upon the tenets of nationalism. It is a drama which selects its materials from the lives of the people of whom Hughes wrote, and directs itself to those people in the belief that they will gain sustenance and hope from the recognition of their strengths, while learning and improving as a result of acknowledging their weaknesses. In so doing, the Black dramatist has moved outside the classic conflicts of Black art: the Black man as either savior or victim of the Euro-American society, to the Black man as retainer of those African values—faith in life, trust in man, and commitment to the human spirit—so alien to Euro-American art.

Charlie L. Russell's *Five on the Black Hand Side* is an important play in this direction. What Ellison did for the African American novel, what McKay, Toomer and Hughes did for African American poetry, is what Russell has accomplished in the African American drama. Using comedy as his medium, he has managed to turn Black drama inward, focusing upon the conflicts between one Black man and another. Though the full impact of his comic genius can best be appreciated when viewed upon the stage, in the monologue of Fun Loving, one is introduced to the humor and wit so characteristic of Black speech: "They call me sweet Peter Jeter, the womb beater, the baby maker, the cradle shaker. The deer slayer, the buck binder and woman finder. I'm known from the gold coast to the rocky shores of Maine. Dig? ... I ain't giving up nothin' but bubbly gum, and hard times. And I'm fresh out of bubble gum. I'm the man who walked the water and tied a whale's tail in a knot. I taught the fish how to swim, crossed the burning sand, and shook the devil's hand."

The major conflicts, however, lie beneath the comic veneer: that between Black men and Black women, Black fathers and Black sons, and between a commitment to individualism and a commitment to Black unity. Each mandates a life style outside that vouchsafed by the Euro-Americans: "... All I'm asking you to do," Gideon chastises his brother, Booker T., "is to be a man. You can't be into a Black and white thing at the same time. It won't work. ... You've got to choose, man. Fence straddling is a dangerous game."

Among other things, *Five on the Black Hand Side* is about choosing: Mr. Brooks must choose to respect his family or to continue to dominate them; Mrs. Brooks must choose either to assert her humanity or to acquiesce in her own subjugation; the children must choose rebellion against paternal tyranny or adherence to old, submissive patterns of conduct.

Although in the old Euro-American situation comedy, Mr. Brooks would have emerged as the villain, Russell understands all too well the society in which his characters live. The villain in *Five on the Black Hand Side,* although never referred to, needs no introduction. He is always there, lurking beneath the surface, influencing the lives of the people in the drama. Booker T. Brooks, Sr., proprietor of a small Harlem barbershop, represents one form of reaction—in both name and thought—to that outside force; Gideon, whose name is too obviously symbolic, represents another. With humor and comedy, insight and love, the dramatist is concerned with bridging the gap between the two, bringing the father closer to the position of the son; guiding the proponent of the Black middle class toward integration—with nationalism. When, at the end of the drama, Booker T., Sr., acquiesces to the written demands of his wife, vowing greater tolerance for her ideas, a greater respect for her humanity, a dons a dashiki, this is not farce, not forced incident, but a realistic depiction of the movement toward unity occurring within Black families in this, the latter half of the twentieth century. Committed to collective struggle, to the principle of unity, Russell's is no more a denigrating attack on the Black middle class; rather, he evidences a strong belief in their propensity for change, and thus, in the propensity of Black people to change.

It is this which forms the central thesis of this important comedy, just as it is this which forms the central thesis of the works of the younger poets and novelists. The literature in which entertainment and protest were the author's major concern failed in this respect: entertainment sought to suggest that change was, at best, impossible, while protest argued that change depended upon the actions of the white society. For Charlie Russell, as for his contemporaries, change is possible only within the Black community. Thus, the art of the new dramatist, poet, and novelist alike, must direct itself to those problems, obscured all too often in the day-to-day confrontation with the Euro-Americans. It is their resolution which will produce the moral, ethical, and humanistic Black nation. Its ingredients are all exemplified in *Five on the Black Hand Side:* love, commitment, collective responsibility and struggle.

But, if Russell is capable of understanding and sympathizing with the Black middle class, he is no less capable of understanding and sympathizing with others in the Black community—those whose actions are inimical to the best interests of the community. In Act II—The Barbershop Scene—one of the best executed scenes in contemporary drama, ranking in clarity and technique with Ellison's depiction of the Golden Day Saloon in *Invisible Man,* Russell parades before his audience a numbers writer, a pimp, and a junkie. Although he understands and sympathizes with these characters, he is unwilling—unlike some of his more ambitious, less talented contemporaries—to pass them off as representatives of the Black community; nor does he romanticize or glamorize them. Instead, he again opts for change: "Man, when we get control of our community, that's the first thing we should deal with."

The primary emphasis of *Five on the Black Hand Side*—and this is true of Black literature in general, at this period—is change. Change involves a commitment to reality, a recognition of the historical devices used to transform African people into what Willie Branch has defined as "An American Negro, something made and manufactured in America." It is also a commitment which recognizes the existence of addicts and pimps, Black capitalists and Black individualists. But, too, it is a commitment which recognizes the truer, more enduring images and symbols of Black life: Black workers and students; courageous Black mothers and fathers; committed men and women in every area of life. It is a reality which consists of oppression and tyranny, but of hope and struggle as well. Only in recognizing the totality of that reality can the way back be found; can the transformation from Negro to African be completed; can the Black artist create an enduring art.

The function of the literature of African American people is to induce change by reminding us of the realities, both of the past, and of the present, by reminding us of the unity which produced the era of Frederick Douglass, the commitment of Marcus Garvey and Malcolm X, the love which gave us Harriet Tubman and Sojourner Truth, the courage which produced Imamu Baraka and Don Lee; by reminding us of the age-old commitment of our ancestors and their progeny to a world based upon morality, honor, and love; a world possible of re-creation only by those whose lives and actions have been dedicated, not to the destruction of human dignity throughout the world, but to its elevation.

Five on the Black Hand Side is a valuable work in this direction. In execution and technique, but above all, in language and theme, it is a drama based upon the realities of Black life, and dedicated to the meaning of a people's history and culture. As such, it opts not for "nauseating mimicry," but for a way out of Euro-American tyranny. Neither minstrel entertainment nor protest designed to affect white liberals, it is a commitment to the most profound meaning of Black life in America; to life over death, to energy over stagnation, to love over hate; in short, it is a commitment to those principles which mandate the creation of the new nation.

CHAPTER 34

Forerunners: Black Poets in America

by Woodie King Jr.

(1981)

Introduction

In too many instances, Black writers in America have written in response to out-side pressures, have attempted to create a literature in accordance with the actions or reactions of a white majority. For this reason, it is not too far wrong to suggest that until quite recently theirs has been a literature of reaction. Richard Wright was among the first to note this tendency, and in the essay "The Literature of the Negro in the United States" he traces the history of Black poetry from Phillis Wheatley to Margaret Walker and concludes that a trend away from "strictly racial themes," as shown in the works of many poets, was due to improvement in the condition of Black people. If the literature of the future, he warned, returns to preoccupation with racial themes, this will indicate that Blacks "are suffer-ing . . . old and ancient agonies at the hands of our white American neighbors." Conversely, continuation of a literature that assumes ". . . the common themes and burdens of literary expression, which are the heritage of all men," means that "a humane attitude prevails in America towards us [Blacks]."

Two major tendencies distinguished the literature of reaction. First, it was a service literature, offered as evidence that Blacks were not an inferior people, and regarded by many practitioners—James Weldon Johnson, Jessie R. Fauset, and Angelina W. Grimké come readily to mind—as an instrument designed to articulate the grievances of the Black middle class. Second, it was viewed by some as an instrument of catharsis, the vehicle to produce an awareness of the crippling effects of "our old and ancient agonies" in the minds of "our white neighbors." The practitioners, which include Wright and the school of protest writers he inspired, believed that literature could produce changes in the attitudes of whites sufficient to cause positive changes in the Black condition.

Belief in the possibility of American redemption is central to the proponents of each position. Even the most militant—and Claude McKay is a good example—appealed to America, and in so doing, often ignored the varied dimensions of the Black experience. In making the argument for tolerance and consideration, too many Black writers, then and now, exaggerated the conditions of their Black subjects and, in many cases, accepted arguments based upon Black inferiority and white superiority. Such characteristics are endemic to Black writing as a whole, yet they are nowhere more discerning than in the area of Black poetry. The first recognized Black poet in America, Jupiter Hammon, gives thanks to God and white men alike, in stilted eighteenth-century diction, for rescuing him from supposed barbarism:

> O come you pious youth! Adore
> The wisdom of thy God
> In bringing thee from distant shore
> To learn his holy word.
> Thou mightst been left behind,
> Amidst a dark abode;
> God's tender mercy still combin'd,
> Thou hast the holy word.

Wheatley, the first American woman poet of renown, copies Hammon's sentiments, while improving upon his poetry:

> 'Twas not long since I left my native shore,
> The land of errors and Egyptian gloom:
> Father of mercy! 'twas thy gracious hand
> Brought me in safety from those dark abodes.

Lester P. Hill, a poet of another age and time, uses the couplet form to convince his "white neighbors" of the continual devotion of Blacks, despite their ordeal:

> We will not waver in our loyalty.
> No strange voice reaches us across the sea:
> No crime at home shall stir us from his soil.
> Ours is the guerdon, ours the blight of toil,
> But raised above it by a faith sublime
> We choose to suffer here and bide our time.

Appeals to whites, and catalogues of our ancient agonies, also form the unifying theme of militant poetry. "Throw the children into the river," writes Fenton Johnson, "civilization has given us too many/It is better to die than to grow up and find that you are colored." Lines from McKay's sonnet make the point more strongly:

> Your door is shut against my tightened face,
> And I am sharp as steel with discontent;
> But I possess the courage and the grace
> To bear my anger proudly and unbent.

The eternal note of Black despair is voiced even during the period of Black Power and Black revolt. Carl Wendell Himes, Jr., writes:

> there he stands. see?
> like a black Ancient Mariner his
> wrinkled old face so
> full of the wearies of living is
> turned downward with
> closed eyes. his frayed-collar
> faded-blue old shirt turns
> dark with sweat & the old
> necktie undone drops
> loosely about the worn
> old jacket see? . . .

There are few models for such poets in the history of the Western world. They are descendants of those who underwent cultural shock, who were separated by brutal wrenching from one culture and denied the right to immerse themselves completely in another. Though the separation from the old culture was not complete—vestiges remained in the animal tales, in some lines from the spirituals, in ditties and anecdotes, and in certain religious practices—still, the Africa of their fathers, seat of the culture which had nourished a race, was deemed inferior by the most eminent of Western scholars. The reaction of Blacks in general and Black poets in particular was to search for a sense of identity, of cultural security in a hostile and strange environment.

Disassociated from one culture and denied entrance into another, they were torn between love and hate toward the land that had enslaved their fathers. This accounts for the ambiguity of much of their verse, for the simultaneous outpouring of anger and hope. There is anger in the poetry of James M. Whitfield:

> America, it is to thee,
> Thou boasted land of liberty—
> It is to thee that I raise my song,
> Thou land of blood, and crime, and wrong,
> It is to thee my native land,
> From which has issued many a band
> To tear the black man from his soil
> And force him here to delve and toil
> Chained on your blood-bemoistened sod,
> Cringing beneath a tyrant's rod . . .

There is hope in the despondent appeal of Langston Hughes:

> Let America be America again,
> Let it be the dream it used to be.

Let it be the pioneer on the plain.
Seeking a home where he himself is free.
(America never was America to me.)

The single line refrain intruded into the format of the poem does not obviate the poet's desire to be one with the culture that denies him, or his wish to redeem the America that "lies deep in the heart of me." Whitfield and Hughes are examples of Black poets prevented by a love–hate relationship with America from recognizing (or admitting) its true nature. Neither could accept the fact that the culture upon which they had been so "crudely grafted" offered no sanctuary, would force them, in time, to seek to step outside even the cultural no man's land into which it had consigned them. We are not nationalists because of the devil, writes Imamu Baraka, we would be nationalists if no devil ever existed. Those not able to articulate their grievances in such terminology, nevertheless, when forced finally to confront reality, would be forced also to renounce the dream of "an America yet to be!"

The poetry written before such an epiphany, however, is a romantic poetry, oftentimes evidencing nothing so much as the poets' ignorance of the facts of history. Therefore, at one and the same time, Black poets pointed out some of the realities of the world in which they lived, while, in the denouement of either singular poems or volumes, they prophesied a Canaan to be, an America redeemed and born anew. Look into the poetry of such romantics from Hammon to Hayden, and the lessons of the Middle Passage, the reality of slavery, the attempt by some men to dehumanize others, seem unlearned. Seldom do their lines vibrate with the cries and curses of those to whom the white God never came, seldom do unnamed, unlettered men and women, who never dreamed the romantic dream, appear as characters in their verse. Personages like Harriet Tubman and Frederick Douglass appear, to be sure, but others of lesser stature and attainments are almost always excluded. Outside the spirituals, seldom is there displayed the universal desire of men, not to be one with tyranny, but to escape it, not to co-exist with evil, but to destroy it. The experiences of those who passed through the nightmare of American history have seldom been accurately recorded by those who function as their amanuenses.

Hope, it appears, was destined to flame eternally in the breasts of Black poets. They held to optimistic views concerning America even in moments of greatest anger and bitterness. Men like W. E. B. Du Bois, capable of uttering such violent curses as those from "A Litany of Atlanta,"—"I hate them, Oh!/ I hate them well/I hate them Christ/As I hate hell/If I were God/I'd sound their knell/This day!"— were also capable of sounding this hopeful chord: "If somewhere in this whirl and chaos of things there dwells Eternal Good, pitiful yet masterful, then anon in His good time America shall rend the Veil and the prisoned shall go free." This is not simply schizophrenia. It is, rather, an attempt by men to confront a hostile society; it is an example of the human quality, peculiar to poets, which causes men always to envision a world different from the one that exists; it is the inability of men, daily under the gun, to evaluate objectively the situation they are in.

Thus their hope and optimism is not so much misfounded as misdirected. They were intent upon remaking America, upon redeeming a land and people beyond redemption; therefore, they paid little attention to the viable culture of their ancestors, failed to delineate the varied dimensions of Black life, wrote too few odes to nameless Black heroes, and discovered too little of value in the Black experience. With Wright they believed that Blacks were metaphors of the American condition; and with Wright again, they believed that Blacks, symbolizing pained and desperate men, were paradigms for men everywhere. That Blacks were metaphors of mankind in a truer, much more fundamental way escaped their imaginations. Yet the courage evidenced by those who survived the Middle Passage, by those who maintained stoic dignity and defiance in the face of oppression, denotes Black people as metaphors of the universal human condition: ". . . the Negroes' most powerful images of hope and despair," wrote Wright, "still remain in the fluid state of daily speech. How many John Henrys have lived and died on the lips of Black people? How many mythical heroes in embryo have been allowed to perish for the lack of husbanding by alert intelligence?"

The answer, unfortunately, is far too many. Many Black poets, in accepting the arguments of white nationalists from Thomas Jefferson to Norman Mailer that they were a people sans culture, eternal victims, mere appendages to the culture of the West, ignored the positive aspects of Black life and assaulted the minds of white Americans in an attempt to validate their own humanity. Men and women who succumbed to images and symbols created by others, they seemed unable to fashion newer, more positive ones from their own experiences, were unable to resolve the dichotomy between hatred and love of America, and attempted to write not a racial poetry, but a poetry of reaction.

For what is racial poetry? It is not merely poetry that takes as its subject matter themes and individuals of particular races. If this were so, all the poetry of the Western world from *Oedipus Rex* to *The Ring and the Book* would be racial poetry. It is not poetry that merely catalogues man's suffering and travails, that denotes only his despondent condition; it is not poetry directed to those outside the race, not poetry of facile optimism, hopeless dreams, or romantic longings. Instead, racial poetry concerns itself with the varied dimensions of a people's lives, notes their strengths and weaknesses, creates new images, metaphors, and symbols from their history, and in so doing, erases the artificial line constructed by Western critics between racial and universal. Poetry which deals realistically with Blacks in America is universal in the truest sense of the term.

In the critical statements and poetry of Blacks in the sixties and seventies, there is cognition of this fact. Black art, argues Ron Karenga, must be functional, collective, and committed, must "expose the enemy, praise the people, and support the revolution. . . ." "We must," asserts Don L. Lee, "destroy Faulkner, dick, jane, and other perpetrators of evil. It's time for Du Bois, Nat Turner, and Kwame Nkrumah. . . . Black artists are cultural stabilizers; bringing back old values, and introducing new ones." Etheridge Knight is the prophet of a new world and a new poetry: "Unless the Black artist establishes a 'Black Aesthetic' he will have no future at all. To accept the white aesthetic is to accept and validate a society that will not allow him to live. The Black artist must create new forms and new values, sing new songs (or purify old ones); and along with other Black authorities, he must create a new history, new symbols, myths and legends (and purify old ones by fire)."

The distance in perception between the poets whom Wright discussed and those of the sixties and seventies is great indeed. The former lived and wrote before the emergence of the Black Power revolution, before the murder of Martin Luther King, before sophisticated attempts by the robot-like men of the Nixon administration to return America to antebellum times. They could believe, therefore, that change was possible, that the time would arrive when men would no longer be forced to create a poetry out of oppression, that America, in Hughes's words, might be America again. Their younger disciples, on the other hand, have witnessed the holocaust reborn, faced universal white resistance as they struggled for manhood rights, have known the indiscriminate murder of Black people from Mississippi to New York, have borne witness to the transformation of white liberals from allies to rednecks, and have begun a movement designed to take Blacks outside American history and culture.

Through the efforts of Imamu Baraka, Askia Muhammad Touré, Don L. Lee, Sonia Sanchez, Etheridge Knight, Johari Amini, Mari Evans, Larry Neal, Willie Kgositsile, Raymond Patterson, and James Emanuel among others, a true racial poetry is being created. It is a poetry that has as its objectives the creation of a new people and a new nation and the destruction of images and symbols that enslave; it is a poetry that demands a revolution of the mind and spirit that calls, with Baraka, for the greatest of man's creations: "We want a Black poem. And a Black world/Let the World be a Black Poem."

These young men and women are indebted to the poets of the past, to those discussed by Wright. Before they could make their presence felt among Black people, the dreams held by older poets had to be sorely tested, the dichotomy between love and hate confronted and resolved, the choice made between illusion and reality, between dedication to the pragmatics of American history and continual commitment to the absurd and impossible. The perceptions of the younger poets, therefore, were sharpened by the works of their predecessors, even by the works of such poets as Hammon, Wheatley, Dunbar, and Johnson, as well as Hughes and McKay. They were sharpened and expanded, however, in a much more meaningful way by a group of poets whom editor Woodie King has labeled "the forerunners." These are the poets who came to prominence, mainly, after the Renaissance years, who bridged the gap between poets of the twenties and those of the sixties and seventies. They began the intensive questioning of the impossible dream, the final assault upon illusion that produced the confrontation with reality, the search for paradigms, images, metaphors, and symbols from the varied experiences of a people whose history stretches back beyond the Nile. With few exceptions, they are the literary godparents of today's Black poets.

They are included in this volume, *The Forerunners,* and their presence makes this a unique collection of poetry, indeed. The book looks back to the past and ahead to the future. It is composed of love poetry and religious poetry, of protest poetry and poetry of resignation. There is poetry of Africa—the motherland— poetry of angst, and poetry of joy. There is angry poetry whose measured lines assault the ear and tender poetry more singsong than lyrical, which soothes and instructs as well. Most of the poems are written in blank verse, though sonnets and ballads are well represented. The editor has brought together in a single volume a variety of poems that exhibit mastery of form and content. There are the staid, timeless lines of Arna Bontemps:

> The years go back with an iron clank,
> A hand is on the gate,
> A dry leaf trembles on the wall.
> Ghosts are walking.
> They have broken roses down
> And poplars stand there still as death.

There is the questioning of Robert Hayden in the idiom peculiar to the surrealists: "Ars Longa Which is crueller/ Vita Brevis life or art?" The speaker in one of Russell Atkins's poems is nostalgic for a world outside "industries' shadows" where "(. . . sudden trees.)/ flowers, a wheedle of them?/*cannabis sativa* burning/ somewhere near/the volumed/dun?" Owen Dodson forwards the Black man's eternal question to his God: "God, why have you ruined me,/What have I done unto thee . . . ?" Margaret Walker implores the Old Testament God in the sentiments of the first slaves: "Pray for second sight and the inner ear. Pray for bulwark against poaching patterns of dislocated days; pray for buttressing iron against insidious termite and beetle and locust and flies and lice and moth and rust and mold."

The strength of the collection lies in its selectivity. In choosing representative poems from the works of older poets, the editor has managed to foreshadow many of the themes of today's Black poets. Margaret Walker, Gwendolyn Brooks, Frank Marshall Davis, Arna Bontemps, and Sterling Brown speak with a modernity echoed in the works of their younger colleagues: Sam Allen, Lance Jeffers, Naomi Long Madgett, Dudley Randall, and Jay Wright. The themes of such poems as "A Black Man Talks of Reaping," "Dancing Gal," "Old Lem," and "At Home in

Dakar" bear striking resemblance to those of such poems as "Black Soul of the Land," "Black Woman," "On Getting a Natural (For Gwendolyn Brooks)," and "My Friend." Here in one collection are the themes of love and strife between Black men and women, themes which deal with the holocaust from several perspectives, images, metaphors, and symbols that depict the beauty and grandeur of a people. Lance Jeffers, one of the most talented poets represented in the volume, searches in the past for images and symbols:

> Give me your spine, old man, old man,
> give me your rugged hate,
> give me your sturdy oak-tree love,
> give me your source of steel.
> Teach me to sing so that the song may be mine
> "Keep your hands on the plow: hold on!"
> One day the nation's soul shall turn Black like yours
> and America shall cease to be its name.

With metaphorical clarity and Black insight, Gwendolyn Brooks is at one with the poets of the seventies in her portrait of Lincoln West, "Ugliest little boy/that everyone ever saw," who finds dignity and strength when realizing the uniqueness of his color and features, when realizing that among all Blacks, he was "the real thing." "When he was hurt, too much/stared at—/too much/left alone—he/ thought about that. He told himself/'After all, I'm/the real thing.' It comforted him." Like Mari Evans and Sonia Sanchez, Naomi Long Madgett celebrates the beauty of Black women and poses the question sounded in their works:

> Where are my lovers?
> Where are my tall, my lovely princes
> Dancing in slow grace
> Toward knowledge of my beauty?
> Where
> Are my beautiful
> Black men?

The Forerunners has made Wright's contention in "The Literature of the Negro in the United States" obsolete. The continuance of oppression against Blacks by white Americans has not caused these poets to continue the tradition begun by their ancestors, one which resulted in a poetry of reaction. Most of them utilize the racial idiom, and thus their poetry is racial in the most positive sense of the term. This is due, however, not to the fact of continual oppression, but rather, to the poets' commitment to Black people, coupled with the realization that poetry written in reaction to the whims and fancies of other men is a facile poetry at best, one which makes impossible the creation of positive images and symbols. These young poets have realized that the songs of the fathers must be updated by the sons, that time and circumstances demand an ever-changing poetry. More importantly, however, they have discovered that to be universal means to step outside the parochialism of the American society, and that to be a good poet as well as a relevant poet entails as great a concern for race as it does for the mastery of craft.

It is this that distinguishes them from the earlier poets and makes them one with their younger counterparts of the sixties and seventies. Hammon, Wheatley, and Dunbar, among others, accepted all too readily the stereotypes of Blacks handed down from the Americans; they believed with their white contemporaries that Blacks were inferior, destined to be the eternal wards of superior, more human men. Their poetry is adorned with too many aunts, uncles, and mammies, too many Christ figures and apologists. Those whom Woodie King has labeled "the forerunners" have looked closely at Black history and discovered truer paradigms. Such are found in the portraits of Old Lem, depicted by Sterling Brown; in the nobility and beauty of the men and women in the poetry of Naomi Long Madgett and Gwendolyn Brooks; in the dignified Africans who so moved Margaret Danner; in the images of courage and determination which effuse the poetry of Lance Jeffers.

These are the poets who, long before Askia Touré and Don L. Lee, recognized the most profound of truths: To control the image is the responsibility of Black writers, for paradigms of positive import can only be created by Blacks freed from the pretensions and hypocrisy of Western culture. They have realized that three centuries of American oppression have rendered all definitions by whites concerning Blacks irrelevant; come to believe with Frederick Douglass that each white man is barred, due to culture and experience, from painting representative portraits of Blacks. They have realized, too, that in a country where oppression is ingrained in institutions and traditions, only the insane among the oppressed are willing to accept mirror images from the oppressor.

The poets, midwifed by the Black Power revolution, are aware of such facts, and thus, they have moved to bury the contemptuous, obscene images of Blacks handed down from Western scholars, poets, and critics. They write a poetry which speaks of strong Black men and women; they find positive images in the holocaust, sift through Black history for monuments of a past of rebellion and revolution. Theirs is a revolutionary poetry, directing itself to Black people, demanding changes in the way that Blacks perceive themselves, and calling far the construction of a new world, based upon a value system hewn out of the Black experience.

Theirs is a true racial poetry, and their debt to the forerunners is great indeed. For it was these poets who broke with the tradition of the past, who dared to cross the Rubicon between acceptance by Americans and defiance of American values and customs, who dared to challenge the right assumed by the oppressor of defining the life style of the oppressed, who argued that a people with a unique history could not sing their songs in a strange and hostile land, and who urged that Blacks, writers and laymen alike, must move outside American history. Langston Hughes remains one of their patron saints; it is not, however, the Hughes of the romantic dream whom they admire, but the Hughes of *The Panther and the Lash*, who realized, finally, that salvation for Blacks is possible only through the efforts of Blacks.

Though there are those in this volume who tend to eschew race, who write a facile poetry of little meaning, who attempt to lose the Black experience in abstraction and surrealism, for the most part *The Forerunners* is marked by those who have turned inward in order to better illuminate the experiences of a people. Listen to Sterling Brown in the twenties and Askia Touré in the sixties, and note that the tradition continues unbroken from the forerunners to their younger colleagues:

> Today they shout prohibition at you
> "Thou shalt not this"
> "Thou shalt not that"
> "Reserved for whites only"
> You laugh.
> One thing they cannot prohibit—
> The strong men . . . coming on
> The strong men gittin' stronger.
> Strong men . . .
> Stronger. . . .

*   *   *

> In this land we will rise, we will rise
> As the pyramids of Africa rise to find the fathers of the
>   Sphinx
> We will rise as a pine tree, tall and proud, rises under
>   bloody
> Southern skies to kiss the moon
> We are the new!
> We are the rivers of the Spring breaking through
> The cold white ice of dying winter.

CHAPTER 35

Great Gitt'in Up Morning:
The Story of Denmark Vesey

by John Oliver Killens

(1972)

Introduction

Twenty-five years ago John Oliver Killens published *Youngblood* (1954) his first novel. A landmark novel, coming in the year of the landmark decision of the Supreme Court concerning school integration. In terms of composition, scope, and vision, it has achieved the eminence of a classic. It is a Southern novel, in the way that the author is Southern, a product of the red loam colored hills and earth of Georgia, of hard, dry, rain-forgotten soil, of sun-baked days and breeze-cooled nights, a product, too, of the first African home away from home. From this terrain and from the experiences occasioned by the arrival of the first Black man on Southern soil in 1614 have come, cascading down the years, portraits of courageous men and women, who pitted their strength against the worst of the Southern nights and passed down to their offspring a heritage of dignity and heroism.

Youngblood captures the essence of such men and women, and in doing so, makes this very Southern novel, one of far reaching import, important and meaningful for Black people everywhere. To read Killens' first novel is to be in touch with history yet to come, to feel, intuitively in 1954 that the time of chaos and turbulence is near.

There were few such prophets during the Eisenhower years of the nineteen fifties. America was undergoing the grand inquisition of the McCarthy years, subjecting thousands of its own citizens to an ordeal surpassed only by the trials and purges occasioning the French revolution. Though Blacks like Paul Robeson, Langston Hughes, W. E. B. Du Bois, and Richard Wright were victims of the hysteria of those times, for the most part, the Black community remained relatively quiescent. Martin Luther King was a Southern Baptist minister, content to minister to his flock; Malik Shabazz was in prison listening to the message of the Messenger; Rosa Parks ambled home day after day from her job sitting un-complainingly in the segregated sections of the buses of Montgomery, Alabama. Stokely Carmichael and H. Rap Brown were students, studying the contradic-tions inherent in the American society, and Fannie Lou Hamer was raising her children in a South ruled still by plantation owners, nightriders, corrupt police, and politicians.

But there were thunder clouds in the seemingly calm sky of the Eisenhower years. The Southern states declared massive opposition to the Supreme Court decision and gave its police forces/mobs the power to stop the implementation of the court's decree by any means necessary. Lynchings and murders of Blacks increased tenfold and to the rostrum of victims were added the names of Mack Parker, Emmett Till and Medgar Evers. The hysteria with which the American right wing had waged warfare against "subversives" during the McCarthy years, was transferred to the coming war against an older more established group of "subversives"—Blacks. The barricades were erected between those who would deny to men and women the dignity of their humanity and those determined to achieve it, no matter the cost. And though few—and Killens was among the very few—realized it at that time, the barricades were being erected not only in the social, political, and economic areas of American life, but in the cultural as well.

Successful revolutions must always be attenuated by cultural upheaval. It is a lesson that the Chinese, the Vietnamese, the Angolans, and the Cubans knew very well. Before the new order can be brought into being, the "new man" must be born, and this birth can take place only when the death of the old images and stereotypes has occurred, only when the reality of the enslaved has been substi-tuted for that of the enslaver.

Writes Herbert Marcuse: "Reality is other and more than that codified in the logic and language of facts. Here is the inner link between the dialectical thought and the effort of avante-garde literature; the effort to break the power of facts over the word, and to speak a language which is not the language of those who establish, enforce, and benefit from the facts." The coming Black revolution needed a new language system, new images, and symbols, and the writers courageous enough to create them would be in dire opposition to those who maintained hegemony over America's cultural life.

The academics and critics, white and Black, were loath to accept portraits of Black men and women, not validated by those who comprised the American cultural superstructure. Wrote Negro critic Blyden Jackson: "Negroes are more literate now than they ever were. They earn more money. They are better housed. They dress better. They certainly look better. And none of these changes came over night. Yet, during all the long years while a race was acquiring strength and consolidating hard-won gains, Negro literature has been perpetuating a literary fallacy. The prototypic Negro hero has been not only bitter, but broken." There is little room in the cultural cathedral of those like Jackson for Malik Shabazz, H. Rap Brown, Fannie Lou Hamer or Rosa Parks, nor for Joe Youngblood.

The Youngbloods, father and sons are the archetypes of the courageous young warriors of the sixties. But they are important also in another respect: they are symbolic not only of new people but of a new cultural value system. They do not attempt to "assert their humanity," for they begin with the knowledge that their humanity is assured. They are bitter men to be sure, but bitter against those who maintain the system of human bondage. They demonstrate love and affection for each other and for other Blacks, assert the prevalence of strong family ties and the determination of men and women to take their places at the barricades with those who seek a saner, better world. Added to their importance as new images, therefore, this dimension makes the Youngblood family heroes in a novel that speaks through the Black experience in a Black idiom. It is a novel telling us, not so much what we were and are, but what we must become. It is this that makes *Youngblood* a historical as well as fictional success and elevates its author to first rank among our historical novelists.

The historical novel has been a difficult genre for Black writers; few have mastered the form; Du Bois in *Dark Princess* and *The Quest of the Silver Fleece*; John A. Williams in *Captain Blackman,* Ernest Gaines in *The Autobiography of Miss Jane Pittman,* Brenda Wilkinson in *Ludell,* and Killens in *Youngblood.* The reason is not that the genre presents problems in terms of composition or construction, but that the novelist must be imbued with a sense of what Richard Wright called perspective: "Perspective for Negro writers will come when they have looked and brooded so hard and long upon the harsh lot of their race and compared it with the hopes and struggles of minority peoples everywhere that the cold facts have begun to tell them something."

To perceive the racial experience in this way means that the Black writer in America must undergo cultural purgation, must cleanse him or herself of the cultural values created by those who establish, validate, and enforce the facts. The failure perception has led to the mediocre novels of the present times, those written by writers whose perspective on Black life and the Black experience differ little from that of Norman Mailer: ". . . The Negro, not being privileged to gratify his self-esteem with the heady satisfactions of categorical condemnation, chose to move instead in that other direction where all situations are equally valid, and in the worst of perversion, promiscuity, pimpery, drug addiction, rape, razor slash, bottle-break, what have you, the Negro discovered and elaborated a morality of the bottom. . . ."

The value system based upon atavism and sensationalism, enunciated first in the writings of Thomas Dixon and Carl Van Vechten and reissued in modern terminology by Mailer, forms the nucleus of the thematic structure of all too many recent novels by Black writers. Their perspectives and perceptions differ little from those of their white tutors and supporters, and thus their works are

not history but anti-history, novels designed not to challenge those who maintain hegemony over images, symbols, language, and reality, but to enforce their
assumptions, to sanctify their visions of the world and to assure them that the
time of Black rebellion has long since passed.

Wrote a white critic concerning one such recent novel in tones of jubilation: "It
has perhaps become redundant to say of a book grounded in the (B)lack experience that it is a violent and angry book. The statement is a reaction against white
oppression. It . . . is refreshing and ironic to come upon a book of this character
that . . . aims these emotions in a new direction." The new direction was against
Black people.

There are Black writers, however, who retain their sense of perspective and
though few in number, their impact has been as severe as the lion's roar in a
silent jungle. John Killens is among that small minority. Always he has insisted
on traveling the road others dared not transgress; as a result, he has consistently
produced books in which perspective and vision combine to remind us of what
is timeless and enduring in the human condition. There is something about us,
he tells us, that is good and ennobling, and those of us who remember this are
to be counted among the blessed. This is the essence of *Great Gittin' Up Morning,*
first published eighteen years after *Youngblood.*

"Because so little is known of his early and personal life," writes Killens of
his subject, Denmark Vesey, "I have taken fictional license in some of the early
chapters." This does not mean, however, that the early life of Vesey as recreated
by the writer has no foundation in fact. The writer knows a great deal of the early
lives of Black revolutionaries from Douglass to Malik Shabazz; he knows, too,
that the revolutionary is distinguished by his absolute refusal to accept the world
as ordained by those who proclaim themselves earth's vice regents. It is not too
far wrong to suggest that Vesey's upbringing was similar to that of revolutionaries everywhere and that his beliefs accorded with those held by Douglass, Mao,
Che, Stokely, and Rap: ". . . He hated slavery with all the anger his young mind
and heart and soul could muster. If there was ever a spirit not meant to be in
bondage, it belonged to him. His was a spirit meant to fly with sea gulls and soar
the eagle's flight."

Before the day of the slave catcher, the young child lived in his African village
and learned enough in the brief span of time to regard the eagle as the paradigm
of freedom. The symbol did not die after he was stolen from his Africa and transported to the island of St. Thomas, undergoing the terrible voyage through the
middle passage, silent witness to thousands of deaths by starvations and brutality.
And he retained his fondness for the symbol even after, at age fourteen, he was sold
to a second master, from whom he took his last name, and was later transported
to America, to Charleston, South Carolina. But he retained remembrance also of
the holocaust he had witnessed: "The stench of blood and human flesh was ever
in his nostrils. His ears would hold forever the sound of the slave breaker's lash

and the cries and weeping of the slaves. He saw women raped before their men, felt everything, died a million deaths and swore a million oaths that he would someday strike a blow for freedom."

The revolutionary begins by hating personal tyranny and injustice; before long, however, he moves to make his condition that of all the enslaved and commences to hate tyranny and injustice everywhere. The freedom he demands for himself, he now demands for every man. At the age of fourteen, young Vesey had already begun the trek toward revolution.

He realized, long before Lord Byron and Douglass, that he who would be free must himself strike the blow, and thus he began to educate himself, committing the first daring act of his career. Learning to read and write, for slaves, were offenses punishable by beatings, banishment further South, and death. When Vesey set about to read "everything he could get his hands on," he struck his first blow against slavery, committed his first revolutionary act. In so doing he was defining the boundary line beyond which oppression could not go—enslavement of mind as well as body—and preparing himself for the rebellion yet to come. If Black people, to paraphrase Richard Wright, ever really understood the nature of their oppression, they would rend the country apart. Education enabled Vesey to understand not only the nature of oppression but the flimsy pretexts upon which the institution of slavery rested. The pretext, Black inferiority and white superiority, was illogical, irrational, and absurd. The uneducated man had known this intuitively, had felt it; the self-educated man knew it empirically.

And he remembered even after he was able to purchase his own freedom with money won in a lottery: ". . . he had a greater devotion to freedom. He worshipped it, he idolized it, it had to him become a religion, and he had become a religious fanatic. Freedom and justice. He could not bear for anybody to be denied freedom or justice." The millennium is reached. The revolutionary springs full blown; his own freedom not withstanding, he will accept nothing less than the absolute: freedom and justice for all humankind.

"Is there a God, Frederick?" Sojourner Truth once queried Frederick Douglass. "Yes," Douglass thundered in reply, "and because there is, slavery must end in blood." Douglass arrived at this perspective after years of dedication to moral persuasion, but Vesey knew from the very beginning that slavery could be ended only by violent conflagration. In reaffirming this view, he discovered that he was not alone. Other Black men thought and felt as he did; there were others who had adopted the eagle as a symbol of freedom. In such men as Ned and Rolla Bennett, Mingo Harth, Peter Poyas, Monday Gell, and Gullah Jack, Vesey found a dedication to the absolute, a love for freedom and justice and a hatred of despotism to equal his own. Each of these men were in accord with the proposition that they had a human right to be free, "To overthrow the government if need be. To liberate (themselves) by any and every means that come to mind and hand. Even if it comes to killing every white man in the Charleston district and for miles and miles around."

The well drawn out plan of these men and their collaborators, men and women, the plot to besiege the city of Charleston and to free the slaves, and their betrayal by a "house slave" and eventual capture by the South Carolina militia is now history.

The insurrection that Vesey dreamed of as a child and sought to bring to birth as a mature man was aborted, and gallant and noble men died upon the gallows as a result. The aborted revolution, however, does not detract from Vesey's status as a revolutionary of the first rank, nor is it the most important aspect of his life. Success cannot be evaluated in the currency of slave masters and their descendants who write history. In a world of injustice, where men and women seek to validate the sanctity of the human spirit, it is not so much the cold facts of history that are important, but ofttimes, the archetypal hero, produced from the chaos and conflicts of which history is made and remembered.

Thus for Killens—and rightly so—the insurrection that never was is of less importance than the life of the archetypal hero, whose hunger for freedom and dignity make him one of the most important of Black paradigms. Here was a sensitive man who hated violence, a man of peace who hated war; he was a man of love, forced by the exigencies of slavery to become a rebel. But he was also a man who hated deeply, and thus he was a complete revolutionary, one who realized that men in bondage must opt only for the absolute, that to be free one must be willing to go to the bitter end.

It is the insight and ingenuity of Killens that makes for this portrait, which imbues this giant of a man with the twin emotions of love and hatred. For far too many Black writers in America, love is viewed as the universal solvent, the cleansing cream that might wipe out the remaining vestiges of slavery and oppression. Thus, those who openly and avowedly profess their hatred, like Vesey, are labeled by those who establish the criterium for truth as Black militants, Black racists, etc.

Killens knows, however, and this is the salient fact of *Youngblood,* and *And Then We Heard The Thunder,* as *Great Gittin' Up Morning* as well, that the revolutionary hates with an all-consuming fire; he hates dictatorship and demagoguery; he hates the ravaging of man by man; he hates a system and those who man it that keeps people throughout the world in poverty, servitude, and economic slavery; he hates the fact that some people live in mansions while others live in rat-infested shacks, that some lay claim to more of the world's natural resources than others; in short, he hates a world in which violence and murder by those who control the machinery of war make a world of love impossible.

The revolutionary, therefore, attempts to make the impossible possible, and this is the sum total of the life of Denmark Vesey. He is a symbol of endurance under fire, a reminder to men everywhere in bondage of the determination of the human spirit to be free; his very presence in history reminds us that there is a demarcation line, a limit to oppression, that men are still willing to die not only for their own liberty, but for that of others as well. Such men and women have always been with us; few have been able to find amanuenses of the talent, commitment, and determination of a John Killens. In a country that insists upon drinking the same intoxicating wine as that drunk by the people of Charleston during the planning of the Day of Reckoning and deluding themselves also that "our Negroes are a happy lot," such antithetical portraits of Black men and women as Vesey and those who followed him are not wanted. And like the house slave who betrayed the insurrection, so, too, do many at the present time betray truth by continuing to produce plays and novels designed to allow Americans to hold fast to their illusions.

Killens has always been a notable exception; his has been one of the major voices shouting eloquently, even before the sixties, sometimes alone, sometimes in concert with others, but always forcefully and clear, that the eagle was not made for iron and chains, but freedom; that slavery of any kind is illogical, and immoral, and its acceptance, no matter the rationale, unnatural. This is the lesson of Vietnam and Cuba, of Watts and Detroit, of Angola and Mozambique; and it is the lesson of *Great Gittin' Up Morning*.

CHAPTER 36

Great Black Russian: A Novel on the Life and Times of Alexander Pushkin

by John Killens

(1989)

Introduction

Alexander Sergeievich Pushkin was born in Moscow on May 26, 1799. He was descended, on his mother's side, from Hannibal, an Abyssinian prince, who became a ward of Peter the Great. Hannibal served his Czar so well that he became a confidant and favorite, was revered at the court, and began the aristocratic Pushkin lineage. In an unfinished work, *The Negro of Peter the Great*, Alexander Pushkin pays homage to his illustrious ancestor. Though his father did not possess as distinguished a lineage as his mother, he was also descended from the Russian nobility. Perhaps more important for Pushkin's development as a poet was his father's literary ambitions. As a result, the household was often filled with various writers, including Pushkin's uncle, who had a reputation as a minor poet. Among those who also visited the Pushkin household were such leading Russian writers as Karamazin, Zukovsky, and Dmitriev. Though by the time of his birth the family had lost much of its wealth and Aristocratic pretensions, he and his brother and sister were educated in the tradition of the nobility. Pushkin had a private tutor and access to his father's personal library, where he early became acquainted with the masters of French and German literature. His voluminous readings, in addition to attendance at the literary soirées given by his father and presided over by his uncle, began his interest in writing poetry. By the time he entered the Lyceum—a school established for educating the children of the nobility for important state positions—he had begun to compose his own verse. His early efforts were patterned after the compositions of classic writers, Russian and French, and centered around such youthful themes as lost love, the pursuit of pleasure, alienation, and occasionally such political pieces as "On the Return of the Emperor-Czar From Paris" (1815) and "Liberty: An Ode" (1817). Such offerings won him respect and acclaim. Derzhavin, Russia's "greatest eighteenth-century poet," praised his accomplishments, and he was invited to join Arzamus, a respected literary society. When he graduated from the Lyceum and took up his post as a foreign affairs officer in Petersburg, he had already acquired a sizable reputation as a writer.

He was also renowned as a rebel. The pursuit of wine, women, and song was characteristic of the young men of the nobility, and Pushkin found comrades as enamored of each as he was. Yet his own appetite for sensational and atavistic behavior seemed obsessive. His actions not only appeared fatalistic, as John Killens intimates, but the many duels fought and the many more contemplated suggest an excessive challenge to authority. The source of this need to engage in combat with those in power may be traced, on one level, to his lifelong feelings of alienation from his parents. Later in life he became convinced of his father's hostility toward him, and he was never really certain of his mother's love. Thus he grew into manhood, harboring intense feelings of alienation, uncertainty, and despair. Such feelings led to participation in radical causes and membership in radical groups. He supported the emancipation of serfs in Russia and of slaves in America, and he opposed the absolute power of the Czar. His activities led to involvement with a radical group, The Green Lantern, and to friendship with many members of the Decembrists, a revolutionary group so named because of the aborted attempt to overthrow the Czar in December of 1825. He lent his powerful voice as a poet to such groups and their efforts. Among the poems he produced in the interest of liberal causes were "The Country Side," which denounced serfdom, and "Christmas Fairy Stories" and the "Ode To Freedom," which attacked tyranny and despotism everywhere. He writes in "Ode to Freedom": "Tremble you tyrants of the world? And you degraded slaves, give ear / be strong, take courage and arise."

His activities with radical groups and his political poetry soon brought him into conflict with the authorities and precipitated his first exile from Petersburg. He was sent first to Southern Russia, where, after three years of riotous living, he was allowed to move to Odessa, a cosmopolitan city near the Black Sea. Here he wrote some of his most important works. He began *The Gypsy*, wrote the first chapter of *Eugeny Onegin*, and finished *The Fountain of Bakshisarai*, *The Prisoner of the Caucasus*, and *Gabriliad*, an "irreligious" poem depicting a sexual liaison between God, Gabriel, and Mary. Later, he would deny authorship of the poem. He soon came into conflict with the Governor General of Odessa, Count M. S. Vorontsov. His continual pursuit of the Count's wife intensified hostilities between the two, and Pushkin was dismissed from the foreign service. He was exiled to his mother's estate, at Mikhailovskoye, near the village of Pskov. Here he was placed under the supervision of his father, with whom he was frequently, sometimes violently, at odds. When he discovered that his father reported upon his activities to the Czar's secret police, he broke all contact with the older man. His relationship with his sister and brother, who also lived at the estate, was good, and their friendship helped him to confront the loneliness and alienation of his exile. In 1825, two events occurred that helped to release him from the boredom of Mikhailovskoye.

In November of 1825, Czar Alexander I died, and on December 14, the Decembrists attempted to take advantage of the confusion brought about by the question of succession. They began a short-lived revolt in Petersburg, which was soon crushed. In what was seemingly an unusually harsh act, the new Czar, Nicholas I, sentenced many of the conspirators to death and exiled over a hundred to Siberia. Most were either friends of the poet or avid readers of his poetry. Yet, because of his exile, he was safe from accusations of actual complicity, though suspicion about his involvement persisted. When he wrote a letter to the new Czar, asking permission for health reasons ("a kind of aneurysm"), he lied to end his exile and go "to Moscow, to Petersburg, or to foreign lands," and surprisingly his request was granted. Nicholas' motivations were twofold. He wanted to demonstrate that his extreme action against the Decembrists was not motivated by cruelty and vengeance, that he was a merciful and compassionate Czar. To end the exile of the man quickly becoming Russia's best known poet and, perhaps, secure his services for his regime might enhance his image in the eyes of his subjects. At the least, he would be better able to keep watch on the poet's activities were he near the court. Pushkin was summoned to Moscow, where, in a meeting with Nicholas on September 8, 1886, he impressed the Czar with his intelligence and honesty. He admitted his friendship with many of the radicals of the Decembrist movement and acknowledged that were he in Petersburg at the time, he would undoubtedly have been among "the rebels"; however, he would not now, he agreed, provide any form of opposition to the new regime. After calling him the "most intelligent man in Russia," Nicholas ended the poet's six-year exile and he was allowed to resume his social and literary life in Moscow.

The Czar's largesse was not given without conditions. The poet's works were to be carefully scrutinized before publication and travel restrictions were imposed. From time to time he was called upon to defend certain poems—the atheistic *Gabriliad* for example—and he had to account for his actions time and again to the Czar's secret police, who were charged with monitoring his movements. Yet, he was back in Moscow, back in the social setting of which he was so enamored. Once again, he became a popular figure at the court and the opera houses, and he continued to enhance his reputation by publication of such works as *Boris Godunov, Count Nulin,* and *Poltava.* After awhile, however, he began to tire of the constraints upon his life, the harassment by the Czar and his emissaries, and even the social life of Moscow. He appealed to the Czar to allow him to become part of the foreign mission, with duties in Paris or even China, but was rejected. On his own, without permission, he journeyed to the Caucasus, where he spent time with his brother's troops on the front line in a war against the Turks. Upon his return he was severely chastised by the chief of the secret police. During this period he became increasingly morose and despondent, and his constant bouts with depression may have led to his surprise marriage to Natalia Nikolaevna. Though she was purportedly one of the most beautiful women in Russia, friends and critics of the poet were bemused by such a seemingly incompatible marriage. Natalia had little cognizance of his literary achievements and ambitions, was not interested in the arts, and was obsessed with the social activities at the court of Nicholas—activities with which Pushkin had become bored. Her family had neither money nor titles, and she consented to marry only after the poet had engaged in persistent, sometimes embarrassing pursuit. After marriage, though she eventually bore him four children, she continued to cause him embarrassment. At numerous balls and parties—many of which she cajoled him into attending, some which she attended accompanied only by her sister—she was the stellar attraction. Flirtatious and naive, she encouraged the attentions of many men at the court, including the Czar. Over the years, Pushkin increasingly found himself compromised by her actions but was powerless to restrain her from pursuing her social aspirations. Gossip, which had begun early in the marriage concerning her purported liaisons, intensified. She was said to be romantically involved with not a few suitors, but when she encouraged the attention of d'Anthes-Heckeren, a handsome young French foreign missionary and the adopted son of the Dutch Ambassador, the poet was forced to act. After receiving anonymous notices informing him that he had been chosen "coadjutor of the Order of Cuckolds and historiographer of the Order," he challenged d'Anthes to a duel. The duel was twice postponed, but on January 27, 1837, the two men faced each other. D'Anthes, a good shot, fired first, wounding the poet, who managed to fire his round, inflicting only a slight wound in his opponent. Pushkin was rushed back to his home, where he struggled to regain his strength, only to succumb two days later. News of the poet's death produced an upsurge of fever and passion, and crowds thronged the streets of Petersburg, surrounding the Pushkin apartment and showing signs of possible political action. Fearing the possibility of a riotous demonstration, the civil authorities held a secret funeral service, moving the ceremony from the large church for which it was slated to a much smaller one and allowing attendance by invitation only. On February 6, 1837, Pushkin was buried in Svyatogorsk Monastery, near Mikhailovskoye, near his mother and great-grandfather, "The Negro of Peter The Great."

Pushkin's reputation as the founder of Russian literature is secure both in his homeland and on the continent. Praise for his works and his rebellious spirit have come from Gogol, Turgenev, Wordsworth and Matthew Arnold. Gorky wrote of his countryman: "Pushkin is the greatest master in the world. Pushkin, in our country, is the beginning of all beginnings. He most beautifully expressed the spirit of our people." Though his works are little known in America, his reputation is also secure among one very prominent group of Americans—Black intellectuals—who have long looked upon his literary successes with admiration and respect. Du Bois cited accomplishment in Russian literature as proof that Black men, free of racial bias, could develop their genius to its fullest, and

Richard Wright cited the achievement of the Russian poet as proof of his theory that Blacks who lived in a congenial racial climate could produce literature, void of a "racial content." Pushkin, wrote Wright, "was at one with his culture."

In *Great Black Russian: a Novel on the Life and Times of Alexander Pushkin*, John Oliver Killens moves beyond the summary praise of both European and Black American intellectuals. He refuses to reduce such an important poet to simply "the beginning of all beginnings" or a vehicle to counter racist claims to moral and intellectual superiority. Instead, Killens has adopted as a starting point for his own exploration of the life and times of this Russian writer Dostoevsky's tribute to Pushkin, over twenty years after his death, that without him "we should have lost, not literature alone, but much of our irresistible force, our faith in our rational individuality, our belief in the people's power, and most of all our belief in our destiny."

The Pushkin of John Killens's imagination is a multidimensional character. Anguish, pain, torment, hope, the search for love are all aspects of his character. The young boy who was despaired of his mother's love because he hungered for it so much is the mature man who wishes to transform fantasy into reality. "My mother loves me. Poor woman, she doesn't know how to express herself to someone like me. And who can blame her? I'm not easy to get along with." These conflicting emotions concerning his mother remain ever present and contribute to his varied feelings of compassion and concern for others, to his constant bouts with depression, and to his feelings of alienation and despair. And a contributing factor also, indeed, a most important one in the development of this poet as man and writer, is the overwhelming impact made upon him by his African ancestor. This fact is often overlooked in the works of academicians who write about Pushkin or downplayed in discussions of his life and works. In a compilation of Pushkin's poetry, one such academic never mentions the fact at all; and a "respected scholarly" work, published in 1970, also ignores the fact of Pushkin's ancestry. But the poet himself was fascinated by his great-grandfather, as his unfinished story "The Negro of Peter The Great" demonstrates. Realizing this concern, after careful and meticulous research, Killens, the novelist, depicts Hannibal as a central figure in the development of his great grandson. Writes Killens: "He [Pushkin] had lain there in his terrible loneliness and thought about his great-grandfather, the friend of the great Czar Peter . . . and the tall Black man with dark eyes . . . came to his bedside and talked with him about the times gone, when he himself was a boy in faraway Africa, a young Ethiopian prince."

The prodigious gifts of the poet are part of the heritage bequeathed by his ancestor, "the African blood" impacting upon his emotional and moral character twofold. The poet who loved human freedom and who despised chains and shackles everywhere, "Alas, where'er my eye may light / It falls on ankle chains and scourges / Perverted law's pernicious blight / And tearful serfdom's fruitless surges," is the poet of rebellion and revolution. But the poet who hungered for his mother's love, who, perhaps, saw reflections of his mother in every woman he intimately knew—and there were many—is the poet of extreme passion and sensitivity who often recoils at his own behavior, and who seldom hesitates to take responsibility for his actions. When he exercises a "master's prerogative," seduces and then impregnates a young servant girl, "He still felt guilty toward her. . . . He was no better than the very bastards [the nobility] he despised and wrote against. He said, 'I'm a devil. Stay away from me.'"

The young girl realizes what Killens enables the reader to realize, that Pushkin is not a devil, but man, one driven, as are all men, often by forces beyond their comprehension or control. He suggests in the case of Pushkin that among these forces were his ancestry and his need for love, and that because of the strong influence of each, the poet is neither the complete revolutionary, as, perhaps, is Kyo in Malraux's *Man's Fate,* nor the writer at one with a society in which his ancestry is of little consequence to his countrymen. Killens, the poet, realizes that the mythical life is never lived, that somewhere between the myth and legend of the man, and the fact and reality of the man, is the man of worth and substance. Thus, Pushkin is able at one and the same time to censure the relatives and friends of the Decembrists for their vacillations after the aborted uprising against the Czar, while himself courting the very Czar who sentenced some of them, his friends, to death and exile. He is capable of denouncing those who lie in order to achieve favor at the court, while in denying authorship of several of his own poems, he rationalized his own fabrications: "I do not owe the imperial court the . . . truth. The only things I owe it are damnation and exposure." Pushkin's explanation of and attempt to understand his complex character, however, are no rationalizations. "A writer," he muses, must suffer many contradictions, among them loneliness, the need for quiet and space, and "the absolute need for people, people to love, to know, to love with, to be happy with, to suffer with." Every time a writer begins a new work, it is "like falling in love again."

Not surprisingly, outside of heredity and the quest for parental affection, Killens discovers that the animus for Pushkin's complex personality, as well as his prodigious talent, lay in his continual belief in the energizing power of love. I have written of Killens elsewhere as the poet of love, for the key to the complexity of his own characters, from the novels from *Youngblood* to *'Sippi,* is the love they possess for themselves, for Black people, and for humankind. It is progressive this love, beginning first with the self and moving on to embrace one's culture and race. Afterward, one is capable of love of the oppressed everywhere. Such love, which moves beyond the Platonic, must be carved out of the tumultuous, turbulent world in which men and women must live. But the achievement can be made and the effort is not, as the existentialists suggest, a lonely and solitary one, but instead, a quest in which the very sensitive are aided by their ancestry, history, and sense of commitment to the elevation of humankind. Such men and women, Killens has argued, include Frederick Douglass, Sojourner Truth, Fannie Lou Hamer, Malcolm X, and Martin Luther King Jr., among many thousands gone, who through love of freedom and hatred of oppression sought to redirect the course of human history. Pushkin is the newest star among Killens's constellation of such lover/warriors and is different from the Pushkin conceived in the minds of either academic scholars or Black intellectuals. To ignore the impact of Pushkin's ancestry, Killens realizes, is to ignore an important source of his artistic and moral strength. But to suggest that the absence of racial conflict produced the climate necessary to write literature about the cares and concerns of all humankind is false. Killens has argued that Black literature of necessity addresses such concerns, for Blacks remain, as Wright once depicted them, as the metaphors of the twentieth century, and to write about the concerns and struggles of Blacks is to write about those of Everyman.

Killens has carefully integrated fact and fiction and produced a portrait of one of the paramount figures in world literature. He has depicted a man of power and intellect, of sensitivity and concern. He has etched out the contours of the life of a writer and universalized his experiences so that they bear resemblance to those of writers everywhere. He has draped over the shoulders of this nineteenth-century Russian writer the cloak of his own concerns and fears about our ability to love and to hope and to create a better world. He has shown us a Pushkin who, for most of his life, believed in justice, compassion, and freedom, and who, like Byron and Goethe, two literary models, was enamored of revolution as a means of liberating men and women from serfdom and slavery as well. He has shown us a Pushkin imbued with a sense of romanticism, and it may well be that the strongest link between the nineteenth-century Russian poet of African descent and his twentieth-century counterpart is the romanticism shared by both men.

For Killens is among the last of our romantic poets. He believes fervently in the promise of humankind; he believes that Black men and women can vaunt the barricades erected out of the experiences of many holocausts and point the way for the oppressed of the twentieth century, for the men and women in Angola, Mozambique, South Africa, and Nicaragua, as well as for Blacks in America. Despite the rhetoric of current prophets of despair, he believes that love is possible between Black people and Black people, and that this love has enabled millions to survive the American racial Armageddon. In all of these concerns, he is, like Pushkin, "the people's poet," one for whom concern with people is more important than wealth or fame. It is this concern which enables both him and the subject whose life he so carefully researched and ably presented in fiction to remain vibrant forces in the daily lives of revolutionaries/romantics everywhere. When he visited Moscow and was taken on a tour which included the shrine to Pushkin, he stood looking down at the crypt of this Black Russian poet. At that moment, two centuries of history merged, and one poet reached across the vast expanse of time and distance to embrace another. *Great Black Russian: a Novel on the Life and Times of Alexander Pushkin* is the result of this encounter. The novel is a great effort and a tremendous achievement.

CHAPTER 37

Black Expression: Essays by and about Black Americans in the Creative Arts

(1969)

Preface

Although the Negro novelist has made a breakthrough of sorts into the long barricaded halls of the universities, the Negro critic remains outside, much like Shelley's nightingale, singing to cheer his own sweet solitude. As writers of fiction, Richard Wright, James Baldwin, and Ralph Ellison are studied in more college classrooms today than any Negro writers heretofore; and yet, each of them has written competent criticism—a fact unknown to those who appreciate their creative efforts.

If, then, Wright, Baldwin, and Ellison are neglected as critics, the censure is much more severe in the case of such competent, professional critics as Alain Locke, Stanley Braithwaite, and Saunders Redding, to name but a few. Not only have these critics contributed to the understanding of Negro literature, but they have also contributed those ideas without which, to paraphrase Matthew Arnold, no creative epoch is possible. Yet, in the America of today, renowned, as one critic has remarked, for its great criticism, Negro critics have died the death of public and academic anonymity.

One may advance several reasons for the academic neglect of the Negro critic, yet three stand out with more prominence than the others. First and foremost is the incontestable fact that Negro literature has never been considered an integral part of American literature. Second, and an outgrowth of the first, is the consensus among Americans, Black and white, that whites are more capable of rendering objective, unbiased opinions about Negro literature than Negroes. (This idea pertains to every facet of Negro life. Books and magazine articles abound with self-appointed experts on the Negro—the majority of such experts being white.) And third, the persistence of the myth, in colleges and universities, that Negro critics lack the sensitivity and perception necessary for literary criticism.

In 1940, Richard Wright's *Native Son* was hailed as "A great American Novel." In 1953, Ralph Ellison was awarded the National Book Award for *Invisible Man*.

Gwendolyn Brooks won the coveted Pulitzer Prize for Poetry in 1950, and in 1956, James Baldwin was hailed as the "greatest American essayist since Ralph Waldo Emerson." Despite these accomplishments, however, Negro literature remains an unwanted and unacknowledged appendage to the vast body of American literature.

In part, this results from the effective use of the term "protest literature," which is bestowed upon any work by a Negro author. It is as if white critics were capable, en masse, of undergoing the experiences of a John Howard Griffin, of viewing the Negro world from within. Thereby drawing the conclusion that anyone relegated to permanence in such a world cannot help but scream, yell, and shout.

However true this may be, in much of Negro literature, the shout of racial protest is missing. In much of the poetry written by Phillis Wheatley during slavery, under conditions which necessitated protest, neither shout, yell, nor scream was heard. And in many contemporary Negro novels, the search for racial protest is unrewarded. Where is Baldwin's protest against the racial situation to be found, for example, in *Giovanni's Room?* Or in Willard Motley's *Knock on Any Door,* or *We Fished All Night?* Or in the novels of Frank Yerby, novels made conspicuous by their total neglect of Negro life experiences? Evidence of such protest is hard to come by, for to argue that the condition under which the Negro lives mandates a literature of protest is one thing; to argue that the Negro author will obey such dictates is another.

However, the most important reason for the inferior status of Negro literature stems from the social mores deeply imbedded in the American psyche. A nation incapable of recognizing Negroes as other than inferior beings—hewers of wood and drawers of water—has been unable to transcend the myths used to buttress the arguments of slaveholders and modern-day segregationists. Even so gifted a writer and liberal thinker as Norman Mailer can today be found parroting the most popular of such myths: ". . . the Negro . . . could rarely afford the sophisticated inhibitions of civilization, and so he kept for his survival, the art of the primitive . . . he subsisted for his Saturday night kicks, relinquishing the pleasures of the mind for the more obligatory pleasures of the body."

Such concepts have led to certain corollaries: Negroes are unlikely to produce important literature, or to undergo the kinds of experiences, universal in character, which form the basis of competent literature. For if one views the Negro through the sociological microscope, his inferiority mandates that his progeny, too, will be inferior. The old myths, therefore, remain. Black is inferior, of a poorer quality than white; Black people as a result are different beings, existing in narrow worlds, enclosed by petty experiences—experiences unrelated to the national character.

Viewed in the light of such deeply ingrained concepts, Negro literature is simplistic, immature, and unimportant. A distinguished editor of numerous anthologies remarked caustically, when asked why no Negro writers were represented in his latest work: "I never thought about it." Neither, it seems, have other anthologists, for anthologies today are noticeable by their omission of selections by Negro writers. Well might Robert Bone lament: "For it is a fact that Negro poets are virtually unknown among the teachers of American literature. Their poems appear but rarely in the textbooks and the anthologies; and their voices are seldom heard in the high schools or the college classrooms."

An outgrowth of the concept of the inferiority of Negro literature is the widely held belief that Negroes are incapable of objectively criticizing efforts by other Negroes. Such a task, therefore, can best be performed by whites. Thus, a major publishing company, seeking an editor for a collection of Negro writings, settled upon a white man who had little or no previous literary experience. Again, the most publicized study of Negro literature remains Robert Bone's *The Negro Novel in America,* whereas Saunders Redding's equally perceptive *To Make a Poet Black* and Hugh Gloster's *Negro Voices in American Fiction* have long been out of print, with no new editions in sight.

But Negro critics have seldom been partial to their brother writers. Indeed, some of their polemics are reminiscent of the days of John Dryden and Thomas Shadwell, of Alexander Pope and Lewis Theobold. For example, neither Baldwin nor Ellison has been reticent in attacking *Native Son.* John Killen's attacks on *Invisible Man* have been vehement, and no more scathing an attack has been made on any literary work than that by Saunders Redding on *Another Country.* Far then from being partial, Negro critics have assaulted the works of other Negroes with a vengeance that makes Samuel Johnson's critique of the works of Thomas Gray judicious by comparison.

However, the oft-stated argument that Negroes lack the sensitivity and perception indispensable to the critical appraisal of literature is of far more import than the preceding ones, if for no other reason than that such arguments are vigorously set forth by members of the academic community. In an article, "American Negro Poetry: On the Stage and in the Schools," critic Robert Bone is the Danton of the literary establishment. Bone writes of two Negro critics, Pearl Thomas and Carolyn Reese: Miss Thomas ". . . is . . . a birthright critic, miraculously schooled in Negro literature by virtue of her race alone." And Miss Reese ". . . cannot deal with Negro poetry because at bottom, she has failed to acquire the necessary skills."

Bone's argument is that these critics approach literature from a sensitive and perceptive vantage point, sharpened primarily by their racial experiences, which to Bone are inadequate. What is demanded is a knowledge of the critical tools sanctioned by the academic establishment. Writes Bone: "For the poet . . . teaches us to recognize our murderous and self-destructive feelings and to master them through form." Ralph Ellison has said something of the same: "Since fiction is always a collaboration between writer and reader . . . if a moral or perception is needed, let them [the readers] supply their own. For me, of course, the narrative is the meaning."

Through form, through the aesthetic presentation of the work of art, the writer communicates with the reader, allowing the latter to share aesthetically the varied nuances of the writer's experience. Form thus becomes a *deus ex machina,* a mechanical construction leading to "a heightened appreciation and awareness of life." Another way of stating the same argument is that form is the most important element in a literary work, while content is only ancillary, a necessary appendage, yet useless as a monitor or approximator of life. Literature is, then, reduced to mere artifact, timeless symbols of enduring beauty, much like the artifacts of Yeats' "Byzantium," appealing to man's natural propensity for beauty, and thus to paraphrase John Keats, truth. In the final analysis, art is a luxury; the sole prerogative of the aristocracy—a new aristocracy born of the academies—to be judged and evaluated upon those canons established by the aristocracy whose needs it serves.

The Misses Thomas and Reese, like Negro critics in the main—and there are exceptions—begin from an entirely different concept of the function of Negro literature. They are one with critics from Aristotle to Tolstoy who have demanded that literature, above all else, be moral; and with Samuel Johnson they would argue that the academic critics "seem to think we are placed here to watch the growth of the planets, or the motion of the stars . . . what we [have] to learn [is] to do good and avoid evil."

This emphasis upon a moral literature may appear medieval to many in the context of the amoral atmosphere of the twentieth century. For the Negro, however, and for the Negro writer, the emphasis upon morality, a clamor for men to do justice and avoid evil, has been the hallmark of his struggle in America, and his most fervent pleas to his country have been couched in moral terms. None of America's minorities believes more in the American creed; none has staked more upon the Constitution; none has depended more upon man's natural instincts for justice and tolerance; and none has shouted with more patience, with more passion, with more eloquence—white man, listen! The Negro has been concerned with the problem of life, in a physical and moral sense, in a society in which Negro life has been the most expendable commodity. Such a concern is a moral one, for "the question how to live is itself a moral idea."

In this context, the Negro critic approaches the work of art from a moral perspective, believing with Matthew Arnold that "It is important to hold fast to this; that poetry is at bottom a criticism of life; that the greatness of a poet lies in his powerful and beautiful application of ideas to life—to the question: How to live."

This is not to imply that the Negro critic eschews aesthetics. All realize, of course, that aesthetics are a necessary requirement of art. Most are opposed to the naive, unmeaningful, critical formulas vouchsafed by the academic community. Criticism which attaches importance to the investigation of the contortions of lines, the hidden meanings of punctuation marks, the ambidextrous usage of words may be of value to the "New Aristocracy," yet completely worthless to men and women seeking an affirmation of life in positive terms.

Again, criticism based upon the search for metaphysical themes—Who am I? What is my identity? What is my relationship to the universe, to God, to the existential other?—is of no value to a Negro community daily confronted by the horrors of the urban ghetto, the threat to sanity and life in the rural areas of the South, and the continual hostility of the overwhelming majority of its fellow citizens.

Though convinced of the importance of aesthetics—a point which has never been seriously contested—Negro critics are wary of theories applicable only to a nonexistent golden age. Believing with Robert Lehan that "the writer is the last remaining hope for the modern world . . .," the Negro critic has demanded that the writer concentrate on life, that life, despairing, laughing, hoping, and dying, in the ghettos of this country. To be sure, the Negro critic has used his Negroness as a vantage point, a point which enables him, unless lie has been quite lucky indeed, to view the American scene from a moral perspective. In so doing, his insights and perceptions have been sharpened to deal morally with that material which is, or which should be, the preoccupation of the Negro writer. And what Gwendolyn Brooks said with regard to the Negro poet is applicable to the Negro critic: "Every poet has something to say. Simply because he is a Negro, he cannot escape having something important to say."

Here, too, Robert Bone's statement is applicable: "By virtue of his deeper insight lie, the Negro writer, can exorcise the demons that threaten his people from within." But it is equally true that he can exorcise those demons which, today, rend the American society. For the Negro writer is America's conscience, and the Negro critic must be the conscience of them both.

This role of the Negro critic as moral adjudicator has never been more necessary than at present. And no period of Negro literature has demanded that the Negro critic exercise his critical sensitivity and perception for more moral reasons. For today, a dialogue persists in the community of Negro writers which threatens the moral foundation upon which Negro literature has in the main been predicated.

Alain Locke planted the seeds of the dialogue in 1925 in his introduction to *The New Negro*. Wrote Professor Locke: ". . . It is the Negro problem rather than the Negro that is known and mooted in the general mind. We turn therefore . . . to the elements of truest social portraiture, and discover in the artistic self expression of the Negro today a new figure on the national canvas. . . . In these pages . . . we have . . . commented upon self expression and the forces of determination. So far as he is culturally articulate, we shall let the Negro speak for himself."

The idea that the Negro should speak for himself was not new. Though much of early Negro literature was marred by propaganda, still Frederick Douglass, W. E. B. Du Bois, James Weldon Johnson, and Langston Hughes spoke from that deep wellspring of Negro experience which represented the extent of Negro culture of that time. What was new, however, was Locke's insistence that the time had come for Negro writers to turn from moralizing, from attempts to force their just cause upon the conscience of the nation. Because attempts to make white men listen had aborted, the New Negro was admonished to forgo such attempts and to turn inward to self expression.

To do so, however, called for a new kind of literature, and a new Negro to write that literature. Albert Barnes characterized both the literature and its creator: "The later Negro has made us feel the majesty of nature, the ineffable peace of the wood and the great open spaces. He has shown us that the event of our everyday American life contains for him a poetry, rhythm, and charm which we ourselves had never discovered. . . . His insights into realities have been given to us in vivid images loaded with poignancy and passion. His message has been lyrical, rhythmic, colorful. In short, the elements of beauty, he has controlled to the ends of art." And perhaps Stanley Braithwaite stated the argument more succinctly "Negro poetic expression hovers for the moment, pardonably perhaps, over the race question, but its highest allegiance is to poetry. . . ."

This philosophy has been stated anew by Negro writers today. Ralph Ellison has written: "If *Invisible Man* is 'free from the ideological penalties suffered by Negroes in this country,' it is because I tried to the best of my ability to transform these elements into art." And, demands Ellison, "I can only ask that my fiction be judged as art; if it fails, it fails aesthetically." James Baldwin, theoretically at least, was certain of the saving grace of art: For the only concern of the artist was "to recreate out of the disorder of life that order which is art."

Not until 1940 were these arguments, first set forth by the proponents of the Negro Renaissance, effectively challenged. The challenge came from Mississippi-born Richard Wright who, as artist and critic, transformed a monologue into a dialogue by presenting, dramatically, forcefully, and persuasively, the other argument. Wright argued, in essence, that conditions in America had not changed to the degree that the Negro could desert the race question, engage in an art for art's sake endeavor, or wander free in the sunny utopia of abstraction in an attempt to desert the harsh reality of being Black in the twentieth century. "The grinding process of history," wrote Wright in 1945, "had forged iron in the Negro's heart [and therefore] we heard a new and strange cry from another Negro." And this cry came from the pen of Claude McKay, the *enfant terrible* of the Negro Renaissance, in bitter, vehement protest, in the militant poem, "If We Must Die."

Though certainly not antagonistic to artistic principles, Wright realized that an era of oppression was not one in which "art could be the only consideration." Negroes capable of ignoring the brutal, inhuman treatment of other Negroes were, according to Wright, Negroes "who recorded the feelings of a Negro reacting not as a Negro."

So central a part does this thesis play in Wright's critical theory that he returns to it in 1956: ". . . The fact of separation from his native land has now sunk home into the Negro's heart; the Negro loves his land, but that land rejects him. . . . Here we can witness the emergence of a new type of Personality." That personality was George Moses Horton who: ". . . was an emotionally trapped man; he lived in a culture of which he was not really a part; he was a split man believing and feeling something which he could not live." . . . Horton's cry for freedom was destined to become the lament, was to roll down the decades swelling, augmenting itself, becoming a vast reservoir of bitterness and infrequent hope.

But Richard Wright died in 1960, and no other Negro writer of his stature has arisen to enjoin the dialogue, presented today by the new proponents of a Negro Renaissance. The New Negroes of the nineteen sixties, apropos of their namesakes of the nineteen thirties, have according to Herbert Hill. ". . . made the creative act their first consideration. . . . As the Negro writer moves beyond anger, he develops a new concern for the writer's craft, for literary discipline and control and seeks an involvement in the larger world of art and ideology."

The Negro critic remains, then, to present the other argument. He must, like Richard Wright, take an active part in the dialogue, not as a Lycurgus dispensing arbitrary laws and rules, nor as a Polonius brandishing answers and solutions, but instead as an engaged participant, fully respectful of both sides of the dialogue. His criticism must be guided by a temperament which allows him to explicate the work of art in terms of its contribution to the alleviation of those problems which have confronted humanity for too long a time. This entails a sensitive and perceptive awareness which can only, in part, be conditioned by the academic establishment, Robert Bone's cry of despair, therefore: "But you really must know Ezra Pound, Hart Crane, and Charles Olson if you hope to understand Melvin Tolson, Robert Hayden, and LeRoi Jones," is presumptuous; for the understanding of such poets depends equally upon a critical perspective conditioned by the many-faceted experiences of the Negro in the turbulent American society.

On this point, the Negro critic and the university will remain at odds. If the day ever arrives when Negro literature is accepted as an integral part of American literature, the Negro critic will still remain invisible. For his is the predominant voice in American criticism which calls upon the Negro writer to dedicate himself to the proposition that literature is a moral force for change as well as an aesthetic creation. In so doing, he risks not only continued invisibility, but denigrating charges that he does not know enough, coupled with insistent attacks upon his credentials as a critic.

This cannot he helped. Though the moral argument has little relevance in America at present, still the Negro critic must demand that the Negro writer articulate the grievances of the Negro in moral terms,. for the time is far distant when the Negro writer can cry out in sweet delirium with John Keats:

> Away! Away! for I will fly to thee
> Not charioted by Bacchus and his pards
> But on the viewless wings of Poesy. . . .

CHAPTER 38

Oak and Ivy: A Biography of Paul Laurence Dunbar

(1971)

Introduction

The year was eighteen ninety-two. Snow covered the narrow unpaved streets of Dayton, Ohio, hiding the shingled houses under a blanket of gleaming whiteness. A messenger, a scarf pulled tightly around his neck, a package tucked securely under his arm, walked up to the stoop of the house belonging to Matilda Dunbar and her son, Paul. Matilda watched the messenger arrive. She reached the door at the first ring, opened it wide, ushered the young man inside. Before he could say, "Package for Mr. Paul Laurence Dunbar," she had taken it from his gloved hand.

The package was from the United Brethren Publishing House in Dayton and contained copies of Dunbar's first book of poems, *Oak and Ivy*. The messenger was unaware of this; however, he did know that the package contained something of importance. All the way over, while plodding through the snow, he had wondered what the package held and who the man was to whom it belonged. Watching the old woman fondling it so carefully, he asked hurriedly, as though afraid that the words might not come at a slower pace: "What is this Dunbar? Is he a doctor, a lawyer, a preacher?"

Matilda smiled. "Paul," she replied, her eyes lighting up, "why Paul is just an elevator boy." She paused, the lights seemed to glow brighter in her eyes. Finally, she continued with a burst of pride, "And . . . and a poet!"

An elevator boy and a poet! For the rest of his life and long after his death, Dunbar would be known by these two terms. Biographers would write warmly about the early days when he operated the elevator in the Callahan Building, where he composed some of his best poems while being frequently interrupted to pick up passengers on a distant floor.

He was a poet long before he became an elevator boy—some would say that he had been born a poet. This was not quite true, although he began rhyming words at the age of six. Some of his biographers would say much later that he was a great poet, but this also was not true. He might have been a great poet if he had been allowed to write the kind of poetry he wished to write. A few years before his death, while visiting a fellow poet, James Weldon Johnson, he seemed to recognize this fact himself. "I have kept doing the same things over and over," he told Johnson. "I have never done the things that I wanted to do."

There was sadness in this statement, and he expressed it often in his lifetime. He believed that he was held down, kept from fulfilling his promise by an unseen fate like that which controlled the lives of his characters in his novel, *The Sport of the Gods*. However, the fate that controlled him was not invisible. It was composed of many forces and many people, and it had operated to make him an elevator boy against his wishes. Before accepting the position at the Callahan Building, he had tried to gain work more fitting for a high school graduate.

He tried factories, warehouses, and even newspapers, many of which had published his poems while he was still a student at Central High School. He asked for positions such as clerk, accountant, or receptionist.

At each place, the employer or a representative gave him the same answer, implied if not always spoken, "We have no jobs of this kind for Negroes." Dayton, in the nineteen hundreds, was a small town. People knew one another, and hardly anything of importance occurred that did not reach the ears of the townsfolk.

Almost everyone knew of Paul Laurence Dunbar. They knew he had been the only Black student enrolled at Central High School; that he had been elected president of the senior class; that he had served as editor of the school paper, and that he was considered to be one of the town's most promising young men. Still, they turned him down with the words, "We don't hire Negroes for this kind of work."

During slavery, Dayton had held no men in bondage. With the exception of the Dunbar family, there were few Black people in the town. Most of the townsmen knew of Black people only through knowing the Dunbars, who were respected as good citizens. Yet these men believed the myths that other men had spread about Black people. Myths that said that Blacks were simple, childish creatures who had to have special homes, special eating places, special seats on public transportation, and special jobs.

What did it matter if Dunbar had been a good student? Was he not still a Black man? Of what importance was it that he wrote poetry? Did not poetry contain rhythm, and did not all Black people have an abundance of rhythm? Moreover, did he not write dialect poetry, and was not dialect the language of a simple, childish people?

Dunbar did indeed write dialect poetry; and in it he catered to the worst of the Southern myths. He wrote of simple slaves who loved their masters, of childish people whose only desire was to go coon hunting, to take the banjo down from the wall, to serve their white masters and mistresses with loyalty and devotion, and to party from "sun down to sun up."

He knew, however, that very little of what he wrote in dialect was true. How could he believe in the simplicity of Black people when there had been such men of the race as Frederick Douglass, Henry Highland Garnet, and Nat Turner? Such women as Sojourner Truth, Harriet Tubman, and Mary Church Terrell? Had he been free to write often of such people in pure English, his poetry would have been far different from what it was. "I never wanted to write dialect," he confessed to James Weldon Johnson; and in poem after poem he despaired over the fact that others dictated the route that his youthful imagination was to take. A clue to his feelings on this point may be found in the poem, *Misapprehension:*

> Out of my heart, one day, I wrote a song,
> With my heart's blood imbued,
> Instinct with passion, tremulously strong,
> With grief subdued;
> Breathing a fortitude
> Pain-bought.
> And one who claimed much love for what I wrought,
> Read and considered it,
> And spoke:
> "Ay, brother,—'t is well writ,
> But where's the joke?"

The joke was missing in a great deal of Dunbar's poetry. Though he wrote of love, nature, and death, the white world ignored these, praising him and making him famous for what he called "jingles in a broken tongue." Few noticed the "note of sadness" that crept into much of the poetry he wrote in standard English. Like Thomas Gray, the English poet, much of his poetry is about death, the thought of dying, and the wish to die. In a letter written to a friend in 1894, he expressed such a wish openly: "There is only one thing left to be done, and I am too big a coward to do that."

He continued to live and to write poetry, short stories, and novels. And he lived in a world in which men, not free themselves, continued to restrict his freedom. They not only forced him to write about Black people, but in addition, they forced him to write about Black people as they wanted Black people to be. He acquiesced because, as he said, "I had to get a hearing."

The hearing cost him dearly. To be sure, it brought fame and fortune; but it also brought despondency, heartbreak, and pain. His sickness, his alcoholic problems, the breakup of his marriage—all resulted from the terrible price he had to pay to get a hearing. In a country where Black poets and writers suffer under the impulses and control of other men, none suffered so much as Dunbar. The extent of his pain may be measured in the lines from *Conscience and Remorse:*

> "Good-bye," I said to my conscience—
> "Good-bye for aye and aye,"

> And I put her hands off harshly,
> And turned my face away;
> And conscience smitten sorely
> Returned not from that day.

But his conscience did not stray far. It came back again and again to haunt him and to force him to fight against those who had restricted his freedom. During those times he wrote poems like *The Haunted Oak,* which describes the lynching of a Black man; short stories like *The Lynching of Jube Benson,* which assails the act of lynching; and novels like *The Sport of the Gods,* which reveals the true nature of the plantation system. In poems and stories like these, he gave the lie to all he had written of the wonderful life "wey down souf" during slavery.

However, such times were too few. The poems and stories of that kind were inadequate compensation for his suffering. When he died at the age of thirty-four, he had outlived his creative talent by ten years. To millions who read his works, the terms by which his mother announced his calling—elevator boy and poet—were adequate to his career. Others were not so easily satisfied. They knew that he might have been described as a great poet and that this recognition had been denied him because of his color. The nation had painted a picture of him to which it demanded that he conform. That picture was to stand for all of his people, and it was one of a simple-minded child, a buffoon.

He was not a buffoon, nor was he an entertainer; and he spent the best years of his life attempting to convince people of this fact. The failure of this attempt and the tension between being a poet and an entertainer formed the major conflict of his life. "Most men," wrote Henry David Thoreau, "live lives of quiet desperation." And although Dunbar's life was seldom quiet, it was extremely desperate. It was a life filled with disappointment and dashed hopes; a life in which the great battles were lost—those with his publishers and critics, and those with love and death.

Despite his shortcomings, or perhaps because of them, he won acclaim in the eyes of millions of Black men. They, too, led lives of quiet desperation. They, too, had been forced to sell their souls in order to survive in a country which constantly deemed them unworthy. They, too, had suffered a loss of freedom. Of all his poems, perhaps the one they admired the most was that in which he put into words not only the terror of his own life, but of theirs as well:

> We wear the mask that grins and lies,
> It hides our cheeks and shades our eyes,—
> This debt we pay to human guile;
> With torn and bleeding hearts we smile,
> And mouth with myriad subtleties.
>
> Why should the world be over wise,
> In counting all our tears and sighs?

Nay, let them only see us, while
    We wear the mask.

We smile, but, O great Christ, our cries
To thee from tortured souls arise.
We sing, but oh the clay is vile
Beneath our feet, and long the mile;
But let the world dream otherwise,
    We wear the mask!

CHAPTER 39

Richard Wright: Ordeal of a Native Son

(1980)

Introduction

To paraphrase Michel Fabre, the distinguished biographer of Richard Wright, to Americans of the nineteen seventies Richard Wright remains unknown and unread. This was true of the late sixties and early seventies despite the fact that from 1940, the publication date of *Native Son,* until his sudden death in Paris in 1960, he was the most famous Black writer in the world. His books have been translated into many languages, and millions throughout Asia, Africa, Europe, and the Middle East have shared, vicariously, the experiences of a Mississippi Black boy. Yet his reputation did decline in the early nineteen sixties, and this may be attributable to a number of factors. Among them were a rising militancy and determination to achieve human rights in America, which led to a search for political, not literary, writers; the popularity of such younger writers as James Baldwin and Ralph Ellison, whose works in comparison to those of Wright appeared moderate in tone and theme; subtle efforts by magazines and critics, with an impetus by the government, to render Wright's attacks on American foreign policy and racism negligible by diminishing his reputation; a self-imposed exile that kept him out of the country and away from the ferment generated during the civil rights crusade; and the reluctance of college and high school teachers to deal with the explosive acts of racism contained in most of his works.

However, in the past five years there has been renewed interest in Wright and his works. A number of critical articles have been written about his books in prestigious journals. *American Hunger,* the last half of the autobiography *Black Boy,* published in 1945, has been released, and a revised edition of the stage adaptation of *Native Son* has played before New York audiences. A new play is slated for Broadway, at least one other biography is headed for publication, several doctors' theses are in the development stage, and plans are under way to release some of his as yet unpublished work. Black intellectuals who ignored him in the sixties today eagerly search through his works, seeking answers as to why and how the civil rights revolution of the sixties went astray; young college professors are inclined to honestly confront his commentary on the debilitating effects of American racism and his death-stilled criticism of the United States government. Today, more and more Americans are reading of his life and trials, of his ordeal as a sensitive Black intellectual in a racist society.

Those who read *Black Boy* confront the man shorn of the writer's mask. They discover that by the time he was fifteen, he had known of the lynching of a stepuncle and the brother of a neighborhood friend; that he had spent time in an orphanage, had known poverty and hunger; that he had witnessed the paralyzing of his mother, her being rendered an invalid for most of her life; that he had personally experienced Southern brutality. He joined the Black migration heading North before his twenty-first birthday, hoping, as he implied in the closing pages of *Black Boy,* to discover the new Canaan. The relative freedom of the North enabled him to become a writer, and he was to create some of the most exciting literature in America. Yet Canaan was always to elude him. Before his success as a writer, he encountered poverty and hunger again, racism and exploitation Northern-style, and authoritarianism in the Communist Party. The pattern of his life seemed not to have altered greatly in many respects, even after the publication of *Native Son* made him world famous. He was involved in an unsuccessful marriage and in frequent altercations with leaders of the Communist Party, and was harassed by agents of the Federal Bureau of Investigation. He divorced his first wife and married again in 1944, and in 1945 he broke publicly with the Party. In 1947, with his wife and daughter, he went into self-imposed exile in France.

If again he sought Canaan, again he was disappointed. His exile afforded some relief from racism, but his fierce sense of independence and his well-earned reputation intensified the conflict between himself and agencies of the American government, which sought to force him to mitigate his attacks upon American domestic and foreign policy and to inform on old comrades and friends in the Communist Party. This aspect of the government's campaign began even before he went into exile, and one of the reasons for his so doing was to escape the pressure brought upon him to be an informant. In France, on a passport granted by the State Department, which had the power to rescind it at any moment, he underwent an ordeal as severe as that he had previously recorded in *Black Boy* and *American Hunger.* It may well have been the strain and stress attending this ordeal which brought about his sudden death.

Rumors concerning his confrontation with agencies of the American government fueled my own interest in Richard Wright. During a trip to Paris in 1971, one of Wright's close friends informed me that Wright had been a special target of the Central Intelligence Agency and the Federal Bureau of Investigation. These agencies, the friend remarked, were responsible for his death. Such rumors were rife on the Left Bank, both among Black expatriates and French intellectuals, but, at the time, I gave little credence to them, simply because I could not believe that a writer was important enough to incur the wrath of the government. But, as the biographies of Wright began to appear—by John A. Williams, Constance Webb, and Michel Fabre—each of whom spoke of government harassment, the rumors took on for me some semblance of credibility. Later, reading Chester Himes's comments in *Amistad One* and his autobiography, and reading Wright's private papers and letters (housed at the Beinecke Rare Book and Manuscript Library at Yale and at the Schomburg library in New York), I was then disposed to think of the rumors as having some validity.

If they did, then here was unexplored terrain, an ordeal undergone by Wright as severe and intense as any before, a dimension of his life that might serve to place his life and works in a new perspective. At the least, some of the intriguing yet unanswered questions concerning his relationship with the Communist Party and African nationalists abroad might be clarified, as well as the extent and nature of his involvement with the government. Fortunately, in undertaking this assignment, I had a research tool not available to past students of Wright: investigative files from government agencies interested in his activities.

The Congress of the United States passed the Freedom of Information Act in 1966 and the Privacy Act in 1974. The former allowed access to previously classified documents compiled on American citizens by various government agencies, and the latter allowed American citizens access to their own files, if any existed. On July 7, 1976, I wrote the Department of Justice requesting theretofore classified documents pertaining to Richard Wright. This request triggered a response by other agencies, and in December of 1977, I received the first document from the Department of State. In April, I received a substantial number of documents from the FBI, and in June, two documents from the CIA. The largest number of documents—187 pages out of a possible 227—came from the FBI. These reflect the fact that information concerning Wright, as well as actions to be taken against him, were forwarded to the FBI. Thus, in these files were found documents from the United States Information Service, the military intelligence units of the Army and the Navy, and the Foreign Liaison Service, which supplied security agencies of other governments with data.

The documents are unusually legible, though deletions of names and information are frequent. Of the total number of pages in the FBI file, thirty-nine have been deleted according to provisions contained in the Freedom of Information Act, which range from the interests of national security to the desire to protect agents and informers. Deletions of entire paragraphs and sometimes a number of pages occur in some documents, making clarification of certain events almost impossible. This is particularly true of documents originating with the Foreign Service and forwarded to FBI Headquarters in Washington from Paris during the last years of Wright's life.

Access to this new research tool forced the realization that none of my college training had prepared me to analyze the material at my disposal. I was taught to examine old and obscure tracts, to balance the thesis of one critic against that of another, to gather evidence for or against one set of postulates and to enunciate findings supported by the proper number of authorities and an abundance of footnote material. My graduate training had taught me to look at the works and lives of men and women as if they existed in a social and political vacuum. This methodology served well in work done in graduate school on eighteenth-century British literature. If Henry Fielding and Samuel Richardson were objects of interest to their government, I had no way of knowing. But the modern American writer, if outspoken and radical or an advocate of unpopular causes, is very likely to be a subject of investigation by some agencies of the government. The fruits of such investigation may be indispensable to understanding certain nuances of his life, which may well have influenced his work.

To my knowledge, Freedom of Information Act material has not been applied to research on American writers; certainly none has been applied to Black writers. Thus, I was involved in setting a precedent, having no guidelines to follow. The material before me could only be understood if I understood as well the historical context of the forties and fifties, during which the adversary relationship between Wright and the government existed. The contours of the study I had planned was changed: I would need to analyze the period of American concentration upon subversives and the "Communist conspiracy," in the hope that light might be shed on some of the people named in the documents, on some of the events concerning Wright's most important undertakings, and on certain actions proposed against him. Thus, books on history were indispensable; so, too, in attempting to understand many of the codes and much of the terminology contained in the documents, were books on such governmental agencies as the CIA and the FBI.

The absence of guidelines, however, presented the greatest difficulty in another area: How was the material to be presented? The documents lend themselves to dramatic and sensationalistic treatment; here is the material of which good drama and fiction are made. There are portraits of cool, calculating agents, of comical ones whose ineptness is blatant, of paid and volunteer informants, Black and white, including one labeled by an agent as "a psychopath." There are intrigue and suspense, and the drama of good and evil is well stocked with heroes and villains. To treat the material in a theatrical way was tempting; in my judgment, however, to do so would have been erroneous.

First, the story was one-sided, coming from the very agencies that had harassed Wright during his lifetime. Second, some of the material was damaging to Wright's reputation and had to be corroborated as much as possible from his private papers and from interviews with his friends. Finally, there were my apprehension and suspicion, heightened by some of the material, of possible governmental action against the late writer. In two instances, the documents suggest an attempt by the legal representative of the FBI in Paris to make the Baldwin-Wright literary controversy into a political one and pit one Black writer against the other. I was forced then to confront the possibility that the vendetta waged by the State Department against Wright in the last days of his life might persist still among old and unforgiving bureaucrats, and that this writer might be used to impugn Wright's reputation. This concern led to my decision to present the data from the documents in as objective a manner as possible. The documents would speak for themselves. I would editorialize little, analyze and evaluate material only when there were adequate collaborative data from Wright's works, from previous studies, or from his own private papers. Looking at Wright and the documents concerning him from a historical perspective allowed me to place the material in chronological order, in accord with various stages of his life. Presented in this way, the documents assume an overwhelming importance in Wright's career, particularly the last years of his exile.

Even without emendation, the documents provide answers to questions heretofore unresolved by Richard Wright scholars. The 1958 document, for instance, reveals that Wright's sudden break with the Communist Party, after debating with himself about such action for a number of years, came about as the result of a personal altercation between him and Benjamin Davis. The document of 1944, consisting of logs of wiretaps on the phones of important party officials, reveals the concern of the Party over Wright's defection and outlines the campaign eventually waged against him. The documents reveal that problems concerning his passport did not originate in 1945, but began in 1940, when his passport was taken by immigration officials at the Mexican border. The document of 1943 reveals that the initial interest in Wright on a full scale occurred as a result of a memo, from the office of Secretary of War Henry Stimson to the director of the FBI, suggesting that Wright may be guilty of sedition—an offense punishable by imprisonment. Other documents reveal the nature of the operations of the Bureau, including the use of informers, questioning of neighbors, and mail openings. The documents of 1958–60 reveal that the major agency interested in Wright's activities abroad was not, as had been suspected, the FBI or the CIA, but the Department of State. In a letter written to his friend and translator Margrit de Sablonière, Wright corroborated this fact by pointing to the Department of State as his major adversary. If this is so, then assumptions that the CIA and the FBI were solely responsible for his early death might have to be reassessed.

The documents of 1956 and 1958 suggest that the State Department may have been engaged in blackmail concerning Wright. He was forced to sign statements and to answer questions regarding "the Communist conspiracy" before his passport was renewed. In letters to friends, in private conversations, in notations contained in the works of his biographers are revealed his anxieties about returning to the United States. Had he done so, he would have had to face the investigative committees of the Congress, and possibly, courtroom trials. Acquaintances such as Langston Hughes, W. E. B. Du Bois, Paul Robeson, and Canada Lee had undergone terrible ordeals with the House Un-American Activities Committee. Robeson and Du Bois had their passports revoked and their means of livelihood ended. Lee and Hughes were forced to disavow past "subversive affiliations." Wright's treatment, were he to be forced back to America, would have probably surpassed that of Robeson and Du Bois. He did not, like the other two men, have the support of progressives and the members of the Communist Party. Thus he would have had to undergo his ordeal alone.

The documents pertaining to renewal of his passport assume major importance. To Wright's applications were affixed questions pertaining to knowledge that he may have had of former Communists. In the presence of the passport chief and the legal representative, if the files are correct, he produced a statement denying recent Communist affiliation of his own and answered questions corroborating information concerning Communists of his knowledge. At the same time, therefore, when the documents suggest coercion by the government, they also suggest some degree of cooperation by Wright. Other documents also suggest such cooperation, but the most damaging document in this respect, the document of 1956, pertains to the conference of Black and African writers sponsored by the magazine *Présence Africaine*. "On his own initiative," reads the document of 1956, "Mr. Wright called at the embassy to express certain concern over the leftist tendencies of the Executive Committee for the [*Présence Africaine*] Congress. He believed the members of the committee were liberal thinkers and he thought there was a distinct danger that the communists might exploit the congress to their ends." This act allied him with the CIA and the security forces of every colonialist nation, whose interest in the conference was pronounced.

If the motives for his cooperation, either reacting to threats of blackmail or attempting to curry favor with the government in his own interest, are indicated in the document, the degree to which such cooperation occurred is not. Nor are the reasons clear as to why, despite his seeming cooperation, the government agencies never trusted him and continued their harassment. The 1956 document seems to be a watershed for both Wright and the government; afterward, he would announce to friends both in conversation and in print that he was on the attack against the government of the United States. By the time of his death, in 1960, these attacks had intensified.

The temptation to draw conclusions in line with those who believe that the FBI and the CIA were directly involved in Wright's sudden death are great. To do so, however, based upon the facts of the documents, would be wrong. I did not find, nor did I expect to find, evidence to support this assertion, held by a great many of the writer's friends. What I found was a pattern of harassment by agencies of the United States government, resembling at times a personal vendetta more so than an intelligence-gathering investigation. I discovered that the government was guilty of producing anxiety and stressful situations, which would have produced severe hypertension in most men, let alone one so sensitive as Wright. But

I discovered nothing to convince me of FBI and CIA culpability in his death. In fact, late documents show the FBI attempting to call off the investigation.

The role of the State Department, however, is another matter, for it was here that the seeming vendetta occurred. The only document that supposedly originated with the State Department casts Wright in an unfavorable position. Documents filtered through the State Department to the FBI show an inordinate amount of activity on the part of the Foreign Service during the last months of Wright's life. Most of the documents are heavily deleted, so their content is difficult to comprehend clearly. Whether there is any connection between this activity and Wright's death may be known only if the deleted sections of the documents are released.

My own observation, however, is that Wright's death, by heart attack, was caused not by cloak-and-dagger assassins but, as Fabre concluded in *The Unfinished Quest of Richard Wright,* by the constant pressure and tension-ridden situations induced by the ordeal to which his government subjected him. In retrospect, this may well have been a crime of the magnitude of assassination. For nowhere in the documents prepared by the government is there evidence that Wright was engaged in subversive activity, that he attempted to undermine the security of the United States, or that he aided and abetted others in doing so. He was a humanist and writer, a man of principle and independent ideas, a Black man who insisted on speaking out against the assault by governments left and right against the sanctity of the human spirit. He was, as Hoyt Fuller wrote, ". . . an American tugging at the conscience and the submerged sense of reason of America, and America should be proud to have produced him. His going into exile was a gesture of affirmation, testimony to his belief in the preciousness of human dignity and freedom."

CHAPTER 40

Claude McKay: The Poet at War

(1972)

Introduction

In 1922, James Weldon Johnson edited *The Book of American Negro Poetry* with the expressed intention of serving notice upon the American public that Black poetry and poets had an existence of their own. The book remains a classic—one of the most important documents in Black literature; however, it did not fulfill its purpose of educating the American public in the field of Black poetry. The recognition accorded Pushkin in Russia, Plácido in Cuba, and Durand in Haiti differed from the recognition accorded Afro-American poets in *their* native land. Not even during the Harlem Renaissance, a period in which Black poets made a major breakthrough in terms of public acceptance, was the acceptance general and widespread. For public recognition (by Blacks as well as whites) Afro-American poetry would have to await the latter part of the twentieth century.

This is readily understandable. In his preface, with the instincts of the prophet-critic, Johnson pinpoints the problem of Afro-American poetry before 1920: Negro dialect poetry had its origin in the minstrel tradition, and a persistent pattern was set. When the individual writer attempted to get away from the pattern, the fixed conventions allowed him only to slip over into a slough of sentimentality."[1] What the status of Afro-American poetry might have been had there been no dialect tradition is open to conjecture. The chances are that, because of racism, the status would not have been appreciably higher.

The vogue of dialect poetry began with a little-known white Southerner, Irwin Russell, who wrote poems about Negroes in the 1860s. Though a few of these poems were sold to *Scribner's Monthly,* we are told in an autobiographical sketch that he "seemed to lack a market for [his] Negro poetry in the North. . . ."

Russell's fame rests upon the poem "Christmas-Night in the Quarters"; and it is with this poem in mind that Joel Chandler Harris later wrote: "The most wonderful thing about the dialect poetry of Irwin Russell is his accurate conception of the Negro character. The dialect is not always the best—it is often carelessly written—but the Negro is there, the old fashioned, unadulterated Negro, who is still dear to the Southern heart."[2] The image of the Negro to which Harris refers can be found in such lines as these from "Christmas-Night in the Quarters":

> Yes, tell dem preshis angyls we's a-gwine to jine
>   'em soon:
> Our voices we's a-trainin fur to sing de glory
>   tune;
> We's ready when you wants us, an it ain't no
>   matter when—
> O Mahsr! Call yo' chillun and take 'em home!
>   Amen!

The first edition of Russell's verse was published in 1888, nine years after his death. The publication of the book could not have come at a more auspicious moment in history. In 1877, President Hayes, paying off political debts to the South, removed the Federal troops whose major occupation after the Civil War had been the protection of helpless Blacks. The removal of the troops left the Blacks prey to vigilante groups—the Ku Klux Klan, the Knights of the White Camellia, and the Red Shirts. As a result of the rise of such groups, the era of Reconstruction and its aftermath ended by 1885; and North and South alike sought a period of tranquility, a return to a time when the Negro knew his place, indeed, back to that time when he was, in Harris' words, "the old fashioned, unadulterated Negro—dear to the Southern heart."[3]

The fact that such a Negro had no existence in actuality disturbed neither Southerner nor Northerner. The Negro question had to be resolved and the internecine warfare between the races halted, if railroads, factories, and industry were to be built in the South. The age, as Mark Twain had pointed out, was gilded, and the men of the age placed economics above racial strife, petty gain above literary or artistic truth: a docile, clownish, loving Negro was needed, and the writers of the Gilded Age were determined to have one—even if they had to invent him.

However, there was no need to invent such a character, for he was there in the landscape, a part of the Southern dust (and poppy fields), found pictured in old New England folk lore and myth. Samuel Sewall, the crusty old abolitionist clergyman, had written about him long before the invention of the cotton gin. Disparaging remarks had been made about him by the most important personages of the nation, a partial listing of whom reads like a *Who's Who* of great Americans: Cotton Mather, John C. Calhoun, Thomas Jefferson, George Washington, and Abraham Lincoln.

Although the comic darky was portrayed most often in American literary works, he was also a familiar figure in the historical and philosophical tracts of the period. For an affirmation of their stereotypes, the men of the Gilded Age needed turn no further than to the philosophical disquisitions of George Fitzhugh.

Admittedly, writers like Harris and Russell would have written of Blacks had there been no George Fitzhugh; however, without the latter's intellectual underpinning, the characters created and offered as images of reality by the two poets would have been accorded little validity. "The Negro," Fitzhugh writes, three years before the firing upon Fort Sumter, "has neither energy nor enterprise, and even in our sparser population finds, with his improvident habits, that his liberty is a curse to himself and a greater curse to the society around him."[4]

If, then, liberty is the bane of the Black man, shackling him with obligations which he cannot fulfill, what condition would be more suitable to his nature? For Fitzhugh, the answer was not difficult. Slavery was the most natural condition for Black men: "The Negro slaves of the South," he argues with utmost sincerity, "are the happiest, and in some sense, the freest people in the world." What occurred at Appomattox, therefore, was not only the surrender of South to North, but the destruction of paradise—the Southern utopia constructed by such men as Fitzhugh. The Black man was removed from his "Garden of Eden" by Northern troops who could not really fathom his nature, who did not understand that a state of servitude was for him paradise itself. It was, then, to regain paradise, to return to Irwin Russell's old, unadulterated Negro, that the dialect tradition gained credibility, prestige, and acceptance in the nineteenth century.

"Almost all poetry in the conventionalized dialect," writes Johnson, "is either based upon the minstrel traditions of Negro life, traditions that had but slight relation—often no relation at all—to actual Negro life, or is permeated with artificial sentiment."[5] To Harris' argument that in the dialect form was to be found "the accurate conception of the Negro character," Johnson responds by denying the existence of such accuracy either in the real or fictional world.

Whatever the needs of the nation at large, whatever the images of Black men necessary to produce an atmosphere of tranquility, few Black artists were eager to join in gilding this stereotyped lily. The history of Afro-American poetry is not a history of dialect poetry. Even Paul Laurence Dunbar, the most successful practitioner of the dialect form, worked in the medium against his wishes. "You know, of course," he related to Johnson, "that I didn't start as a dialect poet. I simply came to the conclusion that I could write it as well, if not better, than anybody else I knew of, and that by doing so I should gain a hearing. I gained the hearing, and now they don't want me to write anything but dialect."[6]

Among Dunbar's major predecessors—Phillis Wheatley, George Moses Horton, Jupiter Hammon, and Frances E. W. Harper—none wrote in the dialect form. Phillis Wheatley's fame rests upon her poetical contributions written in standard English; her models were the couplet forms of her English and American contemporaries. Hammon's rolling phrases and involutions derive their power from biblical models, and Horton wrote humorous ditties in the styles of the Cavalier poets of England and the Connecticut Wits.

The dialect vogue among Black poets began in earnest with Dunbar. Skillful in executing the form, he not only gained personal fame, but also added a lustre to the medium which it did not deserve. When the most respected literary critic of the day—William Dean Howells—placed his stamp of approval upon Dunbar's efforts, dialect poetry received undue validity in the public mind; and though practiced with more financial success by whites, it became the special prerogative of the Afro-American poet.

At the heart of the controversy concerning dialect poetry is the question of language. A character in a poem, novel, or play is often delineated by the language that he speaks. To accept such characters as they are, even though they often are but shadow images of people existing in the real world, or symbols for a group or race, is to accept, as real people, images as they were constructed in the artist's mind and portrayed by the medium of language. Nowhere does the old adage that a man is known by the language he speaks ring truer than in the area of literature. The language of dialect poetry distorts character and situation alike. Dunbar's dialect poems portray characters who are all of one piece: They are objects of fun; they are incapable of experiencing love or hate; they are not concerned with the Black condition in any but its most superficial forms. They are the metaphors of a race of people who, taken collectively, exemplify in the philosophy of George Fitzhugh, the proposition that God is in heaven, and all is right with Black people in America.

All was not right with Afro-American poetry, however, and a young Black man, only six years old when William Dean Howells celebrated Dunbar's proficiency with the dialect form (in the now famous review in *Harper's Weekly* of June 27, 1896), was destined to prove it. Born in Jamaica, West Indies, in 1890, the son of moderately middle-class Negro parents, Claude McKay published his first volume of poetry, *Songs of Jamaica,* at the age of twenty. Most of his selections in this first book were written in dialect; and on these James Weldon Johnson has commented: "These dialect poems of McKay are quite distinct in sentiment and treatment from the conventional Negro dialect poetry written by the poets in the United States; they are free from both the minstrel and plantation traditions, free from exaggerated sweetness and wholesomeness; they are veritable impressions of Negro life in Jamaica."[7]

At the age of twenty, however, McKay was more wanderer than poet. Interested in "seeing something of the world," he arrived in America in 1912, enrolled in and departed from Tuskegee Institute and the University of Kansas within three years, and performed odd jobs—porter, dishwasher, and cook—before finally settling down to a job on the railroad. The position as a railroad waiter was important to McKay for literary as well as financial reasons. As with his gifted contemporary, Langston Hughes, the wandering from one city to another in different states enabled McKay to sharpen his perceptions of the experiences and living conditions of his people. The nuances of Black life cannot be learned from books alone, and the invaluable knowledge which McKay accumulated through his travels may account, in part, for the difference in tone, spirit, and point of view between his poetry and that of his predecessors. For poetical inspiration and vision, Phillis Wheatley had gone to the classical writers; Paul Laurence Dunbar to the prevailing mythologists of the period. Claude McKay, however, went to the people.

That he learned much is evidenced in the best of his poetry. Of few poets is Alain Locke's declaration about the Black artist more true—that he brings to his verse a race spirit and a race soul. But also, McKay brought a sensitivity sharpened by experiences of other lands and peoples, a cosmopolitan perspective that few of his contemporaries possessed. Moreover, he brought a sense of immediacy to his poetry, an urgency that bespoke the possibility of cultural warfare. Like Richard Wright, he saw the ever-encircling arms of Western civilization tightening like tentacles about peoples of different colors, squeezing from their minds a sense of self, nationhood, and culture. The early part of the twentieth century is marked by nothing more so than by cultural imperialism—an attempt by stronger nations (white) to impose their life styles upon weaker ones (Black). Against this cultural tyranny McKay waged war, using words as his weapons:

> But the great western world holds me in fee,
> And I may never hope for full release
> While to its alien gods I bend my knee.[8]

His war was against images constructed by men of the eighteenth, nineteenth and twentieth centuries who were married to the thought that Black men had no rights, human or cultural, which white men needed to respect. Gifted with keen perception, with an intellect capable of seeing history and the world in three-dimensional configurations, he was the logical choice for the role of warrior-poet of his people. He performed this task well, so well, in fact, that here, during the latter part of the twentieth century, when younger, more determined Black men carry on the war against cultural imperialism, his poetry serves as a living inspiration for those who refuse to bow down at the feet of alien gods.

Notes

Editor's Note: McKay's variously reported date of birth was September 15, 1889, according to the family Bible.

1. Preface to *The Book of American Negro Poetry,* (New York: Harcourt, Brace, 1931), p. 4.

2. *The Literature of the South,* ed. Thomas D. Young, Floyd C. Watkins, and Richmond C. Beatty (Glenview, Ill: Scott, Foresman, 1952), p. 529.

3. Ibid., p. 532.

4. Ibid, p. 33.

5. Preface to *The Book of American Negro Poetry,* p. 4.

6. James Weldon Johnson, *Along This Way* (New York: Viking, 1933), p. 160.

7. *The Book of American Negro Poetry,* p. 165.

8. From "The Outcast."

CHAPTER 41

The Black Aesthetic

(1971)

Introduction

A new note, discernible even to the most biased observer, was sounded in the art of Black people during the nineteen fifties and sixties. "I will go on judging and elucidating novels and plays and poetry by Negroes according to what general powers I possess," writes Richard Gilman, "but the kind of Negro writing I have been talking about, the act of creation of the self in the face of the self's historic denial by our society, seems to me to be at this point beyond my right to intrude."

Some critics, less amenable to conversion than Gilman, would have us believe that only two elements separate the present-day Black artist from his forerunner. One such element is anger! ". . . Negro writers are demonstrating the responsibility of the artist to the disciplines and traditions of art and literature . . .," writes Herbert Hill; "simple protest and anger are not enough and rhetoric will not be useful in masking the inadequacies of literary craftsmanship." The other is Black Nationalism, which, according to Robert Bone, "for all its militancy is politically Utopian."

The element of Black anger is neither new nor, as Herbert Hill would have us believe, passé. The Black artist in the American society who creates without interjecting a note of anger is creating not as a Black man, but as an American. For anger in Black art is as old as the first utterances by Black men on American soil:

> If I had-a my way,
> I'd tear this building down
> Great God, then, if I had-a my way
> If I had-a my way, little children
> If I had-a my way,
> I'd tear this building down. . . .

As old as Frances Ellen Watkins, who made one demand of her undertaker:

> I ask no monument, proud and high
> To arrest the gaze of the passer-by,
> All that my yearning spirit craves
> Is bury me not in a land of slaves.

Nowhere does anger reach more intensive expression than in Du Bois, who strikes a note that has found accord in the breast of contemporary Black artists:

> I hate them, oh!
> I hate them well,
> I hate them, Christ!
> As I hate hell!
> If I were God,
> I'd sound their knell
> This day.

Neither is Black Nationalism a new element in Black life or Black art. In 1838, ". . . some of the delegates [at the National Negro Convention]," writes Philip S. Foner, "were convinced that Canadian colonization was still the most urgent business at hand. Others felt that it was necessary to concentrate upon building a better social order in the United States. . . . One group doubted the efficacy of associating with any set of white abolitionists, and advocated restricting the convention to Negro membership. Another, convinced of the inability to achieve equality for Negroes in existing institutions, favored continuing the establishment of separate schools and churches for the Negro people." This sentiment reaches dramatic form in the fiction of Martin Delany, *Blake, or the Huts of America* (1859); Sutton Griggs, *Imperium in Imperio* (1899); and Du Bois, *Dark Princess* (1928).

Again, animosity against the inept, sterile critiques of American academicians—so prevalent in Black critical writings today—is not new. As early as 1900, Pauline Hopkins realized that art was ". . . of great value to any people as a preserver of manners and customs—religious, political, and social. It is a record of growth and development from generation to generation. No one will do this for us; we must ourselves develop the men and women who will faithfully portray the inmost thoughts and feelings of the Negro with all the fire and romance which lie dormant in our history. . . ." Twenty-two years later, William Pickens was more direct: "It is not simply that the white story teller will not do full justice to the humanity of the Black race; he cannot." William Stanley Braithwaite, an American critic in every essential, quotes from an article in the *Independent Magazine* (1925): "The white writer seems to stand baffled before the enigma, and so he expends all his energies on dialect and in general on the Negro's minstrel characteristics.

... We shall have to look to the Negro himself to go all the way. It is quite likely that no white man can do it. *It is reasonable to suppose that his white psychology will get in the way.*" (Italics mine)

Nevertheless, there is a discernible element in Black art today that is new, and Hoyt W. Fuller has come closest to pointing it out: "The Negro revolt is as palpable in letters as it is in the streets." Change revolt to war, and the characteristics that distinguish the old art from the new are readily apparent. The serious Black artist of today is at war with the American society as few have been throughout American history. Too often, as Richard Wright noted, the Black (artists) "... entered the court of American public opinion dressed in the knee pants of servility, curtsying to show that the Negro was not inferior, that he was human, and that he had a life comparable to other people." They waged war not against the society but against the societal laws and mores that barred them from equal membership. They were, in the main, anxious to become Americans, to share in the fruits of the country's economic system and to surrender their history and culture to a universal melting pot. They were men of another era who believed in the American dream more fervently than their white contemporaries. They saw the nation as a land of innocence, young enough to hold out promises of maturing into a nation of freedom, justice, and equality. The days of innocence have passed. The child has become the adult, and instead of improving with age, she has grown increasingly worse. Yesterday, America was evil personified in her youth; today, she is evil personified in adulthood.

The dimensions of the Black artist's war against the society are highly visible. At the core of Black art in the past was a vendetta against the South. The Black novel, from William Wells Brown to Richard Wright, was concerned primarily with Southern tyranny and injustice. Often the North escaped with no more than a rap on the knuckles. "Northern white people," wrote James Weldon Johnson in *The Autobiography of an Ex-Coloured Man* (1912), "love the Negro in a sort of abstract way, as a race; through a sense of justice, charity, and philanthropy, they will liberally assist in his elevation. . . ."

With the exception of writers such as Dunbar and Chesnutt, who viewed the Black man's exodus from South to North as an exchange of one hell for another, Black writers spoke of the North as the new Canaan, of Northern whites as a different breed of man from their Southern counterparts. Is it any wonder that Black people, falling sway to increasing Southern tyranny, began, in 1917, the exodus that swelled the urban areas of America in the sixties and seventies?

"I've seen them come dark/wondering/wide-eyed/dreaming/ out of Penn Station . . .," writes Langston Hughes, "but the trains are late. The gates open/but there're bars/at each gate." The bars were erected by Northern, not Southern, whites. Black people had run away from white terrorism in Savannah in 1904 and Atlanta in 1906, only to experience white terrorism in Ohio in 1904, Illinois in 1908, and New York in 1935. The evenhanded treatment of Blacks North and

South made little imprint upon Negro leaders who, then as now, were more willing to combat injustices down South than up North.

The task of pointing out Northern duplicity was left to the Black artist, and no writer was more effective in this undertaking than Richard Wright. When Wright placed Bigger Thomas and Mr. Dalton in a Northern setting and pointed up the fact that Bigger's condition resulted from Dalton's hypocrisy, he opened a Pandora's box of problems for white liberals and Negro leaders, neither of whom could bring themselves to share his vision. Dalton is a white liberal philanthropist who, although donating money to "Negro uplift organizations," owns the slums in which Bigger Thomas is forced to live. His control of the young Black man is more despotic than that of the Southern plantation owner over Blacks in the South: for him, the weapons of control are economic, social, and political.

He is more sagacious and dishonest than his Southern counterpart; he has discovered a way to "keep the nigger in his place" without such aids as signs and restrictive covenants. He has constructed a cosmology that allows him to pose as a humanitarian on the one hand, while he sets about defining the Black man's limitations on the other. His most cherished symbol of the Black man is Uncle Tom; and he remains enamored of Nigger Jim, the Black everyboy toward whom he feels paternalistic. Like Theodore Gross, he is able to share with Joel Chandler Harris ". . . the fears, laughter, and anger of the Negro"; and he is equally convinced with Gross that Harris ". . . contributed the most popular Negro characters to American fiction—Uncle Remus, Balaam, Ananias, and Mingo . . ."—characters whom he, too, believes to be representative of the race.

Thomas Nelson Page, Thomas Dixon, and Hinton Helper might create, for Southerners, the image of the Black man as ". . . a degenerate, inferior, irresponsible, and bestial creature 'transformed by the exigency of war from a chattel to be bought and sold into a possible beast to he feared and guarded.'" Dalton, however, will not accept this image. Such portraits of Black men disturb his humanitarian (read sexual) ideal of the Black man. "In an effort to make Hell endurable," Robert Bone writes of James Baldwin, "Baldwin attempts to spiritualize his sexual rebellion. Subjectively, I have no doubt he is convinced that he has found God. Not the white God of his Black father, but a darker deity who dwells in the heart of carnal mystery. . . . The stranger the sex partner, the better the orgasm, for it violates a stronger taboo." Bone's inability to come to grips with the sexual aspects of Baldwin's novels reveals more about Bone than it does about Baldwin.

At the least, it reveals a great deal about the Daltons of the North. In order to protect the Marys of the earth (Dalton's daughter in *Native Son*), they have defined the Black man in the most negative terms possible. To the Northern mind, Nigger Jim and Uncle Tom are opposite ends of the same pole; the young boy and the old man are both eunuchs, paternalistic wards who, one step removed from the jungle, are capable of limited, prescribed salvation. The inability of the Daltons to see the Black man as other than an impotent sexual force accounts for much of the negative criticism by white writers about Black literature; it also accounts for the sexually impotent Black men who people the novels of William Styron and Norman Mailer.

The liberal ideology—both social and literary—of the Northern Daltons has become the primary target of the Afro-American writer and critic. In the novels of John A. Williams, Sam Greenlee, Cecil Brown, and Ishmael Reed, the criticism of Don L. Lee, Ron Wellburn, LeRoi Jones, and Hoyt Fuller, to name but a few, the liberal shibboleths are called into question. The Daltons are brought before the bar of Black public opinion and revealed for the modern-day plantation owners they are.

There is another, more important aspect to this war. The Black artist of the past worked with the white public in mind. The guidelines by which he measured his production were its acceptance or rejection by white people. To be damned by a white critic and disavowed by a white public was reason enough to damn the artist in the eyes of his own people. The invisible censor, white power, hovered over him in the sanctuary of his private room—whether at the piano or the typewriter—and, like his Black brothers, he debated about what he could say to the world without bringing censure upon himself. The mannerisms he had used to survive in the society outside, he now brought to his art; and, to paraphrase Richard Wright, he was forced to figure out how to sound each note and how to write down each word.

The result was usually an artistic creation filled with half-truths. His works were always seasoned with the proper amount of anger—an anger that dared not reach the explosive level of calling for total demolition of the American society—and condescension; condescension that meant he would assure his audience, at some point in the production, that he believed in the principles of Americanism. To return to Richard Wright, he was not ". . . ever expected to speak honestly about the problem. [He had to] wrap it up in myth, legend, morality, folklore, niceties, and plain lies."

Speaking honestly is a fundamental principle of today's Black artist. He has given up the futile practice of speaking to whites, and has begun to speak to his brothers. Ofttimes, as in essays in this anthology, he points up the wide disparity between the pronouncements of liberal intellectuals and their actions. Yet his purpose is not to convert the liberals (one does not waste energy on the likes of Selden Rodman, Irving Howe, Theodore Gross, Louis Simpson, Herbert Hill, or Robert Bone), but instead to point out to Black people the true extent of the control exercised upon them by the American society, in the hope that a process of de-Americanization will occur in every Black community in the nation.

The problem of the de-Americanization of Black people lies at the heart of the Black Aesthetic. "After the Egyptian and Indian, the Greek and Roman, the Teuton and Mongolian," wrote Du Bois in 1909, "the Negro is a sort of seventh son, born with a veil, and gifted with second sight in this American world—a world which yields him no true self-consciousness, but only lets him see himself through the revelation of the other world. It is a peculiar sensation, this double consciousness, this sense of always looking at one's self through the eyes of others, of measuring one's soul by the tape of a world that looks on in amused contempt and pity. One ever feels his twoness—an American, a Negro; two souls, two thoughts, two unreconciled strivings; two warring ideals in one dark body, whose dogged strength alone keeps it from being torn asunder."

In 1961, the old master resolved the psychic tension in his own breast by leaving the country that had rewarded his endeavors with scorn and oppression. His denunciations of America and his exodus back to the land of his forefathers provide an appropriate symbol of the Black man who de-Americanized himself.

His act proclaimed to Black men the world over that the price for becoming an American was too high. It meant, at the least, to desert one's heritage and culture; at the most, to become part of all ". . . that has been instrumental in wanton destruction of life, degradation of dignity, and contempt for the human spirit." To be an American is to be opposed to humankind, against the dignity of the individual, and against the striving in man for compassion and tenderness; to be an American is to lose one's humanity.

What else is one to make of My Lai, Vietnam? A Black soldier has been charged with joining his white compatriots in the murder of innocent Vietnamese women and children. How far has the Americanization of Black men progressed when a Southern Black man stands beside white men and shoots down, not the enemies of his people, but the niggers of American construction?

To understand this incident and what must be done to correct it is to understand the Black Aesthetic. A critical methodology has no relevance to the Black community unless it aids men in becoming better than they are. Such an element has been sorely lacking in the critical canons handed down from the academies by the Aristotelian Critics, the Practical Critics, the Formalistic Critics, and the New Critics. Each has this in common: It aims to evaluate the work of art in terms of its beauty and not in terms of the transformation from ugliness to beauty that the work of art demands from its audience.

The question for the Black critic today is not how beautiful is a melody, a play, a poem, or a novel, but how much more beautiful has the poem, melody, play, or novel made the life of a single Black man? How far has the work gone in transforming an American Negro into an African-American or Black man? The Black Aesthetic, then, as conceived by this writer, is a corrective—a means of helping Black people out of the polluted mainstream of Americanism, and offering logical, reasoned arguments as to why he should not desire to join the ranks of a Norman Mailer or a William Styron. To be an American writer is to be an American, and, for Black people, there should no longer be honor attached to either position.

To paraphrase Saunders Redding, I have been enclothed with no authority to speak for others. Therefore, it is not my intention, in this introduction, to speak for the contributors to this anthology. Few of them may share my views; a great many may find them reprehensible. These are independent artists who demand the right to think for themselves and who, rightfully so, will resist the attempt by anyone—Black or white—to articulate positions in their names.

Each has his own idea of the Black Aesthetic, of the function of the Black artist in the American society and of the necessity for new and different critical approaches to the artistic endeavors of Black artists. Few, I believe, would argue with my assertion that the Black artist, due to his historical position in America at the present time, is engaged in a war with this nation that will determine the future of Black art. Likewise, there are few among them—and here again this is only conjecture—who would disagree with the idea that unique experiences produce unique cultural artifacts, and that art is a product of such cultural experiences. To push this thesis to its logical conclusion, unique art derived from unique cultural experiences mandates unique critical tools for evaluation. Further than this, agreement need not go!

One final note: Less than a decade ago, anthologies on Black writing were edited almost exclusively by whites. Today, there is a noticeable difference: the white academician edits an anthology and calls upon a Black man to write the introduction. The editor then declares that his anthology "represents the best of Black literature" or that he has chosen those works "which rank with the best in American artistic production."

This editor makes no such farcical and nonsensical claims. Represented in this anthology is not the best critical thought on the subject of the Black Aesthetic, but critical thought that is among the best. This anthology is not definitive and does not claim to be. The first of its kind to treat of this subject, it is meant as an incentive to young Black critics to scan the pages of *The Black World* [*Negro Digest*], *Liberator Magazine, Soulbook, Journal of Negro Poetry, Amistad, Umbra,* and countless other Black magazines, and anthologize the thousands of essays that no single anthology could possibly cover.

Many writers whose claim to recognition is equal to that of the other contributors and the editor have been left out of this anthology. This could not be helped. Perhaps it can be rectified. Instead of being content to write introductions for white editors, perhaps our serious Black artists will edit anthologies themselves. If this is done, the present renaissance in Black letters will escape the fate of its predecessor in the nineteen twenties, and endure. Then and only then will the revolution in Black letters gain viability and continue right on!

CHAPTER 42

Bondage, Freedom, and Beyond: The Prose of Black Americans

(1970)

Introduction

In song, poetry, and prose, the Afro-American has told of his experiences in America. In this book we are concerned with the prose, the words of Black speakers addressing crowds of people, the essays and articles in magazines and newspapers published by Blacks and whites, the personal narratives in which men and women relate their experiences.

There are also the personal anecdotes which form a part of the folk prose, part written, part oral. There are the letters, those reminders of times past, of present problems, or of future hopes. And sometimes there is satire, a biting humor in which what is taken for laughter is not laughter at all. Finally, in the twentieth century, there are television talks and interviews. It is not wrong to say that the Black man's prose can be seen as a record of his journey from slavery to freedom.

The record began in 1619. In that year a Dutch ship brought twenty Black people to Jamestown, Virginia. They were not considered slaves. They were indentured servants—workers who were to be freed after a number of years of service. However, by 1670, Virginia, like the other colonies, had legalized slavery. From then on, Black people brought to America were slaves.

There were few slaves in America prior to 1793, the year Eli Whitney invented the cotton gin. This machine made cotton easier to process. The demand for cotton grew, and so did the demand for slaves. As a result, by the end of the century, the slaves had increased to over one thousand times the number landed at Jamestown in 1619.

When "the dark wings of slavery" settled over America, men, women, and children were treated like animals. Families were broken up—mothers were taken from children, husbands were taken from wives. People were forced to work long hours under the hot sun picking cotton. Young Black children grew up under the fear of the overseer's whip. The Afro-American lived under oppression from sunup to sundown.

Like all oppressed people, the Black man rebelled. He had rebelled even before landing in America, as on the slave ship Kentucky, where he mutinied and killed the captain and crew. Other times he chose to starve rather than eat the food of the ship masters. Sometimes he committed suicide by jumping overboard.

The Afro-American continued his revolt in the new world. Some, like Gabriel Prosser, Denmark Vesey, and Nat Turner, called their brothers together to fight bloody revolts. Sometimes, alone, he poisoned his master or overseer. At other times he ran away in the night to join leaders like Harriet Tubman, the brave, Black woman commander who carried many to freedom via the Underground Railroad.

Sometimes he was a different kind of fighter. His weapons were his voice and his pen. Men called him an abolitionist. He fought for the freedom of his brothers in meeting halls, in newspapers, and in magazines. This abolitionist was a strange man. He may have had a college education like Martin Delany and Henry Highland Garnet, or he may have been self-educated like Frederick Douglass and David Walker. He may have been born free like Charles Lenox Remond, or, like William Wells Brown, he may have escaped from slavery to freedom. Yet, whether slave or freeman, he fought equally as hard for his brethren in bondage.

But all Black people were not of one mind about slavery. Sometimes the Afro-American did not protest about his condition or about the condition of his brethren. This Afro-American may have been a privileged slave like Jupiter Hammon or Phillis Wheatley. If so, he may have thought that slavery was not too bad. Or, like Charles Lenox Remond, he may have asked his brothers to depend upon the good will of the American people for the destruction of slavery. Or, finally, like Josephine Brown, he may have found a better life outside of America.

Despite these differences, the Afro-Americans agreed on one point—slavery had to be destroyed. This meant, said Frederick Douglass, that "slavery could only end in blood." The blood began to flow in 1861, North and South, Black men and white men engaged in a civil war. Believing the end of slavery hung in the balance, the Black man fought harder than the others. He fought to lift "the dark wings of oppression" from his shoulders and from the shoulders of his brothers and sisters for generations to come.

In 1865, when the smoke cleared on the battlefield, the Afro-American thought that the new day of freedom had arrived. The Thirteenth Amendment to the Constitution was passed, abolishing slavery forever. Then came the Fourteenth Amendment, declaring that the Afro-American was a full citizen, and the Fifteenth, that he was free to vote. Now, thought the Afro-American, the job is to secure these freedoms.

He got off to a good start. With his vote he elected many of his brethren to important positions in the government. He elected John Mercer Langston, Alonzo Ransier, and John Hyman to the House of Representatives; Blanche K. Bruce and Hiram Revels to the Senate; Oscar Dunn to the Lieutenant Governorship of

Louisiana; and P. B. S. Pinchback to the office of Acting Governor of Louisiana. Moreover, he elected many more of his brothers and sisters to city and state legislatures and to government commissions.

The new day, however, had not arrived. Most Afro-Americans were not as fortunate as their elected brethren. Some were either wards of the Freedmen's Bureau or vagabonds who went from town to town in search of food and clothing. Others, afraid and uneducated, ran back to the plantations of their former masters. To make things even harder, President Rutherford B. Hayes withdrew federal troops from the South in 1877. This left the Afro-American once again at the mercy of his former masters. Almost as soon as the troops left, oppression began again.

Organizations for the oppression of Blacks sprang up overnight. There were the Ku Klux Klan (formed in 1867), the Knights of the White Camellia, the Red Shirts, and many other groups. They murdered and maimed Black and white alike. They began a "reign of terror" in America which has not been equaled since. Alone against this oppression, what could the Afro-American do?

There were many options. He could try to change the hearts and minds of his oppressors. He could emigrate to other countries. By the end of the century, he had reduced his options to two. He could follow the lead of Booker T. Washington, or he could follow the lead of Dr. W. E. B. Du Bois.

If he followed Washington, he would accept segregation in the social, economic and political spheres. If he followed Du Bois, he would fight for every right that was his according to the Constitution. The decision was not an easy one. Some Afro-Americans followed the lead of Washington, others followed the lead of Du Bois. At the beginning of the twentieth century, only one thing was certain— the fight to secure the freedoms won in the nineteenth century would go on in the twentieth.

The Afro-American had been fighting for a long time. He was not fighting for the moon. He fought only for what the Constitution said was rightfully his. Yet, the freedom for which he had fought still was not his. President Kennedy stated this fact in a television address on June 11, 1963, in which he said: "One hundred years of delay have passed since President Lincoln freed the slaves, yet their heirs, their grandsons are not fully free. They are not free from the bonds of injustice. They are not yet freed from social and economic oppression. And this nation . . . will not be fully free until all its citizens are free."

There have been some gains. In 1954, the Supreme Court outlawed segregated schools. Civil rights bills were passed in 1960, 1964, 1965, and 1966. The Acts of 1960, 1964, and 1965 strengthened voting rights; the Act of 1964 also dealt with public accommodations, and the Act of 1966 dealt with public housing.

However, these gains meant little to most Black people. Their condition was not changed as a result of these bills. In fact, the Afro-American of the nineteen sixties felt as left out of the American system as did his brothers in the eighteen sixties. Therefore, he engaged in freedom rides, sit-ins, protest marches, and the rebellions of 1964, 1965, 1967, and 1968. Moreover, he embraced new movements. He joined the Black Muslims, CORE, SNCC, Black Panthers and the Southern Christian Leadership Conference.

He demanded new leaders, and many came to the forefront. There were Martin Luther King, Jr., James Farmer, Malcolm X, H. Rap Brown, Elijah Muhammad, and Stokely Carmichael. Like the earlier leaders, his new leaders were not all of the same mind. Some wanted to fight the battle of the sixties through peaceful, orderly protest; others argued that the battle should be waged "by any means necessary." Still others wrote America off as hopeless—they said that the Afro-American could never gain his freedom here, and therefore urged Black people to seek a homeland of their own.

The Afro-American by the end of the nineteen sixties was questioning the true meaning of America. If America, as the Kerner Commission said, was a racist society, could the Afro-American ever gain freedom in it? America had refused to change in the eighteenth and nineteenth centuries. Would she do so in the twentieth? And what about means and ends? Was integration any longer a desirable goal? And if not, was Black nationalism or separatism the answer?

These questions produced divisions among Blacks themselves. Some were like Dr. King—they were integrationists who believed that all Americans would come to do the right thing. Therefore they kept faith in America. Others were like Stokely Carmichael—they no longer believed in the American dream. They argued that Black men could only be free if they controlled their own communities. This was part of a new concept called Black Power.

The challenge of the twentieth century was clear. The American people were divided on the issues of freedom and justice. There were divisions between white men and white men, white men and Black men, and Black men and Black men. For the Afro-American, it was as if history were being repeated. For if freedom was to be attained, the Afro-American of the nineteen seventies, like the Afro-American of the eighteen sixties, had to put his own house in order first.

This had been done in the past. After periods of disunity, Afro-Americans had come together to unite against the common enemy: injustice, oppression, and poverty. Although the situation was more serious than ever before, the belief was that Afro-Americans would finally unite once again to finish the fight begun by their ancestors even as the first slave ship made its way to America.

The Way of the New World: The Black Novel in America

(1975)

Introduction

Questions concerning the function of literature and the role of the artist in society are as old as the dialogues of Plato. Yet such questions received little consideration from the African-American writer until the twentieth century. Early Black writers, forced into daily combat with an almost completely closed society, believed that the function of literature and the role of the artist were similar: Literature was an instrument to be used in warfare against an oppressive society; it was, also, the medium that allowed the Black writer to serve as interpreter between the Black and white society. The dual roles—that of the writer as combatant and that of literature as a weapon in the struggle for human freedom—have received condemnation over the years from critics, Black and white, and led to accusations such as those forwarded by Allen Tate that the Black writer has been limited "to a provincial mediocrity in which feelings about one's difficulties become more important than [literature] itself."[1]

Most African-American critics have been less dogmatic and more analytical than Tate. If the function of literature is to deal with the conditions under which men live—to analyze the effects of a hostile environment upon the human personality, then the proper label for such works, according to some critics, is "sociology." This attempt to define literature by pointing out what it is not has led Ralph Ellison to argue that "People who want to write sociology should not write a novel."[2] Literature, pure artifact, is thus stripped of all save metaphors, myths, images, and symbols, and presented to us without substance or body, dazzling us not with the concreteness of message, but with the magic of words: ". . . If a moral or perception is needed," writes Ellison, "let them [the readers] supply their own. For me, of course, the narrative is the meaning."

Not surprisingly, the white critics have preferred Ellison's pronunciations to those of Tate, for Black literature has presented obstacles difficult to overcome.

If there is no such dichotomy as Ellison proposes—between sociology and literature—the white critic faces a serious dilemma. The literary artifact must be viewed as something more than form, something more than mechanical construct, which, concerned with the social, economic, and political ideas of the times, mandates the kind of exploration suggested by B. Traven. In a little recognized comment upon his own work, Traven admits that he cannot write about people, places, or things, of which he has little intimacy or direct knowledge: "I must have seen the things, landscapes, and persons, myself, before I can bring them to life in my works. . . . It is necessary for me to have been afraid almost to madness before I can describe terror; I must myself suffer all sadness and heartache before I can visit suffering on the figures which I have called into life."[3]

Despite the differing functions between literature and criticism, Traven's remarks retain their import for both. The critic, the cultivator of the soil in which the best ideas might be nurtured, like the novelist, must possess a pervasive grasp of his subject, must know the landscape, the valleys, hedges, highways, and byways of the human soul. Only such knowledge enables him to evaluate the works of others. Unless one is to view literary criticism as an exact science, James Baldwin's comments in this respect have meaning for writer and critic alike, for one writes out of one thing only, his own experiences.

Ellison, on the other hand, argues that one writes out of other books—a view, which, if correct, defines literature as pure artifact and literary criticism as exact science. This definition gained modern import from the writings of the Agrarian critics of the nineteen twenties and thirties, who sought to establish rules for literary criticism which conformed to criterion established by an intellectual elite, designed to satisfy those for whom literature as history and sociology demanded too great a commitment to the world of practical experience. Those critics, whose chief nourishment has been "other books," turned from Baldwin to Ellison and received a much-needed reprieve. For to evaluate the literary artifacts of Black people from Phillis Wheatley to Don L. Lee entails little more than knowledge of the rudimentary aspects of literary criticism; to evaluate the Black novel, for example, requires only such technical knowledge as that concerning plot, language, setting, and conflict.

These are the major elements in the new criticism forwarded by the Agrarian critics, and their modern-day followers have failed to recognize their limitations. The Agrarian critics did their best work in poetry, a genre which more readily lends itself to verbal gymnastics. In evaluating drama and the novel, the critics failed miserably, due to the complexity of the experiences which these two genres contained—experiences which supersede the form that contains them. Such genres are not autotelic, reach outside of themselves, feed upon the tensions in a universe alive with joy, despair, passivity, and rebellion; one where man, mammoth no longer, pits his feeble strength against the forces of his society, wanders from the planet Earth to the solar system in a neverending quest to attain that which the followers of the Agrarians would deny him—the knowledge of human existence and purpose.

To define literature in terms of pure artifact, therefore, to evaluate it by methods applicable to science and technology, would make of every novel, poem, or play a hodgepodge of gibberish and would reduce each writer to the stature of a player in the witches' chorus in *Macbeth,* who, securely nestled upon his own tower of Babel, cackles ceaselessly, in tongues unintelligible to those who hold no magic key. Not autotelic, the novel, like its sister genres, depends upon the creative genius of the author, which, heightened by political, social, and historical factors, depicts the experiences of man and, reaching beyond form and structure, communicates with men everywhere. The novel is the one genre which attempts in dramatic and narrative form to answer the questions, What are we? and What is it all about?

These are social questions. They comprise such an essential part of the makeup of the novel that the evaluation of such novels requires an understanding of the social, political, and historical forces which produced them. What, asks Ellison, do we know of Sophocles' wounds? The answer is nothing. Yet to know of Sophocles' wounds might shed new light on *Oedipus Rex.* We know something of the wounds of Dostoyevsky, Kafka, and Richard Wright, and as a result their works take on added significance.

Individual wounds are one thing. What does one make of racial wounds, those that make of one Black man a Black everyman, that hold meaning for each member of the race, that allow each Black man, when confronted with injustice enacted against another, to avow that there, but for the grace of some God, go I. What does one make of such wounds buried, covertly or overtly, within the literary format? "I snuck the racial thing in," remarks Frank Yerby. What formula will enable the critic to evaluate literature replete with the effects of such wounds? One turns in answer to the real meaning of Traven's remarks, for to understand madness is to be a bit mad, to understand the Jewish experience, the Russian experience, the Chinese experience, is to be Jewish, Russian, and Chinese. No white man, argues Claude McKay, could have written my books. The message is clear: To evaluate the life and culture of Black people, it is necessary that one live the Black experience in a world where substance is more important than form, where the social takes precedence over the aesthetic, where each act, gesture, and movement is political, and where continual rebellion separates the insane from the sane, the robot from the revolutionary.

The history of Africans in America is one of rebellion and revolution, and the novelist who finds meaning in their survival upon this continent must be cognizant of the social, political, and historical milieu from which the necessity for rebellion springs. This is truer for the critic, who remains the final adjudicator. If he is to adequately separate truth from distortion, to pass judgment upon those who seek to create and recreate the artifacts of the racial past, he must be aware of those forces that have produced a distinctive history and a distinctive culture.

Ignoring their own history and culture, the early Black writers attempted to create a literature patterned upon that of whites. With the possible exception of Martin Delany, the world of the early novelists—William Wells Brown, Frank Webb, and Francis Ellen Watkins—and that of the poets—Phillis Wheatley, Jupiter Hammon, and George Moses Horton—was modeled upon that of such Anglo-Saxons as Pope, Carlyle, Mills, and Byron. They were—Webb excepted—abolitionists, who, in fighting the cause of emancipation, adopted almost in total the mannerisms, language, and world view of their white allies. Influences from masters and abolitionist allies pushed the writers toward romanticism at a time when it was becoming the plaything of adolescents and led them to believe, that is, in the eventual assimilation of white and Black cultures.

As a result, they did not attempt to recreate legends of the past, create symbols, images, and metaphors anew, nor provide literary vehicles by which men, out of the marrow of suffering, might be redeemed in myth if not in actuality; instead, they either accepted the propaganda of their detractors or burned their talents into ashes in attempts to refute them. They became the first proponents of the assimilation philosophy and helped to transform the Gabriel Prossers, Sojourner Truths, and Frederick Douglasses into Uncle Toms, Mingoes, and Aunt Sues. The courageous men and women who set examples for Blacks yet unborn, by stealing away from slavery, murdering masters and overseers, and committing untold acts of rebellion against the slave system, find little recognition in their poems and novels.

Yet, these writers were Black men and women, and in their breasts, if sometimes only feebly, also dwelled the hell-fire of revolt. How then does one account for the failure of their works, for their commitment to the romantic dream, for their inability to come to grips with the fundamental realities of the society in which they lived? The answer is that they were firsts—those who came to maturity in the early decades of the republic. For them, the period between 1800 and 1865 was one in which slavery presented the major conundrum, a solution which was viewed as a solution to the overall problem between Blacks and whites. They knew no world other than that divided through sectional strife, centered around the conflict of slavery, and America, at that period of time, appeared as innocent to them, as it would later to such men as Henry James and Van Wyck Brooks.

America was a nation yet to be born and, despite slavery, the romantic belief was shared equally among the early writers that once slavery had ended, a better world would be erected upon the debris of the old. One finds this sense of innocence in the speeches of Douglass between 1863–65, in the poetry of Wheatley, the novels of Brown and Webb. For these writers, the new frontier lay beyond the boundaries erected by slavery; the new world was to be born on the seventh day of emancipation, the second coming ushered in by the last rifle shot fired in the "irrepressible conflict." Upon such a romantic foundation they constructed literature doomed to extinction in the years following Appomattox, and it is not surprising that during the fateful years of Reconstruction no major work is produced among them. Having failed to interpret American reality, they were jolted by the fact that the demise of slavery did not produce the new society, that the Black man's condition was not appreciably altered. The America seen through the eyes of Thomas Jefferson, Henry David Thoreau, Ralph Waldo Emerson, and Walt Whitman was one which neither they nor their progeny were ever to know.

This failure to understand the country in which they lived produced an unfounded reservoir of hope and faith in America and its people that pervades the Black novel from 1853 to 1962. The American dream, as set forth in legal documents, might become real if only certain blemishes upon the body politic were eradicated. Few questioned the thesis that the blemishes were part of the society's character and being, that the legal documents were the creations of men—Jefferson and Washington—for example, themselves corrupted by the issue of prejudice and racism. Failure to realize such facts led Black people and Black writers alike to visualize a world to be after the apocalypse—a theme which pervades African-American literature.

Each period—slavery, Reconstruction, early and late twentieth century—has its version of the Apocalypse, each its Rubicon which must be forded, crossed, before the period of universal brotherhood, not to mention true creativity, is possible. One Apocalypse gives way to another; one Rubicon is but a tributary stream, flowing, merging eventually with the other. The demise of slavery produced segregation and discrimination; the legal ending of segregation and discrimination produced economic and social problems of a magnitude as great as that of slavery and legal segregation. The first writers, therefore, were pioneers, foraging in the literary underbrush, believing always that reality was not what existed at the moment. They were literary visionaries: Brown, Delany, and Webb of one sort; Charles Chesnutt, Paul Laurence Dunbar, and Sutton Griggs of another. Each maintained a common belief and faith that America, after periods of overwhelming darkness, would lift the veil and eternal sunshine would prevail.

We do not know at what point this thesis first came under serious questioning. Martin Delany in *The Condition, Elevation, Emigration and Destiny of the Colored People of the United States* (1852) evidenced cynicism concerning American ideals and pretensions, some of which pervades his novel, *Blake; or the Huts of America* (1859). After two full-length novels designed to change the thinking of white men in regard to their treatment of Blacks, Charles Chesnutt evidences a sense of hopelessness in his final novel, *The Colonel's Dream* (1905). Paul Laurence Dunbar, more optimistic in fiction than in poetry, nevertheless, interjects a note of foreboding and despair in his final novel, *The Sport of the Gods* (1902). Serious, sustained questioning of American ideals by a sizable number of Black writers does not occur until the late twentieth century, after the Supreme Court decision in Brown versus Board of Education, Topeka, Kansas (1954), the freedom riders, the crusades of Martin Luther King, Jr., and the rebellions in New York, California, Illinois, and Michigan. Re-examination, however, begins during the Harlem Renaissance, when Black writers achieved success in the novel genre, both in terms of technical progress and readership acceptance.

This re-examination, never completed, was spurred in part by the Garvey movement, in part by the Pan-Africanism of W. E. B. Du Bois, and in part by a growing intellectual class, differing in educational attainments from their counterparts in the nineteenth century. William Wells Brown, Frederick Douglass, Jupiter Hammon, and Frank Webb were educated in the university of hard knocks; Alain Locke and W. E. B. Du Bois were educated at Harvard, Langston Hughes at Columbia, and James Weldon Johnson at Atlanta and Columbia. There was, in addition, the factor of time. The second coming was overdue by one hundred years—a long time had elapsed between the nineteen twenties, the beginning of the Renaissance years, and the day in 1865 when Douglass, with a group of well-wishers, awaited news of the issuance of the Emancipation Proclamation. The dream, in short, had been too long deferred. The "Great Migration," which by 1920 resembled a small-scaled avalanche, was important in bringing about re-examination of the perceptions held by Blacks in regard to society, and the exodus of men, women, and children from the South had a profound effect upon Black literature in general and the novel in particular. Unlike some of their more prosperous brothers, those who came north, following the great migration, were driven from their homes as a result of attacks by mobs, economic exploitation, and execution without benefit of trial by judge and jury. Langston Hughes sums up their hopes and disappointments in *The Dream Deferred*: "I've seen them come dark wondering/wide-eyed/dreaming out of Penn Station/ . . . The gates open—but there are bars/at each gate."

The North failed to provide a locale and social climate much different from that of the region which they had fled. Many, as a result, soon came to surrender the American dream, to despair of ever witnessing a second coming upon these shores, and in protest and disillusionment, swelled the ranks of the new prophets— Marcus Garvey, Father Divine, and Bishop Grace. Their newfound disillusionment created new difficulties for the novelist. The yardstick of measurement by which change is recorded must, in the final analysis, be those for whom the system has not worked at all. Yet to accept these as the criterion of measurement is to suggest that the system cannot work, that the world envisioned by the earlier Black writers and intellectuals was impossible of being brought into being.

The intellectuals of the Renaissance period attempted to deal with this difficulty by reverting to romanticism. They argued that the problem was not that American society could not work for Blacks, but only that it had not been sorely tested. Resentful of the dilemma proposed in the persons of the unlettered, primarily dark and poor migrants from the South, they sought to buttress their contention by postulating a questionable thesis structured upon the theory of the blessed and the damned. Initiated early in the novel, *The Garies and Their Friends,* this thesis suggested that the denominator man was more important than the numerator Black, that the society envisioned in the Constitution was possible of attainment by those who equaled their white counterparts in terms of culture and material acquisition.

The theory divided Black men along lines first devised by ingenious slaveholders, and the result of the schism accounts for much of the tension between Black intellectuals and the Black middle class in the nineteen seventies. Reacting, in part, against the division, Langston Hughes in "The Negro Artist and the Racial Mountain" struck a proletarian note in 1925: "But then there are the low-down folks, the so-called common element, and they are the majority— may the Lord be praised." These common folk, distinguished by their unashamed adoration for such Black artifacts as the spirituals and the blues, were those who had either survived the exodus themselves or children of those who had survived. In their refusal to follow the assimilationist route, they were, for the artist, those upon whom a viable literature might be founded, for they held "their own individuality in the face of American standardization."[4]

"The Negro Artist and the Racial Mountain" is among the more significant critical documents written during the Renaissance years. Hughes suggested that the Black writer confront the problem posed by a loss of faith in American society, not by creating divisions, but by rewriting the formula that defined the function and objectives of African-American literature. Return to William Wells Brown and Jupiter Hammon and the function of writer and work alike remain unchanged by most of their early twentieth-century counterparts: Literature is a weapon in the quest for Black freedom, and the author is the interpreter of the ways of Black folk to white folk. Hughes paid scant attention to the first supposition but sought to restructure the second. Empathizing with the new migrants to a degree impossible for most writers of the period, and knowing that their disillusionment had sunk deep indeed, he dreamed of a literature to describe accurately their hopes, fears, and anxieties, one to truthfully depict their experiences. He knew, contrary to Richard Wright's suppositions some forty years hence, that Black people did not understand the meaning of their lives, were not cognizant of the rich cultural and historical milieu from whence they came, and that the Black writer should waste little time and energy in directing his works to audiences composed of whites and the Black middle class.

Thus, despite his difficulty in living up to his own prescriptions, Hughes demanded more important objectives from the Black writer than had been demanded previously. The role of ambassador to the white world was to be exchanged by that of teacher to the Black. The advocate for racial justice and democracy was to become the Lycurgus to the Black masses; the entertainer to whites and the Black middle class was to become the analyzer and explicator of African-American culture here and abroad. Not surprisingly, therefore, Jean Toomer, caroling softly, journeys back to the Southland, the first home away from home, though despairingly, Countee Cullen broaches the question, "What is Africa to me?" Rudolph Fisher and Claude McKay look with critical eyes upon a Harlem struggling to be born; Arna Bontemps views the history of Haiti and America; Langston Hughes describes, in fiction, the ways of white folks.

Yet, literature directed toward explicating the lives of "the low-down folk" held dangers which the Renaissance men could not foresee. To deal truthfully with the history, culture, and sociology of the Black masses is to deal openly with anger and resentment expressed in unabashed terms. To accurately analyze the life style of the poor and embittered Blacks who followed Marcus Garvey and Sufi Abdul, the writer had to attack the false premise upon which the middle class and the romantics had structured their cosmology. From the vantage point of the migrants, America was desperately in need of revolution, and the writer who sought to function as their amanuensis would have to record this desire for violent change. That *Native Son* (1940) is the most celebrated novel of the post-Renaissance years evidences the Black writer's disregard of the dangers inherent in accepting a new function for the Black writer.

Native Son remains the most controversial book written by an African-American. Attacks upon the novel and its author have ranged from the hysterical utterances of Communists, to the bemused, bewildered comments of white liberal critics, and to the apologia of such Black writers as James Baldwin and Ralph Ellison. The Black and white critics—the Communists excluded—have this in common: an unbending faith in the American dream and an assumption that, despite the failure of Americans to live up to the ideals of justice and equality, hope should still spring eternally in the breast of the African-American. *Native Son* is not a novel for the hopeful or the faithful, but one which results from the inability of men to fulfill the tenets of their own tables of the law. It was written during a period of history wherein mass murder symbolized the moral depravity of Western man. It was written at a time when the incarceration of men of different skin color, ideas, and religion was the rule, in Europe and America as well. It is a novel which illuminates the reality of its time.

It succeeds, also, on a much more fundamental level, undoing the work of Black novelists heretofore, pointing out the dangerous consequences of romanticism and unlimited faith in an America of the future, and calling for a total restructuring of the society along egalitarian lines. It mandates that Black people forsake abstractionism and dedicate themselves to the possible. It avers that if Bigger Thomas, Black everyman, is to be saved, he will not be saved in an integrated country in which each man walks the path of justice, equality, and brotherhood. Such postulates were difficult for the ideological descendants of Frederick Douglass to embrace. To accept Wright's thesis in total means to forgo the attempt to achieve the integrated society. It means, moreover, that Blacks who seek a sense of their own self-worth must dedicate themselves either to nihilism or revolution. For the most part, the Black writer walked the ambivalent line between Wright's postulates and those adhered to by Douglass' ideological kinsmen, despite Wright's own insistence that if the African-American writer was to serve as a "purposeful agent" of his people, he would have to create those values by which they were "to live and die."

Yet, Wright and his followers, Chester Himes, William Gardner Smith, and Ann Petry, were the first Black literary iconoclasts, modern-day Zarathustras, determined to bury the old dead god and his ideas. By nineteen-sixty, they had succeeded in changing the course of the African-American novel, moving it in the direction that the younger writers of the Renaissance had wanted it to go. After Richard Wright, the novel of outright assimilationism and romanticism no longer appealed to a Black reading audience. The novel that functioned as a vehicle for allaying the fears of whites and Blacks of some affluence was now the novel which depicted unadorned truth. When Chester Himes, writing of the hatred which each Black man feels for his white countryman, assumed that much the same hatred forms part of the psychic makeup of the Black writer as well and suggested that the real question for the writer was "How much does this hatred affect the Negro's personality?" he was signaling the end of the age of ambiguity and ushering in the age of truth—the age of the new Black writer.

Before such a new writer could emerge, there were old plants to be plowed under; confrontations with old ideas and theories were necessary. Men who wage warfare with words must be conscious of the meaning of their existence. It is this that Richard Wright might have said to such detractors as James Baldwin, this that Langston Hughes might have said to the Black bourgeois writers and their representatives who opposed him in the nineteen twenties—that to confront reality was to step outside of the realm of hate and fear, to posit a world far different from that vouchsafed by the Americans. The first step toward transforming reality is to admit the reality that exists at the moment. For only when Black men have moved beyond romanticism and acknowledged the Bigger Thomas in their character, then and only then can the novelist truthfully explicate the world of Black folks. It is this, in part, that the writers of the seventies have accomplished. They are indebted to Baldwin and Ellison in the same sense that the former are indebted to Attaway, Wright, and Himes, who in turn are indebted to the younger writers of the Renaissance. For the most part, each contributed to the steady eroding of the romanticism and futile faith which plagued their predecessors; each managed to purge himself of the hatred which consumed the works of many of the most talented of Black writers. Acknowledging the existence of the Bigger Thomas living constantly in his skull, the Black writer was capable of seeing newer visions, of moving back into the past, of coming to grips with the terrors and joys of those for whom visions of the river Jordan in days gone by were as bold, stark, and immediate as a newborn day.

In short, he embarked upon a new direction, and in so doing, repudiated the idea that the novel should be as vehicle for protest. He moved beyond the example of Richard Wright, seeing, more clearly than Du Bois, that the problem of the twentieth century centered upon power, not race. In the quest for power, the protest novel is a useless vehicle, and the author who addresses himself to the power broker in obsequious, piteous pleadings and cajolings emphasizes his powerlessness. "I do not," wrote Richard Wright, "write for Black people, but for whites," because whites know nothing of the problems confronting Blacks, whereas Blacks do. Read differently, the statement suggests that whites have the power to determine the destiny not only of the country, but of Blacks as well. The events of the nineteen sixties, however, evidence the fact that the white majority no longer has such frightening power.

On a hot summer night in 1965, the borough of Manhattan erupted in violence. Led by the young and the more defiant, men, women, and children took to the streets to articulate their grievances in terms almost too realistic for the printed page. Past and present merged as Molotov cocktails symbolized centuries of hostility transmitted from one generation to another. Before the decade of vengeance and redemption was over, Watts, Hough, Detroit, and Chicago had added their names to a period of American history different from any that had preceded it. In the ashes and rubble of the major urban centers of America, the Black power revolt had its genesis, and "the Black Aesthetic," its cultural and literary arm, was an outgrowth of the same historical events.

Had the rebellions of the sixties not taken place, Black literature in general, and the African-American novel in particular, may not have continued along the road paved by the younger members of the Renaissance, might have veered sharply from the path prescribed by Wright and his followers into art for art's sake, abstractionism, or surrealism. The baptism by fire and blood produced the catharsis, violent in nature, that gave birth to a new literary Renaissance.

Traditional plots in the Black novel, situations, and character became anachronistic. Form, as defined by the Europeans beginning with Cervantes, refined by Henry Fielding and Tobias Smollet, and brought forward as an accomplished instrument by Jane Austen, James Joyce, and Marcel Proust, was no longer the form which the serious Black novelist deemed necessary of emulation. The Blacks who came north in the early part of the twentieth century had undergone almost complete alteration, recognized and transformed the Bigger Thomases in their skulls, and arrived at a sense of political and social awareness which mandated new literary forms. The novels of the early writers, based upon the Euro-American tradition in form and content, became obsolete; such novels as *Invisible Man* hailed for formalistic innovation were more important in terms of content and message. (For many of the younger writers, Ellison's novel, in terms of form, was a refinement of the genre handed to the Western world by Cervantes.)

These younger writers were now able to divine the real forces at work in the society, to understand the power that dominated the lives of Black people in ways that Wright could hardly imagine. The symbol of the twentieth century, wrote Wright, is the man on the corner with a machine gun, and Imamu Baraka asks, "Will the machine gunner please step forward?" At long last, form and structure were recognized as little more than cousins to content, and the Black novelist, machine gunner in the cause of mankind, prepared to move forward in the most monumental undertaking of the twentieth century—the task of redefining the definitions, creating new myths, symbols, and images, articulating new values, and recording the progression of a great people from social and political aware-ness to consciousness of their historical importance as a people and as a nation within a nation—a task which demanded, in the words of poet Don L. Lee, that Black people walk the way of the New World.

Notes

1. Allen Tate, "Introduction" to *Libretto for the Republic of Liberia.*

2. Robert Bone, *The Negro Novel in America* (New York, Yale University Press, 1959), p. 153.

3. Lawrence Clark Powell, "Who Is B. Traven?" in *New Masses: An Anthology of the Rebel Thirties,* ed. By Joseph North (New York, International Pub, 1969), p. 304.

4. Langston Hughes, "The Negro Artist and the Racial Mountain," in *The Black Aesthetic* (Garden City, N.Y., Doubleday & Co., 1971), p. 177.

The Way of the New World:
The Black Novel in America

(1975)

Afterword

Despite a decline in the interest of Black literature and attacks aimed at Black Aestheticians by whites and Blacks, the Renaissance continues. To label Killens, Williams, and Gaines as Black Aestheticians would be erroneous; to suggest, however, that they and their contemporaries have been influenced by, and have influenced, the writings and ideas generated by the Black Aesthetic movement would not. It is due largely to the efforts of such men that, after a century of adhering to the dictates of white propagandists, the novelist has been freed from the tendency to follow those who would lead him either down the road of protest literature or into the elitist sanctuary of literature for art's sake. Both directions represented dead ends and neither led to a realistic confrontation with the problems facing Black people in the American society.

This is not to accept Baldwin's argument, in his celebrated attack upon Richard Wright, that the protest novel was a useless vehicle in producing societal change. Though a direct cause-and-effect relationship between work and situation is impossible to discern, the influence of the protest novel upon changes in the social order, and in the actions of men and women, can be proved in the impact of such novels as *Uncle Tom's Cabin, The Leopard's Spots, Germinale,* and *The Jungle.* Baldwin's criticism holds, however, in the case of protest novels written by Blacks. Conceived as an appeal to the conscience of whites, the dismal failure of the novel to bring about substantial changes has been registered by works from *Clotel* to *Native Son.* The fault lies not in the genre itself, but upon the flimsy premise upon which the writer based his protest—that Americans wanted and desired an egalitarian society in which man opted for truth and beauty over narrow interests, material gain, and selfish pursuits. Most whites, themselves victims of imagists from the cotton barons to the men of Richard Nixon's crime-ridden administration, were incapable of empathizing with the problems of Blacks, could not accept that collective guilt of a nation which to ensure its own survival relegated a race of people to the status of subhumans.

Despite its failure in this regard, however, the Black protest novel was necessary; it was a genre which had to be offered and surpassed; for at its best it revealed the absurdity of the American creed, pinpointed the oneness between white liberal and white bigot alike, succeeded in proving the futility of addressing appeals to white conscience in demonstrating how far distant in vision and expectations whites were from Blacks and how narrow and parochial American thought which conceived of the world as little more than the creation of Anglo-Saxon civilization. Most important, in so educating Blacks, the protest novel vouchsafed the most important of all truths: that change in the Black condition is possible only through the efforts of Black people themselves. Such changes demand the commitment of all Blacks and, most specifically, the Black writer; they demand a commitment not to literature for art's sake, but to literature for the sake of Black people.

Literature for art's sake, which has its genesis in the Harlem Renaissance, might have died a natural death had the Black novelist and poet been free of the need for recognition from a white literary world and the paternalism and condescension which accompany such recognition. Nothing could be more ludicrous than the attempt on the part of an oppressed people to validate the existence of *ars poetica* in America. Such a golden age, where art flourished for the sake of art has never been—not even in that ancient Greece which Matthew Arnold and Archibald MacLeish forwarded as their example. That men have at all times desired such a millennium is irrefutable. Who among us is not overawed by the beauty of which Plato spoke; what human being not aesthetically stimulated by the elegance of style, the proportion and symmetry of line, the pageantry and mixture of color in a superb painting? Who cannot derive compassion and feeling from a deeply felt chord, from the purity of sound, the perfection of rhythm and movement of a well-orchestrated musical rendition, and who does not feel inwardly fulfilled at a lyrical verse, at the staccato movement of words and lines in a Baldwin essay, or the solemn dignity of a Proustian passage? What human being cannot be, does not desire to be, moved by that which is beautiful, that aesthetic sense which distinguishes man from other animals?

To argue the affirmative is not to make the case for literature for art's sake. Man's capacity to appreciate the beautiful, to cultivate a wholesome, healthy aesthetic sensibility, depends upon the security of the environment in which he lives, in the belief in his own self-worth, in an inner peace engendered by his freedom to develop to the extent of his abilities. In a sharecropper's shack in Mississippi, a rat-infested ghetto in Harlem, or a mud hut in Vietnam, a portrait of the Mona Lisa, the strains of a Brahms concerto, the soothing lines of a Keats or a Countee Cullen are ludicrous at best, cruel at worst. In order to cultivate an aesthetic sensibility, given an oppressive society, the first prerequisite is that the oppression must end; to pave the way for the possibility of an ars poetica, the oppression must end; in more concrete terms, before beauty can be seen, felt, heard, and appreciated by a majority of the earth's people, a new world must be brought into being; the earth must be made habitable and free for all men. This is the core of the Black

Aesthetic ideology and forms the major criterion for the evaluation of art: How much better has the work of art made the life of a single human being upon this planet, and how functional has been the work of art in moving us toward that moment when an *ars poetica* is possible for all?

This thesis is not shared by all Black writers. Many continue to exhibit a spirit of elitism, to see literature only in terms of belles-lettres; such writers are ofttimes more zealous than their white colleagues in calling upon the Black writer to create literature which adheres to often nonexistent criterion governing form and structure, to attempt to create a "universal art," and to write novels which eschew social commentary. Such Black writers and critics there are; yet sane men shun their pretensions and look back to the time of Brown and Delany in an attempt to fashion ideas of what the work of art must mean for a people whose liberation has not yet come.

In so doing, the flaws of Black writers of the past are revealed: These have little to do with the argument that their art was not universal or was marred by social commentary; their major flaw was that the literature they produced failed to deal adequately with the central problem confronting any oppressed people—that the symbols, images, and metaphors which substantiate a sense of self-worth and achievement were controlled, manipulated, and defined by outsiders, by those who continued that oppression of the mind begun by their ancestors. Here lay the great battlefield for the Black writer, and it is in waging war upon this battlefield that the Black novelist of the present time has brought the literary artifact to its greatest height of maturity. By refusing to accept the images and stereotypes of white liberals and white bigots alike, like Killens, Gaines, and Williams he attempts to recreate and create those paradigms which have been the major defining characteristics of a courageous and heroic people. He has, like Dunsfords, come back to the Harlem of the mind to discover those images of a people which testify to the greatness and inviolability of humanity everywhere.

Yes, the Renaissance continues, thanks mainly to the Black Aestheticians of the sixties and seventies who moved to gain control over the history and culture of Black people. Not only did they explode the myth that whites were more capable than Blacks of evaluating Black literature, but the establishment of publishing institutions like Third World Press, Jihad, Broadsides, and Emerson Hall; the success of such magazines as *Black World, The Black Scholar, Liberator,* and *Black News;* and the founding of such educational institutions as The Institute of the Black World and Malcolm X University were attempts to maintain hegemony over the cultural artifacts of a people.

Nothing would be more desirable than to end this study on such a positive note, to herald the arrival of the Black writer in the persons of Killens, Gaines, and Kelley as constituting a final victory over white nationalism, to pronounce once and for all the death knell of the old stereotypes, images, and metaphors which enslaved the minds of generations of Blacks. Yet to do so would be to engender false optimism. For white nationalism is not dead, the attempt to control the images, metaphors, and symbols of Black life is as much a part of the present as of the past. The stereotypes of Harris, Page, and Dixon, of Van Vechten, Mailer, and Styron live again in movies and television fantasies written by Blacks, performed in by Blacks, and supported and sustained by Blacks. The list is almost too numerous to mention: *Superfly, Melinda, Shaft, Coffy,* "The Flip Wilson Show," "Sanford and Son," and "The Red Ball Express" represent only the most flagrant examples.

These, the new imagists, because for the most part they are Blacks, are more immune from criticism than the imagists of old. They ignore criticism from the Black community and are content to exist as the ventriloquist dummies of their more sophisticated masters irrespective of the damage wrought by their actions. One thinks of the novelists, of Charles Chesnutt and Sutton Griggs, of Richard Wright and William Smith, of Ann Petry and Zora Hurston; they were men and women who, despite flaws in perception which often limited their vision, believed in the sanctity of the Black spirit, who sought, through their art, to elevate a race of people. These were no scavengers, ignoring the worth and dignity of a people; they were not brainless narcissists unable to realize that their own dignity and sense of achievement were tied in, inseparably, with that of their people. They would have held no truck with those who created and performed in the *Superflys* and the *Melindas,* would not have joined with those who, here, in this period of the twentieth century, attempt to recreate the stereotypes of old—the darky entertainer, docile child, or brute Negro. Like John Killens, they were dedicated to preserving the historical artifacts of a people and would have demanded films based upon the lives of Frederick Douglass, Malcolm X, Sojourner Truth, and Harriet Tubman, films that reveal the dignity of a people whose travels have extended from the middle passage to twentieth-century America.

There is no correlation to be made, however, between the Black sycophants of the present time and the novelists, past and present, and thus, the renaissance wrought by the Black Aestheticians, the new sense of historical vision in the works of Black poets and novelists, the progress made in gaining control over the images, symbols, and metaphors of Black life are threatened by men and women of little talent and far less intelligence, whose objective is not to inform but to disparage, not to create positive images, but to recreate negative ones of the past, to glamorize the hustler and the hipster, to elevate ignorance and downgrade intelligence in a world in which intelligence, knowledge, and understanding are paramount for a people who must yet break the bonds of oppression.

And thus there is little cause for optimism. One is gratified, of course, at the progress of the Black novel from 1853 to the present, and the maturity of the novelists support Fuller's assertion of a new Black Renaissance; one knows, however, that the final battle against the imagists continues, and that the new propagandists are more often Black than white; one watches their "artistic" offerings, listens to their infantile rationalizations, is dismayed at their inability to dedicate themselves to what is noble and beautiful in a race of people; and one, despairingly, recalls the lines from a Baraka poem, "Will the machine gunner please step forward?"

PART 5

Book Reviews

A Black Aesthetic must develop, authors are saying with mounting
emphasis, because of racism in the literary establishment. Black writers
object vigorously to the domination of white publishers, white editors,
and white critics over the public acceptance and interpretation of
their works . . . White critics are simply not wanted, not only by many
of the Young Blacks, but also by some of their older, more charitable
contemporaries . . . The task of listing credentials for the Black critic
is approached only obliquely. The essayist's usual failure to distinguish
between Black author and Black critic is either an oversight or an
implication that imaginative creation and reflective evaluation can, in
their opinion, temporarily be exercised by the same faculties.
—James Emanuel, *Blackness Can: A Quest for Aesthetics*

Although the major venue for conscious, culturally committed, and nationalistic African American literary criticism in the sixties and seventies was *Negro
Digest/Black World,* Gayle also wrote numerous, wide-ranging book reviews for
the *New York Times* (until his infamous 1972 letter where he both resigned and
articulated his criticism of unchecked white biases), *The Nation, Black Scholar,*
and the like.

This section, "Book Reviews," contains some of Gayle's most pertinent review
essays in which he judges the value of works by black authors such as Gayl Jones,
Ishmael Reed, Gwendolyn Brooks, George Cain, William Demby, and Brenda
Wilkinson according to the new standards and criteria set by the Black Arts
Movement, as well as trenchant critiques on the qualifications of white critics
reviewing the work of black writers. Per the latter, his letter of resignation as a
book reviewer for the *New York Times*—in which he scathingly indicted and
found unacceptable what he viewed as the publication's racial double standard by
which white literary critics were allowed to continuously put forth racist reviews
of black writers when any and all culturally based reviews submitted by black
critics were deemed not publishable—was extremely significant because he questioned whether or not white critics were qualified to establish any of the criteria

for black literature and rejected their tendency to group all black writing into one category. He concluded the letter by stating, "[It may be] appealing and satisfying to your constituency, of course; to black critics, however the statement can only be viewed as condescending and insulting. Such it is to this writer, who, preferring to deal with honest racists rather than condescending white liberals kindly requests that his name be deleted from the list of reviewers for your magazine."

CHAPTER 45

Two Views of . . . 'Winesellers' . . . A Yea Say

(1976)

What the Wine-Sellers Buy

Ron Milner's *What the Wine-Sellers Buy* is Black domestic drama at its best. Ably produced and directed, the play eschews the themes and conflicts of yesteryear: There is neither Black nihilism, despair, and hopelessness, nor the mock-epic battle between pitiful Black and ruthless white. Masochistic whites and catharsis-seeking Blacks must search elsewhere for such fare. Rather, *What the Wine-Sellers Buy* is drama of instruction, demanding both rational understanding and a sensibility capable of intense emotional involvement.

The wine-sellers dispense illusion to small segments of the Black community. Thus, they symbolize the ancient conflict between reality and illusion. For Milner, illusion is personified in the character of Rico the pimp, a Mephistopheles beyond even Goethe's imagining. Reality, on the other hand, is represented by Laura Carlton and her suitor, Jim Aaron. At the center of the conflict is State Carlton, Laura's adolescent son. He must choose—either to emulate the pimp or to achieve manhood through hard work, intellect and perseverance. The decision is ultimately a moral one with import for the entire Black community. To choose intelligence over ignorance, perseverance over hustling, reality over illusion, is, finally, to choose life over death.

The dispensers of illusion are Milner's target. Like other contemporary Black playwrights, he has declared war on the twin evils which beset segments of the Black community, hedonism and sensationalism. Thus, *What the Wine-Sellers Buy* is a drama of power and intensity, of bold, stark realism, with neither sentimentality nor self-pity.

Aided by a singularly talented cast, Ron Milner has brought to the Beaumont theater at its best: humorous yet profound, emotional yet intellectual, immediate yet timeless. It is a total experience.

CHAPTER 46

Coming Home

by George Davis

(1973)

There is one central question which the Afro-American literary historian asks about *Native Son:* Given the ability to analyze, rationalize, and discourse upon the Black condition, what might Bigger Thomas have revealed about the nature of man and society? The world as seen through Bigger's eyes is, in reality, a world-vision filtered through the eyes of Richard Wright. Although we do not question the exactness of the world view which Wright presents, sometimes, in our deeper consciousness, we wish to know what Bigger himself actually thought.

The answer to our questions is determined by the form of the novel itself. A thinking instead of a feeling Bigger Thomas would mandate drastic alterations in the form of *Native Son.* Such changes would transform it into a very different novel from the one that exists. However, those of us who would not surrender *Native Son* as it is, though we ask questions concerning certain of its aspects, cannot, on the other hand, ask of him—indeed, demand of him—is that he bring the same sense of determination, heightened awareness, and dedication which characterized his predecessor, and that, in so doing, he move to create the form which will best enable him to explicate the Black situation.

This is to refute the assumption of Black critics and academicians that the form of the Afro-American novel was defined once and for all by Richard Wright, and that since publication of his first novel, the form has remained immune to experimentation. Inherent in this assumption is the idea that only white writers like Jerzy Kosinski and Jan Wurlitzer are free to experiment with new forms and techniques, while the Afro-American novelist is bound by the design bequeathed him from the past. Such assumptions have led novelists from James Baldwin to Cecil Brown to launch attacks upon Richard Wright and *Native Son.*

The attacks should not have been leveled against Wright. Unlike his ardent supporters (Irving Howe and Robert Bone), Wright realized that the hallmark of Afro-American creativity is the ability of the writer to impose his own sensibility upon varying forms, to change the artifact into something new and distinct by bringing to it nuances of the Black world view. Such creativity has produced the spirituals, the blues, jazz, the poetry of Don L. Lee, Mari Evans and Askia Muhammad Touré, and the novels of Ishmael Reed, William Melvin Kelley, and George Davis.

The goal of the Afro-American novelist is to create a new form. Like Black unity, however, this cannot be accomplished instantaneously. The process of creating new forms demands that over a long period of time the writer read other writers, select from them, imitate them, and then, if he is daring enough and talented enough, develop his own technique and style. Constant experimentation with old forms is necessary; the Afro-American writer, working upon those forms handed down from writers of the past, improving upon them, due to the imposition of the Black consciousness, will eventually present a form which is uniquely Afro-American.

Something of this process takes place in George Davis' first novel, *Coming Home* (Random House, $5.95). Like *Yellow Back Radio Broke-Down* and *Dunsfords Travels Everywheres,* this finely written novel imposes a Black sensibility upon a European form without surrendering neither the vigor and energy of the Black life style nor the concern and preoccupation of the Afro-American novelist with the human condition. Influences upon the novel vary from William Faulkner's *As I Lay Dying* to Jean Toomer's *Cane.* Moreover, the novel owes much in terms of form to American and Afro-American drama, for barring the stream-of-consciousness sequences, the characters are continually on stage. Each reveals himself through mental soliloquies; the author, like the Deistic God, having propelled a universe into motion, has retired into contemplative seclusion.

The universe inhabited by Ben, Childress, Damg, Rose and Stacey is a complex one. Each character is a psychological study in himself, and his interactions with others in this universe, where mind is more important than emotions, produces the conflicts which encompass the novel's twin plots. Childress and Ben, both Black, are pilots in the United States Air Force based in Thailand. Childress, soon to be discharged from active duty, plants Communist literature in the quarters of his ex-girlfriend, Damg: "I'm not gon let a Harvard-trained nigger inherit the best whore in Thailand . . ."

But Ben does inherit Damg. Somewhere along the way he also inherits a conscience, which leads to his questioning the validity of his part in the war. His decision to stop bombing the Vietnamese, and the hoax perpetrated by Childress, lead him to join the army of deserters streaming toward sanctuary in Sweden. Childress, however, does not escape unscathed. Ironically, the hoax meant to imperil the careers of Damg and Ben boomerangs, casting aspersion on the character of Childress, who, now a civilian, kills a policeman in self-defense: "Lieutenant Childress," remarks an investigating officer, "is a Black militant, a Black racist with the avowed purpose of overthrowing the government of the United States."

Childress' shadow hangs ominously over the novel, influencing the thoughts and actions of Stacey, the white pilot who chose to room with the two Black officers. After being jailed and charged with murder, Childress is aided by Stacey's girlfriend. The thought of his girlfriend with constant contact with the Black ex-pilot conjures up paranoic visions of sexual orgies and sadistic episodes for the white lieutenant. Unable to deal with the figments of his own imagination, the pilot, while on a bombing mission, leaves himself open to enemy ground-fire, ending his life in a vitriolic outburst of patriot and anti-Black rhetoric.

The Vietnam War is the center of this universe. It is the cataclysmic event which directs and controls the actions and thoughts of people as far away as Thailand, Washington, D.C., and Schenectady, N.Y.: "I wonder why there could not be some kind of divine law that says men can only come to another man's country as tour-ists, and not as colonizers or exploiters. But when white men come to countries where people are just sitting on natural resources—just living and having babies and trying to be happy—they called them lazy or backward or uncivilized. They hated them and used them and justified whatever they did to them by invoking some kind of divine right of commerce. Discovered them, Christianized them, annihilated them or tried to make them into tools—hoes and cotton pickers and brooms and shoeshine rags—for the great march to civilization."

The war also serves as a metaphor for the more intense, longer war waged by Black men upon American soil. Aspects of this war are vividly depicted: that between Black men and Black women, symbolized by the marital difficulties between Ben and Rose: "I was too busy wanting to be white," admits Rose, "too busy wanting to be like them"; that between Black men and the society, symbol-ized by the conflict between veteran Childress and a white policeman: "Then this big white ugly cop come up and told me to get moving, like that. So I told him to wait a minute until I finished reading my leaflet. And he said, 'Get your black ass moving. Now.' I said, 'Man, I got a constitutional right to be here just like everybody else.' And the sucker draws his pistol and tells me, 'This is all the constitution you need!'"

There is, finally, the war waged between the Black man and himself, symbolized by Harvard-educated Ben, who realizes at long last that his position—particularly in war to "protect democracy" for yellow men, alongside men who had for cen-turies denied the same to Black men—was an untenable one. This interconflict is resolved when the pilot refuses to participate in the charade any longer. Stepping outside of American history and values, he demonstrates the deep and abiding respect of Black men, historically, for the human spirit.

Coming Home is a war novel of the first rank. Not only does it explore the ac-tions, thoughts, and reactions of Black men who no longer dissociate the war in Vietnam from the war in America, but the novel also repudiates propagandists, white and Black, who ascribe heroism to those who commit acts of atrocity against a valiant and patriotic people. The true Black heroes of the Vietnam War are those whose sentiments are akin to those of an army infantryman: "I shot a kid, man. I shot a little Vietnamese in the back, man. The night before I lef the Nam . . . I ain't never gon kill no more innocent people, man."

Such sentiments, which illustrate a continuing concern for the human condition, have sustained Black people in America since the arrival of the first slave ship and have helped to distinguish them from the Anglo-Saxons. This distinction, between those who work to erect the New Jerusalem upon this earth and those whose very existence is a threat to decency and sanity, is the material of Afro-American novels as various in form as *Native Son, The Free-Lance Pall Bearers, The Man Who Cried I Am,* and *Blueschild Baby.* What this means is that form, the soil upon which our novelists sow the seeds of Black liberation and Black Awareness, is fertile, indeed. *Coming Home* adds emphasis to this assertion.

CHAPTER 47

An Open Letter to the Editor of
the *New York Times Book Review*

(1972)

Dear Mr. Leonard:

Those who followed the lead of Imamu Baraka and Hoyt Fuller in developing the concept of the Black Aesthetic were well aware of the opposition which awaited them from the American literary establishment. Such opposition, calculated and defensive, was initiated by critics from *The Saturday Review* and *The New York Review of Books,* in separate reviews of the anthology, *Black Fire,* edited by Imamu Baraka and Larry Neal. "Our Mutual Estates," written by Theodore Gross and published in *Antioch Review,* was another broadside, attacking those who questioned the arrogant premise put forward by white critics and reviewers that they were more qualified than Blacks to evaluate the cultural artifacts of Black people. The most recent and perhaps the most insidious of the literature in defense of this position is your article, "No Franchises Available" (*The New York Times Book Review,* Sunday, February 13, 1927).

Those who benefit most from America's racist institutions are duty bound to respond to attacks against those institutions. Nowhere is this more true than in the area of literature, where white critics and academicians have done more to create and popularize negative images, myths, and symbols concerning Blacks than the vigilante apparatus established in the South after reconstruction specifically for that purpose. The objective—to secure the Black man in the national psyche as one having no rights which white men are bound to respect—has been pursued simultaneously by political machines and the literary establishment, the latter surreptitiously functioning as Delphian oracle for the former.

In terms of candor and honesty, the politicians have stood head and shoulders above the critics and academicians. Acting upon a mandate given him in 1968 by racist constituents who sought to re-establish the *status quo* between Blacks and whites which existed in past decades, President Nixon moved forthrightly to satisfy this constituency by opposing busing to achieve integration, cutting back on expenditures for anti-poverty programs, solidifying his alliance with Wallaceite forces throughout the country, and choosing justices for the Supreme

Court who, he believed, would invalidate the judicial decisions of the past, many of which had tended to favor Blacks. One applauds the honest man, though one may disagree with him.

Honesty is a word which has little relevance, it appears, among the members of the white literary establishment. Take the contradictions in your own statements, for example: "We all have to live in this culture; if we are to understand it, much less change it, we must absorb, and comment on, and argue about, the witness of the victims. Consciousness works two ways—forward, projecting itself into the future; . . . and backwards, projecting itself into the past, understanding what it has done and what has been done to it. Writers of every color and sex, expand consciousness."

The "plain niceties" are obscured, however, by the following paragraph: "It is, moreover, patently absurd on the part of patronizing whites or aggressive Black aestheticians to assume that all Black writing is the same, batched up according to the same secret soul recipe, seeking Africa, scourging Europe." The fact that this statement does not reflect the thought or philosophy of Black aestheticians is, one surmises, of little consequence, inasmuch as the freedom to expand consciousness which you so liberally grant to "writers of every color and sex," does not apply to the proponents of the Black Aesthetic.

Moreover, the tone and tenor of the article itself supports the argument made by many of us that the attempt to expand white consciousness has met with dismal failure. Leaving aside the commentaries of present-day Black aestheticians, whose separatist politics differ radically from your integrationist ones, neither in your article nor in those which echo your major arguments is recognition granted to Black men whose politics and literary pretensions closely resemble yours, and yet, who voiced, in almost the same terminology, the words of their younger, brighter successors.

It was Frederick Douglass, not Hoyt Fuller, who declared that, "Negroes can never have impartial portraits at the hands of white artists. It seems to us next to impossible for the white man to take likenesses of Black men, without most grossly exaggerating their distinctive features"; William Pickens, not Imamu Baraka, who wrote that, "it is not simply that the white storyteller will not do full justice to the humanity of the Black race, *he cannot*"; William Stanley Braithwaite, not Don L. Lee, who pointed out that, "The white writer seems to stand baffled before the enigma, and so he expends all his energies on . . . the Negroes' minstrel characteristics. . . . We shall have to look for the Negro, himself, to go all the way. . . . No white man can do it. It is reasonable to suppose that his white psychology will get in the way"; Richard Wright, not Carolyn Gerald, who argued that, "Each day when you see us Black folk upon the dusty land of the farms or upon the hard pavement of the city streets, you usually take us for granted and think you know us, but our history is far stranger than you suspect, and we are not what we seem." Finally, [it was] not a Black man, but B. Traven, a white man, who admitted, "I can't shake anything out of my sleeve. . . . I have to know the humans I tell about. They must have been my friends or companions, or adversaries . . . if I am to describe them."

To expand the consciousness of those interested in the Black experience, however, is an act which you suggest can best be performed by a critic like Morris Dickstein, "who is white and Jewish" (this appears to be the proper combination for expertise on any subject relating to Blacks) and therefore, is capable of "a calm, thoughtful look at Black writers from Richard Wright to George Cain." His article, "The Black Aesthetic in White America," is viewed as "a breath of fresh air in a locked room gone stale from fulminations."

To label such sentiments as racist would be the height of irresponsibility unless one understands the invidious comparison implicit in your comments. Consider: the proponents of the Black Aesthetic are all Black, the opponents all white. The proponents argue for "the fried-chicken-franchise approach to creativity," whereas the opponents believe that "criticism . . . never should have been a summary court to dispatch or pardon books and writers." The proponents are all irrational and intemperate, the opponents all "calm and thoughtful." To those who have desired a rational, intellectual debate centered "upon the concept of the Black Aesthetic, such *ad hominum* arguments amount to little more than McCarthyism disguised as literary criticism.

Those who seriously undertake the task of criticism realize that there are various dimensions to a work of art, and that true clarity is possible only when the writer, armed with precise critical tools, is capable of presenting the extra dimension. To suggest that one "who is white and Jewish" can supply the added dimension necessary to the evaluation of a literary artifact produced by a Black writer is evidence of arrogance surpassed only by that of those academicians who refused to acknowledge the ineptness of the prevailing appraisals of Jane Austen's works, works deemed "superficial and mundane" by white males who, through arrogance and ignorance, were incapable of explicating them.

There are, however, constituencies to appease; those who believe that the white reviewing media, "out of guilt and a sense of historic redress, automatically assign Black titles to Black critics," despite the fact that few of these titles *actually* find their way to Black reviewers (one looks in vain for a Black face among the pages of *The New York Review of Books,* while *Partisan Review,* and *Antioch Review* prefer articles written by incompetent white critics to those written by knowledgeable, competent Black ones. And certainly the limited amount of space accorded Black titles in your own magazine can hardly be deemed overpatronization).

Your constituents, college professors and critics who have suffered loss of prestige, not to mention commissions, because their expertise in the area of Black culture seemed unwanted by *their* magazine, will find much to praise in your declaration that, "Ultimately you may want a Flaubert to review a Monique Wittig, an Ellison to review a Faulkner [How many books by white authors have actually been reviewed by Black critics in *The New York Times?*], a Joan Didion to review a James Dickey." Questions concerning the credentials of those to perform these tasks remain unanswered, however, for they are questions which argue that in the area of literary criticism, one has the obligation to know his subject and to know it well.

Most appealing and satisfying to your constituency, however, will be the rationale offered for assigning titles to Black reviewers over the years: "How to reflect this variety, tension, contradiction, historical grappling, either in the pages of a reviewing medium, in the mind of a single critic, or in the consciousness of a nation? Inevitably you begin with Blacks reviewing Blacks . . . you want to open some doors in a forum that has been predominately white and male; speech as spoken, rage according to its decibel level, witness insisting on its pertinence—let them in." Appealing and satisfying to your constituency, of course; to Black critics, however, the statement can only be viewed as condescending and insulting. Such it is to this writer, who, preferring to deal with honest racists rather than condescending white liberals, kindly requests that his name be deleted from the list of reviewers for your magazine.

Addison Gayle Jr.,
New York City

CHAPTER 48

Ludell: Beyond *Native Son*

by Brenda Wilkinson

(1976)

Brenda Wilkinson's novel is a remarkable accomplishment and bears comparison with an earlier novel—it, too, a remarkable accomplishment—*Native Son.* I make the comparison despite the fact that Richard Wright, the author of *Native Son,* is a literary legend, a writer tested in three genres, whose reputation was forged in the political, social, and literary hell of America during the nineteen thirties, nineteen forties, and nineteen fifties, while Ms. Wilkinson, on the other hand, is not yet into her thirties, has written only a few poems, one short story, and now her first novel.

Still, there are comparisons to be drawn between the older and the younger writer, and the age difference between them may account for the fact that *Ludell* seems an extension of *Native Son* rather than an antithesis of it. Both writers were transplanted Southerners—Wright from Mississippi, Wilkinson from Georgia. Both write in the naturalistic idiom, though Wilkinson has the better eye for detail and is more proficient in handling dialogue. In their first fictional offerings, both writers demonstrated awareness of the varied tensions prevalent in the Black community and both sought to explicate the lives of those who lived there, with equal candor and sincerity. More important, both writers arrived on the literary scene at a time when the Black novel seemed to have lost its moorings, when competing philosophies regarding its function had led to the kind of internecine warfare among Black novelists and critics that marred the achievements of the writers of the Harlem Renaissance.

During the Harlem Renaissance—the period of Black creativity between 1922, the publication of Claude McKay's *Harlem Shadows,* and 1940, the publication date of *Native Son*—the Black novel reached maturity in terms of structure, form and acceptance on the part of readers. Not surprisingly, therefore, the serious critical debate concerning the nature and function of Black literature in general began in earnest.

The novel, as viewed by the old guard (James Weldon Johnson, W.E.B. Du Bois, Jessie Fauset and Alain Locke) functioned primarily as the uplift vehicle of the

Black middle class; in portraying artificial, near-white characters who possessed the mannerisms, language and status of the men and women of the novels of Jane Austen, Anthony Trollope, and Henry James, the old guard sought to inform white America that assimilationism had worked for some, though not all, Blacks. "The party line" was pronounced in Ms. Fauset's introduction to her novel, *The Chinaberry Tree:* "But of course there are breathing spells, in between spaces where colored men and women work and love and go their ways with no thought of the [race] problem . . . What are they like then? So few of the other Americans know . . ." The question, "What are they like then?" leads to a description of characters now legion in the lexicon of the Black middle class: the professional man, the upward-bound striver, the socialite, and the patriot, differing in no major essentials from other Americans, for they are simply "dark American[s] who wear [their] joy and rue very much as does the white American . . . it is the same joy and rue."

Such assimilationist pronouncements came under attack from the younger members of the Harlem Renaissance (Rudolph Fisher, Claude McKay, and Langston Hughes), and Hughes pinpoints the thought of his colleagues in his celebrated article, "The Negro Writer and the Racial Mountain": ". . . There is for the American Negro artist who can escape the restrictions the more advanced among his own group would put upon him, a great field of unused material ready for his art. Without going outside his race . . . there is sufficient matter to furnish a Black artist with a lifetime of creative work . . . But to my mind, it is the duty of the younger Negro artist . . . to change through the force of his art that old whispering 'I want to be white' hidden in the aspirations of his people, to 'Why should I want to be white? I am a Negro—and beautiful.'"

By 1940, the views of the younger writers were ascendant; the novel had begun explication of the lives of those whom Hughes labeled, "the low-down folk." In this accomplishment, however, the younger writers midwifed a litter of new stereotypes: the romanticized pimp, the forlorn prostitute, the ostentatious "sweetman," and the social parasite. Whether such characters were an improvement over those offered in the literature of the old guard is open to conjecture; spurred on, however, by such novels as *Nigger Heaven, Not Without Laughter, The Walls of Jericho,* and *Home To Harlem,* those who would have the Black novel function as an instrument for entertainment, escapism, and naïve romanticism succeeded very well.

But neither school realistically confronted the Black community. The old guard only succeeded in perpetuating the ideal of assimilationism, deeming human worth measurable solely according to criteria established by white Americans. The younger writers were only successful in giving visibility to and romanticizing the least desirable elements in the Black community; without intending to do so, they suggested that hustling, parasitism, and exoticism were major characteristics of a Black way of life. For older and younger writer alike, the hulking, demonic figure of Bigger Thomas, the Black Frankenstein monster, was buried deep in the literary subconscious, relegated to eternal darkness and invisibility.

The publication of *Native Son* ended the debate among the Harlem Renaissance writers by redefining the function and nature of the Black novel. The entrance of Bigger Thomas onto the literary stage demolished the stereotypes of both schools, though those offered in the writings of the younger members, with seemingly indestructible resilience, would reappear in the nineteen fifties in such books as *Manchild in the Promised Land* and *Another Country,* and would stake out new territory in Black movies and television shows. Devoted more to the realities of Black life than its predecessors, *Native Son* depicted men and women trapped in the hell of racism and deprivation; it portrayed a sensitive young man, neither exotic nor parasitic, who craved not the supposed joy of jazz or Harlem night spots, but the opportunity to move freely in a world which appeared to him as one long elevator shaft—the place, where, ironically enough, he throws the dead body of his second victim, the Black Bessie Mears.

That *Native Son* marked a significant break with the traditional form and theme of the Black novel is evidenced by the caliber of the men and women who began to model their own fiction after Wright's accomplishment. The old guard of the Harlem Renaissance had found their paradigms in the works of Carl Van Vechten, Gertrude Stein, and Jean Toomer. William Attaway, Ann Petry, Chester Himes, and William Gardner Smith, who comprised the Richard Wright school of writers, followed their leader into paths charted by Theodore Dreiser, Hart Crane, and Fyodor Dostoevsky. In their novels, the Dostoevskian man came to represent an important dimension of Black life. Their canvases were painted in dark gray colors, and upon their landscapes men walked in hatred and rage, immobilized by an inability to stamp their humanity upon a racist society.

There are arguments against the Wright school. Among the most important is that they were unable to conceive of "reality" as constantly shifting, changing dramatically from one generation to another; Wright's last novel *The Long Dream;* retains, still, the vision of Black life lived during the terrible period of the holocaust. Indeed, Wright and his followers seemed ignorant of that tradition of which James Baldwin spoke so eloquently: ". . . The fact is not that the Negro has no tradition, but that there has as yet arrived no sensibility succinctly, profound, and tough enough to make this tradition articulate . . ."

The members of the Wright school, however, were moral warriors who believed that the novel should function as an instrument for improving the human condition. Ralph Ellison's statement concerning his own novel, ". . . If a moral or perception is needed, let them [the readers] supply their own. For me, of course, the narrative is the meaning," was met with derision, probably by Wright and, as we know from *Amistad I,* by Chester Himes. For here, and more explicitly in his other critical works, Ellison makes concessions to the academic proponents of an "art for art's sake" theology, notwithstanding the fact that nothing in the lives of Blacks people suggest that their writers should dedicate themselves to such specious theories. Such a dedication would mean that the Black writer had leaped outside the history of the society in which he lives.

Invisible Man, therefore, fails to become the model for the post-Wright generation of Black writers, for such novelists as John A. Williams, John Killens, and Louise Merriwether. For it depicts the Black man alone, a character more Kafkaesque than Dostoevskian, existing in a world exemplified more by the paintings of Jackson Pollock than by the writings of Theodore Dreiser. In such a universe, the terror of modern man becomes "universal," not specific, and the lives of Black people are threatened by demons more omnipresent than those of American racism.

The truth of the matter, however, is not that racism has become less threatening, but that Black people, like the post-Wright school of Black writers, have come to accept it as one of the eternal givens of American society. Such acceptance mandated that the Black writer redirect the search for identity away from the computerized mechanistic culture of the West and toward the culture peopled by those whom Frantz Fanon labeled "the wretched of the earth." After the abortive push for equal rights in the nineteen sixties, the return of white liberals to support of the *status quo,* the acceptance of the Nixon–Agnew formula for re-establishing the past pattern of Black–white relationships, it was clear to the younger writer of sensibility that the Black novel could achieve universality only by depicting the style of life, the heroism, and the courage of those who remained outside the American nightmare and were able, therefore, to offer 200 years of fateful encounters within the Diaspora as models for that three-quarters of the world that is neither white nor Western.

But the failure of the civil rights struggle in the nineteen sixties left a legacy of despair, now being articulated by some of the most promising Black novelists. Unable to surrender the quixotic dream of an egalitarian America, and more apt to blame the failures of the nineteen sixties upon Black people themselves rather than upon the white majority, they have produced works which re-create the stereotypes of old and depict a universe in which the major antagonists are Black men and Black women. These novels—*Sula, The Last Days of Louisiana Red* and *Corregidora*—are, basically unhealthy works, suggesting the inability of the authors to accept their own identity and their own humanity.

The attempt to establish a new tradition in Black fiction based upon such narcissistic offerings, therefore, makes Brenda Wilkinson's novel, *Ludell,* of immediate importance. The novel negates the mythology accepted by the writers of the Harlem Renaissance that Black life is artificial or sterile, sensationalistic or atavistic. It argues fervently against the assimilationist contentions of the post-Wright school that Blacks have imbibed the worst characteristics of the West in which they have dwelled for so long.

Like Wright's short story, "Big Boy Leaves Home," *Ludell* is primarily a novel about children. These young innocents, existing in the South, the first African-American home away from home, are such because they have not yet become inoculated with the values of the West. Theirs is an innocence much like that whispered in the poetry of Claude McKay and Mrs. Paul Laurence Dunbar; unsullied by too close association with the white world outside. But, the universe of this novel is alive with innocence, which emanates from the community even in the persons of the stern schoolmistresses, and it is highlighted by the love and care that each Black person exhibits toward the other characteristics of Black life, from the days of slavery until the present time.

Here, as John Killens, Louise Meriwether, and George Cain realized, is the *sine qua non* of the Black tradition, the determining mark of Black heroes and heroines from Frederick Douglass and Harriet Tubman to Fannie Lou Hamer and Martin Luther King, and it is such characteristics, love and caring, that form the organizing principle of *Ludell*. As is traditional in the Black community, the grandmother in this novel steps in to care for the young child, when the child's mother joins the migration heading North. Here, in this Southern land of so much pain and misery, containing a heritage or Black people of so much brutality, Black families love and care for one another, support one another, encourage one another, give sustenance to one to another. In the person of Mis Hattie, tough field boss of an itinerant cotton crew, love and caring is elevated to an all-encompassing metaphor. When Ludell, a member of the work crew, becomes ill and is unable to pick her day's quota of cotton, Mis Hattie ". . . suggested that everybody give her some cotton, since she'd taken sick—and they all had, but no one was supposed to mention it."

Such incidents, as Wilkinson knows, are neither rare nor confined only to the South. They are daily occurrences among Black people and comprise those many unsung episodes which render facile and self-serving the works of those who would use the Black novel as a vehicle for resolving their personal conflicts and who seek to paint the Black world in the time-sanctioned stereotypes of hatred, unmitigated rage, and brutality. Such novels have received a hearing in the past few years only because they appeal to the sensibility of white liberals and the Black middle class, groups who are largely incapable of fathoming the depths of the currents running strong and swift within the Black community. *Ludell*, a novel of substance, suggests that their short-lived vogue, among Black people, is ended, and that the Black novel will return to an explication of the ethics and values which have assured Black survival in this society.

The Black writer, Richard Wright wrote more than thirty years ago, must create "those values by which his people are to live and die." The word, "create" obscures this important definition of the function of Black literature. Far more to the point, the job of the Black writer is to articulate those values, germane to the success of a people in forestalling the final *Götterdämmerung,* and among them has been a communal love and caring unsurpassed and unparalleled by other racial groups in American society. The function of the novel, then, is to return to the values of racial compassion and concern as defined in the fiction of the pre-Harlem Renaissance writers, in the works of Martin Delany and Sutton Griggs; and in this respect, *Ludell* is an important contribution. For this novel reminds those in the Black community—who need reminding—that the Sulas and Corregidoras, the Superflys and the Melindas, are images of men and women who live in large measure not in the Black community, but in the fitful, fanciful imaginations of those who after so many years regard themselves, still, as the bastard children of the West.

CHAPTER 49

Onyx Magazine: The Politics of Survival

(1971)

When Professor William E. B. Du Bois initiated his studies of Black life and culture at Atlanta University in 1897, his objective was to create an atmosphere for scholarship and research, and to construct tools of criticism with which Black people could rewrite and restructure their history. With the exception of Frederick Douglass' *The Life and Times of Frederick Douglass,* William Wells Brown's incomplete history, *The Rising Sun,* Du Bois' *The Suppression of the African Slave Trade,* polemics by Martin Delany and David Walker, and a few fugitive tracts, the history of slavery, Reconstruction and its aftermath was written by whites—the majority of whom were unsympathetic.

There were genuine historical accounts of the lives of Black people which covered each of these periods. They were tucked away in the pages of Black magazines— *The North Star, The Anglo-African,* and Douglass' *Paper,* to name but a few. By the twentieth century, however, these documents had been banished to the archives of selected libraries and replaced by the works of such white historians as Charles Beard, John W. Burgess, and Albert Taylor Bledsoe. These historians not only distorted Black history, but in attempting to make American history palatable to white Americans, they transformed fact into fiction and succeeded only too well in erasing, even from the minds of the victims, the injustices of the past.

The practice of historical erasure and manipulation of historical fact continues unabated at the present time. Despite the prolific publications about Blacks, the attempt to distort what *was* and to substitute what *was not* is a common practice among members of the white intellectual establishment. What else is one to make of the inaccurate, nonsensical account of Black Nationalism written by Theodore Draper? Or the abstract, obscure polemic against the life and history of Richard Wright which comes from the untutored mind of Edward Margolies? Is there anything more in the novels of Black life written by men of such shallow intellect and perverted understanding as William Styron and Shane Stevens than an attempt by the descendants of the plantation owner to determine the life style of the descendant of the slave?

To paraphrase Don L. Lee, during the forties, when white Americans were incarcerating Japanese-Americans in concentration camps; during the Nazi period, when East Europeans were subjected to similar treatment at the hands of Germany—treatment surpassed only by that which Blacks have received from whites in America—there should have been Japanese writers, Jewish writers, Hungarian writers, etc., to monitor the events and to pass down this record of man's inhumanity to specific racial and ethnic groups. That the victims themselves should have written this history, exclusively, is a point which needs no emphasis. To prevent a repetition of the holocaust, the children of the victims must be cognizant of unblemished truths.

For this reason, *Onyx Magazine* ($1.00, P.O. Box 414, New York 10031), edited by Charles L. Russell, is an important and welcome publication at this time. As new Black publications appear daily—many funded by whites who continue to control those who will define the Black experience—Black critics must establish a set of criteria in order to distinguish the authentic from the false. One such criteria might well be: "What does the publication contribute to the building of nationhood?" Or further, in this period of preparation and discussion: "What does the magazine contribute to an elucidation of the dichotomy between various elements of the Black community who have not agreed upon priorities or methods at the present time?"

I believe that in these areas *Onyx Magazine* succeeds. A record of the "First Annual Black Cultural Conference," held in 1968, the publication offers a historical account of where we, as a people, were in terms of ideological differences two years ago. The magazine contains six parts, each dealing with a specific subject: Part I presents a statement of purpose; Part II consists of pertinent opening remarks; Part III is a replay of a panel discussion; Parts IV and V, reports from workshops; and Part VI, a summation of the reports of many workshops.

Within this framework, ideas and challenging questions are raised by a number of individuals, some—Harold Cruse, H. Rap Brown, Larry Neal, Toni Cade, Barbara Ann Teer, and Sam Anderson—well known for their work in the struggle. Others, less well known but equally effective, contribute penetrating analyses of a number of Black issues. Harold Cruse sounds the keynote: "Our cultural essence became so institutionalized in American society, so endemic to the folkways of white and Black thinking, that Black people themselves were seduced into accepting the situation as a normal state of affairs. . . . Often, he [the Afro-American] did not respect himself or what he had in terms of cultural uniqueness." And later: "There's something about the white ego which feels that its cultural standards must be superior to everybody else's, that its standards must prevail at all times."

The meaning is clear. As Larry Neal remarks during the panel discussion, we are at war, and the war must be waged on many fronts. The issue confronting the panel concerned the nature of the warfare, and the opposing viewpoints were represented by various members. H. Rap Brown vigorously argued one point of view: "The role of the vanguard group is to bring down the repression. The role of the political culturalists is to define that repression, to make clear the repression that is happening." Toni Cade, although she would not disagree with this, argues the point for cultural nationalism: "Every nationalist movement has been accompanied by a cultural revival. In the beginning, the artists reject old colonial myths that are no longer useful. Perhaps simultaneously or soon afterward, the culture—particularly the literature—becomes a literature of unity in which the novels, poems, drama are used to establish priorities or to reevaluate the past and make it usable to live with; and very rarely, literature is used to predict the future, to profess what we have not seen or heard."

Miss Cade is talking about the politics of survival. Over the last two years, the debate between cultural nationalists and political nationalists has intensified. Few of the proponents of each position seem to realize that each movement is necessary, but that neither alone is sufficient. True to Miss Cade's analysis, the cultural revival must recreate the past, reevaluate the old values and ideals, and point out the pitfalls and errors of the preceding generations. That the artist has failed somewhat in this endeavor can be seen in light of the fact that there exist, now, in the seventies, Black groups, professing revolution, who seek alliances with whites. A cursory examination of the American past shows that such alliances, instead of benefiting Blacks, have proved the truth of the old Russian proverb that he who rides the back of the tiger usually ends up inside.

"Everything is political," remarks a workshop participant, and the statement is certainly true. The political objective of the Black struggle must be the complete and total dismantling of the American apparatus; however, this cannot be accomplished until Black people are convinced of the sincerity of those who purport to bring about revolution in their name. Having been saddled for so long with Whitney Youngs, Roy Wilkinses and Bayard Rustins, Black people are wary of political movements which, thus far, have produced few concrete changes for them. Perhaps the best statement on the debate between the political and cultural nationalists is that made by Marvin X and quoted by Charles Russell: ". . . The Black man makes no distinction between art and politics—they are one—and everything is everything."

A magazine, most of whose contents are transcribed from tape, is certain to have faults, and *Onyx* has its share. The debate which follows Rap Brown's provocative presentation called for more discussion than the magazine presents, and one can only assume that Cruse's reply was lost in transcription. The same criticism holds true for the workshop presentations in which informative, challenging dialogue appears, to this reader, somewhat incomplete.

Despite these flaws, *Onyx* is a welcome addition to its sisters already on the stands—*Black World, Liberator, Amistad* and *Journal of Black Poetry,* to name only a few. Such magazines reinforce Du Bois' undertakings at Atlanta during the last years of the nineteenth century, and help to present the historical record without knowledge of which no race can survive. For if Black history teaches us nothing else, it should teach us this: The war that we as a people must wage is not against each other, not against our opposing ideologies, but against the American system. Such a system, with its total disregard for humanity, is a threat to the well-being and peace of mankind; it has neither a moral nor an intellectual justification for continued existence.

CHAPTER 50

Reviews

Flight to Canada, Ishmael Reed. New York: Random House.
Eva's Man, Gayl Jones. New York: Random House.

(1976)

Black Women and Black Men: The Literature of Catharsis.

The year, 1974. The place, Caracas, Venezuela.

I sat in the International Hotel, situated deep down in a valley, surrounded by giant mountains composed of overgrown evergreen trees and other dusky, tan-brown foliage, of what species of plants I do not know. From my vantage point—a table close to the window of the hotel dining room—the mountains appeared. Not as the conglomeration of forests that they were, but as mounds and mounds of richly colored rock, piled high atop one another. The aluminum shacks that constitute part of some of the worst slums in the world and dot the mountainsides like nauseating pimples were on the other side, turned away from the hotel—so as not, I imagined, to embarrass the guests.

I had come to this place of sunshine and tranquil beauty, not only to escape the dust and grime of New York City, but also to distance myself from the Americans, to fuel my energies once again, for those instantaneous wars, which still, despite the apologists, most Blacks must be prepared to wage daily against the country in which they live. For three days I had walked among the people of Caracas, made friends with a few, became relaxed, contemplative. Thus, I was unprepared to confront the woman who appeared at my breakfast table on this particular morning, shortly before I was to go once again up into the Venezuelan mountains. She was American, mulatto, a buyer for a Los Angeles dress shop, taking a little vacation from "the pressures," as she called it. The "pressures" that drove her to seek respite in Caracas, however, were different from those that had driven me. It was not the United States, she related, which was oppressive to her—a country she defended with the vigor of a Ronald Reagan; no, her strife and anguish, the chaos that resided within her breasts, resulted from a broken marriage and a "few other" relationships with Black men, in which she had been wounded, hurt, and transformed from a trusting loving human being into a vengeance-seeking Lucretia Borgia.

She recounted tale after tale of horror and suffering, listing grotesque incident after grotesque incident; and as she told her tale (tales), her face underwent marked changes. She had begun the first recital with a sullen, pensive look; after relating the first of her misfortunes, this look became thoughtful and deliberate, and a smile formed around the corners of her mouth; when she finished the last of her recitals and concluded loudly, affirmatively—"I'll never trust another Black man—the smile had spread to her entire face, bringing with it a beautiful look of euphoria. Angry, I arose abruptly, said goodbye out of courtesy, and headed for the hills. I was angry, not so much at what she had said, but at the fact that I had been used. A modern-day Ancient Mariner, Black and female, had sought me out, used me as an object for catharsis, in an attempt to purge herself of those manifold demons riding herd-like across her psyche. In so doing, she had sought to negate my humanity.

I am reminded of this incident upon reading two recent novels, *Flight to Canada* by Ishmael Reed and *Eva's Man* by Gayl Jones. There is something in the works of these two writers of the same Ancient Mariner quality; there is the same need for catharsis, for ego-gratification, and the same theme which ran through "the buyer's" monologue is evidenced in these two novels and others, so recently acclaimed by Black and white critics. Reed, of course, is an anomaly, and if much of his fiction, *The Last Days of Louisiana Red* and *Flight To Canada* proves anything, it is that Black women have no monopoly on demons, real or imaginative. These two novels demonstrate that like "the buyer" in Caracas, like Blacks in general, male and female, the web of folklore which has circumscribed much of our relations with each other from the days of slavery till the present time, have been impervious to the best efforts of conscientious men and women to tear it down. Thus Reed's central argument, as developed in both "Louisiana Red" and *Flight to Canada* may be summed up thusly: Since the days of slavery, collusion between Black women and white men has existed in America. The major objective of this collusion has been the castrating of Black males and the thwarting of manful rebellion. The argument is dramatized in specifics in "Louisiana Red" and symbolized in *Flight To Canada*. In the latter novel, the brunt of the symbolic burden falls upon the character, Barrucuda; an asexual mammy, she is allied with Swille, the sadistic, degenerate slaveholder and Southern baron. She is, as the name implies, a man eater, the natural ally of white men, faithfully doing their bidding, serving as an arm of their power, putting down revolt, chastising other slaves. At the end of the novel, Swille dead, Barrucuda inherits his storehouse of sado-masochistic paraphernalia—whips, chains, etc.

This is not history, but anti-history, a grotesque distortion to be sure; yet, the theme of collusion, though minus the power implications suggested by Reed, is one in which a great many Black males believe. Such collusions, if such they are, more often than not are unconscious and designed to serve noble ends. Certainly, those thousands of mothers, like Wright's mother in *Black Boy,* who punish and abuse their sons for standing their ground against whites, are seeking to save their children, not to affect an alliance with white men. Likewise, those female writers—Lorraine Hansberry and Alice Walker are examples—who in their works depict Black males as helpless victims, overwhelmed by an all-powerful male dominated white society, are not guilty of collusion—in the sense that Reed suggests. Yet, tempered though they may be, bred of unconscious motivations as they assuredly are, such acts serve to enforce the morals, values, and myths of the American society—in short, to keep Black men in their places.

There are more direct forms of collusion, however, some not so motivated by innocence that have surfaced in much of the recent fiction by Black women writers. The new Ancient Mariners burn with the desire to tell their tales of horror, to unburden their tormented souls, to gain their cathartic moment of euphoria. Their stories are simple and direct: Black men are brutal, uncaring, irresponsible beasts, the *sine qua non* of evil in the universe. The more dramatic of these offerings have been those by Gayl Jones. One may disagree with the overall view presented in her two novels, *Corregidora* and *Eva's Man*—and I do—but her tales, like those of the young woman whom I met in Caracas, contains truths that must be honestly confronted.

The depiction of Black women by Black male writers has bordered upon the ridiculous and the criminal. Some Black men—far too many—brutalize Black women, physically and mentally; some Black men—far too many—exploit Black women, sexually and economically; many Black men—far too many—fear independent, intellectually superior Black women; and far too many Black men achieve catharsis venting their rage and anger at white racist America by sadistically abusing Black women. All of this amounts to truth, and it is truth that must be told again and again, not only by women writers, but male writers as well. It is a truth, springing from the soul-felt pain of women who have felt the sting of double lash—that of the society and that of Black men—which needs no supporting rationale. There are no excuses! The behavior of Black men toward Black women cannot be justified by reference to "The Oppressive Nature of the Society," or the difficulties of making it in "White America." Further, it is behavior of which no male is innocent; those of us who have not screamed and screamed loud about the brutalities are as guilty as those who commit them.

The cry of anger, race, and pain shouted with such a deafening crescendo by women writers is legitimate; it has the validity of many personal experiences. Most women can identify with some of the experiences undergone by Eva: sexual molestation—as a child—by male members of the family, sexual advances by older men, the fixation upon young girls as sexual objects by growing young males, the sado-masochism exhibited by males in too many sexual encounters. Were these the major dimensions of *Eva's Man* and the earlier *Corregidora*, one would be pained by the revelations, hurt by comprehending the things that Black people still do to one another, but one would not be turned off, would not believe that he had encountered yet another Ancient Mariner, seeking not to instruct, to educate to help Black men to resurrect themselves, but one who sought, instead, to gain a personal release from pain, a private catharsis, which could only be achieved when the Black male had been rendered impotent. The agent of this male-destructiveness, Eva, then becomes like the American society in general— dedicated to the destruction of Black men as men—and one with whose pain we cease to identify; she is transformed in the course of the novel into the Barracuda who Reed depicts in his fiction.

Take the basic outlines of the story. Eva, like the woman around her, has undergone a history of sexual abuse at the hands of Black males. Climaxing such a history, she is picked up by Davis, taken to his hotel room, and virtually imprisoned. The symbolism is apparent and reaches back to *Corregidora:* the white society (male dominated) imprisons Blacks, denies them freedom of movement, the freedom to expand their consciousness, to be themselves. Black males treat Black women in much the same fashion; thus, Black males differ little from white ones. Reacting against such a history, Eva, in rebellion, subsequently poisons her mate and bites off his penis. Death is not enough to atone for the evils committed by Black men; the Barracudas demand nothing less than the total destruction of manhood, the reduction of the Black male to eunuch.

The novels of Reed and Jones prove that we remain the victims of the myths of others. Reed believes that the world turns upon the axis of power, and that at the center of this axis, is the white male; Jones, that the world turns upon sexuality, and the center is controlled by forests of Black penises which must be chopped down before the liberation of Black women is possible. The paranoia and fear of the writers cannot be easily dismissed; yet, the catharsis they seek in the revelation of their tales of hurt, of their distortions of history, should not be gained at the expense of the reader. For these are not *their* myths, but those borrowed from a racist society. Only in the diseased minds of the Americans is there a supposed equation between power and manhood; if such were really true, one would be forced to the ridiculous conclusion that Gerald Ford is entitled to the appellation man, and that Malik Shabazz is not. Manhood, as Fanon knew so well, must be described as the relentless warfare waged by courageous men against those who use power to oppress and enslave.

It is here that Reed's charges of collusion between Black women and white men in the utilization of power become ironic and inward. Obsession with the power of white males has led him, not only to make this charge, but in his public statements as well as his fiction, to adopt the American societies' rationales and justifications for its continual treatment of Blacks, even ofttimes using the sanctimonious hypocrisy of its language; "Perhaps the civil rights movement," he writes in *The New York Times,* in phraseology that would warm the heart of a Daniel Moynihan, "lost its steam because people noticed that Blacks weren't practicing civil rights among themselves." There are other footpaths, as Frank Webb knew so well, leading toward assimilation than the straightening of one's hair and the bleaching of one's skin.

Collusion, then may be too strong a word! Compatibility, however is not. For there is such between the thoughts of these two novelists, concerning Black people and those of racists past and present. Writes John Leonard about *Eva's Man:* ". . . It may be said that whites took everything away from Blacks but their sexuality and the distortion of that sexuality is responsible for Eva." In other words, we are a primitive people, defined totally in terms of our sexuality; this is our essence, or elan vital, that which drives us, which makes us enemies of each other, the pariahs of civilized America. Look at us and understand that the Freudian theories concerning the incomplete development of libido are true; ours is the world of instinctual gratification, where sex, not power, not humanity, reigns supreme. But not only this, for there is a hidden joke: (All discussions by whites concerning the sexuality of Blacks must be tempered with a joke) the joke is the myth of our sexuality, for even this—our supposed lifeline—is distorted, unhealthy.

Racist critics not withstanding, the literature of catharsis leads to such narrow interpretations. Read the novels of Jones and Reed and we are ignorant of another world outside, unaware, even that Black unemployment in American is double that of whites, that Black people are committing suicide in ever increasing numbers, that the prisons are heavily populated with Blacks, that Black children grow up mentally and physically stunted, that Black people live in substandard housing, go to bed hungry at night, are attacked and assaulted by white mobs from Kentucky to New York. Such "elemental mundane facts," we are led to believe, are insignificant when measured against the evils perpetrated upon some Black women by some Black men and vice versa. Not surprisingly, therefore, the literature of catharsis has made its authors the darlings of the white literary establishment. Writes a reviewer of *Eva's Man:* "It has perhaps become redundant to say of a book grounded in the Black experience that it is a violent and angry book. The statement is a . . . reaction against white oppression. It . . . is refreshing and ironic to come upon a book of this character that . . . aims these emotions in a new direction."

The Americans, wrote Richard Wright over two decades ago, have never been able to accept my truth. The reason is that Wright's truth, no matter the shortcomings, differed from that white Americans wanted to believe. It is far easier for them to accept the truths promulgated in the fiction of Jones and Reed—for such truths, unlike those of Wright, are to be found in the works of Thomas Nelson Page, Carl Van Vechten, William Faulkner, Norman Mailer, John Updike, Bernard Malamud, and William Styron: They are self-serving truths that buttress the illusions about America and Black people held dear by those whose extol the American system in salubrious terms from church pulpit to the oval office.

But there are truths and there are truths, I recalled, as I went each day up into the mountains of Caracas, passing the many-colored men and women, their manner proud and undefeated, though many of them dwelled in the worst of poverty. I discovered that the conflict between the sexes, that etched out so hysterically by the "Buyer" from Los Angeles, was present here, too, that the war between men and women was the one true universal conflict of the ages. But these people were poor, if not hungry, and thus they recognized that there were also other wars; against man's injustice to men and women, against an oppressive economic system which made no distinction between males and females. And I knew then that catharsis had not worked for my breakfast guest; no, no more than it had worked for Coleridge's Ancient Mariner.

Neither does it work for Reed and Jones. For catharsis achieved by spewing forth anger and rage in an attempt to demolish one sex or another, while ignoring the realities of one's existence, is impossible. These authors, after all, still live in a racist society, are buffeted whether they admit it or not by racist forces. And their works reflect their tacit recognition of this fact: Black males as well as Black females are grotesque caricatures in the novels of Reed. Neither possess the attributes of humanity. The women in Jones' novels are as twisted as the men are brutal—sexually perverse Barracudas whose only chance for happiness is in a universe where sexual gender is nonexistent.

But I know, too, that rationalization can never take the place of reality, and the reality for Black people is as stark as that for the inhabitants of Caracas. A major war rages upon this globe at this very hour, and this war is not so much between men and women, as it is between the oppressed and the oppressors. In this country, it is a war between Black people and Americans, a continuation of that begun in the time of Douglass and Sojourner Truth, one of which few Blacks are unaware.

It is a war against evil and injustice, against those who seek to stifle the aspirations of the human spirit. Here in America, it has taken the toll of some of our most courageous men and women; it has caused untold frustration and despair; it has led to cynicism, nihilism, and resignation. Yet determined men and women continue to fight it, to ask from the oppressor no quarter, to demand the liberation of *all* the enslaved. These are valiant warriors; they are to be found throughout this country, Black men and Black women, who, even at the height of this war, retain compassion and pity for those Ancient Mariners among them, whose search for catharsis have forced them to join the archenemies of humankind, who have become one with the forces of reaction and anti-man.

This writer has no such compassion, will join in no appeals to lure the prodigals back to the fold. At this juncture of history, the battle lines are being drawn, wherever Black people are, in Africa, the Caribbean, South America, the United States, and one must choose for himself which side of that line he stands on. No, my compassion is not to be wasted upon writers, who, after all, must take responsibility for what they write. But for those many Black people, men and women, who have reached adulthood without a beautiful, fulfilling, wholesome relationship—if only for a fleeting hour—with a member of the opposite sex, I have the greatest of compassion—and pity.

CHAPTER 51

What We Must See—Young Black Storytellers

edited and an introduction by Orde Coombs

The Hungered One—Early Writings

by Ed Bullins

(1971)

If Afro-American literature should take a "sharp turn toward strictly racial themes" wrote Richard Wright, we will know that Blacks are suffering "old and ancient agonies" at the hands of white Americans. If, on the other hand, Afro-American literature turns toward "the common themes and burdens of literary expression which are the heritage of all men," we can assume that a humane attitude dominates American racial relationships. The assumption that the function of Afro-American literature is to educate white Americans, change whites attitudes and shape white opinion is central to this argument in particular and to Wright's literary credo in general.

Young writers of the present decade (Wright's article was written in the nineteen fifties) would disagree with Wright's premises and conclusion. Having undergone experiences in the urban ghetto that he could only have imagined, the Afro-American writers of today realizes that his art is not determined by the diastole and systole of American history. Instead, it is shaped by the halting and infrequent changes in the Black man's condition; the "old and ancient agonies" will always be with us, but the function of art is to bring awareness to the disfranchised, the alienated, the frustrated, and the desperate everywhere. *What We Must See,* edited by Orde Coombs, and *The Hungered One,* by Ed Bullins, substantiate the thesis.

A collection of 16 short stories, *What We Must See* deals with subjects that are relative to the here and now. "Rites Fraternal" deals with the freedom rites of the sixties; "Etta's Mind," "Waiting for Her Train," and "Miss Nora" with the experiences of Black women in a male-dominated society; "A Proper Burial" and "Second Line/Cutting the Body Loose" with death and despair; "The Blue of Madness" with alienation and suicide. Many of the stories focus on the problem of drugs: "The Fare to Crown Point," "Harlem Transfer," and "After Saturday Night Comes Sunday."

Among the writers, four are seniors in terms of literary accomplishment. Not surprisingly, therefore, the best stories in the collection—"Miss Nora," "Harlem Transfer," "After Saturday Night Comes Sunday," and "Waiting for Her Train" are written by these four accomplished artists who have mastered the mechanics of short fiction. "Harlem Transfer" by Evan K. Walker (winner of the Conrad Kent Rivers Memorial Award) is the most compelling selection in the book.

"He shot the Browning Automatic Rifle down into the crowded street, and the people did not move. . . . He shifted his position in the window and aimed the BAR at a hustler outlined against the dirty grey snow near the curb." With these opening lines the story begins, and before it ends, the protagonist kills a drug peddler, a police lieutenant, and holds a police department at bay. For those who relish the term, the theme is "universal" (vengeance and redemption) highlighted by Black experience. Failing to obtain help from the police (the lieutenant is an accomplice of the peddler) and a Negro organization after his son becomes an addict, the protagonist, an ex-veteran, declares war on the Black man's newest and most dangerous enemy—the drug dealer.

Sonia Sanchez's "After Saturday Night Comes Sunday" also deals with the drug situation. Here is depicted the plight of Sandy, a Black woman, wife of an addict, who must cross the Rubicon between hope and despair, not once in her lifetime, but each hour of each and every day. In experimenting with the language, Miss Sanchez takes us back to Jean Toomer: "That wuz it she that. Stop talking and write what you have to say. Nod yo head to all of this madness. But rest yo/tongue and nod yo/head and use yo/hands till you git it all straight again." Both stories are excellent in terms of form and content, and in each there is concreteness of character, unity of plot, instantaneousness of situation, and fidelity to language. ("Miss Nora" by Lindsay Patterson and "Waiting for Her Train" by Audrey M. Lee are also of high quality.)

Few of the other contributors exhibit the technical proficiency of those cited above; the reason is, perhaps, that they have not read enough and, thus, do not know enough. The world of Afro-Americans is a multi-faceted one that can be properly illuminated only by a sensitivity heightened by influences beyond the ghetto walls. To know the ghetto, the life style of Black people, our language culture and customs is necessary for the writer, but far from sufficient. What is needed, in addition, is a mastery of craft which can be attained only through stern discipline, hard work, and a knowledge of "the best that has been written and spoken" in the long history of mankind.

Knowledge of craft and technique distinguishes the collection of short fiction by Ed Bullins. Reading like an odyssey of one man's experiences of the world, the book—divided into two sections, "The Absurd One" and "The Hungered One"— contains 21 stories. Bullins, a playwright, uses dramaturgical skills to create and enrich moods, painting a broad canvas upon which his characters move with the uncertain grace of men thrust into an incomprehensible world.

There are the surrealistic stories that abound in myth and symbolism: "The Absurd One," "The Hungered One," and "The Reluctant Voyage." There are satires, reminiscent of Rudolph Fisher and George Schuyler, such as "The Rally, or Dialect Determinism," "Support Your Local Police," and "The Messenger." In between are stories of love and hate, of the eternal search for meaning in a world which, absurd for most men, is even more so for Blacks.

"Dandy or Astride the Funky Finger of Lust" is one such story. A panegyric on warfare between Black man and Black man, the story is a character sketch of Dandy (the Northerner) in pursuit of Marie Ann (the Southerner). Carefully executed flashbacks allow us to perceive Dandy as a young man, to distinguish the Dandy of the North from the Dandy of the South. There are, Bullins seems to be telling us, values still left in the Southland—the first home away from home for most Blacks—that must be remembered and treasured. "He Couldn't Say Sex" equals "Dandy" in terms of force and power. The protagonist, forbidden early by his parents to talk about things sexual, searches for a sense of meaning in a world in which sex is all pervasive. The confusion of this nonpromiscuous Black male (negation of the stereotype) results from living in a country that has degenerated to the point where sex is its most important commodity.

The language in the book is first-rate. Although appearing, at time, to be giving stage directions to his characters ("The father comes into the room and looks about the empty walls; he stoops and lifts the upturned campaign poster, wedging it under his arms, making his arm a banner and blindfold across the eyes of the candidate"), Bullins is capable of investing scenes and episodes with imagistic and metaphorical language. "But the word oozed off syrupy July pavement filling his muggy playstreets in asphalt thick waves. The word was scrawled indelibly across his ghetto-sooted mind; its imagery sloughed off his broiled Black sheen in cascades of lust. The word settled in the depths of his quick haunches and tight thighs." The word is sex.

The two books have this in common. They evidence the fact that the battle once waged by the Afro-American writer for the conscience of white America now lies elsewhere. As editor Orde Coombs writes (more accurately than Wright): "These brothers and sisters have gone beyond pleas and execrations. For if in our lives we have seen tragedy . . . if in our lives we have known bottomless despair, we have also seen us moving together as a people." In this respect, Afro-American literature, as presented in these two volumes, is germane to the tumultuous, chaotic world in which we live at the present time.

CHAPTER 52

Blueschild Baby

by George Cain

(1971)

In 1968, the search for a "Black Aesthetic"—a critical criterion that distinguishes the writings of Blacks from those of whites—was initiated. At that time, the application of the concept was more apparent in poetry than in fiction or drama. Langston Hughes, Jean Toomer, and Gwendolyn Brooks offered new and exciting ways of dealing with Black life in terms of form, symbolism, and imagery; and their young successors —Imamu Amiri Baraka, Don L. Lee, James A. Emanuel, and Nikki Giovanni—in experimenting with style, precipitated a revolution in Black poetry.

The Black novelist lagged far behind. Although there were models to follow— *Blake, or the Huts of America,* (1859), *Imperium in Imperio* (1899), and *Dark Princess* (1928)—they were neglected in deference to *Ulysses, The Naked and the Dead, For Whom the Bell Tolls,* and *Light in August.* Based on such models, the Black novel served only to provide white critics with an excuse to perform literary gymnastics and aided in the perpetuation of Anglo-Saxon ethics and values. In attempting to say so much to whites, it has said little of relevance to Blacks.

Blueschild Baby, an autobiographical first novel, is a welcome exception. Written in language that is an integral part of the Black community—a language that abounds in colorful in-group symbols and metaphors ("Everybody and thing here is a warm memory of a time when all was new impressing indelibly on consciousness.")—the novel reveals a world that only Black people can fully comprehend.

The style is vigorous, original, and poetic—rhythmic conglomerations of words pressed so closely together that they reveal the "tom-tom of revolt" in the Black soul with a force and power excelled only by the blues: ". . . Know how a Black man feels all the time. That pressure he exists under all the time till it becomes second nature, a part of him. Walking around wary of the word or gesture that will set in motion an act that will end his life. . . . This is what charges the air of Harlem and lets you know you're there, not the stink or sound, but the tension that lies over all like a cloud ready to bust."

The "tension that lies over all" is the key to the novel. It grips the lives of George Cain's associates in the "junky world" (Sun, Fats, and Jose) and his middle-class aspiring parents who flee Harlem only to find that in the "safe suburbs" they are "surrounded, hounded, and harassed by the white mob." It is ever-present in the life of Nichole, his discarded white mistress and in that of Nandy, the Black woman who helps George redeem himself by surviving 72 hours of living hell (the time it takes to kick the habit). In that time George Cain, former addict, emerges phoenix-like from the ages, as George Cain Black man.

In those works that explicate the Black Aesthetic, whites are depicted as major antagonists because they are such in the lives of most Black people. They are portrayed neither as sympathetic Christ figures nor as superhuman devils. In *Blueschild Baby*, George Cain, like many young Blacks at the present time, simply wishes to get away from them. Rejecting their inhumanity, he turns to drug addiction only to discover that their reign extends even there. This discovery signals his moment of truth.

Evaluated in the terms so dear to white academicians—form, concreteness of character, organization of plot, usage of stream of consciousness, etc.—*Blueschild Baby* ranks high indeed; however, for those attuned to the Black Aesthetic in casting well deserved censure upon the theology of the integrationists and in opting for Black unity instead of Black and white togetherness, the novel represents a major breakthrough for the Black writer. For this reason, it is the most important work of fiction by an Afro-American since *Native Son*.

CHAPTER 53

Love Story Black

by William Demby

(1981)

> She had taken off her Chinese embroidered robe and revealed her
> wasted child-like body as in an ancient ritual of puberty, shyly, a
> profound sense of the rituality of what she was doing. And she lay back
> on the divan, and in the dawn light or sunset glow . . . she placed a
> cushion under her head and in the innocence and frenzy of first love
> she touched my fingers tentatively and then seized them with the force
> of the passionate grasping to life that is both birth cry and death rattle
> and motioned me to hurry, hurry, hurry . . .

So William Demby concludes *Love Story Black,* one of his best novels. The
hurrying is necessary, both for Mona Pariss and Edwards, the novel's narrator. Both—the one-time famous black singer, "now pushing ninety" years old
and the interviewer, writer, professor of English—are about to undergo a love/
religious ritual in which the myth becomes first truth, then understanding, then
revelation: Edwards recalls a nightmare/myth in which he has encountered an
old woman in a hut; he seeks water and the answer to a riddle: "I have come millions of miles over the desert of time with a riddle . . ." The old woman in the hut,
"the prophetess," will surrender the answer, reveal "the meaning of the riddle, if
I make love to her—"

Love Story Black is then a novel about making love, about truth and revelation,
birth, rebirth, and death, and though the symbolic import of the novel is borne by
Mona Pariss, the tale is as much of the young professor as it is that of the of the
old woman. Edwards, who teaches courses in Chaucer and in Black Literature,
like the author, has lived abroad and written novels, which as both his employer
and a student inform him are outside the black tradition. If his detractors are
to be believed, Edwards and his fiction are Europeanized; thus the writer must
undergo his own odyssey, seek a clue to many riddles, search for clarification,
meaning. He does not find either when he travels to Africa with a middle class
black woman, his fiancée, who deserts him for an African guerilla fighter. Ironically, what he finds in Africa is not the mystery of his roots but sickness. The

answer to the riddle, not so much identity, but the meaning of identity, can be discovered only through Mona Pariss.

Mona is the not so grim ferryman, capable of ushering others across the river Styx, because of the learned lessons of her own tragic experience. In her youth, she became infatuated with "Doc," itinerant minister, railroad porter. She was Doc's discovery. It was he who started her on the road to international acclaim and success. Yet what she wanted most from the preacher, he could not deliver. ". . . He told me this weird story," she relates, "about how he never did it with girls, and that a young girl like me would be better off staying a virgin all her life . . ." The advice is not so much a lie as it is a rationale. Doc, as Mona is to discover, has been castrated. Thus, for almost ninety years, she lives the agony and suspense of the experience that never was. There is some small recompense gained, when in exchange for the interview that stretches over time, she orders Edwards to lie naked with her in bed.

Neither Edwards nor the reader is aware of the coming consequences of this act. Neither could have foretold that Edwards, coming back to America after desertion by his fiancée in Africa, would return to Mona Pariss to complete the last of the interviews, disrobe yet another time and become the surrogate lover, mistaken by the old woman for "Doc" of long ago, and fulfill the demand of the prophetess of the nightmare/myth. Yet the thematic import of the novel demands an ending no less existential, mysterious, or satisfying. For the love of Mona Pariss is a child-like love—love at first sight—terrifying and wonderful in its evocation. It is like a religious conversion, passionate, instantaneous, soul-consuming. It is a love that has transcended time, one infused with need and desire, becoming— and this is not too strong a word—a conflagration, sweeping Mona to death and Edwards to a new birth. Hers, however, is what Albert Camus would have called a happy death.

The symbolism in *Love Story Black* is as telling as that demonstrated heretofore by Demby in *Beetlecreek* and *The Catacombs,* revealing the writer's continuing preoccupation with life, death, and love. These have remained his trinity: these givens in the life of every human being. Life as Demby knows must end in death; neither life nor death is meaningful without love. Love makes both acceptable and one gathers from this work, that Demby pities those who have never achieved it. For Camus's doctrine, "I rebel, therefore I am," Demby would proclaim I love, therefore I am, thus raising the existential equation beyond romanticism to touch the most profound longings and utterings of the human soul. Such are exemplified in the life and times of Mona Pariss and the old woman herself, in her quest and in her achievement, exemplifies humankind at its best.

PART 6

Autobiographies

The move from Negroness to Blackness has been a slow/painful/
upward journey of the twentieth century, a journey still not completed.
The voice of Blackness in the wilderness of North America awoke the
Black man from the sleep of his forgotten identity. He awoke angry
and startled at those who had put him to sleep. In the beginning of this
Black literature, anger overshadowed self-identity. But when reason
lit the darkness of this new world, the energy of anger turned inward
toward themes of Black love, respect, and Black nationhood.
—Sonia Sanchez, *"We Be Word Sorcerers"*

Although autobiographical facts may be irrelevant to some critics/writers, Gayle's autobiography served as a candid introspection of himself, his childhood, his attitudes, and his actions toward his father and mother.

Section six, "Autobiographies" includes an excerpt from Gayle's autobiography, *Wayward Child: A Personal Odyssey*, which includes revelations of his conflicts with various aspects of his childhood and early life, in particular his relationship with his father and the "mulatto" class in Newport News; a rare 1972 interview with Saundra Towns in which he expounds on the function of black literature, writers, and critics; and a number of autobiographical essays, including the "The Son of My Father" and the two-part "Black Fathers and Sons."

This section concludes with "The Children of Bigger Thomas." The character of Bigger Thomas from Richard Wright's *Native Son* represented in Gayle's eyes a black sense of humanity, and Wright represented for Gayle writing that spoke to and for the masses of black people, those speechless "twelve million black voices."

CHAPTER 54

Addison Gayle

Interviewed by Saundra Towns

(1972)

The following interview, with critic Addison Gayle, took place at Mr. Gayle's home in New York on June 6, 1972. In the midst of his most recent work, a history of the Black novel, Mr. Gayle paused to answer questions ranging from literature to politics.

Q: *Why don't we begin by talking about the novel? Is the novel obsolete? Has the novel, for Blacks, any viability as a form?*

A: I think that white critics who say that the novel is becoming obsolete are correct, as far as the novel as written by whites is concerned. It is becoming obsolete because the function of the white novel is being duplicated now by movies, television, etc. If you examine the white novelist, and I suppose that among the most popular are Norman Mailer, Saul Bellow, and John Updike, you find a common denominator running through their novels, and that is a sense of decadence, a sense of futility, a sense of hopelessness, a sense of man being overwhelmed by his society and by the environment. Now you can pick that up out of any good Bergman film. You can get that out of any decent foreign film. At that point, the white novel does not inculcate a sense of morals, does not redefine definitions because it can't. The definitions have already been defined by white people. The white novel in America has nowhere to go. The Afro-American novel, on the other hand, has a great deal of viability because the job of the Afro-American novelist is to redefine definitions, to inculcate a system of values which will replace the values that have prevailed in this society, values which Blacks have never fully incorporated.

The function of the Afro-American novel is the liberation of Black people; the Afro-American novel will endure. I suppose that Black novelists are fortunate in that as Black people we have not had all of the things that America has given to white people. Our horizons are still high. We can still see some reason for living, some reason for being, if only to challenge all of these concepts that the Americans have handed down to us all of these years. So the novel for the Afro-American is a very important form. The problem and the danger is that just as you have Black screen writers—and what's the idiot's name?

Q: *Van Peebles?*

A: Van Peebles is a perfect example! Simply imitating whites and doing the sex-violence bit a little better. The chance is that you'll have Black novelists talking about the malaise in the Black community, the hopelessness, the futility. At that point, the novel will have nowhere to go because it won't be a Black novel then, it will be a white novel.

Q: *Are you saying that if Black writers are true to their culture, the truths that they produce in their novels will not be the same truths that white novelists have produced in theirs? In other words, when you talk about "horizons," you're not simply saying that because Blacks are "more primitive," or "less civilized," that they can still aspire . . .*

A: Oh no! What I'm saying is that for Black people, having lived in this country and having undergone all that we have, it is impossible for us to accept the world as decadent. Our whole existence has been one in which the world is a place of limitless possibilities. We continue to look at the world in that way. If you are white in this country, you soon run out of steam; you run out of goals; you run out of objectives; and you run out of any reason for living.

That's what's the rule for white kids on the campuses, for white people in general. As horrible as all of the oppression and everything has been, what it has done for us is to inculcate a kind of fighting spirit which breeds a kind of optimism, which says that there is a reason for living. The white novelist can only say that "*My* reason for being is to inculcate a sense of how dismal the world is." Whereas the Black novelist can say that "*My* reason for being is to change the world, to change the world vis-a-vis the relationship of the world to Black people."

You know, Ellison, in *Invisible Man,* talks about America as being a land of limitless opportunities, a kind of New Frontier. I think that what he means, or what he should mean, is that for Black people, it is a world to be conquered, by going through or by going beyond the white experience. If we simply want to be white folks, then the world is as dismal and as hopeless and as futile for us as it is for them. But if we're going to be true Black folks, if we're really going to be true to our culture, to our history, then the world is one of limitless possibilities.

Q: *I don't want to belabor the point, but I could see argument being presented that the reason that Blacks see the world as one of limitless possibilities is because they've never had anything.*

A: Well, that depends on what you mean by "anything."

Q: *They've never had the affluence that whites have had.*

A: O.K. But I think it's a good thing, in a sense, I think if one understands what the affluence has done to white folks, then one could argue that it's a good thing that Black folks haven't had it. But I'm not talking about affluence, I'm talking about a humane, spiritual quality. I'm talking about people who can still walk around and call each other brothers. I'm talking about people who can say we have a common goal; we have a common cause; we have a common unity.

White folks don't talk about unity. They talk about alliances. The Russians want to ally with the Americans; the Americans want to ally with somebody else. Always to do somebody else in. But Black folks are the only ones who have this spiritual kind of unity thing. And *that's* what I mean. I don't mean optimistic in terms of Black folks becoming affluent. I mean optimistic in terms of believing in the human condition. I think we believe in the human condition because we've seen so many examples of it—at work! We've seen guys living, mothers living and existing in Mississippi and South Carolina, etc. We've seen guys living in Harlem and Watts and *not* becoming drug addicts. We've seen people who have not allowed themselves to be done in by this white system. When you see people like that walking around every day, it gives you a tremendous degree of optimism in the human condition. On the other hand, what does the white novelist have before him? He has a Nixon; he has an Agnew. He has decadence, and therefore he sees decadence. You know, it's a very interesting thing. Even though they're stereotypes; even though they're the worst possible symbols and images that one can have, the people who are alive, who are viable, even in the novels of Mailer and Updike, are Black. They're horrible stereotypes, but they're the only people with energy, the only people with vitality.

Q: *Then would it be correct to say that out of the experience of living in this country, what Blacks have created is a way of looking at the world which is quite different from, and also more lasting, than that of whites?*

A: Certainly. A completely different way of looking at the world. I think it's in *Another Country* that Ida says to Vivaldo, "If you had to take everything Rufus had to take, you couldn't have existed." Well, that's true. If white folks had to take in this country what Blacks have to take, I doubt if white folks would be around very long.

The species might become extinct—which wouldn't be a bad idea. That kind of experience necessitates a different kind of vision. You see the world differently. The Black guy, the Black writer, who pushes it through in this country, with everything that this country puts on Black writers, the cat who doesn't sell his soul, who maintains his integrity—Richard Wright for example—has a vision of the world, of how the world works, and has a foundation of courage under him that a Mailer could never have. And so, sure, two completely different ways of looking at the world.

Q: *Well, given such a situation, what kind of novels do you see emerging? That is, what kinds of novels do you think Blacks ought to be writing now?*

A. Let's look at the novel traditionally. I suppose that traditionally the novel has had two functions, the functions that Fielding talked about: to instruct and to entertain. What some people did—the Proletarian writers and the Marxist writers—was to argue that it was more instruction than entertainment, that the novel had to instruct. Now you know, the Afro-American novel, as I said before, and I can't say this enough, is simply one tool in a whole system of attempts to redefine definitions, to inculcate new values, to create new myths, symbols and images. What this means is that the Afro-American novelist must be part politician, part sociologist, part historian, and part novelist. Because he must look toward the day when the Afro-American novel will be a completely different form from what the novel is today. If one is going to redefine definitions, then one needs an instrument that is different from what we call the novel today. Something that will get to Black people quicker, and that Black people will grasp more easily than by reading a three-hundred-page novel. But the function of the novel, the function of the Afro-American writer as I see it, is a political function, and that is the liberation of the minds of Black people in this country. It's a weapon, and I make no bones about it. Call it propaganda, call it what you will. It's a weapon. Just as a painting is a weapon, just as a Molotov cocktail is a weapon. The functions are different, but it's certainly a weapon.

The only function, it seems to me, that the Afro-American novelist can have is to produce the kinds of awareness of our own particular strengths, of our own history, of our own culture, that will enable us to create the nation-state.

Q: *A nation-state?*

A: Yes. I mean within this country. United as we are by culture and history, a separate people. And that's what we are. I would think one of the functions of the novelist is to inculcate a sense of our separateness. I don't know what's wrong with that, since the function of the novel from William Wells Brown to Ralph Ellison has been to inculcate into us a sense of our togetherness with the rest of America.

You know, when people ask, "My God! What's wrong with the Afro-American novelist these days? What are these Black Aestheticians talking about? They're talking about making literature into propaganda!" Well, hell! Black literature has always been propaganda. The truth is that all literature is propaganda. But Black literature has been designed to inculcate into Black people a sense of their unity with this country. Now, when we're saying, "No. That's not the job of the novelist. The job of the novelist is to inculcate into Black people a sense of our separate historical mission in this country," we come under attack. But that's the function of the novel: to inculcate a sense of our uniqueness, our cultural strengths, our historical courage that has enabled us to survive in this country.

Q: *What you are saying is very interesting, and it brings up still another point, which, again, many white aestheticians argue, and that is that if the novel is going to have a political function—and when they make this point they always refer to the*

Marxist writers of the thirties—if the novel is to be primarily a political instrument, then it ceases to be art. And at that point it will not have any lasting value.

A: Yes, well, you see that, of course, depends upon one's definition of art. My definition of art is based upon whether or not the work is effective in producing awareness in Black people. Call it what you will, if it's a peanut butter can and it convinces some Black kid that he doesn't have to become what the American society says he has to become, it's art. I don't think of art as white folks think of art: a painting that you hang on your wall and invite your friends to come and look at—to show them that you've gone down to a museum and bought something you don't understand. Or books that white folks and the Negro middle class put on their bookshelves, and never open, by the way, and won't understand. Art for them is decoration. Wherein art for me depends upon its effectiveness.

Q: *It's functional?*

A: Sure. I'll call an Afro-American novel very bad, even if it is well written, and conforms to all the "structural and technical" aspects of the genre, but doesn't produce anything for Black people. I think *Invisible Man* is a great novel, structurally, technically, etc. But I don't think it's as important as *Blake; or The Huts of America,* because *Blake* would convince some kid that he has Black heroes whom he can emulate. Wherein what *Invisible Man* would convince him of is that he is a very screwed-up individual, wandering around in the American society, trying to find his identity. At that point, *Blake,* to me, is much more important as an art.

Q: *Well, in line with that, you said about one novel, George Cain's* Blueschild Baby, *that it was the most important novel since* Native Son. *Now, I suppose that many people might take issue with that. Could you explain why you said it?*

A: Sure. And once again, it's essentially what I think of art. *Native Son* dealt with a very fundamental problem vis-a-vis Blacks in the American society, and that is, what is the extent of the American oppression upon Blacks? And you must remember that *Native Son* was not long after the Harlem Renaissance, where you had your Negro assimilationists telling white folks that "there are only a few of those Bigger Thomas niggers running around. Most of us are nice, upstanding Negroes who want to become middle class, who want to become American."

At that point, I think what *Native Son* said was that you have a hell of a lot of embittered, rebellious Blacks running around this country, and you had better do something about your country before these Blacks begin to do something about it for you. By the same token, *Blueschild Baby* comes about at a time when the most important problem confronting Black people in this country is drugs. And what you get is George Cain taking a very different tack. Not saying "Look, America, you do something about this problem," but saying "Black folks, here is your problem, you do something about it." At that point, it is a damn important novel because it moves in the direction that Black people have been moving in, and that is from a dependence upon society's changing to Black people changing.

Q: Then, in terms of fulfilling the needs of the Black Aesthetic, it becomes very important.

A: Certainly. At the heart of the Black Aesthetic is the political argument that as Black people we must go it alone in this country. We've moved away from the Richard Wright position that the American society will change. That's a politically untenable position to hold.

Q: Since we're talking about the Black Aesthetic, let me ask you a few questions along that line. There was an article in a recent issue of The Nation in which this young white critic says that he recognizes the feasibility of the Black Aesthetic, and that it is as important a movement as the Transcendentalists and the New Critics. He ends his article by saying that although the Black Aestheticians may not want to have anything to do with this country, this country certainly wants them. In essence, that's how the argument goes. How do you see the Black Aesthetic faring in this country? Do you think that it will be co-opted by the literary establishment?

A: No. Once it becomes co-opted by the Establishment it ceases to be a Black Aesthetic. The Black Aesthetic is antithetical to everything that the American literary movement is, to what it means. The idea that America wants the Black Aestheticians is very ironic. It's the old liberal credo: We intelligent, right-seeing white folks really appreciate you Black folks who are outcasts, and we want you to come into the fold. Wherein the importance and the viability of the Black Aesthetic—of course, I can't speak for all Black Aestheticians—is that many of them no longer want to be a part of America, let alone the American literary mainstream. Because that way lies death.

Of course, some Black writers will naturally go that way because that way lies money. But the Black Aesthetic has as its fundamental thesis that there are cultural streams dividing Blacks from whites in this country. At that point, the idea that the Black Aesthetic will become simply another literary movement misses the point. We're not talking about literary movements in that sense at all. The Black Aesthetic will exist until the liberation of Black people is assured, because the Black Aesthetic is as much a political movement as it is a literary one. I think of the Black Aesthetic as nothing more than the cultural arm of Black Nationalism.

Q: If we talk about a Black Aesthetic, and subsequently, about changing the definitions by which Black people define themselves, then, inevitably, we have to talk about how one gets to the Black audience. Now, one of the problems that comes up with the novel, as you, yourself, have pointed out, is that few people have time to sit down and read three or four hundred pages. So how do you see this whole business of consciousness-raising coming about? What I have in mind is some of the dramatists who have been saying that Black theater should replace the Black church in the community as the institution around which Black people should congregate. What is your response to that idea, and what do you think about drama and poetry—certainly more immediate forms—as opposed to the novel?*

A: O.K., look. There are Black audiences and there are Black audiences. There's a Black audience who'll respond to sidewalk drama. That Black audience gets sidewalk drama. There's a Black audience who'll read novels—and I'm talking about the kids in colleges where Blacks are teaching—these kids get the novel. There is a Black audience that will respond to poetry in bars and poetry in churches. These Blacks get poetry in bars and in churches. There are Black audiences who will respond to film.

What I'm getting at is that I don't think that the different practitioners of the genre should be at war with each other as to which is going to get the audience. I think all are necessary. Once again, that's the literary mainstream. They keep arguing about who is the most important, the poet or the novelist. All Black artists are important. Everybody can't be a poet; everybody can't be a novelist. But there's an audience for all of these forms. I think that the thing to do is to produce one's work and get to that audience that one can, instead of worrying about whether or not the dramatist is going to get this audience or not.

If the message gets through and is effective, it doesn't matter whether the message is carried by the poet or the dramatist or the novelist. It's the message that's important. We're talking about some twenty million people. Certainly there are people who will deal with the various forms. I would think that if you're talking about reaching the greatest number of Black people in the shortest period of time, you're talking about some form of oral literature. But that doesn't mean that John Williams should stop writing novels.

Q: *Then, your advice to the Black artist would be, be true to yourself, that is, produce what you can produce best?*

A: Sure. And, I don't know, if you produce and if you have some means of getting your work to the people, I think you'll have results. But you can't think about taking over the church because the church has its function. One doesn't want to replace the church, one wants to make the church more viable.

Q: *In line with what Cleage is doing in Detroit?*
A: Certainly.

Q: *But can we talk for a minute about this whole business of the artist? In a recent issue of* Black World, *it was mentioned that there is supposed to be some kind of feud between various enclaves of Black writers. What do you make of that?*

A: It depends on the magnitude of the feud. If it's a thing where one guy is upset because someone wrote a bad critical review of his book, that's one thing. If the feud concerns objectives, then that's another thing. There should be no feud between Black writers concerning objectives. Even those Black writers who argue that what they want to do is to create art that will last, and want to be in the literary mainstream, shouldn't be feuded with; they should simply be ignored. One should not argue with Ralph Ellison; one should ignore him. The situation is too perilous at this point for Black writers to be feuding with each other about objectives. The objectives, as I see them, have to do not with the writers, but with Black people.

Because no Black writer in this country, and I don't care who he is, is free until Black people are free. And that is the objective: to free Black people mentally, spiritually, and physically. Now, if the feud concerns that, then it shouldn't be, because I feel that if you're Black and you live in this country, it seems an *a priori* decision to arrive at. You don't have to be very bright to see that. So I don't know why people would argue about that. Now there may be feuds about how one fulfills these objectives. But that shouldn't be a feud, that should be a discussion—a discussion between people of different points of view. It should never get to the point of feuding. I would think that a great deal of the feuding between Black writers is really a kind of holdover from what the American literary establishment so often does. It causes a great many of these feuds by picking *its* favorite Black writer, and then *its* favorite Black writer begins to assume that he is *the* favorite Black writer. And at that point you get jealousy and you get elitism. You get all kinds of things which have nothing to do with the real objectives. But once again, you don't feud with people like that; you ignore them.

Q: *Yes, but is it, perhaps, inherent to the profession of writing that one must think that he is "better" than other writers? And if that's so, doesn't it make the task of actualizing a Black Aesthetic almost impossible?*

A: No. You see, you must remember that these are *Black* writers you're talking about. And no Black person in this country, whether he's a writer, an ambassador, or a college president, is any better than any other Black person. And if you don't believe me, let said "Better Black Person" stand up on the corner of Forty-Second Street and try to get a cab to take him to Harlem. At that point, it's kind of ridiculous. What those Black writers have done is to adopt American characteristics, just as the Black middle class has adopted American characteristics. But what kind of nonsense is that, that you're better than other Black writers? Your books don't get displayed any more than any other Black writer's; your books don't get advertised any more than any other Black writer's; you don't get any larger advances than any other Black writer. How are you going to be better than any other Black writer? If you're better, then something should happen for you.

Q: *Then the Black writer who defines himself as part of an elite is really fooling himself vis-a-vis the situation in the country?*

A: Certainly. He's sick. He's as sick as the Black middle class. As I said, I have a test. If you tell me that you are Black and you're better than I am, I will not argue with you. I will simply say to you, "Well, Mr. Better Blackman, let us walk down to Forty-Second Street. I will put you on this corner; I will get you a white cab driver. Now the cab driver will tell me that he's not going to take me to Harlem. Now, since you are better than I am, I want to see him take you." He won't take him, either, right? I will perform another test. I will say "Mr. Better Blackman, you go and get an apartment in Forest Hills, since you're better than I am." But they won't have him there, either! Now, I don't know. How is he better? How is one Black guy better than another? And don't tell me that he's better than I am because he's not on welfare. Don't tell me that. Because the reason that he's not being driven to Harlem is not because he's on welfare. If you look at him, you don't know if he's on welfare or not. And he's not denied an apartment in Forest Hills because he is or is not on welfare. It's because he's Black. Elitism is something that Black folks can't afford.

Q: *Yes, I see. Then the Black artist, too, must redefine himself, must, in a sense, throw off the role that Western society has traditionally assigned him. And what of the critic? What is his function?*

A: That's a good question. I don't know whether I can answer it or not. The function of the Black critic is, I suppose, to create arguments, to create conflict. That is, I think the critic, himself, should have an objective in mind as to what a particular form—novel, poem, or play—should do. He should applaud or censure the writer who does or does not approach that objective. I think the objective of the writer and the objective of the critic are the same—that is, the liberation of Black people.

The critic, then, must point out to the writer how far he has gone in approximating that objective, where he has fallen short in doing it, even as to how he may do it. But, basically, with the objective in mind. The function of the Black critic is to create conflict by presenting ideas, and challenging ideas, and to evaluate the work of art in terms of whether or not it approaches the political objective.

Q: *But isn't that very difficult? And very complicated?*
A: Why?

Q: *First of all, you're asking for a tremendous amount of knowledge on the part of the critic.*

A: I certainly am! I'm asking that he know American literature. I'm asking that he know American history. I'm asking that he know politics. I'm asking that he know Western culture inside out. I certainly *am*.

Q: *But will the Black critic address himself to the structure of the work, as well?*

A: Well, look. If a work is effective—once again, let's return to that—if a work is effective, then I don't know why the problem with structure. If the objective is to inculcate a sense of awareness in Black people, if that objective is met, then why does one worry about structure? Structure, after all, is what the critic says it is.

Q: Well, it seems to me—and maybe this is all wrong—that if you're talking about a Black Aesthetic creating new definitions, new values, new images, etc., mustn't you be concerned about what the vehicle is going to be for conveying these things? Mustn't the vehicle be different from the traditional Western vehicle, and if it's not different, do we then say that the writer is not conforming to the Black Aesthetic?

A: No. I think that, ultimately, Carolyn Gerald is right, and one is talking about new forms. But I think we also must remember that new forms are not just created overnight. New forms take years to reach fruition. And so I think that it's true that there will eventually be new forms, but I think that the form is of less importance than the content, or as I keep calling it, the message.

The form is the delivery system, while the message is the thing delivered. Now, that doesn't mean that you have a faulty delivery system. My point is that if the delivery system is faulty, then the message won't be delivered anyway. I think the difference between myself and the American critics is that they want to make something mystical and abstract out of a delivery system. Now, if the content is faulty, it doesn't matter what kind of delivery system you have.

You can have the most perfect structure in the world. Look, *Finnegan's Wake* is perfect, structurally. It's a great, beautiful novel. *Crime and Punishment* is completely chaotic. Dostoyevsky has no sense of organization and structure. Yet which is the better novel—even the white folks admit it! But it's very interesting what they do. When it's white novels that are concerned, then form becomes subsidiary to content. When it's Black novels that are concerned—and I can understand it because they can't deal with the content—content becomes subsidiary to form. I keep seeing it in that sense.

Q: O.K. A broader question, then, vis-a-vis this whole question of criticism. Is there a need for more Black critics? Is there a need for more Black literary criticism by Black critics? I'll tell you why I raise the question. Students of mine have complained, repeatedly, about not being able to find literary criticism on Black novels, on Black poetry. I always refer them to your Black Expression, *and I know that Margolies has something—you know, there are certain things around by whites. But, is there a dearth of this kind of criticism by Blacks?*

A: Oh sure; certainly. And I think for two reasons. One reason is that Black critics, heretofore, with the exception of very few, have been much more willing to criticize *Moby Dick* than *Native Son*. Second, it's much easier, I suppose—and one can get into an argument with the novelists about this—to become a novelist than it is to become a critic.

I'm afraid a critic has to know so damn much. I don't even like to think of myself as a critic because I don't know that much. But a critic, a real Afro-American critic, should be steeped in American literature, American history, the literature of Europe as much as possible, the history of Europe, Black literature, Black history. He should know the literature and history of Africa. All of this should be his domain.

You know, a writer does not write out of a vacuum, and I'm afraid the Afro-American critic has to have some sense of the writer's total involvement with the world outside of the Black community, since all of our writers have been involved with that world. Take Richard Wright, for example. Suppose all you've read, or all you know is Afro-American literature; well, Wright didn't know very much about Afro-American literature. He knew Dostoyevsky, he knew Turgenev, he knew Mencken, he knew Faulkner. So a whole perspective is cut away from you. I suppose John Williams is probably one of the most widely read of the writers. John reads everything. Well, you're going to be pretty hard put to evaluate a novel by John Williams if you don't know very much. Third, I suppose, is that writers are kind of funny people. They're egotistical as hell. They like for people to recognize them at parties. They like for people to say, "Hey! I read so and so of yours." And very few people read critics. You know, the Afro-American critic has, in a sense, just been discovered. But it's a very interesting thing. Even Black folks would go to white critics for their evaluation of Black writers. There've been Black critics. There've been Black critics as far back as Benjamin Brawley in the nineteen twenties. Some of the best criticism about Black books came out during the nineteen twenties.

Saunders Redding has been writing damn good criticism for some fifteen or twenty years. How many Blacks know Saunders Redding? And you know, it's due to the establishment on the one hand, but it's also due to the fact that a hell of a lot of Blacks would much rather read the Sunday *New York Times Book Review* than *Black World*. Yes, there are Black critics—not so many as one would like—but there have always been Black critics. When I started doing *Black Expression* (and it's interesting, I started doing that when I was in college), I did a paper on Baldwin, and the guy said to me, "You can go ahead and do it"—I was doing it for a term paper—he said, "You go ahead and do it. I just don't think you'll be able to find enough criticism on it." What he was saying was that I wasn't going to find enough criticism on it in general, not even Black criticism. And I found a hell of a lot of criticism. If you notice, there are articles in the book all the way back to the twenties. There has been Black criticism. There hasn't been enough. But I'll say again that one of the things very important to understand is that a critic must know a great deal, must know a hell of a lot.

Q: I certainly would think that with Afro-American literature becoming, at present, a part of the curriculum at high schools and colleges, there would be more and more of a demand for Black criticism.

A: I'm not sure that that's true. Once again, another reason, I suppose, why there haven't been very many Black critics is because the media have been controlled by whites who would much rather have white folks telling them what Black folks think than to have Black folks telling them what Blacks think. And I don't think that's going to stop. *The New York Review of Books* is going to continue to allow incompetent white men to write reviews of Black books.

That doesn't bother me. My thing is that one day we Black people will get to the point where we won't read the *New York Review of Books*. We'll read *Black World*, instead. At that point, we'll get Black people reviewing Black books instead of getting the *New York Review of Books* with incompetent white people reviewing Black books. It doesn't bother me that they don't allow Blacks to review Black books. It bothers me that Black people continue to buy the *New York Review of Books* instead of *Black World*. If you must, buy the *New York Review of Books* to find out what the whites are doing, but then buy *Black World*.

Q: *You're talking about Black people supporting their own institutions.*
A: Sure.

Q: *You mentioned, and I was going to bring the point up, that it doesn't matter to you that whites do the reviewing of Black books in* The New York Review. *You just recently resigned, if one can speak so, as a reviewer for the* Times. *What prompted that move—well, of course, one has read the letter—but would you amplify your reasons for doing it?*
A: Look. John Leonard wrote an article in which he said, in so many words, that the whole Black literary revolution had gone too far; that Black writers had been demanding that Black books reviewed in *The New York Times* be reviewed by Blacks because whites didn't know enough to review them, and that *The New York Times* was going to call a halt to this movement; was going to let it be known that the *Times*'s policy was that there is no distinction between a Black reviewer and a white reviewer; that a Black reviewer can review white books—even though none are ever reviewed by Blacks—and a white reviewer is just as equipped to review Black books as is a Black reviewer—which is racist and strikes at the heart of the Black Aesthetic. I don't make any bones about it.

Somebody asks me "What kind of nonsense is this that white folks can't review books by Blacks?" It's not nonsense. To me it's perfectly logical. There are various dimensions to a work of art, to a work of literature. Take a novel. There are various dimensions. There's the personal dimension; there's the dimension which comes out of particular experiences, as Eliot calls it, "of the race," and so on.

Now, the white critic can only bring to a Black novel *some* of those dimensions. He might bring a kind of knowledge of the historical tradition of the novel. He cannot bring to that novel any of the experiences of being Black in America which went into its making. At that point, he is an inept critic. He has to be.

It seemed to me, to get back to the point, that Leonard was saying that the Black Aesthetic has no viability, is not legitimate, and it is not legitimate, strangely enough, not because it's intellectually unsound, but simply because the people who propose it are Nationalists. It seemed to me, at that point, that he was attacking not only the Black Aesthetic Movement, but Black Nationalism as a whole. I think what infuriated me *most* was the point that Black critics were incapable of reviewing Black literature anyway, because they take the "fried chicken-franchise approach." Wherein what you get from white critics, and in particular—and I quote him—from "Morris Dickstein, who is white and Jewish," are very valuable explications. Now to me that was an insult.

And I did not feel that I could write for a magazine which could hold, as editorial policy, the argument that Black critics were not capable of evaluating Black literature. After all, my position is that Black critics are the *only* ones capable of evaluating Black literature. It was contrary to my principles.

Q: Yes. Another interesting thing about that Leonard statement was that the critics he tried to discredit—surreptitiously, if you will—were some of the best writers that we have in the Black community. You know, people like yourself, and Ishmael Reed, and Toni Morrison. . . .

A: Sure. I happen to know something about the history behind that article. I know what's been going on vis-a-vis *Black World* and the *Times*. The article was an out-and-out attack upon statements—accurate statements—that had been made by Hoyt Fuller. An out-and-out attack. At that point, it seemed to me that the attack was not only against Hoyt Fuller, but it was against every Black critic who had ever written for the *Times*.

Q: Are you saying that you took it as a personal affront?

A: No! What I'm saying is that it was an attack against Hoyt Fuller in particular and Black critics in general, and at that point, it seemed to me that it was contradictory to my own position. After all, I support the Black Aesthetic. An attack upon the Black Aesthetic, an attack upon Hoyt Fuller, is an attack, basically, upon a critical movement which opts for the liberation of Black people. My analogy, I suppose, would be my going to another country and joining an organization and finding out that that organization is really that country's version of the Ku Klux Klan—and remaining in the organization. I would equate the *Times*, in my better moments, with the Ku Klux Klan.

Q: Since we're talking about the Times, *what did you think of the review of Chester Himes's autobiography—which appeared in the same issue as your letter, by the way?*

A: I think the attack was malicious. I think it was a personal, malicious attack which only points out that one can do what he wants to do with a book review. I think that it really emphasizes what many of us have talked about when we suggest, in a sense, that criticism can really be the tool that one wants it to be. If you want to give a book a bad review, you can. If you want to give it a good review, you can. I think that the review, as Julius Lester pointed out later, was a personal, malicious kind of a review. The autobiography disappointed me in some instances, but only because there is so much more that I would have wanted to learn from the book.

And that may be my problem instead of Himes's. But I certainly would have wanted to know much more about Himes's association with Wright, Ellison, and people like Bill Gardner Smith than I get from the book. I would like to know much more about the novels: what he was going through when working on them; what kinds of problems he had with the novels; how he may have changed a scene here or a scene there. I'd simply like to know more about the basic process of his creating as many novels as he did. I don't get a sense of that, and I don't get a sense of Himes, the artist, in the autobiography. I liked it simply because it tells you a great deal about Himes, the man.

Q: *He's supposed to be writing a sequel to it.*

A: Yes. I would hope that the sequel would do some of that. I'd certainly like to know more about Himes, the artist, the artist in the act of creation.

Q: *Yes. Well, James Baldwin, too, has just published a new book, a group of autobiographical essays. . . .*

A: I liked *No Name in the Street.* One of the reasons is that I think that of all the writers, the one who shows the greatest propensity for growth is James Baldwin. You read Baldwin's *Nobody Knows My Name,* and you read *No Name in the Street,* and you see the tremendous distance that Baldwin has traveled. The Baldwin who began, in a sense, by attacking Richard Wright, by arguing, in a sense, that he did not want to be a Negro writer, he wanted to be a writer, by talking about the possibilities of Black men and white men one day creating the great society, is the Baldwin who, in *No Name in the Street,* has come to realize at least some of the things that young writers are saying in the seventies. And that is that if one is Black and if one puts his hope and faith in the resurrection or changing of the American society, then that is an act of futility. That if salvation is going to come, it's going to be brought about by Black people, themselves. And I think, at that point, it's showing the tremendous growth of Baldwin. Tremendous kinds of revelations come out of the book. He has made almost a ninety-degree turn, after meeting with Malcolm, and after being involved with the Panthers, and after attempting to get his friend out of jail. You see the workings of a tremendous mind through tremendous problems, to arrive pretty close to the position that a hell of a lot of the young people are at today. I think he's not all the way there, you know, but closer, I think, than any other Black writer who started where he did. His whole thing was that Wright, in presenting Bigger Thomas, had pulled a hoax on the American society. And then, of course, embracing the Panthers, who are a kind of fulfillment of everything that Wright talked about in *Native Son.* That shows the tremendous growth of the man. So, I liked the book. I think it's one of his most important.

Q: *He's certainly a beautiful writer. One reads him, and if one has any aspirations toward writing, he has second thoughts. You know, you think to yourself, "My God, what could I possibly say?"*

A: Sure. The white critics will attack him, if they have not already, by arguing that the book is disorganized; it's not structured. Of course, if you read Baldwin, you're much more interested in what he has to say than in whether or not period follows semicolon, follows colon. Once again, it's what he has to say that is important.

Q: *In other words—if we can go back to this business of structure for just a moment—you're not saying that one should ignore structure, but simply that structure should not be more important than content. That you don't damn a book simply on the basis of structure?*

A: Right! The white critics don't! I think that's my point. When I read some white critic who has damned *Crime and Punishment,* or damned *The Trial,* then I'll say "Hurray!"

Q: *Yes, Kafka is a very good modern example. You know, he's taught in all Contemporary European Literature courses as one of the best of the West's modern writers. And yet, structurally, he's impossible. Structure isn't even discussed in relationship to Kafka, which is very interesting.*

A: Sure, sure.

Q: *You know, we've been talking about Black writers who, it seems to me, represent a certain stage in Black intellectual thought. Both Baldwin and Himes are expatriates. What I've been noticing with growing interest is that during the sixties and seventies you don't get Black writers leaving the country the way they did—well, let's say from Wright's time on.*

A: Yes. That reminds me of one young writer—and, gee, I don't remember his name—who recently left the country and came back. He said "I got to Europe to discover that everything was happening in America." And everything that was happening in America was happening because Black folks are here. Now I think the difference is, as I said before, Black writers in the past didn't want to be any different from white writers. Well, if you are a white writer in America, or his counterfeit, then you are attempting to see the American society through his eyes. So, what you see is a decadent society. There's no energy; there's no life. If you are a Black writer, then things are going on in the Black world.

This is where your energy is. This is where your vitality is. This is what the guy was pointing out in the article in *The Nation,* by the way. He was saying that it is with Black writers that things are happening. And that's because things are happening with Black people. There's no reason for the writer to go to Europe. If he's going to deal with what's happening, then he'll stay.

Q: In other words, the contemporary Black writer is not looking to white society for inspiration. He looks to Black people, and there he encounters a wealth of inspiration.

A: Certainly.

Q: And that's positive. Because surely our writers, our artists, are extremely important people in terms of guiding us. If they don't forsake us, then there's hope.

A: Not only that. We are important to our writers. Because, in a sense, we breathe into our writers. If our writers want to be white writers—and I don't mean white in color—but if they want their art to "live," if they want to create the great artistic masterpiece, then I'm afraid they're in trouble. After all, there's nothing in the American society that would inspire one to create the great masterpiece.

Q: Certainly. You only have to think about some contemporary writers. To go back to the novel, again. Think about Jerzy Kosinski, who won the National Book Award a few years ago. His books are so incredibly sterile; his vision of the world is such an arid, pessimistic one that you read him and wonder "Well, what else is there to say?"

A: Sure. Look at the writers that people might agree on as great writers. Take a Dostoyevsky; take a Tolstoy, for example. These were men writing about viable societies. The Russia of Dostoyevsky was a viable society. The American society is over-fat, over-affluent, over everything. The greatest thrill these days, for white folks, outside of the T.V. set, is violence and sex. And so their writers simply depict this. But, my God! What is coming out of the Black community? Viability.

And then, of course, not only the viability and energy that exist now, but all of that untapped history and culture that were simply ignored before. You know, a John Williams, in *Captain Blackman,* goes back to deal with a whole period of Afro-American history. You can't find that in the American society because there's nothing as exciting in American history as a Nat Turner revolt, or a Denmark Vesey revolt, simply because, in the latter cases, you have people who are really competing against overwhelming odds. When America depicts her heroes, she picks George Washington, who commands troops instead of being anywhere in the line of battle; Thomas Jefferson, who sits on his estate and hurls out indictums. But, there's Frederick Douglass, on the firing line. There's Martin Delany on rostrum after rostrum. There's a Harriet Tubman, going down and bringing people out from slavery. The tremendous energy, vitality, and greatness in that history! In Black history alone, there are ten or fifteen epics, just waiting for the Black writer to write them.

Q: So that one of the many untapped sources that the young Black writer could turn to would be history. You do that in Oak and Ivy, *the biography of Paul Laurence Dunbar. That is, you draw tremendously upon the history of the time. And certainly we haven't gotten much of that.*

A: Sure. But look, we're only talking about a hundred or so years ago. You don't even have to go back that far. Where's the novel that's going to treat a Malcolm X, H. Rap Brown, Stokely Carmichael—tremendous material for the novelist? You don't find that in white America. What do you find? A few beatniks, a couple of hippies, a few SDS'rs. You know, affluent suburban white kids, playing at revolution, who can go home whenever the revolution gets tough.

Q: Yes . . . Let me ask you about an issue that comes up whenever two or more Black people get together. There's tremendous controversy—aggravated, I tend to think, by the Women's Lib Movement—between Black men and Black women. Many of us as children were told of the "evils" of Black men, and I would imagine that the same was true for Black men as boys. And so we begin as enemies, and I mean in a sense far more serious than that suggested by the "battle of the sexes." I suppose that another aspect of the dilemma would be the kind of outcry that's being heard from many Black women at the fact that all of the most "desirable" Black men are being co-opted by white women. All of these things, it seems to me, feed into this controversy.

A: Once again, I think it's a controversy which has nothing to do with what should be our real objective, and that is the liberation of Black people. Black men are not going to be liberated in this society until Black women are liberated. Black women are not going to be liberated until Black men are. I think that what has happened in the past is that Black men and Black women have drawn upon white mythology for certain images of each other and have proceeded to deal with one another as though each were those particular images.

You see, one cannot very easily censure one side without censuring the other side. Black males accepted the American mythology that the closer the woman approached Anglo Saxon norms, in terms of hair, skin color and form, the more desirable she was. Black women, in turn, accepted the mythology that the closer the Black man approached the Anglo Saxon norm—Cary Grant and John Wayne—the more acceptable he was. What you got then, of course, were people dealing with each other in terms of symbols and images instead of dealing with one another as human beings. The repercussions were tremendous.

For example, Black women, who now are enraged because white women have found Black men appealing and attractive, in a sense, are being hypocritical, because about fifteen years ago, quite the opposite existed. That is, Black women were more prone to be in positions where they were propositioned—and many accepted—by white men. I know, you don't like that.

Q: No, I don't think it's entirely true.

A: Anyway, what has happened now is that Black men, who have not represented the Anglo Saxon image for Black women, have become, in the eyes of white women, attractive; at which point, they have become attractive for Black women. Which is simply saying that Black women have found out that Black men are attractive because white women have told them so. And the same goes for Black men.

I think the difference is that Black men have not yet found out—a great many of them—that Black women who do not approach the Anglo Saxon norm are beautiful. I think that if the problem is going to be resolved that there has to be a realization of some truths. One of those truths happens to be that it is not the Black woman's fault; it is not the Black man's fault. The entire structure of this country is dedicated to the proposition that Black men will never be men. One can say "Well, that's not my fault. I didn't bring it about." That is the reason for being of this system—to emasculate Black men. What that means, it seems to me, is that there must be a tremendous kind of understanding by the Black man of what is going on vis-a-vis him and this system. And, there must be the same kind of understanding on the part of the Black woman of what is going on between him and the system. If that understanding is there, then Black men and Black women will realize that they are not each other's enemy, but that the system is the enemy of both of them.

Q: Yes. I just want to take issue with a couple of your points, though. Although, all in all, I think that you are right. But in answering the question, I think that you overlook a couple of very crucial things. One of them is that certainly Black women have been equally victimized by this system. Very often Black men argue that Black women have always had it easier in this society than they have because, after all, she has always been able to get a job. I find that a superficial argument, because if you examine the dynamics of giving the Black woman a job while the Black man is denied one, all that does to the woman as an individual, to the woman as a person, is to trap her between the devil and the deep blue sea, so to speak. What it means is that she is put in opposition to her man. After all, she has the job; she is doing what he should do.

On the other hand vis-a-vis the white woman, she is still in an inferior position because she has to do what the white woman does not have to do. It seems to me that if one looks at that situation carefully, the only thing that has been done is that the antagonism between the Black man and the Black woman has been accelerated so that she does not, in fact, have it easier, at all.

In addition, the Black woman's sense of her identity is being stripped, too. Because if the archetype of the male is the person who goes out, makes the money, protects and takes care of the home, and thereby is able to define himself as a man, then the Black man has certainly been deprived of his manhood. On the other hand, if the archetype of the woman is the one who stays home, is understanding, loving, etc., toward her husband, takes care of the children, etc., then the Black woman has equally been denied her identity.

A: O.K. I agree with you. Only I don't make the argument that Black women have had it easier because they've had jobs. I say that they've had it easier because the entire paraphernalia of this country—its educational institutions, its courts, its political structures—have not been aimed at the Black woman. It has been aimed at destroying Black men as men. Let me give you this example. Take Vietnam. The Americans are not attempting to destroy the South Vietnamese; their objective is to destroy North Vietnam. South Vietnam and North Vietnam are parts of Vietnam, but the concentrated fire power of America is against North not South Vietnam. Now certainly the South Vietnamese are being hurt. But I think it is much easier for a South Vietnamese to exist in Vietnam than for a North Vietnamese.

Q: Yes, but I think that the part of the analogy that you are overlooking is that South Vietnam, at this point in time, is autonomous . . .
A: Well, not really, but O.K.

Q: Whereas in the situation of Black men and Black women, theoretically, Black women are dependent upon Black men, so that through a kind of chain reaction, if you will, what happens to Black men, happens to Black women.
A: I agree. The point is that I agree with you. I'm not so sure that, historically, Black women have agreed with you. I'm not so sure that Black men have agreed. I think you're right. I think that if Black men and women can understand that the system, in destroying Black men, also destroys Black women, then we won't have any reason for the controversy. And you ask me when it will be resolved. It will be resolved at that point. It, will be resolved at the point where Black women and Black men realize that the enemy is not each other, it's this country. But, unless you've got that realization, the controversy is never going to be resolved.

And until you can somehow change people's perceptions, change this kind of adhering to white images of what Black folks ought to be—I still think that's the crux of the problem. My God! Take any Black college, and the Black males are ridiculous. I'm certainly not going to excuse the kinds of things that Black men have done to Black women over the years. It's been terrible. What happens so often when people are oppressed is that they begin to see *each other* as the real enemy instead of the oppressor. And you know, the situation in this country is very clear. Black people have one oppressor, and that's this country. There are Black people who, in collusion with this country, oppress other Black people. And they are both male and female. But the real enemy is not Black people, it's this country.

Q: I'm glad that you said that. Particularly the point that you made about under-standing one another within the context of the group experience. I certainly agree with you. It seems almost impossible to have meaningful and lasting relationships if you don't understand the dynamics of being Black in this country, if you don't, quite simply, understand the experiences that have made the person. Which brings up another point. It seems to me that the position of Black people in this country

*is so extremely complex that what needs to happen before we move on anything
that happens in the country at large—and I'm thinking now, in particular, of the
Women's Lib Movement, to which many Black women have begun to adhere—is
that that movement or idea be examined in terms of its feasibility for Black people.
Do we need to have a structure that will do that?*

A: I think we do. I think we certainly need an overall structure that, in a sense,
will help us, as Black people, do the things we ought to do anyway. And that is to
put always, before anything, the interest of Black people. None of that nonsense,
"I am an American; my country comes first." None of that nonsense about "I'm
much more concerned with the man than I am with his color," when talking about
politics. Our question is very simple: is it or is it not good for Black people? And
we need some structure to help us to arrive at these very fundamental questions.
As you said, to analyze every movement. If this movement is good for Black
people, how is it good for them? And act on it at that point. Not, "Is it good for
me?" Is it good for Black people. That has to be the credo. That's what the Black
Aesthetic is all about.

*Q: Which sort of suggests the need for—and I don't want to sound elitist—really
serious attention to learning and a genuine appreciation for knowledge.*

A: Sure. And an appreciation for a rational approach to problems. Look, our
situation in this country is so serious that we just can't afford to deal with problems anymore from that shoot-from-the-hip kind of approach. Problems have
to be analyzed and solutions have to be found.

The primary thesis from which to approach every problem is, "Is it good for
Black people?" We need people for whom this will be a major preoccupation. I
think the Institute of the Black World has begun a fundamental, pragmatic approach to the problems that confront us. We certainly need an institution of that
sort. And for all the endeavors that we become engaged in, the question should
be, "Is it good for Black people?"

*Q: Which brings up another issue—the role of the intellectual. You know what
the traditional role of the intellectual has been in Western society. What do you
see, given the magnitude of the task facing Black people, to be the role of the Black
intellectual?*

A: Well, you know, here again it depends, basically, I think, on temperament.
My question would be, "What have you done for Black people, lately?" That's
the question that should be addressed to everybody. Now, I don't think the intellectual can be satisfied with just sitting at his desk and putting his name to
something. I think he has to do much more than that. What that much more is,
I don't know.

What that much more is will depend upon what he is capable of doing and
will depend upon what he does best. I don't suggest that the intellectual go and
start a drug rehabilitation program because I don't know whether he can do that

or not. He can certainly talk to addicts. He can do that. He can certainly become involved in the kinds of things that may be along his line. For example, he can become involved in Black magazines; he can become involved in starting creative writing groups. I think he should become involved. But I don't argue the point which I think is Cleaver's point, that the Black intellectual has to be out in the street behind the barricade because ain't nobody behind a barricade. Now, if you get to the point where there are barricades, there's no question about where he ought to be. But there are no barricades. Nobody's "behind the barricade" in that sense.

I don't think that he can be content to just sit at his desk and send out articles, etc. I would suppose the best answer to that would be that he should do what Black folks call upon him to do, and Black folks will call upon him. If he's doing any work, Black folks will call upon him. I don't think he should sit down and wait, but I think part of it is doing the things that Black folks call upon him to do.

Q: In line with the whole business of doing things that Black folks call upon one to do, I know that recently you were invited to speak at a prison in Ohio. What were your reactions to that experience?

A: Look, you know, if I had a lot of money (and people assume that I have money; I don't have any), if I had a lot of money, I would sponsor forums for Black writers and Black artists to go to the prisons. Because the experience at Chilicothe was a tremendous one. Here you have a group of Black people in prison—studying Black history, Black culture, Black literature, tremendously aware politically, socially, and historically—who only want Black folks to come. And I think it should be an obligation for Black artists to go to the prisons, to read their poetry, to give lectures, to become involved with those particular things that are going on in the prisons in their locale. And I think that's tremendously important.

Q: Do you see a lot of potential in that population?

A: Oh, there's a tremendous amount of potential. I sat there, listening to these damn articulate guys. It's very interesting. Any of them, you know, could have been my best buddies. The only difference between them and my buddies is that they were in the prison. Tremendously interesting, exciting kinds of guys. Tremendous potential there. It's a kind of situation in which, once again, Black folks can do something for Black folks.

Q: Yes. When you look at those men, you realize just how perilous the position of Black people in this country really is. Because, as you pointed out, any one of them could be you. When you are a Black man, there is almost no separating line.

A: Sure. The difference between being in prison and out of prison, if you're Black in this country, is usually a matter of luck.

Q: I think James Baldwin brings that out very well in No Name in the Street. *But just one last question. There seems to be an interesting kind of activity going on in the Black community. Things like the new position taken by* The Amsterdam News, *here in New York. The* Gary Convention. *The fact that Black professionals have begun to form kinds of interest groups. How do you interpret these movements?*

A: I see it as a kind of revelation which comes about over a long period of time, compelled by the kinds of things that happened during the fifties and the sixties, things which convinced us—and it's interesting that we needed any convincing—that one could not depend upon America. You see, the problem with the integrationist theory is that it has always depended upon America, upon America changing. Well, what happens if America does not change? Things continue as they are.

And I think that what happened after the 1954 Supreme Court decision, after the freedom rides, after the sit-ins, after Martin Luther King, was the awareness that, "Look, you'd better get out and do it yourself, because this society is not going to change." I think that what that means is that you find this tremendous kind of energy which would not be possible if one sat back and waited for this society to decide to change.

If you're an integrationist, then you don't have to do very much because one day the American society will "change"; white folks will realize that we're all brothers under the skin, and the Great Society will be there the next day. At that point you don't have to do very much. All you have to do is keep clean, make sure you have good manners, save your money, and one day you'll be welcome as one of the overall American middle class. But, if the society is not going to change—and, after all, it's been manifested in the attacks against the Supreme Court decision, the "white backlash," the many incidents which have happened in the North (Forest Hill is only one example), the attacks by liberals upon the people in Ocean Hill—Brownsville who attempted to educate our children—all of these things have convinced knowledgeable blacks, blacks with any degree of insight, blacks with any degree of sanity, that this society is not going to change. Despite all of this, there are still blacks adhering to the dead, decadent doctrine of integration; men like Roy Wilkins and Kenneth Clarke who suggest that the society will change. But I think that most black people don't have time, anymore, to think in terms of the society changing. We're about doing things ourselves which is the way it ought to have been all along.

CHAPTER 55

I Endured

(1967)

In 1966 at the commencement exercises of the University of California, attired in black cap and gown, tassel pushed to the right, I arose at the deep-throated command, voiced by a tired, bored chancellor—"Masters of Arts, arise!" Slowly, almost unbelievingly, I had arisen with the other recipients of the Master's degree to the applause of guests, parents, students, and faculty members.

The distance between this step and the first, taken six years before, seemed, then, more than a thousand miles. Set down with others of Black skin, in the jungle of the ghetto, I had been expected, to paraphrase James Baldwin, to perish. I had not. I had traveled the thousand miles; and perhaps I should have felt elated.

Perhaps! But if so, the elation did not come. Maybe the company of my fellow graduates had something to do with this. I discovered, then, that I did not like their company; perhaps this had always been so, but now I felt my discomfort more than ever. Most of the graduates were white; and those who were Black seemed Black in skin color only: they seemed, as Richard Wright once remarked to an African, "to be more Anglo-Saxon than the Anglo-Saxons." To these graduates, the ceremony had meaning, it proved something to them about themselves. They had joined the elite of the nation, and become numbered among the chosen few of the world who had completed five or more years of college, who had survived the ascent to the top of the ivory tower.

Out there stood a world, waiting for them. "I have a world about me," wrote Wordsworth in the "Prelude"; "It is my own, I made it." My fellow students did not have to make their world, they had only to fit in, to become a part of one already in existence. They were blessed, for the making of worlds can be a frustrating experience; thus most men forgo the frustration and settle for the world as it is.

Yet, for Blacks in general, and for me in particular, this entailed settling for a world made by others. It meant dwelling forever in the house of the magic mirrors, having distortions flashed upon your mind so often that soon the only reality you knew was that contained in the mirrors. Tennyson has his lady of Shalott lament, shortly before viewing Camelot from her isolated castle for the first time in twelve years: "I am half sick of shadows." But the lady had only lived in her castle for twelve years; suppose she had lived there for a lifetime, knowing nothing but shadows, would she have been able even to recognize Camelot, let alone look down upon it?

"Congratulations," the girl beside me remarked, as once again we took our seats. I smiled and turned away. The program called for more speeches, more music, and more applause; the band was to play a selection from Brahms, the president of the graduating class was to speak on "The Future of the College Graduate." I sat and smiled for a long time until, quite suddenly, the smile turned into a short cynical laugh.

"I endured!" I remarked through my laughter. The girl who had spoken before looked at me strangely; the handsome dark Negro on the other side of me shifted uneasily in his seat. I laughed again, silently, as again the thought came to my mind—"I endured." But then, just as quickly, another thought came to push the first away and to silence the laughter altogether. *But many perished in the struggle, many more worthy than you!* To how many of us does this thought come, and how many are haunted by it? What does Ivan Karamazov care if ninety-nine babies live, so long as one must die?

There are many who died, but two come readily to mind. Amos, short and Black, orphaned at the age of three, possessed an incredible propensity for remembering the most important facts and details. Almost verbatim, he could recall the important points in the Fourteenth, Fifteenth, and Sixteenth Amendments, and if called upon, the dates on which each amendment was ratified. Bernice, Black and skinny, with short hair and soft eyes, was a child prodigy who read Dickens at five years of age.

In the summer of 1965, after receiving my bachelor's degree, I was back in Newport News, Virginia, visiting my family. On one of those frequent trips to the ice cream store with my young sister, I met Amos. Amos looked older than his thirty years. His cheeks were sunken, and there were deep lines carved in his face. His skin, once so beautiful in its Blackness, was now ugly and coarse, covered with dust and grime. "Doc Gayle," he said, extending a dirty hand to me. I grasped the hand, returning his hearty greeting. We talked for a while. "I should've left when you did," he repeated over and over, "I sure wished I had left when you did."

Embarrassed, I attempted to convince him that my leaving had not made that much difference. I was lying and he knew it. No, there were no guarantees if one left to go North. One could perish as quickly in the streets and ghettos of New York as in the ghettos of Newport News. But he knew that survival for Negroes in this country is mostly a matter of luck; and one is more likely to be lucky up North than down South—at least the chances of lightning striking are better.

Finally we broke away from each other, he, walking in the opposite direction, head down, shoulders bent. Watching him amble out of sight, I remembered that Booker T. Washington, in his autobiography, *Up From Slavery,* had written: "Our greatest danger is that in the great leap from slavery to freedom we may overlook the fact that the masses of us are to live by the production of our hands, and fail to keep in mind that we shall prosper in proportion as we learn to dignify and glorify common labor and put brains and skill into the common occupations of life. . . ."

These "common occupations," agriculture, mechanics, and the domestic services, were to be performed by those who "without strikes and labor wars had tilled [the] fields, cleared [the] forests, built [the] railroads and cities, and brought forth treasures from the bowels of the earth. . . ." In Washington's view, working with one's hands was the essential characteristic of a Black laborer, and dignity was accorded those who succeed in bringing forth better crops or making better bricks than their neighbors.

Amos could see little dignity in making bricks or tilling fields, and the possibility was that he never would. Dostoyevsky's Grand Inquisitor offered bread to the masses in opposition to the freedom offered by Jesus Christ. But when the Grand Inquisitor was dishing out his bread, Amos was not there. If he could have chosen, he would have chosen the freedom of Christ instead of the bread of the Inquisitor. Yet he could not choose; there were for him only two alternatives: to fly into some nameless future, or stay and go to the shipyard. Against his will, he was to be part of the Black waves which constitute that Black ocean of men which Booker T. Washington had implored white industrialists to dip their buckets into.

Now, mentally and spiritually, he was dead. What had flashed so brilliantly in him just twelve years ago, was gone, gone beyond recall. He had wanted to be a lawyer, and he could have been one; now he was a laborer, and he didn't want to be. Somewhere in the plight of the Black boy who wanted to be a lawyer and the Black man who was a laborer against his will is the awful truth of this country. But, too, it is a testimony to the power of the philosophy of Booker T. Washington which has held sway for so long over the minds of so many Negroes in every walk of life.

Thank God I did not see Bernice, this one time sweetheart of my memories, who had wanted to be an English teacher, who had taught me things about Huck Finn, Pip, and Bigger Thomas that I never learned in high school. But I heard of her fate from the gossip-vine. She had married one year after completing high school, and the next year the babies had begun to come. There had been little Freddie, and a year later, Janet, and two years later the twins, Loretta and Michael. The following year, no babies came, but the husband left, and the next year Bernice was in jail, picked up for shoplifting. *How many perished in the struggle, many more worthy than you?* "Why," shouted Ivan Karamazov, "did the baby have to die?"

One consults the philosophers! There is, to interpret Hegel on a simplistic level, a divine spirit moving through the universe, and those who are in touch with this divine spirit are masters of men. The acorn, to subject Aristotle to the same simplistic interpretation, is destined from birth to be an oak tree. But Man, constantly changing, evolving, creating his essence as he goes through life, comes out of Sartre's "Existentialism." "Man must surpass himself," says Nietzsche's Zarathustra. Where is the right and where is the wrong? Was Amos destined like the acorn? Was Bernice, because she was not in touch with the divine spirit, doomed to die the death of disillusionment and despair? How could either of them have created their essence in a world which would forever deny their existence?

There is a section, "The Parable of the Laws," in Kafka's novel, *The Trial*, in which the protagonist is told the story of a man who came to the court of the laws, waiting to gain entrance. The man is told that he cannot enter at the moment. Thus he waits, finally dying at the feet of the guard in front of the door, which the guard proceeds to shut forever. The man could have entered the door at the right moment, but when was the right moment? The man could not know himself, and there was no one to tell him. Who should have told him? Who was responsible for his knowing? And who is responsible for Amos and Bernice, who had to settle, against their will, for one world because the doors of another had been closed to them? Who should have prepared them for that moment when the doors of American society would crack ever so slightly? Where does the responsibility for their death lie?

One's first response is that the responsibility rests with the individual. Lastly, it is the individual who must be the arbitrator of his own destiny. It is he who must cut through the jungle of chaos and confusion in which modern man finds himself. For the Negro, this is more true. Living in a Kafkaesque world, where all experiences are magnified out of proportion, where every daily occurrence borders on the grotesque, where communication on any real and meaningful level, even with those closest to him, is impossible, the Negro must seek in the Blackness of his own being for his own truth.

"If ever I can say to the fleeting moment," laments Goethe's Faust, "verweile doch, du bist so schön"—remain, so fair thou art—then will the bargain with Mephistopheles be fulfilled. It is the Afro-American, this modern day Faust, who is forever seeking some fleeting moment—when all that this white world represents will no longer menace him, no longer threaten him. But the Negro must break the Faustian pact himself. There is no God standing ready at the call to rescue him. His God died on the day the first Black man was enslaved, the very hour the chains were put about the arms and ankles of the first Black slave, and the agonizing wail, torn from the slave's throat each time the whip cut into his Black flesh, was but the dying wail of his God.

But here, we are far from the kind of responsibility that Booker T. Washington talked about. Washington continues in his "Autobiography": "In this address

I said that the whole future of the Negro rested largely upon the question as to whether or not he should make himself, through his skill, intelligence, and character, of such undeniable value to the community in which he lived that the community could not dispense with his presence. I said that any individual who learned to do something better than anybody else—learned to do a common thing in an uncommon manner—had solved his problem, regardless of the color of his skin."

Here we have the origin of the bootstrap philosophy. The individual must make himself. This is his responsibility. He must pull himself up by his own bootstraps. Washington presupposes a hostile environment on the one hand, but on the other, one tolerant enough to recognize merit. There is a point, supposes Washington, at which all men meet; and this point is reached when one man recognizes that his brother, too, is lost in the wilderness, yet that he is willing to cut his way out, depending only upon his own strength and power. Rugged individualism and the survival of the fittest: and it is common to all men to recognize the fittest.

From Sophocles to Strindberg, men have inwardly cheered the victor. What does it matter to the Roskolnikovs of the world if Napoleon murdered millions of people on his way to fame? What history calls the victor to account? Each Negro is personally responsible, therefore, for making "himself of value to the community." Pull yourself up by your own bootstraps! This statement has been a blessing to those of us who hope to compensate for our own inadequacies. One wants to deny that his success in life, whatever that may be, was due to the fortuitous winds of fate which happened at that lucky moment to be blowing his way.

We want to believe that the "A" we received in English was a reward for brilliance; and we refuse to accept the fact that being the only Negro in a classroom in a predominantly white college, we began with "B" before the class commenced. The fact that the firm for which we work in the sixties turned down Blacks in the fifties is only—we like to believe—because no Negro of our caliber appeared before.

We have endured. We have pulled ourselves up, and the question that runs uppermost through our minds is "Why have other Negroes not done the same?" "Look," said a young Negro chemistry major, "those same slums down there. I lived in them, too!" He didn't say it, but the remark was there, in his chest, waiting to burst out: "And I came out of them, why can't they?"

We ask, therefore, why couldn't Amos and Bernice pull themselves out of the slum which was their own minds? The Bootstrap Philosophy presupposes at the outset that one has boots. And in a metaphorical sense, these boots are character, intelligence, and skill. But these are not inherited; they are acquired, and once acquired they must be developed. Thus, our question now: Who is responsible for the development of these characteristics, granting that they have been acquired?

One argues that it is the family, perhaps because the Black family has been made the scapegoat for the ills of Negroes. Every mother and father is responsible for his children, and upon them initially rests the responsibility for the development and growth of the child. (One's mind, however, runs off into all kinds of analogies. One thinks of the American Constitution, and one supposes that Mother America is responsible for her children, responsible, at least to the degree of starting them out upon the race on an equal footing. But the Constitution has ceased to be an important document in one's life, and so one hurries from the analogy.)

The truth is that the Black family, in many ways, is ill equipped to assume the responsibility for the development and growth of the child. The father is so burdened by the daily task of survival that, even were he equipped, his energy is all but dissipated in the struggle for life itself. The mother fares little better. Her life is one crisis after another, the first beginning when she gives birth to her first Black child. Yet too, the Negro family is more than likely to be under the influence of the Booker T. Washington philosophy. "There's nothing wrong," Bernice's mother once told us, "with doing a good day's work. I clean Miss A's house, but the Lord don't frown on it 'cause it's honest work.

Honest work it was, and neither of us would argue the contrary. In justifying her own life, however, the old woman was attempting to justify her daughter's life also. There is nothing wrong with being a cleaning woman or a shipyard worker; not every man wants to be a lawyer, a doctor, a teacher, or even a writer. But conversely, not every man wants to be a laborer, and it is here that the Washington philosophy is most pernicious. The assumption is that Blacks are suited only for the most menial of tasks, delegated forever to be the servants and coolies of those who are to build the romantic empire. But more important, such a philosophy removes freedom of choice and substitutes a rigid form of determinism.

"There are more valuable people and less valuable people," remarks the Jewess in Bertolt Brecht's play, *The Private Life of the Master Race:* and we Blacks—dare I say it?—are guilty of using the same categorical division among ourselves that the society at large has used against us. Amos and Bernice were less valuable people because they were poor and Black. In the Negro school, this was enough to seal their fate. Had they been Black and middle class, or light-skinned and poor, this kind of determinism would not have been operative. There would have opened to them an entirely different universe. Their teachers would have felt a sense of responsibility and taken upon themselves the burden of doing what the family could not do. The boots would have been polished and the straps tightened; somehow a scholarship to college would have been found for them.

"I hope," Amos had confided, "I can get a scholarship." Graduation time came and passed, and although Amos graduated number one and Bernice number two out of a class of sixty-one, no scholarship was forthcoming for either of them. Sometime later, during the summer, one heard rumors that Barbara, whose mother was a teacher, had gotten a scholarship or that Arthur, whose mother was president of the P.T.A., had gotten a scholarship. One never found out whether the rumors were more than just that; but one knows that neither Bernice nor Amos received a scholarship of any sort.

Amos went to work in the shipyard to save money to enter Hampton Institute; but the wages paid Negro workers at that time were very little, and by summer's end, what he had been able to save was not enough to even pay for his books for one semester. Yet doggedly, he plowed on, intent on enrolling the next semester; again, the money was not adequate. Semesters came, went, came again, and Amos clung to his dream; but after each semester had passed, the dream became a little less substantial, a little more distant, until soon it had drifted deep into the reservoir of that subconscious where all our unfulfilled dreams eventually end.

Even had they have gone to school, Amos and Bernice may have died mental and spiritual deaths. This we will never know. But they did not go, and somehow the responsibility is not altogether theirs. In a sense, they died because people who should have cared did not, because they were doubly cursed: both Black and poor. They died because the people who could have done most to help them were locked like prisoners within the dungeons of their own egotistical selves.

All of our teachers had problems. They had believed Booker T. Washington and had, according to their estimates, pulled themselves up by their own boot-straps. They had made themselves valuable to their communities, learned to do something better than anybody else—"learned to do a common thing in an uncommon manner"—and yet they had not solved the problem of color. Perhaps they realized now, the intent of Vardaman's blast against Booker T. Washington: ". . . I am as opposed to Booker T. Washington with all his Anglo-Saxon reinforce-ments as I am to the . . . typical little 'coon' Andy Dotson, who blacks my shoes every morning."

Here were the Negro teachers, symbolically being linked to the descendants of Andy Dotson, when all their lives they had been trying to get away from Andy Dotson. Where was the justice in a world which could not recognize a man capable of putting distance between himself and his less fortunate fellow man? What could the teachers do to put more mileage between themselves and Andy Dotson? As quickly as possible they had moved away from the Andy Dotsons of the ghettos; they had forbidden their children to play with the Andy Dotsons of the world; objected when their daughters dated one; protested when one sought to identify with them; joined the white citizens in outrage when one of those Andy Dotsons rioted and destroyed the property of their country; cheered when the criminal Andy Dotson was finally caught in the act of pillage; what more could they do?

"I used to go to the old cowboy and Indian movies," wrote James Baldwin, "and I would always applaud the cowboys until I found out that the Indians were me." Why couldn't our teachers realize that for all their Anglo-Saxon reinforcements, the Andy Dotsons of the world were them?

This is an unfair question, in that it should not be put to the teachers alone. Most of us have tried to kill the Andy Dotson in ourselves in order to prove to the world that we are a separate species. But the ruse has not worked. The cowboy, to paraphrase a French nihilist, draws his six shooter, and fires madly into the crowd at random, and each of us dies an Andy Dotson.

Unable to move beyond their personal sickness, these teachers acquiesced in the death of two young people who did not have to die. It is not important to fix responsibility—for we are all responsible—but we must realize that these young people did not have to die. Until we realize that many more worthy than we have perished in the struggle through no fault of their own, the phrase "I endured" becomes nothing more than the final curtain of a tragedy, where all the actors lie upon the same stage, gored and bleeding to death.

CHAPTER 56

The Son of My Father

(1970)

I am compelled to state here, in the beginning, that the thoughts recorded in this book are mine alone and that I do not, nor have I attempted, to speak for any other Black man in American society. I make this statement in the hope of sparing some other Negro the moments of frustration and anger which I experience when some "Negro Leader" on television, bright lights illuminating his unscarred countenance, proceeds to tell America in impassioned tones what I think, believe, and want.

Such utterances by Negro Leaders have produced severe traumas for me, causing me to hurl notebook, pen, and pencil at my television set, shout obscenities at the unhearing figure before me; and finally, not too long ago, when I had almost reached the breaking point, I scribbled a note to one of these leaders asking that on future occasions he preface his remarks by stating that: "I speak for every Negro in America, except Addison Gayle." The letter accomplished nothing, for three weeks ago this same leader was on television again, informing the public that he, not other Negro Leaders, spoke for me.

America is at that desperate stage when, feeling the threat from her long-neglected citizenry, she needs some supporting, sustaining voice to assure her that the neglected are still, despite all, hopeful, passive, and restrained. Nations, like men, are wary of truth, for truth is too often not beautiful, as Keats believed, but very painful and very discomforting. It is not comforting to be reminded that those who sow the wind shall reap the whirlwind, not even when the whirlwind appears so visibly, as in frequent summers of discontent when desperate men have belied the vocal protestations of their leaders.

No Negro in America speaks for me; neither do I speak for any one else. It would, perhaps, be too great a shock to find compatibility between my thoughts and those of others, for unlike Narcissus, a mirror image would cause me untold discomfort. I am, I know, a desperate man, a cynical man and, perhaps, according to Freudian psychology which can in no way explain me, a sick man. Some of my friends would add, quickly, a mad man. I do not object. Perhaps to be sane in this society is the best evidence of insanity. To repress all that I know, to keep hidden in my subconscious all that I feel, may inevitably force me to those acts of desperation which I am capable of viewing here, frankly and honestly with a certain objective detachment.

This is to say that the very act of recording these thoughts may provide that catharsis which will enable me to retain control of that demon within my breast which allows me no respite in twentieth century America. One wonders what fate might have befallen Dostoyevsky had he not created Roskolnikov or Demitri? What might Baldwin have become, had he not been capable of traducing Bigger Thomas in print? And Wright, Bigger's creator, what might he have been were not the fearful portrait of Bigger etched upon his subconscious mind, displayed upon that canvas of the psyche in garish, brutal colors?

The end product of writing should be revelation for both the writer and reader. I have no quarrel with those who argue that poetry "should not mean but be." I simply call them liars, and let it go at that. I hold no breach against those who argue that Black literature, in the main, has not conformed to those artistic rules and canons established by the academicians. I know that such tools are important to them. For they are incapable of understanding Black literature without the aid of these instruments of dissection with which they are most dexterous.

Literature, however, and Black literature in particular, should afford revelation and insight into truth when created under conditions favorable to free, honest expression. For the Afro-American, solitude is the most necessary condition, for Blacks are abominable liars, especially, in those cases where an audience is concerned. This is not to suggest that Black writers are not also liars—indeed a great many are the most notorious liars of all. But, alone, secreted only with his thoughts and a desire to honestly record those thoughts, the Black writer may, at least, blunder into an awareness of truth.

This truth, then, will come as a revelation, and I have little doubt that mine will—especially to those who, over the years, have professed to "know" me. They will discover, sometimes painfully, that they have not known me at all; yet, this is primarily because I have not known myself. For example, I did not know—or would not admit, which is the same thing—how vehement was my hatred even toward those whom I professed to love most passionately.

If however, those who remember me will recall my unspoken nuances—the quick bowing of my head, the slight raising of my eyebrows, the smile which has never really been a smile, the uncomfortable habit that I have of moving from place to place whenever alone in a room with white people—then they can begin to piece together the puzzle of our relationship and to make some sense out of what I write here. When I say that I hated, I am uttering my first verbal truth with full cognizance of its import, and if not a revelation to others, this is indeed, a revelation to me. This is my first positive statement to white people, and because it is the truth, I do not apologize for it. I only regret that I did not, or could not, make it before.

Perhaps I did not really hate before! Perhaps, despite everything, I retained enough of my mother's Christian preachments to think of love as the universal solvent, the cleansing cream which America needs but apply to the ugly, pock-marked blemishes upon its white-hued surface. Perhaps I believed that one could not create a world of hatred because invariably that world became a suspicious one, an isolated one, and, finally, one so infected by disease that life, any life trapped within it was worthless. Or, perhaps, I was too much of a coward to hate: too timid, too meek.

And this despite the fact that I owe what some people call my success to hatred. Six years ago, I worked as a porter at a government establishment in Brooklyn, New York. After four years, I left that job and three days later began to assault the pavements of New York City searching for another. My odyssey began early on a Monday morning, on a dismal, overcast day in May when the streets of New York seemed most indifferent—a day much like those which I had cherished in the Virginia town where I was born.

Long before, on such days, I had searched for jobs in Virginia with less trepidation, with less overt fear than that which plagued me as I searched for employment in New York City. To state for the nth time that the Afro-American's life in the South in comparison with his life in the North is in many ways more comfortable if not more compatible is to state what is general knowledge. For there is comfort in honesty, in knowing that the perils one faces are blatantly visible, not cloaked with the time-honored garb of hypocrisy and deceit. The South is nothing if not honest, and Blacks who hate it the most, grudgingly admit to its honesty.

The indictment against the North, however, stems from its dishonesty, its hypo-critical facade which has engendered more frustration in the Black intellectual than all the perverted acts perpetrated upon Negroes by those creatures who inhabit the hinterlands of the South. In the South, the Negro is, when visible, merely a Negro, an accursed son of Ham destined, like a mute, to be the stanchion of stubborn support for a romantic, idyllic utopia where class and race are so structured as to allow for a well-ordered society. Here, only the Blacks speak of equality. The whites hurl the correlative word, "place"; for there is a place for the Negro in Southern society—albeit, a place at the bottom of a rotten cesspool—yet a place where being Black, though a stigma, is legitimate. The Negroes are still considered as a people, and brotherhood means loyalty to one's own race.

In the North, on the other hand, the Negro is conceived of as an instrument, a non-being, the noble savage, who must, in whatever way possible, be civilized; scrubbed clean of his heredity; robbed of his propensity for Blackness; the last vestige of tribalism erased from his mind. Like the missionary, the Northern white seeks to bring the savage within the confines of Western civilization with far more potent weapons than guns and Bibles: higher horizons programs, civil rights commissions, urban renewal, and cultural centers for Black youth.

There is more truth in the South than in the North, more honest feeling in the man who knots the rope about your neck, more honest conviction in the mob which howls for your blood. In the North, one falls into that absurd world where impotent men gather unto themselves other men as children, intent on guiding them, on leading them to that coming paradise, that enchanted land of freedom and equality, notwithstanding the fact that paradise is only paradise if one finds it himself.

Here in the North, rhetoric and practice come into conflict: it is no surprise that the great rhetoricians of America are Northerners, for here rhetoric is the most celebrated avocation. From the politician in the highest echelons of government to the freshman college student come the wail of discontent, the table-thumping oratory, the endless reports of committees, civil rights groups, civic organizations, all attesting to the deep concern, the great sympathy felt by men of the North, more sophisticated, more liberal, for their fellow citizens who happen to be Black.

Such people believe their own rhetoric, and it is their rhetoric which sustains them. They conceive of rhetoric and practice as one and the same. The college chairman who heads a committee to improve conditions in the ghetto, and yet neglects to improve the conditions in his college so that more ghetto residents may attend, is equating rhetoric with practice. The politician who, although voting for civil rights bills, cautions Afro-Americans not to move too fast is equating rhetoric with practice. The college student who demands tolerance from others toward Blacks and neglects to make such demands upon his parents and neighbors is equating rhetoric with practice.

The Negro, therefore, recognizing the conflict, capable of differentiating between rhetoric and practice, yet unable to divine the motives for the great disparities which he knows to exist, is incapable of finding a bearing, a central point in an absurd world where men are victims of their own rhetoric. It is the frustrations engendered by such conflicts which drive Black people to acts of frustrations, to acts of violence, ofttimes, as in the case of a friend, to suicide.

The Negro, the world's greatest dissimulator, is unable to survive in a world where dissimulation is the norm, hypocrisy the accustomed and accepted mode of behavior. Better to be entrapped in a web of practicality where men take the word "place" as the God-ordained condition of twenty-five million people than to be enmeshed in a web where men are convinced that their manifest destiny lies in mesmerizing the natives by their spellbinding, hypnotic oratory. The first web can be cut; its strands can be severed; at the least, men never tire of attempting to rip it apart. The second web, however, is non-corporeal, having no body, no structure, no substance. It is impervious to assault, except that of the most violent nature; for the Messiah is incapable of differentiating between rhetoric and practice until such time as those who see truth in men's actions, not in their words, nail him, shamelessly and without guilt, to the cross.

It is not long before the Negro who journeys from South to North is called witness to his moment of truth. Epiphanies are almost daily occurrences. There is so much to be revealed. There are so many thousands of shapes, forms, and symbols through which revelation may come. The first epiphany often occurs in the North when the Negro first faces his hoped-for employer. Contrary to most reports, on fast arriving in the North, the Southern Black is not incensed by the ghetto—this comes later—for the Northern ghetto has always held mystical, romantic connotations for him. Here it is that the tenuous tie with the North, perfected through the years by the mass exodus of his ancestors, is most secure. Few Blacks in the South have neither friends nor relatives in Northern ghettos. Thus, neither the filth and stench of the ghetto, nor its chronic violence can rid the newcomer of that compulsion to dwell among his own in the Harlems, Wattses, Houghs and Bedford Stuyvesants of the North.

Discrimination, Northern style, is encountered when the newcomer searches for his first job and is brought face to face with his first Northern employer. The encounter is more likely than not to be traumatic, reinforcing the subdued antagonism engendered by the South, intensifying it to the point wherein this antagonism gives way to a hatred which given birth, feeds upon itself like a cancerous cell until the victim is either consumed or miraculously made whole—himself consuming that which would destroy him.

Early in the morning on that dark overcast day, I checked out five jobs, all of which had surreptitiously vanished before I arrived. My sixth stop was the corner of Delancey Street and Broadway, a combination restaurant and newsstand which, according to *The New York Times*, "Wanted: a man to do light portering, some clerking." It was the "light portering" which caused me to be hopeful, for such job descriptions in the South are usually synonyms for Negroes.

I was met at the door of the shop by a dark-hued white man who, mistaking me for a customer, commented on the state of the weather. Smiling, I proceeded to point out the true nature of my business which was not to buy wares but, instead to sell my labor. No sooner had I mentioned the ad than the man abruptly turned his back to me, and walked quickly to the other end of the store, informing me through a running monologue with himself that the job was taken. However, his actions, not his words, convinced me that he was lying. All morning I had been turned away from jobs, always with a smile, a sympathetic murmur of sympathy, unbelievable to be sure, yet unchallengeable on any save intuitive grounds.

This man had made it impossible for me to believe him. I left the store, went across the street to a drugstore, waited a few minutes, and dialed the number listed in the newspaper. The man himself answered the telephone. Mimicking James Mason, I asked if the job listed in the morning paper had been filled. The answer was no. I asked if I could come over to see about the job. I was told to come at once. I went to the store a second time. This time the man met me, rage breathing from every pore of his nostrils, his ugly face contorted into the most weird design.

"Yes?" He growled.

"I came for the job." I announced.

"There ain't no job!" He replied.

"I just called, and you said there was one," I answered, "You said come right over."

Briefly, a flicker of surprise came to his eyes, but he recovered quickly. "You didn't call here," he said. "That's a lie, there ain't no job." He turned on his heels and went to serve a customer who had come in.

I stared after him for a few minutes before finally walking out of the store. There was a big lump in my stomach. My hands shook noticeably. In facing him with what I knew to be the truth, in forcing him to acknowledge his own lie, I had, perhaps, scored a moral victory. Yet I was still without a job because a man who did not know me, had decided *a priori* that I should not have one. The moral victory was far less sustaining than my growing hatred.

Floyd Patterson, in his first fight with Ingemar Johanssen, was knocked to the canvas again and again, only to rise yet another time. Many were awed by the tenacious courage displayed by the champion, the refusal to stay down, to say die. I was not amazed, for I too had learned early to absorb merciless punishment, to pick myself up from the canvas of a ring in which the fight can only end in life or death.

Like the ex-heavyweight champion, I was on my feet searching for another job less than fifteen minutes after absorbing a crushing blow to my psyche. This time I intended to shape the odds nearer to my liking. I decided to buy a job.

The headquarters of the job-buying market is a narrow street at the southern tip of Manhattan, some few feet from the Hudson River. On this narrow street, occupying an entire block, are an assortment of dilapidated office buildings housing numerous agencies which legally traffic in human flesh. Sometimes as many as five agencies are in one single building. Each agency occupies a large room, two at the most, partitioned into two sections. One section, the larger is usually, though not always, furnished with folding chairs; in the other section, beyond the partition, neat, middle-aged businessmen (white) and their assistants sit at wooden desks surrounded by telephones.

Throughout the day, from opening time at eight o'clock in the morning to closing time at five o'clock at night, people of all races come to these partitioned offices offering themselves as saleable commodities. On any given day, one will find a small number of white applicants, a large number of Puerto Rican applicants, and a great number of Black applicants.

I chose one of the smaller agencies which had emptied, somewhat, at that hour of the day. A number of people were still present. Some were waiting, I suppose, for clarification of job offers. Some women were checking to see if the prospects for domestic work tomorrow were brighter than prospects today. Standing along the two walls of the agency were older Negro men, in whose faces the tragedy of a people was stenciled in bold, heavy lines, watching each new arrival suspiciously, their ears attuned to the ring of the telephone; they smiled condescendingly each time the eyes of the agent swept their paths; for the agent was their savior, able to reward them with a half day's work, enabling them to fight off the D.T.'s, hunger, or eviction yet a little while longer.

I was met by an assistant, a charming, brown skinned girl of about twenty-one, heavily rouged, her hair in a pompadour, her false eyelashes flickering as if in amusement. We smiled at one another, and she communicated her nervousness by smoking her cigarette almost to the filter, leaving her long fingers stained a deeper brown than her skin. Like me, she, too, lived at a fever pitch of desperation; though she, like some omniscient spectator of Dante's Hell, watched men, women, and sometimes teenage children stacked before her eyes, no longer human, but instead objects to be auctioned away for one week's salary—the legal requirements of the agency. She had dwelled among these hollow men and women so long, these mechanical men and women of Kafka's novels, that she had become almost hollow and mechanical herself. I pitied her, even as she pitied me.

She helped me to fill out several forms, and after I had completed them, she motioned me to a folding chair, took the forms, and deposited them on the desk of a short, fat white man, whose bald head seemed a comic distraction in this place where laughter would have been an unforgivable crime.

Not too long after, I sat in a chair at the desk, staring at the man's bald head, listening to him describe a job recently referred to his agency. The job was located in a restaurant on Broadway, two blocks from City Hall. The prerequisites were for a young man who had some experience at handling a cash register, and who would not balk at long hours. I satisfied the agent that I met all the requirements, after which he brought out a number of papers upon which I scribbled my signature. The assistant gave me a card bearing the agency's letterhead and the name of the man I was to see, and smiled at me knowingly; I quickly left that little room, which smelled like something akin to death.

The restaurant was located in the basement of a large hotel which, at that time, was undergoing alteration. I passed several Black workers: plasterers, hod-carriers, and porters, one of whom pointed the way to the manager at the door of the office—he, seeing me approaching, had come from behind a glass enclosure. He was young, blond, his face clean of blemishes, his body thin, athletic in appearance. His movements seemed impetuous, quick, and determined. I handed him the agent's card.

Hardly had he finished reading the card, before, without hesitation, almost as if I were not present, he blurted out: "But why did they send you? We don't hire Negroes."

We recoiled one from the other! He because he had said what he did; I because he had said it so blatantly. He was, I suppose, an honest man, and instinctively, he uttered the truth which needed no supporting rationale. I never thought for a moment that he hated me, nor that he thought much about me at all; this was not necessary to justify the irrefutable statement: "We don't hire Negroes."

It was the look of consternation on my face which made him offer me car-fare, which prompted him to tell me that he was sorry. He looked after me with sympathetic eyes, as I, having spurned his offer of carfare, backed away as one fighting to sleep through some horrible nightmare. I walked away, almost in a state of shock. In this shocked state, I telephoned the agency, reported what had happened, hung up the phone, and boarded the "A" train for Brooklyn.

When finally I reached my stop in the heart of Bedford Stuyvesant, the ghetto to which I came now for some solace, for some semblance of myself, some tes-tament of myself as a human being, I left the subway, bypassing the bars along the way, where I would find that human misery by which to measure my own. I avoided those who knew me, even at that moment when I wanted their affection the most. I avoided them because I did not want them to see me cry. Crying is an act which one should perform only in private, for crying is a private way of groping for truth. Once inside of my apartment, I removed the phone from the hook, locked my door, fell across the bed, and cried.

On the bed, clawing and clutching at the pillows, my breath coming in quick, short gasps, my nose filled with mucus; my mouth hot, dry. I twisted, shouted, and screamed almost in convulsion; the tears gushing from my eyes; my body burning as if seared by some scorching, burning flame; with my fists I flailed the pillows; with my fingernails I tore at my hair, drew blood from my skin like some hurt, wounded beast in orgasm. I surrendered my soul to that Faustian devil who hovers over the Black male, in pain, in ecstasy, in total to complete, everlasting hatred.

In time I would come to understand that it was not only the acts of discrimina-tion, not only the feelings of rejection, not only the soul-rending words, "We don't hire Negroes"; but, instead, the motivation for the surrender to Mephistopheles was simply that white men had made me cry, had forced me to that point where I would seek a baptism in my own tears, a baptism which would cleanse me of any sense of responsibility to them, any sense of affection for them, any sense of respect for them. The ultimate pain which any man can inflict upon another is to force him to tears.

"God gave Noah the rainbow sign/No more water, the fire next time," chanted a now forgotten Black slave. For me the water had come to give birth to that fire which would consume me, almost completely. Sparks from this fire propelled me to college, forced me to attempt, naively, to wreak vengeance upon those who had forced me to reveal my soul in all of its nakedness. Instructors who knew me as a conscientious, hardworking student had no cognizance of that demon within which forced me on; nor could they know that the mere sight of them, their whiteness, was enough to trigger that demon into action. Riding the wings of the demon, I pushed my way through curricula foreign to me, spent entire nights writing and rewriting term papers; stood Buddha-like as my instructors attempted to convince me of their dedication to the human spirit.

Some were kind enough to single me out, to invite me to their homes. They questioned me about my hopes, my expectations, and about race relations. Always, I lied to them, partly out of fear, but partly, too, out of the belief that were I to tell them the truth, to relate even one tenth of my truth, they would expel me from school and have me locked up in the nearest hospital for the mentally insane.

Others spoke of me in laudatory terms: They told me that I was the kind of Negro whom they would "not mind living next door to them"; that I should be a "spokesman for my people"; that I was proving that any man with initiative could prosper in this democracy. They refused to see me as other than a phenomenon, a testament to all that their rhetoric had portrayed. I was the emancipated Negro, shrived of the sin of Blackness because I had proved that I could absorb the wisdom of Shakespeare, Plato, and Emerson. I was the transformed savage, having been rescued from the jungle of the ghetto and stripped of the ghetto facade; now I was almost human, ready to be welcomed, even if half-heartedly—for the savage can never be completely transformed—into middle-class senility, impotence, and death.

Students, on the other hand, were worse than instructors. If the instructors believed me to be intellectually resurrected, the students considered me to be socially resurrected, capable now of association on an almost equal level with them. I was *the Negro* to have at social gatherings. I avoided most of these and went only when I was bored with school work. I was the Negro who talked on their terms, voiced their discontents, and gave words to their frustration.

To them I told as much of the truth as possible, until I discovered that they sought this truth, eagerly, masochistically, as authoritative evidence, facts from the donkey's mouth, with which to substantiate the ever-changing tenor of their own rhetoric. To be sure, they dreamed of the new Canaan, but one from which I, as an individual, would be excluded. When I entered their new world, I would enter as mind, as intellect, divested of that corporeal form, body, bedecked by a Black skin. Believing in the power of rationality, these students saw me in terms of intellect only; for to them, intellect was unlimited. I, however, could not live by intellect and intellect alone; for there was, within my breast, an irrational demon which often propelled me to irrational acts. I could not, therefore, accept their compact, for unfortunately, sometime ago, I had signed the most binding compact of all.

"I fall upon the thorns of life," wrote Shelley, "I bleed!" And sometimes one wishes that the bleeding would be over and done with; and if not this, then that some tourniquet might be applied to stop the flowing blood once and for all. On the other hand, perhaps it would be best if the blood gushed profusely, like a water hose, pushing out the impurities quickly, allowing one only the intoxicating moment of release, an ecstatic descent into a dream world, where there is no life, and thus, no pain.

"Verweile doch, du bist so schön," she called after me. Standing by the plane, tall, slender, deep blue eyes, blonde hair cut short about her neck, tears in her eyes, she watched as I walked slowly, unsteadily up the ramp. The fleeting hour was fleeting all too quickly, and never again would we see one another, never again walk the same sandy beach together; never again share the same world.

Her world had been as strange to me as my world was to her. Few of us, like Malcolm X, make the trip to Mecca where one meets people of different skin color whom one cannot reject outright. Yet many Negroes find their personal Meccas; and there, though color is never irrelevant, there is perhaps something better—one is indifferent to color.

She was my Mecca. Here color was not negated, but simply ignored. Together we found the new Canaan, and yet, I knew that I could not live in it. Too many Blacks were outside, too many Blacks whose tortured faces continued to move before my mind like so many accusing mouths; and we both knew that one day, I would have to acquiesce to the painful utterances of those mouths, desert Canaan, and return to the ghetto not, as my father had hoped, to save the people, but to die with them.

We arrived, therefore, at some definition of our life together, found some way of memorializing all that had been, and we stumbled upon the concept of the fleeting hour (die fliegende Stunde).

"Verweile doch, du bist so schön," we chanted night after night together (remain, so fair thou art), for fair those hours were indeed. Two human beings caught in a historic trap, one incapable of destroying a vicious, binding compact, desiring always to be victim, rather than victimizer; two people living for a short span of time in a peace, a serenity to which no words can give form and body; two lovers who, were there some merciful God, would have been allowed to perish then and there.

It was the hour, however, which would perish; not we. Cowards, we would continue to live, to be hurled again and again upon those sharp, jagged thorns which drained us of life-giving blood. Soon the magic of the words, the spell of the incantation, "verweile doch, du bist so schön," would mean little more than an epigram for an essay or a poem. Like Keats, we had spent our allotted time with the nightingale, drunk of hemlock, and tasted of mirth and flora; and yet even such memories were doomed to death in the atmosphere to which I was compelled to return.

The Negro, I have written elsewhere, is timeless; and this is so, for time stopped for us the moment the good ship *Jesus* unloaded its first cargo in the New World.

Since that moment, we have sat atop the jagged thorns of life convulsing, like so many tortured animals, from wounds inflicted by weapons as diverse as whips, pistols, ropes, and rhetoric. Yet rhetoric is perhaps the most bludgeoning weapon of all. We have been enslaved anew by rhetoric: that of our own prophets as well as that of the missionaries. We fear our own emotions, seek to check them, to subdue them in obedience to some man-made laws which we should neither respect nor honor.

We have chanted love thine enemy, when every fiber of our being has cried "death" to those who despoil us; we have preached forgiveness, when not even the most pious among us can forgive that brutal past from which we sprang; we have sung hymns to a God who, in his infinite mercy, has forsaken us as readily as he forsook his first son; we have dreamed of "a fleeting hour" when even that was not enough to assuage the wounds of the past. Hollow men, we have not dared consider the admonition of Ralph Ellison's invisible man: " . . . maybe freedom lies in hating."

But if not, perhaps freedom lies in realizing that one hates. Perhaps all that is left the Black man in America is a revelation, an awareness of himself; and perhaps the key to that conundrum posed by the Black poets, the answer to the question of identity lies in an exploration of one's true emotions, starting at that elementary first principle of denigrated humanity: "I hate."

I begin this book cognizant of the war which goes on constantly within my soul. It is a fierce war and, no doubt, a destructive one. Yet this war must be fought out to some conclusion before I can begin to wrestle with the problems of men in general. That things which have happened to me, have happened also to others, I have little doubt; yet in happening to me, they have left wounds upon my psyche, and pain others cannot imagine.

I am, I suppose, a stranger, one who has sought a personal truth, hoping to be more enlightened by it than his audience; a stranger, who believes that men live always with some demon within their breasts which can only be exorcised by a dedication to those frightening realities which exist at the moment; a stranger, who has always believed that mankind would be better off today had it accepted as savior the choice of that mob which shouted "Give us Barabbas," instead of accepting one who, from the cross, could only issue his pitiable, feeble moan: "Father forgive them, for they know not what they do."

CHAPTER 57

Excerpt from *Wayward Child: A Personal Odyssey*

(1977)

My days and nights changed little during the next four months, in which I moved always close to mental catastrophe, buttressed by alcohol and tranquilizers. My journal of the period—I managed to keep one, though I wrote only occasionally—is filled with notations on my lack of appetite, my long periods of sleeping, waking, and sleeping again, the decrease of my work output from twelve hours to half an hour daily, from twenty pages to one, and is capped by the admission of June 21, 1973: "Life in a flux, I am, I know, a sick man. I must unravel my life . . . I must become well."

At the age of forty, believing myself to have reached the feverish pitch of crisis, I went into therapy. The therapist, Raphael Rosell, was from South America. He had hypnotic eyes, a perpetual smile playing about the comers of his mouth, and hair cut short atop his head. I had long maintained a reservation about psychoanalysis, believing that only the weak sought such assistance, that I could deal with emotional problems by retreating into isolation. Raphael was an unorthodox therapist; the relationship he attempted to establish between himself and his patients was not that of father and son/daughter, but that of one friend to another. After two months, we had established a relationship moving along those lines, and I had become much calmer than I had been over the last year. Thus, having established a working relationship, the bulk of our work began in the fall of 1972.

At the beginning of September, three weeks before I was to begin work at school again, the topic between us was feelings. I remember sitting in the easy chair, watching him unwrap, moisten, and then light a panatella. Finally, he turned to me, eyes flashing hypnotically: "Well, my friend, how are you?"

I responded automatically as usual, "Fine."

"Any thought about what we talked about last time?" I reached for my pipe, lit up, drew heavily. Last time and the time before, the subject has been the same—feelings. I had written the session up in my journal, and then forgotten about it. "I didn't come to any conclusions," I replied.

"Well, what do you think, if anything?"

"The same. I don't trust feelings. You can't live by them."

"Why are you so strongly against feelings, against being, as you call it, emotional?"

I relit my pipe. The answer was ready, yet the formulation and articulation of it was not for the therapist, but to be recorded in my journal. There I answered truthfully the questions I avoided during therapy. I had written of the last session: "It was feeling and emotion that sent me here to analysis in the first place. Having lost control, almost completely, for the second time in my life, I had come close to destroying myself." Fondling my pipe in my hand, I turned to Raphael, said, "Look, emotions, feelings, they are damn private things . . . things inside. . . ."

He picked up the abrupt change in my voice. "Why are you so hostile?"

"Hostile?" I responded. I laughed nervously. "Why is it when I don't give you an answer you want, I'm hostile?"

He narrowed the distance between himself and me, bent closer. "Look, whenever we get on this subject, you'd like to tell me to go fuck myself, wouldn't you?"

I hesitated, thought, "Yes, I would." I stared at him without answering.

"Why don't you?" he persisted.

"Why should I?" I queried uncomfortably.

"You should if you want to. Why are you afraid to be angry, to let go, why so tight?"

I retreated by taking a long time to light my pipe. My mind went back to Walter, to the figure standing over top of him, me, to the animal I had become, and there was momentary panic at the thought of being angry with Raphael, of leaping the narrow space between us, of seizing him by the throat. I shuddered at the thought.

Placing his hands on my shoulder, looking directly into my face, he said softly, "We always come back to it sooner or later. There's all this feeling down there and, I think, a hell of a lot of anger, too. You fight it, control it. Look, you've got marvelous control. But maybe you don't have to use all that energy controlling it. If we can find out what it is, why it's there. . . ."

"All right!" I cut him short. "I know what you're saying; but, I don't want to come—as you call it—in touch with my feelings."

"Why not?"

"Because I did about four months ago, and I ended up here."

"Addison," he interjected briefly, "cut the bullshit. Maybe you had a nervous breakdown, were about to have one. I thought so at first. Maybe you thought you could make things up to your wife by having a nervous breakdown. Now, I'm not sure whether you would or not—I mean have had a breakdown."

The answer rolled defiantly from my lips: "You're damned right, I wasn't going to have a breakdown!"

I was surprised that he seemed to believe me; I did not think I believed myself.

"Why?"

"Because . . . because . . . Look, I just wasn't!"

"You mean you were going to control your feelings come hell or high water?"

The panic showed through my response. "Look, will you get off this stuff about feelings? I've told you, in this white people's country, Black people don't walk around with their feelings on their shoulders. You'd better be thinking most of the time."

Agitated, he threw up his hands. "The white people again. I talk to you about *your* feelings and you start talking about white people."

Laughingly, I remembered that he once called me the artful dodger. I had made him uncomfortable now. Not being a Native American, he knew about the racial situation only second-hand. In this area, I was the expert. "Because," I replied, "if you want to talk to me about feelings or anything else, you have to come to racism in this country. I know that damn much. Let your feelings go, laugh, be happy around white people and they try to take advantage of you; exhibit your anger, let out the rage, get in touch with your feelings, as you call it, and you end up killing one of them. No, if you're a Black man in this country and you want to survive, you keep it inside."

His voice became soft, slightly sarcastic. "But, Addison, you are scared to death of Black men, too. But look, I'm not talking about the political situation, not about Black men or white men, but about you—why all the control, why so tight?"

There was a kindness, almost a pleading tone in his voice, in his eyes. The seriousness was there, too. I looked away from him, out at the East River. A boat passed by. White clouds and blue sky appeared in the distance. Suddenly I felt very tired, moved my eyes back to his face, said, more softly now, "Because I didn't want to have a nervous breakdown."

"Why not?" he asked softly, tenderly.

"I didn't want to lose my mind," I said.

"What do you think will happen, if you lose your mind?"

"I don't know."

"Have you ever seen anyone, known anyone to lose his mind?"

"I don't know."

"What do you think happens when people lose their minds?"

"They become like children."

"What's wrong with being a child?"

The boat had disappeared. The river was calm, peaceful. "Children are helpless; they can't protect themselves and nobody else will do it for them. In this world, you'd better be able to protect yourself."

That night, I wrote in my journal: "Raphael is not a bad person, but I should stop going to see him. Yes, he was right, I am afraid of Black men too. So what? He knows it and I know it. Why doesn't he explain it? Why do I have to do all the work? He makes me damn uncomfortable; first about being in competition with my father, now about feelings. I don't know what he means—get in touch with your feelings. What the hell do I do? Do I push a switch, turn a button? And what does it matter if I keep my feelings to myself? Why should I make a public disclosure of them? Why should I use them the way women do—to blackmail people, to cause guilt, gain pity? And he knows that I am not a machine, that I have feelings. Yes, I *do* feel pain, love, remorse. I do!"

One of the most crucial sessions, as I saw it, occurred later, near the end of the month, after I had settled back into the routine of teaching. Back again in the soft easy chair, I looked away from Raphael, out again toward the East River. The sky was dark, a trickle of rain fell on the tall buildings some few yards from the window. Raphael puffed on his cigar; I lit my pipe.

"Well." He waved the cigar in, my direction—the cue for me to begin talking.

I rested the pipe on the metal ashtray. "I had . . . a funny kind of experience—in class today."

"Do you want to talk about it?"

I did. I looked past his eyes, flashing alive now, to a blank spot on the wall near the window. I was back in the classroom. I was teaching the novel *Native Son*. I moved from the desk to the blackboard, wrote the words "gratuitous murder" on the blackboard. I explained the meaning of the term to the class: "For years Bigger lived with pent-up rage inside of him, hatred, a wish to murder. Remember our discussion of *Germinal*, and the coal miner Bonnemort. The situation is analogous: all of their lives these men were brutalized by society, all of their lives, they longed for revenge. The longing is part of their blood, flows in their veins, as the energy that drives them from day to day. Murder is the organizing principle of their lives, their subconscious lives, and if they live long enough and circumstances arise, one day they will give way to their passions, commit murder—out of rage and hatred." I had moved to the far side of the room, near the window. I was about to begin further explication of Bigger's crime when, suddenly, I felt faint, dizzy, my legs began to wobble, my heart pounded faster, faster, and, talking rapidly, I moved to my desk, flung a question out to the class, with trembling hands lit my pipe.

"How long did this feeling last?" asked Raphael. "Not long. Maybe a minute, maybe less."

"Has it happened before, in class?"

"Yes, a long time ago."

"Did the students know?"

"No, I covered it very well."

"What do you think triggered it off?"

"I don't know."

"Could it have been the story?"

"I don't know why. I've taught this novel, God knows how many times."

"Did something happen before class? Yesterday, even that morning?"

He paused, relit the panatella. I took advantage of the break to relight my pipe. The rain fell more heavily, water bounced from the roofs of tall buildings; the East River seemed to have disappeared under a cloak of darkness. I remembered that I had once thought of drowning in that river.

"We've been talking all along about feelings," Raphael began again, "emotions, rage, and anger. Is that what the novel is about?"

"Yes."

"Could there be some connection there?"

Thoughtfully, I puffed on the half-lit pipe. There was, I supposed, a connection, but I didn't know how to explain it. "At the end of the novel," I said, "Bigger Thomas goes to the electric chair. I think that I might have thought about that."

"I don't understand."

"Well . . . if you were Black in the South and you committed a crime against white people, you went to the electric chair. That's how it was. Almost everybody in our neighborhood had heard of someone who had gone to the electric chair. So if you were a bad boy, the old people would say that you were going to the electric chair."

"And you were told this?"

I remembered the Madonna, her shrieks, her screams, the dreaded words. "Yes, a lot of times, by a lot of people."

"Why, what did you do?"

"Nothing really. I was kind of hardheaded, smart, thought I was different."

"So what?"

"So, sooner or later, they thought I would end up in the electric chair. My family, teachers, older people in the neighborhood. They were trying to protect me, I guess."

"From what?"

"From white people. I guess they thought that if I continued being different, sooner or later, I would get into trouble."

"You hated them then? Now you're protecting them?"

"I never hated them all."

"No, but a lot of them, you thought they were your enemies."

"I understand them better, now."

"Or you're ready to forgive them?"

I lapsed into silence.

"Well, all right. But you said they wanted to protect you? Couldn't it have been that they didn't want you to be different?"

"It might have been."

"And so if you were different, you would be punished?" He paused, looked down at the space near my feet, brought his eyes slowly to mine. "And being different means to be an individual, saying what you want to, doing what you want to, acting for yourself? Right?" He did not wait for my reply, his eyes narrowed, became slits, hard. "In other words, to be different meant to be white. White people were smart, white people could talk back, say what they wanted, do what they wanted, be different. If Black people like you—not mulattoes, though that's another thing—we call them *assimillados*—do this, they are acting like white people. Is it possible you were being punished, being mistreated, harassed, for acting like white people?"

The pipe rested in the metal ashtray. I thought about his summation, rolled the words around in my mind. Is that what my father had recognized, years ago, when he had asked me why I wanted to be white? But also, did being an individual mean being white? Did not wanting to be ugly, not wanting to be Black, wanting to be mullato, did this equal wanting to be white? "Maybe," I answered Raphael and myself, affirmatively, "maybe I was acting like white people."

"And you still are, aren't you?"

I was surprised by the question. I had thought, since Seattle, that I had moved outside of the patterns of old, had at least wanted to. "Do I?" I asked, unsure.

"Well . . . think about it. You're a professor in a white university. You're a writer, internationally known. You wear expensive clothes, live in a white neighborhood. You lecture at well-known white colleges, sit on committees, people come to you for advice, help, who knows?—all of these are things that white people do, aren't they?"

The answer of course was yes. I thought of a co-worker, who wanted to be a full professor, and I was amused; I had never expected to be a professor at all— assistant or associate, let alone a full professor. Such jobs were those white people dreamed of. Nothing in my experience made me want to strive for such positions. I had become an associate professor by accident, not by design.

Alone with my journal the next night, I tried to put the pieces together. "My father had been right, after all. He had known, perhaps, much better than I, that the mulattoes were not the real targets, as I had believed. He had known. And had expected me to know that they had had no real power. They were surrogates, wielding power at the behest of others; their arrogance was a counterfeit arrogance, based not so much upon just desserts, but upon the benevolence of white people. They were not the rose, had only been close to the rose, and for me, to go beyond them, to achieve victory over them, to defeat them meant to want to be what white people were, what they symbolized. It meant, finally, to want to be white. This meant moving outside of one set of patterns and trying to live within the rules of another. And there was no middle ground; each option meant betrayal, each had its own rules of punishment. Very well. I no longer have to accept either option. I have more realistic images now. I know much more of Frederick Douglass and Martin Delany, of W. E. B. Du Bois and Henry Highland Garnet, of Harriet Tubman and Sojourner Truth. *And if I were a betrayer before,*

I am no longer, and I will no longer feel guilty; I am not a white man; I am a Black man."

If, as I had believed, the chances of mental disaster had been outstanding in the spring and summer of 1972, here, in the winter of the same year, they were minimal. I was still afflicted by short bouts of depression, but they were neither of long duration nor very severe. The very thought of suicide became abhorrent to me, and gradually I became less of a recluse, willing to move outside the isolation and alienation I had once coveted so much. I accepted my appointments to committees, both in the university and in the college itself as something more than formal positions, and worked enthusiastically at committee assignments. I wrote more surely and steadily, and by October, I had finished work on the history of the Black novel. I accepted positions on Black magazines as a contributing editor that I would not have accepted before, and I dated often with a passion almost completely lacking in the past.

Two days after Thanksgiving, however, an incident occurred which sent me once again into severe despair and made me seek a session with Raphael outside our normal schedule. David Lorrens had committed suicide. The official statement would always announce his death as an accident, would explain that his car had veered uncontrollably, forcing him into the crash which ended his life. Not long after I had left Seattle, David had suffered an emotional breakdown, had been forced into intense psychiatric treatment; for the past year his mental state had been kept in check by tranquilizing drugs.

I received the news of his death with stunning uncertainty. What did it all mean? How had it happened? Could it not also happen to me? Later that night, in an attempt to bolster my courage, I had written lines of bravado: "Every man must find his own nirvana; and no man can guide him there." The words could not mask the guilt I felt, however, the belief even that long ago, in the shadow of the white mountain, I might have said something, done something, to prevent his catastrophe. I remained away from school the next day, broke a date for the following night, walked again down by the East River. I thought of my father and of my former classmates in Virginia, now the breathing dead, and I realized anew how vulnerable we all were, how prone to overwhelming disaster. There were, I knew, no guarantees in life, no one was absolutely secure from calamity, but I knew also that for us, the strain and stress of living in this white country enhanced our odds twofold. Later, during the week, after having been unable to down the despair on my own, I called Raphael, made an appointment, told him about David, about my observations.

"Isn't it possible," he asked, after lighting the panatella, "that your depression has to do with you as much as David?"

"If you mean," I admitted, ashamed, "that I thought it might happen to me, too, sure."

"No," I don't mean that. "That's normal; but something else."

I could think of nothing.

He moved from the leather chair, retrieved an ashtray, came back to stare directly at me. "All your life you wanted to be a big shot; now you're a big shot, and it bothers the hell out of you."

I do not like the term "big shot," it grates on my nerves, conjures up despicable images. "I came to talk about David," I said angrily.

"Like hell. Look, cut out the bullshit. You came to talk about you. Let's talk about you." He waved away my interruptions. "You've been scared shitless all your life. If you're so goddamn scared, how do you protect yourself? And never mind the bullshit about white people—you wanted to protect yourself from every goddamned body."

"Why the hell are you so fucking uptight?" I interjected, forcefully.

"Who says I'm uptight?"

"You act like it."

"So what? Don't I have a right to be uptight?"

"Look." I extended a forefinger.

"No! You look! If I'm uptight, what the hell does it mean to you? Except maybe you think it's your fault that I'm uptight?"

I sat bolt upright in the chair. Of course I thought it was my fault. I thought I had offended him, made him angry.

"Like all big shots," he went on, "you wanted to be feared, and liked. And so when I don't smile at you, talk rationally to you, have a bad day, curse, it means that I don't like you. But what the hell should any of this have to do with you? I have my own life, my own problems, frustrations, everything that you have."

I sighed, turned away from him. I did not need him now, at this point in therapy, to spell it out for me. He had his own problems: so did the Madonna, Rosalie, Yvonne, Ruth, my father, David.

"Now you see"—his voice became soft, compassionate—"what we've been getting at. All those defenses you erected as a child are still there. The needs too. How does a poor boy, Black or white, protect himself? He becomes a big shot. No one can touch him then. But if his defenses and needs remain the same, he can never be secure even as a big shot. He is still frightened; he thinks that something can still happen to him. In your case, there's something else: you not only had to save yourself; you had to save everybody: Rosalie, your mother, your sisters, your race, oppressed people, all your girl friends, David, God know who else."

"Look," I shouted, not sure of what I wanted to say, "Look. I think you're crazy. Some of that stuff—the big shot thing—there may be some truth in some of that. But that saving stuff . . . Look, I'm a writer; I don't like to see people unhappy, abused, persecuted; there's not much I can do. I do what I can."

He scowled, brought his face close to mine. "You're not being honest. That's the old rationale. You wanted to save people because you thought you were responsible for them. And because of that, people have tricked you all of your life.

You call it blackmail. But it worked both ways. I won't try to trick you—you've been tricked enough. But why the hell do you think you're responsible for what happened to other people? To Rosalie, your mother, your father, to David? You knew them for only a small part of their lives. You're like those mothers who come in here filled with guilt about their children, as if the children weren't open to other influences, as if what happened to them wouldn't have happened anyway. No, Addison, my friend, what happened to the people you know may have been bad, but you're not responsible. You're not."

"To assume responsibility for others," I confided later in my journal, "means to relieve the individual of responsibility for his own life, to seek to foster dependence and thereby control. People become abstractions, are transformed into objects of manipulation, are robbed of their humanity. Did I eve really believe it was my fault that David committed suicide, that Rosalie suffered? Or did I need to convince myself that I believed this? And how could I have made things different for either of them, how could I have dictated to them what their needs were, should have been, told them how to resolve their own conflicts? Neither would have listened to me, nor I to them. Both acted out of the patterns of their lives, confronted the terrors of living in the ways they knew best. In the battle against conflict they were their own best allies, and nothing that I could have done would have altered the outcome of their private wars. No, I could not save them. Only they could save themselves.

"I could offer solace, sympathy, compassion, comfort. But I could not fight their wars, could not save them; no, no more than I could save the Madonna. How could I make her pain more bearable—was it ever as unbearable as I had imaged? And if I were incapable of saving her, what right did I have to censure her, to think of her as my betrayer? Had she no life beyond what she had brought into being, no needs that were not secondary to mine, no right to exist but as an appendage to me?

"But what did all of this mean now for me? What good did it do to understand the past patterns of my life? What was I supposed to do? I could not, perhaps, radically alter them, even though I wanted to. The defenses I had erected during childhood had worked. I did not go to the electric chair. To be sure, fear propelled me through a great many experiences, but had it not been for that fear and anger, would I have come through, survived? So what if for most of my life I had shied away from close relations, feared rejection, sought instead isolation, alienation? Had I not done so, would I have been able to get through school, would I have acquired the discipline necessary to write? But further, if not for the terror of living, could I have continued to live?

"Raphael talks about happiness. But what does this mean? I am not as unhappy now as I was before; not in such a continual state of panic. What happened to me in that Brooklyn precinct house could very well, I know, happen again, but if it did, somebody would take notice; my friends would write about it, make an issue of it. And so what if I used my status and reputation to protect myself? Everyone needs protection and it is difficult to get from inside only. Even Raphael. He is proud of being a psychologist, defines himself, at times, in this way. And then there are the white people I am always meeting, who attempt to impress me with their credentials, informing me of the books they have written, the positions of importance they hold.

"And if this is the norm for white people, why not for Black people? Being a writer and professor does not make me better than other Blacks, but it offers a minimal kind of protection that I had never had before. Addison Gayle the writer and professor differs from Addison Gayle the porter and orderly because the former can wrap himself in a cloak of security that the latter would be denied. And why should I not wear this cloak, so long as I do not lose sight of the basic reality: Whenever the racial Armageddon comes, the common denominator for the writer and the porter is the Blackness of the skins of both."

Crises like that generated by David's death were almost nonexistent over the following months, and those that did occur, involving chance meetings with Rosalie, or disappointment over a romantic affair, no longer rekindled the old despair. I was helped along toward emotional recovery by the kind words being written about me by friends (even the unkind ones, by enemies, delighted me) and others engaged in the area of Black literature. Lecture invitations came steadily now, along with job offers from major colleges. My book *The Black Aesthetic* had been translated into Japanese and became, according to one critic, the manifesto of a new critical movement in American literature. My sessions with Raphael had become more philosophical than analytical, devoted more to how I would handle myself in the future than to what had happened to me in the past. "Whatever happened to you back there," he had said, "I can help you understand, but neither I nor you can undo. Besides . . . we both know, don't we, that much of the past was manipulated by you, perhaps because you had to, but nevertheless, it was."

Looking back into the past from this vantage point, it was not difficult to conclude with him that I had been either ingeniously my own best ally or my worst enemy. I, too, doubted seriously now if much of what had happened to me, if much of what I had considered crisis, had happened at all, been crises at all. Certainly, I had remained functional through everything, had never been completely immobilized, had used anger, fear, anxiety toward constructive ends. No, the past could not be undone, and I am not sure that I would want to undo it, that I would not, if given the option, relive it all over again. But it could be understood, and the way for me to do this was to do what I liked doing best—to write—this time to write about the past.

In 1971, after I had signed the three-book contract with Doubleday, the editor, Loretta Barrett, and I had decided that a series of personal articles, similar to those that I had compiled for *The Black Situation*, would constitute one of the books. Those articles had dwelt upon aspects of my past, had been autobiographical, but most of the essays had dealt with other topics, with literature, with the social and political aspects of the Black situation. In March of 1973, with the first book in the series, *The Way of the New World,* now behind me, and buttressed by the new more positive image of myself, I decided to write not a series of articles, but an autobiography in narrative form. During our March session, I effusively related my plans to Raphael.

"Maybe I'll begin with Seattle, with David and Rainier—I still see the mountain as a kind of rite of passage, see David as very important in everything. Then I'll use flashbacks, move backward to reveal as much of the truth as possible, try to place things in a rational, chronological order, move up through my life as an adult, come up to now, to the present."

"Are you a little scared?"

"I'm a lot scared. Not so much of confronting myself, but of confronting other people."

"How will you deal with that?"

"I don't know! I suppose I'll use images and symbols; words that say one thing and mean another."

"But you don't like that, do you?"

"No, it's dishonest. Writers, at least, should be honest."

Cynically: "Tell the truth, no matter what?"

"Well . . ." I thought of Leslie Berger. "Sometimes," he had said, "you hurt people by being honest." "As honest," I said, "as I can be."

"Do you see any dangers or rather, problems?"

"Only that much of it will be said, I guess, to people who thought they knew me; but I don't think on the whole, it will be sad."

"But your life has been, well, if not sad, certainly not very happy. The first book, as I remember, *The Black Situation,* that was sort of sad."

I recalled his comments after I discovered that he had gone to the library at the beginning of our sessions and read the book without my knowledge: "It was very touching." And I remembered the exchange that had followed:

Me: "I think it's funny."

Raphael: "Funny! I don't see a damn thing funny about your life!"

"If my life had ended," I continued explaining about the autobiography, "two years ago, last year, maybe my life would have been totally unhappy. I don't think so, but maybe you could say that it would have been. But nothing that has happened to me has not helped me. Everything, as I see it, has brought me to this point. Look: I've already lectured at four colleges this year. Three weeks from now, I go to a week-long seminar in Atlanta; two weeks after that I lecture again at the Sorbonne. If I hadn't had the kind of experiences I've had, hadn't undergone what I did, I might not be doing those things."

"On the other hand, you might not have had to . . ."

I repeated the words so often spoken between us, "Prove myself?"

"Yes."

"Maybe not. But maybe if I didn't have to prove myself, I wouldn't have lived. And I've lived. If I died today, I would know that I've lived. And, you know, I'm so sure that I want to be cured of what's bothering me. I don't want to be so afraid, and I'm not so much anymore. I'm not so uptight anymore. But being Black in this country means to always be prepared for war; I don't ever want to lose that attitude."

"You're ready to leave therapy now, aren't you?"

I lowered my head guiltily. "I suppose so."

"Why don't you?"

"I don't know."

"You're not so dependent on me. You never were, on anybody. I think that you could do very well without me. If not, you can always come back."

"I don't have to make up my mind now, do I?"

"Of course not, my friend. Whenever you're ready."

We remained silent. I avoided his eyes.

"Do you agree with me now," he changed the subject, "that you're different from other people not because you're Black, but because you're a writer?"

"Well . . ." I began hesitantly, relieved that we were moving to already covered ground.

"Don't think of being different as being weird or better than someone else. That's part of your hangup. Things are either one way or another. Think of different as having a sensitivity, an insight that maybe other people don't have. Maybe artists are different from other people, maybe you are different because you do something with your hangups, make them work for you."

This subject had constituted one of our most heated sessions. Afterward, I had written in my journal: "Why does Raphael want to make me less Black? I am not different from other Black people, only luckier. The feeling, the sensitivity is there, in each of us, but it comes out in different ways. Had I remained at the Brooklyn Army Base, never moved outside, I might have gone to jail or, worse, the electric chair. The anger and rage that goes into writing might have pushed me into other directions, might have made me a real Bigger Thomas. In becoming a writer, I simply rebelled in a much more socially acceptable way. This constitutes a difference, if at all, in terms of degree: The man who can murder on the printed page can do so time and time again and need not fear jail or death.

"But writing is not all about anger and rage, death and murder. It is also about love and compassion, about living and hoping. It is about morality and justice, about positive relationships between one human being and another, about beauty and splendor, about success and victory, about empathy and feeling; it is an attempt to make sense out of the absurdity of one's experiences. It is, to quote Baldwin, an act of love. And, in this sense, maybe Raphael, with Freud, is right; perhaps those who see, simultaneously, both beauty and ugliness, hatred land love, who feel anger and rage at the injustices leveled against people by others, who wish to interject a new sense of morality into the world, maybe such people are different. Maybe I am, in a sense, different from other people."

Still, sitting there looking at Raphael, it was difficult for me to voice aloud what I had written in my journal. I banged my pipe out in the metal ashtray, nodded in agreement, said by the shake of my head that I conceded my difference.

"Do you," he moved on, "think that you can deal with Rosalie now, truthfully, I mean, with your marriage, in a book?"

I avoided giving him a direct answer. We debated the question for the remainder of the session, but he knew as well as I that the real answer was not for his ears, but for the blank pages of my journal. That night, a bottle of wine at my elbow, I wrote: "The real problem is not so much Rosalie, but the guilt. The breakdown or near breakdown occurred because of the picture I had in my mind of myself. I thought of myself as a criminal, as one who had committed a crime. Yet, even if this were so, did the punishment fit the crime? Should I have been reduced almost to insanity for terminating a relationship? Suffering, I suppose, was natural, but at some point the suffering need end, the world had to be put back together again, life had to continue.

"And so it had to be for both of us. But I prolonged the suffering in my own mind. I conjured up fantasies of her in which she underwent the most terrible experiences—psychological, even physical injury—and all the time I was certain that none of this could happen to me, that I could not really be forced across the threshold of insanity. I could not allow such strength for her, could only view her as a pitiable child, destroyed by my criminality. I imbued her with my own feelings, molded her, made her a surrogate of my imagination. But she is a woman of tremendous strength. She has lived, survived, and her world has not come to an end. She set about with determination to put her world back together again, while I have only begun to do the same. And yet both of us stepped outside of our histories, breaking with traditions that had mentally enslaved us. We both came to realize that life was, above all, chaos and tumult—whatever order could be imposed, would be imposed by the individual. Two lovers, even, could determine the destinies not of each other, but of each singly, and this could be done only by facing the horrendous ordeal of the past.

"*Four months ago I could not call your name without feelings of self-pity, self-hatred, guilt and despair. Today, however, I can write about you, picture you not as abstraction, but as a human being; and instead of a sense of guilt, now, I feel a sense of loss for what might have been. But I know what there was, sometimes, despite all else. I recall still the gaiety and laughter, the dreams and the hopes; and then I am alive with the sense of living, of self-worth, of good feeling; and it is then that I realize that I have crossed the Rubicon.*"

CHAPTER 58

Black Fathers and Their Sons

Part I

(1970)

"I am sorry," wrote a friend, "for using a letter to you as an excuse for shedding so much sickness." Our weekly letters had been therapeutic nostrums for both of us. In these letters we breached that barrier between truth and half truth which always stood between us in any meaningful dialogue with the white world. We had flaunted our sickness, owned up to it, offered no apologies for our despair, our feelings of hopelessness, of hatred, of bitterness. For the first time, perhaps, we had acted as men: that is, vomited forth our truth, as every man must inevitably do.

For a long time, however, this was difficult. We had not trusted each other at first. Meeting in a graduate classroom of a large white university, we were both suspicious as to how the other had gotten there. How many timid-Negro grins had we bestowed on white professors in our respective undergraduate schools? How many of those white professors had we succeeded, using our Black skins as artillery, in frightening out of a grade? How many other Blacks had we left pulsating on the floor, as we hurriedly trampled over them for academic favors?

But more important: How many roles had we been forced to play? On what day, Uncle Tom, on what day, the Militant New Negro, and which of these roles had stuck with us, subconsciously clung to us, undiscernible to whites, yet glaringly revealed to any Negro? These things we had to find out about each other before either of us could be free to indulge his sickness.

For Negroes, to even engage in speculations about whites demands serious scrutinization of one's audience. If one's view is liberal, one is open to the charge of Uncle Tomism. If one's view is hostile, one is censured as militant. Each censure carries the same punishment: ostracism. Thus, Negroes in first meetings with one another must invariably wade through hours of meaningless dialogue, pretend the role of devil's advocate, quote profusely from both sides of the race question until one finally arrives at a decision as to the stand of one's companion.

My friend and I were diametrically opposed, and yet, despite this, we were united in our mutual unhealthy frame of mind. He had been brought up in the Booker T. Washington tradition: taught to believe that one could solve the problem of color by building a bigger ranch house than his neighbor. His parents had demanded of him that he excel, that he always come in first in the race, and those occasions on which he ran a poor second, he was severely chastised. His early life was one of continuous libraries, concerts, and weekly sermons at an educated Baptist minister's church. At thirteen years of age, he read Dickens, Tolstoy, and Emerson. At sixteen, he wrote his first essay: "A tribute to Abraham Lincoln."

At seventeen years of age, he graduated from high school, first in a class of one hundred and fifty, and four years later, he graduated from college, *summa cum laude*. Now, for the first time in his life, he was away from home, away from the watchful and protective eyes of middle class Negro parents, in a situation where firsts were as common as grains of sand.

My life had been entirely different. Exactly what my philosophical orientation was is difficult to tell. I was torn between two conflicting ideologies, and like Faust, I was inseparably bound to both proponents of these ideologies. My mother was immersed in the dogma of Christianity, and my father was submerged in the dogma of Karl Marx.

Somewhere in the early stages of my existence they had decided that each was to have a crack at me. I was subjected to Jesus Christ at nine o'clock on Sunday mornings, after which I was free to leave church and go to the vacant lot, next to a poolroom, where my father ministered every Sunday to the irreligious masses. It was as though I were Adam in the Garden of Eden and Gabriel and Satan were wrestling for my soul. At the outset, my mother had the inside track. Having been bribed (a dollar if I read it from cover to cover) into reading the Bible, I shared much of my mother's enthusiasm for Christianity. The stories of the creation and the revelation held a fascination for me, although I suppose that even then I was being unloyal to my mother's teaching: I had more than an underdog's sympathy for Satan, and I was more convinced that Judas was a victim of historical determinism than a conscious villain.

Nevertheless, my fondness for my mother coupled with her bribes early won me to her side. My father did nothing outwardly to counteract her influence. Shrewder than my mother and more pragmatic, he knew that the philosophy of Christianity, when confronted by the realities of my own experiences, would be proved untenable on its own merits. "No thinking Negro," he once remarked, "can remain a Christian." More principled than my mother, he offered no bribes. He bought me books written by Negroes, and instead of coaxing me to read them, he put faith in his evaluation of my own inquisitive nature to propel me in that direction in a way which a monetary bribe could not.

As a result, by the age of thirteen I had read *Souls of Black Folk* by W. E. B. Du Bois, the autobiographies of Frederick Douglass and Booker T. Washington, poems by Langston Hughes, the Carter G. Woodson series on Negro Life and History, and novels by Richard Wright, Claude McKay, and Jessie Fauset. In addition, from his well-stocked collection of Russian literature, I read, on my own, the Russian Masters: Pushkin, Gogol, Tolstoy, Chekhov, Turgenev, Dostoyevsky.

None of my reading of this material was accompanied by lectures from my father. Whereas my mother had thought it necessary to illustrate the truth of the Bible through symbolism and metaphor, my father, on the other hand, was content to let me arrive at my own truth. He had no doubt, in his own mind, as to what that truth would be. Convinced of the wrongness of the cause of Christianity and knowing that, as a way of life, Christianity could not survive the test of time, he felt that automatically, through despair, I would gravitate toward Communism as he had.

The road to Communism lay in a process of elimination, wherein one discarded capitalism in favor of this higher truth. It was as though he conceived of the world of the Negro as being enclosed only by these two philosophies. Capitalism, he stressed, was irrelevant to the Negro. In a world composed of bourgeois elements and proletarian elements all, despite the claims of the petit-bourgeoisie among them, were members of the proletariat. "Communism," he once wrote, "means, in a simplistic sense, the dictatorship of the proletariat. We Negroes are the proletariat; all we need is the dictatorship."

Thus, the route to truth led through the negation of the philosophy of Christianity (to him capitalism and Christianity were one and the same) to a cleansing, as he used the biblical phrase, of one's "sinful soul." Like Keats, he saw truth as beauty and, to paraphrase Samuel Coleridge, Communism as the divine ventriloquist through which that truth was made manifest: It became word, then flesh, then spirit. Despite his pragmatism, in this sense he was as romantic as my mother; although his romanticism had been manufactured out of a sense of despair.

A Negro intellectual in the thirties, his only choice was escapism or despair. Negroes were lynched at the rate of one every week; Black children in the schools, both segregated as in the South and integrated as in some parts of the North, were then, as now, cast like refuse upon the junkheap of American society. Race riots in which men, women, and children were brutally murdered and maimed were common occurrences in the North and South. Furthermore, the depression had hit hardest at the Negro, especially those in urban areas. Black men, often with children at their sides, stood in lines awaiting the dispensing of foodstuffs—sacks of meal, small white navy beans, and slabs of fat back (white, salted meat)—forced to bow and scrape before the white overseers of the program, or more frequently, to relinquish their position in line to late-arriving whites.

Despite personal knowledge to the contrary, the Negro intellectual was forced to ask, in his private soul, with W. E. B. Du Bois, suppose all that they say about us is really true? Suppose the descendants of Thomas Nelson Page and Thomas Dixon, who argue that the Black man's inferior position in the world is due to biological laws, the laws of nature immutable and unchangeable unless through the process of complete assimilation—suppose, after all, this is true.

Surely the objective evidence pointed to the Afro-American's inferiority. The lowest I.Q. scores were made by Blacks. The slowest students in the school system were Black. Black people had not built the great cathedrals, designed the mammoth bridges, discovered the great cures for disease, written the immortal literature. No Afro-American sat in the high councils of government, nor occupied any real seat of power. Furthermore, no Black then, as now, was out of the reach of white power: neither the uncontrolled fury of the lynch mob, nor the controlled fury of a racist policeman.

Confronted with this wall of insurmountable facts, the Negro intellectual was forced to look within, forced to take the excursion into self where truth reigned undistorted. Whatever calm, whatever peace was to be found by rejecting the outer reality and clinging to an inner subjective reality which could not be proved, either to the bigoted skeptics or more important, to one's loved ones: wife and child. Proudly, Ulysses remarks in Tennyson's poem by that name: "I have become a man!" Such a statement could not have been passed on from a Black father to his son. For the Black Telemachuses were wise children. They knew where the seat of power lay, knew their oppressors, and knew and resented the helplessness of their fathers.

The father was impotent, if not cowardly, in their eyes; somehow the father was blamed for the present, held responsible for the past, and dismissed as an important element in whatever the future would bring. At that level, it was impossible to understand him and easy to hate him. It was not important to the child that the father had not built the great cathedrals or created the great literature. What was important, however, was that the father had not torn down the signs which read "white" or "black" on the walls of public rest rooms, on public drinking fountains, and on buses and street cars. Moreover, the father had given them legality, had, in effect, acquiesced in his own emasculation by peaceful, passive compliance.

My father, I believe, felt this dual contempt—one from the outside world, the other from his son—more than most. At times, he would look at me with disdain, perhaps reading something in my eyes that I could not imagine to be there. Though we were the best of friends, and I loved and respected him deeply, he knew that in reality we were enemies. I was the young Hamlet who sooner or later would be forced to thrust the dagger into his heart, forced to stamp out his life in order to be free of the guilt which I felt, and would feel, so long as he lived. For me, he would have had to die to become a man; take a hammer, go forth and rip down those infamous signs, be shot in the process, in order to give life to me.

He knew what I felt for he, too, had deserted the God of his father. "My father," he once remarked, "was a weak, spineless man asking the white God to do the things that he didn't have the courage to do himself." He knew that these were the words which I would eventually hurl at him. Out of his despair, like his father, he had taken unto himself a God, asked it to perform miracles, to open the gate to the promised land, to smite his enemies, to release his children from bondage, to let his people go.

After having seen the world go down in death, doom, and destruction, he had accepted a new God, in an attempt to assure himself that life would go on, that order would once again be restored, that optimism was not yet dead. And in this respect he was like my mother. Neither could believe in futility, neither could postulate an existence devoid of the props, the machinery of infantile optimism; each in his own way placed more faith than he should have in the human species, in man, in his ability to transcend, to treat his fellow man as another human being with Christ, or as an integral part of any possible society with Marx.

Both veered toward this common faith and belief in mankind, and both, at this point, believed in conversion. The sinner could be saved, the oppressor redeemed, the executioner transformed. Mankind had, despite historical evidence to the contrary, the inner strength and conviction to build the great society in which all men would live free and unmolested by outer forces. Neither believed in a complete philosophy of nihilism, neither would have supported the argument of Turgenev's Bazarov that I don't know what comes after, and I don't care, I only know that what exists now must be destroyed. Neither would go that far, neither would throw optimism to the winds in exchange for complete negativism; neither would believe the fallen angel to have fallen below the level of redemption. For both, this was an area beyond their comprehension, and for this reason perhaps, both would awaken to the sad truth that in the quest for my soul both would be losers.

True to her Christian upbringing, my mother took the fact of my betrayal with stoic suffering. Sometimes now, I suppose, she still prays for me, hoping that the prodigal will—if not return to the house of his God—at least find peace. My father, on the other hand, took defeat very hard. Partly it was due to the guilt which he harbored for having forsaken his own father; partly it was because he was shrewd enough to know that every Black Hamlet, like himself, had held a knife poised at the breast of a father, and that only by acquiescing in the death of the father could the son be free. But more important, in rejecting his philosophy, I was, in a sense, rejecting his attempt to convince me of his manhood, telling him in effect that he was not at war with society, but instead engaged in a mock skirmish in which no decisive victories could be won. I was throwing all his theories into disrepute, telling him that the process of negation was an unsure one, that a Communist heaven was as bad as a Christian one, and that perhaps, the alternatives to both heavens was hell.

At sixteen years of age, I unsheathed the dagger. Having been selected as a finalist in an oratorical contest, I chose as my subject, "The Myth of Gods." In the speech I attacked Christianity, democracy, and Communism, saving my heaviest criticism for Communism. "Just," I said in words which would rankle within my father's conscience, "as Christianity was spawned by white men, so will Communism or any ism be spawned by white men; to believe, then, that one will work, when the other will not, though both have the same mother is to be unrealistic;

no gods spawned from the brains of white men can do other than enslave Black men; we must, therefore, rid ourselves of all the white gods, regardless of what names they go by." I had opened the wound. In the audience, my father looked up at me, frowned, and shook his head. That night, alone in the living room, the wound was opened further. "You can't go through life hating every one," he said, "believing in nothing; your speech was a speech of hatred. You denigrate the human race, all of it; this should not be. You must never lose sight of what is good in men, of what is beautiful in the human spirit. Life is a challenge, not a formula already set down for someone to build a paradise upon; no, one must work for paradise; one must work for a good world; and one must believe in people, for people will make this world."

"You sound like Momma," I retorted. "And this is your problem: Your God is no Blacker than hers, your paradise no nearer than hers, your prophets no more accurate than hers. Perhaps both of you need Gods; perhaps all the Black people in this country need Gods; but I don't. I don't need any Gods; for having forsaken Momma's God, I have forsaken all Gods."

We would continue to be friends, although the bond of father-son had been irreparably severed. His world was as dead to me as was the world of my mother. I was orphaned, with nothing to comfort me, to warm me, but the dagger of my mind. I was alone, a voluntary outcast, alienated from those whom I deeply loved, at an age when no young man should be alone. Unlike Faust, I had refused to sell my soul, perhaps, because I believed neither in God nor the devil. Furthermore, I believed, as my father had said, in nothing. Like Bigger Thomas, my life, to quote Baldwin, "was surrounded by hate." However, more sophisticated than Bigger Thomas, I did not release my frustrated hatred by killing—perhaps I would have undergone a healthy catharsis by doing so. But I did not. I moved in a world of shadows, incomprehensible to anyone but me. I sought for values within, conscious of the fact that I would have to make my own, that there was no blueprint for me to follow.

I knew what every Hamlet knows: that the values by which the father lives are untransferable, and if the Hamlet is Black, this is even truer. Each Black child must dig his own way out of the mud and stench of twentieth-century life, must create his own values. and no Black father can hand his values down to his son. I believe that my father, too, recognized this, despite the fact that he could never bring himself to admit it. Like all revolutionaries, he was committed to revolution only on his terms. To argue that the social order needed to be destroyed was to him indicative of one's intelligence and progressivism; on the other hand, to suggest that his blueprint for the reconstruction of society was not the right one was to indicate reaction and ignorance.

Moreover, to suggest, as I had done, that the father was not, and could not be, the guiding light, the shining beacon heralding the advent of the son into the world, was treacherous. And for this he never forgave me. It was not that he became rude or antagonistic toward me; he simply became indifferent. He read my essays on Negro novelists, scrutinized my short stories, and listened to my recitals of speeches on the American Democracy for high school classes. Yet all of this he did as a critic, completely objective, holding his opinions within. By the time I graduated from high school, we had become almost totally estranged. Communication had broken down; it was as if we were separated by a gulf which transcended the years, a gulf spanning the very history of the Negro's relationship to society and his fellow man. We had found out things about each other, things of the spirit, which had made us incompatible as father and son.

Despite his radicalism, for him the spirit of the times and of his soul was the spirit of Western humanism emanating from the Greek city state to the present day. Urbane and sophisticated, he would have fitted into the turbulent times of the eighteenth century, not as a Black man but as a white man. For him, therefore, it was not a search for identity but simply being able to hold onto his identity against those who would rob him of it. A leader, he was as far from his followers in temperament, hopes, fears, and anxieties as the pretender to the British throne from his fellow countrymen, and it was to his credit that he refrained from evidencing disgust or contempt for followers who would not make good citizens, even in his own utopia.

My argument against him was that he had misjudged both the spirit of the times and the spirit of his own soul. How he could adhere to the philosophy of the enlightenment was beyond me; and how he could have sacrificed his integrity in clinging to an identity vouchsafed by a society which was but the result of a tradition which he should have hated and despised I could not understand.

Long before James Baldwin and Lorraine Hansberry, I had decided that I did not want to be integrated into a burning house. More specifically, I wanted to be instrumental in setting that house aflame, in watching it burn to a crisp. My spirit was more than revolutionary, for each revolutionary is necessitated by the dogma which produces him to present an alternate plan, to build a better mousetrap than the one which he would displace.

No such strictures bound me. Having decided through empirical evidence—the day-by-day experience of being Black in America—that my condition was the worst, my interests were simply in ameliorating that condition; if my condition were indeed the worst, then no plan was necessary, what came after was academic. The country should be set to flames, gutted from one city to another, and the survivors should sit atop the dying embers and dream of the new society. But the dream was possible only after—not before—the Apocalypse had occurred.

These are the views which earlier separated me from my father, and later separated me from my friend in graduate school. Like my father, he, too, was more "Anglo Saxon than the Anglo Saxons." His world was the world of Jefferson, Emerson, Hemingway, and Faulkner by way of default. He studied these men, and in studying them formed a mystical union between himself and them which gave him a badge in the society. He never questioned the fact that he was wed to corpses, that the thoughts and ideas of his heroes were thoughts not applicable to millions of Black men, and therefore not applicable to him. He had never been able to think in such terms.

Like my father, he thought, in terms of a cosmology which included all mankind, irrespective of the fact that other Blacks were not included in this select club. The exclusion of his brothers did not bother him, however. What bothered him most of all was the fact that they (other Negroes) remained as a constant embarrassment to him. The rioting by Black people throughout the country cast him in a new light, made him visible to his white friends who had previously found his disquisitions on Wordsworth, Pope, and Shelley to be illuminating. Now they wanted his opinions on Negroes, on the riots, on the possibility of wide-scale violence between Black and white.

Against his will he was called upon to interpret the Black revolution, and none of his friends realized that he was incapable of doing so. The gulf between himself and the Black rioters was a very wide one, widened over the years by his family and friends, each attempting to convince him that the concept of Negritude was a joke, that man was an individual, and that no man's fate was inexplicably bound to that of another. He had, because of this, become a man with no allegiance, a man with no real identity, estranged in a society where the words individuality and brotherhood constantly clash with one another.

Yet, in being called upon to interpret a new phenomenon, one of which he knew very little, he was destined, in the course of his explorations, to confront the realities of his existence as a Black man in the American society. For the first time he was forced to examine the concept "Negro Intellectual" and see behind the concept the vicious categorization in microcosm of what was more full blown in the life of the average Afro-American. For a "Negro Intellectual," like a "Negro Leader," was a special brand of Negro, yet, Negro nonetheless. The teachers who had singled him out as a "brilliant young Negro" were paying him a left-handed compliment, creating for him a special class in order to be able to more accurately distinguish him from the all-inclusive class into which his Black skin had placed him. Yet over and above him stood that class for which all of his training had prepared him, toward which his mother and father in their constant cajolings had pushed him, to which on the strength of intellect, accomplishment, and ability he duly belonged.

He therefore realized, for the first time, how complete his rejection really was, and too, he realized the extent of his alienation. He was, to paraphrase Mathew Arnold, a wanderer between two worlds, one he wanted dead and the other he was powerless to bring to life. Somehow fate had cheated him. He was equipped to be white in everything but skin color, and to the deepest part of him, he desired to be white. He was convinced that Western civilization was God's greatest gift to man, and that only those capable of being a part of Western civilization were deserving of the appellation civilized. Unlike James Baldwin, he would have had no perplexing problems in looking upon the Chartres Cathedral. He would have taken it for his own, mainly because of his ability to interpret its beauty, gazed upon it with the scrutiny of a scholar, and felt a common bond between himself and its creator.

Yet he would awaken to the horrible reality that the Chartres Cathedral was not for the likes of him. No knowledge of the great works of antiquity—of Aeschylus, Homer, Sophocles, Milton, Chaucer—could compensate for his Black skin. The society had created one measuring rod by which to gauge him, one criteria by which to determine his worth, one set of guidelines to define his humanity, and in so doing relegated him forever and despite all to a special niche in its own cosmological scheme.

And none of his "firsts" could help him! How many times must he have sat—as all Blacks sometimes sit—alone in seclusion with his private soul and reflected on the contradictions inherent in this society. He had been told that diligence, application, and perseverance were the pathways to dignity and recognition as a human being. Manhood, he had thought, was to be earned by testing oneself against those supposedly one's equal, beating them in those pursuits supposedly their private domain. This he had done, and his brilliant record supported the assertion. He was not only good enough to be among them, but in most cases good enough to be above them.

Yet day by day he was threatened by those same monsters which beset every Black man in America: His dignity was affronted by the corner clerk, called into question by a taxicab driver, denied by a white laborer on any public transportation, and annihilated by any racist policeman. He was as helpless, as trapped, as victimized as any Negro, in any ghetto, in any part of the country; yet, he was limited in a way in which they were not. He was not free to burn down buildings, to man the rooftops and snipe at his oppressors, to wield the broken bottle, to hurl the cold, crumbling brick. Still holding to the dream, he was unable, like Bigger Thomas, to even blunder into manhood by taking another life, by being destructive, by releasing the pent-up emotion now beginning to come to the surface of his conscience.

The society which had conditioned him to believe that he was different, that he was not like other Negroes, that he was a special case, had helped to transform him into a sick, frustrated, neurotic young man: a Dr. Jekyll–Mr. Hyde personality in which the two opposing identities could not always be precariously balanced. As Dr. Jekyll, he yearned for recognition from white America, courted its approval, desired its benevolence; as Mr. Hyde he desired destruction, courted violence, and wished for, perhaps, self annihilation. The key to his survival, then, would lie in his ability to maneuver between these two roles, to shift identity at will, yet to be always conscious that he was shifting roles, to insure that he would. not inadvertently become Dr. Jekyll forever—an identity which could only lead to further confrontations with reality—nor become Mr. Hyde for all times—a role which would lead him to either cut his throat or dedicate himself to nihilism.

Like my father, perhaps he was destined to become a piteous old man existing on a dream because to let go of the dream was to court disaster. He, too, saw salvation in terms of a white God, irrespective of the facts of history that all white Gods had succeeded in betraying their Black subjects. Neither he nor my father would allow himself the luxury of complete, everlasting hatred, the surrender of the soul forever, for eternity, to that Mr. Hyde part which dared to thunder forth the incontestable statement: this is the worst.

Idealists destined for senseless martyrdom, theirs would always be the world of inaction, of stagnation, of frustration. They shouted for freedom when what they really wanted was respect; they clamored for equality when what they really sought was recognition. If the scholars bred in the tradition of Western civilization were to write their epitaphs, they would accord them special niches among the martyred. For me, however, they have written their own epitaphs. They were children in a world which cries out for men; they were dreamers in a world in which only the nightmare has reality; they were liars in a world which needs truth; they were conservatives at a time when revolutionaries are necessary; they were martyrs, and like all martyrs, they deserved their crosses.

Yet, in his last letter, my friend had begun to realize the extent of his sickness, and this may yet save him from the cross. However, he had only reached purgatory: the realization. Heaven, the acting upon the realization, lay some many years in the future. Perhaps, like my father, he will never get to heaven; perhaps he will remain for the rest of his life in purgatory, warring with shadows instead of concrete, material things—I do not really know. I stopped writing to him because I could not communicate with spirits in purgatory; we were too far apart, too great a gulf separated his purgatorial world from my heavenly one; yet that he could ever reach my heaven is doubtful. To do so he would have to be born again, undergo the transformation from adult to childhood and begin the long road upward. He would have to find his identity not in Western civilization but in that mutilated species of humanity which Frantz Fanon has called the wretched of the earth. In short, he would have to become Black in mind, body, and soul.

Thirteen years ago, I sat in my father's small book-filled room looking up at this tired man who, I knew, still bore the scar of my dagger. We did not look each other squarely in the face, perhaps because he realized that there was no longer an equality between us. The roles had been changed. I was on my way to becoming the man that he had never been able to be, free in a way far beyond his wildest expectations. He was old, decrepit, and dispirited, clinging to life with that same selfish tenacity with which he had clung to his dream: that tomorrow the world would be better, and thus a good place in which to die. "I hope," he said to me, hardly above a whisper, "that when you finish your education, you will go out and help your people, educate them, as I have tried to do."

"No," I replied, staring at him, searching for those eyes which he kept hidden from me; "No, I will not try to educate them; they will educate me. Perhaps they will teach me to make fire-bombs, and give me the strength and courage to throw them at the nearest slum building. I will go to them, not to teach, but to learn—to learn the things that no white God could ever teach me."

We said nothing more after that. Now and then he attempted to scan my face, to catch me unaware, and look into my eyes, but he could not bring himself to make the face-to-face confrontation. He would probably have liked to assure himself that I was not really his son, that I was some stranger, sent to betray his faltering eyesight. Even then he could not forgo illusion in an attempt to deny reality. He saw not me, but a shadow, and that shadow was unreal, incomprehensible, and strange. I left shortly after kissing him on the cheek and grasping his hand in a pretense at affection. I did not see him alive again; he died six weeks later, the world no better nor worse than the day he was born.

CHAPTER 59

Black Fathers and Their Sons

Part II

(1970)

I did not cry at my father's funeral. Standing between my sister and aunt, trying not to look at the waxen figure before me, I folded and unfolded my arms, stared down at my feet and up at the faces of Black people who had come to say goodbye to him. The reason that I did not cry had nothing to do with our recent estrangement. We needed each other too much to have remained estranged for long. There was no question of my love for him, for I loved him very much even though he did things which pained me deeply.

I was not sorry that he was dead! That may not have been my expressed opinion at the time, for I was young and not yet so cynical. I realize now that not only was I not sorry that he was dead, but I looked upon his death as a blessing. I am no longer young, and I am now quite cynical. In this respect, I am different from my father. I cannot recall his ever uttering a cynical remark. In fact, he reserved his bitterest criticism for cynics. "They are men who believe that reality is fixed and cannot be changed," he often said, "and when one reaches that conclusion about the world, he can never change anything; he is better off dead."

Perhaps I believed that a great deal depended upon whether one considered reality to be worth changing. My father, on the other hand, assumed that a world in which men were victims of institutions and governments needed changing; and he would accept neither oppressors nor oppressed as fixed realities in a world ruled by men. Both oppressed and oppressor, he believed, were the products of corrupt governments and institutions, and he would not allow governments or institutions to define reality for him. A student of Jean Jacques Rousseau, he believed in the innate goodness of man. He saw the city-state as the first community of man to be organized around a political leader. Corruption set in when, out of a desire to unite their community with God, the religious scribes attributed divine power to the political leader. The king was anointed, and at that moment man lost the privilege of defining reality for himself. For the duty of the king, to paraphrase Plato, is to define reality for his subjects.

In my father's peculiar cosmological system, however, the king was not responsible for encroaching upon the freedom of his subjects—the system that spawned the king was culpable. Power corrupts to be sure, but whether the corruption is absolute or relative depends upon the allegiance one owes to his fellow man. The power of the king was not vouchsafed by the people. It was his by divine right. Therefore, the king's allegiance was not to the people but to the divine order of things. The solution was not complex. Behead the king and destroy the divine order. Thus, power would pass to the people, and they, free to construct their own universe, would set about defining themselves.

My father had been drugged by the opiate of Marxism. He was a romantic in a world where mankind metes out its harshest punishment to romantics and martyrs. He was the forerunner of those who today shout "Power to the people," although he was far more honorable than they. He sincerely wished to see power placed in the hands of the masses; even though he realized that the moment the masses obtained power, intellectuals like himself would be among the first to be assigned to the wall.

Part of our difficulty with one another stemmed from his romanticism. He was so romantic about people and the world around him that for a long time I believed him to be mad. A forceful orator, he was often called upon to speak on behalf of the Communist Party; but, privately or publicly, his speeches always contained references to the coming revolution in which the American people, rising as one, would throw off oppression and unite under the banner of brotherhood. He did not believe in separatism, and although he often castigated "Mr. Charlie" with the vehemence of a Malcolm X, his was a dream in which Black, yellow, brown, and white men walked shoulder to shoulder in unity.

We are indebted to Franz Fanon for predicting the coming war between the haves and the have-nots, between the machine men and the natural men. My father reached a similar conclusion in the nineteen forties. In his speeches he argued that the have-nots would engage the haves in a bloody revolution and that the have-nots, who outnumbered the haves, would finally win. Like some Black militants at the present time, he believed in an alliance of Black and white radicals, and his allegiance to the Communist Party was due, in part, to the fact that it made such an alliance possible.

This constituted the most irrational and romantic aspect of his philosophy. Even at the age of nineteen, I was suspicious of alignments with white people. When I questioned his judgment on this point, he was quick to answer that "many white people were more revolutionary than Black people," which proved nothing to me except that, even in the area of revolution and rebellion, whites were accorded a greater degree of freedom than Blacks. He was so obsessed with the desire to remake the world, to march at the head of an integrated revolution, that, unlike Richard Wright, he failed to understand the full implication of the American-Soviet pact in 1942. In an act of expediency, the Communist Party decided to "lay the Negro question aside" at a time when one Black man was lynched in

America every day. Today, the Communist Party is the greatest opponent of Black Nationalism.

"Those who ignore history are doomed to repeat it," wrote Bismarck. The statement was meant for those who survive history, not those who perish. The children of men who have survived the holocaust, who managed to come through unscathed, soon forget that they are descendants of victims, that oppression was leveled against their fathers, and pledge undying fealty to God and country.

The reason is clear. Each man recoils in horror at the idea that the term victim might be applied to him. No man wants to be a victim nor admit that he is one. To be Emperor of Rome is far more satisfying than to be impaled upon the bloody nails of the cross. The children of victims begin to fantasize about oppression: Tyranny was always directed against some other people, some other race, some other group of dissenters. The chances are that such people brought damnation upon their own heads. They pushed the government too far, contested the wrong decisions of the majority group, or, more likely, deserved the punishment they received.

I remember a Japanese professor, an expert on brain disease working with monkeys which he had come to prefer to people, standing in his laboratory at the University of California, the tears running down his face, asking "Why did they lock me up? They took me out of school and locked me up. Why me?"

He addressed the question to me. The Indians could have given him a better answer. These first victims of American oppression evidence how far Americans will travel along the road to racial genocide. The Indian population once outnumbered that of many nations in the world today. That population has been depleted like the herds of buffalo which once supplied the Indians with food. Today, the children of the holocaust live on the largesse of the children of their persecutors, packed on reservations, hungry men in a land of affluence. To those who deign to listen, the folklore and dances of the Indian people tell of persecution unsurpassed in the annals of human history.

Theirs, however, is the history of the victim, and men want no part of it. Like the Japanese professor, they are content to live secure in the belief that times have changed, that the new Americans are different from the old, that the tyrant has reformed; until one day the bubble bursts, reality transplants illusion, and one is forced to ask the question "Why me?" The answer given by the historian is not likely to be the true one. The victim lives history, seldom does he write it. Those to whom this task is entrusted are usually master distorters, more concerned with appearance than actuality. If one reads American history textbooks, for example, *The Epic of America* by James Truslow Adams, he is likely to wonder why the Indians were not slaughtered to the man. They were savages incapable of building the great society, uncultured, uncivilized, content to allow the wealth of America to remain underground. Stumbling blocks in the path of progress, they deserved their fate; and a nation ordained by God to establish life, liberty, and the pursuit of happiness on earth, measured out their fate with the barrels of many rifles.

Are men ignorant of such facts of history as the genocide of the Indians? Not ignorant, naive! In the nineteen forties, when the symbol of man's reality was the concentration camp, when one Black man was lynched every day, my father remained convinced that Black people would not be exterminated *en masse* by white Americans. Naiveté knows no time barrier. Today, when the American government exploits South Americans, napalms Vietnamese, and keeps half the world in ignorance and poverty, some Blacks refuse to believe that they will fall victim to similar acts of persecution.

"Black people," I wrote at the age of nineteen, "are a people alone; we have no allies and no friends. We face the darkness alone." My father, upon reading these words, became very angry. He realized that I was challenging his concept that each man, but for corrupt governments and institutions, would be his brother's keeper. He answered me in the usual way, that is, he flaunted his knowledge and ridiculed my ignorance. "What do you know," he shouted, "what do you know about allies? I know about allies! I know that we have allies! Look at Russia, look at China, look at the workers in every country of the world." I did not reply. There are those illusions which men must retain in order to hold on to their sanity. Had there been no Marx, he would have become as devout a follower of Christ as he became of the author of *Das Kapital*. As it was, he believed that the Marxian truth was the truth for all men, and the fact that men acted out of motives of greed, hate, and prejudice did not deter him from a belief that governments and institutions, not people, were to blame.

His romanticism prevented him from realizing the most profound truth of all: the victim is a man alone, and he will perish or survive according to his own ingenuity or resources. This statement is more true for the victim in America than for those in most other countries. The tendency for the victim to confuse himself with the oppressor in America is very strong. Most Black militants are honorable men, far more idealistic and moral than the gentlemen of the N.A.A.C.P. They are committed to ending racism, and they are also committed to a world order in which each man will be free to choose his own destiny. They interpret freedom to mean release from economic oppression, from the burdens of war, and from the excesses of local and national police power.

Dig deeply into their rhetoric and you will unearth a world in which men of all ethnic, racial and religious groups live together in a communal society, share communal affluence, and sup from a communal trough. They prophesy the day of the coming millennium when the existence of the millionaire and the hungry man will have come to an end, when no man will live in a mansion or in a rat-infested tenement, when no man will possess more of the earth's bounties than his neighbor. One would imagine that men who hold such thoughts, who see such visions, would have little trouble in recruiting followers, especially among Black people for whom dreams and visions are necessary artifacts of life.

The majority of Blacks, however, are more comfortable with the program of the N.A.A.C.P.—with accommodation instead of solution: let us make our pact with Mephistopheles, on our terms if we can, on his if we must. Every man wants the good things of life, even if to attain these he must sell a pound of flesh or his brother. What is needed, runs the rhetoric of the N.A.A.C.P. spokesmen, is not a new system but a new technician, one who will retune the old system, remove the bugs, and make it work for the majority of the people.

Ivan Karamazov is anathema to the men of the N.A.A.C.P., who have managed to grow fatter in a country where other Black men grow angrier. Only the subversive thinks in terms of all or nothing, of saving all men or no men. Nothing in the history of mankind argues the fact that all men can be saved or are worth saving. The race belongs to the swift; the spoils to the victor. We are again with Pavlov and his dogs, and he who seeks to be rewarded must respond to the sound of the right bell. Unlike Black militants, the men of the N.A.A.C.P. do not think of replacing the bell with another whose sound will ring true for all men. Among the beneficiaries of the spoils system, they seek to keep it intact with only slight modifications here and there.

A poll in the June 30, 1969, issue of *Newsweek* shows that the majority of Black people support the N.A.A.C.P. There is no reason to distrust the polls. Few Blacks see themselves as victims; fewer still are dedicated to dismantling the oppressive American apparatus in total. Men who make five thousand dollars a year, own cars and television sets, and are daily reminded of starvation in Biafra, poverty in Haiti, and apartheid in South Africa, are inclined to support the American system, not destroy it.

How then is Christ to be reconciled with the devil? One must, at least, convince each that the same tyrant rules them both, that the rewards lavished upon one today may be replaced by punishment tomorrow. One does not appeal to morality! Both Christ and the devil have lived in the world too long, have become too sophisticated to accept appeals based upon morality. Therefore, one leaves morality to the ministers and appeals to his comrades on the basis of self interest. Whether my Black neighbor likes me as a person or not, my interests and his are the same. The guard who leads me to the concentration camp today, will come back for him tomorrow. If he did not know this before, the events of the last year have done much to educate him.

In the presidential campaign of 1968, Richard Nixon and Spiro T. Agnew dedicated themselves to the task of eliminating crime in the streets and restoring law and order. Undoubtedly this job could have been better performed by George Wallace. Americans, however, are gentle assassins; they would rather starve a man slowly than kill him outright. They elected a sophisticated stand-in for George Wallace as president, and a model closer to the original as vice president. The turn to the right at the national level was accelerated at the local level. In the mayoral primary elections of 1969, the citizens of Minneapolis nominated a policeman, in Los Angeles they nominated a racist, and in New York they nominated a fascist.

The people, came the message from the White House, are getting fed up with disturbances on the nation's campuses, demonstrations, and crime in the street. Backlash is a phrase created by sensation-seeking journalists. The American people are not bigots and racists, are not opposed to Blacks having their rights. Let us bury the Kerner Commission report in the archives along with the Myrdal report; nations are not obligated to accept the findings of men who study them. Sane men, however, do not adhere to the existence of a backlash. Frontlash is a less sensational phrase, but far more accurate a description than the former. What has happened in the country at large is a national regurgitation of long submerged hate. The American cool and poise is eroding under duress. The true national character is emerging in all of its hideousness. Black militants did not create bigotry in America; their actions have not transformed men into fascists overnight. Those who today call for "putting the nigger in his place" did not issue the demand yesterday, for yesterday the nigger was content to stay in his place. This is no longer the case. Beginning with the Black Power movement in 1966, Black people initiated a sustained, vigorous drive to eradicate "special places" from the institutions of American life. This meant, in the words of the Black Panther slogan, that white Americans would move over or be moved over. Having grown accustomed to patient, passive, compliant Blacks, the American white middle class, secure in its own place, looked for a hero to return the nation to sanity, to reinstitute the status quo, to bring back the "We shall overcome years," to put the nigger back into his place. Heroes are difficult to come by in the American society, and thus, the white middle class was forced to dig back into the past, to manufacture one out of old, discarded timber. In 1969, Richard Nixon became the 37th president of the United States.

Those who elected him president with the belief that he would "put the niggers in their places" are not, it appears, to be disappointed. The school desegregation guidelines and the voting rights bill are being amended in ways calculated to mini-mize their effectiveness. Anti-poverty programs are being overhauled and many may be scrapped altogether. Black Nationalist organizations are being infiltrated, militant Black leaders harassed, and, in some cases, jailed. The concentration camps are being made ready, and no Black man can be sure that before long he will not be one of its inmates.

We have come close to racial Armageddon. The scripture applies to men and nations alike: Those whom the gods would destroy they first make mad; and America is going through a night of madness. Police departments purchase the heavy machinery of war, shopkeepers arm their help, old ladies in Dearborn, Michigan, take target practice, Jewish youths in Brooklyn form defense leagues, citizens in Chicago join vigilante groups, and the children of former victims prepare to make war upon the victims of the present. "And we are here," wrote Matthew Arnold, "as on a darkling plain/ Swept with confused alarms of struggle and flight,/ Where ignorant armies clash by night."

For Black people, there are no darkling plains. "Let us not die like hogs," wrote the Black poet Claude McKay in 1927, and the statement holds true today. We do not want to die at all. Only the insane are eager to exchange life for death. Pain is unbearable, but death is unknowable, and men would rather take their chances with the unbearable than with the unknowable. No, Black men do not want to die. But if die we must, then die we will. And we will not die like hogs; we will not be annihilated without taking a fair toll of the oppressor; we will not cleanse this earth with our blood alone; we will not be lined against the wall without offering strong resistance; we will not march to the concentration camps singing "We shall overcome." We will die! And we will die alone. But we will not die passively, on our knees, shouting to some impotent Jesus, "Lord, forgive them for they know not what they do."

I remained beside my father's grave long after the others had gone. I would miss him in the years to come. I seldom obeyed his counsel, but I was glad that he was around to give it. In fighting so continuously against him, I prepared myself for that much more vicious war with this country. When I left his grave late that night, I still had not cried.

And why should I have cried? The father who died was more fortunate than the son who lived. He lived for fifty-six years, and during this time, his only major disappointment was his son. He lived at a time when hope was still possible, when the chances of an end to the American racial nightmare were a probability, when the world seemed ready to steer clear of nuclear catastrophe. At the time of his death, he still clung fervently to his belief that mankind was moving toward creating a society in which the haves and the have-nots would share the world's abundance together. Many times the world disappointed him, but it never gave him cause to be bitter. He saw the rise of new Black nations and he saw Black men governing those nations. He saw strides taken in the area of human rights in America, and he was convinced that these strides foreshadowed the day when race would have no part in American life. He died as he lived, neither disillusioned nor despondent. In twentieth century America, he lived as a romantic and died—a romantic still. In light of such accomplishments, to have cried at his funeral would have been irreligious.

CHAPTER 60

The Children of Bigger Thomas

(1968)

Shortly after having been appointed an instructor of English at the City College of New York, I wandered into the faculty dining room and sat alone, taking a seat far away in the corner and hoping, despite my Black skin, to maintain a sense of anonymity. I had scarcely seated myself and placed my order, however, when a young lady, herself a new appointee, calmly walked over and sat at my table in a chair directly facing me.

Though the waitress had already taken my order, I continued to stare at the menu. Finally the silence became embarrassing. Then my guest spoke—some nonsensical amenity, mistaking me for an old-timer.

"No." I replied, "I'm very much new."

"Oh!" She answered. "I'm new too; in Social Science, and you?" "English," I replied, looking away from her blue eyes.

"Oh, one of those." She pursed her lips. "I was always a poor English student. Are you full-time?"

"Yes," I answered. "Very full."

The waitress came to take her order. I lit my pipe and stole a glance at my dinner partner. She was young, perhaps twenty-one or two, with close-cropped hair and a fine Nordic chiseled face. She looked like a caricature of the white liberal.

We talked about literature. Yes, she too had disliked Henry James. She had never been able to see much in Tolstoy. Kafka was too frightening. Hesse was frightening, too, but in a more optimistic way. And then, suddenly, almost unnoticeably, somehow sneaking into the conversation was the name of James Baldwin. "I think Baldwin's great, though I don't agree with everything he says," she said.

I nodded my head. First sideways, then up and down.

She continued. "I don't believe that all Negroes are as pessimistic as Baldwin. Take *The Fire Next Time*. It's chilling—I mean, almost frightening. You feel, I guess, if you're a Negro, like cutting your throat; at least I would."

The waitress came with our meals. I started on the soup, avoiding the eyes of my guest. I wanted to avoid her, to get up and move away. She was coming too close, moving in on me. Somewhere along the line we would cross over into that Netherland, where I hope never to have to confront white people. I preferred no dialogue at all, but since one was forced upon me, I wanted to restrict the dialogue to literature.

Literature is a nice, neutral topic. Men may argue about it without becoming involved in the perilous search for truth. One may wander in the dead world of Fielding, Dickens, or Hemingway and remain on common ground. Thus, too, one should be able to argue about James Baldwin. Yet I knew from past experience that this was not so. James Baldwin was like the transitional phrase in grammar—a bridge to another idea; and invariably this other idea involved the wishes, hopes, anxieties, feelings, thoughts, and beliefs of other Black people.

This constitutes the most difficult part of any dialogue with white people. Like Saunders Redding, "I have been clothed with no authority to speak for others." A mere statement of this fact, however, has never been enough to silence my white friends. For despite this admonition, I am asked to give my views, to say what I think, and at this point we are both in the Netherland.

The Netherland is my own private Gethsemane, that place in which I rid myself of that Ancient Mariner complex which has plagued me throughout most of my adult life. Perhaps most Afro-Americans have a compulsion to tell their truth, to lay down the burden of falsehood under which they have labored for so long, to rip away that "minstrel's mask" which has been one of the telling characteristics of the race. All, however, are aware of the inherent danger in giving way to this compulsion. During slavery and for many years after Reconstruction, giving freedom to such compulsion meant quick and brutal physical punishment. Today, the punishment may be less swift and often not physical, but even so, it is just as (if not more) brutal.

In a play by LeRoi Jones, *The Dutchman,* one finds the modern prototype of the Black Ancient Mariner. The protagonist, Clay, at one point in the play finally vomits forth (literally vomits) his truth in a long, rambling monologue. The speech is a severe indictment of the American society. As a result, Clay is knifed by the white girl Lula, and thus given the punishment meted out by a white society for daring to tell a truth it had not wished to hear.

Therefore, to confront the truth is to journey into the Netherland—that strange place reserved for crackpots, irresponsible Afro-Americans, and troublemakers. Here are Blacks who have long ago forgotten the admonition of Ralph Ellison's Doctor Bledsoe: "What's the matter with you, boy? Don't you know we always lie to white folks?" Here are those who have chosen alienation, chosen isolation, become dangerous in the eyes of white people, and militants or Black Nationalists in the eyes of other Afro-Americans.

Yet we are all, consciously or unconsciously Black Nationalists at heart, whether we think in terms of Senghor's "Negritude" or Frantz Fanon's *Wretched of the Earth,* or of the Black Power philosophy. For this reason, Nathan Hare concludes his book, *The Black Anglo Saxons*, with a plea for the Black middle class to return to the mainstream of Afro-American thought and culture, knowing that inevitably the society will force them to do so.

It is within this Netherland that I live. Here, beneath the facade which others have draped over me, deep down in the Blackness of my soul, is the real me, not invisible but merely incomprehensible. And I have been able to remain incomprehensible for years by not allowing white people to get too close to me, by holding them always a slight distance away. They have never really needed me anyway; they have had experts who have given them sufficient data concerning me, and this data has then been authenticated by Negro "leaders." S.C.L.C., for example, has told them that I am passive, and Roy Wilkins has assured them that I only want the things that other Americans want.

Due in part to what these Negro "experts" have told them and to their own propensity for taking their truth as the truth for all men, white people have codified my life in terms of their own. They have separated me from the Blacks who riot, differentiated me from those in the ghetto who did not pull themselves up by their bootstraps, bestowed upon me the honorific title of "Negro Intellectual."

This does not mean that they are incapable of dealing with me on human terms; it means, simply, that they wish to be the definers of these terms, which means in turn that they desire to define humanity for me. "We are all Americans," a professor recently remarked to me, becoming very perplexed when I offered no rejoinder. I had none to offer. We could not have talked on common ground. We could not have arrived at a definition of American which would have suited both of us. Certainly he would not have accepted my definition, for he had decided *a priori* that being an American meant to possess a certain state of mind and that I, like him, possessed this mental state. What confusion I might have introduced into his life had I told him that for me being an American is definable by the nebulous phrase "born in America." For this is all. This is the sum total of what it means to me to be an American.

The professor would not have understood. We operate, to paraphrase Redding, on two different planes of awareness. From his private heart, the professor looks at the world projecting upon it his own reality, shaped and molded by his own experiences. I, too, look at the world seeing reality in terms of my experiences; yet I know that nothing he has experienced has made it necessary for him to include me, and everything I have experienced has made it impossible for me to exclude him. Despite our Anglo-Saxon similarities, therefore, we are far apart. I am much closer to the people of Africa, of Asia, of South America than I am to my colleagues with whom I hold discourse upon Locke, Stendahl, Dostoyevsky, and Emerson.

I am closer to the Afro-American in the ghetto than I am to the "responsible Negro" in the suburbs, many of whom have developed all the instincts of chicanery and hypocrisy practiced by the majority race. Being admitted now to coffee shops which previously had closed their doors to me has only heightened my suspicion of all coffee shops. Like W. E. B. Du Bois, I also wander in the world of Sophocles, visit the Inferno of Dante, travel the gamut from the seduction of Gretchen to the "Walpurgis Nacht" with Goethe, visit the coal mines of southern France with Zola, live in old and changing Russia with Chekhov, ride the river boat with Mark Twain, and hunger for solitude with Henry David Thoreau. But I am never more at home than those times when I walk the streets of Harlem, seeing in Harlem misery and despair, ugliness and brutality, and yet hope, zest, and courage for life. Its people are the last existentialists, each and every one a modern-day Sisyphus relegated to a lifetime of pushing his stone up a hill, alienated in an oppressive universe—a universe devoid of either sense or reason. Yet daily these proud people confront this nonsensical world. They are defiant, and in their defiance there is a beauty which none of their poets has succeeded in capturing.

They are the measuring rod by which I determine my own essence. I can only find my identity among them. It is their perspective which holds true for me, their perception which determines the real me behind the facade. Now, perhaps, after the civil rights era, I am a part of the psyche of my white friends. To other Black people, however, I am a part of their entire lives, their anxieties, fears, and desperations. They realize, even if I sometimes forget, that the master's degree is not a stream separating me from them. Like Elijah Muhammad, they know where my sympathies lie, know where home is for me; and they know, too, that my manhood can only be defined in terms of their manhood.

Unlike white people, Black people have no illusions concerning me. They pierce the veil of my defenses and tear down the walls of my reserve. White people, on the other hand, are content to hold to their illusions about me (since the illusions constitute their reality), and allow me my defenses. They are made comfortable by my reserve. If I am reserved, I will not give the lie to their illusions, disrupt their sense of an orderly world, or challenge their theories concerning Blacks.

A communication gap exists between white and Black Americans, mainly because they have been listening to the wrong prophets for too long. The late Martin Luther King was one such prophet, who in his twisted metaphysics depicted an Afro-American such as has never existed upon the earth, except by accident—an Afro-American capable of enduring great suffering, of undergoing the most extreme hardships, of confronting the most horrible persecutions, while looking forward to that great getting-up morning when he and his progeny will walk the golden streets of a free land.

Most Afro-Americans are cognizant of the fact that if the spilling of Black blood could redeem "fallen America," America would have been redeemed long ago, for during slavery and since enough Black blood has been spilled to cleanse even hell itself.

Neither King nor his supporters were disturbed by the fact that there was no such Afro-American. For them, the telling point was that there should be. To paraphrase Richard Wright, the Black man is America's metaphor, and that metaphor should project an abstract image, bearing as little discernible resemblance to reality as possible. If, however, the metaphor is that of a Christ figure, then the Afro-American is the worst representative. No one who really knows us can imagine a people more different in every respect from the historical Jesus. Cleansed of the romantic epithets of the Negro prophets, the Black man is revealed to the discerning eye as a hating, fearful, trapped Bigger Thomas.

From Jesus Christ to Bigger Thomas, however, is a step which the white liberal mind cannot take, for it entails a realistic confrontation with the problems which face this country shorn of the useless verbiage, the abstract rhetoric, and the myths which now surround them. But if the Afro-American is to be understood—and only such an understanding can prevent that fire next time—then the metaphors will have to be reshaped, true images will have to be constructed from real, solid foundations; romanticism will have to be foregone, and Bigger Thomas must be enthroned in that spot once reserved exclusively for Jesus Christ.

"I have known many Bigger Thomases," Richard Wright notes in his essay "How Bigger Was Born," and most Americans, likewise, have known many Bigger Thomases. Some of the Bigger Thomases of the world, as Wright accurately saw, are white; in America, however, the overwhelming majority are Black, if only because Black people in this country have been more limited in freedom, more fearful of outside forces, more suspicious of other people, and more inclined to repress the rage which always bubbles within.

Bigger Thomas, born in a Chicago slum where he lived in a one-room hovel with his mother, brother, and sister, was relegated because of the color of his skin to a life of despair and futility. Given a job by a white liberal who owns the very slums in which he is forced to live, Bigger accidentally kills the liberal's daughter. In addition, he murders his own girlfriend, not gratuitously but by design, setting up the interesting angle that Bigger was responsible for only one murder—that of his Black girlfriend, a fact which has practically no bearing on the outcome of his trial. Caught by police, Bigger is tried and, despite pleas from his Communist lawyer, sentenced to die. He dies without repentance, without atonement for the death of the white girl.

Is there, then, something in the life and trial of Bigger Thomas which makes Wright's character a fitting image of the twentieth-century Black man in America? Of the critics who have dealt with this aspect, James Baldwin is, perhaps, the best known. Baldwin's criticism, however, attempts to constrict the image of Bigger Thomas to that of an isolated Black in a Chicago slum, though one reading *The Fire Next Time* may at times confuse Baldwin himself with Wright's creation. Basically, Baldwin's argument is that "all of Bigger's life is bound by hate and fear," and that this should not be. Man, if one reasons with Baldwin, should have freedom of choice, the moral and mental (if not physical) stamina to ward off those ever-seducing, enslaving arms of society. Man is not the sum total of his environment, but the environment is the sum total of man. In this analysis, man is the arbitrator of his own destiny, irrespective of the more powerful forces which attempt to interpret that destiny for him. Like Sartre and the existentialists whom he pretends to disdain, Baldwin sees the Afro-American as a free being moving in a nondeterministic environment, capable with Goethe's Faust of hailing the fleeting hour, of caressing it, of making it his own.

Faust figure the Black man may be; however, for him the fleeting hour comes about either at the whim of other men in the American society or not at all. Mephistopheles vouchsafed a freedom to Faust which the Afro-American has never possessed and does not now possess. Far from being the arbitrator of his own destiny, the Afro-American is subservient, regardless of his status, to some higher court of law, not divine but human. To argue, therefore, that Bigger's life should not be bound by hatred and fear is far different than to argue that it is.

One imagines that what bothers Baldwin is his inability to totally commit himself one way or another. To be dedicated to mankind (whatever that means) is perhaps a noble endeavor, but one as abstract and idealistic as the dedication to a comprehensive moral law which guides all men. Humanity begins at home; the struggle begins with that group and in that place where humanity has been most severely traduced and most emphatically denied. That group is the Black Americans and that place, despite the apologists, is America. The white press has portrayed Baldwin as "the metaphor of the American Negro," a portraiture which does little justice to Baldwin and gross injustice to Afro-Americans. Baldwin's preoccupations with "humanity and universal mankind" earn him instead, to be far more accurate than the white press, the appellation "metaphor of a white Hamlet."

In Notes of a Native Son, Baldwin argues that it was Wright whom he had to destroy before he could succeed as a writer. This is not true. What Baldwin felt impelled to destroy, indeed what threatened him far more than his ambivalence concerning his position in the cosmological scheme of Western civilization, was the ever-present, hulking, hating murderous image of Bigger Thomas in Baldwin which propelled him to Paris, formed the basis for his argument in The Fire Next Time, caused him in some moments to strike out at white America. And it is Bigger who haunts him still, making him an alien, never completely secure in this country where, as in that adolescent age of his rebellion, he may be called upon by forces antithetical to his nature to commit murder.

I can muster no sympathy for the Baldwins of the world. Their attempts, no matter how well intentioned, to destroy the image of Bigger Thomas have succeeded in increasing the confusion of whites, in instilling suspicion into Afro-Americans and wrenching the American problem from its proper perspective, forcing it into a universal, metaphysical arena to which it belongs, if at all, only incidentally. Of all the earth's wretched, the Black American is the most wretched despite protestations of affluence from the Black middle class.

Though it may be true that Black Africans, as Roy Wilkins has reminded us, lack the material comforts of life—cars, homes, television sets—and are, for the most part, sentenced to the straw mat, the bush and the tree-thick jungle, still, despite all, the Black African lives in a land where manhood is possible, where mutual respect between men is possible, where hatred, fear, and suspicion do not have to be ever-present shadows never obliterated even by the shade, but forever lingering even in those places where there is no light.

Sometime ago I sat in on a play entitled *A Tribute to Patrice Lumumba*. The play consisted of a number of scenes tracing the life of the ex-Congolese premier from birth to death. In the opening scene, a young woman, holding a baby in her arm who was supposedly the infant Lumumba, walked proudly across the imaginary Congo landscape and addressed a crowd of imaginary Congolese with the words: "Today is born unto you a manchild!"

No one can imagine the images of pain and despair which those words called up in me, one destined never to be a man in any real sense of the term until that moment when I decide that of those two dreadful alternatives—life and death— death may be the more attractive of the two. Yet Lumumba's mother could have and may have made such a statement; for every African mother—even those of Rhodesia and South Africa—may so hail their sons. Whether he becomes a man or not, for such a child the pathway is open, uncluttered by a legacy of enmity and fear whose roots stretch back over two hundred years.

The African child, then, may wait for the biological laws of evolution, those laws which determine manhood in a physical sense, to take their course. Juju man the African may be, but he needs none of this juju to acquire manhood. The Black American needs some kind of juju, some kind of Black magic, some powerful potion to effect that transformation which the biological process, due to centuries of mutation, can no longer effect. White people have thwarted the laws of biology as far as the Black man is concerned, cast doubt upon the laws of Darwin, and prohibited the Black child from becoming a man. In vain now would one, like some Diogenes, search with a spotlight—not with a lantern—among Afro-Americans for a man. The species is almost extinct, and if one listens to the timid cries of some of the Negro leaders, resurrection of the species in the future seems impossible.

But we too are culpable. We have done much to bring about our own destruction. We have attempted to deny our heritage, and in so doing, destroyed our chances at manhood. We have accepted the metaphors created for us by the majority members of the society, just as we have accepted the leaders whom they have granted to us. We have accepted their truth long beyond that point wherein it becomes dangerous to do so, and in accepting their truth and their prophets, we have acquiesced in the negation of our manhood. We have attempted to destroy the image of Bigger Thomas, and such an attempt has led to confusion and frustration. For in reality, deep inside, away from the searching eyes of our white liberal friends, we are full-bodied Bigger Thomases, capable of resurrecting our manhood in that *Götterdämmerung* of chaos and violence which is the only recourse left to us by a castrating society.

Yet we live with Bigger Thomas, our psyche, only in the Netherland. Here we allow that Bigger part of us free reign, allow his terror, his bitterness to soothe us, to placate us, to transform us from the hollow men of everyday reality into the flesh-and-blood men which we can only become in our imaginations. Here we curse Gomorrah and pine for the fire and thunder of the coming year of our lord, knowing that such will not bring us redemption, but instead that wished-for vengeance, that moment of supreme fulfillment when those who have defiled us for so long will be burned and seared by a power, some power at long last, which they can neither control nor harness.

Indeed! We are monsters in the Netherland. We give no quarter; we hunger and thirst not after righteousness but after death, doom, and destruction . . . castigating, castrating, defouling, torturing, murdering those whom here we acknowledge as our enemies, as our oppressors, as, even, the unwanted guarantors of our destinies. Here Bigger Thomas is no fictional character, no unacknowledged stereotype, no object of shame and insult. We have left our magic mirrors behind, stripped off our masks, confronted ourselves, and in so doing, surrendered our soul in tears, in pain, in ecstasy, in total to that demon-within which affords us no peace, grants us no respite, vouchsafes us no life.

But the demon offers us our only chance to regain our manhood and to break free of the stultifying heritage of the past. The demon offers us freedom, the only kind of freedom which is desirable and the only kind of freedom which may itself free us forever. This freedom is truth: the freedom to tell other Americans what we are, what we believe, what we are capable of—not through abstract metaphysics, clumsy phraseology or theological pronouncements, but through the sounds of anguish and despair, the shouts and screams of those for whom manhood is an intangible abstraction. There is still some validity in the old cliché "the truth will set us free."

My dinner companion paused; the fork midway between her waist and breasts.

"But," she continued, "Baldwin is much better than LeRoi Jones. I mean, Jones is so frightening—so much bitterness, so much hatred. . . ."

I smiled. "Bigger Thomas," I said.

"Bigger . . . ?" she quizzed.

"Thomas. A character in Richard Wright's *Native Son.*"

"Oh, yes," she said quickly, not getting the point. "I heard about it. I mean, I didn't read the book, but I know something about it."

"He killed a white woman," I announced, coldly.

"Oh!" She smiled weakly, placing her fork back on the plate.

Leaning across the table, I leered at her. "He killed her, and cut her body up, and threw it into a furnace."

The smile disappeared from face. "Oh," she managed. "So that was the story?"

"Story?" I ejaculated. "Hell no, that was the truth!"

She was no longer eating. She scanned my face but found no trace of a smile, no hint of the lie I was telling. "There was no reason either," I continued. "At least, no visible reason. They were sitting down to dinner one day in a large restaurant, and he simply reached out with a knife and stabbed her. Then he grabbed her quickly, before anybody could see that she was hurt, and threw her over his shoulder and walked out."

I picked up a table knife and grinned at her. She looked around, smiled timidly, finally uttered an excuse and left, most of her dinner still untouched.

SELECTED BIBLIOGRAPHY

Criticism

"Black Writer's Views on Literary Lions and Values." *Negro Digest* 17 (Jan. 1968): 32.

"The Critic, the University and the Negro Writer." *Negro Digest* 17 (Jan. 1967): 32.

"Cultural Nationalism: The Black Novel and the City." *Liberator* 9 (July 1969): 14–17.

"Cultural Strangulation: Black Literature and the White Aesthetic." *Negro Digest* 18 (July 1969): 32–39. Reprinted in Baker, *Black Literature in America,* 369–373; Gayle, *The Black Aesthetic, 38–45.*

"A Defense of James Baldwin." *CLA Journal* 10 (March 1967): 201–208.

"The Function of Black Literature at the Present Time." In Gayle, *The Black Aesthetic,* 383–394.

"The Harlem Renaissance: Towards a Black Aesthetic." *Mid-continent American Studies Journal* 11 (Fall 1970): 78–87.

"Langston Hughes: A Simple Commentary." *Negro Digest* 16 (Sept. 1967): 53–57.

"The Negro-Critic: Invisible Man in American Literature." *Record* 70 (Nov. 1968): 165–171.

"An Open Letter to the Editor of the *New York Times Book Review.*" Reprinted in *Black World* 21 (May 1972): 92–94.

"Perhaps Not So Soon One Morning." *Phylon* (1968). Reprinted in Gayle, *Black Expressions,* 280–287.

"The Politics of Revolution: Afro-American Literature." *Black World* 21 (June 1972): 4–12.

"Under Western Eyes: A Review Essay." *Black World* 22 (July 1973): 40–48.

Edited Collections

The Black Aesthetic. Garden City, N.Y.: Doubleday, 1971.

Black Expression: Essays by and about Black Americans in the Creative Arts. New York: Weybright and Talley, 1969.

Bondage, Freedom and Beyond: The Prose of Black Americans. Garden City, N.Y.: Zenith Books, 1971.

Nonfiction

The Black Situation. New York: Dell, 1972.

(Anthology): Gayle, *Bondage, Freedom and Beyond.*

(Periodicals): *Black World,* January 1971; July 1973; *Journal of Human Relations,* Second Quarter 1967; *Negro Digest,* July 1969.

"Making Beauty from Racial Anxiety" by Addison Gayle Jr. 29–34. In Stephen Caldwell Wright (ed. and preface). *On Gwendolyn Brooks: Reliant Contemplation.* Ann Arbor, Mich.: University of Michigan Press, 1996. xi, 277 pp. (book article)

"Cultural Strangulation: Black Literature and the White Aesthetic" by Addison Gayle Jr. 207–12. In Angelyn Mitchell (ed.). *Within the Circle: An Anthology of African American Literary Criticism from the Harlem Renaissance to the Present.* Durham, N.C.: Duke University Press, 1994. xii, 530 pp. (book article)

"Should the Canon Be Revised?" by Addison Gayle Jr. *Magazine of the Graduate School and University Center* 5, no. 2 (Fall 1991): 20–27. (journal article)

"Gwendolyn Brooks: Poet of the Whirlwind" by Addison Gayle Jr. 79–87. In Mari Evans (ed. and pref.), Stephen E. Henderson (introduction). *Black Women Writers (1950–1980): A Critical Evaluation.* Garden City, N.Y.: Anchor-Doubleday, 1984. xxx, 543 pp. (book article)

"The 'Negro-to-Black' Conversion in Contemporary Afro-American Autobiography: Two Patterns" by Sigmund Ro. Trondheim working papers 1 (Fall 1982): 22–45. (journal article)

"Blueprint for Black Criticism" by Addison Gayle Jr. *First World* 1, no. 1 (1977): 41–45. (journal article)

"Two Views of Winesellers" by Addison Gayle Jr. *Black World,* 25, no. 6 (1976): 95–97. (journal article)

"The Function of Black Criticism at the Present Time" by Addison Gayle Jr. 37–40. In Houston A. Baker, Jr.,. *Reading Black: Essays in the Criticism of African, Caribbean, and Black American Literature.* Ithaca, N.Y.: Cornell University Africana Studies and Research Center, 1976. 58 pp. (book article)

"Literature as Catharsis: The Novels of Paul Laurence Dunbar" by Addison Gayle Jr. 139–51. In Jay Martin. *A Singer in the Dawn: Reinterpretations of Paul Laurence Dunbar.* New York: Dodd, Mead, 1975. 255 pp. (book article)

The Way of the New World: The Black Novel in America by Addison Gayle Jr. Garden City, N.Y.: Anchor, 1975. 339 pp. (book)

"Reclaiming the Southern Experience: The Black Aesthetic 10 Years Later" by Addison Gayle Jr. *Black World* 23, no. 11 (1974): 20–29. (journal article)

"Debate: The Black Aesthetic (Defender)" by Addison Gayle Jr. *Black World* 24, no. 2 (1974): 31–43. (journal article)

"Under Western Eyes" by Addison Gayle Jr. *Black World* 22, no. 9 (1973): 40–48. (journal article)

"The Politics of Revolution: Afro-American Literature" by Addison Gayle Jr. *Black World* 21, no. 8 (1972): 4–12. (journal article)

"Cultural Hegemony: The Southern Writer and American Letters" by Addison Gayle Jr. *Amistad: Writings on Black History and Culture* 1 (1970): 3–24. (journal article)

"The Harlem Renaissance: Towards a Black Aesthetic" by Addison Gayle Jr. *Midcontinent American Studies Journal* 11, no. 2 : 78–87. (journal article)

"Cultural Strangulation: Black Literature and the White Aesthetic" by Addison Gayle Jr. *Negro Digest* 18, no. 9 (1969): 32–39. (journal article)

"Richard Wright: Beyond Nihilism" by Addison Gayle Jr. *Negro Digest* 18, no. 2 (1968): 4–10. (journal article)

"A Defense of James Baldwin" by Addison Gayle Jr. *College Language Association Journal* 10(1967): 201–208. (journal article)

Short Stories

(Periodicals): *Black World,* May 1970; *Negro Digest,* May 1967.

INDEX

NATHANIEL NORMENT JR. is an associate professor and chair of African American studies at Temple University. He is the editor of *The African American Studies Reader, Readings in African American Language,* and the author of numerous articles in scholarly journals.

The University of Illinois Press
is a founding member of the
Association of American University Presses.

Composed in 10.5/13 Adobe Minion Pro
at the University of Illinois Press
Manufactured by Sheridan Books, Inc.

University of Illinois Press
1325 South Oak Street
Champaign, IL 61820-6903
www.press.uillinois.edu